Entertaining Satan

Entertaining Satan

WITCHCRAFT AND THE CULTURE
OF EARLY NEW ENGLAND

JOHN PUTNAM DEMOS

New York   Oxford
OXFORD UNIVERSITY PRESS
1982

Library of Congress Cataloging in Publication Data
Demos, John Putnam.
Entertaining Satan.
Includes index.
1. Witchcraft—New England.   2. New England—
Social life and customs.   I. Title.
BF1576.D42   974'.02   81-22463
ISBN 0-19-503131-8   AACR2

Printing (last digit): 9 8 7 6 5 4 3 2 1

Printed in the United States of America

To Virginia,
Partner in all things

Preface

This book is the end of a very long inquiry. The book itself spans a good six years in the writing; the inquiry goes back two decades. My first term-paper, as a beginning graduate student in 1960, was about witchcraft, and, in a sense, I have lived with witchcraft ever since. I have loved this project, and hated it, by turns. I have frequently forsaken it for other interests, and just as frequently been "reconciled." Like an old and tested companion, it has become almost a part of me.

Witchcraft is, of course, an old, old chestnut of historical interest and study; but that was not my motive in setting out. (Indeed, the "popularity" of the subject felt to me then, and still feels, faintly like an embarrassment.) Two factors, separate but overlapping, served to justify an effort of *re*study. One was an overemphasis in previous writings on a few sensational episodes—with the Salem trials of 1692–93 making the single most obvious case in point. Witchcraft, I could see at the outset, belonged to the regular business of life in premodern times; or at least it belonged to the belief system, the value structure, the predominant psychology of those times. To explore its everyday presence and meaning, and thus to right the balance of research, seemed a worthy scholarly objective.

But there was a second, and deeper, objective, to which terms like "system" and "structure" directly referred. My coming of age, professionally speaking, coincided with a general growth of interest in "interdisciplinary history." Efforts of intellectual bridge-building—demographic history, historical sociology, psychohistory—marked a new fashion in research. And such bridges seemed especially apposite to witchcraft. More than most "old" subjects, this one might yield new forms of understanding when re-examined in the clear light of social science. For social science was itself much taken with witchcraft. A large academic literature, especially in anthropology, canvassed materials from numerous cultures around the world—and furnished exemplary models to historians.

The range of this literature reflected an important social fact. Witchcraft is widely found, across time and space, amidst a variety of otherwise disparate circumstances; it qualifies therefore as a problem of transcultural significance. To study it is (or should be) more than an exercise in parochial reconstruction. Comparison, contrast, pattern, even "laws of human behavior": such are the alluring possibilities that beckon scholars to witchcraft.

At least they beckoned me. And my plans for the project were fashioned accordingly. My first outlines were organized around a series of interpretive questions, lifted more or less wholesale from the social science literature. My notes from that early stage bristled with "analytical models" and "conceptual schemas," with "functions" and "costs," with "manifest" and "latent" tendencies. The outlines were clean and symmetrical; the notes seemed expansive enough; hence the prospects looked generally bright. But before many words had been committed to paper, I knew that something was seriously wrong. Briefly stated: my study, if continued along the same track, would be long on concepts, but distressingly short on human detail. The *people* were slipping through the scholarly cracks.

Back to my research files. Days of confusion. Restless nights. Conversations with friends and colleagues. (I especially remember one with a novelist of long acquaintance, which helped me to recognize how close are the imaginative worlds of history and fiction.)

I began to write "stories" about witchcraft—true stories of specific episodes for which my evidence was especially full. Stories of everyday experience in all its nettlesome particulars. Stories which put individual men and women (sometimes children) right at center-stage. Stories with beginnings, and middles, and ends.

Throughout this passage I saw—I *felt*—the historian's old dilemma: history as art *versus* history as science. If the barricades should ever go up, I know now which way I'll jump. But better by far not to have to choose.

At any rate, this book declines to choose. Science is not renounced, only scaled down. Again and again, science has given me questions— and (less often) something like answers. (In one memorable instance scientific theory led me to search for, and then to find, important new evidence.)* My initial outlines are there in the summary chapters that conclude each major part of the study.

Yet the other chapters are truly the core. They are my stories, grown now to "case studies." Their descriptive bare-bones have been fleshed out with elements of background, of context, and (at least occasionally) of overt interpretation. Fortunately, the records of witchcraft overflow with revealing detail. To go through the records is to see far more than a simple set of episodic plot-lines. Witchcraft was by definition something quite extraordinary, but it touched many other things entirely ordinary. It thus supports—it virtually demands—a style of cultural portraiture both broad and deep.

Clearly, such portraiture must *evoke* as well as analyze. And this is where the "art" comes in. For me, personally, witchcraft study has been evocative in the fullest possible sense. Indeed the word seems insufficiently strong. Through witchcraft I have come to know scores of people who lived and died centuries ago. (Sometimes I wonder, a little morbidly, how many of my contemporaries I know as well.) Rachel Clinton, John Godfrey, Elizabeth Garlick, Eunice Cole, Elizabeth Knapp and Samuel Willard, Mary Parsons and Sarah Bridgman, Elizabeth and William Morse: all have figured hugely in my thoughts and feelings, and even (once or twice) in my dreams. I think I would recognize them, and know just what to say to them, should I meet them in some otherworldly byway years hence.

An author's hubris, certainly. But I want to express my hope that this is more than a witchcraft book narrowly construed. I want readers to share my own experience of knowing the common folk and common life of a distant time.

And now, one final consideration, introduced some years ago by Marion Starkey in the preface to her fine account of the Salem trials,

---

* This experience—of a sort rarely vouchsafed to historians—merits a brief retelling. The details of Elizabeth Knapp's "possession" (see Chapter 4) seemed, in the light of modern psychoanalytic theory, to imply some anomaly of idealized "introjects" (the internal representations of parents based on experience in earliest childhood). More specifically: they suggested that Elizabeth's father, though a respected community leader at the time of her possession, must once have been a figure of doubt and shame for her. A subsequent search for evidence on the father's prior career discovered telling (and hitherto unknown) details: some involvement in petty crime, a conviction for public "drunkenness," and, finally, an indictment for adultery (all when Elizabeth was aged one to four). In short, this was exactly the sort of thing which theory would—and here did—*predict*.

The Devil in Massachusetts. Witchcraft research, wrote Starkey, is "bad business . . . it makes you superstitious." She felt "impelled to report" several misadventures attending her work on Salem: for example, "a small hurricane . . . [that] brought every tree in the yard crashing against the house" on the day she began, and a "plague of lightning" when she finished. I feel similarly impelled. My report runs less to misadventures (though I cannot forget the basement flood that nearly destroyed my research notes) than to fortuitous author-subject connections. Here is still another viewpoint on my "motives" in the study.

I discovered, early on, a genealogical connection. In the famous trials at Salem, one family—the Putnams—spurred the prosecution beyond all others. Puritans through and through, early settlers, farmers, stalwarts of the village establishment, and, finally, "accusers" of others more fortunate and forward-looking than they—the members of this family earned for themselves a special niche in witchcraft history. My maternal ancestors, hitherto known to me only through photographs in an old family album (and my own middle name), were Putnams, too. Westerners, in recent generations. But—I learned—New Englanders before that. Salem? Yes, the line runs straight back. The witch-trial Putnams? The very same. I recall thinking, on the afternoon when I scaled this family tree, that my project would have an aspect of personal closure—even, perhaps, of exorcism.

And there was more. The remarkable drama of Elizabeth Knapp's "possession" (recounted at length in Chapter 4) was set in the Massachusetts town of Groton. But her life began, and was powerfully molded, in another community well to the east—Watertown, my own place of residence for the past dozen years. And where in Watertown was the Knapp home located? A careful map from an old town history disclosed the answer: the Knapps and I are next-door neighbors.

I suspect that many writers, at one stage or another, feel joined by fate to their particular topics and projects. But when the topic is witchcraft, such feeling grows unusually—albeit "superstitiously"—strong.

Watertown, Massachusetts   J. P. D.
May 1982

Note

In quotations from original sources, throughout this book, spelling and punctuation have been "modernized," in order to enhance readability.

Acknowledgments

I must acknowledge, in the first place, a variety of significant debts to institutions. My research and writing in this project was supported by fellowships from the Center for Psychosocial Studies (Chicago), the John Simon Guggenheim Memorial Foundation, and the Charles Warren Center for Studies in American History (Harvard University). I was hospitably received and ably assisted, as I pursued the trail of witchcraft, at the New England Historic Genealogical Society, the Massachusetts Historical Society, the Connecticut Historical Society, the American Antiquarian Society, the Connecticut State Library, the Massachusetts Archives, the Connecticut Valley Historical Museum, the Forbes Library, the Essex Institute, the Cornell University Library, the Ann Mary Brown Memorial (Brown University), and the Houghton Library (Harvard University). All these places turned up relevant primary documents, which I have gratefully read and used. In addition, I have been aided by staff-persons in various public offices: e.g. the courts of Essex, Middlesex, and Suffolk counties, Massachusetts; the town offices of Ipswich, Salem, and Northampton, Massachusetts, Hampton, New Hampshire, and Wethersfield, Connecticut. Two portions of the present work have been previously published in a slightly different form: Chapter 2, in the *William and Mary Quarterly* (3rd series, XXXIII, April 1976), and Chapter 10, in *Uprooted Americans: Essays to Honor Oscar Handlin*, Richard Bushman *et al.*, eds. (Boston, 1979).

My personal acknowledgments are another story; given the longevity of the project, they amount to a virtual roster of "significant others" throughout my adult life. Near the start I benefitted from various forms of cross-disciplinary exchange; I think especially of discussions with my philosopher father, Raphael Demos, my anthropologist aunt, Dorothy Lee, my psychologist friend, Carter Umbarger, and (another friend, another anthropologist) Robert LeVine. Since then there have been many more discussions of great individual and cumulative value to me. Ann Gordon, Anna Ornstein, Robert Middlekauff, and Mary Dunn (twice!) have commented on one or another piece of my witchcraft work, in the context of professional meetings. Draft-chapters have been read and criticized by Stanley Katz, David and Sheila Rothman, Alexander Keyssar, Rudolph Binion, David Fischer, Kai Erikson, Kenneth Keniston, Ernest Wolf, John Fitzpatrick, Silvan Tomkins, E. Anthony Rotundo, and Ellen Rothman. Members of the Group for Applied Psychoanalysis, the American Civilization colloquium of Brandeis University, and the Center for Psychosocial Studies have heard me out on my subject, and have helped to sharpen my thinking. To all these individuals and groups I am, of course, deeply thankful.

Three more people have read the entire manuscript; to them my thanks are compounded proportionately. Sheldon Meyer, editorial director of Oxford University Press (New York), has given me quiet encouragement and wise counsel over many years—and, not least, has been patient to a fault. Curtis Church has bestowed on my every word the benefit of his fine editorial instincts. Virginia Demos has endured the project, nourished it, and improved it in ways too numerous to recount; my debt to her is expressed on a separate page. I should also mention Alison Demos, an infant when I first tried to write about witchcraft and a proofreader by the time I finished—and Moira Demos, creator of a fine "poppet" which has hung over my desk and guided my hand for the past five years.

Finally, this seems an appropriate place to put the names of four persons whom I feel privileged to call my teachers: William R. Taylor, Oscar Handlin, Erik H. Erikson, and the late Heinz Kohut. Teachers, but for whom . . .

Contents

FOUR HISTORY

Entertaining Satan

Introduction

"It is known to all men," wrote John Higginson in the spring of 1698, "that it pleased God some few years ago to suffer Satan to raise much trouble amongst us. . . ." Higginson was senior pastor in the town of Salem, Massachusetts, and he referred, of course, to a long chain of legal proceedings with which the name of Salem has ever since been linked. Their beginning, he noted,

> was very small, and was looked on at first as an ordinary case which had fallen out before at several times in other places, and would be quickly over. Only one or two persons belonging to Salem Village, . . . being suspected, were examined, etc. But in the progress of the matter, a multitude of persons both in this and other neighbor towns were accused, examined, imprisoned, and came to their trials . . . where about twenty of them suffered as witches; and many others were in danger of the same tragical end.[1]

But if the Salem trials have been "known to all men" from Higginson's time to our own, the "ordinary cases" make another story. Salem was unique in its quantitative dimensions—witch-hunting gone wild—and for that reason alone has exercised a disproportionate hold on the public imagination. By contrast, witchcraft apart from Salem, witchcraft before and after the "tragical" years of 1692–93, has been little remembered. The result is an impoverished, not to say distorted, view of a germinal phase in our people's history: Salem appears as a brief and dark chapter in that history, an utterly bizarre throwback to the "medieval" superstition from which the first generations of colonial settlers had presumably escaped. Presented thus, it stands apart from the main lines of early American experience.[2]

John Higginson knew better. A septuagenarian by the time the Salem trials began, he was a longtime student of witchcraft, "ordinary" and otherwise. He had observed it at first hand, had written and preached about it, and had helped to shape attitudes toward it among the two generations of his parishioners.[3] He and they knew witchcraft as an ever-present danger—and a not infrequent reality—in their common social experience. Moreover, they dreaded it terribly. "Witchcraft," said Higginson, "is one of the most awful and tremendous judgements of God which can be inflicted on the societies of men."[4]

"Awful" and "tremendous": the words were immediately resonant for all whose Puritan piety ran deep. At the same time, specific manifestations of witchcraft could be small of scale and intensely personal in substance. Records from witch trials touch repeatedly on the routine exchange of services and favors, on seemingly innocent conversation, on local encounters of an everyday kind. Here witchcraft met and joined with other strands of belief in supernatural influence—fortune-telling, astrology, healing charms, love potions and powders, to mention only a few. "Magic" of all sorts was a lively presence for seventeenth-century folk, in New England and elsewhere.

Thus did witchcraft cut a long arc through the cosmology of the pre-modern world, from the grand doctrines of "learned divines," at one end, to the practical concerns of village farmers and artisans, at the other. No single set of case-records yields a view of the full span; but two brief *vignettes* may serve to introduce certain of its leading features.

> Windsor, Connecticut. An autumn day in the year 1651 . . . A group of local militiamen is engaged in "training" exercises. Suddenly, there is an accident: a young recruit—one Thomas Allen —cocks his musket and inadvertantly knocks it against a tree. The weapon fires, discharging a bullet which strikes another trainee. The victim, an older man named Henry Stiles, is mortally wounded.
>
> A few weeks later the "particular court" of the colony meets in regular session. On its agenda is an indictment of Thomas Allen: "that . . . [thou] didst suddenly, negligently, carelessly cock thy piece, and carry the piece . . . which piece being charged and going off in thine hand, slew thy neighbor, to the great dishonor of God, breach of the peace, and loss of a member of this commonwealth." Allen confesses the fact, and is found guilty

of "homicide by misadventure." For his "sinful neglect and care-less carriages" the court orders him to pay a substantial fine. In addition he is "bound to good behavior" for the ensuing year, with the special proviso "that he shall not bear arms for the same term."[5]

But this is not the end of the matter. Presumably, Stiles's death remains a topic of local conversation—and three years later it yields a more drastic result. In November 1654 the court holds a special session to try a case of witchcraft—against a woman, Lydia Gilbert, also of Windsor: "Lydia Gilbert, thou art here indicted . . . that not having the fear of God before thine eyes, thou hast of late years, or still dost, give entertainment to Satan, the great enemy of God and mankind, and by his help hast killed the body of Henry Stiles, besides other witchcrafts, for which, according to the law of God and the established law of this com-monwealth, thou deservest to die." The court, in effect, is con-sidering a complicated question: did Lydia Gilbert's witchcraft *cause* Thomas Allen's gun to go off, so as to kill Henry Stiles? Depositions are taken from eyewitnesses and others with infor-mation bearing on the case. . . .[6]

(Unfortunately, these depositional records have not survived to our own day. But probate documents show that Stiles was a boarder in the home of Lydia Gilbert—and her creditor as well. Perhaps there was trouble between them, even some open dis-plays of anger? And if so, perhaps their neighbors suspected in Goodwife Gilbert a vengeful motive toward Stiles?)[7]

In due course the trial jury weighs the evidence and reaches its verdict—guilty as charged. The magistrates hand down the prescribed sentence of death by hanging.[8]

(Again the extant records break off abruptly. They afford no information about reaction in the community at large—always an important matter. But, based on what is known of such reaction in similar cases elsewhere, it is reasonable to imagine one more act in the unfolding drama.)[9]

On a Sabbath, shortly after the trial's conclusion, the pastor of the Windsor church devotes his sermon to a question that presses painfully on the minds of his parishioners: *Why has this terrible scourge of witchcraft been visited on their little com-munity?* The pastor's answer is neither surprising nor pleasant to hear, but it carries a purgative force. *The Windsor townsfolk are themselves at least partially to blame.* More and more, in recent months, they have strayed from the paths of virtue: overvaluing secular interests while neglecting religious ones, tippling in ale-houses, "nightwalking," and—worst of all—engaging one another in repeated strife. In such circumstances the Devil always finds an opening; on such communities God necessarily brings retribution. Thus the recent witchcraft episode is a lesson to the people of Windsor to mend their ways.

Lydia Gilbert was not the first witch to have lived in Windsor, nor would she be the last. And Stiles's death was but one of many attributed to so-called *maleficium*. For New Englanders of that era, the happenstance of everyday life was part of a struggle of cosmic dimensions, a struggle in which witchcraft played an integral part. The ultimate triumph of Almighty God was assured. But in particular times and places Satan might achieve some temporary success—and claim important victims. Indeed he was continually adding earthly recruits to his nefarious cause. Tempted by bribes and blandishments, or frightened by threats of torture, weak-willed persons signed the "Devil's Book" and enrolled as witches. Thereafter they were armed with his power, and obliged to do his bidding. God, meanwhile, opposed this onslaught of evil—and yet He also permitted it. For errant men and women there was no more effective means of "chastening."

In a sense, therefore, witchcraft was part of God's own intention. And the element of intention was absolutely central, in the minds of all who took part. When a man lay dead from a violent accident on a training field, his fellow-townspeople would carefully investigate how events had proceeded to such an end—the weapons involved, the actions of individuals, the immediate context and circumstances. But, in addition, they sought to understand the *why* of it all—the motives, whether human or supernatural (or both), which lay behind the events. The same was true for other forms of everyday mischance. When cows took strangely ill, when a boat capsized in a sudden storm, when bread failed to rise in the oven or beer went bad in the barrel, there was cause for careful reflection. Witchcraft would not necessarily provide the best explanation, but it was always a possibility—and sometimes a persuasive one.

It could indeed be *most* persuasive when linked to some nexus of personal antagonism. Had the sufferer (the "victim") quarreled recently with another villager? And had the terms of their quarrel been unusually harsh—perhaps including curses or threats of future harm? And did the other party have a previous reputation for dabbling in the "black arts?" Affirmative answers might open the way to charges of witchcraft, while negative ones would likely close it off. Victims rarely suspected *maleficium* without having a specific person in mind. Witches, moreover, were not the only source of human suffering. Personal malice (apart from witchcraft), error, incompetence, the Devil's own machinations, and the inscrutable ways of "divine providence" also took their toll. To explain any particular misfortune was to choose among all these alternatives; and clues to the "right" one came from a whole course of *antecedent* experience.

Occasionally, to be sure, there were palpable signs of "diabolical" influence.

Boston, Massachusetts. October 1688 . . . A tall man alights from his horse and hurries along a pathway toward a small house. A door opens to admit him and quickly closes again. The visitor is the Rev. Cotton Mather, a young but already eminent clergyman of the town. The house is occupied by the family of a mason named John Goodwin.[10]

Immediately upon entering, Mather becomes witness to an extraordinary scene. On the parlor floor in front of him two small human forms are thrashing about. A girl of thirteen (named Martha) and a boy of eleven (John, Jr.) are caught in the throes of agonizing "fits." Their bodies contort into strange, distended shapes. Their eyes bulge. Their mouths snap open and shut. They shriek uncontrollably. From time to time they affect the postures of animals, and crawl about the room, barking like dogs or bellowing like frightened cows. Their father and several neighbors look on in horror, and try by turns to prevent serious damage to persons or property.

Mather waits for a moment's lull; then he opens a Bible, kneels, and begins to pray aloud. Immediately the children stop their ears and resume their shrieking. "*They* say we must not listen," cries the girl, while hurling herself toward the fireplace. Her father manages to block the way; briefly he catches her in an awkward embrace. But she reels off and falls heavily on her brother.

Soon it is time for supper. The children are temporarily calmer, and come to the table with their elders. However, when food is offered them, their teeth are set as if to lock their mouths shut. Later there are new troubles. The children need assistance in preparing for bed, and they tear their nightclothes fearfully. At last they quiet and pass into a deep sleep.

Mather sits by the fireside and reviews the history of their affliction with the distraught parents. The family is a religious one, and until the preceding summer the children were unfailingly pious and well behaved. Martha's fits had begun first, John's soon thereafter; indeed two still younger members of the family have been affected from time to time. A physician was summoned, but could discover no "natural maladies" at work.

The parents recall an episode that had directly preceded the onset of Martha's fits. The girl was sent to retrieve some linen from a laundress who lived nearby. Several items had disappeared, and Martha complained—intimating theft. The laundress indignantly denied the charges, and was joined in this by her own mother, an Irishwoman named Glover. Goodwife Glover was already a feared presence in the neighborhood; her late husband, on his deathbed, had accused her of practicing witchcraft. Now she poured out her anger on young Martha Goodwin. The girl has not been the same since.

Late in the evening, having listened with care to the entire story, Mather prepares to leave. John Goodwin explains that several neighbors have been urging the use of "tricks"—countermagic—to end his children's difficulties. But Goodwin himself prefers a strategy based on orthodox Christian principles.

In this Cotton Mather is eager to cooperate. He returns daily to the Goodwin house, and on one particular afternoon he is joined by fellow-clergymen from all parts of Boston. Then he invites Martha Goodwin into his own home for a period of intensive pastoral care. (Martha's younger brother is taken, at the same time, to the home of the minister at Watertown.) Their afflictions continue, though with lessened severity.

Meanwhile the courts intervene, and Goodwife Glover is put on trial for her alleged crimes. Her house is searched, and "poppets" are discovered—small images made of rags, believed to be instrumental in the perpetration of witchcraft. Eventually she confesses guilt and raves wildly about her dealings with the Devil. The judges appoint six physicians to assess her sanity; they find her *compos mentis*. The court orders her execution.

On her way to the gallows Goodwife Glover declares bitterly that the children will not be cured, for "others had a hand in it as well." And, in fact, the fits suffered by Martha and young John increase immediately thereafter. Winter begins, and suspicion shifts to another woman of the neighborhood. However, the new suspect dies suddenly, before she can be brought to trial. At last the children show marked improvement, and by spring they are virtually their former selves. Meanwhile a triumphant Cotton Mather is working long and late in his study to complete a book that will soon be published under the title *Memorable Providences, Relating to Witchcrafts and Possessions.* A central chapter presents some carefully selected "examples," and includes the events in which Mather himself has so recently participated. The Goodwin children will be leading characters in a local best-seller.

Goodwife Glover was relatively rare, among those accused of witchcraft in early New England, in confessing guilt. Only at Salem did any considerable number choose to convict themselves, and there, it seemed, confession was the strategy of choice if one wished to avoid the gallows. Were Goody Glover's admissions, in effect, forced out of her? Was she perhaps seriously deranged (the opinion of the court-appointed physicians notwithstanding)? Did she truly believe herself guilty? Had she, in fact, sought to invoke the power of the Devil, by stroking poppets with her spittle—or whatever?

There is no way now to answer such questions, for the evidence comes almost entirely through persons who believed, and prosecuted, the charges against her. It does seem likely, in a society where virtually everyone accepted the reality of witchcraft, that at least a few persons would have tried to practice it. In a sense, however, it no longer matters whether specific individuals were guilty as charged. What does matter is that many of them were believed guilty, and that this belief was itself efficacious. As anthropologists have observed in cultures around the world, people who think themselves bewitched are vulnerable to all manner of mischance. They blunder into "accidents"; they lose their effectiveness in work and social relations; at least occasionally they sicken and die.

These patterns of belief and behavior will receive extended consideration below.[11] The resultant "cases"—i.e. occasions when action was taken *against* witchcraft—are summarized here in a preliminary way. As Higginson implied, they were generally of limited scope—with "only one or two persons" accused—and "quickly over." At least the trial proceedings would be quick; often enough there was a prelude, and an aftermath, lasting considerably longer. Before there was a witch there must be victims and accusers. (In some instances the victims *were* the accusers; in others they were different people joined by bonds of family or friendship.) Private suspicion would lead first to *in*formal efforts of redress: by physicians, by ministers, and possibly by local adepts in counter-magic. Precisely because they were informal, these endeavors left comparatively few traces for a historian to follow; he can establish their existence, and feel their importance, without fully grasping their substantive contours. Occasionally (perhaps often?) suspicion of witchcraft led no further. But there was, of course, another alternative—litigation in the courts. When this step was taken, witchcraft became an official, and fully public, affair. And because the courts kept written records, it is possible even now to scrutinize the particulars.

Witchcraft was a capital crime in every one of the New England colonies, as it had been in Old England from long before.[12] The crime was defined as "solemn compaction or conversing with the Devil" (in the Fundamental Orders of Plymouth Colony), as "fellowship by covenant with a familiar spirit" (in the "laws of judgement" of the first settlers of Southampton, Long Island), or simply as "giving entertainment to Satan" (in a common form of indictment).[13] Interestingly, the statutes stressed the bare fact of diabolical connection, without reference to the use of such connection in causing harm. In practice, however, there *must* be harm—enough to warrant the effort and expense of a formal proceeding. Thus witch trials began with a complaint by (or on behalf of) the supposed victims.

Complaint led next to a gathering of evidence at the local level. Most commonly, this process had two parts: the taking of sworn depositions from qualified witnesses, and an "examination" of the accused by community officials. Once gathered, the material was forwarded to those higher courts which alone held authority to try capital cases. Henceforth procedure was strictly prescribed and scrupulously observed: indictment by a grand jury; full consideration of the written evidence (and, whenever possible, a personal reaffirmation of testimony by the deponents themselves); verdict by a special "jury of trials"; sentencing by the magistrates. Some features of witch trials seem highly repugnant today—for example, the use of elaborate and intimate body-searches for "witches' teats" (nipple-like growths thought to permit the suckling of satanic "imps" and "familiars"). But in the context of the times such procedures were not extraordinary. Contrary to popular belief, physical torture was *not* used to extract confessions.[14] Testimony was taken on both sides, and character evidence favorable to the defendant was not uncommon. Guilt was never a foregone conclusion; indeed, many juries seemed reluctant to convict. And when they did vote a conviction, the magistrates might decide to intercede, by withholding "consent" to the verdict, overturning it on technical grounds, or sending the jurymen back for additional deliberation.[15]

As noted, all such proceedings were written down. A good many of the trial records have since disappeared, but from those that survive one can estimate the scale—the *quantity*—of witchcraft in early New England. Excluding Salem, the total of cases through the end of the seventeenth century was 93.[16] This figure divides almost evenly between the two leading areas of settlement—with 50 in Massachusetts (including Plymouth and what would later become Maine and New Hampshire), and 43 in Connecticut (including what was at first the separate colony of New Haven). In all instances it is possible to discover at least the filing of a formal complaint; unfortunately, in some, little or nothing can be learned of subsequent developments. Court records also disclose another category relevant to the present study: civil suits for slander, where the substance was allegations of witchcraft. (In effect, these were witchcraft cases with the roles of plaintiff and defendant turned around.) Here the total is 26, 17 from Massachusetts, 8 from Connecticut, and 1 from Rhode Island. Thus, when both categories are added together, there are more than a hundred cases with a direct claim to attention. The outcomes of these cases (in so far as known) cover a broad range. A clear majority were acquittals of one sort or another; however, 16 "witches" (5 in Massachusetts, 11 in Connecticut) were found guilty and put to death. A handful of additional convictions were reversed by the magistracy; still other convicts, at least a few, managed to escape before sentence could be passed or carried out.

In order to have a final picture of all New England witchcraft in the seventeenth century the results of the Salem trials must, of course, be counted in.[17] And this brings the totals to 234 "cases" (indictments and/or complaints filed) and 36 executed "witches." The figures permit comparison of witchcraft—or, rather, concern with witchcraft—in New and Old England. To be sure, allowance must be made for differences of population, differences in the time-periods covered, and generally incomplete data. Still, the comparison is worth making, if only by way of approximation. Alan Macfarlane's careful study of witchcraft in the county of Essex during the Tudor-Stuart era provides one standard of measure. Over a span of 120 years, Macfarlane found, the roughly 100,000 people of Essex produced some 650 indictments for witchcraft, resulting in 74 known executions.[18] When the standard is widened to include England as a whole, the numbers become less firm. C. L. Ewen, an early and important laborer in this field, concluded that the total of executions for the whole country was something under a thousand.[19]

Table 1.   Witchcraft cases: Old vs. New England

	Years Covered	Popula- tion	Indict- ments	Execu- tions	Annual rates (per 100,000 pop.) Ind.	Ex.
England	1542–1736	4,000,000				
Ewen est.			—	1,000	—	0.13
Macfarlane est.			2,000	300	0.26	0.04
Essex co.	1560–1680	100,000	650	74	5.42	0.62
New England	1630–1700	50,000	234	36	6.69	1.03

Note: The figures for England are derived from C. L. Ewen, *Witch Hunting and Witch Trials* (London, 1929) and A. D. J. Macfarlane, *Witchcraft in Tudor and Stuart England* (London, 1970). The population estimate of 4 million for England as a whole is a very rough "average"—between the lower numbers of the start of the period (mid-sixteenth century) and the higher ones at the end (early eighteenth century). The Essex estimate of 100,000 is taken directly from Macfarlane (p. 8). The New England figure of 50,000 is reached by another effort of averaging (between a low of 10,000–20,000 in the 1630s and a high of almost 100,000 at the end of the century). It hardly needs saying that this makes a crude sort of numbers-game; but as a way of obtaining *gross* rates of witch-hunting, it should be admissible.

Macfarlane, by revising and refining Ewen's data and melding them to his own, suggests "a total of 2000 persons tried . . . and some 300 execu- tions."[20] These estimates may be taken as upper and lower bounds for the actual totals; both are presented in the accompanying table.

Again, it is necessary to acknowledge the limitations of the data, and thus of the comparisons themselves. But from the two columns of "annual rates" this much seems clear: New England was at least as active as Old England in finding and prosecuting witches—and prob- ably a good deal more so. Interestingly, the figures look most nearly equivalent when New England is matched with the county of Essex alone.   Essex was beyond doubt a center of witch-hunting within the mother country; and Essex supplied a disproportionately large comple- ment of settlers for the new colonies across the sea. The linkage is sug- gestive, to say the least.

New England witchcraft invites comparison with still other parts of the contemporaneous world. The numbers become increasingly prob- lematic the farther afield one looks; but surely witch-hunting was *more* common—and far more devastating—in many of the German states, in the Swiss Confederation, in France, and perhaps in Scotland.[21] On the other hand, it appears to have been less common in Italy, in Spain, and in the Low Countries.[22] And it was downright *un*common in other parts of British America. A few full-dress trials, occasional slander suits, no executions whatsoever—thus the record of the southern and middle colonies.[23] In sum: if one imagines a spectrum of premodern communities, arrayed from the most to the least deeply preoccupied with witchcraft, early New England holds an intermediate position. To this should be added an important qualifier about *time*: New England's contribution to witchcraft history came relatively late. Its earliest cases coincided with the last real peak of English witch-hunting, and Salem was virtually the *finale* for "panic witchcraft" anywhere in the West.

But quantitative summary carries us only across the surface of our subject. The *qualities* of witchcraft are the heart of the story. In one broad aspect they are everywhere similar: they express a tendency to "project," to "scapegoat," to extrude and expel that which individuals (or groups) define as bad. The tendency is transcultural. (Indeed, one might almost call it universal, by including a good many settings where witches are known by another name.) The content, however, is highly specific to particular times and places. Diversity is the rule in the fantasies, the generative circumstances, the contingent values, the interpersonal structures—which support and reflect any given "system" of witchcraft belief.

Precisely because the data are so richly variegated, there is no single method of arranging them for cultural analysis. The questions they invite, the answers they may (with effort and luck) be made to yield, are of many sorts. A fundamental divider splits virtually the entire range, into "sociological" and "psychological" sections.[24] And both of these have their subsections. Moreover, when time and change are figured in, there are still more permutations. Some studies deliberately narrow the field, pursuing one pathway and one goal to the exclusion of all the others. But the present work, for better or worse, assays a multidimensional approach.

Part One offers a sampling, and summary, of witchcraft *biography*. The central figures are the "witches" themselves. A pair of life-histories (Chapters 1 and 2) are presented in detail; Chapter 3 attempts a group-portrait or profile. The organizing questions are those of behavior, and character, and developmental sequence. How were individual New Englanders recruited for the role of witch? Or—to put the matter somewhat differently—what sorts of people were most vulnerable to accusations of witchcraft? Did the accused display common attributes of age, sex, marital and family status, social position, and so on? In short, this opening section asks *who* the witches were, and *why* they were.

Part Two shifts the focus to victims and accusers of witches, and proceeds chiefly by way of *psychology*. Witch beliefs in general, and witchcraft accusations in particular, are examined in relation to key strands of inner preoccupation. Again, there are two case-studies (Chapters 4 and 5)—one of a single victim, the other of a small group of victims/accusers—followed by an overview of the whole (Chapter 6). Separately and together, the chapters ask why certain persons felt themselves to be targets of witchcraft, and why such feeling was credible to others. The issue here is *motive*, in a highly personal sense. What sorts of internal distress were liable to prompt accusations of witchcraft? And why did the substance of accusation take one form rather than another? What indeed does witchcraft study reveal about the deeper levels of experience—about emotions, drives, unconscious pressures and conflicts —in New Englanders at large?

Parts One and Two are centered on individual persons (or *the* individual as a generalized type), whereas the later sections describe communities. Part Three, organized under the general rubric of *sociology*, relates witchcraft to the shapes and structures of group-life in early New England. Seen from this vantage point, witchcraft cases formed an integral part of social experience. They expressed, and epitomized, recurrent lines of tension in the group. They might even perform "functions" for the group—sharpening its boundaries, reinforcing its values, and deepening the loyalty of its membership. Thus Chapters 7 and 8 present two separate communities closely involved with a witch trial. And Chapter 9, another overview, addresses the same themes in a more comprehensive fashion. Succinctly put, this part asks what forces and features of community life were liable to support—and, in some degree, to generate—specific projects of witch-hunting.

When all else is done, there remains the important issue of timing. And this is the burden of Part Four—on *history*. Communities are again the chief "unit of study," but now from the standpoint of movement and change. Witchcraft cases were not evenly distributed across the years; rather, they came and went, waxed and waned, in somewhat ragged sequence. To study this sequence over time is to plot a line between recurrent "peaks" (widely bruited suspicion, formal trial proceedings) and "valleys" (intervals when concern with witchcraft lessened). Thus Chapters 10 and 11 unfold a pair of "community histories," with witchcraft and other elements of local experience at least partially joined. The latter is, of course, a crucial point—i.e. *which* other elements, and *what* manner of joining. Chapter 12 explores the same theme for whole colonies or regions, and broaches the largest, most difficult historical problem about witchcraft: its decreasing salience after the seventeenth century. Part Four, in sum, asks why witchcraft cases occurred in certain times, and not in others.

Biography, psychology, sociology, history: four corners of one scholar's compass, four viewpoints overlooking a single field of past experience. Each captures part, but not all, of the whole. There is overlap, to be sure, and some redundancy. The route from one point to the next is never smooth; the pace is slow; the process, inherently toilsome. Yet the field itself is studded with luminous nuggets of information. To see all this from *different* sides is to move at least some way toward full and final comprehension.

ONE
Biography

"If ever there were witches, men and women in covenant with the Devil, here are multitudes in New England."

The Rev. Samuel Parris (1692)

1

"A Desolate Condition"

As the witchcraft drama of 1692 moved outward from its initial setting in Salem Village, one of the new characters added to the cast was an Ipswich woman named Rachel Clinton. Hers was not an especially conspicuous role, but she did suffer arrest, trial, conviction, and imprisonment for a period of several months. She regained her freedom only as part of the general reprieve of January 1693.

A variety of Ipswich residents were summoned to give sworn depositions against her; three of these have survived.[1] Mary Fuller testified about a recent occasion when "Rachel Clinton came to our house and charged me with raising of lies of her." A heated argument had developed—in the midst of which came news that a girl in a neighboring house (belonging to the deponent's brother) had "fallen down dead . . . as she, the said Rachel, passed by." This report proved exaggerated, but the girl "continued for the space of three hours" to be unable to move or speak. At length Mary Fuller asked her to "hold up her hand if Rachel was the cause of it, and she did. And when she could speak, she said, 'a woman with a white cap passed by and struck me on the forehead.'"

Another witness, Thomas Boreman, described a disturbance of some time previous in the Ipswich meeting-house. "Some women of worth and quality" had accused Rachel Clinton of "hunching them with her elbow" as they went to their seats for Sunday services, and had asked Boreman to refer the matter to the town selectmen. Boreman did as requested; then, while riding home the same night, he encountered a strange animal which appeared at first "like a cat" and then "something like a little dog." Further along, he noticed "on my right hand . . . a great turtle, that moved as fast as I rode." At this point he "thought of Rachel Clinton [and] the little creature and the turtle vanished away."

A third deponent, William Baker, recalled a time "about ten years ago" when a quantity of beer had mysteriously disappeared in the house of "my master Rust." On the day it was brewed "Rachel Clinton came there, and met with some small affront"; immediately thereafter "the said Rachel went backward and forward six or seven times up and down the lane that leads to our house." When Goodwife Rust "went down to see whether the beer worked or not," she found the barrel empty—"and neither was there any appearance of wet upon the floor." Subsequent usage showed the barrel to be entirely leak-proof, so the various people involved drew what was (for them) the only plausible conclusion.

These materials demonstrate that neighborhood suspicion of Rachel Clinton long antedated her trial in connection with the Salem outbreak. And there is further evidence bearing on the same point. A stray document, recently located in the manuscript holdings of a university library, strongly implies an *earlier* trial of Rachel Clinton. Headed simply "Witchcraft 1687," it reads as follows:

> The deposition of Thomas Knowlton, aged 40 years, sayeth that about three weeks ago [when] Mr. John Rogers and his wife were gone to Boston . . . Rachel, the wife of Lawrence Clinton, that is now suspected to be a witch, went to Mr. Rogers' house, and told Mr. Rogers' maid that she must have some meat and milk. And the said Rachel went into several rooms of the said house. . . . And when she saw me come in, she, the said Rachel, went away, scolding and railing, calling me . . . "hellhound" and "whoremasterly rogue," and said I was a limb of the devil. And she said she had rather see the Devil than see me. . . . (Samuel Ayers and Thomas Smith, tailor, can testify to the same language that Rachel used or called the said Knowlton.) And after this the said Rachel took up a stone and threw it toward me, and it fell short three or four yards off from me . . . and so came rolling to me, and just touched the toe of my shoe. And presently my great toe was in a great rage, as if the nail were held up by a pair of pincers. . . . And further the said Thomas Knowlton testified and saith that about three months ago my daughter Mary did wake and cried out in a dreadful manner that she was pricked of her side with pins, as she thought. Being asked who pricked her, she said she could not tell. And when she was out of her fits, I . . . asked her whether she gave Rachel any

pins; and she said she gave Rachel about seven. And after this she had one fit more of being pricked.[2]

The various testimonies presented so far recount five separate episodes, involving dozens of people, and spaced in time through a full decade. Evidently, then, Rachel Clinton's reputation for witchcraft was both widespread and enduring. The historian is bound to inquire about the source of such a reputation; and, in doing so, he commits himself to a painstaking search through masses of local and genealogical records. But in this case the palm is distinctly worth the effort. For the story of Rachel Clinton has a coherent plot-line, a wealth of vivid detail—and not a little pathos. It would be unreasonable to ask for more, in the reconstruction of obscure lives from three centuries ago.

In the spring of 1635 a ship named *The Planter* prepared to sail from London for New England. Among its passengers was the family of one Richard Haffield, "currier," age fifty-four. Before departure Haffield presented a certificate signed by the minister and mayor of his home-town—Sudbury, in county Suffolk—attesting to his "conformity to the orders and discipline of the Church of England."[3] The certificate also contained the names of his wife Martha, age forty-two, and his five daughters—Mary, seventeen; Sarah, fourteen; Martha, eight; Rachel, six; and Ruth, three.

Here the documentary record of Rachel Clinton, née Haffield, begins; we learn at once the approximate date, and the likely place, of her birth. To this can be added certain valuable details about her family and childhood, gleaned from evidence given years later in legal proceedings over the settlement of her parents' estate. Witnesses testified, from personal knowledge, that her mother, Martha Haffield, had been a "maid-servant . . . about the time she was married"; that Martha's own parents (named Mansfield) "were very poor and were not able to give her any portion that was known to their neighbors"; that Richard "had a son and two daughters by a former wife" named Judith; that Martha bore Richard's three youngest children; and that she (Martha) was "very abusive and unreasonable" toward her stepdaughters (Richard's surviving children by Judith), "both in want of necessary apparel and other ways, as also in many hard words and blows."[4]

These genealogical particulars may be hard to follow (see chart on p. 23), but their thematic import seems clear. Little Rachel passed her early years in a rather turbulent and fractured household. The father, in remarrying, had chosen someone of lesser status. The mother apparently recognized this discrepancy, resented it, and took it out on the children of the socially superior first wife; as a result the family group was sharply divided. To this awkward situation the mother may have brought some personal pathology all her own. We are told that her neighbors were inclined to "wonder" at her "strange and forward behavior"; we know, too, that in later life she was officially judged insane.[5]

Was it, perhaps, the father's role to mute the tension which infected this entire *ménage*? If so, his death in 1639 was a loss of multiple dimensions. His will can be read as an attempt to head off conflict among his heirs. The children of his two wives were mentioned under separate headings, as recipients of specific properties; the basic portion for each daughter was set at £30.[6] Much later, an old friend would recall the deathbed scene: Richard Haffield, "being moved . . . to give his two eldest daughters something more than he did his other daughters, which he had by this wife, he answered, 'I dare not; I have given them all portions alike, and what is left [is] to be divided among them.' "[7] Yet this even-handed policy was of no avail in what followed; court records show that Haffield's estate was still being litigated more than fifty years after his passing!

It was, apparently, a considerable estate—by one account, "above £500." When Haffield came to New England, he brought with him both "goods and ready money, and afterwards he sold a good estate in land, left him by their grandfather."[8] His initial holdings in Ipswich were well above the average grant for early settlers there.[9] These facts need emphasis, because the subsequent story of the Haffield family, and especially of Rachel, is a story of declining fortunes. From comfortable beginnings, events moved them fitfully down the social scale. In Rachel's own case the end-point was deep and embittered poverty.

The process was a gradual one, however, and there is no evidence of hardship in the years immediately following Richard Haffield's death. It appears that his widow managed to conserve the family resources, letting some of her land out to tenants, spinning cloth for occasional sales, and asserting the rights of "commonage" that accrued to all of the early settlers.[10] When, in 1653, the youngest Haffield daughter (Ruth) was summoned to court for "excess in apparel," she was discharged on proof "that her mother was worth two hundred pounds."[11] This action is interesting for two reasons. The culture at large affirmed a scale of social distinctions, marked by laws about the clothing appropriate to different statuses. The Haffields dressed in the manner of the wealthy— and, as the court concluded, did so legitimately. On the other hand, some of their neighbors must have questioned their claims to this pref-

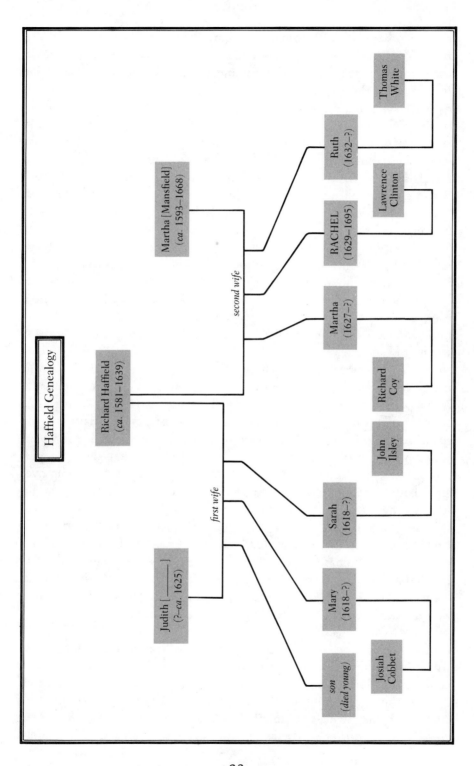

Haffield Genealogy

Richard Haffield (*ca.* 1581–1639)

first wife — Judith [————] (?–*ca.* 1625)

second wife — Martha [Mansfield] (*ca.* 1593–1668)

son (*died young*)

Mary (1618–?) — Josiah Cobbet

Sarah (1618–?) — John Ilsley

Martha (1627–?) — Richard Coy

RACHEL (1629–1695) — Lawrence Clinton

Ruth (1632–?) — Thomas White

23

erence; otherwise Ruth would not have been "presented" in the first place. Thus the episode has an ambiguous meaning, at once confirming the family's original position, and suggesting that there was now room for doubt on the matter.

We should notice, in passing, one event that did *not* occur in the period following Richard Haffield's death: his widow did not remarry. It was very much the norm in colonial New England that men and women who lost their spouses should marry again after a "decent" interval. This was true for people of varying ages (including some in their seventies and eighties), and especially so for the wealthy. Cultural tradition and practical circumstance converged in discouraging the maintenance of households headed by a single adult.[12] Martha Haffield was forty-six when her husband died, and her control of his estate should have made her an attractive prospect. Yet she remained a widow until her own death almost thirty years later. Perhaps this was a reflection on her personal qualities, but we have no way to be sure. It meant, however, that Rachel passed her later childhood in a household without a father, indeed without males of any age. In this respect her experience was highly atypical.

Further evidence on the family's history in the 1640s and 1650s is extremely limited. On one occasion the widow Haffield was brought to court, tried, and convicted of "taking the name of God to witness to a lie, first affirming to John Fuller and his wife that her daughter did strike her, and after[ward] denying to them [that] she said so."[13] Here was a hint of continuing tension within the household—though surely no more than a hint. Perhaps, after 1645, the total situation improved since both stepdaughters were married by then. This reduced the household to the widow and her three natural children. In time, of course, the latter would also reach a marriageable age. Martha (eldest of the three) became the wife of Richard Coy in 1650, and Ruth (the youngest) married Thomas White in 1654. Rachel, however, remained single for another twelve years—if only one could learn why! She and her aging mother continued to live together, in a "little house" on land "near the mill-dam" purchased from the town of Ipswich in 1655.[14]

At this point the narrative must jump ahead a full decade. Beginning in rapid sequence after 1665, events engulfed the Haffields in bitter controversy. The pivotal developments were: (1) the widow's certified insanity, and eventually her death; (2) Rachel's belated marriage; (3) a protracted struggle over the family inheritance. Luckily, there are copious records of all this, records which illuminate both structural and emotional features of the unfolding sequence. Long rent by internal tensions, the Haffield family now exploded in conflict. No one emerged unscathed from this chain of domestic fission, but the injury to Rachel was particularly severe. In a real sense she would never recover.

There is reason to think that the mental condition of widow Haffield had deteriorated gradually over a period of several years. In May 1666 the local magistrates, meeting at Ipswich, made temporary provision to deal with the matter. A court order directed that Thomas White, husband of the widow's daughter Ruth, receive the rents from her farm and apply them to her "maintenance," and that two of her neighbors provide "so much of linen or other goods as she needs for her present supply."[15] Several months later the magistrates extended and clarified these measures. Declaring the widow officially *non compos mentis*, they gave Thomas White sole charge of her affairs, "to be as a guardian to her, . . . and to receive and recover her estate, . . . and to act and do for her as she might have done being *compos mentis*."[16] White wasted no time in acting on his new responsibilities. Scarcely two months had passed when he, as "guardian to Martha Haffield, widow," brought suit against one Robert Cross, "for withholding or refusing to deliver £21 or thereabouts in gold, which was illegally taken from the said Haffield and conveyed to the said Cross by Lawrence Clinton for his time."[17] The resultant litigation continued for nearly three years, and eventually reached the highest court in the colony.

The dispute revolved around the following events. In 1665 (or perhaps a little earlier) a young man named Lawrence Clinton appeared in Ipswich as a servant to Robert Cross.[18] A liaison developed between Clinton and Rachel Haffield, and soon enough there were plans for marriage. Since Clinton had contracted to serve Cross for an additional three and one-half years, he was obliged to offer compensation "for his time." Clinton himself had no ready cash, but his fiancée did. Thanks to her, Cross received the sum of £21, and released his servant forthwith. It seems, however, that questions were raised about the legality of these arrangements, and so magistrate William Denison summoned all of the principals to his house for a public "examination." Memories would differ, later on, as to what precisely was said at this meeting, and evidently no written record was kept. But in any case a Clinton-Haffield wedding followed soon thereafter. At the age of thirty-six Rachel was finally married—and to a man fourteen years her junior![19]

The match would doubtless have provoked comment on this latter account alone, but the payment for the groom's "freedom" was the real sticking point. There were two opposite versions of what had happened.

According to Cross and Clinton, Rachel had volunteered to pay, out of funds that were fully her own. Cross had been somewhat reluctant to agree to the deal, "for a servant was of more concernment to him . . . than the money," but yielded eventually to Clinton's "very urgent" pleadings. Thereupon he told Clinton: " 'I will go with you to Rachel Haffield and know whether you came by this money honestly.' Which accordingly we did. And my wife told my master that he need not question me about it, for she gave it to me to buy my time of him, and that it was her own."[20]

Rachel's right to dispose of this money was, in fact, a critical issue, and the defense sought to deal with it in a variety of ways. Several witnesses testified about the earlier "examination" before magistrate Denison: for example, "This deponent . . . heard [Rachel] say that the money which she gave Lawrence (now her husband) was her own. . . . And being demanded where she had the money [from], she said that her mother gave it [to] her."[21] Others recalled the widow Haffield as saying explicitly that "she had given [Rachel] all her money long ago, to dispose of as she sees occasion."[22] There was also evidence of a more circumstantial kind. The Haffields' tenant reported that he had regularly made his rental payments to Rachel.[23] According to another man, "it was commonly received that Rachel had the disposing of all her mother's affairs," and, on specific occasions, the widow "was denied that which she desired, except she would bring her daughter Rachel to engage for it."[24] This, presumably, was the pattern interrupted by the court order of 1666 giving official powers of guardianship to Thomas White. A final part of the evidence concerned Rachel's own reaction to all this. One man recalled an impromptu visit to her house, when

> I found her very sad, and weeping, and crying. And she said . . .
> "my brother [in-law] White goes about to undo me every way."
> First, she said he would have had her . . . [say] that she stole the
> money, which was her own. And when he could not make her say
> so, then would have had her . . . [say] that her husband did steal
> it . . . "which, if I had [done], I must have lied against my knowl-
> edge. But he [i.e. Thomas White] is a cheating rogue, and [he]
> goes about to undo me. He keeps my portion from me, and strives
> to get all that I have."[25]

The case for the defense was necessarily elaborate, because of one vital gap in the evidence: there was no written deed of gift to Rachel from her mother. By the same token, the task of the plaintiff seemed comparatively easy. Perhaps because he was confident of a favorable judgment, Thomas White brought few witnesses and concentrated on the single question of Rachel's right to the money. To the defense account of the Denison hearing was counterposed the following: "Rachel Haffield acknowledged . . . that the gold which she gave to Lawrence Clinton was not given her by her mother; but it being under her own custody, she thought that she might dispose of it according to her pleasure." On a different occasion, moreover, the witness had "heard . . . the widow say [that] if her daughter Rachel had disposed of any of her money for her own use, she had stolen it from her; for she never gave her any."[26] This was the extent of the plaintiff's case. Ownership could not be established without a deed, and mere "custody" conferred no right to "dispose of" property.

The local jury accepted this argument, and rendered judgment for the plaintiff, whereupon Cross appealed to the Court of Assistants in Boston.[27] Of this latter action no record survives, but evidently the initial verdict was *reversed*. For within a year Thomas White had reopened the proceedings on a plea of "review."[28] This time the burden of proof had shifted. Most of the evidence from the first trial was presented again, but White added significant new testimony to his side of the case. His aim, very clearly, was to depict the entire sequence as resulting from a deal between Robert Cross and his servant Clinton. In the process, Cross had been substantially enriched, Clinton had obtained his "freedom," and Rachel had served as a witless dupe—or so the argument went.

The Denison hearing figured prominently in this testimony. Just before it began, Rachel had become doubtful about proceeding to marriage ("she feared it would prove an uncomfortable business, and if she had the money again she cared not for the man"); so Cross and his "friends" used the occasion to stiffen her resolve. "Goodman Cross spoke much to the praise of his man, and said he had rich friends in England," and then "urged Rachel to give . . . a peremptory answer whether she would have Lawrence Clinton or not." These tactics offended the magistrate, who "bid them go out of doors and not woo maids in his house," whereupon the struggle was continued elsewhere. Rachel returned with her sister to their mother's house, and shortly thereafter Robert Cross appeared. There was a report (presumably a ruse) that Lawrence had taken ill and wanted Rachel at his side. At first she declined to go, but then changed her mind. "And so at last"—as Ruth White testified— "she was got from me, and was married; and then Goodman Cross came with [Clinton] to my mother's house, and would have had them to take possession of the house, notwithstanding [the fact that] the magistrates had given my husband possession before. And Goodman Cross seemed to me to be the leading man in the whole matter, and . . . the chief instrument to bring it to pass. . . ."[29]

But the most vivid testimony of all came from Rachel herself. Apparently reversing her earlier allegiance, she now flung bitter charges at the Cross family—and at her own husband:

> This deponent sayeth that Robert Cross, Senior, did much solicit me to be married to Lawrence Clinton, and also did labor hard with the worshipful Mr. Symonds to marry us together. He told me that [Clinton] was a man that deserved a maid worth a bushel of gold. And also Robert Cross, Senior, said that he would give me a better portion than ever my father did. And also he sent his son to persuade me to be married to Lawrence Clinton. Further this deponent sayeth that Lawrence Clinton said that he had an uncle worth thousands, and he would make him his heir, and that he had fifty pounds in gold to come in Capt. Pearce's [ship], and that he had a mother at Boston. And also he told me a thousand lies more to delude me, so as to be married to him and to cause me to put money into his hands. Further, this deponent sayeth that Robert Cross, Senior, threatens this deponent that in case the money now in controversy were taken from him again, then he would sell her and her husband Clinton for servants.[30]

These testimonies notwithstanding, the jury sided with Cross. White appealed to the General Court, but eventually dropped the case short of a definitive ruling.[31]

In fact, the suit against Cross was just a limited setback for Thomas White, for he was still guardian of widow Haffield and the bulk of her property. He continued to act vigorously in exercising this authority. According to Rachel, the "small cottage" in which she and her mother had lived for years was abruptly sold on White's orders, their "household stuff" confiscated, and the widow herself "translated to the said White's, where . . . she is in as bad a condition as before."[32] Martha Haffield did not long survive this "translation." A brief notice in the "Wenham Burials" recorded her passing on March 22, 1668.[33] With this the struggle among her children and heirs entered a climactic phase.

The stakes remained high, by any standard. The family farm alone was assessed at £300. The widow's personal property, which included such items as silver spoons, brass kettles, and elaborate linen goods, came to another £50.[34] From this total, however, Thomas White extracted various sums against the expenses of his guardianship: "£22 per year for the keeping and attending of his mother[-in-law]"; £12 in court costs "in suing for the gold"; £1. 10s. for "fetching her goods to Wenham" (i.e. to White's own house); £2. 10s. in burial charges[35]—to mention only a few. A will, written some six years earlier when the widow was still of sound mind, spelled out her wishes as to the "unencumbered" parts of her estate. Rachel was to have ownership of the farm, provided she would share the income (earned from rental) with her sisters Ruth White and Martha Coy. Personal belongings were similarly divided. Meanwhile the two stepsisters—Mary Cobbett and Sarah Ilsley, children of Richard Haffield by his first wife—were cut off with a mere ten shillings apiece.[36]

Predictably, there began a new round of legal proceedings. Carefully pursuing a two-sided approach—suits in the county court, and petitions to the General Court—the Cobbetts and Ilsleys sought to break the will as written. They had never received so much as "one penny" beyond the £30 portions expressly specified in their father's will; yet an equitable division of his property would have yielded a much larger sum.[37] Apparently their stepmother, as the official "executrix," had simply declined to probate the will for all these years, and had now effectively excluded them from her own line of inheritance. This seemed all the more unjust, because—so the plaintiffs contended—a large part of the estate had come into the family from *their own* mother. Their claims were considered, and reconsidered—but were rejected each time.[38] Principles of equity notwithstanding, the courts find no breach of law here. The estate was reserved, then, for the widow's own daughters, and its precise disposition thereafter is not recorded. However, there is reason to think that Thomas White retained overall control. We know the court named him as his mother-in-law's executor. And we know, too, that in 1695—White having died, and the task of "administration" being *still incomplete*—his wife Ruth was appointed to succeed him.[39]

This was, in truth, the *finale* in a lengthy familial saga reaching back to Richard Haffield's death more than half a century before. There were many individual participants, and several different sideplots, along the way; but, seen whole, the outline of events is clear. The prize sought from all sides was Richard's considerable wealth. In the first phase his widow and executrix, Martha [Mansfield] Haffield, managed to shut out his two eldest daughters. A field of five potential claimants was thereby reduced to three. Following Martha's death, Thomas White used a similar position (and the same strategy of delay) to win special advantage for *one* of the remaining three. Thus in 1695, having outlived all of her siblings, and with the estate somewhat shrunken but still largely intact, Ruth [Haffield] White emerged as her father's principal legatee.

Rachel Clinton was, of course, an unfortunate loser in all this. It is not clear that she ever received her rightful inheritance.[40] On the contrary, we find her, at about the time of her mother's death, beseeching the court for aid, "being destitute of money and friends and skill in matters of law." Her petition made a long and sorrowful tale. Her "portion" from her father had been wholly withheld by her brothers-in-law, "upon pretence of improvement." The house in which she had lived was gone, and likewise many of her belongings. As a result, she had "neither home nor hearth to shelter herself, not so much as from the extremity of the weather, unless by intrusion into . . . [Thomas] White's family, where she hath little welcome." She needed immediate "relief," so that she would "not be forced to wander from house to house like an Indian or brute beast."[41]

Rachel's petition also made reference to her "carriage [i.e. conduct] . . . in respect of some late passages," which she attributed to the "distracting" effects of her current situation. In fact, one of these "passages" has a place of its own in the Court Records (March 26, 1667): "Rachel Clinton, complaining to Mr. Symonds that John Clarke had lain with her, and upon her trial denying it, the sentence of the Court is [that] she shall be whipped."[42] Which was the truth—her initial complaint or her subsequent denial? Either way, the matter reflected poorly on Rachel. And there is a further question to ask: where was Lawrence Clinton in all this? Why was he nowhere mentioned, either in his wife's petition for "relief" or as part of her previous troubles at court? Moreover, why was he obliged (immediately following Martha Haffield's death) to surrender "all his rights and interest that he . . . may have by her will."[43] Had he perhaps quarreled with Rachel and left her (or *vice versa*)?

Some evidence from two years later weighs in *favor* of this probability. In the summer of 1670 Lawrence was presented, tried, and convicted by the court "for attempting to abuse or ravish Mary Knowlton." At the same time he was "enjoined to allow his wife two shillings per week towards her maintenance, and to carry it himself to her, and, further, . . . to live with his wife, as duty binds him, or at least to lodge with her one night in a week."[44] But to "enjoin" was one thing, to enforce was another; and during the next several years the court was obliged again and again to attend to this matter. In 1671 Rachel complained that her husband was not providing regular maintenance. The court sentenced him to prison "till he hath paid her 40 shillings for times past," while ordering Rachel herself "to entertain him as her husband when he comes to her."[45] In 1672 Lawrence was presented for "not living with his wife . . . according to law."[46] (He was also tried, by the same court, "for oppression in his labor, in taking 16 shillings for three days and [one] half work at Mr. Baker's house, painting a room, and receiving his dinner every day.")[47] In 1674 there was a new presentment, of both spouses, for not living together, and Rachel complained once more that her husband "hath not provided for her."[48] And in 1676: precisely the same sequence yet again.[49]

There was still more to come. In September 1676 the court convicted a maidservant named Mary Greeley of "committing fornication with Lawrence Clinton."[50] According to the testimony of her friends, Greeley had said "that she was afraid that she was with child . . . because . . . Lawrence Clinton had lain with her upon a sabbath day when her master and dame was gone to meeting."[51] The Ipswich Town Records noted the subsequent realization of her fears: "Jacob, son of Mary Greeley, born the first of April, 1677."[52] The court affirmed paternity to Lawrence and ordered him to "pay 20 pence per week in corn toward the keeping of the child";[53] thenceforth the boy was known as Jacob Clinton. By the succeeding autumn Lawrence's ardor had found a new object. Accused of fornicating with one Mary Wooden, he "confessed the fact in open court"; both parties were sentenced to be "severely whipped."[54]

Shortly thereafter Rachel petitioned for divorce. The court "could not grant it"—whereupon Rachel asked for new assurances of her "maintenance," and the court ordered "the said Lawrence to pay her 50 shillings upon demand."[55] Meanwhile Rachel was pursuing extra-marital interests of her own. She and a certain John Ford were imprisoned on "suspicion of uncleanness and other evil practices." Witnesses (including Lawrence Clinton!) reported finding the two of them together in a compromising situation: Ford "in bed, [with] his upper clothes off," and Rachel standing nearby. They denied having been intimate—"sometimes they sat up; sometimes she went to bed, so he sat up in the chair; and sometimes he went to bed, and she sat up"—admitting only to "unlawful familiarity." The court bound them to good behavior, and ordered them "not to come to each other by night or day unless in the company of some other discreet person, under penalty of being imprisoned."[56]

Perhaps this order was effective; there is no evidence of any further

liaison between Rachel and John Ford. Indeed there is nothing to connect her in a friendly way with *any* other member of the community.
From henceforth Rachel was entirely alone. The court abandoned its
long-standing efforts to force Lawrence to live with her, or even to give
her regular support. A terse directive in 1681 put an end to her oft-
repeated complaints: "Rachel Clinton . . . desiring that her husband
provide for her, was allowed 20 shillings—she to demand no more of
him."[57] Perhaps, this once, Lawrence was willing to pay.

In the same year Rachel renewed her efforts to obtain a divorce. A
plea filed with the General Court in Boston recounted her plight with
the usual sort of pathetic detail: her early prospects of holding a "good
estate"; the "fair promises" of Lawrence to be "a loyal and faithful husband to her"; his subsequent "wasting" of her property; his readiness to
"break the bonds of wedlock" by wooing "a young woman, whom he got
with child . . . and [afterward] married . . . at Providence"; her currently
"desolate condition"; her "daily fears" that Lawrence might try to take
what few and meagre possessions she still retained. The court was always loath to allow a divorce, but in this case the circumstances must
have seemed overwhelming. In October 1681 Rachel's petition was
quietly granted.[58]

And what of Lawrence during this same period? Apparently he remained in Ipswich until about 1680; the town had tried, in 1673, "to
give [him] warning that they will not accept him as an inhabitant among
them,"[59] but in 1678 his name appeared on a list of Ipswich men who
had taken the oath of allegiance to the king.[60] He worked here and there
as a day-laborer, and was occasionally in court for minor offenses (fraud,
debt).[61] He continued his relation to Mary Wooden; in 1678 she bore
his second out-of-wedlock child, a son named Lawrence.[62] But not long
thereafter Lawrence and Mary Wooden left Ipswich for good. In
February 1681 they were married at Providence, Rhode Island—even
though (as noted above) Lawrence was still the legal husband of Rachel.
From Providence they moved on to Newport, where Mary had a daughter—and died. Lawrence married yet again (a widow named Morris)
and fathered six more children, most of whom would eventually settle
in Connecticut. From these irregular beginnings sprang a long line of
Clintons, most of them substantial Yankee farmers and professional
people.[63]

If Lawrence paid further heed to Rachel, the fact is not recorded;
almost certainly their divorce broke contact forever. Meantime Rachel
struggled along, however she could. According to local tradition, she
lived her final years in a hut on Hog Island near Ipswich Harbor.[64] She

left occasional traces in the Town Records, appearing sometimes as "Clinton," sometimes as "Haffield," but most often simply as "Rachel."[65] The confusion as to surname, and the familiarity implicit in the use of a given name, marked her as a town fixture. She became, as well, a town charge. The selectmen's account for 1686—to take only one example—included the following entries:

> To Joseph Quilter, for a load of clay
>   for Rachel Clinton .... £oo. 02. oo
>
> To John Newman, for a day's work
>   for Rachel .... oo. 02. 06
>
> To Daniel Ring, for Rachel, for wood
>   and mending her house .... oo. 10. oo
>
> To Philip Fowler, for two days' work
>   he got done for Rachel's house .... oo. 09. oo[66]

And so her life drew near its close. The date of her death does not appear, but on January 7, 1695 administration of her estate was granted to Ruth White of Wenham.[67] There was little to administer except debts—most of which were owed to the Whites in any case.

The witchcraft depositions, presented earlier, record the manifest strain in daily contacts between Rachel Clinton and her fellow townspeople during her later years. Perhaps *they* begrudged her need for public support; perhaps *she* felt that this support was insufficiently generous. Significantly, in at least two instances her supposed witchcraft stemmed from unsuccessful attempts to beg food and/or drink from neighbors. Yet this dependence on public and private charity will not by itself account for Rachel's reputation as a witch. It was only in the context of her whole life-history that her needs assumed a menacing aspect. She was indeed a special sort of beggar. She had belonged to one of the first families of Ipswich—first in both a chronological and a social sense. Years before, the court had affirmed that her sister (thus Rachel as well) was entitled to wear the finery of "gentle" folk. There are, moreover, hints of this theme in the witchcraft testimony itself. Note that Rachel was accused of jostling "some women of worth and quality" as they went to their seats in the meeting-house. Consider, too, that seating arrangements in a New England meeting-house were determined by reference to status; the town saw to it that spatial and social "place" were carefully interconnected. In her younger days Rachel would presumably have joined the "women of worth and quality" near the front. But now?

The begging, and its attendant difficulties, exemplify a larger pattern that lay behind the designation of many supposed witches. What stands out in Rachel's life, virtually from beginning to end, is a series of *profound disturbances in human relationships*. These events deserve a final review. Her experience as a child was very probably marred by the resentments and anxieties of her "strange and forward" mother; within the family a sharp fault-line divided her from her older stepsisters. Her father died when she was only half grown, and her mother never remarried. Rachel herself remained single until virtually middle age. When finally she did marry, her husband seemed a patently inappropriate choice (an indentured servant, very much her junior). Moreover, the match required an extraordinary maneuver whereby *she* paid the full cost of her fiancé's "freedom." This precipitated a bitter family quarrel, which only worsened following her mother's death. As a result Rachel became permanently alienated from her sisters and brothers-in-law. Meanwhile her marriage went rapidly to pieces. She and her husband lived together for no more than a few years, then drifted steadily apart. The courts tried hard to reunite them, and to ensure that Rachel had financial support, but with little apparent result. Lawrence Clinton was repeatedly involved with other women, one of whom he married while still (from a legal standpoint) husband to Rachel. Rachel, too, was suspected of carrying on an extramarital affair. Eventually she obtained a divorce, and from then on lived alone and in poverty. Her relatives took no interest in her plight, so she depended increasingly on public assistance. Evidently, there was no one left for her, no family, no friends; her relations to others had ended uniformly in loss and betrayal and failure.

What was the effect of all this on Rachel's inner life—and outward behavior? Did she not show to the world the character of an embittered, meddlesome, demanding woman—perhaps, in short, the character of a witch? Did she not "scold" and "rail," threaten and fight? Was she not capable of reviling her social betters with epithets like "hellhound" and "whoremasterly rogue," or of deliberately "hunching" them as they moved past her in church? To be fair, this picture was drawn by her neighbors and antagonists, and it may be considerably skewed. Certainly Rachel had another view. Whenever the record allows her to speak for herself, she appears as a pathetic object of misfortune and malevolence —one of life's casualties, a victim.

There is, in any case, no need to choose between these contrasting impressions; *both* expressed the truth of her experience. With Rachel, victim and victimizer were two halves of the same whole. Simply put: events combined against her, depriving her of wealth and dignity, and she responded out of a deep, angry despair. But was there *more* than mere "response" on Rachel's part? Was there also some veiled complicity—such as one often finds in habitual victims? The question must be asked, even though the records will not support an answer. Judgments of this sort are extremely difficult even when face to face with living people, not to mention a historical specimen from three centuries before.

Perhaps, then, Rachel helped to make life happen; still, what sticks in the mind most forcibly is all that happened *to* her. Every culture has its whirlpools of callousness, of cruelty. Most people manage to steer around such places, but, inevitably, a few are pulled into badly exposed positions. So it was in this instance. Beyond all doubt, Rachel Clinton was an easy mark for social predators; it is hard *not* to believe that Robert Cross and Lawrence Clinton plotted to defraud her. Moreover, in the struggles that followed, her own relatives acted no less selfishly. Once the lines were drawn, her situation rapidly became untenable. Caught in the midst of a vicious tug-of-war, reeling first to one side and then to the other, from this point forward she was merely a pawn. Women like Rachel were fitted to the role of "witch" at least in part because they were so profoundly *vulnerable*.

2

"Peace with No Man"

In the long roster of early New Englanders accused of witchcraft, John Godfrey invites attention for one special reason: he was *male*. To be sure, other men were accused at various times (and four or five were executed), but most of them were husbands of female "witches."[1] Thus —given the overall prominence of women in witchcraft cases—it seems probable that the charges against these men arose as a secondary or derivative matter.

But John Godfrey cannot be fitted to this pattern, for he had no witch-wife; in fact, he had no wife at all. What was it that made him suspect anyway? Why should this particular man have been singled out for such special disfavor from virtually all of his masculine peers? Does his career perhaps reflect an intensification of certain themes which, in the lives of women, created a strong presumption of guilt? Is this, in short, an instance of witch-behavior in "pure culture"—or as pure as we are likely to find?

> [William Osgood, of Salisbury, deposed that:] in the year '40, in the month of August, he being then building a barn for Mr. Spencer [and] John Godfrey being then Mr. Spencer's herdsman, he on an evening came to the frame where diverse men were at work and said that he had gotten a new master against the time he had done keeping cows. The said William Osgood asked him who it was. He answered [that] he knew not. He again asked him where he dwelt. He answered [that] he knew not. He asked him what his name was. He answered [that] he knew not. He then said to

him, "How then wilt thou go to him when thy time is out?" He said, "The man will come and fetch me." . . . I asked him, "Hast thou made an absolute bargain?" He answered that a covenant was made [and] he had set his hand to it. He then asked of him whether he had not a counter covenant. Godfrey answered, "No." William Osgood said, "What a mad fellow are thou to make a covenant in this manner." He said, "He's an honest man." "How knowest thou?" said William Osgood. John Godfrey answered, "He looks like one." William Osgood then answered, "I am persuaded thou hast made a covenant with the devil." He then skipped about and said, "I protest, I protest."[2]

This episode, recounted nearly twenty years after the fact, marks the first certain appearance of John Godfrey in New England. The place was Newbury, Massachusetts, then a community barely five years old. The deponent, William Osgood, was a young carpenter and millwright who would later become a founder of the town of Salisbury. "Mr. Spencer" (another John) was a local gentleman and heir to a large estate in Newbury; both Godfrey and Osgood were temporarily in his employ.

Of Godfrey's background and origins nothing definite can be learned. Even the time of his birth is in question. Twice later on, in the course of legal proceedings, he made reference to his age: in 1660 he deposed "aged about 40 years," and in 1661 "aged about 30 years."[3] Imprecision (or ignorance) as to chronology was not unusual among the early New Englanders, but *this* discrepancy seems particularly large.[4] As such, it accords nicely with other will-of-the-wisp elements in Godfrey's personal history. Upon reflection, the first estimate seems far more plausible, since by 1640 Godfrey was established as a "herdsman" and this was normally a job for a young man, not for a boy. Thus 1620 will serve as a best possible approximation of the year of Godfrey's birth.

Actually, there is one very early notation of the name John Godfrey— on a passenger list for the ship *Mary and John*, which left London for New England in March 1634.[5] We cannot be sure that this emigrant and the later "witch" were one and the same, but the probability seems strong; for John Spencer, and others prominent in the founding of Newbury, were also among the passengers for this sailing. Most of the group had come from a tier of counties on or near the south coast of England (Dorsetshire, Somersetshire, Berkshire, Hampshire, and Surrey),[6] and it is tempting to think that John Godfrey's roots were likewise in that part of the country. Perhaps, then, his beginning in New England was as a boy in his mid-teens, fresh from a springtime voyage, unaccompanied by family, and "bound" in service to a gentleman from the region of his birth. If so, it was a beginning that held no forecast of the unusual career that lay ahead.[7]

If the Osgood deposition is creditable, then John Godfrey was suspected of conniving with the Devil at least as early as 1640. There is no other, comparable information from this period, but it is worth noticing the first court cases in which Godfrey joined as a principal. In the summer of 1642 he sued Richard Kent of Newbury for slander, and Kent was found "greatly criminal." In 1649 he won a similar complaint against Richard Jones of Salisbury.[8] Depositions from these cases do not survive, hence the substance of the slander remains unknown. But allegations of witchcraft seem an obvious possibility. At a minimum, such events reveal Godfrey as someone about whom others were tempted to speak in strong and sharply hostile terms.

There were additional cases during the 1640s in which Godfrey appeared as *defendant*: in 1648, for "subborning a witness"; in 1649, for "lying"; again in 1649, for some unspecified charge.[9] Gradually, it appears, his position outside the normative bounds of his community was solidified. Yet for most of the next decade (1650–58) he did not come to court at all. Scattered references in land deeds (and in later legal proceedings) show him moving out of Newbury, and appearing briefly in Rowley, Haverhill, and Andover, but otherwise he left no tracks.[10]

The absence of Godfrey's name from court dockets during this long interval is all the more striking in light of the pattern that developed immediately thereafter. From 1658 until his death in 1675 Godfrey was in court at least once each year, and, in some years, many times. As suit and counter-suit piled one on top of the other, his record of legal actions became extraordinary even by the standards of a highly litigious society. Most of these actions dealt with property—land, money, bonds, wheat, corn, rye, oxen, sheep, cloth—and most involved relatively small values. Nearly all of Godfrey's opponents at court were other Essex County residents, of modest wealth and status. Taken as a whole, the records depict a man continually at odds with his peers, over a host of quite specific, personal, and mundane affairs.

In the spring of 1658 Godfrey lodged a suit for debt—his first of this type—against one Abraham Whitaker of Haverhill, and within months he had begun additional actions against other persons from Haverhill.[11] It appears that these cases were in some way interrelated—and that Godfrey's position was fully supported by the verdicts. Almost immediately, however, the issue of witchcraft was raised—and formally presented to the court. The exact sequence is unclear, but evidently there were two actions pressed more or less simultaneously. A petition, signed by eleven persons and submitted at Ipswich in March 1659, alleged that "diverse [persons] of esteem with us, and, as we hear, in other places also, have for some time suffered losses in their estates and some afflictions on their bodies also."[12] Moreover, these events, which defied explanation by reference to "any natural cause," had usually followed "upon differences had betwixt themselves and one John Godfrey, resident at Andover or elsewhere at his pleasure." Under the circumstances an official inquiry seemed necessary. Unfortunately, there is no record of the court's further proceedings in this matter, but almost certainly Godfrey was indicted, tried in Boston, and acquitted.[13] Meanwhile the accused was mounting a counter-suit, on grounds of slander, "for charging him to be a witch." A local jury sustained this complaint, "notwithstanding [we] do conceive that by the testimonies he is rendered suspicious."[14] Thus was Godfrey vindicated in the short run—but clearly put on notice for the future.

A variety of depositions, from either or both of these actions, survive in the files of the county courts.[15] Twenty-four different witnesses are included here, and probably there were others whose testimony has disappeared. Careful tracing of these people shows a considerable geographic spread—no less than six different towns were represented[16]—but clearly the most detailed, and most telling, evidence came from residents of Haverhill. The four men with whom Godfrey was concurrently involved in property suits all participated in the witchcraft inquiry—one as a signer of the original petition, the other three as deponents. And yet there was more to this than the simple extension of a personal quarrel. If Godfrey's debtors played a significant role, so, too, did others who had no such immediate interest in the outcome. If some witnesses were people of small means and humble status, at least a few held leading positions in their community. William Osgood, who recalled for the court that curious episode on "Mr. Spencer's" farm long before, was among the wealthiest inhabitants (and most frequent office-holders) in the town of Salisbury. And Henry Palmer, a comparably important figure at Haverhill, also entered the lists against Godfrey.

The full corpus of testimony supplied many particulars on the difficulties that Godfrey experienced (or caused?) in his personal relations. Henry Palmer, for instance, recounted an episode "3 or 4 years since" when he had been serving as a selectmen at Haverhill. Godfrey "did often speak to me to join with the rest of the selectmen to hire the said Godfrey to keep the cows at Haverhill." When refused, Godfrey "showed himself much displeased," and soon thereafter cattle from the herds of both Palmer and his son-in-law vanished "quite away."[17] A similar sequence, described in a deposition from Elizabeth Whitaker, throws more light on Godfrey's personal style—or at least the style attributed to him by his adversaries. Since the details are presented with special vividness, this document is worth quoting at length:

> I being at my father's house, one day [there] came in John Godfrey, and my father entertained him and gave him victuals and [bedding?]. And the next morning after, as the said Godfrey was [*illeg.*] a pair of shoes, he fell out very bitterly with me, and told me that my husband owed him more than he was worth and also that all the cloth I had was his. Then said my father to him, "That is not true, Godfrey, for she had them clothes of me when she was married." Then Godfrey rose up in a great rage and knocked his head against the manteltree and threatened my father and I that we should neither of us get nothing by it before that summer passed. Then presently upon it I went and gave my father's three swine some meat, and the swine was taken with foaming and reeling and turned around and did die. Then, after this, when I came home, the said Godfrey came [on] a Sabbath day in the morning next after Salisbury court, and demanded charges for witnessing that week before at Salisbury court. And my husband told him [to] come another time and he would pay him. Then, as Godfrey stood at the door of the house, my husband and my brother was driving our oxen out at the barn. Said Godfrey, "Where are you going with them oxen?" Then said my husband, "I have hired my brother to keep them in the woods today." Said Godfrey, "I will keep them for you, if you will." Then said my husband, "No, my brother shall keep them." Then said Godfrey, "One of them oxen should never come home alive anymore." And that day they were lost, and one of them did never come home alive anymore. And the next day, when my husband was gone to look [for] the oxen, the said Godfrey came to our house and asked for my husband, and I told him he was gone to look [for] his oxen. Said Godfrey, "If Abraham had hired me, I would have looked [for] them and brought them home. For," said Godfrey, "he may seek them, but he will not find them." And when my husband came home, I told him what Godfrey had said, and my husband went that night to seek Godfrey to hire him. But Godfrey went away, and I saw him no more till after the one of the oxen was found dead. And after this, upon Godfrey falling out and threatening, we had many strange losses in our swine and cows and calves, and sore weakness of my body [such] that I could not go up and down all summer.[18]

The abrasive, grasping qualities so prominent in this account of Godfrey appear throughout the testimony presented against him. Indebtedness, threats, angry accusations, and "losses" of property or health: such were the central ingredients of an oft-repeated sequence.

And yet this sequence deserves a second look. Consider Godfrey's response—"one of them oxen should never come home alive anymore"— when his services as cowherd had been refused in favor of Whitaker's brother. Were those his exact words? Or had they been slightly altered, in the process of recollection, so as to exaggerate the element of danger? Even if correctly quoted, they leave room for varying interpretations. Perhaps this was simply a petulant reflection on the brother's competence, with the implied meaning: "your brother is such a poor herdsman that probably he will lose one of your oxen." If so, there was a vital difference between what Godfrey *meant* and what Whitaker *heard*—and it was precisely the difference between a casual (and defensive) slur and a *bona fide* threat. There is no way now to recover the intent behind such a remark, and Whitaker's interpretation of it was, in any case, what counted most at Court. But it is important to recognize the possibilities for misunderstanding and subtle distortion that must have attended any dealings with a reputed witch.

Two other aspects of the evidence seem worthy of comment, for what they suggest about Godfrey's character and social circumstances. First, there was something odd, and disturbingly suspect, about his conversation. It was not merely his frequent resort to "threatening" statements (though this was an obvious, and important, count against him). There was also his tendency to say things that would startle, or confuse, or annoy his listeners. His comments to Osgood about his "new master" have the look of deliberate provocation.[19] The same could be said of another episode reported at court, involving a visit by Godfrey to the house of an Andover resident named Job Tyler.[20] According to the Tylers, an odd-looking bird came in their door together with Godfrey. Efforts to catch it proving unsuccessful, the bird then "vanished" quite suddenly. And Godfrey "being asked by the man of the house wherefore it came . . . answered 'it came to suck your wife.' " There were, moreover, times when Godfrey was given to "speaking about the power of witches." For example:

> The said Godfrey spoke that if witches were not kindly enter-
> tained, the Devil will appear unto them and ask them if they were
> grieved or vexed with anybody, and ask them what he should do
> for them. And if they would not give them beer or victuals, they
> might let all the beer run out of the cellar. And if they looked

steadfastly upon any creature, it would die. And it were hard to
some witches to take away life, either of man or beast; yet when
they once begin it, then it is easy to them.[21]

Repeatedly, then—and in all sorts of ways—John Godfrey flouted his
community's standards of discreet conversation.

Another recurrent theme in the testimony on Godfrey is his special
association with *cattle*. He was, of course, an experienced "herdsman":
he had worked in this capacity during his servant-years, and later he was
hired for a time to "keep the cows" at Haverhill.[22] Yet all did not go
smoothly here. As noted above, Godfrey was forever putting himself
forward as a herdsman, and was often rebuffed. His interest in cattle
seemed beyond doubt, but there was something strange about it. Perhaps,
indeed, he was *too* interested. One witness reported a curious incident
when Godfrey,

> hearing her call [her] calf, . . . [asked] what it was she called. She
> told him, this calf. He asked if she gave it milk still. And, as the
> calf was drinking the milk, the said Godfrey stroked the calf on the
> back, calling it "poor rogue" and "poor rascal," and said it was
> very fat. And that night it died, and we could none of us find any-
> thing it ailed.[23]

Another witness described rumors that Godfrey had "come to places
where some cattle were bewitched . . . and said, 'I will unwitch them,'
and presently they were well."[24] Here, then, was a truly remarkable,
even supernatural, talent, and yet it could not be trusted. *Un*witching
and *be*witching were too closely related—in cow-keeping, as in any
other activity. When joined in a man of bad temperament, such powers
assumed a highly menacing aspect. It was no coincidence that most
of the damage attributed to Godfrey's witchcraft involved domestic
animals.

What seems most striking about John Godfrey's life following the
witchcraft litigation of 1659 is his immediate return to the same community, to a familiar network of personal relationships, and to a highly
similar pattern of activities. It was almost as if nothing had happened.
A court case in September brought judgment against him "for not performing a summer's work." Witnesses testified that Godfrey had engaged
to work for Francis Urselton of Topsfield "when he came out of Ipswich
jail," had taken money, and had then reneged on his own part of the
arrangement.[25] But never mind this outcome; the important thing is that
someone had wished to hire Godfrey in the first place. An accused witch

—formally acquitted of the charges against him, but "rendered suspicious" by much testimony—was considered employable!

With the Urselton case Godfrey began a new and intense round of legal involvements.[26] The matters at issue were largely as before: land, cows, crops, and debt. Most of his opponents were drawn from the circle of his neighbors and associates (if not exactly his *friends*) in Haverhill, Andover, and the immediate surround. In 1661, for example, he initiated a complicated suit for debt against his old adversary Job Tyler. His own claims included payment for twenty-seven days of labor on Tyler's farm, for many additional errands, for back loans, and much more. Meanwhile a counter-suit by Tyler alleged debts on Godfrey's side as well, mainly for "washing, dress, and diet [during] a summer." Witnesses spelled out the particulars, viz.: "Moses Tyler deposed that his mother dressed John Godfrey and washed his clothes above twenty weeks in one year, and that his father found Godfrey's diet for eleven weeks, which was never satisfied."[27] The Tylers, be it recalled, had supplied damaging evidence against Godfrey in the witchcraft inquiry. Yet here are all parties, just a short while later, with their lives densely intertwined. The evidence makes clear that for a period in 1661 Godfrey had been working as Job Tyler's hired man, and, most probably, staying in Tyler's house. For whatever reasons, the Tylers had taken into their home a man whom they themselves regarded as a witch.

The following year Godfrey became involved in new litigation, with still another Haverhill family. His chief antagonist this time was one Jonathan Singletary, age twenty-two, son of a modest "planter," recently married, and father of an infant daughter who had died soon after birth. The records depict Singletary (the name looks French in derivation, and was occasionally written "Singleterre") as a young man overwhelmed by sudden adversities. Repeatedly in debt and in trouble during these years, he would subsequently leave the area altogether for a new start in the colony of East [New] Jersey.

The earliest Godfrey-Singletary litigation involved the latter's use of a certain bond, but this was soon followed by various claims for debt ("50 shillings in silver" and "£8 in wheat and corn"). The depositional evidence revealed a tangled skein of interaction between the two men, in which Singletary was consistently at a disadvantage. (The same evidence offers some pithy examples of Godfrey's speech style—for instance, this comment on a debt of corn allegedly withheld from him by a friend of Singletary's: "I had rather it were in a heap in the street and all the town hogs should eat it, than [that] he should keep it in his hands.")[28]

As a result of all this, Singletary was temporarily jailed; his father made a further (unsuccessful) attempt to settle with Godfrey; and, finally, accusations of witchcraft were made.[29] As before (in 1659), there is no certain record that Godfrey was formally tried on this charge, but the probability seems strong.[30] We do know, in any event, that Godfrey once again sued for slander, "for calling him a witch, and saying 'is this witch on this side of Boston gallows yet?' "[31] There is only one substantial deposition that survives from the case, a statement by Singletary, recounting a bizarre experience during his stay in Ipswich prison.[32] Sitting alone, late one evening, he heard loud noises, "as if many cats had been climbing up the prison walls . . . and . . . boards or stools had been thrown about, and men [were] walking in the chambers, and a crackling and shaking as if the house would have fallen upon me." Almost immediately his thoughts ran to witchery, and, more especially, to an acquaintance who "upon some difference with John Godfrey . . . [had been] several nights in a strange manner troubled." Whereupon Godfrey himself appeared in the doorway (having magically unbolted the lock), and said:

> "Jonathan, Jonathan." So I looked on him [and] said "What have you to do with me?" He said, "I come to see you; are you weary of your place yet?" I answered, "I take no delight in being here, but I will be out as soon as I can." He said, "If you will pay me in corn, you shall come out." I answered, "No, if that had been my intent, I would have paid the marshal and never have come hither." He, knocking of his fist at me in a kind of a threatening way, said he would make me weary of my part and so went away.

Soon he was back, and the discussion continued in a similar vein. At last, Singletary took a rock and lunged at his tormentor, "but there was nothing to strike, and how he went away I know not, for I could . . . not see which way he went." There was only one means of explaining such an episode—at least from the standpoint of the "victim."

There is no doubt about Godfrey's *next* trial for witchcraft. Prosecuted during the winter of 1665–66, this case is duly noted in records still on file from the Court of Assistants in Boston.[33] The initial complaint was lodged by Job Tyler and John Remington. Eighteen witnesses were summoned (from whose testimony seven depositions survive). The indictment charged that Godfrey had "consulted with a familiar spirit" and had "done much hurt and mischief by several acts of witchcraft to the bodies and goods of several persons." The jury's verdict was an obviously reluctant acquittal: "We find him not to have the fear of God in his heart. He has made himself suspiciously guilty of witchcraft, but not legally guilty according to law and evidence we have received." The magistrates "accepted" this decision, but aimed a back-handed swipe of their own at Godfrey, in obliging him to pay all the costs of the trial. (There were substantial expenses for those who had come to Boston to give evidence.)[34]

The depositions were a mixture of old and new material. The Whitakers and Tylers recounted their various misadventures with Godfrey, going back a full ten years, and presumably other witnesses did likewise. But John Remington had a fresh contribution—and a telling one, as the proceedings unfolded. A carpenter who had moved to Haverhill from Andover some five years before, Remington testified concerning an injury recently sustained by his fifteen-year-old son. Unsurprisingly, the point of departure here was a quarrel with Godfrey over the care of the family cows. Remington had decided to "winter" his herd on land some miles distant from his home, and apparently this had provoked John Godfrey to "great rage and passion." Indeed, Godfrey had sworn that "he should have cause to repent it before the winter was out." The actual tending of the animals was "for the most part" left to John Remington, Jr., and it was he (allegedly) who suffered the consequences of Godfrey's anger.[35]

Riding home alone through the woods one day, the boy noticed sudden signs of apprehension in both his horse and his dog. Soon there appeared, in the middle of the path, a crow, "with a very great and quick eye, and . . . a very great bill." Young Remington "began to mistrust and think it was no crow," and "as I was a-thinking this to myself," the horse fell heavily "on one side" with the boy's leg underneath. Eventually he reached home—though not without further harassment from the pseudo-crow—and recounted the experience to his parents. Two days later Godfrey visited the house and began the following conversation (as recalled by John, Jr.):[36]

> He asked me how I did, and I told him, pretty well, only I was lame with the horse falling on me. Then said Godfrey: "Every cock-eating boy must ride. I unhorsed one boy the other day, and I will unhorse thee, too, if thee rides." . . . Then said I: "I am not able to carry victuals on my back." Then said Godfrey: "tis a sorry horse that cannot carry his own provender." Then said Godfrey to me: "John, if thee had been a man, thee had died on the spot where thee got the fall." Then said my mother: "How can thee tell that? There is none but God can tell that, and except thee

be more than an ordinary man, thee cannot tell that." Then Godfrey bade my mother hold her tongue; he knew what he said better than she. And [he] said: "I say again, had he been a man, . . . he had died on the spot where he fell."

John Remington, Jr. had witnessed the original quarrel between Godfrey and his father, and the power of his own *fear*, while he carried out his duties with the herd, can easily be imagined. Weeks later his father testified that "the boy is very ill . . . and swells in the body every night [so] that I fear he will die of it."[37] As to Godfrey's motives in all this, there is much less clarity; but the bitter comment—"every cock-eating boy must ride"—suggests his long-standing concern to protect his particular vocation. (If boys did *not* ride, perhaps there would be more work for a herdsman?) Godfrey's reference to "unhorsing" seemed, of course, directly incriminating, and most suspicious of all was the statement that but for his age young Remington would have died on the spot. This was knowledge not vouchsafed to "ordinary" men. No suspected witch could afford to make comments that even hinted at such knowledge.

Acquitted in such a narrow and grudging way, Godfrey had little to look forward to in the spring of 1666. At least twice (probably three times) he had faced the possibility of conviction and death on the gallows; few, if any, of his peers believed in his innocence; and his notoriety extended throughout Essex County—perhaps beyond.[38] Indeed, his name had become something of a byword, mentioned in situations where Godfrey himself played no direct part whatsoever. A lawsuit from Newbury in 1668 produced the following bit of testimony: "He [the defendant] further said that he could have as good dealing from a Turk or pagan or Indian as from Mr. Newman [the plaintiff]—yea, saith he, from Godfrey himself—with many such like words."[39] In a separate case, several months later, a defendant was alleged to have slandered a county magistrate, by asserting (among other things) that "he was as bad as Godfrey in usury." (When the deponents had asked "what that Godfrey was," they were told that "he was an evil-looked fellow, and that he was a great usuror; and if he came before a judge, his looks would hang him.")[40]

It is striking, too, that some men not particularly involved in Godfrey's legal and business affairs could feel, and express, a bitter rage when confronting him in person. One particularly violent episode was described in court by a local constable:

I, going to Job Tyler's house to serve an attachment, did take John Godfrey with me. And when I came to the said Tyler's house, John Carr being there said, "What come you hither for, Godfrey, you witching rogue? I will," said John Carr, "set you out of doors." This deponent said to the said John Carr, "Let John Godfrey alone." The said Carr said he would not, but said, "What had you to do, to bring such a rogue with you?" And the said Carr immediately ran his fist in the said Godfrey's breast, and drove the said Godfrey up against the chimney-stock which was very rugged. Then I charged the said Carr to be quiet and let the said Godfrey alone. But the said Carr said he would turn the said Godfrey out of doors and kick him down the hill. And again this deponent charged the said Carr to let the said Godfrey alone, and so Carr did forbear, and called the said Godfrey many bad names.[41]

Much of this had been true long before, yet now one senses a cumulative effect that was new and compelling. The records of the late 1660s suggest a changing set of relationships—a different balance of forces—as between Godfrey and the people among whom he lived. Whatever his difficulties in the earlier phase, there had been no mistaking the force of his aggressive energy, his determination to fight on, his ability to outmaneuver opponents, and the *apprehension* he aroused on all sides. But after 1666 he seemed an altogether less menacing, and more vulnerable, figure.

There was, for example, a marked tilt in the record of Godfrey's court appearances. The vigorous and frequently successful plaintiff of former years was cast more and more in the role of defendant. (In the period 1660–64 he had appeared 13 times as defendant and 34 as plaintiff; for 1665–69 the comparable figures were 19 and 23.) Moreover, Godfrey could no longer be sure of obtaining fair treatment from the legal process itself. The court docket from the late 1660s contains several notations like the following: "John Godfrey vs. Henry Salter. For refusing to give him an acquittance as promised for a deed of sale of land at Haverhill. Verdict for the defendant, but the Court did not accept the verdict."[42] (What this meant, more precisely, was that the magistrates in charge detected prejudice in the decision of the jury.) Similarly, court and community officers sometimes balked at executing judgments in Godfrey's favor. His only recourse in such cases was a further appeal to the magistrates: for example, "John Godfrey vs. Abraham Whitaker. For refusing, though the marshal's deputy, to levy executions against John Remington and Edward Yeomans."[43] Thus the same court which had once served Godfrey as a forum for the exercise of his peculiar talents now became the protector of his weakness.

But protection from this source was incomplete and inconsistent, and Godfrey's troubles continued to mount. In 1669 he was accused of "firing" the house of a Haverhill neighbor, and causing the death (by burning) of the neighbor's wife.[44] Convicted on all counts by the county court, he eventually won a reversal through an appeal to the Court of Assistants in Boston. Also, during these years, he was twice convicted of theft,[45] and once for "subborning witnesses . . . by hindering persons from giving evidence and sometimes instigating some to give false evidence."[46] (The penalties in the latter instance included a fine of a full £100.) Still other cases traced a line of personal deterioration. There were repeated fines for drunkenness,[47] for "taking tobacco in the streets,"[48] for "cursing speeches,"[49] and for "prophaning the sabbath."[50] Godfrey had never cared much for the social and moral conventions of his community; now, one feels, he no longer cared for himself.

There was one final court case of special interest here. In 1669 Godfrey filed suit against Daniel Ela (still another resident of Haverhill), charging defamation "for reporting that he, the said Godfrey, was seen at Ipswich and at Salisbury at the same time."[51] On this occasion, in contrast to the earlier ones, there is no hint of a criminal charge against Godfrey; the comments attributed to Ela were a matter of personal conversation. Indeed, the word witchcraft is not mentioned in any of the documents from Godfrey's own suit, though the implication was very clear.[52]

Some of the testimony simply confirmed that Ela had spoken as alleged, but a far larger portion aimed to show the *grounds* for such a statement. Ela called as defense witnesses several persons who had seen Godfrey in Ipswich, and others who had seen him in Salisbury, on the particular day in question. Moreover, there were reports of similar occurrences in the past. A deposition from one John Griffin may stand for the rest:

> About seven years ago the last winter John Godfrey and this deponent went over Merrimac River on the ice . . . to Andover— Godfrey on foot, and this deponent on horseback, and the horse was as good a one as ever I rode on. And when I was at Goodman Gage's field, I saw John Godfrey in the same field a little before me. . . . But when I had ridden a little further—not seeing Godfrey or any tracks at all (and it was at a time when there had fallen a middling snow overnight)—I ran my horse all the way to Andover. And the first house I came into at Andover was Goodman Rust's

house, and when I came in I saw John Godfrey sitting in the corner, and Goody Rust told me that he had been there so long that a maid that was in the house had made clean a kettle and hung on peas and pork to boil for Godfrey. And the peas and pork were ready to boil, and the maid was skimming the kettle.[53]

This picture of wintertime life in early New England conveys a homely charm that is strengthened by the passage of three hundred years. The fresh snow, the river crossing, the fast ride on horseback, the snug house, the peas and pork warming in the fireplace: here are all the ingredients of a vintage Norman Rockwell painting. But, more important, there is a calmness, a "factual" tone, an absence of dread and loathing, *in the participants themselves*. In fact, the same quality characterizes most of the other evidence presented in Godfrey vs. Ela, and sets this case apart from all of the earlier ones. That a man should be capable of appearing in two places simultaneously, or of outracing a fast horse, seemed literally incredible, but it was not equivalent to magical acts of destruction against life or property. And it is *most* significant that none of the witnesses in 1669 imputed such acts, or threats to perform such acts, to John Godfrey. There was, in this final public consideration of his alleged witchcraft, much less at stake; as a result the proceedings were both less intense and less involved.

Following the conclusion of this case—a conclusion, incidentally, which favored the defendant—six years of life remained to John Godfrey. There was no significant change in his experience during these years, at least nothing that the extant records can be made to reveal. Suits and counter-suits over questions of property, minor criminal offenses, a restless moving about: so his life wound down. The end came in the summer of 1675, apparently at Boston. There is no certain record of Godfrey's death,[54] but legal documents from the settlement of his estate are pertinent. In September 1675 the court appointed a school-teacher named Benjamin Thompson, of Charlestown, Massachusetts, as his administrator; it appeared, too, that Thompson would be his chief beneficiary.[55] But this arrangement was soon challenged by others with a claim on Godfrey's property. Though there was no will, a statement signed with the dead man's mark appeared to undermine Thompson's position. It affords as well a last look at Godfrey's personal style:

That whereas there was formerly a deed of gift of my estate, drawn from me John Godfrey unto Benjamin Thompson of Charlestown. . . . [I declare that this was] done by fraudulent means, myself and most of the company being drunk at the same time. He engaging to pay unto me for my yearly maintenance the full and

just sum of ten pounds in silver, the which was never paid to me
to the value of one farthing, though the said ten pounds was yearly
engaged to be paid during my life. . . . All that he ever did for me
[was], once when I was in Boston prison, he was an occasion of my
being let out. The truth of which, I being in perfect sense and
memory, I do protest upon my soul before God as I am a dying
man. . . .[56]

The estate was not large, but included personal effects, several oxen,
and a hundred acres of land in Haverhill. Additional papers showed
death-bed bequests to two men (not including Thompson) who had
assisted Godfrey during his terminal illness. The issue dragged on in the
local courts for at least two years, and its final resolution went unrecorded. Probate litigation was not uncommon in colonial New England;
but it seems particularly fitting, given all we know about the *life* of
John Godfrey, that his *death* should have occasioned one more quarrel.

We have managed to follow John Godfrey through some thirty years
of his personal history. The picture is necessarily incomplete—less a
filled canvas than a collection of fragments—but certain thematic continuities do come clear. The following summary is an effort to stress
these continuities more forcefully than has been possible heretofore.
They are presented as six distinct, although obviously overlapping, attributes of Godfrey's life and career. Taken altogether they go far toward
explaining Godfrey's singular position (given the sociocultural context),
and the logic of his "selection" as a potential (or actual) witch.

   1. It is striking, first of all, that John Godfrey was without family,
and virtually without relatives of any kind, during all his years in New
England. The only person who *may* have been his kin was one Peter
Godfrey of Newbury; but even here the evidence is limited to a shared
surname and a modest amount of personal contact.[57] Was Peter a
younger brother? a cousin? a nephew? Perhaps, but the records do not
say. Apart from this single possibility, there was no one at all: no parents,
no spouse, no children. Life-long bachelors were an extreme rarity in
colonial New England; in this respect alone John Godfrey must have
seemed conspicuous.

   The singular fact of Godfrey's bachelorhood suggests a further hypothesis which, while highly speculative, forges links with other bits and
pieces of his life. Was he homosexual—perhaps not actively, but
"latently," so? Consider the following: Godfrey's pursuit of work as a
herdsman meant that he was continually presenting himself to men, and
displaying his talent for their "approval." And there was a "passive" side

to this; he was, in effect, saying "choose me." Often these approaches involved him in "triangular" situations, in which the "object" of his attentions was a mature man. (His "rival" in such instances was usually an adolescent boy. The bitter reference to "cock-eating boys," quoted in the deposition by John Remington, also comes to mind here.) Moreover, the pattern of multiple litigation with a variety of men in his community —a pattern which seems to have a compulsive aspect—may reflect a defense against homosexuality. The strategy would be the one known to psychoanalysis as "reaction formation": i.e. in order to suppress a culturally forbidden wish to *love* other men, ego *attacks* them continually. Finally, the bitter, tenacious style in which he waged his personal battles has a distinctly "paranoid" cast—and homosexuality has long been associated with paranoia, in psychiatric theory and practice.[58]

2. Lacking family, he also lacked a *home.* Many plots of land passed through his hands, either from regular sales or in payment of debts; but he did not maintain any settled habitation. His domestic arrangements were quite haphazard, and in part he depended on others. Thus one glimpses him staying overnight at the Whitakers in 1656; spending the summer of 1661 at Job Tyler's; eating a meal, in 1668, at the home of Matthias Button ("he said to Goody Button . . . 'woman, weigh me out some meat,' and she arose and gave him meat and brought in water"); declaring in court, in 1669, that "his usual abode was at Francis Skerry's in Salem"; and spending his last days, in 1675, under the care of a certain "Dr." Daniel Weed and Richard Croade.[59]

3. By the standards of his time and culture John Godfrey was extremely *mobile.* His life seemed to violate the usual gravitational forces —social ones for certain, perhaps physical ones as well. The following is a list of his places of residence arranged in chronological sequence (though probably not a complete list, since some of his movements went unrecorded):

1640:	living in *Newbury* (as "Mr. Spencer's herdsman")
1648:	called "of *Andover*"
1649:	called "of *Newbury*"
1652–53:	probably living in *Rowley*
mid-1650s:	living in *Haverhill*
1657:	called "of *Dover*"
1658:	called "of *Newbury*"; then "of *Haverhill*"
1659, 1661:	called "of *Andover*"
1666:	called "of *Newbury*"
1668:	called "of *Ipswich*"; then "of *Newbury*"

> 1669:   called "of *Salem*"
> 1671:   called "of *Haverhill*"
> 1675:   probably living in *Boston* (at time of death)

Many of the early New Englanders changed residence during the course of a lifetime, and in some instances there were several such changes. But few people felt comfortable with this pattern, for their own values consistently affirmed stability. And virtually no one amassed a record of movement to approach John Godfrey's.

There is little doubt that this record was consciously recognized, and condemned, by Godfrey's peers. The petition which opened the witchcraft inquiry of 1659 referred to "John Godfrey, resident of Andover or elsewhere at his pleasure"[60]—a quite unique notation. In later years his liability for Sabbath-breaking was described in terms of "travelling from town to town."[61] But most striking of all in this connection was the evidence presented in Godfrey vs. Ela, the defamation case of 1669. The defendant's statement that Godfrey had been seen in two places at the same time found credence with many witnesses; such a feat seemed quite plausible from a man whose reputation for moving about was already beyond question. The testimony of John Griffin (quoted above) shows that this reputation had long encompassed some "supernatural" elements.

The three aspects of Godfrey's life considered so far have an important underlying affinity. The dearth of kin, the casual dependency on others for bed and board, the frequent changes of residence: these are all manifestations of an extreme *rootlessness*. Perhaps it seemed, to those who knew him, that John Godfrey was scarcely touched by the elemental ties which controlled the lives of "ordinary men." And being thus unbound, what might he not think, and feel, and do? The answer was manifest in three additional elements of his character: his abrasive interpersonal style; his grasping, importunate spirit; and his extraordinary contentiousness. These things, too, formed an overlapping triad of signal consequence.

4. Of Godfrey's manner in dealing with others, the surviving evidence yields an entirely consistent picture. He was rough, provocative, and unpredictable. He paid little heed to accepted conventions; he would try, for instance, to collect debts on the Sabbath when "good" men were otherwise preoccupied.[62] He cursed; he threatened; he was given to sudden "rages." He never once admitted fault—never, so far as one can tell, allowed himself those moments of ritual self-abasement so familiar to the Puritans.

5. The spirit behind the style was equally plain. Time and again, the

records show Godfrey *grasping* for something—whether for work as a herdsman, or for property, or for revenge. Many of his demands seemed excessive in amount and inappropriate in character, but he never stopped pressing. Jonathan Singletary, petitioning the court for relief from Godfrey's incessant claims, expressed a widely held view: "still he goes on with me, as with many other poor men, and saith he is resolved utterly to undo me, although he undo himself also."[63] There is a quality of relentless pursuit here, no matter what the cost or consequences. With Godfrey, so it seemed, a wish became a need and finally an imperative demand.

6. Conflict was the normal condition of John Godfrey's life. His instincts were deeply combative, and he made little effort to curb their expression. Once again Jonathan Singletary can serve as spokesman for views that were widely held in the community. "Why do you come dissembling and playing the Devil's part?" said Singletary, midway through his quarrel with Godfrey at Ipswich prison. "Your nature is nothing but envy and malice, which you will vent though to your own loss, and you seek peace with no man."[64]

It was, of course, in court that Godfrey's "nature" found its appropriate outlet. Beginning in 1658 his involvement in litigation of one sort of another was virtually continuous. This pattern has been sampled rather extensively in the preceding pages; what remains now is an overall summary, a score-sheet of court cases in which Godfrey participated as one of the principals. The total of such cases is simply staggering—132 by a conservative count. (This figure is the sum of actions explicitly noted on a court docket. Almost certainly there were additional cases for which records have since been lost.) In 89 of these cases (some 67 percent of the total) Godfrey appeared as plaintiff; in 30 he was the defendant in a civil suit (23 percent); and in a further 13 instances he was indicted on criminal charges (10 percent).[65]

The matter of *outcomes* also deserves notice. When Godfrey brought suit against others, a verdict for the plaintiff was returned in 55 percent of all cases. (The other 45 percent included verdicts for the defendant, non-suits, and cases reported without reference to result.) When others brought suit against Godfrey, plaintiff was victorious only 30 percent of the time. He was, then, not only an aggressive litigant (far more appearances as plaintiff than as defendant), but also a notably successful one (a high rate of "favorable" verdicts, relative to that of opponents).

Godfrey's combative instincts remained active to the end of his life, but they became in a sense less consequential. He continued the vigorous pursuit of his interests in the courts—but more and more often he was himself a defendant. His rate of successful prosecutions did not fall significantly—but only because the magistrates reversed several decisions by juries which seemed prejudiced against him. His involvement in petty misdemeanors increased—but he was less subject to charges of witchcraft. And, to the extent that his reputation as witch hung on, his accusers showed less fear, less anger, less deep-down dread. There developed around him a new balance of forces, which perceptibly reduced his social influence. From malevolent foe to clever trickster, from witch to eccentric: such was the direction of the change.

The foregoing list of significant themes in the life and career of John Godfrey yields a final opportunity to assess his position in the larger history of New England witchcraft. He was in some ways distinctive even among accused witches—for example, in his gender, and in his detachment from family and kin.[66] (The hints of latent homosexuality suggest a further area of possible singularity.) But at least as striking overall are the various traits and experiences which Godfrey shared with others accused of "familiarity with the Devil." The blunt, assertive style; the appearance of envious and vengeful motive; indeed, the unrestrained expression of a whole aggressive side: in all this Godfrey epitomized the character which New Englanders expected in their "witches."[67] Of course, this character was manifest in a *social* context; always and everywhere, witchcraft charges reflected chronic disturbance in human relationships. And this part of Godfrey's experience is documented for us with truly remarkable clarity.

In another sense, however, "witches" and their accusers interacted on a deeply reciprocal basis; disturbances and disharmony were themselves an epiphenomenon, the paradoxical sign of an inner bond. Here, too, Godfrey's case is instructive. Even in moments of bitter antagonism he and his peers were inextricably joined. Theirs was a relationship of functional dependence, with implicit gains for each side.

For average folk in Essex County Godfrey's presence was frequently adaptive, helping them to relieve and resolve significant elements of inner tension. He offered, most conspicuously, a ready target for anger, a focus of indignation. An attack on Godfrey was understandable, even commendable, if not quite legitimate in the formal sense. Moreover, his special malign agency served to explain and excuse a variety of misadventures which must otherwise have been attributed to personal incompetence. When cows were lost or food was spoiled, when a boy was injured in a fall from a horse, the people involved could fix the blame on witchcraft. There was a kind of comfort here. Finally, and most

broadly, John Godfrey defined for his community a spectrum of unacceptable behaviors. Like deviant figures everywhere, he served to
sharpen the boundaries between "good" and "bad," "moral" and "immoral," "legitimate" and "illegitimate."[68]

Meanwhile Godfrey himself seems to have derived covert gratification
from the special notoriety he gained as a "witch." His response to accusation, and even to formal indictment, was to continue the very pattern of
activity which had brought him into difficulty in the first place. He
became in this way a man of consequence, someone known (and feared)
through the length and breadth of Essex County. His compulsive involvement in conflict implies as well a psychological need on Godfrey's
part. Something deep inside urged him insistently to challenge, to provoke, to contend.

Even as he tested the normative frontiers of his community, Godfrey
was never far from its organizing center. Thus to describe him as an
"outsider"—a common sociological view of accused witches—would be
substantially misleading. He was, after all, a familiar participant in a
variety of everyday situations. At one time or another he had his bed
and board from many of his neighbors, he worked alongside (and for)
other men, he accompanied the constable in serving attachments, and
so on. Indeed it might well be argued that he was a special sort of *insider*,
so deeply did he penetrate the thoughts and feelings of his peers.

And did they, for their part, have a sense of this underlying affinity?
Godfrey was not an "ordinary" man by the standards they customarily
applied, but could they feel confident that his life and behavior were
totally at variance with their own? Did his rootlessness, for example,
serve in the end to separate him from the mass of his fellow–New
Englanders, or did it merely exaggerate a central tendency in their lives
as well? Had not many of these men and women undergone, quite
willingly, a process of uprooting beyond anything experienced by most
of their English contemporaries? And did they not feel repeated temptations to move about in the American "wilderness," as new towns were
established and new lands opened to settlement?[69] There was, too, the
matter of John Godfrey's conduct toward others. Aggressive, angry,
grasping he certainly seemed; but were the others entirely free of such
traits themselves? Their sermons, their charters, and their private devo-
tions affirmed harmony and "peaceableness" as pre-eminent values; but
the records of their courts and governments told a different story. Petty
disputes among neighbors, and "heart-burning contentions" within whole
towns or religious congregations, were endemic to the history of early
New England.[70]

These pathways of identification suggest how fully John Godfrey and his neighbors served and used—one might even say, needed—each other. They afford, moreover, a new point of approach to questions which otherwise seem particularly baffling. Recall that John Godfrey was suspected of practicing witchcraft during a span of at least fifteen years. Two or three times he was prosecuted on charges that might have brought the death penalty. After each trial, no matter how narrow his escape, he returned to the same locale and was re-incorporated into the same network of ongoing relationships. The problem of John Godfrey simply would not go away. Perhaps now we can begin to understand why. For this was a problem deeply rooted in the collective life of the community, and in the individual lives of its various members. It is not too much to say, in conclusion, that there was a little of Godfrey in many of the Essex County settlers; so his fate and theirs remained deeply intertwined.

3

Witches:
A Collective Portrait

To investigate the witches as a biographical type is no easy task. With rare exceptions (e.g. John Godfrey and Rachel Clinton) the record of their experience is scattered and fragmentary. Much of the surviving evidence derives from their various trial proceedings; in short, we can visualize them quite fully as *suspects*, but only here and there in other aspects of their lives. We lack, most especially, a chance to approach them directly, to hear their side of their own story. Most of what we do hear comes to us second- or third-hand, and from obviously hostile sources.

It is hard enough simply to count their number. Indeed, it is impossible to compile a complete roster of all those involved. We shall be dealing in what follows with 114 individual suspects.[1] Of these people 81 were subject to some form of legal action for their supposed witchcraft, i.e. "examination" by magistrates and/or full-fledged prosecution. Another 15 were not, so far as we know, formally accused in court; however, their status as suspects is apparent from actions—for slander —which they themselves initiated. A final group of 18 (some not identified by name) are mentioned elsewhere in writings from the period.

Yet these figures certainly *under*-represent the total of witchcraft suspects in seventeenth-century New England. The court records are riddled with gaps and defects; it is possible, even probable, that important cases have been entirely lost from sight. Consider this single, sparse entry in the records of the "particular court" at Hartford, September 6, 1649: "Thomas Stanton, plaintiff, *contra* Joan Sipperance, in an action of slander to the utter undoing of his wife's good name and almost taking away her life, to the damage of £200."[2] What sort of slander, besides witchcraft, might literally take away life? Yet without additional evidence—the depositions, the warrants, and so forth—we cannot properly add Goodwife Stanton to the suspect-group.

The unofficial (i.e. non-legal) materials are more limited still. There is, for example, an interesting letter written in 1684 by the Rev. James Fitch, the minister at Norwich, Connecticut.[3] Its main subject is a "remarkable providence"—in fact, a sequence of possession behavior—experienced by a certain "maid" of the town. Other, similar cases produced accusations against identifiable witches; but none are mentioned here. Was this element actually missing from the Norwich episode? Or did the Rev. Fitch choose to omit it for one reason or another? (Clergymen frequently urged "discretion" as to the naming of particular suspects; Cotton Mather, on at least one occasion, "charged the afflicted that they should cry out of nobody for afflicting of 'em.")[4] Notice, too, a tantalizing entry in the diary of a Harvard College tutor: "(1684) 21.1 . . . It was reported of Nathaniel Gove in Cambridge that the Devil appeared making a noise like a bird after . . . him."[5] Was there no witch to be implicated here? Again, the materials are not sufficient for an answer.

The Salem trials, though not a central part of the present investigation, throw additional light on the problem of unrecorded witches. The events of that notorious "outbreak" may be viewed as expressing two rather separate processes. There was, first, an explosive release of intramural pressures and tensions—the murderous climax to twenty years of village factionalism.[6] This, however, accounts for only a portion of the charges heard as the trials went forward. Many of the accused were not residents of Salem; indeed, some twenty-two *other* towns were eventually represented in the proceedings by one or more defendants. A few had been prosecuted for witchcraft on an earlier occasion. (For example: Susannah Martin of Amesbury, and Rachel Clinton of Ipswich.) Most were in court for the first time, at least in this connection. Yet the depositions clearly show that local suspicion of these persons was both widespread and long-standing. Episodes from one, two, even three decades previous repeatedly found their way into the official record:

> [Case of Sarah Wilds of Topsfield] John Andrew . . . and Joseph Andrew . . . testifieth and saith that in the year 1674 we were a-mowing together and one of us broke our scythe, and . . . we went to the house of John Wilds, senior . . . and . . . saw some-

thing about as big as a dog glance from a stump or root of a tree along by . . . the oxen. . . .[7]

[Case of Dorcas Hoar of Beverly] Mary Gadge . . . testifieth and saith that about nine years ago . . . being at the house of John Giles . . . and Dorcas Hoar being there also, the said Hoar told her that her child was not long-lived, . . . and about a month after that time her said child was taken sick and died suddenly. . . .[8]

[Case of Mary Bradbury of Salisbury] Samuel Endicott . . . testifies that about eleven years since, being bound upon a voyage to sea with Capt. Samuel Smith, . . . just before we sailed Mrs. Bradbury of Salisbury, the prisoner now at the bar, came to Boston with some firkins of butter of which Capt. Smith bought two. . . . And after we had been at sea three weeks . . . it stank so and ran with maggots, which made the men very disturbed about it, and [they] would often say that they heard Mrs. Bradbury was a witch. . . .[9]

It appears, in sum, that the trials begun at Salem struck an immediately responsive chord in many of the surrounding communities. Suspicions that had festered, locally and informally, for years now yielded a full panoply of legal proceedings. Had the Salem trials not occurred as and when they actually did, these suspicions might well have *remained* informal, i.e. outside the historical record. And the larger point, in the present context, is that some indeterminate number of New England witches can no longer be identified. *Trials* and *suspects* conform to no single profile; indeed their relation, one to the other, recalls the familiar "tip-of-the-iceberg" metaphor.

But if our list of 114 is only the tip, its substantive and structural features still merit investigation. There is no reason to imagine any considerable difference between the known witches and their unknown counterparts.[10] The former are presented here, as a group, in their leading biographical characteristics. Their (1) sex and (2) age have an obvious claim to attention. Thence the focus moves, successively, to their (3) background and early life, (4) marital and child-bearing status, (5) pattern of family relationships, (6) overall record of social and/or criminal "deviance," (7) occupational history, and (8) social and economic position. A final question concerns their (9) personal style and character, and their specific experiences as witches—that is, as objects of formal and informal sanction at the hands of their cultural peers.

Sex

There was no intrinsic reason why one sex should have been more heavily represented among New England witches than the other. The prevailing definitions of witchcraft—the performance of *maleficium* and "familiarity with the Devil"—made no apparent distinctions as to gender.[11] Yet the predominance of women among those actually accused is a historical commonplace—and is confirmed by the present findings.

Females outnumbered males by a ratio of roughly 4 : 1. (See Table 1.) These proportions obtained, with some minor variations, across both time and space.* (See Tables 2 and 3.) Furthermore, they likely *under*state the association of women and witchcraft, as can be seen from a closer look at the males accused. Of the twenty-two men on the list, eleven were accused together with a woman. Nine of these were husbands of female witches, the other two were religious associates (*protégés* of the notorious Anne Hutchinson). There is good reason to think that in most, if not all, such cases the woman was the primary suspect, with the man becoming implicated through a literal process of guilt by association. Indeed this pattern conformed to a widely prevalent assumption that the transmission of witchcraft would follow the lines of family or close friendship.[12] (There were at least two instances when a woman-witch joined in the charges against her own husband.)[13]

Of the remaining eleven male witches five seem to have been young persons given to reckless and boastful talk of supernatural power. Caleb Powell (see Chapter 5) was a seaman who claimed special acquaintance with "astrology and astronomy and . . . the working of spirits."[14] James Fuller of Springfield was brought to trial because he "did . . . most wickedly call upon or pray to the Devil for help . . . at several times"; he admitted having spoken so, "but denied the truth of it, saying he had belied himself," and was ordered whipped for his "wicked and perni-

---

* There was some tendency for the proportion of males to increase during periods of large-scale "witch-hunting." There were two such periods in early New England: 1662–63 (in the river towns of central Connecticut), and 1692–93 (the Salem "craze"). In the former case the portion of males among those charged was 36 percent (4 of 11), in the latter 27 percent (38 of 141). The reason for this increase (as compared with the otherwise prevailing norm) is relatively easy to see. Whenever concern with witchcraft was especially strong, charges spread not only from one prime suspect to another but also to members of their immediate families. In short, the husbands of accused witches were liable to be implicated in a secondary way, and also (but less often) their male children.

Table 1.   Sex of witches, overall[a]

Male	22	(20%)
Female	90	(80%)
Not Known	2	

Table 2.   Sex of witches, by decades[b]

	Males	*Females*	*NK*	*Total*
Before 1640	0	1	0	1
1640–49	3	6	0	9
1650–59	7	28	1	36
1660–69	9	17	0	26
1670–79	1	9	0	10
1680–89	1	19	1	21
1690–99[a]	1	10	0	11
Total	22	90	2	114
Salem 1692–93	38	103	0	141[c]

[a] Not including those accused at the Salem trials.
[b] Each witch has been classified in the decade when she (he) was *first* accused. Subsequent accusations of the same person are not included here.
[c] See Paul Boyer and Stephen Nissenbaum, eds., *Salem Village Witchcraft: A Documentary Record of Local Conflict in Colonial New England* (Belmont, Calif., 1972), appendices, 376–78.

Table 3.   Sex of witches, by colonies

	Male	*Female*	*NK*	*Total*
Mass. Bay	9	45	1	55
Conn.	10	31	1	42
New Hamp.	0	6	0	6
Other	3	8	0	11
Total	22	90	2	114

cious, willful lying."[15] Hugh Croasia of Fairfield, Connecticut, was brought into court for making similar statements, and confessed that in some of them he "lied" and about others "he was not sure himself."[16] John Bradstreet of Rowley was reported to have said "that he read in a book of magic, and that he heard a voice asking him what work he had for him; he answered, 'go make a bridge of sand over the sea, go make a ladder of sand up to heaven, and go to God and come down no more.' "[17] Bradstreet, like Fuller (and also like Robert Williams of Hadley, whose case is less fully documented),[18] was acquitted of witchcraft—but convicted and punished for lying.

In four more cases men were accused of witchcraft, as part of some family or neighborhood quarrel. In a sense such accusations were incidental to other events and circumstances; they were also transitory and limited to those few individuals most immediately involved. William Graves of Stamford was charged with bewitching his married daughter in the time of her child-bearing—and while he and she (with her husband) were bitterly at odds over her "portion" of inheritance.[19] William Browne of Gloucester was accused of a similar crime against his neighbor Goodwife Prince, who was concurrently his antagonist in some (unspecified) local dispute. (Neutral parties urged that Browne's threats of harm be discounted, "knowing what manner of man [he] was"; Goody Prince "would put it out of her mind, but could not." Eventually Browne was convicted not of witchcraft but of "diverse miscarriages.")[20] William Meaker of New Haven was charged by Thomas Mullener with bewitching his hogs, in the aftermath of still another personal quarrel. (Meaker sued for defamation and won.)[21] Thomas Wells of Ipswich was repeatedly embroiled with his neighbors Cross and Brabrook: they accused him of having said, among other things, that he could "set spells and raise the Devil, he offering himself to be an artist." (He "utterly denied" this, and no formal charges were pressed.)[22]

To summarize: twenty of the male witches were rendered suspect either by "association" (with an accused woman) or else in a distinctly limited way (as part of a larger sequence of hostilities). In a sense the charges against all these persons were *secondary*. Two men alone remain from the original group: John Godfrey of Andover (and elsewhere) in Massachusetts, and Henry Wakely of Wethersfield, Connecticut. Their careers are considered at length in other parts of this volume—and they do seem to qualify as witches of a *primary* kind.[23] But, viewed in context, they were truly exceptions. The rule in early New England was that witches were women.

Significantly, it has also been the rule elsewhere. Recent studies in European witchcraft, while uncovering much regional and period variation, agree on this one point—the primacy of women as suspects.[24] Anthropological research finds the same tendency in a host of otherwise extremely variable premodern cultures. There are, to be sure, some special cases—individual settings in which men are accused at least as frequently as women—but not many. The great mass of the evidence, from whatever quarter, declares a profound connection between witch-craft and womanhood. To see this clearly is to broach another "level" of understanding: perhaps the forces at work here have transcultural and transhistorical dimensions. It is the usual instinct of a historian to ground interpretation in the parochial arrangements of a particular time and place, and often enough this instinct serves him well. But he should never assume interpretive sufficiency in such terms. There are some elements of social experience which do seem to have a much broader (even "universal"?) resonance.

An easy hypothesis—perhaps too easy—would make of witchcraft a single plank in a platform of "sexist" oppression. Presumably, the threat of being charged as a witch might serve to constrain the behavior of women. Those who asserted themselves too openly or forcibly could expect a summons to court, and risked incurring the ultimate sanction of death itself. Hence the dominance of *men* would be underscored in both symbolic and practical terms. Male dominance was, of course, an assumed principle in traditional society—including the society of early New England. Men controlled political life; they alone could vote and hold public office. Men were also leaders in religion, as pastors and elders of local congregations. Men owned the bulk of personal property (though women had some rights and protections). Furthermore, the values of the culture affirmed the "headship" of men in marital and family relations and their greater "wisdom" in everyday affairs.[25] Cer-tainly, then, the uneven distribution of witchcraft accusations and their special bearing on the lives of women were consistent with sex-roles generally.

But was there *more* to this than simple consistency? Did the larger matrix of social relations enclose some dynamic principle that would energize actual "witch-hunting" so as to hold women down? On this the evidence—at least from early New England—seems doubtful. There is little sign of generalized (or "structural") conflict between the sexes. Male dominance of public affairs was scarcely an issue, and in private life there was considerable scope for female initiative. Considered over-all, the relations of men and women were less constrained by differences of role and status than would be the case for most later generations of Americans. It is true that many of the suspects displayed qualities of assertiveness and aggressiveness beyond what the culture deemed proper. But these displays were not directed at men as such; often enough the targets were other women. Moreover, no single line in the extant materials raises the issue of sex-defined patterns of authority. Thus, if witches were at some level protesters against male oppression, they themselves seem to have been unconscious of the fact. As much could be said of the accusers, in their (putative) impulse to dominate.

Two possible exceptions should be noticed here. Anne Hutchinson was suspected of performing witchcraft, during and after her involvement with "antinomianism." And the ecclesiastical proceedings against her affirmed, among other things, the "natural" subordination of women to male authority. (Said Governor Winthrop at one point: "We do not mean to discourse with those of your sex.")[26] Similarly, the convicted witch Anne Hibbens had been "cast out" of the Boston church for a variety of reasons, including this one: "she hath [violated] . . . the rule of the Apostle in usurping authority over him whom God hath made her head and husband." (According to John Cotton, the pastor, "some do think she doth but make a wisp of her husband.")[27] Yet even in these cases there was no clear line of connection between the (alleged) witchcraft and the flouting of conventional sex-roles. With Mrs. Hutchinson heresy remained the central issue throughout. With Mrs. Hibbens many years elapsed between her trial of excommunication (1640) and her conviction for witchcraft (1656). It is also well to remember numerous other New England women who would seem to qualify as sex-role "deviants." Their sins were many and various—assault on magistrates and constables,[28] "wicked carriage and speeches" toward husbands,[29] physical violence against husbands (and others),[30] sexual harassment and abuse of men[31]—yet most of them would never fall prey to charges of witchcraft.

And one final point in this connection: a large portion of witchcraft charges were brought against women *by* other women. Thus, if the fear of witchcraft expressed a deep strain of misogyny, it was something in which both sexes shared. It was also something in which other cultures have quite generally shared. These considerations will lead, in a later chapter, to another, rather different way of understanding the predominance among witches of women.

Age

How old were the accused? At what age did their careers as suspected witches begin? These questions are difficult to answer with precision, in many individual cases; but it is possible to create an aggregate picture by analyzing a broad sample of age-estimates. In fact, Tables 4–6 present four separate aggregates, based on varied materials and following somewhat different procedures.

Table 4.   Age of witches (excluding Salem)

Age[a]	A. Entire group[b]			B. Major suspects[c]		
	Male	Female	Total	Male	Female	Total
15	0	1	1	0	0	0
20	1	1	2	0	0	0
25	0	4	4	0	2	2
30	0	2	2	0	0	0
35	0	5	5	1	1	2
40	3	8	11	2	5	7
45	4	12	16	1	11	12
50	3	14	17	3	9	12
55	2	8	10	0	6	6
60	0	8	8	0	3	3
65	0	3	3	0	0	0
70	0	1	1	0	1	1
75	0	1	1	0	0	0
NK	9	22	31	2	5	7
Total	22	90	112	9	43	52

[a] Ages computed by taking midpoint in estimated range and rounding to nearest multiple of 5.

[b] Includes all known suspects, except two (for whom sex is not known); ages computed to year of legal proceeding.

[c] Includes only principal defendants in a formal prosecution (not secondary defendants and/or plaintiffs in suits for slander or defamation); ages computed to year of earliest known suspicion.

Table 5.   Age of witches (Salem group)[a]

Age-cohort	Male	Female	Total
Under 20	6	18	24
21–30	3	7	10
31–40	3	8	11
41–50	6	18	24
51–60	5	23	28
61–70	4	8	12
Over 70	3	6	9
Total	30	88	118

[a] Includes all those accused, in the trials of 1692–93, for whom some age-data is obtainable; arranged by ten-year cohorts. Reprinted from John Demos, "Underlying Themes in the Witchcraft of Seventeenth-Century New England," *American Historical Review*, LXXV (1970), 1315.

Table 6. Age of witches (Salem group: special sample)[a]

Name	Residence	Age 1692	Yr. first accused	Age first accused
Bridget Bishop	Salem	55–60	1678	41–46
Mary Bradbury	Salisbury	75–80	1672	55–60
Martha Carrier	Andover	45–50	1685	38–43
Sarah Cole	Lynn	ca. 47	unspec.	40–45?
Rachel Clinton	Ipswich	63	1682	53
Mary Esty	Topsfield	58	1687	53
Dorcas Hoar	Beverly	ca. 57	1678	ca. 43
Elizabeth How	Ipswich	55	1682	45
Susannah Martin	Amesbury	67	1669	44
Mary Parker	Andover	ca. 62	1684	ca. 54
Ann Pudeator	Salem	50–60	"some years ago"	40–50?
Wilmott Reed	Marblehead	ca. 55	1687	ca. 50
Susannah Roots	Beverly	ca. 67	"some time since"	50–60?
Sarah Wilds	Topsfield	ca. 63	1676	ca. 47

[a] Includes those for whom there was a clear pattern of suspicion antedating indictment at Salem in 1692–93.

Table 4–A presents data on the entire group of known suspects; 4–B narrows the pool so as to include only those who qualify as major suspects. These two tables also express different modes of computation: the first is based on the year of formal proceeding (i.e. an "examination" or indictment in court, the filing of a suit for slander or defamation, or, in a few cases, some other notice of suspicion), whereas the material in 4–B is linked to the year of earliest known suspicion. The distinction is easily clarified with a specific example. Goodwife Elizabeth Morse (see Chapter 5) was prosecuted for witchcraft in 1680; her age at the time was between sixty and seventy. However, the depositional evidence against her recalled events dating back as far as sixteen years previous; hence her reputation as witch began when she was much younger (not more, and possibly, less, than forty-four to fifty-four).

The results, from both tables, converge on one time of life in particular: what we would call "midlife," or simply "middle age." The years of the forties and fifties account for the great mass of accused witches, whether considered at the time of prosecution (67 percent) or of earliest known suspicion (82 percent). It seems necessary to emphasize these figures in order to counteract the now familiar stereotype which makes witches out to be old. In fact, they were not old, either by their standards or by ours. (One victim, in her fits, was asked pointedly about the age of her spectral tormentors, and "she answered neither old nor young.") Contrary (once again) to currently prevalent understandings, the New Englanders construed the chronology of aging in terms not very different from our own. Their laws, their prescriptive writings, and their personal behavior expressed a common belief that old age begins at sixty.[32] All but a handful of the witches were younger than this. Indeed, substantial majorities of both the groups considered above were age fifty or less (72 percent of the general sample, and 78 percent of the "major suspects").

Additional material, derived from the Salem trials, is presented in Table 5. Age-estimates for some 118 of the persons accused in those trials yield a profile generally consistent with the other findings. (One notable difference involves the cohort under twenty. But most of these young people were accused in a secondary way, i.e. because their mothers were already, and more substantially, implicated. Under panic conditions, blood-lines would serve as "conductors" of suspicion; hence the indictment of both children and adult men in unusual numbers.)

Because of their sheer extent, and also because the records have been so fully preserved, the Salem trials afford a special opportunity to analyze the age of witches. Some of the accused (as noted already) had been longtime targets of local gossip and suspicion. A special sample of fourteen forms the basis for Table 6. The reputation of each one is described in the depositional material; moreover, there is at least some evidence as to their ages. Most were in their forties or fifties when first suspected, and the rest were only a little older. (This may actually *under*state the length of their careers as witch, given the possibility of additional data now lost and the likelihood that the earliest suspicions would not yield an immediately identifiable result.)

Here, then, is still another convergent body of evidence pointing to midlife as the time of maximum vulnerability to charges of witchcraft. And one can scarcely avoid asking *why* this should have been so. What, for a start, was the meaning of midlife in that time and that cultural context? One point seems immediately apparent: midlife was *not* seen as one of several stages in a fully rounded "life-cycle." Early Americans spoke easily and frequently of "childhood," "youth," and "old age"— but not of "middle age."[33] The term and (presumably) the concept, so familiar to us today, had little place in the lives of our forebears centuries ago. Instead of constituting a stage, midlife meant simply manhood (or womanhood) itself. Here was a *general* standard, against which childhood and youth, on the one side, and old age, on the other, were measured as deviations. Early life was preparatory; later life brought decline. The key element in midlife—as defined, for example, by the Puritan poet Anne Bradstreet—was the exercise of power, the use of fully developed capacity. The danger was *mis*use of power, the besetting sin an excess of "vaulting ambition."[34] In fact, these conventions gave an accurate reflection of experience and behavior. In the average life the years from forty to sixty enclosed a high point of wealth, of prestige, of responsibility for self and others.[35] This pattern can be demonstrated most clearly for *men* in midlife (from tax-lists, inventories, records of office-holding, and the like); but it must have obtained for women as well. A middle-aged woman was likely, for one thing, to have a full complement of children in her care and under her personal authority. The numbers involved could well reach eight or ten, and in some families there would be additional dependents—servants, apprentices, other children "bound out" in conditions of fosterage. With female dependents the authority of the "mistress" was particularly extensive; significantly, it appeared as an issue in at least one of the witchcraft cases. Listen to the words of Mercy Short, "in her fits" and addressing her spectral tormentors:

> What's that? Must the younger women, do ye say, hearken to the elder? They must be another sort of elder women than you then! They must not be elder witches, I am sure. Pray, do you for once hearken to me![36]

Beyond the cultural insistence that others "hearken" to her, a woman in midlife would enjoy considerable prestige in her village or neighborhood. She was likely by this time to be a church member—and, if her husband was well to do, to have a front-row seat in the meeting-house. Indeed, her status reflected her husband's quite generally, and his was probably higher than at any time previous. The point, in sum, is this. Midlife was associated, in theory and in fact, with power over others. Witchcraft was a special (albeit malign) instance of power over others. Ergo: most accused witches were themselves persons in midlife.

If this seems a bit too simple, there are indeed some additional—and complicating—factors. The accused were not, on the whole, well positioned socially. (See "Social Positions" later in this chapter.) Their personal access to power and authority was, if anything, below the average for their age-group. They can therefore be viewed as representative of midlife status only in a very generalized sense. Perhaps it was the discrepancy between midlife norms and their own individual circumstances that made them seem plausible as suspects. Perhaps a middle-aged person who was poorly situated (relative to peers) could be presumed to want "power"—and, in some cases, to seek it by any means that came to hand.

To suggest this is to acknowledge elements of *dis*advantage—of deficit and loss—in generating suspicions of witchcraft. And one more such element must be mentioned, at least speculatively. Most of the accused were middle-aged women; as such they were subject to the menopausal "change of life." The old phrase sounds quaint and slightly off-key to modern ears, but in traditional society menopause brought more—at least more tangible—change than is the usual case nowadays. Its effects embraced biology, psychology, and social position, in roughly equal measure. This process will need further, and fuller, consideration in relation to the putative victims of witchcraft;[37] for the moment we simply underscore its meaning as loss of function. The generative "power" of most women was by midlife visibly manifest in a houseful of children; yet that same power came suddenly to an end. There was a gap here between one mode of experience and another—past versus present—an additional kind of unsettling discrepancy. Was it, then, coincidental that witches appeared to direct their malice especially toward infants and very young children?[38]

And was it coincidental that one particular suspect chose to date her beginnings in witchcraft to the time of her own menopause? The woman in question, goodwife Mary Osgood of Andover, confessed in court "that about 11 years ago, when she was in a melancholy state and condition . . . she made a covenant with the Devil. . . ." Subsequently, however, she wished to recant this statement, and was interviewed (while still in prison) by the Rev. Increase Mather:

> Being asked why she prefixed a time, and spake of her being baptised [i.e. by the Devil], etc. about twelve years since, she replied and said that when she had owned the thing, they asked the time, to which she answered that she knew not the time. But being told that she did know the time and must tell the time, and the like, she considered that about twelve years before (*when she had her last child*) she had a fit of sickness and was melancholy; and so [she] thought that *that time might be as proper a time to mention as any,* and accordingly did prefix the said time. [Italics added.][39]

Mary Osgood was born in about the year 1635. Thus, when brought to trial at Salem in 1692, she was some fifty-seven years old. But at the time she "prefixed" for her covenant with the Devil she was forty-five, had recently borne her last child, and was emotionally depressed. In terms of the interpretation proposed here, this was indeed "as proper a time to mention as any."

Background

The most severe of all the deficiencies in the source materials relate to the early life of the witches. In what circumstances did they grow up? Was there something distinctive about their various families of origin? Were they orphaned, sent out into servitude, subject to illness, raised by disabled or insensitive parents, to any extent beyond the average for their cultural peers? Unfortunately, the material to answer such questions is not extant. In only one case—that of the unfortunate Rachel Clinton —can we gain some sense of beginnings. Rachel's experience suggests the possibility that early-life discontinuity may have contributed something to the making of witches; but there is no way to be sure.

Several cases, however, show some direct extension of the suspect-role from parent to child. Jane Walford of Portsmouth was prosecuted for witchcraft on two separate occasions (1656, 1669); years later (1682) her daughter Hannah [Walford] Jones was similarly charged. (In the latter case Goodwife Jones was reported to have said to her principal accuser: "If he told her of her mother, she would throw stones at his head." He, for his part, "affirmed that the above named Goody Jones and *all her generation* [i.e. her own progeny] were accounted witches.")[40] At least three times a mother and daughter were accused together: Winifred and Mary Holman, at Cambridge, Massachuetts, in 1659;[41] Winifred Benham, "senior," and her daughter Winifred, at Wallingford, Connecticut, in 1697;[42] Mary Staples, Mary [Staples] Harvey, and Hannah Harvey, at Fairfield, Connecticut, in 1692. (The last of these was actually a three-generation alignment: mother, daughter, and granddaughter.)[43] There were a few additional instances in which either the family tie cannot be certainly demonstrated, or the accusation of the younger party appears insubstantial.[44]

These cases imply the genetic transmission of witchcraft (so to speak). Yet they do not add up to a large sum. The children seem to have been less seriously implicated than their mothers; the latter were usually the prime suspects. In fact, the principle of guilt by association operated less strongly between generations (parent-to-child) than between spouses (wife-to-husband). More husbands, than children, of witches were themselves formally charged—and, when charged, they were more liable to suffer conviction and death.

It is significant, moreover, that many children of accused witches went on to useful, even successful, lives. Thus four sons of the Windsor witch, Lydia Gilbert, became substantial citizens of Wethersfield and Hartford. (Two were frequent officer-holders.)[45] David Lake, the younger son of Alice (convicted and executed at Dorchester in 1651), was a leading man in the town of Little Compton, Rhode Island.[46] Erasmus James, Jr., son of Jane (perennial suspect in Marblehead), rose from humble beginnings as a carpenter to the status of "merchant and shipwright"; eventually he was a local selectman, his name prefixed by the honorific "Mr."[47] The sons of Mary [Bliss] Parsons of Northampton attained various forms of civic prominence, while her daughters married prominence (e.g. merchants and ministers).[48] Other cases display a more modest range of outcomes. But there are no signs anywhere of lasting and disabling stigma, and few enough of even casual suspicion.

Other elements of "background" deserve investigation. Were the witches anomalous in their ethnic and/or religious heritage? On this the evidence is clearer, and it supports a negative answer overall. An early suspect in the Hartford trials of 1662–63 was Dutch—Judith Varlet, daughter of a merchant and relative by marriage of Governor Peter Stuyvesant of New Netherland. (A leading victim in the case was given to "Dutch-toned discourse," when overtaken by fits.)[49] The widow Glover, convicted and executed at Boston in 1688, was Irish and Catholic, and at her trial could speak only in Gaelic.[50] Elizabeth Garlick of Easthampton apparently had one Huguenot parent.[51] And Mary Parsons was the wife of a "papist" before her ill-starred second marriage and trial for witchcraft at Springfield.[52] But otherwise the witches seem to have been of solidly English stock and mostly "Puritan" religion. (A few were Anglican, but probably not more than half a dozen.)[53] There were of course, non-English, non-Puritan folk scattered here and there throughout New England: Irish, Scots, Dutch, French; Catholics, Quakers, Baptists, Jews. Their peculiarities (from the mainstream viewpoint) are noticed at occasional points in local and personal records; but, with the above-mentioned exceptions, they did not arouse suspicion of witchcraft. No less was true of the Indians. From the start English migrants to the New World regarded the native peoples as "Devil-worshippers."[54] Yet this did not mean *witches* in the usual sense. Indians were brought to trial in colonial courts, on numerous occasions and for various crimes—but not for this one. The point, again, is the inward direction of witch-hunting among the New Englanders. The worst work of the Devil they looked for—and found—among their own kind.

Marriage and Child-Bearing

But what of the families in which witches lived as adults, the families they helped to create as spouses and parents? The marital status of the suspect-group is summarized in Table 7. The results on this point seem generally unremarkable: there are no clear departures from the pattern of the culture at large. The portion of widows (10 percent) looks normal for the age-group most centrally involved, given the prevailing demographic regime. The never-marrieds (another 10 percent) include those few young men who virtually courted suspicion and also the several children of witches accused by "association." (John Godfrey was the only person past "youth" in this particular sub-group.) There was but one divorcée.[55]

In sum, most witches were married persons (with spouses still living) when brought under suspicion. Most, indeed, had been married only once. Four were definitely, and two probably, in a second marriage; one had been married (also widowed) twice previously. Perhaps a few others belong in the previously married group, assuming some lost evidence; however, this would not alter the total picture. Again, the witches seem little different in their marital situation from their cultural peers.

As part of their marriages the accused would, of course, expect to bear and rear children. But in this their actual experience may have differed somewhat from the norm. The pertinent data (vital records, genealogies, and the like) are flawed at many points, and conclusions must be qualified accordingly. Still, with that understood, we may ponder the following. It appears that nearly one in six of the witches was childless—twice the rate that obtained in the population at large. (See Table 8A.) Moreover, those who *did* bear children may have experienced lower-than-normal fecundity (and/or success in raising children to adulthood). In numerous cases (23 out of 62) the procedure of family reconstitution yields but one or two clearly identifiable offspring. Meanwhile, relatively few cases (7 of 62) can be associated with large complements of children,

Table 7.   Marital status of witches[a]

Married	75	(79%)
Widowed	9	(10%)
Divorced	1	(1%)
Never Married	9	(10%)
Not known	20	

[a] At time of trial proceeding and/or seriously felt suspicion.

Table 8A. Children of witches[a]

	Males	Females	Total
Had children	7	55	62
Did not have children	3	9	12
Not known	1	10	11
Total	11	74	85

Table 8B. Children of witches (sub-group)[b]

1–2 surviving children	23
3–5 surviving children	32
6 or more surviving children	7

[a] Sample includes all those witches known to have been married. It does not include unmarried suspects, or those whose marital status cannot be ascertained.

[b] Includes only those witches known to have had children.

i.e. six or more per family. (See Table 8B.) Fuller evidence would surely change these figures, reducing the former and raising the latter; but it would take a quite massive shift to bring the witches into line with the child-bearing and child-rearing norms of the time.*

Connections between witchcraft and children emerge at many points in the extant record: children thought to have been made ill, or murdered, by witchcraft; mothers apparently bewitched while bearing or nursing children; witches alleged to suckle "imps" (in implicit parody of normal maternal function); witches observed to take a special (and suspicious) interest in other people's children; witches found to be predominantly of menopausal age and status; and so on. These themes will appear and reappear in the chapters that follow. Thus the witches' own child-bearing (and child-rearing) is a matter of considerable interest. And if they were indeed relatively ill-favored and unsuccessful in this respect, their liability to witch-charges becomes, by so much, easier to understand.

* A cursory investigation of local demography for seventeenth-century New England suggests the following broad patterns. Some 5 to 8 percent of couples were childless. Another 5 to 10 percent managed to raise no more than one or two children to adulthood. Some 60 to 70 percent produced six or more offspring (surviving to adulthood).

Family Relationships

There is another, quite different way in which the witches may have been atypical. Briefly summarized, their domestic experience was often marred by trouble and conflict. Sometimes the witch and her (his) spouse squared off as antagonists. Jane Collins was brought to court not only for witchcraft but also for "railing" at her husband and calling him "gurley-gutted Devil."[56] Bridget Oliver and her husband Thomas were tried, convicted, and punished for "fighting with each other," a decade before Bridget's first trial for witchcraft. (A neighbor deposed that she had "several times been called . . . to hear their complaints one of the other, and . . . further [that] she saw Goodwife Oliver's face at one time bloody and at other times black and blue, . . . and [Goodman] Oliver complained that his wife had given him several blows.")[57] The witchcraft trials of Mary and Hugh Parsons called forth much testimony as to their marital difficulties. Mary was alleged to have spoken "very harsh things against him before his face . . . such things as are not ordinary for persons to speak one of another." Hugh, for his part, "never feared either to grieve or displease his wife any time"; once, by his own admission, he "took up a block [of wood] and made as if . . . [to] throw it at her head."[58] A second Mary Parsons (whose career is fully described in Chapter 8) also quarreled frequently with her husband. The estrangement between Sarah Dibble and *her* husband was so bitter that he actively encouraged suspicions of her witchcraft; moreover, his general "carriage" toward her was "most inhumane, [e.g.] beating of her so that he caused the blood to settle in several places of her body."[59] There was similar evidence about other suspects, including several of those tried at Salem.[60]

In some cases the lines of conflict ran between parents and children. The Marblehead witch Jane James was chronically at odds with her son Erasmus; at least once the county court undertook an official arbitration of their differences. (On a separate occasion the same court examined and fined Erasmus "for giving his mother abusive language and carriage.")[61] As noted previously, the witchcraft charges against William Graves seem to have developed out of a longstanding dispute with his daughter and son-in-law.[62] Susannah Martin's household was disrupted by violent quarrels between her husband and son; the latter was brought to court and convicted of "high misdemeanors" in "abusing of his father, and throwing him down, and taking away his clothes."[63]

This material cannot meaningfully be quantified; in too many cases the surviving evidence does not extend to any part of the suspect's domestic experience. But what does survive seems striking, if only by way of "impressionism." Harmony in human relations was a touchstone of value for early New Englanders, and nowhere more so than in families.[64] A "peaceable" household was seen as the foundation of all social order. Hence domestic disharmony would invite unfavorable notice from neighbors and peers. A woman from Dorchester, Massachusetts, called to court in a lawsuit filed by her son, expressed the underlying issue with candor and clarity: "it is no small trouble of mind to me that there should be such recording up [of] family weaknesses, to the dishonor of God and grief of one another, and I had rather go many paces backward to cover shame than one inch forward to discover any."[65] Yet the lives of witches —we are speculating—were often crossed with "family weaknesses." And perhaps these belonged to the matrix of factors in which particular suspicions originated.

Such weaknesses may have held other significance as well. The troubles in Rachel Clinton's family (examined at length in Chapter 1) left her isolated and exposed to a variety of personal misadventures: her sheer vulnerability made a central theme in her story. Rachel was doubtless an extreme case, but not a wholly atypical one. Conflict with spouse, siblings, children had the effect of neutralizing one's natural allies and defenders, if not of turning them outright into adversaries. The *absence* of family was also a form of weakness. Widowhood may not by itself have invited suspicions of witchcraft; yet where suspicions formed on other grounds, it could become a serious disadvantage. Case materials from the trials of the widows Godman (New Haven),[66] Holman (Cambridge),[67] Hale (Boston),[68] and Glover (Boston)[69] implicitly underscore their vulnerable position.

The experience of Anne Hibbens (Boston) is particularly suggestive this way. Mrs. Hibbens had arrived in New England with her husband William in the early 1630s. Almost at once William established himself as an important and exemplary member of the community: a merchant, a magistrate, a member of the Court of Assistants. But Anne made a different impression. In 1640 she suffered admonition, then excommunication, from the Boston church; a still-extant transcript of the proceedings reveals most vividly her troubled relations with neighbors and peers. In 1656 she was tried in criminal court—and convicted—and executed— for witchcraft. The long interval between these two dates invites attention; and there is a third date to notice as well, 1654, when William Hibbens died.[70] It seems likely, in short, that William's influence served for many years to shield her from the full force of her neighbors' animosity. But with his passing she was finally, and mortally, exposed.

Crime

Witchcraft was itself a crime, and witches were criminals of a special sort. Were they also criminals of other—more ordinary—sorts? Were they as a group disproportionately represented within the ranks of all defendants in court proceedings? Was there possibly some implicit affinity between witchcraft and other categories of crime?

Again, the extant records do not yield fully adequate information. Some 41 of the accused can be definitely associated with other (and prior) criminal proceedings; the remaining 73 *cannot* be so associated. The difficulty is that many in the latter group can scarcely be traced at all beyond their alleged involvement with witchcraft. Still, the total of 41 offenders is a considerable number, which serves to establish a minimum "crime rate"—of 36 percent—for the witches as a whole. Clearly, moreover, this is only a minimum. To concentrate on witches for whom there is some evidence of *ongoing* experience is to reduce the "at risk" population to no more than 65. (The latter, in short, form a sub-sample among the accused whose offences might plausibly have left some trace in the records; the rest are biographical phantoms in a more complete sense.) This adjustment yields an alternative rate (of offenders/ witches) of some 63 percent.

The two figures, 36 and 63 percent, may be viewed as lower and upper bounds for the actual rate, and their midpont as a "best guess" response to the central question. In short, approximately one half of the people accused of practicing witchcraft were also charged with the commission of other crimes. But was this a notably large fraction, in relation to the community at large? Unfortunately, there are no fully developed studies of criminal behavior in early America to provide firm standards of comparison, only scattershot impressions and partial analyses of two specific communities included in the current investigation.[71] The latter may be summarized in a sentence. The overall "crime rate"—defined as a percentage of the total population charged with committing crimes at some point in a lifetime—was on the order of 10 to 20 percent.* Thus, even allowing for the possibility of substantial error, the link between witchcraft and other crime does look strong.

There is more to ask about the other crime, particularly about its substantive range and distribution. Taken altogether, the witches accounted

---

* The rate for *women only* was much lower, perhaps in the vicinity of 5 percent. And this may be a better "control group" for present purposes, since most witches were female. If so, the disparity between witch-behavior and prevailing norms appears even more pronounced.

Table 9.   Crimes of the witches[a]

Assaultive speech	20
Theft	10
Lying	6
Sex offenses	5
Physical assault	4
Resisting authority	2
Arson	1
Fraud	1
Unspecified	3

[a] Note: This analysis does not include a variety of civil offenses: e.g. debt, breach of contract, and other disturbances of property relations.

for fifty-two separate actions at court (apart from witchcraft itself). Table 9 provides a summary.

The first of the categories in this table includes a dozen slander and/or defamation cases, and several others designated by terms like "filthy speeches," "scandalous speeches," etc. In every instance the issue was the same—that is, verbal attack on other persons. Such offenses appear frequently through the entire corpus of New England court records; but their prominence here is especially striking. Indeed, the total of twenty would rise substantially, given better (i.e. fuller) data. The "unspecified" cases most likely belong to this category, and the witchcraft materials themselves contain additional examples of assaultive speech (which may or may not have been prosecuted as such).

The category "theft" is also prominent in the sample. Ten different witches were prosecuted on this charge, some more than once. (The properties involved were quite various: linens, clothing, "a piece of brass," farm implements, and the like.) "Lying" comes next among these criminal frequencies, with six prosecutions (five of them involving male witches). Close behind are sexual crimes (one adultery, three acts of fornication, and one case of "unclean carriages") and physical assaults (four all told). The numbers for the remaining categories are too small to have much significance.

The overall shape of these figures bears careful consideration. How does it compare with crime distribution in the population at large? Were there some offenses to which the witches seemed unusually prone (in relation to their "average" peers)? Again, firm standards of comparison are lacking; however, a moderately extended sampling of records from several different New England courts yields at least an approximation thereof. (See Table 10).

Table 10.   Crime frequencies,
witches vs. the general population (percentages)

Crime categories	Entire sample[a]	Women only[b]	Witches only[c]
Assaultive speech[d]	27	23	41
Theft	8	4	20
Lying	4	5	12
Sex offenses[e]	13	32	10
Physical assault[f]	22	13	8
Resisting authority[g]	13	15	4
Drunkenness	11	4	0
Other	1	2	4

[a] Includes two different sub-samples from the quarterly courts of Essex County, Mass. (1645–49, 1663–64), and one each from the courts of Suffolk County, Mass. (1672), the "particular court" of Connecticut (1650–55), and the local court whose operations are described in the "Pynchon Court Record" (1650–85).[72] Within each sub-sample all offenses are counted (from the years specified) except for civil suits over property. Total number of cases: 618. The figures express percent of all cases counted.

[b] Includes only *female* offenders within the designated sub-samples. Total number of cases: 93. The figures express percent of all cases counted.

[c] Includes only persons subsequently charged with witchcraft. Total number of cases: 49. (Three "unspecified" cases are excluded.) The figures express percent of all cases counted.

[d] Includes slander, defamation, "filthy speeches," "scandalous speeches," etc. (where the object was another *person*).

[e] Includes fornication, adultery, "lewdness," "lascivious carriages," etc.

[f] Includes assault, battery, and "breach of the peace" (where the issue was physical violence involving two or more persons).

[g] Includes all offenses against duly constituted authority, civil and/or religious, involving some act of *commission*. (However, acts of *omission* are not included—e.g. "absence from public worship," failure to perform the "watch"—as these could express either a conscious defiance of authority *or* laziness, failure of memory, etc.)

The limits of Table 10 must be frankly admitted: e.g. the small numbers involved (especially for the witches), the absence of a true "control group," and the ever-present vagaries of the records. (Note, too, that the mode of comparison is internal to the data itself, that is, crimes compared *to each other* rather than to people or communities.) Still, there are points of emphasis and contrast which do seem meaningful. Crimes of assaultive speech and theft are dramatically highlighted here. Together they account for 61 percent of all charges pressed against the witches, as opposed to 35 percent for the larger sample. Moreover, the fact that accused witches were predominantly female suggests a refinement in the sample population. If men are excluded—if, in short, the comparison involves witches versus *women* offenders generally—then the disparity becomes even larger, 61 percent and 27 percent.

Are there reasons why persons previously charged with theft and/or assaultive speech might be found, to a disproportionate extent, in the ranks of accused witches? Was there something which these two categories of offense shared (so to say) with witchcraft? Such questions point to the meaning of witchcraft in the minds of its supposed (or potential) victims—another topic, for a later chapter. But consider what is common to crimes of theft and assaultive speech themselves. The element of loss, of undue and unfair taking away, seems patent in the former case, but it is—or was for early New Englanders—equally central to the latter one as well. Slander, for example, meant the loss of good name, of "face," of reputation, and thus was a matter of utmost importance. (The evidence against one alleged slanderer, who would later be charged as a witch, was summarized as follows: "She hath *taken away* their [i.e. the plaintiffs'] names and credits . . . which is *as precious as life itself.*" [Emphasis added.])[73] "Filthy speeches" was a somewhat looser designation, but in most specific instances it described a similar threat. Even "lying"—a third category of crime, notably salient for witches—can be joined to this line of interpretation. A lie was, in a sense, a theft of truth, and seemed especially dangerous when directed toward other persons.

In sum, each of these crimes carried the inner meaning of theft. And so, we shall presently see, did witchcraft. Theft of property, theft of health (and sometimes of life), theft of competence, theft of will, theft of self: such was *maleficium*, the habitual activity of witches.

Occupations

As noted, most New England witches were women. And most New England women faced distinct limitations of occupational role. Their lives were governed at all important points by domestic concerns. They were wives, they were mothers, they were "mistresses" of households. Often enough they joined in the productive work of their menfolk; in effect, they served as part-time assistants to farmers, innkeepers, merchants, and craftsmen of various kinds. But they did not undertake such activities in their own right. The world of "occupations" was officially reserved for men—served indeed to identify men, to distinguish them one from another. "John Sweet, of Boston, shipwright . . ." "Daniel Ela, of Haverhill, tanner . . ." "Francis Nurse, of Salem, yeoman . . ." Name, residence, occupation: thus the three-part formula common to all manner of court and probate records. Ordinarily, for women, only the first two parts applied.

And yet there were some exceptions. "Jane Hawkins, of Boston, midwife . . ." "Isabel Babson, of Gloucester, midwife . . ." "Wayborough Gatchell, of Marblehead, midwife . . ."; here was a special *woman's* occupation. That midwife and witch were sometimes (often?) the same person has long been supposed by historians;[74] hence the evidence, for individual cases, deserves a most careful review. In fact, only two people in the entire suspect-group can be plausibly associated with the regular practice of midwifery.[75] Otherwise the witches were not midwives, at least in a formal sense. It is clear, moreover, that scores of midwives carried out their duties, in many towns and through many years, without ever being touched by imputations of witchcraft.

However, this does not entirely dispose of the issue at hand. Witchcraft charges often did revolve in a special way around episodes of childbirth, and some of the accused were thought to have shown inordinate (and sinister) interest in the fate of the very young. Thus, for example, Eunice Cole of Hampton aroused suspicion by trying to intrude at the childbed (later deathbed) of her alleged victims.[76] Others among the accused pressed medicines and advice on expectant or newly delivered mothers, or, alternatively, sought to take from the same quarter.[77] Some may have displayed special skills in attending at childbirth, even without being recognized officially as midwives. (When Elizabeth Morse was tried for witchcraft, witnesses described her part in the delivery of a neighbor. First, she was deliberately kept away. Then, as "strong labor . . . continued . . . without any hopeful appearance," she was "desired to come"—but declined, evidently miffed at not being asked sooner. Eventually she relented, "and so at last . . . went, and quickly after her coming the woman was delivered.")[78] Perhaps, at bottom, there was a link of antipathy: the midwife *versus* the witch, life-giving and life-taking, opposite faces of the same coin.

Recent scholarship of English witchcraft has spotlighted the activities of so-called "cunning folk."[79] These were local practitioners of magic who specialized in finding lost property, foretelling the future, and (most especially) treating illness. Usually they sided with moral order and justice; often enough their diagnoses served to "discover" witchcraft as the cause of particular sufferings. Yet their powers were mysterious and frightening: charms, incantations, herbal potions, a kind of second sight —all in exotic combination. Inevitably, it seemed, some of them would be tempted to apply such powers in the cause of evil. Thus they might move from the role of "discoverer" to that of suspect—in short, from witch-doctor to witch.

Were there also "cunning folk" among the transplanted Englishmen of North America? The extant evidence seems, at first sight, to yield a negative answer. There is little sign that individual persons achieved (or wanted) a public reputation of this sort, as was plainly the case in the mother country. The nomenclature itself rarely appears, and then only as a form of name-calling. ("What?" exclaimed one man of Goody Morse; "Is she a witch, or a cunning woman?")[80] Almost certainly, the religious establishment of early New England set itself against such practice. Puritan leaders, on both sides of the Atlantic, associated it with the Devil—and, on this side, their views carried decisive influence.

And yet, while "cunning folk" did not present themselves as such, some of their ways (and character) may have survived in at least attenuated forms. For within the ranks of witches were several—perhaps many —women of singular aptitude for "healing." Not "physicians," not midwives, and not (publicly) identified by the pejorative term "cunning," they nonetheless proffered their services in the treatment of personal illness. For example: the widow Hale of Boston (twice a target of witchcraft proceedings) ran a kind of lodging-house where sick persons came for rest and "nursing."[81] Anna Edmunds of Lynn (presented for witchcraft in 1673) was known locally as a "doctor woman"; references to her practice span at least two decades.[82] (One prolonged court case showed her in implicit competition with a Boston physician. The physician had tried, and failed, to cure a young girl with a badly infected leg; and when the girl's parents turned next to Goody Edmunds he vowed to "swallow a firebrand" if her treatment proved successful.)[83] Elizabeth Garlick of Easthampton (see Chapter 7) prescribed "dockweeds" and other herbal remedies for sick neighbors.[84] Katherine Harrison (see Chapter 11) played a similar part at Wethersfield; her therapies included "diet, drink, and plasters."[85] A woman of Boston, not identified but suspected in the "affliction" of Margaret Rule "had frequently cured very painful hurts by muttering over them certain charms."[86]

Some specific episodes of "doctoring" were directly joined to witchcraft proceedings. Winifred Holman of Cambridge (accused and prosecuted in 1659–60) offered to treat a child taken strangely ill: "If you will put it into my hands I will undertake to cure it." (When, afterwards, the child's mother became "sorely afflicted," Holman made a similar offer, and "did prescribe some herbs to her.")[87] Mary Hale of Boston sent "a caudle, as she called it," to a young neighbor who had fallen ill; he "refused [at first] to drink or receive the same, saying it would do him harm," but later "by persuasion of some in the room did eat some thereof, and thereupon grew worse and worse until the time of his departure out of this life."[88] The trial of Rachel Fuller of Hampton focused on the events of one morning in particular. The suspect had come without invitation to the bedside of a sick child named Moses Godfrey. Her appearance was extremely strange—"her face daubed with molasses"— and her behavior aroused immediate suspicion. She sought to hold the boy's hand, but was prevented from doing so by his mother. And then:

> the said Rachel Fuller turned . . . and smote the back of her hands together sundry times, and spat in the fire. Then she, having herbs in her hands, stood and rubbed them in her hands, and strewed them about the hearth by the fire. Then she sat down again, and said, "Woman, the child will be well," and then went out of the door."[89]

When little Moses died a few days later, the people of Hampton drew what for them was the logical conclusion. Yet Fuller had presented herself as trying to cure, not worsen, the child's illness. Was she perhaps playing the part—without, apparently, claiming the name—of "cunning woman"?

There are two more persons to mention here, whose careers raise the same question. Margaret Jones of Charlestown was one of the first witches executed in New England. Few details are known of her life prior to her trial (in 1648), but John Winthrop has left us a summary of the evidence which convicted her:

> 1. She was found to have such a malignant touch, as many persons (men, women, and children) whom she stroked or touched with any affection or displeasure . . . were taken with deafness, or vomiting, or other violent pains or sickness.
>
> 2. She practicing physic, and her medicines being such things as (by her confession) were harmless, as aniseed, liquors, etc., yet they had extraordinary violent effects.
>
> 3. She would use to tell such as would not make use of her physic that they would never be healed, and accordingly their diseases and hurts continued, with relapse against the ordinary course, and beyond the apprehension of all physicians and surgeons.

Additional charges included her ability to "foretell" the future, "an apparent teat in her secret parts," and her connection (according to one witness who "watched" her cell in prison) with a "familiar" in the shape of "a little child." However, the evidence of her "physic" seems to have been the leading, and decisive, factor.[90]

Unlike Margaret Jones, Goodwife Ann Burt left discernible tracks in the historical record over a good many years. Her arrival in Boston aboard the *Abigail* from London was noted in a passenger list of 1635. She was part of a family group that included her husband, her son by a previous marriage, and two stepsons. Within a year the Burts were settled in Lynn, where they (and their progeny) remained fixed for the rest of the century. Their social and economic position was quite modest, and they found themselves in court, for small disputes and misdemeanors, rather more often than most of their peers.[91] Ann, meanwhile, acquired a local reputation for doctoring—and, eventually, for witchcraft. The testimony presented at her trial in 1670 was expansive on both counts.

Madeline Pearson saith she heard Sarah Pearson say [that] when her father had her down to Goodwife Burt to be cured of her sore throat, the first night she was there the said Burt put her to bed and told the said Sarah [that] if she would believe in her god she would cure her body and soul . . . and further [Goody Burt said] that her husband did not believe in her god and could not be cured, and that her maid did believe in her god and was cured . . . and the said Burt said to her, "Sarah, will you smoke it?" And giving of her the pipe she smoked it, and the said Sarah fell into her fits again and said that goodwife Burt brought the devil to her to torment her. . . .

Jacob Knight deposed that . . . I boarded in the house of Mr. Cobbet . . . in which house widow Burt lived at that time. . . . [One morning] I went into widow Burt's room to light my pipe, and told her I had a pain in my head, and . . . [then] went [back] into my lodging room . . . and [presently] . . . there was widow Burt with a glass bottle in her hand, and she told me there was something [which] would do my head good, or cure my head, and gave me the bottle in my hand. And when I had drunk of it, I was worse in my head. . . . And . . . the next morning but one . . . going to Salem, I saw a cat . . . and a dog . . . and one before me like unto widow Burt. . . . And the night following . . . I, looking out of the chamber, it being a clear moonlight night, saw widow Burt upon a gray horse in my brother's yard, or one in her shape.

Bethiah Carter . . . deposed that [her sister] Sarah Townsend . . . lived with Goodwife Burt [who] . . . told said Sarah [that] if she could believe in her god she would cure her body and soul. . . . Since then Sarah had been sorely afflicted with sad fits, crying out and railing against me [i.e. the deponent], saying my father carried me to Boston, but carried her to Lynn to an old witch.[92]

The career of Ann Burt joins many elements which elsewhere appear only in isolated or partial forms. Especially striking is her repeated insistence that her patients "believe in her god." The figure of the cunning woman again suggests itself—and again dissolves in the face of finally inconclusive evidence.

What this and other evidence does make clear is a key association: between efforts of curing, on the one hand, and the "black arts" of witchcraft, on the other. Opposite though they seemed in formal terms, in practice they were (sometimes) tightly linked. "Power" in either direction could be suddenly reversed. We cannot discover how many New England women may have tried their hand at doctoring, but we know that some who did so brought down on themselves a terrible suspicion. Among the various occupations of premodern society this one was particularly full of hope—and of peril.

Social Position

There is a long-standing, and reasonably well attested, view of early America that makes the settlers solidly middle-class. To be sure, the notion of "class" is somewhat misleading when applied to the seventeenth century; "status" would be a better term in context. But "middle" does seem the right sort of qualifier. The movement of people from England to America included few from either the lowest or the highest ranks of traditional society—few, that is, from among the laboring poor (or the truly destitute) and fewer still from the nobility and upper gentry.[93] Yet, with that understood, one cannot fail to notice how the middle range became itself divided and graded by lines of preference. The "planting" of New England yielded its own array of leaders and followers, of more and less fortunate citizens. Social distinction remained important, vitally so, to the orderly life of communities.

Later chapters (7–9) will explore all this quite fully and directly; we broach it now to ask one sort of question, as part of our profile of the witches. What was *their* status as individuals, relative to their cultural peers? The answer lies embedded in a welter of local evidence: probates, tax lists, records of office-holding, seating-plans for village meetinghouses, genealogies, court records, and scattered personal documents. From such materials whole populations can be "sorted" by rank, with results that seem generally convincing, though liable to error in particular cases. The sorting attempted here posits three broad social groups— "high" (I), "middle" (II), and "low" (III)—of roughly equal size. Of course, all such categories are a matter of contrivance, conforming to no

Table 11.   Social position of the accused

I. High rank	5
I/II. High/middle	6
II. Middle rank	5
II/III. Middle/low	12
III. Low rank	51
Mobile	7
Up (III→I) (2)	
Down (I→III) (5)	
Total	86

specific historical reality; but they do help to arrange the material for analysis.

Within our working roster of accused witches, some eighty-six can be classified according to this scheme. (For the other twenty-eight there is too little evidence to permit a judgement.) A substantial majority can be assigned directly to one or another of the basic rank-groups. Eighteen more occupy marginal positions (i.e., *between* groups), while seven seem distinctive in their mobility (up or down) and are on that account held for a separate category. The details are rendered in simple form in Table 11. The import of these figures is immediately clear: witches were recruited, to a greatly disproportionate extent, among the most humble, least powerful of New England's citizens. As a matter of statistical probabilities, persons at the bottom of the sorting-scale were many times more likely to be accused and prosecuted than their counterparts at the top. Moreover, when the results of such accusation are figured in, the difference looks stronger still. Among all the suspects in categories, I, I/II, and II, only one was a *convicted* witch. (And of the remainder, few, if any, were seriously threatened by the actions taken against them.) The accused in categories II/III and III present quite another picture. Indeed they account for all convictions save the one above noted, and for the great bulk of completed trials.

Finally, the "mobile" group deserves special consideration. Five of them started life in a top-category position and ended near the bottom (e.g. Rachel Clinton). Two experienced equivalent change but in the opposite direction. None was convicted; all but one, however, were subject to full-scale prosecution. (Moreover, five were tried more than once.) In short; the mobile group, while not numerous, included people whose "witchcraft" was taken very seriously. To interpret this finding is difficult, without comparable information about the population at large. But there is the suggestion here of a significant relationship: between life-change and witchcraft, between mobility and lurking danger. Perhaps mobility seemed a threat to traditional values and order. And if so, it may well have been personally threatening to the individuals involved. As they rose or fell, moving en route past their more stable peers, they must at the least have seemed conspicuous. But perhaps they seemed *suspect* as well. To mark them as witches would, then, be a way of defending society itself.

Character

With the witches' sex, age, personal background, family life, propensity to crime, occupations, and social position all accounted for (as best we can manage), there yet remains one category which may be the most important of all. What were these people like—as people? What range of motive, of style, and of behavior would they typically exhibit? Can the scattered artifacts of their separate careers be made to yield a composite portrait, a model, so to speak, of witch-character?

The case-studies direct attention, immediately and very powerfully, to one quarter in particular. The lives of both John Godfrey and Rachel Clinton were distinguished above all for *conflict*—with peers and neighbors (and, in Rachel's case, with immediate kin), with local institutions, with generally accepted values and precepts. In both cases the pattern was long in duration and pervasive in result; in both cases, too, there was substantial investment from all parties concerned. The balance of responsibility is not easy to sort out: Rachel emerges, in part, as a victim of circumstances beyond her control, and even Godfrey seems in some of his experiences more sinned against than sinner. Yet their own propensities toward conflict are also clear enough. Picture Rachel "hunching" her fellow-congregants "with her elbow," as they went to their seats in the meeting-house, or reviling her neighbors with epithets such as "hellhound" and "whoremasterly rouge." Recall Godfrey's career as a litigant, extraordinary in its qualities (e.g. of bitter, personal feeling) and quite unparalleled in its quantity (at least 132 cases overall).

These two lives epitomize, albeit in extreme form, a central theme throughout our subject. Witchcraft was *defined* in reference to conflict; and most charges of witchcraft grew out of specific episodes of conflict. Hence it should not be surprising that the suspects, as individuals, were notably active that way.

Godfrey's record for court actions was approached, if not equalled, by others in the suspect-group. Thus, for example, Henry Wakeley of Wethersfield was a notably frequent litigant (at least thirty-seven actions) in the years before his indictment for witchcraft.[94] John Black-leach, also of Wethersfield, was also suspected during the general Connecticut witch-hunt of the early 1660s, and was also a principal in numerous suits at law.[95] Of course, these three were exceptional among witches in their gender; their female counterparts were much less likely to go to court. Yet some at least of the latter, when compared to other *women*, also stand out as litigants. Katherine Harrison of Wethersfield launched at least a dozen lawsuits against neighbors just before and just after her indictment for witchcraft.[96] Margaret Gifford of Lynn was repeatedly in court, over a good many years, as "attourney" for her merchant-husband.[97]

Even in the absence of detailed court records it is sometimes possible to reconstruct the contentious bent of a witch's life and character. Once again the case of Boston's Anne Hibbens furnishes especially revealing material. As noted earlier, Mrs. Hibbens was excommunicated from Boston's first church, long before her indictment and trial for witchcraft. At issue in the church trial was her conduct toward several joiners whom she had employed to redecorate her house. A disagreement about price and payment had become a bitter quarrel, and Mrs. Hibbens had pleaded her own cause to the point of giving deep personal "offense." According to the joiners, she had lied, had spoken abusively ("she . . . said that the timbers of the room would cry for judgment against us"), and had generally refused to deal with them "according to the Word [of God]." Worse still was her "divulging and publishing it all abroad." She had spurned all opinions contrary to her own (including those of her husband, her pastor, and numerous duly appointed arbitrators). Thanks to Robert Keayne's eyewitness account of the church's inquiry into this affair, Mrs. Hibbens's personal style can still be scrutinized at close range.[98] In fact, the sympathies of a modern reader may well go out to the accused, as she is seen struggling against enormous communal pressures. However, there can be no doubt about the attitude of her fellow-congregants. Their disapproval, their scorn, their outrage are manifest on every page. Unfortunately, there is no comparable record of Mrs. Hibbens's witchcraft trial in 1656; but one roughly contemporaneous document, William Hubbard's *General History of New England*, includes the following summary:

> *Vox populi* went sore against her, and was the chiefest part of the evidence against her, as some thought. . . . Others have said that Mr. Hibbens losing £500 at once, by the carelessness of Mr. Trerice, the shipmaster, it so discomposed his wife's spirit that she scarce ever was well settled in her mind afterward, but grew very turbulent

in her passion, and discontented, on which occasions she was cast out of the church, and then charged to be a witch, giving too much occasion by her strange carriage to common people so to judge.

Hubbard himself was obviously skeptical about the result of the Hibbens case—and he drew from it a general conclusion: "Many times persons of hard favor and turbulent passions are apt to be condemned by the common people for witches, upon very slight grounds."[99]

That "persons of hard favor and turbulent passions" made likely targets for witchcraft accusations is borne out by other materials from other cases. What follows is a motley assemblage of taunts, threats, and curses attributed to one or another suspect:

Mercy Disborough did say that it should be pressed, heaped, and running over to her.[100]

He [Hugh Parsons] said unto me, "Gammer, you need not have said anything. I spoke not to you, but I shall remember you when you little think on it."[101]

She [Goodwife Jane Walford] said I had better have done it; that my sorrow was great already, and it should be greater—for I was going a great journey, but should never come there.[102]

She [Elizabeth Godman] said, "How doth Goody Thorp? I am beholden to Goody Thorp above all the women in the town; she would have had me to the gallows for a few chickens."[103]

Mercy Disborough told him that she would make him as bare as a bird's tail.[104]

Then said he [Hugh Parsons], "If you will not abate it [i.e. a certain debt in corn] it shall be but as lent. It shall do you no good. It shall be but as wild fire in your house, and as a moth in your clothes." And these threatening speeches he uttered with much anger.[105]

Goodwife Cole said that if this deponent's calves did eat any of her grass, she wished it might poison or choke them.[106]

He [William Brown] said that I was very fair for the Devil and . . . the Devil would fetch me speedily . . . and those that set their hands to the writings were going to the Devil for a New Year's gift, and it should be the dearest day's work that ever I made. . . .[107]

Goody Clawson called to me and asked me what was in my chamber last Sabbath day night . . . and at another time . . . she . . . contended with me . . . calling me "proud slut—what, are you proud of your fine clothes, and you long to be mistress, but you never shall be." And several other provoking speeches.[108]

Apart from documenting specific episodes of this type, the record yields more general impressions of the accused. Thus Elizabeth Godman was (described as) "a malicious one"; Elizabeth Morse had acted out of "the malice and envy of her heart"; Mary Hale yielded frequently to "discontent";[109] and so on. In one way or another these suspected witches revealed the angry center of their otherwise singular characters.

To be sure, most of the evidence on the motives and behavior of witches comes by way of their accusers; what, then, of its relation to "objective" reality? Perhaps such evidence should be viewed as inherently prejudiced, indeed as a reflection of the accusers' *own* character and inner preoccupations. This difficulty can be countered, if not entirely resolved, in several ways. For one thing, at least some of the pertinent testimony derives from situations which had nothing to do with witchcraft. (The life-stories of John Godfrey and Rachel Clinton furnish many obvious examples.) There are also various comments made in court *by* the suspects—in short, self-reports—to much the same effect. (Mary Johnson declared that general "discontent" had tempted her to invoke the Devil.[110] Katherine Harrison apologized for slandering her neighbors with "hasty, unadvised, and passionate expressions."[111] Hugh Parsons admitted that "in his anger he is impatient, and doth speak what he should not.")[112] Finally, there is the simple probability that so much opinion, of such a broadly convergent sort, cannot entirely misrepresent actual experience—the proverbial "fire" burning unseen but rightly inferred behind a cloud of all-too-evident "smoke." Hostile characterization usually finds some truth on which to fasten, even where it also expresses a deeply subjective concern.

From time to time the witches' characteristic "malice" shaded off into something more like mischief. Their conversation was sprinkled with comments likely to shock or startle, comments which often ran to witchcraft itself. John Godfrey was remembered for "speaking about the power of witches."[113] Mary Parsons would talk at length on the same subject, and then excuse herself thusly: "Why do I say so? I have no skill in witchery."[114] Thomas Wells denied charges of setting spells, invoking the Devil, and the like; however, "I does remember that I have discoursed with some of Carrington and his wife which suffered for witches, of Doctor Faustus, and [of] another in England which could set a spell and other acts of witchcraft."[115] Elizabeth Seager, accused at Hartford in 1663, "did adventure to bid Satan go and tell them she was no witch." (Her auditors were plainly aghast. One, "after she had a little paused, said, 'Who did you say?' Then Goodwife Seager said again she had sent Satan to tell them she was no witch. This deponent asked her why she made use of Satan to tell them, why she did not beseech God to tell them. . . . She answered, because Satan knew she was no witch.")[116] Such talk from a suspect seemed thoughtless, if not deliberately offensive; it served to confirm rather than deflect, the charges against her.

Some suspects appeared to favor witchcraft and its alleged practitioners. Elizabeth Godman "would be often speaking about witches . . . without any occasion . . . and [would] rather justify them than condemn them"; indeed, "she said, 'why do they provoke them? why do they not let them come into the church?' "[117] When her neighbor, Mrs. Goodyear, expressed confidence that God would ultimately "discover" and punish witches, "for I never knew a witch to die in their bed," Mrs. Godman disagreed. "You mistake," she said, "for a great many die and go to the grave in an orderly way."[118] Hugh Parsons was suspected of holding similar views. According to his wife he could "not abide that anything should be spoken against witches." Indeed the two of them quarreled while discussing a witch trial in another community: Hugh was allegedly angered "because she wished the ruin of all witches."[119] There were, in addition, postures of support for particular suspects (e.g. Alice Stratton for Margaret Jones, Elizabeth Seager for Goodwife Ayres, Mary Staples for Goodwife Knapp), which would also invite unfavorable notice.[120]

Some of these statements and postures serve to raise a further question. Was the impulse to provoke others through leading references to witchcraft a manifestation of some larger characterological disturbance? Here, indeed, is the germ of an old supposition, that witches have usually been deranged persons, insane or at least deeply eccentric. For New England the situation was largely otherwise. Numerous and varied forms of evidence suggest that insanity was recognized, understood, accepted—without reference to supernatural cause—whenever and wherever it might appear. Thus elderly New Englanders made wills containing special provision for kin who were "impotent . . . in understanding," or "taken with a lunacy," or "so distempered, . . . besotted and stupefied . . . as to be hopeless ever to act in the world."[121] Magistrates assigned power of attorney to women whose husbands had become "distracted."[122] Town officials dealt with the problems created by some who were given to sudden violence (e.g. "a lunatic man" of Andover, described as being so "outrageously mad or distracted . . . that he endangered great hurt or death" to others).[123] *All* such arrangements show a steady, almost matter-of-fact, tone. Consider two more:

> This court considering the case of Sarah Jackson, widow, in attempting to murder her late husband John Jackson, deceased, the fact

being owned by her . . . there being many testimonies presented to endeavor to prove her under some kind of distraction as the cause of that attempt . . . although the said attempt in the nature of it deserves a higher censure, yet finding her to be a woman subject to more than ordinary hurries and temptations, and at times crazy in her head, and subject by her age and sex to bodily infirmity, do only . . . order her to pay as a fine to the county treasury the sum of five pounds.[124]

Whereas Jane Flanders . . . was convicted before this court of being guilty of telling several lies, and for making debate among neighbors, and casting great reproaches upon several . . . the said same Flanders did acknowledge in court that she is often distempered in her head . . . [and] the premises considered, this court doth judge that she shall be disenabled for giving evidence in any case and be bound to her good behavior in the sum of ten pounds.[125]

This last pair of cases seems especially interesting in the present context. The behavior attributed to widow Jackson and Goodwife Flanders is notably reminiscent of that which, under some circumstances, gave rise to witchcraft charges: attempted murder, chronic lying, slander, and other forms of personal contentiousness. Yet here there was an added and special element: the evident "distraction" of the actors chiefly involved.

In what is known of the witch-suspects, this element does not appear. Of outright insanity there are no signs whatsoever, no incoherence of speech, no extreme irregularities of behavior, no very substantial disorder of thought or feeling.[126] To be sure, some portion of the accused behaved at least occasionally in peculiar ways: Goodwife Morse, observed "digging and crabbing the ground with the end of a staff, which I never took notice of any person that acted in the like manner," would make a fair example.[127] But they seem not to have been more than a *small* portion overall. By and large, what stands out about these people is their command of personal faculties, their ability to chart a given course of action, and to see it through.

However disagreeable they seemed to their peers, the suspects were tough, resilient, purposive. John Godfrey was not merely a frequent litigant; he was also a determined and successful one.[128] Anne Hibbens would bend, but never break, in the face of unanimous censure by her brethren in the Boston church.[129] Katherine Harrison countered the animus of her Wethersfield neighbors by way of formal actions at court and informal (personally given) rebuke.[130] Indeed it was this configuration of qualities that made the individuals involved seem not only suspect but genuinely fearsome. Had they been "crazed," "distracted," or "impotent . . . in understanding," their words and deeds would not have counted for very much. In reality, they seemed anything *but* "impotent." Their general ill will, their presumed envies and resentments, their explicit threats to do harm would all be treated with the utmost seriousness, precisely because, in a certain sense, they were *strong*.

Their strength was manifest even *in extremis*, even as accusations of witchcraft jeopardized their names and their very lives. Mary [Bliss] Parsons, "having intimation" of the suspicions against her, "voluntarily made her appearance in court"; when "called to speak for herself" on a subsequent occasion, "she did assert her own innocency, often mentioning . . . how clear she was of such a crime."[131] Elizabeth Clawson, "being reflected on . . . for witchcraft, was examined by the honorable court but doth absolutely and peremptorily deny herself to be any such person."[132] Mercy Disborough made a similar denial, "roundly and absolutely, and without the least stick or hesitancy."[133] Margaret Jones insisted on her innocence, in spite of "great pains [taken by neighbors] . . . to bring her to confession and repentence . . . and so she said unto her death." (According to one account, she was "very intemperate" at her trial, "railing upon the jury and witnesses.")[134] Jones's friend Alice Stratton defended her well after her execution, saying that she "died wrongfully . . . and her blood would be required at the magistrates' hands"; meanwhile the same magistrates were preparing charges against Stratton as well.[135]

The "great pains" used with Goody Jones were apparently standard in cases where the jury had returned a finding of guilt. Confession and repentance would perhaps gain some advantage for the convict in the afterlife of the spirit. There was, too, the issue of her "confederates"; perhaps a last charge of community pressure would serve to draw out the names of additional suspects. This pattern was vividly exemplified in the case of one Goodwife Knapp, executed for witchcraft at Fairfield, Connecticut, in 1653. Following her conviction Goody Knapp was visited by numerous women of the town, all urging her to "do as the witch at the other town did, that is, discover all she knew to be witches." Her response was properly guarded: "she said she must not say anything which is not true, she must not wrong anybody." Yet she also promised some last-minute revelations, to the minister or magistrate, just "before she went out of the world, when she was upon the ladder." Her interviewers were not satisfied; they wanted an immediate "discovery"—and they had a particular suspect in mind. Goody Knapp warned one of them "to take heed the Devil have not you, for she could not tell how soon she might be her companion," and added, "the truth is you would have me say that Goodwife Staples was a witch, but I have sins enough to answer for already, and I hope I shall not add to my condemnation. I know nothing by [i.e. about] Goodwife Staples, and I hope she is an honest woman." The others objected, "Did you hear us name Goodwife Staples' name since we came here?" and "wished her to have care what she said and not breed difference betwixt neighbors after she was gone." To which Goody Knapp replied once more: "Hold your tongue, you know not what I know, I have ground for what I say. I have been fished withal in private more than you are aware of. . . ." Discussion continued in this vein, and the position of Goody Knapp became more and more uncomfortable. She reportedly declared "that a woman in the town was a witch and would be hanged within a twelvemonth." She made tantalizing references to "Indian gods" and "shining things which shine lighter than the day." And when a friend "told her she was now to die, and therefore she should deal truly, she burst forth into weeping and desired me to pray for her, and said I knew not how she was tempted: 'Never, never a poor creature was tempted as I am tempted; pray, pray for me.'"[136]

That some of the accused yielded to such extraordinary pressures seems less surprising than the evident fact that many did not. Only at Salem did confessions, and attendant revelations about alleged confederates, come forth in large numbers. Otherwise most witches seem to have protested their innocence, as Margaret Jones did, "unto . . . death."

Conclusion

From this long and somewhat tortuous exercise in prosopography a rough composite finally emerges. To recapitulate, the typical witch:

1. was female.
2. was of middle age (i.e. between forty and sixty years old).
3. was of English (and "Puritan") background.
4. was married, but was more likely (than the general population) to have few children—or none at all.
5. was frequently involved in trouble and conflict with other family members.
6. had been accused, on some previous occasion, of committing crimes—most especially theft, slander, or other forms of assaultive speech.
7. was more likely (than the general population) to have professed and practiced a medical vocation, i.e. "doctoring" on a local, quite informal basis.

8. was of relatively low social position.
9. was abrasive in style, contentious in character—and stubbornly resilient in the face of adversity.

Of course, few actual suspects conformed to all of the above specifications; and, conversely, many non-suspects could be fitted to half or more of them. A list of this type deals, at most, in probabilities, beyond which lies the irreducible factor of human idiosyncracy.

Moreover: since witchcraft was always a drama of multiple parts, only so much can be learned from any one line of study. Even with a prime suspect in view—one whose resemblance to our witch-profile approached perfection—there could be no "case" until every part was filled. Victim(s), accuser(s), a chorus of witnesses and "bystanders": thus was the cast rounded out. These other roles, and the people who filled them, have the next claim to attention.

TWO
Psychology

"She said that she knew nothing of those things that were spoken by her, but that her tongue was improved to express what was never in her mind, which was a matter of great affliction to her."

The Rev. John Whiting (1662),
on the fits of Ann Cole

4

"A Diabolical Distemper"

Introduction

In their front-line struggle against the Devil and his legions, New Englanders labored under severe handicaps. Theirs was a supremely difficult task because the enemy was so devious, so shrewd, so resourceful in his methods of attack. His strategy was endlessly varied and surprising; he missed no opportunity for destructive intervention in human affairs. He possessed, moreover, the great advantage of being *invisible* to those whom he strove to subdue. The term most frequently applied to him, "Prince of Darkness," served to characterize both his ends and his means. Most of his efforts were cloaked by stealth and subterfuge—seen only in their injurious effects.

Fortunately, there were certain moments when the terms of warfare sharpened, permitting a more open and straightforward confrontation. Periodically, for example, the hand of the Devil fell directly on particular human victims, causing "fits" and other torment of an unmistakable kind. Usually these victims were girls past childhood but not yet fully adult. In their sufferings others could find an epitome of malevolent power. Human behavior, indeed the core of human personality, was shockingly distorted; a daughter, or a neighbor, appeared as one "transformed." Many such assaults had, as their alleged source, some local witch acting at the Devil's behest. Occasionally, however, Satan attacked without intermediaries. "Possessing" his victim from inside, he made of her a literal "demoniac."

Each episode of this sort, though utterly horrifying to pious folk, afforded a fine opportunity to study the Devil from close-up. In an atmosphere charged with anticipation and excitement, whole neighborhoods gathered around, noting every one of the victim's strange "carriages." Physicians were summoned to make a preliminary diagnosis; "natural" causes must be definitely ruled out, before further steps could be taken. Magistrates would also be present, to deal with legal issues as they might arise. But ministers were concerned here, above all others; theirs was the central role in fighting Evil and its specific manifestations. They were the experts, the leading tacticians, the mightiest warriors in supernatural combat.

In a clear case of possession certain procedures were axiomatic: prayers beside the victim when she was "in her fits," earnest conversation with her when she felt temporarily "relieved." Sometimes, indeed, a minister would actually invite the victim into his own household for a period of uninterrupted observation.[1] There were special occasions of fasting and prayer—daylong sessions of intense involvement for all concerned. Ministers came from out of town, hoping both to assist in resolving the case at hand and to deepen their understanding of diabolism in general. Long, painstaking discussions were held among them. The victim was enjoined, time and again, to describe one or another aspect of her experiences. The result was a body of information of quite extraordinary value.

But in order to be maximally useful this information must be publicized; invariably, the ministers themselves rose to the occasion. Their pulpits made an obvious and ready forum. Sermons would provide a digest of the lessons learned from particular episodes of possession. Why had the Devil struck here, rather than in another place? What had been the chief openings for his malign influence? Which forms of godly ministration had proved most effective as counter-influence? Questions such as these demanded the fullest possible consideration. To broaden the web of their communication, the ministers availed themselves of the written—no less than the spoken—word. Those who had observed the Devil's onslaught at first hand were quick to record their impressions for the benefit of colleagues. Manuscript accounts of witchcraft circulated through the ranks of the clergy in various parts of New England.[2] Occasionally these materials seemed worthy of publication. Increase Mather's *Illustrious Providences* was the first such work actually printed in New England; released in 1684, it became thereafter a model adopted by several others.[3] These books were written with a twofold purpose. They displayed most vividly the power of "providence," whether for good or ill, to alter the course of human affairs; in so doing they affirmed, and underscored, belief in the supernatural. At the same time, they were meant to reduce the Devil's influence by holding him up to public scrutiny. As in so many things "Puritan," the issue of *exposure* was central here.

Whatever their contribution to the cause for which they were intended, these writings are a godsend to historians. For evident human interest, for richness of detail, for all they reveal about the intersection of character and culture, they are unsurpassed among extant materials from the seventeenth century. They present a picture that is almost clinical in substance and tone; comparison with psychiatric case reports in our own time does not seem far-fetched. There is, in short, no better window on the inner world of mental and emotional structures that supported the belief in witchcraft in colonial New England.

Description of the Case

In the month of January 1672 the Rev. Samuel Willard finished a treatise of some eight thousand words, entitled "A Brief Account of a Strange and Unusual Providence of God Befallen to Elizabeth Knapp of Groton."[4] Soon thereafter he sent it off to Increase Mather in Boston, and it is found among the Mathers Papers today. There is no way of discovering how many persons saw Willard's manuscript, but Mather himself included a short summary in his *Illustrious Providences*.[5] So it was that the possession of Elizabeth Knapp entered the general fund of knowledge upon which New Englanders drew in their struggles against the Devil.[6]

Wasting no space on preliminaries, Willard's "account" began as follows:

> This poor and miserable object, about a fortnight before she was taken, we observed to carry herself in a strange and unwonted manner. Sometimes she would give sudden shrieks, and if we inquired a reason would always put it off with some excuse; and then [she] would burst forth into immoderate and extravagant laughter, in such ways as sometimes she fell onto the ground with it. I myself observed oftentimes a strange change in her countenance, but could not suspect the true reason, but conceived she might be ill, and therefore diverse times inquired how she did, and she always answered well—which made me wonder.[7]

The time of this beginning was autumn, 1671; the place was Willard's own household. The leading figure in the events about to unfold was Elizabeth Knapp, a girl of sixteen. Sometime during the preceding summer Elizabeth had come to live with the minister and his family as a maidservant.[8]

On Monday, October 30, her "affliction" began in earnest; it continued until at least mid-January, when Willard broke off his narrative. Its features were quite numerous and diverse, and varied sharply in their intensity. Nonetheless, the overall sequence showed important elements of rhythm and patterning visible even through a welter of bizarre detail. There was, in the first place, a series of marked swings—from repeated and violent fits, to quieter periods of "intermission," and back again. It is necessary to describe these with some care.

As experienced by Elizabeth herself, the fits began with painful attacks on her own person: "In the evening [of October 30] . . . sitting before the fire, she cried out 'Oh, my legs!' and clapped her hand on them. Immediately [she cried], 'Oh, my breast!' and removed her hands thither. And forthwith, 'Oh, I am strangled!' and put her hands on her throat."[9] Similar behavior recurred at intervals later on. At one point in early December Elizabeth complained of terrible new "assaults . . . [which took the form of] scratching her breasts, beating her sides, strangling her throat, and she did often times seem to our apprehension as if she would forthwith be strangled."[10]

A second aspect of the fits, clearly related to the first, was sheer motoric frenzy. Viewed through the eyes of the bystanders, there was something appallingly *physical* here. It was as if Elizabeth's body had released a vast store of latent energies all at once, no matter what the cost or consequences:

> From thence to Sabbath day . . . she was violent in bodily motions, leapings, strainings, and strange agitations, scarce to be held in bounds by the strength of three of four . . . violent also in roarings and screamings, representing a dark resemblance of hellish torments. . . .[11]

And again, some days later:

> She was . . . with violence and extremity seized by her fits in such ways that six persons could hardly hold her; but she leaped and skipped about the house perforce, roaring and yelling extremely and fetching deadly sighs as if her heartstrings would have broken, and looking with a frightful aspect, to the amazement and astonishment of all the beholders.[12]

Elizabeth in her fits had become a corporeal bomb, observed in the process of exploding.

These extraordinary behaviors sometimes conveyed an openly destructive thrust. A clear instance occurred in mid-December, when Elizabeth "was hurried again into violent fits . . . striking those that held her [and] spitting in their faces. And if at any time she had done any harm or frightened them, she would laugh immediately."[13] Yet an attack aimed outwards at the available human targets was easily turned back on the self. In introducing one such episode, Willard speaks of Elizabeth "using all endeavors to make away with herself and doing mischief unto others."[14] Indeed the self-destructive impulse had been present almost from the beginning. Two nights after her first severe seizures, she was "suddenly thrown down into the midst of the floor with violence, . . . and with much ado was . . . kept out of the fire from destroying herself."[15]

Here, then, were the standard ingredients of Elizabeth Knapp's fits: painful sensations of attack, expressions of wild, physical abandon, overtly destructive behavior toward self and others. To these must be added certain forms of perceptual and verbal disturbance. Her eyes were "always, or for the most part, . . . sealed up . . . in those fits."[16] And often, during the same periods, she was rendered "speechless."[17] (She described her subjective experience of the latter difficulty in these terms: "When she was taken speechless, she feared as if a string was tied about the roots of her tongue, and reached down into her vitals, and pulled her tongue down—and then most when she strove to speak.")[18] Occasionally, her speech was disordered rather than wholly inhibited, and she would repeat "diverse words, sometimes crying out 'money, money,' sometimes 'sin and misery,' with other words."[19] But she could never, while thus afflicted, converse with others in a reasoned way. At the same time, her understanding remained intact, "for when she came out of it, she could give a relation of all that had been spoken to her."[20]

As the weeks passed, her fits were elaborated and extended in various ways. New, and increasingly bizarre, features appeared alongside the usual repertoire. During one stretch she "barked like a dog, and bleated like a calf, in which her [vocal] organs were visibly made use of."[21] (Here her sensory powers were heightened rather than diminished, for "whenever any [person] came near the house, though they within heard nothing at all, yet she would bark till they were come into the house.")[22] On another occasion, "she got her a stick, and went up and down, thrusting and pushing here and there."[23] On a third, "her tongue was for many hours together drawn into a semicircle up to the roof of her mouth, and not to be removed (for some tried with the fingers to do it)."[24] Finally, there was an extraordinary moment when the Devil "entered" Elizabeth directly, and spoke, as it were, "through" her. (Of this, more later on.)[25]

The fits, as noted previously, alternated with distinct "intermissions."
During these periods Elizabeth remained relatively calm, rational, and
at least outwardly amenable to human influence. She was able not only
to hear and to understand, but also to respond in kind. Still, there were
lingering signs of *malaise*. Immediately after the cessation of her fits, she
felt anxious, contrite, self-accusatory, and openly "melancholy." Thus,
for example,

> On Tuesday [November 28], about 12 of the clock, she came out
> of a fit which had held her from Sabbath day. . . . And then her
> speech was restored to her, and she expressed a great, seeming
> sense of her state. Many bitter tears, sighings, sobbings, complain-
> ings she uttered, bewailing of many sins aforementioned, begging
> prayers, and in the hour of prayer expressing much affection.[26]

Often, at such times, Elizabeth would recount her spiritual failings in
considerable detail. She spoke of her "disobedience to parents," her
"profanation of the sabbath," her resentment against "burdensome" labor,
and the fact that "she was neither content to be at home nor abroad."
She was willing, even eager, to declare how "unprofitable [a] life she
had led, and how justly God had thus permitted Satan to handle her."[27]

But these moments of open remorse yielded, quite regularly, to a far
more impassive state. Elizabeth's mood turned flat and distant; Willard
called it "a sottish and stupid kind of frame . . . [when] much was
pressed upon her, but no affection at all [was] discovered."[28] More, she
showed "an extreme senselessness of her own estate." Far from willingly
reproaching herself, she said that "she had no trouble upon her spirits,
. . . [and that] Satan had left her."[29] Of course, this seemed particularly
distressing to the ministers. It was as if Elizabeth had drawn a curtain
against their influence, and they had no effective means to pull it aside.
She turned from their prayers, and their earnest pleadings, with blasé
indifference—"her tears dried up and her senses stupified."[30]

One further aspect of the intermissions deserves special emphasis. It
was during their "active" phase that Elizabeth managed to talk most
fully and coherently about her personal transactions with the Devil. She
acknowledged, from the outset, frequent and varied contact: meetings,
conversations, arguments, "struggles." And she admitted her own complicity in all this. She was sure that her general mood of "discontent"
had invited the Devil's attentions in the first place;[31] and she recalled
from years earlier her interest in knowing him quite fully. ("She acknowledged . . . that when she came to our house to school, before such

time as she dwelt with us, she delayed her going home in the evening till it was dark, . . . upon his persuasion to have his company home; and [she said] that she could not, when he appeared, but go to him.")[32]

For his own part, the Devil had one central purpose in approaching her: he wished to gain a new follower for his infamous cause. Time after time he appeared before her, carrying "a book, written with blood, of covenants made by others with him."[33] Always he urged that she add her own name to the list. As means of "persuasion," he mixed offers of gifts and favors with long harangues, threats, and actual violence. In exchange for a commitment he would give "largely to her—viz., such things as suited her youthful fancy, [including] money, silks, fine clothes, ease from labor, to show her the whole world, etc."[34] Often he volunteered to help with her household chores "and once in particular to bring her in chips for the fire, [and] she refused; but when she came in she saw them lie by the fireside, and was afraid."[35] At times he tried a different approach, using "many arguments" to convince her that her sins were already irremediably great.[36] (Once, after urging others to repentance, she declared sadly that "it is too late for me.")[37] He also "assaulted her many ways," "sat upon her breast," and forced her to view the "hellish shapes . . . [of] more devils than anyone . . . ever saw men in the world."[38] It was this latter treatment which—according to Elizabeth—caused most of the wild behavior in her fits.

Her flashes of destructive impulse could also be ascribed to Satanic agency. Repeatedly the Devil had urged her "to murder her parents, her neighbors, our children, especially the youngest—tempting her to throw it into the fire, on the hearth, into the oven."[39] Indeed he had given her a "bill-hook" to use in attacking Willard himself; "but coming about it, she met me on the stairs, at which she was affrighted." (Willard recalled this meeting quite distinctly—in particular, the "strange frame in her countenance" and her obvious efforts "to hide something"; but at the time he had no reason to suspect her truly murderous intent.)[40] Suicide was a further part of the Devil's persuadings. Once Elizabeth was on the verge of drowning herself in a well, "for, looking into it, she saw such sights as allured her, and was gotten within the curb, and was by God's providence prevented."[41]

The full span of Elizabeth's possession, as recorded in Willard's narrative, was an even three months (October 16–January 15). Within this period she experienced some eighteen days of "extreme" or "violent" fits. There were perhaps sixteen additional days with fits of "moderate" in-

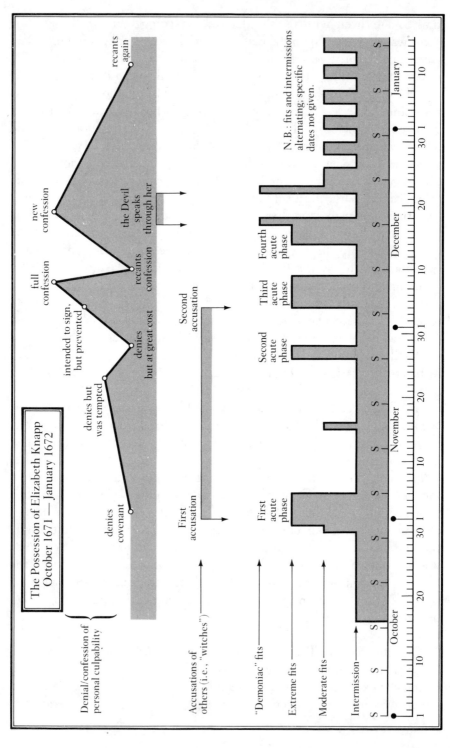

The Possession of Elizabeth Knapp
October 1671 — January 1672

Denial/confession of
personal culpability

recants
again

new
confession

full
confession

intended to sign,
but prevented

denies but
was tempted

denies
but at great cost

recants
confession

the Devil
speaks
through her

denies
covenant

Accusations of
others (i.e., "witches")

First
accusation

Second
accusation

"Demoniac" fits

First acute
phase

Second
acute
phase

Third
acute
phase

Fourth
acute
phase

N.B.: fits and intermissions
alternating; specific
dates not given.

Extreme fits

Moderate fits

Intermission

October   November   December   January
1   S   10   S   20   S   S   30   S   10   S   20   S   S   30   S   10   S   20   S   S   30   S   10

tensity. The remainder of the time (roughly fifty-eight days) comprised her intermissions. These different kinds (or intensities) of experience were not, of course, randomly distributed. (See chart.) Indeed the fits were grouped into four main clusters—truly the critical periods in the entire sequence.

First Acute Phase

The earliest of Elizabeth's severe seizures began, as noted, at the end of October, and lasted through the evening of November 4. Significantly, their onset coincided with Samuel Willard's absence from his household on a trip that would last several days. Still, there was no lack of volunteers to attend the "miserable" victim in her hours of torment. On the second day she was "observed by diverse" (persons from outside the Willard household); by the fourth day she was performing "in the presence of many." She asked that the pastor in the neighboring town of Lancaster come to pray with her, and her wish was immediately granted. Willard himself returned home on Friday, November 3. His efforts to deal with her proved totally futile at first; indeed whenever he "came in [her] presence, she fell into those fits."[42]

From the very outset all her attendants sought to fathom the cause of Elizabeth's behavior. The most obvious possibility, and the one that first occurred to the victim herself, was affliction by local witches. Thus in the midst of these early seizures Elizabeth "seemed to impeach one of the neighbors . . . as though she, or the Devil in her likeness . . . had come down the chimney [and] stricken her." The woman so designated was sent for at once and subjected to an ancient test for witchcraft. She, along with others from the crowd that stood by, was made to *touch* the victim—whose eyes remained "sealed up" all the while. The initial result was *positive*, for Elizabeth "knew her very touch from any other, though no voice were uttered, and discovered it evidently by her gestures." Yet this by itself did not warrant formal charges, and further tests proved contradictory. Willard's narrative becomes uncharacteristically vague at this point, noting only the conclusion: "Afterward God was pleased to . . . justify the innocent—even to remove jealousies from the spirits of the party concerned." There were prayers all around, and Elizabeth complained no more of "apparition or disturbance" from this particular source.[43] The lack of specific information about this outcome is regrettable, for it set the entire case on a new and distinctive track. Later Elizabeth would try once more to pin the blame on local witchcraft, with an equally unsuccessful result.[44]

Her attempted accusation having been turned aside, Elizabeth "used many tergiversations and excuses" (to gain time?), and presently "broke forth into a large confession." This became the first of her many sessions of self-reproach. However, she drew the line when "pressed to declare whether she had not consented to a covenant with the Devil . . . [and] with solemn assertions denied it." To be sure, her chronic state of "discontent" had served to arouse his interest, but she had utterly rejected his urging to "sign the book." Then why, others wished to know, did her fits continue? Because, she replied, the Devil was using every means, including physical torture, to break down her resistance.[45]

On Sunday, November 5, a "physician" came to examine Elizabeth, and offered a medical diagnosis. He declared that "a main part of her distemper . . . [was] natural, arising from the foulness of the stomach and corruptness of her blood, occasioning fumes in her brain and strange fantasies." The patient was directed to take "physic" (i.e. medicine), and was sent home to her own parents.[46] These measures produced an immediate and salutary effect; Elizabeth grew much quieter, and "gave some hopes of recovery." Indeed, she enjoyed a lengthy intermission, occasionally "exercised with some moderate fits . . . yet not with extremity." There was one difficult day (November 15) when Willard had arranged a special prayer meeting for her. Her fits began to re-intensify, but abated again the following night.[47] Meanwhile, she was questioned repeatedly about her contacts with the Devil. She added to her former statements an account of two journeys by horseback when the Devil "accompanied her in [the] form of a black dog with eyes in his back." She still denied having "verbally promised to covenant with him," but "acknowledged that she had some thoughts so to do." The latter was a significant admission; among other things, it encouraged Willard to press for further changes in her story.[48]

Second Acute Phase

On Sunday, November 26, Elizabeth was seized with violent new fits, which lasted virtually without interruption for more than forty-eight hours. The physician now "contended that her distemper was diabolical, refused further to administer, [and] advised . . . extraordinary fasting; whereupon some of God's ministers were sent for."[49] From this point forward Willard and his colleagues were completely in charge. On Tuesday, November 28, Elizabeth came out of her fits, into the usual forms of self-reproach. This, in turn, was succeeded by a new spell of quiet distraction and passivity—and then, six days later, by more fits. Thus, the wheel of her "distemper" came full circle once again.[50]

Third Acute Phase

The pace of the treatment effort quickened. Ministers from neighboring towns came and went, and local onlookers maintained an almost constant vigil; Willard complained that "there was no room for privacy."[51] From all sides Elizabeth was pressed for new admissions, and step-by-step she gave her ground. On December 4 (concurrent with the renewal of severe fits) she allowed that once "after many assaults, she had resolved to seal a covenant with Satan . . . [and] he presented himself and desired of her blood, and she would have done it, but wanted a knife." Again, on a later occasion, she had been ready to yield, but was "prevented—by the providence of God interposing my [i.e. Willard's] father." (The details of this encounter are somewhat obscure.)[52]

Having reached the brink of a terrible confession, Elizabeth drew back temporarily and sought to throw the blame elsewhere. In the midst of a particularly violent fit, she suddenly "cried out of a witch, appearing . . . in the form of a dog downward, with a woman's head." She proceeded to name another Groton neighbor as the source of all her agonies, declaring "that if the party were apprehended, she would forthwith be well, but never till then." In accordance with established procedure, the woman she accused was brought immediately to the scene. Elizabeth responded with

> unusual shrieks, at the instant of the person's coming in, though her eyes were fast closed. But having experience of such former actings, we made nothing of it but waited the issue. God therefore was sought to, to signify something whether the innocent might be ac-quited or the guilty discovered; and He answered our prayers, for by two evident and clear mistakes she was cleared, and then all prejudices ceased, and she never more to this day hath impeached her of any apparition.[53]

For a second time Elizabeth had tried, and failed, to identify a witch from her own community. Later she would claim that the Devil had purposely "deceived her concerning those persons impeached by her." He had assumed "their likeness" while tormenting her, and had told her "that they bore her a spleen, but he loved her and would free her from them."[54] In this way Elizabeth excused her "mistakes," but scarcely re-solved her larger predicament. With no witches to accuse and prosecute, the focus of inquiry narrowed to the issue of her own guilt. Very soon the pressure would become too much for her.

On Friday, December 8, Elizabeth "did, first to one, and afterwards to many, acknowledge that she had given of her blood to the Devil, and made a covenant with him."[55] In personal conference with Willard, she spelled out some particulars. (For example, she was illiterate and could not write her name in the infamous book, but the Devil guided her hand.) The "contract" was for seven years: "one year she was to be faithful in his service, and then the other six he would serve her and make her a witch." Later she grew remorseful—so she claimed—and wished to nullify the entire agreement. This enraged the Devil, and he tried to make her sign again, "which she refused to do . . . whereupon he struck her"—beginning her most recent fits.[56]

Quickly, Elizabeth regretted having confessed to so much. On Saturday, December 9, she returned to a "stupefied" state, and by Sunday she was eager for a chance to recant. She sent urgently for Willard, and "with tears told me that she had belied the Devil in saying she had given him of her blood, etc." She sought to change her story so as to reassume an earlier position, admitting some "persuasions" toward a diabolic pact, but not the actual deed. Willard was neither sympathetic nor believing: "I declared a suspicion of the truth of the relation, and gave her some reasons." A day later, at a private conference between the two of them, he rebuked her "preposterous courses" and declared that "it was no marvel . . . she had been led into such contradictions."[57]

Fourth Acute Phase

Soon Elizabeth was overtaken by new fits, the most angry and destructive she had yet experienced. It was now that she lashed out openly at her various caretakers. But this was only a prelude to the central episode in the entire case—an episode which, for Willard, resolved any lingering doubt "whether she might properly be called a demoniac, or person possessed of the Devil."[58] For at last Satan directly revealed himself "by speaking vocally in her." The sequence began while most of the townspeople were at Sabbath services. (Elizabeth had remained at home with "a little company.") First, her body assumed "amazing postures"; then a strange, "grum" voice erupted from somewhere inside her. Her father and a neighbor rushed back from the meeting-house, and were greeted with a string of invectives from the Devil-in-Elizabeth. Willard arrived a short while later; his first-hand impressions merit full quotation:

> The first salutation I had was, "Oh! you are a great rogue." I was
> at first something daunted and amazed . . . which brought me to
> a silence . . . in my spirits, till at last God heard my groans and
> gave me both refreshment in Christ and courage. I then called for
> a light to see whether it might not appear a counterfeit, and ob-

served not any of her organs to move. The voice was hollow, as if it issued out of her throat. He then again called me a great black rogue. I challenged him to make it appear [so]; but all the answer was, "You tell the people a company of lies." . . . I answered, "Satan, thou art a liar and a deceiver, and God will vindicate His own truth one day." He answered nothing directly, but said, "I am not Satan; I am a pretty black boy [and] this is my pretty girl. I have been here a great while." I sat still and answered nothing to these expressions. But when he directed himself to me again—[saying] "Oh! you black rouge, I do not love you"—I replied, "Through God's grace, I hate thee." He rejoined, "But you had better love me." . . . I seeing little good to be done by discourse, and questioning many things in my mind concerning it, I desired the company to join in prayer unto God. When we went about that duty and were kneeled down, with a voice louder than before he cried out, "Hold your tongue, hold your tongue; get you gone, you black rogue; what are you going to do; you have nothing to do with me," etc.[59]

The effect of all this was at once terrifying and enormously seductive. Samuel Willard had assumed his rightful place as spokesman for the forces of God, but it was not easy to keep eager bystanders from jumping into the fray. Some "put on boldness to speak to him," in spite of the minister's explicit advice to the contrary. How often, after all, did ordinary folk have a chance to test their wits—and their courage—in open disputation with the Devil? The course of the exchange, thrust and counter-thrust, became increasingly disordered, and the Devil resorted to outright "blasphemy." With a final admonition to the crowd "to be wary of speaking," Willard took his leave. And there is no further record of this extraordinary scene.[60]

Subsequent events were anti-climactic. On the following Tuesday (December 19) Elizabeth made a new confession, declaring that "the Devil entered into her the second night after her first taking [i.e. fit] . . . at her mouth, and had been in her ever since."[61] On Wednesday she demanded to be taken to Boston in order that a large "assembly of ministers" might pray with her. (But hard winter weather made any such plan impractical.) And on Friday there were particularly severe fits, including a second performance by "the same voice" from somewhere inside Elizabeth.[62] After the New Year her condition appeared to stabilize. The pattern of fits and intermissions became almost routine, and her seizures were somewhat "abated in violence." Still, there was no sign of fundamental improvement, and no clear prospect of recovery. "Thus, she continues . . . to this instant . . . followed with fits," wrote

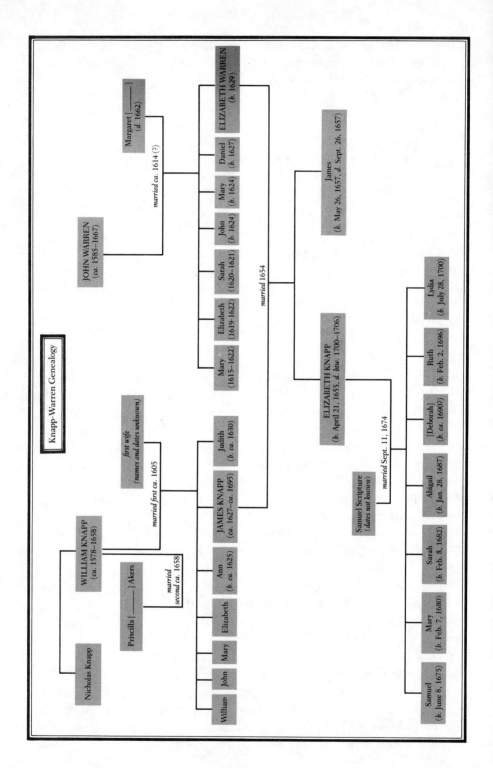

Knapp-Warren Genealogy

Willard on January 15.[63] Unhappily for latter-day students of witchcraft, the pastor broke off his running narrative just here. How, and when, and where the case was finally resolved—these things we will never know.

Background of the Major Participants

The drama described herein was played to a large audience, but the principal actors were only two: the "demoniac"-girl and her clergyman-therapist. To a large extent, the development of the case depended on the formal structure and inner dynamics of their relation to one another. It seems necessary, therefore, to learn as much as possible about their personal and family histories, both before and after the events which joined them in such compelling fashion.

The Knapps and the Warrens

Like most seventeenth-century families, the Knapps have left only modest traces for the historian to follow. Elizabeth's paternal grandfather, William Knapp, reached Massachusetts in 1630; his brother Nicholas arrived at about the same time. Both men belonged to a party of migrants recruited and financed by Sir Richard Saltonstall as the nucleus for a settlement at Watertown. William was by then at least fifty years old, married, and the father of several children.[64] He was evidently a carpenter by trade; called "old Knapp," he appears in the Watertown Records as late as 1652, performing contracts for repairs on the meeting-house and the construction of an animal pound.[65] His wife, meanwhile, was licensed to keep a "house of entertainment" [i.e. a tavern].[66] Fragmentary information suggests that this family possessed no more than an average amount of property relative to the full range of their fellow-townspeople.[67] And their social position was equally modest. William Knapp was never an officeholder, at either the local or the provincial level. At least three times he was summoned before the General Court for offenses against the law—for swearing, for speeches against the governor, and for selling beer without proper authorization.[68] He died at Watertown in 1658, "aged about 80."[69]

William Knapp raised at least three sons; the one who concerns us here is James, born in England about the year 1627.[70] His first appearance in contemporaneous documents comes from a list of Watertown men who took an "oath of fidelity" in 1652.[71] Four years later he reappears, in a far more substantial and significant context. Married by this time, James Knapp was formally charged in the court of Middlesex county with the grievous crime of adultery.[72] A Watertown widow named Mary Davis had recently died in prison while giving birth to a bastard child; she attributed paternity to Knapp, "constantly affirming the same, in her health and right mind, as also to her death."[73] The further handling of this case is not recorded, though evidently there was no conviction.[74] In 1657 James was back in court, confessing to drunkenness,[75] and in the same year he was fined for violating certain town ordinances.[76] Meanwhile his older brother, John Knapp, was convicted on several counts of "diverse flagitious practices and thefts," and given a heavy punishment.[77] (James himself was implicated in some of the "thefts," though not, apparently, prosecuted for them.) And their aging father, William, was judged "so enfeebled in his understanding" as to be unable to manage his affairs.[78] This was, in sum, an unusually difficult period for the whole clan.

Yet gradually James's fortunes began to improve. Last noted at Watertown in 1661 (as a recipient of payment "for the stocks"),[79] he went the next year to join in a new settlement at Groton, thirty miles to the northwest. He received land there as an original proprietor; and, with the exception of one brief period during King Philip's War, he remained a Groton resident for the rest of his life. His land holdings, and his share of a local "rate" made in 1681, suggest that his economic position was above average, but distinctly below the level of the most wealthy.[80]

James Knapp made his greatest mark at Groton through extensive public service; few if any of his contemporaries appear in the town records as frequently as he does, in various positions of official trust. In 1665, when James was not yet forty years old, he was chosen as a selectman, and he was re-elected to this office almost every year until 1692.[81] He also served on numerous *ad hoc* committees—to seat the meetinghouse, to supervise construction of a gristmill, to negotiate town boundary lines.[82] Called "corporal," and later "sergeant," in various official documents, he was a leader in the military "training band" of his community.[83] The sum of this evidence reveals a quite exemplary career. Moreover, given the absence of special distinction in his family line, his checkered past, and his relatively modest wealth, James Knapp must have earned his honors chiefly by way of energy, talent, and (reformed) character.

James Knapp's wife was born Elizabeth Warren, in England in about 1629.[84] She, too, was raised in Watertown, but beyond this her life is virtually undocumented. Fortunately, her family can be traced at least in part. Her father, John Warren, was a cardmaker from Nayland, county Suffolk. There, in 1629, he was prosecuted by the church authorities for refusing to kneel at communion; the following year he joined the first great Puritan hegira to New England.[85] He was forty-five years old, married, and the father of four young children. The family settled at Watertown, where John Warren soon achieved local prominence. The land records of the town attribute eight different lots to his ownership, comprising a total of nearly two hundred acres.[86] Twice in the early years he was chosen as a selectman, and he held other offices as well.[87] After 1650, however, his position in the community was distinctly altered. His religious views, especially his opposition to infant baptism, placed him outside the orthodox mainstream, and led to various "presentments" and prosecutions in the courts.[88] He was apparently friendly toward the Quakers (dreaded heretics, in the eyes of the Massachusetts establishment); at least once he was suspected of harboring such persons in his house, contrary to law.[89] By the end of his life John Warren's nonconformity was a fact well attested in both old and New England.

James Knapp and Elizabeth Warren were married in Watertown in 1654. Their first child, a daughter whom they chose to call Elizabeth, was born on April 21 of the following year. In May 1657 a new baby arrived—a son named after his father. However, the town records note the death of this child barely four months later, and there were no more children born to the Knapps thereafter.[90]

What can be learned of Elizabeth Knapp's early years? Her father's (alleged) misconduct must have thrown a cloud over her little *ménage*. And this was followed, likely deepened, by her infant brother's death. As to her mother, there is no hard information; but a fragment from a contemporaneous diary suggests important—and highly plausible—possibilities. The source is the Boston merchant John Hull, the time "about 1658," the substance as follows:

> There was a woman of [illeg.], Knapp; pretending to rail, and being troublesome, she was sent to prison. Sometimes she would hate Quakers, sometimes plead for them; sometimes weeping tears, she could, out of herself, speak not a word to any; sometimes weary others with much speaking.[91]

Was this Elizabeth [Warren] Knapp? The absence, in Hull's notation, of a given name forbids certainty; but the chances do seem strong.[92] Perhaps, then, this family drama presented not only an adulterous father but also a seriously disturbed mother. (And perhaps the *two* developments were interconnected.)

Willard's "Brief Account" provides some additional scraps of information: (1) Elizabeth lived for a time in the neighboring town of Lancaster —presumably as a maidservant, and perhaps in the household of Simon Willard (Samuel's father); (2) she moved in with the family of the younger Willard (in Groton) some weeks previous to the onset of her fits;[93] (3) she had been going regularly "to our house [i.e. Samuel Willard's] to school, before such time as she dwelt with us."[94] This evidence makes a cumulative point of some interest. Elizabeth was, from a certain age, largely under the care and tutelage of adults other than her own parents.

In the fall of 1674 Elizabeth was married to a man named Samuel Scripture. Curiously, their wedding is noted in the records of Cambridge, but their life henceforth was centered in Groton.[95] Scripture first appears in the records of Groton in January 1673.[96] There is, in fact, no prior indication of his presence anywhere in New England—nor of others with the same surname. Apparently he was a complete outsider, perhaps a new immigrant from England. His position at Groton was modest from the start. He ranked in the lower half of taxpayers in 1681.[97] He served occasionally as a minor office-holder: as fenceviewer, hogreeve, surveyor, and (once) constable.[98] He was a soldier in King Philip's War.[99] But there was nothing here to distinguish him from the average yeoman-householder. Certainly, his career made quite a contrast with that of his notably prominent father-in-law.

Samuel and Elizabeth [Knapp] Scripture lived together as husband and wife for at least twenty-five years. During this time Elizabeth bore at least six children.[100] The last of these arrived in the year 1700, and by 1707 Samuel was having children by a second wife (named Sarah).[101] Evidently, therefore, Elizabeth did not survive much past the beginning of the new century. All things considered, her life after 1672 seems quite unextraordinary—or at least unrecorded. Supremely notorious at one point in her girlhood, she soon returned to the ranks of ordinary folk in a small, rural community.

The Willards

Samuel Willard, our second major protagonist, was born at the pinnacle of New England society, and remained there throughout his life. His forebears were gentlefolk from the counties of Sussex and Kent in old England. Simon Willard, father of Samuel, came to Massachusetts in 1634 as a man of twenty-nine. Dignified from the first with the title "Mr.," he was granted a large homestead at Cambridge. After just two years, however, he joined with the Rev. Peter Bulkeley in founding the new town of Concord. Here he became at once a justice of the peace, and a deputy to the General Court. In 1654 he was made an Assistant of the Bay Colony, and he retained this high office until his death twenty-two years later. He was also a military leader for the entire province, earning the rank of "Major." His wealth was very great by the standards of his time; his "estates" at Concord, and later at Groton, ran to many hundreds of acres. He fathered seventeen children, by three different wives. As much as any man in early New England, he qualifies for the term "patriarch."[102]

Samuel was the sixth child of Simon; his birth, at Concord, occurred on the last day of January 1640. He spent four years at Harvard, graduating in the class of 1659.[103] He began his preaching at Groton in 1663, and was ordained there in 1664.[104] In the same year he married Abigail Sherman, herself the daughter of a distinguished New England clergyman. The birth of his own children began in 1665, with the arrival of a daughter named Abigail. A son (Samuel, Jr.) was born in 1668, but does not seem to have survived infancy. A second daughter arrived in 1669.[105] If, then, we stop the record of Willard's life at the time when Elizabeth Knapp came into his household, we find a young (thirty-one-year-old) clergyman of excellent pedigree, well established in his first pulpit, married, and the father of two small daughters.

His career thereafter fulfilled the promise implicit in his birth and early achievements. He continued his ministry at Groton until March 1676 when the town was devastated by a sudden Indian attack. The survivors fled for the duration of King Philip's War; most would eventually return—but not Samuel Willard.[106] Temporarily located in Charlestown (where both his father and his wife soon died), Willard began to preach at the Third Church in Boston; in 1678 he was appointed its pastor. This was known as a particularly liberal church, its membership policies framed by the Half-Way Covenant. The congregation included a large portion of Boston's merchant elite. Here Willard would become, in time, a recognized leader of the ministry at large. His reputation was that of a "moderate"; he accepted the need for some adjustment of ecclesiastical practice to meet the evolving circumstances of New England life. (In this he was a natural opponent, and rival, of Increase Mather.)[107] He was prominent in various church synods of the later seventeenth century, and he served for a time as acting president of Harvard. His death, in 1707, was much lamented throughout New England. His successor in the Third Church eulogized him as "a star of the first magnitude," and few of his contemporaries would have challenged this assessment.[108]

Discussion of the Case

In the concluding section of his "Brief Account" Samuel Willard returned to the critical problem of *interpreting* Elizabeth Knapp's possession. There were, in fact, at least five ways of accounting for such
episodes. The first was sheer fraud and fakery. Were Elizabeth's seizures
"counterfeit" rather than "real"? Willard dismissed this possibility, citing
"the great strength appearing in them . . . [which is] beyond the force of
simulation." A second line of explanation emphasized "natural"—as
opposed to "diabolical"—causes; however, the local physician had rendered definitive judgment on that score. Willard noted that the key
episodes, though similar in some respects to "the actings of convulsion,"
were significantly different in others. Furthermore, the victim's overall
physical condition had remained surprisingly good through the whole
period in question. A third possibility was, of course, the malign activity
of witches; but here, too, the evidence had proved contrary. Twice
Elizabeth had tried to direct suspicion toward women of the community,
and both times the accused had been "cleared." With these explanations
discounted, two alternatives remained. Either Elizabeth was the innocent
victim of terrible pressures brought by the Devil alone, in an effort to
force a commitment from her, or else there was a prior "pact" between the
two of them, of which her "distemper" was somehow a manifestation.[109]

Elizabeth, understandably, advanced the former interpretation, but
the Rev. Willard (and most of those he spoke for) apparently inclined
toward the latter one. As previously noted, the overall tendency of the
minister's "treatment" procedure—his public comments, his prayers and
exhortations, his leading questions—was to bring the unfortunate girl to
a confession of personal guilt. This matter deserves emphasis for what it
reveals about the interest of the *community* in such events. Actually, the
"innocent victim" explanation has much surface plausibility, while the
notion of "diabolic covenant" sits rather awkwardly with the observed
facts. (Why would a willing servant of the Devil be obliged to suffer
such grievous "tortures" at his hands?) From this an important inference
follows. It seemed preferable, in the minds of Willard and his followers,
to associate the evil they opposed with a *human* agent—witches, most
likely; but if not witches, then the so-called victim herself. The Devil
was always implicated as an ultimate source; but still there must be
some*body* whose guilt could be more immediately discovered.

So it was that the townspeople of Groton sought to locate the root of
Elizabeth Knapp's "distemper" inside herself. And we, too, will yield to
a similar inclination. However, the terms of our inquiry—our own effort

to understand this extraordinary sequence—are necessarily different. From fits and demonic possession we move to "conversion symptoms" and "intrapsychic conflict." It is an abrupt transition, and yet a necessary one. We should not shrink from concluding that Elizabeth Knapp was truly ill—by our standards, if not by theirs.

The psychiatric concept of conversion affords an appropriate starting point. The fits, and their behavioral content, are surely recognizable in this light even to laymen. The literature of clinical psychiatry is full of cases evincing symptoms immediately analogous to the bizarre actings of Elizabeth Knapp. In this literature a conversion is understood as the somatic expression of psychological conflict.[110] Like many other symptom-formations it presents a compromise between an unacceptable impulse (or affect) and "defenses" intended to exclude the impulse from consciousness.[111] As such it is a form of body language, which can, in turn, be retranslated into its original psychological content. Almost by definition, conversion harks back to infancy, when *psyche* and *soma* are hardly differentiated. (Thus archaic, even "primitive," elements are to be expected.) In the language of clinical psychoanalysis, the pathogenic conflicts are typically "pregenital";[112] indeed, there is often a deep "oral" substrate. Moreover, two of the most important (and ubiquitous) psychic defenses can be traced to the same developmental source-point. "Projection"—the process of attributing one's own unacceptable motives and feelings to others—is modelled on the infant's instinct to "spit out" whatever he finds unpleasurable. "Introjection"—the incorporation into the self of forces which, when coming from outside, are felt as a threat to the ego—reinstates the infantile experience of "taking in."[113] Here, then, are some of the leading structural features usually attributed to conversion. By themselves, however, they say nothing either about the *motive* which may be implicated in a given experience of illness or about the *meaning* of particular conversion symptoms.[114] With this we must return to the substantive material from the case of Elizabeth Knapp.

In some respects Elizabeth's motives lay close to the surface of her manifest behavior. Indeed the element of self-display is quite transparent. Girls of sixteen did not ordinarily occupy a position of special prominence in the day-to-day life of communities like Groton; yet here was Elizabeth, for weeks on end, very much at the center of the local stage. The metaphor of theater suggests itself quite naturally; every witchcraft case was, in part, a public drama. The enactment of elaborate roles, the presence of attentive spectators, the fundamental interest in seeing and being seen —all these elements point in a single direction. It is worth emphasizing that Elizabeth herself *sought* public attention, and that her demands were scaled higher and higher as time went along. Clearly she welcomed new additions to her audience, for Willard notes that she would "always fall into fits when any strangers go to visit her—and the more go, the more violent are her fits." There was, moreover, her request to be taken to Boston for special presentation to "an assembly of ministers."[115] Boston was the biggest stage that New England could offer her, and its clergymen were the most distinguished of potential reviewers.

None of this is meant to imply literal "staging" on Elizabeth's part; we have no reason to doubt Samuel Willard's judgment that Elizabeth's troubles were "real." (From the standpoint of modern psychiatry this is equivalent to saying that her symptoms had an unconscious origin.) But the place of her dramatic proclivities in the total shape of Elizabeth's personality remains in question. Are they best understood as a "secondary gain," i.e. as simple reinforcement of more fundamental gains derived from the relief of other (and "deeper") problems?[116] On the contrary, the pattern of display seems in this instance so insistent as to command a place at the core of our interpretation. Here is a motive of exhibitionism that qualifies as "primary" in itself—a *source* of conflict, rather than an artifact or increment thereto.

Closely linked with this exhibitionism, Elizabeth's behavior also expressed an implicit strain of *dependency*. Like many forms of conversion, her symptoms simulated illness, as recognized within the framework of contemporaneous medical knowledge—thus the call for a physician, and the initial confusion between organic and demonic diagnosis.[117] Violent and repulsive as it was, her pathology conveyed a desperate message to those around her: "Take care of me, for I can no longer take care of myself!" In this way Elizabeth divested herself of responsibility for her every act and impulse.[118] If others would not intervene, she might throw herself into the fire; indeed, whole squads of caretakers were needed to "hold her down." In a somewhat distorted form her plight mirrored the dependency of an infant, at the mercy both of his own disorganized impulses and of the environment. In each case the need for external regulation is paramount to survival. From a clinical standpoint, the reference of this dependency is an oral one; its developmental source is the earliest period of life, when the mouth serves as the conduit of vital nurturant supplies. Thus the details of Elizabeth's behavior signify a "regression" of a fairly extreme kind.

A third aspect of this behavior that also carried the force of motive was violent and pervasive rage. The danger implicit in Elizabeth's fits came through to her audience in many ways. Cherished values, affectionate relationships, established routines—not to mention life and limb

—were immediately at risk. The Devil was, above all, an engine of terrible wrath. Sometimes he worked *upon* Elizabeth, inflicting the tortures she enacted so vividly; occasionally he went *inside* her, and made her own personality the vehicle of his destructiveness. It is no long leap of psychiatric hypothesis to say that all this rage expressed a conflict deep within Elizabeth herself.

Exhibitionism, dependency, rage: these were among the leading inner forces which fueled her illness. But what of erotic motives and conflicts —the source, after all, of those "classic" hysterias which Freud studied and treated while building the foundations of psychoanalytic theory?[119] This is a more complicated question. On the one hand, Elizabeth Knapp did show special interest in the Rev. Willard (and perhaps in other clergymen of comparable stature); moreover, her developmental position, i.e. as an adolescent girl, might well support an interpretation emphasizing repressed sexual wishes. Perhaps this was a simple "anxiety hysteria," fueled by libidinal energies (newly strengthened after puberty) and structured by a revival of the infantile "family triangle."[120] If so, Willard was merely a stand-in for her own father, the object of her original "oedipal" wishes. Still, father figures come in many shapes and guises, and so the evidence demands our further scrutiny.

In fact, there was no clear hint of erotic aims in any of Elizabeth's behavior toward Willard—no direct overtures, certainly, and little enough that might be interpreted as disguised (or symbolic) manifestations. Again and again, Elizabeth conveyed the wish that Willard attend to her and care for her; occasionally, too, her underlying rage turned in his direction. But her overall posture toward the minister had a strange, flat, two-dimensional quality. She did not treat him as a center of independent initiative, let alone as a fancied "love object." For his part, Willard grew exasperated with her manipulative ways. Coming and going as her whim directed, he failed utterly to establish a solid, affective basis of communication with her. When she was "in her fits," he was no more than the leading member of her audience; when she reverted to her "sottish and stupid" frame, his margin of influence was small at best. And yet, plainly, she wanted him there. Indeed in her periods of grief and remorse Elizabeth fastened on the minister with a desperate intensity, as if in hopes that he might save her from herself.

Willard was trying to "treat" Elizabeth's illness in the only way he knew, and his efforts can profitably be compared with treatment settings in our own day. Clinical psychoanalysis, for example, depends fundamentally on the development of "transference"—the tendency of every patient to reproduce elements of his earliest affective states in his current relation to the therapist. (Indeed, transference is a ubiquitous phenomenon; highlighted in the patient-therapist context, it nonetheless colors all our lives everyday.) The substance of transference in specific cases is as infinite and varied as human experience itself; however, current theory recognizes two main structural variants.[121] The *libidinal* transferences, first studied by Freud, reinstate triangular relationships among children and parents—most conspicuously, the oedipal configuration. Founded on early loves and hates, they may well seem "primitive" in their leading features; however, they invariably show an intense subject-and-object quality. The "other" (i.e. the transference object) is experienced as an independent person—and "cathected" with "drive-libido."

A second, quite different category encompasses the so-called *narcissistic* transferences. Here the resurrected past displays a far more constricted aspect. The patient's inner self is the exclusive center of activity, and the therapist is approached as a mere adjunct or appendage. There is little opening for true affective states such as love and hate, which presume a basic I-and-thou differentiation. But gradually these transferences unfold their own psychic configurations. An archaic self, inflated with grandiosity, asserts unbounded claims of omnipotent strength and irresistible beauty. Alternatively, this same self displays a primordial connection to an "idealized other," an internal figure of perfection.[122] The transference develops either in a "mirror" form (the therapist as reflector of the patient's grandiosity) or in an "idealizing" form (the therapist as sustaining source for the patient's otherwise empty self). In both cases the object is valued chiefly as a source of narcissistic supplies, and the central issues are those of control.

The foregoing excursion into clinical theory returns us by a natural route to the evidence on Elizabeth Knapp. For it should now be evident that her relation to her own "therapist"—the Rev. Willard—approximates the narcissistic, rather than the libidinal, transferences. The patterning of this relationship through time, as well as its qualitative aspects, bear out the comparison. Recall that her fits began when Willard had left home on a trip of several days—in short, when the "narcissistic object" had abandoned her. It is reasonable to speculate that her symptoms expressed a disguised aim to bring the minister back. She needed his regularly available presence to maintain the integrity of her all-too-fragile self.

Still more persuasive in this regard are the events of two months later. Gradually, as time passed, Elizabeth had admitted guilt over her own willingness to consort with the Devil. On December 8 she had given a full confession, which, within a day or two, she greatly regretted.

Urgently, she sent for Willard; tearfully, she sought his support for a new statement of her essential innocence. But, as noted above, he was a good deal less than forthcoming; indeed, he rebuffed her entreaties outright. Elizabeth reacted like many patients jolted by an unwelcome turn in the transference relationship; her symptoms multiplied and worsened. Within a few days she produced fits in which her destructive motive became more open and direct than at any previous time. From this she proceeded directly to the gripping scene where the Devil spoke inside her. And what did the Devil say? For the most part, he attacked the "great black rogue" who repeatedly "deceived" the townspeople and told "a company of lies." The villain here was none other than Samuel Willard himself. The "reviling terms" heard on this occasion left an especially deep impression, since they "were such as [Elizabeth] never used before. . . . Yea, [she] hath been always observed to speak respectfully of me."[123] One might well infer, with respect to this episode, that Elizabeth had achieved two aims simultaneously. She rebuked one distinguished mentor (who had recently disappointed and "deceived" her), and announced in shocking terms her connection to another. For better or for worse, Elizabeth had found a new "narcissistic object"; drawing upon *his* strength and sustenance, she gave her most memorable performance.

To summarize the argument thus far: Elizabeth Knapp was a deeply troubled girl, whose leading symptoms may be regarded as somatic conversions. The underlying conflicts lay mainly in the narcissistic realm—thus the blatant exhibitionism of her various "fits." Libidinal tensions in general, and oedipal ones in particular, seem to have played a subordinate role. (However, sexual factors need not be ruled out entirely; the upsurge of drive energies that normally accompanies adolescence may well have contributed to the larger disorganization of the inner "self.")[124] The narcissistic transferences toward the Rev. Willard displayed a mixed character. There was considerable readiness to idealize this pre-eminent figure in the local community, and at critical points Elizabeth looked to him to rescue her from her deepening predicament. At other times she expected only "mirroring," from Willard no less than the rest of her audience. But this alternating pattern is consistent with the "regressive swings" typical of the analysis of narcissistically fixated patients. (More specifically, such patients often move from a base-line in the idealizing transference to temporary positions of archaic grandiosity.)[125]

Elizabeth's symptoms may now be more closely examined. Their meaning cannot be definitely ascertained without a full record of associated thoughts and feelings, but there are grounds at least for some speculation. Her "speechlessness," for example, may be understood as a signal instance of compromise between unconscious aims and defenses. The need for life-giving sustenance is too admixed with angry, "biting" impulses; the wish to take in quickly becomes the wish to devour. As a result, the apparatus of "oral" interaction is temporarily shut down. Elizabeth is prevented thereby from hurling savage, blasphemous words at her caretakers and (in fantasy) destroying them with her voice.[126] At the same time, however, her destructive wish finds a secondary (i.e. disguised and deflected) outlet. For, by not talking with those who stood by, she manages in effect to discount their existence; at the level of unconscious process this is a form of (omnipotent) annihilation. Other symptoms express the same problem of "oral rage." Her sense of being strangled is a somatic epitome of the *defensive* process—the repression needed to hold herself back. The opposite side of her conflict—the destructive aim—is more nearly represented in her bizarre simulation of an angry dog.[127] Unable for long periods to speak, she managed instead to bark!

It is worth recalling here that Elizabeth's anger was articulated quite fully in a cluster of vivid fantasies. The Devil urged her repeatedly to attack her benefactors (Samuel Willard and his family), and occasionally to injure herself. At their outer limits her thoughts ran to homicide and suicide. That she described such thoughts as forced upon her by Satan was, again, the work of her own defenses, a "projection" pure and simple.[128] Thus she managed to taste her innermost wishes, while denying personal responsibility for them.

To speculate on the dynamic significance of all this is to return to the theme of narcissism. For patients struggling with deep, intrapsychic lesions—as, indeed, for all of us when confronted with sudden insults to our self-esteem—there is a distinctive mode of aggressive response. "Narcissistic injury" evokes "narcissistic rage"—a wish to hurt that is uncompromising, compulsive, and bent on revenge at all costs.[129] Where other angers are limited by instrumental considerations (the pushing aside of an obstacle to some wish or pleasure), this one seeks total eradication of the source of affront. It can be mobilized readily enough in the present, but in truly pathological cases it resurrects archaic developmental states. When control over a mirroring object is abruptly lost, or when access to the power of an idealized object is obstructed in some way, the abnormally fragile self responds with fury. In the inner world of unmodified narcissism disappointments are experienced as intolerable flaws.

The same fragile self is periodically vulnerable to "fragmentation."

The nucleus of mental parts and functions (formed, under ordinary circumstances, in the first two years of life) may lose its cohesion and come apart.[130] This disintegrative process was vividly represented in the wildest of Elizabeth Knapp's fits. The dramatic surges of uncontrollable affect, the inhibition of some functions (e.g. speech, sight) and the hyperactivity of others (e.g. motoric expression), the whole element of frenzy: here are the outward signs of a breakdown at the organizing center of personality. Indeed, Elizabeth's insistence on playing out her troubles before an attentive audience can perhaps be understood as a desperate effort to *reverse* the trend toward fragmentation: with strong infusions of mirroring, the self might yet manage to hold together. Her sudden sensations of pain ("Oh, my legs . . . Oh, my breast") can be fitted to the same clinical picture. These symptoms mocked medical illness and injury, and invite a diagnosis of hypochondria. Viewed from the standpoint of narcissism, hypochondria is an exaggerated preoccupation with particular somatic (or mental) functions.[131] As such it implies some degree of fragmentation—e.g. a part is detached from the self-nucleus and unduly "cathected" with narcissistic "energy."

For long periods, of course, Elizabeth remained relatively calm and undisturbed by the Devil. (We might say that her tendency to fragment was temporarily neutralized.) Yet these were hardly normal or happy times; she seemed distant and impassive to others, and herself complained of "melancholy." There is an evident correspondence here to states of "narcissistic depletion" frequently noted in clinical case-studies.[132] The patient seems trapped in his own lethargy; he describes feelings of pervasive "emptiness" and "flatness" that he cannot throw off. What he thus reports from his conscious experience is actually the result of an inner stalemate between archaic narcissistic aims and the standards of his ego. To resist the extreme (and potentially disorganizing) pressures of the "grandiose self" requires a literally exhausting feat of repression. Success is achieved only by a massive mobilization of inner defenses; and since these defenses must be constantly reinforced, there is little energy left over for other goals and tasks. So it was—we may surmise— with Elizabeth during her days of "intermission."

Genetic Reconstruction

The task of "genetic reconstruction"—interpreting a patient's current problems and behavior in the light of his past development—is difficult enough for psychoanalysts. A historian must, therefore, be extremely cautious about the claims he makes for his own efforts in this direction.

The data from the early experience of his "subjects" are necessarily limited and fragmentary, and there is usually no indication at all of inner reactions to that experience. Perhaps he can hope to find material that seems *consistent* with his overall interpretation; but firm, "causal" connections can hardly be established. The following discussion, consisting of five lengthy paragraphs on genetic issues in the case of Elizabeth Knapp, will explicitly separate fact and hypothesis. Each paragraph opens with a short biographical statement (in italics) which can be documented by reference to extant materials. From this relatively solid source-point a trail of inference is plotted, toward possible psychological meanings.

1. *Elizabeth Knapp was the first child of her parents. She had one sibling, a brother who was born when she was just two years old and died four months later.* Perhaps, like most eldest children, Elizabeth was invested at the outset with the particular concern of her parents. And probably, like most Puritan children, she was subjected to an increasingly harsh disciplinary regime after her first year of life.[133] Then her brother arrived, replacing her in the infant world of narcissistic indulgence. It is easy to imagine that she felt hurt and angered by this sequence, and that she experienced (quite normal) "death wishes" toward her new rival. His *actual* death, however, must have come as a terrible confirmation of these wishes. Thus she learned an early (unconscious) lesson: her anger was too dangerous, too effectual—and must be entirely suppressed. Henceforth a whole sector of her inner life was denied contact with outward reality; there was no opportunity for its gradual modification through growth experiences. Raw, infantile rage remained an underground pressure on Elizabeth's subsequent development, insistently demanding a suitable outlet. Years later, when the Devil overtook Elizabeth, he urged her to murder "her parents, her neighbors, our [i.e. the Willards'] children, especially the youngest." The families of James Knapp (as of 1657) and Samuel Willard (as of 1671) show a marked demographic correspondence: husband and wife, both roughly thirty years old, and two small children. Hence the notion of attacking "especially the youngest" seems more than a little resonant.

2. *There were no more children born to Elizabeth Knapp's parents. She was raised, in effect, as an only child.* It is important to stress the extreme rarity of this familial configuration in colonial America. Most couples had at least six children (and some twice that many); a few were completely infertile (for biological reasons); but virtually none raised a single child and no more.[134] Perhaps this imposed special burdens on Elizabeth, as the sole carrier of the family's aspirations into the future.

Whatever pathogenic forces were operating in this household, their effect was concentrated on a very small circle of members. The position of the mother deserves our particular consideration. The death of her little son, painful enough in itself, was compounded by her inability to conceive another child. Of course, infant mortality darkened the experience of many New England families, but time and the care of new babies helped to soften the sense of loss. The Lord gave, and took away, and gave again. Yet for Goodwife Knapp there was a pattern as distinctive as it was inexplicable: the birth of two children, the loss of one, and then—barrenness. This felt all the more painful in a culture which took child-bearing so much for granted.

3. *During her earliest years Elizabeth Knapp's father was suspected of committing adultery, and fathering an illegitimate child. This was, in fact, a period of unusual trouble and misfortune for the whole family.* (See the table of Knapp Family Chronology.) The indictment for adultery is truly a singular and stunning datum. Among hundreds of cases, spanning twenty years in the operations of the county court, James Knapp was the only defendant so charged; conviction could have brought the death penalty. Knapp, it seems, was *not* convicted; yet probably a residue of doubt and suspicion lingered long thereafter. Why had the widow Davis insisted, to the time of her death, that Knapp was her paramour? If her charge could not be proved, neither could it be *un*proved. Recall, too, these additional aspects of family shame and difficulty: James Knapp (a year after his indictment for adultery) confessing to drunkenness; his brother John convicted as a thief; their father judged officially incompetent; John Warren (Goodwife Knapp's father) pursued by the courts for religious deviations, and thus detached from his once-prominent position in the community.[135] The sequence must have disheartened them all; but perhaps, again, it bore down with special force on Elizabeth [Warren] Knapp. And then, the final blow—the death of her only son, and her subsequent childlessness. Is it unreasonable, given all these circumstances, to think that she yielded increasingly to depression and despair? (As noted above, there are strong grounds for identifying her with the "troublesome . . . woman" whose derangement was pointedly described by a diarist of the time.) And is it incautious to imagine that she became deeply absorbed in her own sorrows and failed to provide consistent, empathic mothering for her one surviving child—and, finally, that this child suffered lasting hurt as a consequence?[136]

4. *James Knapp became a leader of the new community at Groton.* This seems important, in the present context, for the contrast it makes with the record of Knapp's experience before he went to Groton. Per-

Knapp Family Chronology, 1654–58

Summer 1654	James Knapp and Elizabeth Warren married.
Summer 1654	Elizabeth (Warren) Knapp's parents prosecuted for religious nonconformity.
July 1654	Elizabeth Knapp, Jr., conceived.
April 1655	Elizabeth Knapp, Jr., born.
Summer 1655	Illegitimate child conceived by widow Mary Davis.
Spring 1656	Illegitimate child born to widow Mary Davis; paternity attributed to James Knapp.
June 1656	James Knapp prosecuted for adultery.
August 1656	James Knapp, Jr., conceived.
December 1656	William Knapp (father of James) declared *non compos mentis*.
April 1657	James Knapp prosecuted for drunkenness and violation of local ordinances.
April 1657	John Knapp (brother of James) prosecuted for theft; some complicity attributed to James.
May 1657	James Knapp, Jr., born.
September 1657	James Knapp, Jr., dies.
1658 (?)	Elizabeth (Warren) Knapp apparently insane (?).
Summer 1658	William Knapp (father of James) dies.

haps he moved *in order* to make a new start; here, at any rate, lies a sharp boundary line in his personal history. Having crossed the line, he may have "over-compensated" for the past, insisting on unusually rigorous standards of conduct. This posture would find additional confirmation in the checkered course of other lives well known to him (father, brother, father-in-law). Goodness, success, and social prestige—he might well have concluded—were inherently precarious. His relation to his own household must have developed accordingly; as a father, he would be watchful, formal, and rather severe. And what of the likely response to such a father, from a child already vulnerable in fundamental ways? One imagines a good show of outward conformity—but without any strengthening of inner self. The child, moreover, may have remembered something which most of her Groton neighbors had forgotten (or never known in the first place). Her father was now a pillar of the local establishment, a model of public and "Puritan" virtue; yet years before his position had been quite different. When the Devil spoke from inside

Elizabeth, he railed at the Rev. Willard for "deceiving the people." But was there someone else of whom Elizabeth herself—at least her unconscious self—might have wished to say the same thing?

5. *After her earliest years, Elizabeth Knapp was sent to live and work as a servant in various foster households.* At first glance, there is nothing here to distinguish Elizabeth's experience from that of hundreds of other New England children; "indentured servitude" was an accepted route of socialization (and formal tuition) in the culture of pre-modern times.[137] However, it seems at least mildly surprising to find this arrangement applied in the case of an only child. Is it possible that Elizabeth's parents were conscious of some difficulty in their intrafamilial relations? Did they conclude, as a consequence, that Elizabeth would be better off under another family's roof? These are tantalizing, but quite unanswerable, questions. Equally speculative is the issue of Elizabeth's probable reaction to being thus "bound out." Was she inwardly resentful? Did she experience a renewed sense of disappointment in the (less-than-idealized) parental object? If so, she gained substitutes of far greater stature. And right here the evidence does offer some suggestive clues. During the intermissions in her fits Elizabeth reported that the Devil had sought to win her allegiance by offering lavish inducements—"money, silks, fine clothes, ease from labor, to see the whole world." This seems, in retrospect, a list of envious wishes thrown up from Elizabeth's unconscious, and its contents point straight to the Rev. Willard. Certainly Willard had money—a good clerical salary, and a very large family inheritance. Like all New Englanders of the highest rank, he possessed and wore finery—"silks," for example. (The notorious "sumptuary laws" prohibited such clothing to lesser folk; and this category presumably included the Knapps, at least as of 1671.)[138] Did he also enjoy "ease from labor"? From the perspective of a sixteen-year-old, it may well have seemed so; clearly the work of clergymen diverged from the menial norms of the community at large. Moreover, clergymen had more frequent occasion to travel than most of their peers—though few would claim to have "seen the whole world." Here, then, is the power and the glory of Samuel Willard, as viewed through the eyes of Elizabeth Knapp. It was toward this fount of strength that she directed her "idealizing" propensities. But her position, as his servant, was intrinsically difficult; she was in, but not of, the family. Under ordinary circumstances, her wish for closeness to Willard could only be disappointed. And so, unconsciously, she created some *extra*ordinary circumstances, inviting thereby a greater share of his attention.

The foregoing speculations may now be summarized and arranged in rough chronological sequence. In the earliest stages of her life Elizabeth Knapp missed those forms of parenting that are most essential to inner development. Her budding self never achieved secure "cohesion" because she was not adequately *recognized*, or *affirmed*, or *empowered*, by the people closest around her. Her mother was disabled, by a string of personal and family sorrows, from responding to the needs of a small child.[139] Her "grandiose" yearnings, wholly typical in one so young, were ignored or rebuffed; driven underground, they survived in archaic form to present her developing ego with a constant threat of disruptive intrusion. Even so Elizabeth might have salvaged her growth by drawing on the strength of the second parent. But James Knapp was not a fit object for idealization; badly tainted by trouble and scandal during his years at Watertown, he remained a clay-footed figure even after he had obtained prominence at Groton. Meanwhile the birth and death of Elizabeth's little brother froze her infantile rage so as to make it inaccessible to the influence of subsequent experience. As an older child, she looked in vain for someone new to idealize. Her relation to the Rev. Willard proved especially hopeful in prospect—and bitterly disappointing in actual result. Her eventual "possession" wove together all these threads of narcissistic imbalance: rage, archaic grandiosity and the demand for mirroring, attachment to a figure of eminence. And its motive, from start to finish, was a desperate pitch for remedial "supplies."

Conclusion

In its origins the ordeal of Elizabeth Knapp was personal, and private, and highly idiosyncratic. But its consequences were altogether public. A community, too, was powerfully "possessed." *She* needed and valued her audience of Groton townsfolk. *They* felt rewarded and gratified by her performance. Indeed they were more than mere audience. Time after time they stepped onstage as actors in their own right: questioning Elizabeth around specific points of her experience; evaluating, prodding, and encouraging her; and even disputing directly with her Devil. Thus they helped to plot the course of events, and to speed or retard its pace. Their own investment in all this merits special consideration.

The "entertainment" value of witchcraft episodes has been much noticed by scholars, and its importance in the Knapp case seems beyond doubt. Elizabeth's recurrent "fits" made a uniquely gripping spectacle: Willard's account noted "the amazement and astonishment of all the beholders."[140] The number of "beholders" is hard to estimate: Willard mentioned gatherings of "diverse," "the company there present," "the presence of many"—and complained that "there was no room for privacy." Perhaps most (even all?) residents of Groton contrived to observe at least some part of the unfolding sequence, and ministers (among others?) came from farther afield. Clearly, too, there was much agitated *talk* and discussion. When Willard preached on the affair, he noted a variety of local response: "a great deal of enquiry . . . about the devil's agency"; questions asked in a "spirit of censure"; even some "jocund" and "frothy" remarks. The interest, the excitement of it all, seemed palpable.

But, as noted already, the townspeople of Groton were not just "beholders" eager to be entertained. Elizabeth's experience touched them in far deeper ways. They sought from it (and largely obtained) an affirmation of their values, their loyalties, their very identity. Willard's account repeatedly suggests the importunate, "pressing" quality of their interest:[141]

> diverse [people] . . . pressed upon her to declare what might be the true and real occasion of these amazing fits. . . .
>
> being pressed to declare whether or not she had consented to a covenant. . . .
>
> she was demanded a reason why she used those words in her fits. . . .
>
> much was pressed upon her, but no affection at all was discovered. . . .
>
> some . . . pressed that there was something yet behind not discovered by her. . . .

And how fully, how handsomely, she responded! She began with "self-condemnations" (a catalogue of her personal sins), and moved on to her direct encounters with the Devil. There were base "promises" (of "money" and "ease" and "great matters"). There were horrible "temptations" (to murder, to suicide, to theft, to idleness, to blasphemy). And there was the matter of the "covenant" itself. Had she, or hadn't she, signed the Devil's book—and bound herself formally to his "hellish" cause? Willard professed not to know the answer. ("Her declarations have been so contradictory . . . that we know not what to make of them.")[142] But after the climactic scene in which the "grum voice" spoke from inside her, it may not have mattered. Her status as "demoniac" was then "put out of question." The Devil had made a "full discovery of himself," and for the people of Groton that was quite enough.[143]

To discover the Devil—in a sense both literal and metaphoric—was, after all, their chief goal from the start. Through Elizabeth's possession they confronted the evil (the "promises," the "temptations") which plagued them all. There were many levels of resonance. There was the naming, the locating, the making tangible, of what had hitherto seemed obscure. There was a certain kind of tasting—a vicarious indulgence of forbidden wish and fantasy. And there was, at the end, a decisive act of repudiation: *The Devil is in Elizabeth, not in me. . . . The evil is there, not here. . . .* Thus did the beholders sound their own depths, sorting the good from the bad. They emerged—one imagines—with a stronger, sharper sense of themselves. They were cleansed.

From all this they derived an enormous emotional lift. The "narcissistic gains," so conspicuous in Elizabeth's personal experience, embraced the entire community as well. Listen once again to Samuel Willard, addressing his parishioners:

> Let us consider the awfulness of the judgment itself: this is none of those ordinary dispensations of God's providence which are frequent and usual in the world. . . . It is no common sickness and calamity . . . but it is extraordinary and stupendous. . . . God thus leaves the common track, and comes in so unwonted a way of judgment.[144]

Specialness, singularity; self-enlargement, self-display: the melody is impossible to miss. And it continues:

> There is a voice . . . to the whole land, but in a more special manner to poor Groton. . . . God hath in His wisdom singled out this poor town, out of all others in this wilderness, to dispense such an amazing providence in. . . . Let us look upon ourselves to be set up as a beacon upon a hill. . . .[145]

Indeed Willard's entire sermon can be read as a coming-to-grips with narcissism. "We are . . . above others"; "we have . . . above others"; "us above others": the language is recurrent, and revealing. As shepherd to the local flock, Willard felt concerned lest the exaltation of the moment carry them all too high. "While we judge and censure others," he warned, "we do tacitly justify ourselves, and think ourselves better than others." There was danger that a "tremendous providence" be misconstrued and misused—that it "raiseth, and humbles not, the soul." (Again, the same image.) This, in turn, would be "to forget our sinfulness . . . to forget divine sovereignty . . . to rob God of the glory of His goodness."[146]

"Puritan" sentiments, surely; but did the auditors hear? Did they—

could they—respond inwardly and come down from the heights of their recent experience? At very least it must have made a hard struggle.

For them, for us, for everyone, the impulse to hold the heights is inescapable. Merely to be present on "extraordinary" occasions is self-enhancing; to participate, even in a small way, is to deepen the effect immeasurably. We cherish such moments in memory.

I saw the demoniac.

I heard the Devil speak.

I was there.

5

"Let Me Do What I Could"

Among the more fantastic powers attributed to Satan by the New Englanders were those which enabled him to disrupt the physical arrangements of ordinary households. Stones, sticks, and boards might "by his means" rise from the ground to crash loudly on outside walls and windows, while, indoors, domestic articles of all sorts would suddenly take flight. Falling, shaking, hurtling about, these objects became missiles of destruction: the threat to life and property was palpable. The unseen forces at work were variously characterized, as "poltergeist," as "lithobolia," or simply as "stone-throwing devils."[1]

Such forces made an impressive appearance in the town of Newbury, Massachusetts, during the last weeks of the year 1679. The focus was the house of an elderly couple named Morse, and it was William Morse himself who left the fullest account of the particulars. Three short excerpts may serve to convey the flavor of the whole:[2]

> Thursday night, being the 27th day of November, we heard a great noise without against the house; whereupon myself and wife looked out and saw nobody . . . but we had stones and sticks thrown at us [so] that we were forced to retire into the house again . . . and then the like noise was upon the roof of the house. . . .

> [Four days later] in the afternoon the pots hanging over the fire did dash so vehemently one against the other [that] we set down one that they might not dash to pieces. I saw the andiron leap into

the pot and dance and leap out, and again leap in and dance and leap out again, and there abide. . . . Also I saw the pot turn itself over and throw down all the water. Again, we saw a tray with wool leap up and down and throw the wool out, and so many times. . . . Again, [we saw] a tub his hoop fly off of itself, and the tub turn over, and nobody near it. Again, [we saw] the wooden wheel turned upside down, and stood upon its end, and a spade set on it. . . .

Again, in the morning, a great stone . . . did remove from place to place; we saw it. Two spoons [were] throwed off the table, and presently the table was thrown down. And [I] being minded to write, my inkhorn was hid from me, which I [later] found covered with a rag, and my pen [was] quite gone. I made a new pen, and while I was writing one ear of corn hit me in the face, and firesticks and stones [were] throwed at me. . . . Again, my wife [had] her hat taken from her head sitting by the fire by me. The table [was] almost thrown down again; my spectacles were thrown from the table almost into the fire. . . . [At length] I was forced to forebear writing any more [for] I was so disturbed with so many things constantly thrown at me.

Into this strange and frightening situation came a man by the name of Caleb Powell, later identified as a ship's "mate" temporarily resident in Newbury. According to William Morse, Powell seemed at first wonderfully sympathetic with "our great affliction"; indeed, he proposed to render personal assistance. In making this offer, Powell claimed various forms of special knowledge, including "Astrology and Astronomy and . . . the workings of the spirits, some in one country and some in another."[3] Perhaps he meant only to boast of his wide travel and experience of the world; perhaps he referred to his training in celestial navigation; perhaps, too, he exaggerated a little. Morse, at any rate, heard in such talk distinct undertones of the occult, as did some of the neighbors. A local goodwife would subsequently testify that "Powell said he could find the witch if he had another scholar with him." And there was gossip that his fellow sailors regarded him as something of a "wizard."[4]

Whatever the basis for such opinions, Powell's understanding of the Morses' problem was quite direct and pragmatic. Apparently William and Elizabeth Morse had at some previous time taken into their household their young grandson John Stiles, and it was this boy, in Powell's view, who lay behind their current predicament. According to William's own testimony, Powell said . . . "this boy is the occasion of your grief, for he hath done these things, and hath caused his good old grandmother to be counted a witch." Then said I, "how can all these things be done by him?" Said he: "although he may not have done all, yet [he has done] most of them. For this boy is a young rogue, a vile rogue. I have watched him and seen him do things, as to come up and down."[5]

Moreover, Powell believed he could resolve the problem: he would take the boy temporarily under his own care in order to effect some (unspecified) change. The Morses, though at first "very unwilling," were eventually persuaded to try this plan, and so their grandson went off. The result was prompt and dramatic: "we have been freed from any trouble of this kind ever since."[6]

If Caleb Powell expected appreciation for his efforts with young Stiles, he must have been rudely jolted by what followed. For out of his success the Morses drew a wholly sinister conclusion. Powell had demonstrated a power to clear up their "trouble"; so perhaps that same power had created the trouble in the first place. The witch-doctor might also be the witch; it was all, in any case, part of the same "black art."[7]

Here the chronology of events assumes great importance. To recapitulate: On Thursday, November 27, and throughout the ensuing weekend, the disturbances in the Morse household had become particularly severe. On Monday, December 1, Powell had taken the grandson away, and the "trouble" had abruptly ceased. Then, on Wednesday, December 3, William Morse went to the local magistrate, to lodge a formal complaint against Caleb Powell "for working with the Devil to the molesting of . . . his family"; depositions were given, and the case was continued until the following Monday. Morse used the intervening days to gather further testimony; meanwhile (perhaps on Friday) John Stiles returned to the home of his grandparents, and the former pattern of disturbance resumed. On December 8 the magistrate held a further hearing, with Powell himself present, and a regular prosecution was authorized for the next full session of the county court. Powell was thereupon taken into custody by the constable until he could post bond; failing to do so, he would be "carried to prison."[8]

Why was William Morse so quick to accuse Caleb Powell? The evidence is not conclusive on this point, but it does allow certain inferences. Elizabeth Morse (William's wife) had been for many years the target of neighborhood gossip about witchcraft. (More on this, shortly.) And there is some hint, in the materials on Powell, that such gossip had been

strengthened by the new situation. Note that William's own account of
the case had attributed to Powell the following words: "this boy [i.e.
Stiles] hath done these things, and hath caused his good old grandmother
to be counted a witch."[9] Was there, then, a rising current of suspicion
in Newbury against Elizabeth Morse? And was her husband anxious to
find some alternative "witch" on whom to fix the blame?

The county court would not meet to decide the case against Powell
until the end of the winter, and meanwhile there were further developments. Through most of December the devil remained vigorously at
work in the Morse household; the average of threatened, and actual,
damage remained high. To this pattern was added one new element—
"fits," and other "afflictions," in the boy Stiles. He began periodically
to "swoon"; at other times he was "hurried into great motions" or "violently thrown to and fro." On one particular day he was "very danger-
ously thrown into the fire, and preserved by his friends with much
ado." He experienced painful sensations of pricking and pinching. His
grandparents discovered sharp objects stuck into his body: knives, "an
iron spindle," and "a three-tined fork." He was given to shouting and
"intolerable ravings"; he "also made, for a long time together, a noise
like a dog, and like an hen with her chickens, and could not speak
rationally." He was sometimes unable to take food or drink—"it was
turned out as fast as they put it in"; on other occasions "he did eat
ashes, sticks, rug-yarn." The pattern was not a constant one: twice he
was taken to a doctor's house and was briefly "free from disturbances,"
and there was one longer period (December 26–January 9) when "he
and the house also . . . had rest." But after each of these intermissions
the fits resumed, with as much intensity as before. At some point in the
sequence the boy began to identify Powell as his chief tormentor.
"There's Powell, I am pinched," he would shout, or, when he had been
injured in a ghostly "flight" above the town, "he said . . . that Powell
carried him." So it was that young Stiles joined his grandparents in
their efforts against the enigmatic seaman.[10]

Other information shows, however, that the case was also developing
in a different direction. On January 7 the magistrate took a large number of depositions (perhaps as many as a dozen) from local townsfolk,
all tending to implicate Elizabeth Morse.[11] Some reflected directly on
recent events, but others were quite unrelated. This material was forwarded to Boston for use by the Court of Assistants, where two months
later it formed the basis for an indictment, formally charging Goodwife
Morse with the practice of witchcraft. The constable of Newbury was

ordered to arrest her and deliver her to the prison-keeper at Ipswich; there she would remain until further notice.[12]

Was there some purposeful effort to encourage and organize these judicial actions against Elizabeth Morse? One person had a definite stake in seeing the old woman charged—and, according to subsequent testimony, some of the witnesses were strongly "urged by Powell to say as [they] now saith." (One later withdrew her evidence, and "broke forth in tears, craving forgiveness" from the Morses.) The source of this allegation was William Morse himself, hardly a disinterested party.[13] Still, it does seem plausible that Powell, temporarily freed from prison on bond, should have grasped any opportunity to turn the case against another suspect. His fate and that of Goodwife Morse were directly counterposed.

For Powell the suspense lasted until the end of March, when his own case came to trial. Some seventeen deponents had given evidence, but clearly the major testimony came from William and Elizabeth Morse.[14] It was not quite enough to secure a conviction. The court could find no "evident ground of proceeding further against the said Powell"; at the same time there was too much "ground of suspicion" for an outright acquittal. As a result, Powell would "bear his own shame" and the court costs as well—but, more importantly, he would henceforth go free.[15]

The way was now cleared for the trial of Goody Morse before the next meeting of the Court of Assistants in May. The intervening weeks brought a new flurry of preparations. At Newbury the magistrate took further depositions, which, when added to the earlier ones, made a very bulky file.[16] Numerous witnesses from the town were summoned to Boston to "swear" to their written testimony.[17] The defendant herself was transferred to the Boston jail, and a committee of women was appointed to give her the standard physical examination. ("You are required, at one of your houses, to search very diligently the body of Elizabeth Morse . . . for the finding out [of] some marks, if she hath any, that usually witches have.")[18] The case was tried, and the verdict rendered, on May 20: Elizabeth Morse was found "guilty according to the indictment." Seven days later, "after the lecture," Governor Simon Bradstreet handed down the prescribed sentence of death by hanging.[19]

And yet, it seems, some of the Assistants remained doubtful; for within a few days the court voted "the reprieving of Elizabeth Morse" until its next session in October.[20] Thus began a protracted series of efforts to forestall her execution. When the Assistants met in the autumn they decreed a further postponement—at which the House of Deputies protested: "Relating to the woman condemned for witchcraft, [we] do not understand why . . . the sentence given against her . . . is not executed. Her second reprieval seems to be beyond what the law will allow."[21] Meanwhile Elizabeth languished in prison. At one point during the summer her husband sent to the court a written plea, asking that she be allowed "in the daytime to walk in the prison yard . . . and in the night . . . [to] have privilege of a chamber in the common jail, and be freed from the dungeon which is extremely close and hot in this season . . . and also liberty on the sabbath to go to meeting."[22] The court's response is not recorded, but the petition alone underscores the difficulty of her situation.

In the spring of 1681 William Morse initiated new efforts on his wife's behalf. In preparation for another meeting of the Court of Assistants he submitted a long and detailed rebuttal of charges heard the previous year. Piece by piece he reviewed the depositional materials, offering counter-evidence in some instances and pleading ignorance in others.[23] (It was here that Morse accused Powell of having played the leading part in gathering the original testimony.) A second petition—this one from Elizabeth Morse, though transmitted through her husband—asked for a new hearing on the case. Evidently the condemned woman sought some definite outcome, "whether I shall live or die, to which I shall humbly submit, unto the Lord and you."[24] The House of Deputies gave a prompt and affirmative response, ordering warrants for "her farther trial"; but the Assistants once again demurred. Instead they voted still another reprieve. This time they allowed Elizabeth to return home to Newbury, "provided she go not above sixteen rods from her own house and land at any time, except to the meeting house."[25] These terms hardly seem generous; still, the important thing was to have her out of jail. And once out, she would never return. Her death sentence remained in effect, and her latest stay was only for a few additional months—but apparently the court did not choose to pursue the case any further.

William Morse died two years later, leaving most of his property to his "beloved wife, during her natural life." Elizabeth lived on for some while longer, apparently sharing her house with the family of her youngest daughter. They, in turn, were enjoined by William Morse's will to "take such care of my wife . . . as her need doth require, for her comfortable supply on all accounts"; otherwise they would forfeit their rights of inheritance.[26]

The date of Elizabeth's death cannot be determined; however, something of its manner and attendant circumstances was noted in a treatise on witchcraft published years later by the Rev. John Hale of Beverly. There is, in this eyewitness account, a final, and deeply resonant, pathos:

> In her last sickness she was much in darkness and trouble of spirit, which occasioned a judicious friend to examine her strictly, whether she had been guilty of witchcraft. But she said, no; but the ground of her trouble was some impatient and passionate speeches and actions of hers while in prison—upon the account of her suffering wrongfully—whereby she provoked the Lord by putting some contempt upon His word. And in fine she sought her pardon and comfort from God in Christ, and died so far as I understood praying to and resting upon God in Christ for salvation.[27]

• • •

In those early months of 1680, when the witchcraft investigation turned decisively against Elizabeth Morse, it tapped a deep pool of local suspicion and fear. The testimony given to the court recounted episodes from long before: "about seven years ago," "about sixteen years ago," "about ten years since," "about fifteen years ago," to mention only a few. This material was the heart of the case for conviction, but there was also much evidence of peculiarities in Goody Morse's everyday behavior—"strange actions," such as habitual "digging and crabbing the ground with the end of a staff, which I never took notice of any [other] person that acted in the like manner."[28] And there were many references to gossip and speculation about her alleged witchcraft. One witness had attributed his personal misfortunes to Elizabeth, since she had been so much "talked of for a witch." A second recalled a time when William Morse "began of his own accord to say that his wife was accounted a witch, but he did wonder that she should be both a healing and a destroying witch." One of her neighbors had actually remonstrated with Elizabeth about "the report that went of her as touching her name for witchcraft." Another was quoted as having said of her: "What? Is she a witch, or a cunning woman?"[29]

There was evidence, too, of efforts to use counter-magic against the accused. One instance, recorded in detail, merits quotation here. The witness was recalling the last illness of her mother, a certain Goodwife Chandler, some fourteen years before:

> Her mother . . . when she was ill . . . would often cry out and complain that G[oodwife] Morse was a witch, and had bewitched her . . . One [person], coming to the house, asked why we did not nail a horseshoe on the threshold (for that was an experiment to try witches). My mother, the next morning, with her staff made

a shift to get to the door, and nailed on a horseshoe as well as she could. G. Morse, while the horseshoe was on, would never be persuaded to come into the house. . . . And being demanded the reason, she would not tell me now, and said it was not her mind to come in; but she would kneel down by the door and talk and discourse, but not go in—though she would come oftentimes in a day. . . . William Moody, coming to the house and understanding that there was a horseshoe nailed on the door, said, "a piece of witchery"—and knocked it off and laid it by. Very shortly after [on] the same day G. Morse came in and thrust into the parlor where my mother lay. . . . And my mother complained of her, and I earnestly desired of her that she would be gone, and I could very hardly with my importunity entreat her to do it. The horseshoe was off about a week, and she would very often come in that time. About a week after, my mother, to keep her out of the house, got Daniel Rolfe to nail on the shoe again, which continued so about 7 or 8 days; and at that time she would not come over the threshold to come in, though often importuned to do it. Then William Moody, coming again, took off the horseshoe and put it in his pocket and carried it away; then the said Goodwife Morse came as before, and would go in as before.[30]

This intriguing sequence reveals, among other things, a division of public opinion about the morality of counter-magic. According to one viewpoint, horseshoes over the threshold were themselves "a piece of witchery," and thus hardly less wicked than the practices they were meant to repulse. Still, there was no direct challenge here to the suspicions directed against particular "witches" as individuals.

Indeed, the story of Goody Chandler's illness helps to fill in the picture sketched earlier. Elizabeth Morse had evoked over many years a very special concern. In idle conversation among her neighbors, in situations where she played a direct role, in the dreams and fantasies of those who knew her well, her presence energized a range of unsettling worries. These feelings, visible enough on their behavioral surface but largely obscure in their roots and origins, deserve the closest consideration. To study them is to touch a number of pressure-points that shaped the inner lives of ordinary folk in seventeenth-century Newbury.

What, then, of the *effects* attributed to Elizabeth Morse's witchcraft? The leading targets? The harm done? The "mischief"? There was, for a start, the matter of illness and injury to person. Four witnesses reported such experiences, and blamed them on Goody Morse. The range comprised "bloody flux," persistently "sore breasts," "itching and pricking" sensations, and a general "smiting" in the "lower parts."[31] There was also the illness of Goodwife Chandler described earlier (including "grievous fits"). Two children had died under circumstances that directed suspicion at Goody Morse. (For example: "Goody Morse came to visit him; she stroked up his head, [and] presently after I did apprehend the child grow worse, and in a sore and solemn condition continued until he died.")[32] Finally, there was one report of temporary incapacity (without a physical injury) from a man who "going many days on fowling . . . [could] get no geese" until he had made up an apparent slight to Elizabeth Morse.[33]

Livestock made another target for Elizabeth's alleged witchcraft: literally dozens of farm animals were believed to have been struck down by her means. Thus, for example, a calf belonging to one Zachariah Davis

> fell a-dancing and a-roaring . . . so we put him to the cow, but he would not suck, but ran a-roaring away, so we caught him again with much ado and put him into the barn. And we heard him roar several times in the night, and in the morning I went to the barn and there he was setting upon his tail like a dog, as I never see no calf set . . . before; and so he remained in these fits while he died.[34]

Another calf suddenly lost "the hair and skin off his back," a cow had "dung run out of her side," a mare refused to eat or drink, several sheep foamed strangely at the mouth: so the evidence went.[35] (In most cases such symptoms were but a prelude to permanent disability or death.) Here, indeed, was the largest category among all the "afflictions" laid to Goody Morse. (It should also be noted that some types of property were not thus involved. There was no mention in the testimony of damage to trees and crops, or of spoilage in food or drink, and—with the important exception of the "troubles" within the Morse home itself—household effects remained undisturbed.)

Witches were assumed always to seek opportunities to attack, but occasionally they settled for giving fright rather than inflicting actual injury. Thus Elizabeth Morse was accused of making sudden spectral appearances (e.g. "in the night, coming in at a little hole"), or causing terrible and mysterious noises.[36] More frequently she would harass her victims in the shape of one or another small animal:

> Lydia Titcomb . . . going home from the pond, there flew [something] out of the bushes, in her opinion like an owl; and it came up presently to her, and was turned into the shape of a cat, and quickly after turned into the shape of a dog. Sometimes [it] would

be all black, then [it would] have a white ring about the neck. Sometimes [it] would have long ears, sometimes scarce any to be discerned; sometimes a very long tail, sometimes a very short one scarcely discernible. And in such manner it followed us some time, as if it would leap upon our backs, and frighted us very much, and accompanied us . . . till near the house. And the last time we saw it, we left it playing about a tree.[37]

Everyone who underwent such experiences was severely "frighted." Some simply fled, but others (especially men) tried to strike back. One witness had encountered a strange "white thing like a cat," kicked at it, and succeeded finally in smashing it against a fence (where it "stopped with a loud cry"); he learned subsequently that Goodwife Morse had been treated by a doctor for a "hurt in her head . . . the same night, and same time of night."[38] (Surely this was more than coincidence?)

Occasionally, too, Goody Morse was suspected of having intimate contact with animals. One night, in the prison at Ipswich, the keeper "went near her bedside, and . . . heard a strange kind of noise, which was like a whelp sucking of the dam, or kittens sucking."[39] And a neighbor of Goody Morse had reportedly seen "some small creatures, like mice or rats, run into the house after her, and run under her coats."[40]

A final part of the testimony involved her display of preternatural knowledge and power. On several occasions she had mysteriously gained access to private information—the contents of a letter, the details of a conversation, awkward or embarrassing personal experiences.[41] In each case there was no human source to account for such access. At least once she had tried to foretell the future (predicting the death of a neighbor at sea).[42] Often, too, she had managed to appear, without warning or invitation, at the scene of important personal events. ("I do not remember that I did see her come or go away, but saw her at once, which did make me very much suspect she had bewitched my heifer.")[43] There was an irresistible quality about these incursions, which made her fellow-townspeople feel quite unsafe. There was also a strong presumption of "diabolical" influence.

The varied effects attributed to Goodwife Morse were preceded by events and circumstances of seemingly causal significance. These, too, deserve attention, for they help to answer an important question: what forms of personal contact, which sorts of experience, set the stage for witchcraft? In many instances the victim had previously opposed Elizabeth (or her husband) over some matter of common concern. Stripped to its essentials, the sequence was the one expressed in this bit of testi-

mony from Caleb Moody: "About 16 years ago I had some difference
with the said [Elizabeth] Morse; the next morning one of my best hogs
lay dead in the yard, and [with] no natural cause that I know of."[44]
Occasionally the witnesses recalled an open expression of anger on their
own part. (One had shouted at William Morse and threatened to
"break his bones.")[45] More often they mentioned the anger of the
"witch" herself. ("Goody Morse came out, and was mighty with me.")[46]
Either way there was reason to suspect a motive of retaliation.

A second, and related, category of exchange comprised substantive
requests by Goody Morse, which, for one reason or another, had gone
unmet. Caleb Moody had spurned her plea "late of a Saturday night . . .
to go to Mr. Woodbridge's store to see after her husband. . . . I told her
I did not apprehend any danger of him." The next day one of Moody's
sheep mysteriously "lay down and died."[47] John Mighell had been
hewing shingles for the Morses, and when evening came the work was
still unfinished. Goody Morse urged him "to stay all night," and then,
when he declined the invitation, to "be sure to come again tomorrow."
But he did not return, despite several further pleas, "and at last . . .
word came to me that she was very angry with me, and suddenly . . .
there was a great alteration in my cattle."[48] Still another witness—the
man who was unlucky in his "fowling"—had previously been asked by
Elizabeth to perform some small chores, "which I neglected to do so
soon as she desired." His neighbor Moody then advised that "I would
get no geese until I had finished her work, which accordingly I speedily
did. And afterward I had success, as I used to have formerly."[49]

In other cases there was neither an outright refusal of her request,
nor simple procrastination, but rather a persistent pattern of forgetting.
Zachariah Davis fully intended to bring her the "small parcel of wings"
that she needed, each time he made the trip from his home in Salisbury;
but each time he failed to remember. Goody Morse told him "she wondered at it, that my memory should be so bad"—and retaliated, so
Davis believed, by bewitching his family's cows.[50] On another occasion
Jonathan Haines agreed to bring her "a bushel of malt from her brother
Anthony's," but regularly forgot about it. His mare subsequently became ill, and a friend advised that "I must carry the malt, and then . . .
my mare would be well enough." Haines replied, with evident bitterness, "if it be so, before I will humor the Devil I will lose all that I
have," whereupon his friend undertook to do the errand for him. The
upshot, of course, was immediate and total recovery of the mare.[51]

A final point of suspicion was the experience of some witnesses *after*
they had testified against Goody Morse. A man named Chase was

stricken with "bloody flux" on "the very day" of his testimony, "and so it held me till I came to the court and charged her with it."[52] An elderly woman named Toppan participated in the same "examination"; a short while later "Elizabeth Morse came after her and took her about the wrist, as if she would enquire what was the evidence she gave in against her." That night Goody Toppan "felt a cold, damp hand clasping her about her wrist, which affrighted her very much and put her into a very great and dropping sweat"; she remained ill, and out of sorts, for weeks thereafter.[53]

It appears, then, that a considerable variety of experiences might precede the operation of Goody Morse's witchcraft; but there was, throughout, a common denominator. Her victims had acted in ways which, in *their* view, were certain to make her angry. Open "difference" and disagreement, the failure (whether conscious or unintended) to supply her needs, and testimony against her in the witchcraft case itself would surely invite a vengeful reply. Hence the most immediate and visible *affect* in the witnesses was simple fear. Sometimes such fear drew a clear line of connection between the precipitating event and the alleged affliction—as, for example, in the aforementioned case of the "cold, damp hand" clasping the victim's wrist just as Goody Morse had done a few hours earlier.

But other impulses, other feelings, were also operative here. Indeed, if the witnesses were afraid in a conscious way of Goody Morse's anger, they were also struggling (though less consciously) with anger in themselves. Some of them could experience their own wish for vengeance without quite recognizing it for what it was. The men who struck back when pursued by animal-familiars were releasing some notably violent affect. One, in particular, showed great satisfaction at having delivered a successful counter-blow: he woke his neighbor "and desired him . . . [to] go to such a tree and there I thought he would find a dead cat," and then went "straightaway home and told [his] wife."[54] The use of violence against these "creatures" of the witch expressed a deeper wish to assault the witch herself—deeper, and psychologically inadmissible.

In other witnesses the underlying anger remained well below the surface, visible only in its indirect effects. The instances of "forgetting" are particularly illustrative. Zachariah Davis could not remember to bring Goody Morse her "parcel of wings" despite having them "in my mind a little before I came." (Indeed, this had happened "three or four times" running.)[55] Jonathan Haines had a similar problem: "In the morning I remembered my promise when I came from home, but I forgot it before I came to her brother[-in-law]'s house. And so often-

Table 1.   Elizabeth Morse's victims

Age	Male	Female	Total
10–19	3	2	5
20–29	7	0	7
30–39	8	0	8
40–49	1	6	7
50–59	1	1	2
60–69	0	0	0
70–79	0	1	1
Total	20	10	30

times I did think to bring her malt, but it was always out of my mind, let me do what I could."[56] Something had blocked off these errands in the minds of both Davis and Haines, something that did not yield to purposeful attention. To repeat and re-emphasize the revealing phrase of Jonathan Haines: memory failed, "let me do what I could." We would say that there was unconscious resistance at work here, or, in other words, that neither man was inwardly willing to do as Goody Morse had asked. We might speculate further that the root of such resistance was covert hostility, a wish to challenge and to thwart—indeed to hurt. At some level Davis and Haines were *damned* if they would cooperate with their witch-neighbor.

It remains to ask how these experiences were distributed within the population at large. Does the evidence suggest disproportionate involvement for one group or another? Was there any pattern of gender or age among the victims of goody Morse's witchcraft? The entire list, as reconstructed here, includes 33 persons. There are 22 males, 11 females. Approximate ages (at the time of supposed "affliction") can be discovered for all but three.[57] The details are summarized in Table 1. Leaving aside those five persons less than fully adult (i.e. under twenty years old), the table reveals one marked difference. Most of Goody Morse's female victims belonged to the age-group forty to forty-nine; none were younger than this, two were older. By contrast, the male victims were predominantly less than forty years old, with almost equal numbers in the twenty to twenty-nine and thirty to thirty-nine categories. We may conclude, in short, that suspicion of Elizabeth Morse was especially strong within two demographic sub-groups: middle-aged women (roughly her own peers)[58] and younger men.

Marked as they were by age and sex, these two sub-groups also reported qualitatively different experiences of the "witch" and her *malefi-cium*. The female victims, for one thing, reported much direct inter-action with Goody Morse. They were visited by her, they conversed with her, and on some occasions they fought openly with her.[59] Several of them had accused her to her face of practicing witchcraft; one had discussed the subject at length with her, "endeavoring to convince her of the wickedness of it."[60] The men, on the other hand, had fewer and briefer contacts with Goody Morse. (As noted, the most common occa-sion for such contacts was a request by her for work or other favors.) By and large, they were much less familiar with her in the everyday routine of their lives.

There were, additionally, distinctions of substance in the charges made by the two groups. The women had experienced illness, injury, or threats thereof, to themselves and, more particularly, to their children. Two childhood deaths were attributed (by the mothers) to Goody Morse.[61] In another case a woman, apparently alone in her house with her chil-dren, was frightened by persistent, unexplained noises.[62] And, in an-other, the witness was talking with William Morse about a particular episode of childbirth, in which Elizabeth had played a rather strange part.[63] Two *more* women had been made sick, one of them fatally so.[64] The men were afflicted in other ways. The accusations of cattle-witchery came almost entirely from men—likewise the reports of assault by animal-familiars. However, only one man claimed to have been made sick by witchcraft, and none reported illness in his children.

There are important lines of pattern in all this, connecting age, sex, and inward concern. The one group may reasonably be termed "meno-pausal women." The central threads in their testimony—bodily change, health and illness, children—quite plainly announced their life-course position.[65] Whatever their individual idiosyncracies, they shared the same underlying preoccupation—perhaps, indeed, the same feelings of danger. The men, too, felt endangered, but their concerns ran less to person than to property. Their domestic animals, and above all their cows, were highly susceptible to injury by witchcraft. The threat im-plicit here cannot be fully appreciated without some consideration of context; hence the following brief excursion into livestock history.

Item: Livestock made a particularly valuable form of property for all the people of early New England. They were, moreover, conveniently transferrable property, and this was important in communities without much circulating cash. Unlike land and housing, cattle could be moved about: to repay debts, to furnish "portions," or simply to support their

owners in periods of relocation. At the same time, cattle made a particularly *risky* property. Even in the most attentive hands they could be
lost or stolen, they could sicken or die.

Item: It goes without saying that livestock supplied the New Englanders with essential foods. Cow's milk, in particular, was invested with
life-sustaining significance. But this was not simply a practical matter,
for milk has, in all cultures, a special and symbolic meaning. Presumably, the effect is heightened where cows are milked in plain view each
day—and where infants are regularly nursed at their mothers' breast.

Item: Livestock comprised that group of animate creatures closest to
the experience of humankind. They, too, had moods and feelings; they
were by turns hot and cold, vigorous and tired, healthy and sick. They
and their owners inhabited the same world of everyday sensation. Hence
the variety of *names* given to cattle in colonial New England—"Chip,"
"Spark," "Betty," "Rose"—names which express warmth and a sense of
individuality as well.[66] A scholar of early New England agriculture has
written that cows were "in a sense . . . part of the family";[67] if so, the
affectional ties must have gone quite deep. Perhaps there was even a
kind of identification, a sense of sharing that blurred the species-
boundary.

But even if all this is granted, it remains to ask why young men, in
particular, should have been so sensitive to losses in livestock. Why,
indeed, should not the other leading group of Goody Morse's victims—
the older women—have brought forth similar questions and charges?
Part of the answer lies in their different relations to *property*. Men, of
course, were always the official property-holders in this society, and for
many young men livestock made the first important property owned
outright. Their cows (and other domestic animals) served as the basis
for building an independent livelihood.

However, more explicitly psychological elements seem also to have
played in here. The two victim groups displayed on balance a marked
difference in orientation to the supposed witchcraft. The contrast can be
rendered in graphic form, as is shown in the accompanying chart.
The vulnerability of livestock, in the second case, now appears as part
of a larger paradigm. With the younger men witchcraft was experienced in two ways, both of them rather circuitous: the witch's "familiar"
attacked the victim, or the witch herself attacked the victim's livestock.
With the women there were no intermediaries.

In fact, this contrast mirrored actual patterns of experience within
and between the two groups. In the one case witch and victim shared
a common age and gender; in the other they represented different

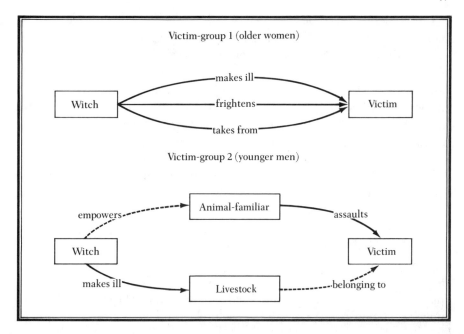

generations *and* opposite sexes. In the one case they shared the same world of everyday experience; in the other their relations were (relatively) formal, delimited, constrained. In the one case witchcraft operated quite straightforwardly; in the other, it came from a greater distance —and by a route more indirect.

Yet there was, finally, a common core of fantasy about Elizabeth Morse *as witch.* All victims absorbed it, acted on it, and gave to it from their own experience. Again and again Goody Morse comes through the words of their testimony as a figure of menacing—even deadly—intrusiveness. She appeared suddenly at awkward moments, utilizing where necessary her special powers of flight. She forced herself on her neighbors in ways ordinary but unwelcome, asking them for favors or simply for paid assistance. When another woman lay sick, she "thrust into the parlor" on one occasion, "rushed in" on a second, and generally "would not refrain [from] coming."[68] (As previously noted, this pattern was altered only in the face of a magical counter-strategy—a horseshoe nailed over the threshold.) When her spirit was transmitted to animal-"familiars," it made these creatures extraordinarily aggressive. (The "great white cat" encountered by one witness climbed upon his chest, seized his "neckcloth and coat," "again was a-coming up upon [his] left side," and finally "came between [his] legs, so that [he] could not well go forward"—rather uncharacteristic behavior in a feline.)[69]

Other actions ascribed to Goody Morse conveyed the same inner meaning. Her success in divining the contents of an important letter was patently intrusive.[70] So, too, was her knowledge of a young man's private life: "James Brown . . . testifieth . . . that I was one night at Salisbury, and the next day was at goody Morse's. She told me of several of my misdemeanors, among the rest of what I did the night before; and I asked her how she could tell of 'em."[71] (Here spoke the voice of adolescent guilt.) At such moments the victims experienced a keen sense of inner violation. Their privacy was invaded, their autonomy compromised; they had lost control of information vital to their lives and reputations. Their integrity as distinct persons was temporarily in doubt.

Nor were these isolated instances. Autonomy, control, integrity: such words describe a central theme evident throughout the testimony against Elizabeth Morse. Time and again Elizabeth's victims proved unable to defend their property from the effects of her alleged witchcraft; in some instances they were helpless even to protect their *bodies*. There was indeed violation here—and of an absolutely fundamental kind.

The story of Elizabeth Morse has one unusual twist. Though long suspected—and finally convicted—of practicing witchcraft, she thought of *herself* as a victim. Indeed, it was only after *maleficium* had invaded her own household that she underwent formal indictment and trial.

Her "troubles" and suffering as victim deserve some final consideration. What, we may well ask, was actually happening in the home of William and Elizabeth Morse during the winter of 1679–80? Whence came the rattlings, the shakings, the breakage, the sudden disappearances that plagued them for days on end? How can we explain the activities ascribed to "stone-throwing devils" in terms congenial to our own, more "scientific" sensibility?

Clearly, the Morses' grandson must have a central place in any such explanation. After all, the phenomena here in question can be directly correlated with the actual presence of John Stiles. When the boy was away (whether with Caleb Powell or at "the doctor's"), the Morses experienced complete relief from their difficulties. As soon as he returned, the former pattern resumed. Was young Stiles moving or throwing objects around the house, perhaps at moments when his grandparents were otherwise preoccupied? Caleb Powell seems to have thought so—as witness the following statement from a neighbor:

> Mary Tucker . . . remembereth that Caleb Powell came into her house and said to this purpose: that he coming to William Morse's

house, and the old man being at prayer, he thought [it was] not fit
to go in, but he looked in the window. And he said he had broken
the enchantment, for he saw the boy play tricks while he [i.e.
Morse] was at prayer, and mentioned some, and among the rest
that he saw him [i.e. Stiles] to fling the shoe at the said Morse's
head.[72]

This account mixes elements of the "real" and the "occult" in a notable way. On the one hand, Powell has seen the boy playing some very
ordinary and unmysterious "tricks"; on the other, he claims thereby to
have "broken the enchantment." There are, in fact, additional hints that
John Stiles was capable of directly assaultive behavior. Once, when
taken to another house nearby, the boy began to fall into a fit. There
were some familiar symptoms—"grievous hollering" and eating of ashes
—but also he "threw a great stone at a maid in the house."[73] Perhaps
here, on a visit to a neighbor, he indulged more openly an impulse
which at home he would try to camouflage.

In short, the forces which so disrupted the Morses' household may
have been human ones, after all. Yet direct intervention by John Stiles
will not account for the entire range of episodes noted in the trial
records. For example, andirons that "danced" in and out of fireplace
pots, or chairs that "did bow often towards me," seem to belong to a
different category. William Morse was himself concerned to rule out
human mischief as an explanation for his difficulties, and sprinkled his
testimony with disclaimers to this effect: "and nobody near it," or "and
[we] saw nobody meddle with it."[74] Indeed the sheer *number* of episodes
recounted by the Morses excludes the possibility of attributing each and
every one to the "tricks" of John Stiles.

The alternative—and complementary—explanation for all this is the
influence of raw fear in the Morses themselves. They were, quite obviously, distressed and frightened by the unfolding sequence. And they
reacted, like most persons struggling with extreme anxiety, by elaborating
in fantasy what was already present in reality: at least some of their
experiences were imaginary. It seems significant that most of the Morses'
difficulties occurred at times or in situations especially conducive to
worry. There was, for example, the morning when William Morse felt
"minded to write" but was prevented from doing so by a string of
bizarre accidents.[75] In fact, Morse began on this occasion to compose an
account of the various "diabolical" assaults on his house—a task which
almost inevitably would make him anxious (and accident-prone?). Most
of the other disturbances noted in the trial testimony came when the
Morses were alone, or at night when they lay in bed in the dark. At

such times they must have felt particularly vulnerable, and perhaps their fear served to create its own objects.

And what of their grandson Stiles? What sort of a boy was he? How can we best understand the behavior attributed to him? We should be careful, in the first place, about ascribing his "tricks" to *conscious*, planful mischief. If he actually did throw a shoe at his grandfather—and if, too, he directly caused many similar misadventures—he may have done so quite unknowingly. The same can be said of his "fits." Such episodes belonged, of course, to a long-familiar tradition (for victims of witchcraft); and in Stiles's case they proved convincing to a variety of careful observers. (If consciously contrived—so the argument goes—they would have been *less* convincing.) "Fits" and "tricks" should, then, be viewed as different parts of the same continuum—the first ostensibly self-destructive, the second destructive to others.

There were further signs of irregularity in young Stiles, both before and during the time of the witch-trials. In the spring of 1680 he was presented in court "for stealing a silver spoon from John Dole"; and "being examined, [he] confessed the fact."[76] He was accused on the same occasion of uttering "wild words" to various friends and companions. According to testimony, he had declared that "he would go to hell"; when asked why he said so, "his answer was because he was not going to Heaven." Furthermore, he "said that he could not read on the sabbath day . . . because the devil would not let him."[77] These things had happened "before the late trouble at William Morse's"; but there is similar material in the trial record itself. Thus one witness, "living near to William Morse's, in the evening, quickly after sunset, saw John Stiles standing by Mr. Denison's cowhouse; and I asked him what was the best news at their house, and he told me that there was several hundreds of devils in the air, and they would be at their house by and by, and they would be at my house anon."[78]

Such fragments of conversation suggest, in Stiles, a special interest in things diabolic. There is indeed a note of attraction, of personal affinity, here, which forecasts his subsequent experience of "possession." But *why* did he feel that he belonged to the world of Hell and devils? Was there something in his life or background with which he could not otherwise come to terms?

In fact, John Stiles has left regrettably few independent tracks for the historian to follow up. This much alone can be determined: His mother was born Hannah Morse, the second or third child of William and Elizabeth. There is no extant record that she was married. (Moreover, the surname Stiles does not appear among the adult population of Newbury during the 1660s and 70s. There were two men by that name living elsewhere in Massachusetts, but both had their own wives and families.)[79] Young John, as we well know, lived for some part of his childhood in the home of his grandparents. And he seems not to have had siblings. When William Morse wrote a will, just weeks before he died, he made substantial cash gifts to only two of his heirs: "my daughter Hannah . . . and her son John Stiles."[80] Such tidbits imply some anomaly of family situation. Why, in particular, was young John so conspicuously fatherless? Two possibilities immediately suggest themselves: (1) his mother may have been widowed when he was very small; or (2) he may have been the unwanted offspring of an illegitimate (perhaps adulterous?) union.

By broadening this inquiry somewhat so as to touch other branches of the Morse line, we discover additional evidence of social and personal deviation. In 1676 a second daughter (Abigail) of William and Elizabeth Morse had borne an illegitimate child. Convicted thereupon of fornication, she was soon involved in lengthy proceedings over the placement of her child in a foster home.[81] A third Morse daughter (Elizabeth) is mentioned in her father's will (along with "her four children") but is otherwise untraceable.[82] There were also two sons (Jonathan and Obadiah), both of whom moved out of Newbury as young men.[83] This picture of the second generation seems, overall, an unusual one. The families of other Newbury settlers (for example, that of Anthony Morse, William's brother) were extending and strengthening their roots in the community. Yet *this* family was dwindling, both in its physical presence and in its moral standing. In fact, there would be no descendants of William Morse living in Newbury beyond the end of the seventeenth century.

Perhaps, then, the members of this family were especially ripe for the "afflictions" which overtook them in the closing weeks of 1679. The evidence, once again, is fragmentary, but it yields a suggestive pattern. Events had converged during a number of years to create an edge of tension and disappointment in the lives of William and Elizabeth Morse. When trouble began, they were quick to magnify it; their worries became self-reinforcing—even, in some instances, gave rise to quite imaginary misadventures. But not all the misadventures were imaginary. John Stiles was, on his own account, ripe for the role he would come to play. Perhaps there were inner resentments (in a youth who had missed the regular care of parents); perhaps there was a sense of unworthiness (joining the disgrace of an irregular birth with the violence of satanic "possession"); perhaps, too, there was a simple wish for attention. Whatever the actual combination of forces, Stiles and his grandparents come through as marginal figures, leading problematic lives.

What might ordinary folk make of all this? How would they connect such a personal and family history with witchcraft? William Morse himself recognized the possibilities. His "humble petition" to the Court of Assistants, in May 1681, concluded with the following disclaimer: "As to rumors of some great wickedness in our house, which should cause the devil so to trouble us, our conscience is clear of the knowledge of any such thing, more than our common frailties."[84]

"Common frailties" or "great wickedness"? That, of course, was the vital question. The accused gave one answer; the accusers and victims, another. To most Newbury townspeople *circa* 1680 the Morse household seemed an especially likely target for the Devil—when he sought, as inevitably he *would* seek, new avenues for his malign influence.

6

Accusers, Victims, Bystanders: The Innerlife Dimension

Introduction: The Primary Victims

"Every man is in certain respects: (a) like all other men, (b) like some other men, (c) like no other man."[1]

This simple yet profound observation, offered many years ago by two eminent social scientists, can be pressed into service in the present context. In certain respects the disposition of individual New Englanders toward witchcraft was quite idiosyncratic. In others it was common to particular groups, large or small. And in still others it touched matters of species-wide significance.

The present chapter deals with psychological issues at the group level. For the most part it speaks to the entire New England "group"— in short, to those preoccupations which all (or, at any rate, most) people of that time and place effectively shared. Still, at some points it reaches out toward the realm of "universals," while at others it explores distinctions within the population. For example, one cannot overlook the presence of sub-groups which occupied rather different positions in relation to witchcraft. The ranks of accused witches were (as noted already) disproportionately filled with women in the middle years. And there was also some imbalance in the proportions of witchcraft-victims—those who saw themselves as objects of attack (and who, in their turn, supplied most of the testimony against the accused). Table 1 summarizes results from an analysis of nine relatively well documented cases. On the one hand, the figures reveal a general susceptibility to "attack" by

Table 1:   Victims of witchcraft by age and sex

		Male	Female	Sex not known	Total
Ages	0– 9	8	6	3	17
	10–19	8	12	—	20
	20–39	49	19	—	68
	40–59	10	18	—	28
	60+	1	2	—	3
	Total	76	57	3	136

witchcraft, embracing both sexes and all ages. On the other, they suggest some differentials in the strength of this susceptibility. Men in early adulthood (ages twenty to thirty-nine) are most clearly over-represented. And women of the middle years (forty to fifty-nine) are also present beyond their numbers in the population at large.

However, bare numbers do not adequately tell the story here: the quality of involvement must also be accounted for. And when one proceeds, case by case, to assess the *forms* of victimization (and of the accusatory responses) the patterns implicit in Table 1 are considerably strengthened. By and large, it was middle-aged women and younger men who supplied the most detailed and keenly felt testimony against accused witches. The qualitative materials also spotlight one other group whose importance is not evident in the numbers alone: girls in the age-range ten to nineteen. In the popular lore of witchcraft this has, of course, been the victim-group *par excellence*. The lore exaggerates, but it does not falsify. When a teen-aged girl succumbed to "fits," other manifestations of witchcraft were usually overshadowed. Among the known prosecutions less than half included this particular feature; but wherever present its impact was extreme.

Here, then, were the leading groups in witchcraft proceedings. In fact, each one has received some special attention in the case-study chapters immediately preceding. Elizabeth Knapp was in most respects a prototype of the teen-aged girl "under affliction"; while the victim/accusers of Goody Morse came predominantly from the ranks of younger men and middle-aged women. There is, however, something more to be said about these three groups. Disproportionately represented among the victims of witchcraft, they must in some sense have felt disproportionately vulnerable. The sources and meanings of such vulnerability belong, indisputably, to the "innerlife dimension."

Women in Midlife

It is easy enough to label the first group as "menopausal women," but
the label itself demands special consideration. When such women complained about the witchcraft of Goody Morse, they showed a marked
preoccupation with body-states, with illness and injury, with morbidity
and mortality in children. And the same tendency appeared in other
cases where women in mid-life came forward as witchcraft victims.[2] If
this seems implicitly "menopausal," then some of it is attributable to
biological processes shared by women of comparable age everywhere.
But other elements were added by the context—both demographic and
cultural. New England wives of the seventeenth century bore children,
at quite regular intervals, for as long as they were able;[3] most had their
last child after the age of forty.[4] The pregnancies came again and again,
until suddenly they stopped, which is to say that menopause was vividly
demarcated in terms of personal experience. At the same time child-
bearing was an assumed and vital function of such women—in their
minds, literally "God-given." No matter what the difficulties and perils
involved, New Englanders accepted the Biblical command to "be fruitful
and replenish the earth"; indeed, the bearing of children shaped their
very definition of womanhood.

How, then, would individual women react to the loss of this central,
life-giving capacity? Unfortunately, the extant records are not of a sort
to answer such questions, but they do allow certain inferences. As
always, menopause was a life-stage of painful transition, but probably
more so *then* than nowadays.[5] Its core was a sense of sudden and profound loss, perhaps even of "robbery." The flow of inner (and outward)
experience broke sharply; life henceforth must proceed in new channels.
The forces that made the change were hard to understand and impossible
to control, obscure yet deeply felt, unseen in their origins but most
palpable in their results. Given all these circumstances, New England
women of middle age might well cast themselves as sufferers, as victims
—even as targets of witchcraft.

There is another, still more speculative point to raise about the vulnerability of such women. Recent research on aging has noticed a pattern
of midlife "crossover"—a tendency in men and women over forty to
reverse, or at least to diminish, their conventional sex-roles.[6] Men give
increasing play to traits and impulses hitherto considered "feminine"—
to "nurturance," to "dependency," to sentiment of all kinds. Women, on
the other hand, move in an opposite direction—toward increasing autonomy and self-assertion. Since this phenomenon appears in a variety of

otherwise different cultural settings, it lays claim to universal developmental significance. And if the claim is accepted, there are intriguing
implications for the present study. New England values were, by and
large, notably uncongenial to personal expressions of self.[7] Yet New
England women in midlife experienced deep, inner promptings of precisely that sort. Individual response must have varied—from greater to
lesser compliance, and even to outright repression. Perhaps the witches
were recruited disproportionately from the former group (those who
yielded most fully to assertive impulse). The victims, by contrast, may
have been those who struggled against the trend—but experienced a
sense of danger, of exposure to unseen forces, in doing so.

Men in Young Adulthood

Autonomy was more obviously a central issue for another category of
victims. Most New England men would, in their twenties and thirties,
assume the status of independent householders.[8] They must take a wife
and begin to father children. At the same time, and as part of the same
process, they must assume control of their own livelihoods (whether in
farming, in a trade, in commercial enterprise, or, more rarely, in an
ecclesiastical "calling"). The process was neither rapid nor entirely
smooth. Average age at marriage, for New England men, was over
twenty-five years; and cultural convention made "youth" last until thirty.
Moreover, it was not always easy to establish the economic underpinnings of independence. The property of young men came, most
typically, from their families of origin (in short, from their fathers),
and sometimes it was given grudgingly, or late, or on terms that fell
short of outright control. There is enough evidence here for one scholar
to propose the term "patriarchalism" as a way of describing the family
system of early New England.[9]

But there was more to all this than the adjustment of property relations vis-à-vis potentially witholding fathers. Young men everywhere, as
they assume an independent status, must break from an emotional
matrix in which they have been sustained and guided through their
early years. Expressed in formal terms, this means the relinquishment—
or at least the drastic realignment—of underlying "infantile" ties. And
among such ties none is more powerful, and ultimately compromising,
than the one which pulls (back) toward mother. The danger is of double-
barreled "regression," to infantile dependence and infantile sexuality.
(Our highly pejorative term "mother's boy" captures both elements.
Such a person continues too long and too much to rely on the support

and approval of his mother, while also retaining her as his primary "love object." As a result he does not—inwardly—grow up.) The opportunity, on the other hand, is to act by and for oneself, to move ahead toward new (age-appropriate and "non-incestuous") loves. Therein lies the route to maturity.

The possible connections to witchcraft are not far to seek. Young men supplied a far larger number of victims than any other category. Moreover, their sense of liability to attack can be interpreted as expressing several convergent strands of inner concern with women of their mothers' generation. In the first place, the witch commands extraordinary power over them and their possessions. (They continue to feel the strength of the "maternal object.") At the same time, they strike postures of resistance and repudiation—refusing the witch's requests for cooperation in routine aspects of everyday experience, and leading the charge against her in the courts of law. (They wish, however they can, to break the "incestuous" tie.) For this the witch grows angry with them, and punishes them severely. (They feel guilty, and deserving of punishment, for what they are about.) But when the witch attacks them, she does so indirectly, i.e. through familiars, or by striking down their cattle. (Distance is still maintained; in fantasy, as in social reality, the "maternal object" must not come too close.) The entire situation is complex and keenly felt—and *vulnerability* is right at the heart of it.

Girls in Adolescence

The third of the leading victim-groups, girls between the ages of ten and nineteen, presents special problems of interpretation. On the one hand, the evidence of their involvement in witchcraft proceedings is remarkably full and vivid; on the other, there is hardly any evidence about their experience apart from such involvement. Girls in their teens left fewer tracks for historians than any other group (young children alone excepted). Boys of comparable age can (sometimes) be followed in schools or colleges; and at least a few older men left autobiographies which made reference to their early years. For girls, however, there is virtually nothing. One imagines them growing up in a family-centered context and absorbed in a conventional round of domestic chores. They certainly assisted their mothers—in tending to gardens and orchards and domestic animals, in cooking and spinning, and in the care of still younger children. Their average age at menarche can be estimated at fourteen to sixteen.[10] Shortly afterward they began to be drawn into courtships, though most would not marry before twenty. Did they form "peer-groups" or some equivalent thereof? Where they much involved with older persons outside their immediate families? What was the balance between internal and external restraints in their everyday experience? On these points the record is mute.

Of course, there are vast differences between adolescence then and adolescence now. The whole context of growth between childhood and adulthood has been transformed, with corresponding changes of inner experience. One result, for example, is a greatly increased emphasis on issues of adolescent "identity." Modern-day teenagers confront a bewildering variety of pathways into adult life (e.g. alternative careers, geographic and social environments, value systems, etc.). And the reality, or illusion, of choice is frequently painful. In this respect the young people of seventeenth-century New England were differently situated. Their choices were relatively few, and some elements of "identity" came to them almost ready-made.[11]

The biological dimension of adolescence is, however, much less liable to change. From the standpoint simply of hormonal and biochemical process, the experience of this age-group cannot have differed very substantially across the centuries. Assuming, moreover, that psychological process is rooted in biology, then it too must show elements of invariance. And it is in exploring such elements that one may reasonably look for help from current scientific theory. The evidence of participation in witchcraft cases is itself compelling. To "interpret" this material is to build a long and admittedly shaky bridge toward what is known of adolescent psychology in general.

The fits of Elizabeth Knapp (see Chapter 4) were in many respects typical for teenaged girls under the influence of witchcraft. Still, no one experience was *entirely* typical, so it is well to review the main, i.e. the most commonly noted, features.

> *Preliminaries*: The victim becomes anxiously preoccupied with her spiritual condition. She discovers ominous signs of God's displeasure toward her—this in spite of her manifest involvement in religious devotions and her outwardly faultless behavior.
>
> *Onset*: Her fits begin with spells of fainting, hysterical crying, disordered speech, and disturbances of sight and hearing.
>
> *Intensification*: The fits become longer, more frequent, and more bizarre in their substantive features. This phase often includes a delusionary confrontation with spectral witches, who seek to tempt, trick, or terrorize the victim into signing "the Devil's book" (that is, making a pact of perpetual allegiance).

The victim offers desperate resistance, herself reviling the witches in the most outspoken terms.

Acute Phase: The fits at peak intensity may include the following elements: (1) excruciating sensations of "pricking" and "pinching" (as if by numberless pins and nails), also of "burning" (by invisible flames); (2) bizarre contortions of body parts: twisting, stretching, unusual postures of extreme rigidity and limberness by turns; (3) frenzied motor activity: rolling on the ground, running about aimlessly, simulated "flying" and "diving"; occasional "barking" or other animal imitation; some impulse to injury of self or others; (4) periods of extreme immobility, amounting to paralysis; feelings of extraordinary pressure on the chest or elsewhere; (5) anorexia: more or less complete inhibitions of eating (sometimes accompanied by a strong wish to eat, but with clenching of mouth whenever food is brought); (6) occasional forced consumption of invisible (and painful or poisonous) liquids when overpowered by the witch; (7) "frolicsome" intervals, mostly without pain; cavorting in a "ludicrous" way, babbling impertinent nonsense; insults and gestures of physical assault toward bystanders, friends, and family.

Intermissions: The victim experiences "quiet" periods, lasting hours or days, and characterized by lassitude, a "melancholy" air, and feelings of self-reproach.

These behaviors constitute a package, a syndrome, a composite picture of a considerable group, which partly reflects the individual experience of each victim, while entirely representing none of them. As such, it does not lend itself to full-fledged diagnostic or "genetic" interpretation of the sort possible in a single case-study. Nonetheless certain themes do come clear, and some of them are very close to the surface.

In the first place, "fits" invariably conveyed a sharp challenge to conventional standards and received authority. The victim might do or say almost anything, no matter how shocking. ("She frequently told us that if she might but steal or be drunk she should be well immediately.")[12] Parental commands were ignored or rejected. ("Upon the least reproof of their parents . . . most grievous, woeful, heart-breaking agonies would they fall unto. If any useful thing were to be done to them, or by them, they would have all sorts of troubles fall upon them.")[13] A minister's prayers brought ingratitude and scorn. ("Her whole carriage to me was with a sauciness that I had not been used to be treated with. . . . She would call to me with multiplied impertinences . . . and hector me at a strange rate.")[14] Ordinary human constraints were rejected, and mocked, when the victims simulated animals. ("They would bark at one another like dogs, and again purr like so many cats.")[15]

A second aspect of these episodes was attention-seeking—or outright exhibitionism. The routines of a household, a neighborhood, even an entire village were temporarily reorganized around the sufferings of the victim. Ministers came from near and far to pray over her; magistrates prepared other forms of public action in her behalf. Her fits were end-lessly recounted in local gossip; they might, in addition, yield material for sermons and books. Affliction of this sort was, in sum, a route to instant fame.[16]

To challenge authority, to court fame: these, presumably, were wishes for which the fits provided ample gratification. But we must also credit the painful side—the hurts, both physical and psychological—of much afflictive experience. Viewed from the standpoint of clinical theory, such hurts look extremely "primitive." They seem random and disorganized, and unmodified by any rational or "censoring" process. Indeed, the fits epitomize an infant's world of sensation. The extreme orientation to body surfaces, the pricks, the pinches, the sudden changes of body temperature: here are the (sometimes inevitable) discomforts of the first period of life. And yet the infant is not merely a recipient of such "torments"; he (she) wishes, in fantasy, to respond in kind. Consider the ingredients of "infantile sadism" as observed by a clinical psycho-analyst:

> All physical functions . . . are drawn in . . . [to] the attack. . . .
> Limbs shall trample, kick, and hit; lips, fingers, and hands shall
> suck, twist, pinch; teeth shall bite, gnaw, mangle, and cut; mouth
> shall devour, swallow, and kill (annihilate); eyes kill by a look,
> pierce, and penetrate; breath and mouth hurt by noise, as the
> child's oversensitive ears have experienced. . . .[17]

Virtually every one of these attacking modes could be matched to par-ticular points in seventeenth-century accounts of fits: in effect, the modern psychoanalytic theorist and the premodern observer of witch-craft have discovered the same thing. Of course, the fits reflected the viewpoint of victims, not agents, of attack; but in the world of uncon-scious process such postures are readily turned around. Indeed, the infant cannot tolerate his (her) own "sadism"; there is less danger in attributing these impulses to other "objects." And so they are "projected" outside the self, where they join company with the actual discomforts mentioned previously and then return to attack.*

In most of us these "primitive" images and fantasies lie dormant far below the threshold of consciousness. Revised and reworked into new structures after infancy, their connection to any actual behavior seems remote indeed. There is, however, one subsequent period of life when they may gain new energy and find new pathways to expression. This is the period of adolescence. Again, in most of us the developmental residues of earliest life remain largely suppressed (or modified and controlled) *even* during adolescence. But for a few with psychic "deficits" of one sort or another, the odds of a breakthrough are much increased.[19]

The central tasks of adolescence, as understood by current psychoanalytic theory, are twofold: first, to shift from the original "infantile" object-ties toward more mature levels of psycho-sexual functioning, and, second, to rework the "nuclear self" around goals, ideals, and a sense of inner "identity" appropriate to the adult life-situation. Both of these tasks, however, entail some return to earlier developmental positions: one must first go backward in order ultimately to be free to move forward. As a leading theorist has put it: "The significant emotional needs and conflicts of early childhood must be recapitulated before new solutions with qualitatively different instinctual aims and ego interests can be found." Thus, "adolescent regression not only is unavoidable, it is obligatory . . . [and] phase specific."[20]

On the side of psychosexual development this means, more specifically, a renewal of both oedipal and *pre*-oedipal issues. And the latter

* In fact, the matter is more complicated still. Infants can only sporadically maintain the boundaries between "self" and "non-self"; and "objects" from their environment frequently obtain a place in their internal representational world. A "bad object," in short, may be experienced as being "inside" as well as "outside." Consider once again, the words of the psychoanalyst: "In our earliest days, but later in life too, when the self feels full of ruthless egoism or hate, . . . intense anxiety arises; the violence . . . raging within, and felt to be uncontrollable, is unutterably terrifying. It is then omnipotently denied and dissociated from the self, but is attributed instead to the persons inside who are the objects of the hate or greed, and are then felt to have provoked hate by their hate. It is they who are felt as bad: envious, robbing, ruthless, murderous. Thus it happens that a good helping person . . . changes shape and turns into a terrifying and dangerous enemy inside one; *one is felt to be possessed of a devil inside* [emphasis added]. . . . The bad objects within thus take their origin from our own dangerous and evil tendencies, disowned by us; characteristically, therefore, they are felt as 'foreign objects,' as an incubus, a nightmare, an appalling, gratuitous, and inescapable persecution."[18]

are of special interest here. Adolescent *girls*, in particular, experience a powerful regressive pull toward the "pre-oedipal mother." This, in turn, calls forth resistances and defenses (to avoid "remaining attached to a homosexual object and thus fatally rupturing the development of femininity").[21] The ensuing tug-of-war may generate all manner of behavioral and emotional stress: the (nowadays) familiar mother-daughter conflicts are only its most visible manifestation.

Our own culture accords a measure of tolerance to such conflicts; but in early New England the situation was probably quite different. The "regressive pull" and its defensive counterparts would obtain fewer chances for expression in everyday behavior; the "phase-specific" struggles were, for the most part, confined to the nether regions of the unconscious. Yet in some few cases they could not be so confined. Outward circumstance (such as a heightened level of public anxiety about witchcraft) and unusually severe inward pressures (in one or more individual persons) combined to "convert" them into behavior: hence the fits of the "afflicted girls." The fits bear the stamp of pre-oedipal regression at virtually every point. The "dependency" theme is unmistakable: the victim lies helpless before the whims of her witch-tormentor. The prevalence of "oral" imagery is another powerful indicator. The mouth becomes a prime conduit of attack (as with biting, but also, by way of implicit referents, the pricking and pinching so commonly mentioned) and of succor (the witch and her imps).

The witch, as represented in these fits, has an entirely negative coloration; but this, too, seems consistent with well-known inner processes. The relation to the pre-oedipal mother is always highly ambivalent; love and need mix uncomfortably with rage and resentment.[22] Moreover, the revival of this relation in adolescence necessarily spotlights the negative side; the victim seeks to ward it off, to repudiate it, or at all events to overcome it.* Her behavior has the characteristic structure of many such symptomatic outcomes in that it expresses a compromise between the original wish and the main line of defense.

---

* No doubt the figure of the witch was invested with some "oedipal" anger as well (i.e. in the adolescent girl, vis-à-vis her mother as possessor of the paternal "love object"). Indeed, the antagonism expressed here included at least three different psychodynamic undercurrents: (1) pre-oedipal rage; (2) a "reaction formation" against pre-oedipal love; and (3) direct oedipal rivalry. The present interpretation accords primacy to the first two elements, owing to the highly "primitive" nature of the symptom-formations. In fact, many young people experience pre-oedipal regression when faced with the (developmentally appropriate but always frightening) revival of oedipal issues near the onset of adolescence.

Occasionally the wish itself, with its loving connotations, rises near to the surface: the witch offers blandishments of one sort or another (for example, "a table spread with a variety of meats and . . . asked her to eat"),[23] and the victim describes herself as feeling "tempted." More often, though, the positive side of the ambivalence is suppressed—converted, indeed, to its opposite. This process, which theory calls "reaction formation," is recognizable in the compulsive and exaggerated character of its result. "Oh, you horrid wretch! You make my very heart grow cold within me!" says a victim to her spectral tormentor, in announcing a theme that she will endlessly belabor.[24] The cold heart, the scorn, the hatred are so emphatically expressed as to invite skepticism: she protests too much. Here, once again, she defends herself against the strength of her own underlying yearnings.*

The biological and biochemical changes which usher in the psychosexual conflicts of adolescence have a similar triggering effect in the realm of the "self"-system.[26] A rapid growth-spurt, the evident signs of sexual maturation, the emergence of new emotional experiences (especially in relation to the opposite sex) combine to foster a sense of inner discontinuity. There are, too, unsettling aspects of *psychosocial* development—a new awareness of the larger human community beyond the home of one's childhood, the community which holds one's ultimate fate. Hence a measure of "diffusion," even in a previously "cohesive self," is normal for adolescence. There is some revival of earlier narcissistic structures, which find outward manifestation in flights of blatantly "grandiose fantasy" and intense episodes of idealization (adolescent

---

* A version of these same inner processes is commonly observed among adolescents of our own day—as witness the following comment by Anna Freud: "Instead of displacing libido from the parents—or, more likely, after failing to do so—the adolescent ego may defend itself by turning the emotions felt toward them into their opposites. This changes love into hate, dependence into revolt, respect and admiration into contempt and derision. . . . The behavioral picture that emerges at this stage is that of an uncooperative and hostile adolescent. . . . The hostility and aggressiveness, which serve as a defense against object love in the beginning, soon become intolerable to the ego, are felt as threats, and are warded off in their own right. This may happen by means of projection; in that case the aggression is ascribed to parents who, consequently, become the adolescent's main oppressors and persecutors. In the clinical picture this appears first as the adolescent's suspiciousness and, when the projections increase, as paranoid behavior."[25] To this familiar sequence the "afflicted girls" of early New England seem to have added one further measure of defense—a "displacement" of the unaccepted impulses (both of the original object-love and the projected aggression) away from the true objects, i.e. the parental figures themselves, onto "witches," spectral and otherwise.

hero worship). An optimal passage through this period leads in the end to reintegration of the self, around the "push" of more realistic ambitions and the "pull" of mature ideals. But where development is less than optimal, the adolescent regression carries a threat of severe pathology. "Diffusion" amounts then to full-blown "fragmentation"; and the clinical picture may verge on psychosis.

The fits allegedly caused by witchcraft always implied fragmentation in their most characteristic features—the violent frenzies, the sudden surges of pain in widely separated parts of the body, the disorganization of functions such as speech, sight, and hearing. There were also implicit elements of "grandiosity" (the victim as *special* target for the forces of evil), demands for "mirroring" (from excited onlookers), "idealizing" attachments to figures of eminence (ministers come to offer counsel and prayers), and periods of "melancholy" intermission (between fits). In different but convergent ways these were the signs of a deeply disordered self.

One additional feature of some (not all) fits was an inability, over long periods, to *eat*. (The problem was sufficiently common for Cotton Mather to conclude: "It seems that long fasting is not only tolerable but strangely agreeable for such as have something more than ordinary to do with the invisible world.")[27] What makes this especially interesting is its apparent similarity to the clinical syndrome known today as *anorexia nervosa*. Here, indeed, is a rare opportunity for directly bridging the centuries with a single piece of symptomatic behavior. The modern-day victims of *anorexia* are also, for the most part, adolescent girls.

According to current authority, anorexic disorders are rooted in a desperate "struggle for individuation." The typical sufferer/patient attempts through her illness to throw off underlying (and initially unconscious) feelings of "being enslaved, exploited, and not . . . permitted to lead a life of . . . [her] own."[28] This feeling derives, in turn, from a long sequence of developmental experience. Outward impressions of the family setting are often quite favorable: the patient has been "obedient, . . . helpful, . . . eager to please, . . . precociously dependable, . . . excelling in school work"—indeed "the pride and joy of her parents." Closer inspection, however, reveals a broad pattern of overcontrol on the one side and overconformity on the other. One or both parents have been "overly helpful" and "overly rigid" in supervising all aspects of the patient's development, and "overly proud" of her accomplishments. The child has reacted with a sunny show of "pleasing compliance," while experiencing an inward sense of ineffectiveness, suffocation, and (deeper still) resentment and rage. The *anorexia* expresses a covert declaration of independence: by not eating, the patient declines further control, and, in real terms, precipitates an agonizing struggle with "authority" (parents and doctors).[29]

This short summary necessarily oversimplifies a large corpus of clinical writing, and the parts relating to familial interaction could not in any case be applied in witchcraft studies. (The data on the families of particular victims are simply too thin.) However, the diagnostic categories do make an interesting approach to certain of the leading themes found in the experience of the "afflicted" girls. As noted above, the fits conveyed a challenge to authority—and so, now, does *anorexia*. Behind the fits lay much "narcissistic" pathology—and in this respect as well *anorexia* seems broadly parallel. Anorexic patients are described as having especially "fragile self-esteem," as feeling "helpless" and "ineffectual"; and these are the most generalized symptomatic features of narcissistic disorders. The patient, in effect, has been used as an extension of the parent's own narcissism (hence the exaggerated elements of control and pride);[30] as a result, her own sense of self, and more especially of *body* self, is precarious. And this, too, is a plausible way of viewing the afflicted.*

The discussion has reached, by a very roundabout route, an area of convergence in the experience of the three leading sub-groups of witchcraft victims. The women in midlife, the cohort of younger men, and now the afflicted girls seem—in different ways and for different reasons—to have marked out a common center of preoccupation. It is not altogether easy to characterize, but such terms as control, autonomy, and self have appeared again and again. And they will reappear, strongly, later on.

Witchcraft and the General Population

Although involvement in witchcraft proceedings was not randomly distributed by age and sex, neither was it the exclusive province of any

---

* There is, in most anorexics, a manifest defect in "the perception, or cognitive interpretation, of stimuli arising in the body." In this connection an "inability to recognize hunger" is the "most pronounced deficiency"; however, the pattern extends to other areas as well (e.g. an indifference to changes in temperature, even of a quite extreme sort). It appears "that such patients experience their bodily sensations in a way that is bewildering and foreign to them"; and they have similar difficulty "in identifying [their own] emotional states."[31] A sense of self that includes seemingly "foreign" elements is the common *residuum* in both anorexic patients and witchcraft victims troubled with fits.

particular demographic group. On a given occasion, persons young, middle-aged, and elderly—male and female—might be found in the ranks of the accusers and/or victims. Seen whole, these events traced very broad horizons of concern.

The remainder of this chapter will proceed accordingly. Distinctions *among* persons are henceforth put out of view; the argument turns on a general psychology of witchcraft, assumed to embrace (in varying degrees) the entire population of seventeenth-century New England. The aim is to pull out recurrent themes and essential preoccupations, wherever they may appear in the material. Thus the focus moves from the visible surface of behavior and feeling to the sometimes invisible world of inner life—from those parts of the witchcraft story which the participants themselves directly articulated, to others which involve inference and interpretation on *our* terms. The issue throughout is the experience of the victims, and of their supporters in the community at large.

More specifically, discussion begins with a summary of (1) the varieties of harm attributed to witchcraft (what the victims suffered), and (2) the prevalent stereotypes of witches (how the victims, and others, perceived them from a general standpoint). In a sense this pair of topics can be seen as embracing *symptoms*, on the one hand, and *fantasies*, on the other. A subsequent section takes a more formal approach, in order to categorize (3) the predominant *affects*, and (4) the major *defenses* associated with experience of witchcraft (what the victims consciously felt, and how they sought to cope with their feelings). This, in turn, is followed by a venture into "depth psychology," organized around (5) underlying "psychodynamic" *conflicts* (the inward, largely unconscious preoccupations of the victims) and (6) the *genetic factors* behind such conflicts (the victims' developmental experience). The chapter concludes by canvassing a number of theoretical viewpoints, in order to integrate the full range of findings.

Symptoms

The fits and associated "possession" behaviors were easily the most vivid of the symptomatic outcomes attributed to witchcraft. Full-blown performances of this sort were largely confined to adolescent girls; but some of the constituent elements appeared from time to time in victims of other ages and the opposite sex. A few examples will serve to illustrate. William Branch, a Springfield freeman in his thirties, testified in the witchcraft trial of Hugh Parsons about a nighttime encounter in his bedroom: "there was a light all over the chamber like fire, and there came a thing upon me like a little boy, with a face as red as fire, . . . and

I felt something like scalding water on my back, and then I heard a voice saying 'it is done, it is done.' "[32] Susannah Toppan, a Newbury woman of seventy-four, joined in the prosecution of Goody Morse, and soon thereafter "in the night she felt a damp hand clasping her about her wrist."[33] Philip Smith, a Hadley selectman of about fifty years old, was made sick as a result (so he believed) of witchcraft; and he "cried out . . . of sharp pins pricking of him, sometimes in his toe, sometimes in his arm, as if there had been hundreds of them."[34] Susannah Trimmings, a woman of about thirty from Portsmouth, New Hampshire, argued with a suspected witch who suddenly "left me, and I was struck as with a clap of fire on the back, and she then vanished toward the waterside, in my apprehension in the shape of a cat."[35] A boy in his early teens, from Branford, Connecticut, was much given to "lies and stealing"; soon the Devil appeared to him "in the shape of a fox" and "carried him away . . . and [among other torments] threw him into a hogsty amongst swine and stopped him up into a hole where they [the boy's parents] after found him."[36]

If, on one side, these bizarre and sometimes delusional experiences approximated the notorious fits, on the other they shaded into physical illness. Witchcraft could surely cause disease—as well as accident and injury. Of course, there were also many "natural maladies" (as compared with supernatural ones): the task was to distinguish between them. So it was that physicians played a direct, if ancillary, role in witchcraft proceedings. Often they were asked to examine a patient/ victim and to provide an initial diagnosis; occasionally they performed *post mortem* autopsies. In many instances lay opinion was also sought (and given); for physicians were not always available, and medical knowledge was not in any case the exclusive province of specialists.

It is difficult, and unnecessary in the present context, to decode the obscure language of seventeenth-century medicine. One general point, however, needs emphasis: virtually any variety of illness might lend itself in a given instance to either a "natural" or a "supernatural" interpretation. (Sometimes indeed *both* interpretations seemed applicable.) This was true of mental and emotional disorders no less than physical ones. New England had its share of mental illness, as noted in stray references scattered through local records: two women of Boston "taken with a kind of raving and madness"; an Andover man called "outrageously mad or distracted" (and "one part off the moon"); a Beverly girl "overcome with melancholy and . . . deeply distempered . . . [so] that her understanding is . . . besotted and stupefied"; a young man of Branford, Connecticut, suddenly "taken . . . with a lunacy."[37] None of these persons seems to have been considered bewitched or possessed or otherwise under supernatural influence.

There was similar elasticity in the category "fits." Again, the records speak randomly, and without signs of special concern, about particular episodes: "hysterical fits"; "convulsion fits"; "violent fits"; "strange fits"; "swooning fits, or hysterical-like, not knowing of it herself."[38] One Sabbath day in 1676 a Boston youth "sank down in a swoon, and for a good space it was as if he perceived not what was done to him; after [he] kicked and sprawled, knocking his hands and feet upon the floor like a distracted man . . . [and] in the night he talked of ships, his master, father, and uncle Eliot." Such behavior seems, on its face, not dissimilar to the pattern of supernatural affliction; yet in this instance other parties detected a more modest cause. According to Samuel Sewall, the youth's "troubles arose from a maid whom he passionately loved: for . . . when [his father] and his master had agreed to let him go to her, he soon grew well."[39] At Salem a young bride experienced "strange fits" whenever her husband approached her sexually. A court, considering her petition for divorce, could not positively determine "whether she dissembled or whether [the fits] . . . were in reality"; however, "it is judged by many of understanding that they were more feigned than fainting."[40] At Hampton, New Hampshire, a minister's son "fell down in a fit" and died the next day—"a sorely afflicting providence" which his family "thought to be occasioned by worms."[41] In still other cases fits were attributed to difficulties in childbirth, to sudden experiences of "fright," to menstrual irregularities, to guilt over "notorious sin," and to the "afflicting hardships of poverty."[42]

Clearly the term "fits" was a broad one, carrying no automatic association with witchcraft. As such, it creates a puzzling interpretive problem: what were the special elements which distinguished the various sub-forms of this behavior? There seems to be no easy answer here; contemporaries themselves could not always agree on particular cases. Thus, for example, the Rev. Samuel Willard carefully analyzed the fits of Elizabeth Knapp in order to prove them "diabolical." (He sought thereby to foreclose alternative interpretations.)[43] And in another case, at Barnstable, a minister reached the opposite conclusion, while explicitly recognizing that there was room for doubt: "Sundry of our poor flock [underwent] . . . a smiting in their intellectuals, in a strange and unusual manner . . . though not according to the form of a diabolical possession, as some may apprehend."[44]

But, again, what *was* "the form of a diabolical possession"? Several factors are implied, if somewhat ambiguously, in the extant records. For example, Willard emphasized "the great strength" of Elizabeth Knapp's seizures; the same was characteristic of other cases as well. Diabolical fits, whatever their specific origin, were uniquely violent, tumultuous, "strong." There were also special touches of the bizarre, though these are hard to identify (and still harder to categorize) now. There was the matter of duration: most witchcraft fits seem to have continued over a prolonged period of time. But last—and probably most important— there was context: a climate of worry and suspicion (antedating an episode of fits), and the victim's own orientation to her (less often, his) suffering. In this regard the sheer availability of a suspect must some- times have proved decisive. Goody Garlick of Easthampton was long rumored to be a witch; thus when Elizabeth Howell (of the same village) succumbed to fits—and named Garlick as her "tormentor"— the odds tipped strongly toward this construction of events.[45] So, too, with Eunice Cole (of Hampton, New Hampshire) and her supposed victim Ann Smith, Mercy Disborough (of Fairfield, Connecticut) and Katherine Branch, Rebecca Greensmith (of Hartford) and Ann Cole— among others.

Where physical illness was linked to witchcraft, opinion and testi- mony emphasized similar factors. The strength of a given ailment was noted in one way or another; likewise, too, the suddenness of its onset. (For example, "About five years ago . . . the child being very well to the outward view, [was] suddenly taken very ill. . . .")[46] Strength and suddenness belonged, in turn, to a larger aura of "strangeness." Illness caused by witchcraft would usually display unique features. An elderly woman was "suddenly taken . . . dreadful sick . . . [with] her thigh and her leg being stiff like a stick"; she ascribed the problem to witchcraft, and explicitly distinguished it from "such infirmities as do accompany old age."[47] A young boy, regarded by his mother as bewitched, was in a visibly "strange condition, . . . for the child's secrets did rot, or were consuming."[48] Another boy "was handled in such a strange manner [when sick] as the doctor said he had not seen the like."[49] A woman, fallen "grievously" ill under suspicious circumstances, "foamed at the mouth"; her daughter "wiped it off, but . . . was very much frighted to see her so."[50] Still another ground of suspicion was illness in the *absence* of any recognizable cause. Thus one man "had a considerable difference with Goody Clawson. . . . [Soon] after my child in an evening was taken very violently with screaming and crying, insomuch that with all haste I opened her clothing and examined her body, but could find nothing that might expose it to that pain and misery."[51]

Some of these illnesses proved fatal; then there would be evidence from the corpse itself. A witness in the Harrison case testified about "Mrs. Robbins in the time of the sickness whereof . . . [she] died": at first the patient had been "stiff so that . . . her arms or legs . . . could not move," yet as soon as she died "her whole body was limber extraordinary."[52] In some instances there was a formal autopsy. A doctor's *post mortem* report on Elizabeth Kelley noted "pliable nerves and joints, . . . pure fresh blood in the backside of the arm, . . . a deep blue tincture . . . [in] the whole skin, etc." and concluded that "experience of dead bodies renders such symptoms unusual."[53] Still, no matter how peculiar the symptoms, the key factor once again was context: attitudes of concern about witchcraft in general, and fears of identifiable witches in particular. In most instances the victim had made quite specific accusations ("In the time of that sickness whereof . . . [she] departed, Mrs. Robbins very much complained against Goody Palmer as one that caused her afflictions").[54] The exceptions were infants or very small children; in their case the accusations came from parents.

Illness and injury to persons (including fits): these were the most fearful harms attributed to witchcraft. And where the affliction proved fatal, to one or more victims, the likelihood of court proceedings was greatest; hence the matter of witch-caused deaths merits particular notice. The largest proportion of such deaths seems to have involved children, and, more particularly, very young children. Our special sample of intensively analyzed cases yields a total of fourteen victims fatally attacked, nine of whom were under ten years old. (Of the nine at least six seem to have been infants.) Quite apart from these statistics, the records imply in many places a dangerous affinity between witchcraft and the very young. The widow Marshfield was suspected of being a witch because (among other reasons) "she hath envied every woman's child in the end till her own daughter had a child."[55] Alice Lake of Dorchester was reportedly enticed into witchcraft "by the devil . . . appearing to her in the likeness, and acting the part, of a child of hers then lately dead, on whom her heart was much set."[56] Katherine Harrison "or her shape" appeared in her neighbor's bedroom "in the night just before my child was stricken ill . . . and I said 'The Lord bless me and my child, here is Goody Harrison,' and the child lying on the outside I took it and laid it between me and my husband; and the child continued strangely ill about 3 weeks . . . and then died."[57] Rachel Fuller visited a neighbor with a sick child, "and said that this would be the worst day with the child, tomorrow it will be well; and the said Fuller took the child by the hand and . . . [the child's mother] snatched the hand from her and wrapped it in her apron."[58] Eunice Cole was charged with concocting schemes against Ann Smith, "all tending to entice her to live with her"; moreover, "it was her design formerly to insinuate herself into young ones."[59] And there is the additional point that accused witches included a disproportionate number of childless women. (Goody Cole was a prime example.)[60] Envy of children, peculiar forms of interest in children, perhaps even a (distorted) love for children: such elements figured repeatedly in witchcraft cases. They always implied danger—and sometimes proved fatal in their evident result.

Another category of afflictions—in our terms, "symptoms"—involved the loss of a capacity or function. Here there was no overt (physical) ailment, but rather a failure to perform as usual. Included among such experiences were one man's disappointment in "fowling" ("going many days . . . I would get no geese"),[61] another's difficulties in fruit-growing,[62] another's errors in his trade of tailoring ("in such a manner he was bemoidered in his understanding . . . [that] seven times he placed the sleeves wrong"),[63] and a woman's periodic "trouble with her wheel, when she set herself to spin for the necessity of her family."[64] Frequently, too, there were problems with the preparation and storage of food. Beer went bad in the barrel, fine cheeses were suddenly spoiled by maggots, an oven was "enchanted" so as to prevent effective baking.[65] Again, the explanation could be—and sometimes was—witchcraft. The implicit psychological gain is easy enough to see: there was no simpler way to excuse error and incompetence.

Livestock presented a perennially inviting target for witchcraft. Cows most especially, but also sheep, pigs, chickens, and horses, were made to sicken and die by witches bearing a grudge against their owners. Interestingly, livestock afflictions seemed to mimic human ones—as, for example, in the matter of fits. Zachariah Davis, a deponent in the trial of Goody Morse, had a calf that "fell a-dancing and a-roaring . . . and there he was setting upon his tail like a dog, as I never see no calf set . . . before; and so he remained in these fits while he died."[66] John Gibson, a supposed victim of witchcraft by his Cambridge neighbor Winifred Holman, had a "brood of chickens which . . . were taken with fits: they would turn their heads upward, and turn around many times, and run about the house as if they were mad, and sometimes pitching towards the ground but not touch the ground."[67] The diagnosis and treatment of afflicted animals also followed the usual pattern for human victims. Witchcraft was associated with certain forms of illness: those in which there was no overt sign of physical malfunction, or those characterized by especially mysterious forms of inner "consuming." Thus a victim in Fairfield, Connecticut, "had 3 sheep [which] died suddenly, and they opened them, and could not find by anything within them the cause of their deaths, and some neighbors said they believed they were bewitched."[68] Meanwhile a New Haven woman, finding one of her chickens dead, "remembered she had heard if they were bewitched they would consume within, and she opened it, and it was consumed in the gizzard to water and worms."[69]

There were many further symptoms, which can only be mentioned here. Some involved the loss by occult means of private information. ("Mary Coleman . . . witnesseth that . . . Goody Cole did repeat the words [that] . . . this deponent . . . and her husband spake together; . . . but these words were never spoken to any [other] person neither by this deponent nor [by] her husband.")[70] Another large group might be categorized as simple—but suspicion-arousing—mischance. Strange animals, regarded as "familiars," appeared at odd moments to plague unlucky victims. Household items were mysteriously lost, and just as mysteriously refound; in some instances such properties (and also their owners) were subject to harm by way of "poltergeists" or "stone-throwing devils." There were sights to perplex, and noises to frighten, and "tricks" to embarrass—all without explanation in terms of "natural" causes.[71]

The symptoms reviewed here seem notably varied overall, but they have in common the element of loss. Injury, suffering, fear: thus was witchcraft *defined*. And yet admixed with the bad there was a kind of good—or at least of gain—from the standpoint of the victims themselves. Witchcraft provided a way of understanding many painful experiences, that would otherwise have seemed inexplicable. To identify the source of one's difficulty was, in effect, to put bounds on it and on the anxiety to which it gave rise. Moreover, understanding implied action. There were ways and means of responding to witchcraft: legal proceedings, prayers, the many varieties of counter-magic. Powerful allies—ministers and magistrates—could be expected to lend their support. And attitudes of sympathy might spread community-wide. To that extent the victim, his friends, and his family need no longer feel helpless and alone. Indeed, wherever a diagnosis of witchcraft was persuasively made, the witch herself became the helpless one. The advantage of action accrued to the victims—who might henceforth play the (very active) role of accusers.

Fantasies

The foregoing "symptoms" were joined to a cluster of vivid "fantasies" about witchcraft—mental pictures that New Englanders of all sorts carried around inside their heads. These, too, pose large interpretive questions. What were the chief traits attributed to the witch as a generic type? What were her (alleged) goals and methods? What was the nature of her special power, and where lay her vulnerabilities (if any)?

But the answers to such questions are not easily found. Were we contemporaries of the New Englanders, or had we a time-machine at our disposal, we might simply try to *ask* them. To a point, at least, they could tell us about their pictures of witchcraft, for many of these were conscious. No doubt others would have to be considered as belonging to the realm of "unconscious fantasy," accessible chiefly by way of clinical interviews, "projective tests," dream analysis, and the like. The modern-day behavioral scientist has a whole arsenal of strategies and "instruments" for dealing with such situations.

As historians we cannot, of course, make a direct approach. And it is hard for us to maintain distinctions between behavior, on the one hand, and mental images (or fantasies) on the other. To be sure, our subjects produced a number of general statements about witchcraft, which do provide something of what we are looking for. Yet there are problems even here. Most such statements come from clergymen whose concern with witchcraft was in some respects atypical. Scholars have long recognized the existence of discrepant kinds, or levels, of witchcraft belief.[72] Among the clergy there was great interest in the literally diabolical elements—the Devil himself, and a vast satanic conspiracy against organized religion (in which witches played subordinate parts). Yet among ordinary villagers and tradesmen these priorities were reversed, with witch*craft* and its immediate manifestations constituting the main interest.

These differences were no less apparent among the New Englanders than elsewhere. The Rev. Deodat Lawson, minister at Salem just before the great witchcraft "outbreak," spoke of Satan in the largest possible terms: "Satan is the grand enemy of all mankind. . . . He is the original, the fountain of malice, the instigation of all contrariety, malignity, and enmity . . . Satan himself . . . and his accursed legions . . . do set themselves by all ways and means to work . . . [mankind's] ruin and destruction forever."[73] And Cotton Mather attributed to the Devil and his "incarnate legions" particular designs against New England—indeed, "an horrible plot . . . which if it were not seasonably discovered, would probably blow up and pull down all the churches in the country."[74] Satan was never, of course, excluded from the consideration of ordinary New Englanders, but his proportions were altogether reduced. A victim under affliction might see him "in the shape of a white calf," "in the form of a black dog with eyes in his back," or "having the figure of a short black man."[75] An accused witch had reputedly met him first as "a fine young gentleman a-suiting to her, and when they were discoursing together, . . . [she] looking down upon his foot, she perceived it was the Devil."[76] As to plots and conspiracies, there was occasional testimony from confessing witches. Goody Greensmith admitted having attended "a meeting under a tree on the green . . . [where] we danced and had a bottle of sack."[77] Mary Parsons recalled a "night I was with my husband and Goodwife Merrick and Bessie Sewell in Goodman Stebbins' lot. . . . We were sometimes like cats, and sometimes in our own shape, and we were a-plotting for some good cheer; and they made me go barefoot and make the fires because I had declared so much at Mr. Pynchon's."[78] It was quite a distance from these modest revels to the "horrible plots against all mankind" of which the clergymen wrote and spoke so fervently.

In the face of such disparate materials, the effort to reconstruct the dominant fantasies of witchcraft becomes unavoidably complicated. Clerical pronouncements must be balanced against ideas and viewpoints imbedded in the popular culture. But the latter are not so easily broached; at many points they can only be inferred from external behavior. This creates some overlap with issues considered in a previous chapter. In short, one cannot entirely distinguish *biography* (the way accused witches actually lived and behaved) from *fantasy* (the way witches were pictured, as a type, in the culture at large), since the evidence in each case is partially the same.

But to recognize these difficulties is at least partly to control them. And the task itself can scarcely be escaped. To anticipate: the figure of the witch displayed at least four leading forms or guises—those of *attacker, envier, intruder,* and *nurse.* She also showed certain vulnerabilities (counter-magic: the witch as *victim*). Inevitably, these aspects meshed and overlapped; and there was coherence, even unity, in the composite that included them all. Only in retrospect can they be separated and evaluated, each one on its own terms.

The witch as attacker. Attack was the very essence of witchcraft in early New England. Traditionally, the legal meaning of witchcraft had embraced a considerable range of behavior; and many particular indictments spoke simply of "familiarity with the Devil" (or some equivalent phrase). Even at the end of the seventeenth century, Massachusetts legislators were defining witchcraft to include the use of "sorcery, charm, or enchantment . . . to tell or declare in what place any treasure of gold or silver might be found . . . [or to] provoke any person to unlawful love."*[79] However, this was a formal account of the matter, and a reflection of the official viewpoint which condemned all things occult as emanating from the Devil. What witchcraft chiefly meant, in practice, was the use of supernatural means *to do harm.* Some writers explicitly distinguished such "malefic witchcraft" from "divining witchcraft" (all other kinds).[81]

The methods, the strategies, the apparatus of malefic witchcraft were extremely variable—and sometimes obscure. A considerable portion of the witch's activity found her assuming the form of a "shape" or "spectre." In this way, presumably, she escaped the usual constraints of body and mind, and obtained powers literally supernatural. Still, the witch in her human form—going about her everyday business—was more than ordinarily potent. Her words, her touch, her look were directly, and destructively, efficacious. Thus when Governor Winthrop summarized the evidence against Margaret Jones of Charlestown, he mentioned first her "malignant touch, as many persons . . . whom she stroked or touched with any affection or displeasure, or, etc. were taken with deafness, vomiting, or other violent pains or sickness."[82] (Other instances of "malignant" stroking and touching are found elsewhere in the witchcraft records.)[83] When Katherine Branch saw the accused witch Mercy Disborough "looking about on her, she immediately fell down into a fit"; and she spoke later of Disborough's "two fiery eyes."[84] (Again, there were looks of a similar sort at other times and in other cases.)[85] The threats of a witch were notoriously dangerous: word preceded deed in a dreaded sequence noticed again and again in the present study.

One additional means of witchcraft bears special mention: the use of "poppets" (sometimes rendered "puppets") or other "images" to represent particular victims. On rare occasions there was physical evidence to introduce at court. ("Order was given to search the old woman's house, from whence were brought several small images, or puppets, or babies, made of rags and stuffed with goat's hair and other such ingredients.")[86] More often the objects could not be discovered—or were visible only to a victim overcome by fits.[87] In any case, the *idea* was the same: the witch would "stick pins into these puppets," or "stroke" them, or otherwise

---

* Rare cases of this type can be found in the court records. In 1674 one Edward Peggy was tried at Boston "for using indirect means by powders or other ways unlawful to engage the affections or desires of womankind to him, and for begetting Ruth Hemingway of Roxbury with child." But neither the indictment nor the verdict (guilty) made any direct mention of witchcraft, and the punishment (a whipping and support payments for the illegitimate child) was relatively mild.[80]

"abuse" them, and her intended victims would fall "tormented" in directly corresponding ways.[88] In one sense the puppet *was* the victim; in another the victim became herself a puppet—linked, as it were, by invisible strings to the hands of the witch. It would be hard to contrive a better figure for representing the power of witchcraft to control and distort every aspect of human activity.

But the use of such power in specific episodes of attack did not by itself define malefic witchcraft. For beyond behavior there lay fundamental considerations of motive. Attack, after all, was a large category including many forms of action, some of which might conceivably be justified by immediate or impending circumstances. Not so with the witch, however; her motives as an attacker were entirely evil. And the foremost, the worst, of these motives was an ever-present *anger*.

Moreover, charges against particular witches invariably stemmed from specific episodes of controversy. The victim and the accused had squared off as antagonists: feeling was engaged, words passed, threats were made (or imagined). To seem unduly angry was to invite suspicion; and, once formed, such suspicion prompted the inference of further anger. The process was effectively circular, but that did not invalidate its results. David Wheeler of Newbury, who for many years had "lived next neighbor to Elizabeth Morse," suffered many "strange accidents"; Goody Morse, he believed, was the "author" of these "by witchcraft . . . through the malice and envy of her heart."[89] Daniel Westcott of Fairfield had initiated "several discourses" with the accused witch Elizabeth Clawson, "concerning her being angry with me." At one point he "told her that she said to the authority she never laid down to sleep in anger, and how could that be when she continued angry with me. She answered, 'what do you think of it?'—but would not answer directly."[90] The same woman was defended by another witness, on diametrically opposite grounds: "he saith that he lived near neighbor to Goody Clawson many years and did always observe her to be a woman for peace, and to council for peace, and when she had provocations from her neighbors [she] would answer and say 'we must live in peace, for we are neighbors.' "[91] Anger and/or "peace": here was a critical dimension of character dividing witches from honorable Christian folk.

In fact, the recruitment of witches involved anger as a precondition. There was a general belief—as one New Haven woman put it—that "a forward, discontented frame of spirit was a subject fit for the Devil to work upon in that way [i.e. of witchcraft]."[92] Confessing witches, and some of the afflicted girls, bore this out. Mary Johnson, executed at Hartford in 1648, "said that her first familiarity with the Devil came through discontent."[93] Elizabeth Knapp, in admitting her own temptations toward the Devil, acknowledged much the same thing.[94] The Rev. Deodat Lawson urged, in a famous sermon, that his auditors be especially vigilant against "giving way unto sinful and unruly passions . . . such as envy, malice, or hatred of our neighbors and brethren. These Devil-like passions . . . do endanger the letting in [of] Satan and his temptations; yea, he generally comes into the soul at these doors, to captivate any person to the horrid sin of covenanting with him."[95] Cotton Mather analyzed the famous outbreak at Salem as follows: "It is not irrational to ascribe the late stupendous growth of witches among us, partly to the bitter *discontents* which affliction and poverty has filled us with; it is inconceivable what advantage the Devil gains over men by *discontent*."[96] (And again: "Have not many of us been Devils unto one another for slanderings, for backbitings, for animosities?")[97]

The Devil himself appears, in the writings of the ministers, as a creature of consummate anger. "Foaming with his [own] wrath . . . [he] seeks rest and finds none." He "relishes no sacrifices like those of human heart-blood, and there is [for him] no music like the bitter, dying, doleful groans, ejaculated by the roasting children of men." Moreover, "it is the true mark and character of Satan's kingdom that it is established, supported, and propagated by malice, enmity, wars, blood, slaughter, and destruction of mankind."[98] Satan's wrath aims at God no less than at mortal men—and God responds in kind. ("The Devil is himself broiling under the intolerable and interminable wrath of God.")[99] And wherever Satan successfully intrudes in earthly affairs, it is "the wrath of Almighty God himself" that opens the way. (The sins of men anger God, who then allows Satan to operate freely among them.)[100] In sum, Satan is *defined* by his perpetual wrath, against God and all his creatures. God, too, is wrathful (always) against Satan and (sometimes) against mankind. Satan's purpose is to stir up wrath among men and women, in order to bring about their eventual destruction. He often finds recruits among persons who are already inclined to anger, and, when covenanted to them, he makes them angrier still. Thus, seen in context, the witch's characteristic "discontent" is but the outward manifestation of a vast and invisible system of diabolical influence. And throughout its workings this system is fueled from a single source—the infernal energy of "devilish wrath."

The witch as envier. Closely associated with anger in prompting the witch's attack was a deep and uncompromising *envy.* Indeed, the two motives formed a kind of tandem—"malice and envy," in the common phrase of the time. In part, the witch was so angry because she was so envious: she could not prevent herself from coveting the possessions and advantages of others. She was needy, and greedy, and forever determined to get what she wanted. She would start by asking; but if rebuffed, she would not hesitate to resort to stronger means.

The grasping quality attributed to witches comes through again and again in the court testimonies. Goody Cole barged in on a selectmen's meeting at Hampton "to demand help . . . for wood or other things"; when refused because "she had an estate of her own," she complained that "they could help goodman Robie, [he] being a lusty man, and [yet] she could have none." (A few days later some of Robie's livestock died "very strangely.")[101] Hugh Parsons had one of four "equal shares in a cow," and particularly wished to have "the root of the tongue"; but it fell (by lot) to one of his partners. Later it mysteriously disappeared from a boiling kettle, and the partner had "ever since believed that no hand of man did take it away, but it was taken away by witchcraft."[102]

Envy, like "discontent," was directly associated with the process of becoming a witch. Potential recruits were plied with "fine promises": for example, "money, silks, fine clothes, ease from labor" (Elizabeth Knapp); a chance to be "big rich" (Mary Staples), to "live deliciously" (unidentified boy) or to "go where there were fine folks" (Katherine Branch); even "an husband" and a guarantee against death (Mercy Short).[103] According to Cotton Mather, the Devil was acutely alert to signs of envious wish: "There is no condition but what has indeed some hunger accompanying it; and the Devil marks what it is that we are *hungry* for . . . [whether] preferments or employments; . . . cash or land or trade; . . . merriments or diversions. . . . The Devil will be sure to suit his persuasions [accordingly]."[104]

The witch as intruder. Another persistent element in the figure of the witch was untoward and unwanted intrusiveness. The very language of the victims (or their supporters) is revealing here. Goody Palmer of Wethersfield was said to have "thrust herself into the company" of the Robbins family where her alleged victim lay mortally ill, despite being "forewarned not to come."[105] Goody Morse had played the same part in a similar scene: "She thrust herself into the parlor where my mother lay . . . [and] I could very hardly with my importunity entreat her to . . . be gone."[106] Goody Hale of Boston had "asked very inquisitively" about the affairs of a young man toward whom she apparently bore a grudge.[107] Goody Cole was discovered by one of her accusers "looking into my house among my cattle . . . I asked her what she did there; she answered, 'what is it to you, sawsbox?' "[108]

Some of these episodes, as described in court, seem to blur the line between actual experience and private fantasy. ("Goodwife Seagar came into [the Mygatts'] house, on a moonshining night, and took [Mrs. Mygatt] by the hand and struck her face as she was in bed with her husband.")[109] But all of them have an underlying melody. Encroachment, pushiness, a stubborn and inappropriate assertion of self: thus the witch in her everyday relations with neighbors. (One woman, considered "suspicious" of practicing witchcraft, was the subject of the following court order: "she must not go in an offensive way to folks' houses in a railing manner, as it seems she hath done, but . . . keep her place and meddle with her own business.")[110]

Indeed, the same theme was implicit in some of the more bizarre "symptoms" attributed to witchcraft. A witch's shape invading her victim's household came, to say the least, as an unwanted guest; an imp or animal-familiar harassing a frightened traveller was patently intrusive. And the "theft" of personal secrets, the knowledge of private conversation or correspondence, carried a similar meaning. Even fortune-telling could be seen as a kind of encroachment—on the future.

The witch as nurse. The image of "nurse" may seem incongruous here; yet in a peculiar, even perverse, way it captures important elements in the fantasy-picture of witchcraft. From the standpoint of clinical psychiatry, such elements expressed a prominent strain of "orality"—a cluster of "primitive" concerns centering on the "bodily zone" of the mouth and its intrinsic "modalities." But for the moment the material can be explored on its own terms.

The witches, the accusers, all the believers in witchcraft, were endlessly fascinated by the relationship which must, in their minds, obtain between a witch and her various "familiars." The latter, of course, were small (sometimes invisible) animals sent here and there to carry out particular projects of *maleficium*. Their connection to their witch-mistress was a very close one: to her they gave their devoted service, from her they received a most intimate form of sustenance. Periodically, she suckled them on "teats" specially adapted to that purpose. Whenever such activity was observed by competent witnesses, it made important evidence for trial proceedings. Here is a typical example: "Mary Perkins . . . saith that many years since, one Sabbath day when Mr. Dalton was preaching, this deponent saw a small creature about the bigness of a mouse fall out of the bosom of Eunice Cole, and [it] fell into her lap, it being of a sad color, and as soon as it was in her lap it ran away."[111] A second witness against Goody Cole recalled another occasion in church when she "did hear a noise like to the whining of puppies when they have a mind to suck . . . [and] to her best discerning . . . the noise

came from under the said Eunice [Cole]."[112] There was similar testimony against Goody Morse ("I went near her bedside, and I heard a
strange kind of noise, which was like a whelp sucking of the dam, or
kittens sucking")[113] and Goody Miller ("I watching with Katherine
Branch . . . [on] the night when said Katherine was in her fit, she looking at the bed said, 'Goody Miller, hold up your arm that the black dog
may suck the better' ").[114] Occasionally the imp took a human form:
"In the prison, in the clear daylight, there was seen in her arms, she
sitting on the floor, and her clothes up, a little child, which ran from
her into another room; and the officer following it, it was vanished. The
like child was seen in two other places."[115]

The witch in the latter instance (Margaret Jones, hanged at Boston
in 1648) "had (upon search) an apparent teat in her secret parts as
fresh as if it had been newly sucked."[116] And the discovery of such
teats was of great moment in witchcraft proceedings. Frequently this
became an official responsibility of special committees of women appointed by the magistrates "narrowly and truly to inspect and search
[the defendant's] body whether any suspicious signs or marks did appear
that were not common or that were preternatural."[117] The resultant
reports showed a careful, almost clinical, attention to detail. In one case
"they found nothing, save a wart on one of her arms."[118] In another
"they found a strange place in her legs being a conjunction of blue veins
which were fresh with blood . . . which was provable where she had
been sucked by imps or the like."[119] In still another: "we find . . . on
her secret parts, growing within the lip of the same, a loose piece of
skin and when pulled it is near an inch long [and] somewhat in form
of the finger of a glove flattened."[120]

Related testimony came from individual witnesses, recalling some
moment of personal experience with the accused. When Eunice Cole
had been "stripped" to receive a whipping for some (unspecified) offense, the local constable noticed "under one of her breasts . . . a blue
thing like unto a teat hanging downwards about three quarters of an
inch long."[121] When John Godfrey, during Sabbath services in the
meetinghouse, "yawned open his mouth," a neighbor observed "a small
teat under his tongue."[122] And when Goody Clawson bore her children,
the midwives who attended her noticed that she "was not, as to the
form of her body . . . as other women ordinarily are."[123]

There was always room for doubt and disagreement in these matters.
Goody Cole, for example, when asked about the "blue thing" under her
breast, "said it was a sore."[124] And Alice Stratton discounted the so-
called "marks of a witch" on her friend Margaret Jones by attributing

them to an injury sustained years before in childbirth.[125] But the most remarkable evidence of this sort came from the execution of Goodwife Knapp at Fairfield Connecticut in 1653. Here the fantasy of the witch-as-nurse was translated into a macabre interest in a corpse; the details merit careful retelling.

Like all such events, the hanging of Goody Knapp attracted a large crowd of onlookers. No sooner had she been pronounced dead and "cut down" from the gallows than a large group of women pressed forward "looking for the marks of a witch upon the body." They proceeded to "tumble the corpse up and down"; then "several . . . said they could find none [i.e. no marks]," and a heated discussion ensued. A certain Goodwife Staples seemed particularly upset: "wringing her hands and taking the Lord's name in her mouth, . . . [she] said, 'will you say these are witch's teats? They are not.' " Witnesses would later remember that she "handled the said teats very much" and "pulled them with her fingers . . . as though she would have pulled them off." Presently Goody Staples "called upon Goodwife Lockwood to come" and reiterated her protest: "Will you say these are witch's teats? I . . . have such myself, and so have you, if you search yourself." Goody Lockwood answered tartly: "I know not what you have, but for [my]self, if any find any such things about me, I deserve to be hanged as she was." There was still more "handling" of the corpse, and more argument. Goody Staples persisted in her objections, although "several of the women cried her down and said they were teats." At length the group was joined by a certain Goodwife Odell, who had "searched" the convict previously with an official (court-appointed) committee. Goody Odell "showed them the marks that were upon her, and said 'what are these?' " and "they all wondered, and goodwife Staples in particular, and said they never saw such things in their life before."[126]

There is, in sum, a kind of paradox here. Prevailing belief ascribed to witches a particular animus against infants and small children. Moreover, a parallel belief declared that witches might directly intervene in the nursing process—for example, by causing acute soreness in the breasts ("there was several little red pimples about her nipple, . . . and her milk all knotty in her breast . . . and she thought she had been bewitched"),[127] or by inhibiting lactation itself. ("Goody Garlick sent to her for breast milk, and presently after her milk dried away.")[128] Yet witches, too, had small creatures under their personal care. They, too, undertook to nurture and protect such creatures, and even to "give them suck." The witch with her imp was a figure—albeit a distorted one—for human motherhood.

Counter-magic: the witch as victim. Powerful, resourceful, devious as she invariably was, the witch was not considered invulnerable. Those whom she attacked might, under some circumstances, respond in kind. Ancient cultural tradition had bequeathed them a rich lore of "tricks" and "remedies"—some of which offered defense against witchcraft (by blunting its intended effects), while others involved counterattack (through hurting the witch directly). By the seventeenth century these practices had become controversial; they seemed in themselves to smack of "witchery." The organized Christian churches increasingly disapproved of their use, and the churches of early New England were no exception. Clergymen throughout the region were inclined to condemn all countermagic as "going to the Devil to find the Devil." The proper way to combat witchcraft, in their view, was through prayer, fasting, and other forms of supplication to God.[129]

And yet, among average folk, the old way survived. Its proposed, or actual, use made a part of many witchcraft episodes (a greater number, surely, than the extant records indicate, since official attitudes were so strongly disapproving). For example, John Goodwin, the Boston mason whose children fell under "some affliction" in the year 1688, was greatly tempted to go this route—"for many did say (yea, and some good people, too) were it their case they would try some tricks. . . ." In the end Goodwin drew back and gained public commendation from the likes of Cotton Mather for his "gracious resolution to oppose devils with no other weapons but prayers and tears."[130] But other victims made a different choice.

Certain of these "tricks" contrived simply to keep witches away. Two instances have been noticed already: a horseshoe nailed to a door, and branches of "sweet bays" laid under the threshold ("it would keep a witch from coming in").[131] Wherever such practices succeeded in their primary aim, there was also the added result that the case against particular suspects deepened accordingly. Indeed, the horseshoe stratagem was described by one witness as "an experiment to try witches."[132]

Additional experiments were meant to draw witches to the scene of their crimes. Many of these involved the burning of substances directly implicated in "affliction." A pudding was thought to be enchanted, and "a piece of it . . . [was] thrown into the fire"; soon thereafter the prime suspect (Hugh Parsons) was heard to "mutter and mumble at the door." Witnesses discounted his professed "errand to get hay," believing instead that "the spirit that bewitched the pudding brought him thither."[133] In another case a sick child's urine was scalded with "embers out of the fire . . . and by the by Rachel Fuller came in, and looked very strangely. . . ."[134] Other such burnings involved a pig's tail, a cow's ear, a lock of a young girl's hair, a woman's cap, a load of apples.[135] There were some interesting variants on this procedure. In one case the victim's urine was bottled and locked in a cupboard, whereupon a suspect appeared and "did not cease walking to and fro about the house." An hour later the bottle was "unstopped," and the woman in question immediately "went away from thence."[136]

The central purpose of the above stratagems was detection; secondarily, they created discomfort for particular suspects. In other episodes of counter-magic these priorities were reversed: discomfort—indeed, real harm—came first, and detection second. Henry Gray, a witness against Mercy Disborough, had a cow that was "strangely taken." He thereupon "sent for his cart whip and whipped the cow, and she was soon well again." The same afternoon Goody Disborough appeared with a painful—and mysterious—injury: she "lay on the bed and stretched out her arm and said to her [neighbor] 'I am almost killed.' "[137] Similarly, Jonathan Woodman, testifying in the trial of Elizabeth Morse, remembered a time when he "met a white thing like a cat, which did play at my legs." Eventually he succeeded in kicking it hard against a fence, where "it stopped with a loud cry." Meanwhile, elsewhere on "the same night and [at] the same time of night" a doctor was summoned to the house of Goody Morse to examine a "hurt in her head."[138] The familiar "experiment" of burning might also have this type of effect. When Goody Garrett found her best cheese spoiled and flung it into the fire, "suddenly . . . Goodwife Seager cried out exceedingly . . . and . . . came into the house . . . and sat wringing her body and crying out, 'What do I ail? what do I ail?' "[139]

The implied premise behind all these practices was an extremely close association among the witch, her familiars, and the various objects of her witchcraft. In a sense the cheese, the cow, and the "white thing like a cat" had become extensions of her own person; hence injury given to *them* meant injury also for *her*. The methods used to "bring her out" carried a similar implication: when materials considered bewitched were burned, she could be compelled to appear before her victims. Indeed, she was now a victim herself. Exposed, embarrassed, and sometimes physically injured by counter-magic, she would henceforth be more and more vulnerable to the special forms of "torment" which New England society reserved for her kind.

But counter-magic expressed the same linkage which, under other circumstances, allowed the witch to act as tormentor; only the direction of influence had been altered. And the larger point about all the "fantasy" materials considered here is the closeness of the relation in which witch and victim were invariably joined. Action by the one brought immediate *reaction* in the other—by way of witchcraft (a touch, a look, a muttered curse) or of counter-magic (involving objects into which the witch had extended her power). Above all else, it was the image of "puppetry" which most vividly represented this fundamental theme in witchcraft fantasy. The strings of control were tight, and direct, and extremely hard to break. And the aura of manipulation enveloped all.

Affects

Just here the line of this discussion reaches a marked turning. From "symptoms" and "fantasies"—those visible behaviors and images about which the records speak quite directly—it proceeds to "affects," and then to "defenses." Important elements of visibility remain; but we must begin to order the materials on principles of our own making. In a word, our viewpoint becomes more openly *interpretive*, more directly informed by theory. Eventually the surface of behavior recedes altogether, as the focus shifts yet again to "psychodynamic" considerations. Hence the overall direction of inquiry is from "outer" to "inner," from "conscious" to "unconscious," from behavior to process. We might, perhaps, have discussed several earlier parts of the chapter with the New Englanders themselves. But such discussion would grow increasingly difficult, or impossible, in what follows.

Modern psychological research has identified eight "primary affects" behind the rich complexity of emotional experience.[140] They are "primary" in the sense of being inborn and intrinsic to the species, grounded in facial and neural physiology, and impervious to any further reduction. They seem to have "functional" importance both from an evolutionary standpoint and for individual adaptation. They frequently appear in combination. And they display, in every case, both a mild and an intense form. The full roster is as follows: (1) Interest/Excitement; (2) Distress/Anguish; (3) Fear/Terror; (4) Anger/Rage; (5) Disgust/Contempt; (6) Shame/Humiliation; (7) Surprise/Startle; (8) Enjoyment/Joy. The first four (as listed here) are powerfully evident in the witchcraft materials, and the next three are moderately so. Witchcraft was, then, a crucible of human affect—notable no less for the range than for the intensity of its expression.

Interest/Excitement. Elevated levels of interest were manifest, first of all, in the gossip that witchcraft invariably inspired. Rumor, suspicion, hearsay: the records afford only passing glimpses of all this, since it had no claim to official recognition. Yet it made, beyond doubt, the stuff of countless village conversations. Where such gossip does appear in the extant records, it is often so tangled as almost to defy comprehension. For example: "Henry Grey, aged about thirty-nine years, saith that he hath been informed by some of his neighbors that Mercy Disborough hath at times discoursed with the wife of Thomas Bennett, senior, and Elizabeth Bennett, her daughter, that the said Mercy said she could not abide the said Henry Grey never since he bought a parcel of apples of her mother Jones and reported that they wanted of measure—which was about 18 years since." (The deponent had experienced mysterious losses among his livestock.)[141]

Interest spread, and excitement deepened, around the time of court proceedings. Thomas Burnham arrived at Springfield just before the trial of Hugh Parsons; local gossip was centered on "strange doings . . . about cutting of puddings and whetting of saws in the night," and Burnham did "hear of it in all places, wherever I come."[142] Personal observation of such "doings" evoked an especially strong response. Fits, for example, drew large and fascinated audiences. When the Devil spoke from inside Elizabeth Knapp, excitement reached such a pitch that the Rev. Willard could no longer exercise his appropriate "ministering" function.[143] Trial scenes were equally gripping—with the examination of witnesses, the defendant's response, the appearance (in some cases) of victims still "under affliction," all before a "great assembly" of onlookers. A finding of guilt would evoke new forms of interest. The convict was subjected to a final flurry of prison interviews around the issues of repentance and atonement, and was pressured to identify her "confederates" in witchcraft.[144] Execution itself was a public and keenly felt affair: there was hope for some last-minute confessions or "discoveries." And even after the witch was gone, she inspired much discussion. Gradually, with the passage of months or years, interest waned (or shifted to new suspects). But witches were more fully remembered than most of their New England peers.

Distress/Anguish. There is no doubting the distress experienced by many who conceived themselves to be victims of witchcraft. Indeed— where there was so much loss, pain, perplexity—anguish would not be too strong a word. Those who were sick or otherwise afflicted in their persons could not easily conceal their feelings. One man plagued by nighttime visits from the "shape" of a witch "groaned . . . as if his flesh had been pulled from his bones."[145] A second seemed "very churly over what he had been" and "cried out, 'Lord, have mercy upon me, the cat hath killed me and broken my heart.' " (The reference was to a supposed imp, in the form of a cat.)[146] A woman and her afflicted daughter had this

exchange: "I . . . asked Betty how she did, and she put out her hand
[and said], 'Oh, mother!'; and she cried, and I cried, and she said,
'Mother, I am bewitched. . . .' "[147] A girl who "complained of witches
as occasioning her sickness . . . said [with] tears running down her
cheeks, 'You tell me [that] it is a fancy that I complain that I am afflicted
by some evil, evil persons, but it is true. . . .' "[148] Mysterious damage to
property, and especially to livestock, also evoked much feeling. A man
who had lost cows, pigs, and oxen to witchcraft (so he believed) allowed
in court that "these things do something run in my mind [so] that I
cannot have my mind from this woman."[149] At least occasionally "these
things" were expressed in dreams or sleep disturbance. Thus one victim
"dreamed that John Godfrey was come . . . in the likeness of a bear"; a
second was repeatedly "troubled in his sleep about witches."[150]

But the distress associated with witchcraft was not confined to victims;
the accused were also—and for very good reason—painfully affected.
When suspicion mounted against Goodwife Seager she "said she was in
great trouble, even in agony, of spirit."[151] When Goody Jones had been
formally indicted, she was observed visiting with her friend Alice Stratton; and "Goodwife Stratton had her bible on her lap, and they were
both of them crying."[152] When a neighbor was "seriously telling Goody
Morse of the report that went of her as touching her name for witchcraft, . . . she seemed to be much affected with it, and fell on weeping,
and said she was as innocent as herself, or the child now unborn, or as
God in Heaven."[153] These descriptions come from testimony by victims
and accusers, who could not avoid seeing the affect of their supposed
"tormentors." In witchcraft cases there was anguish enough for all sides.

Fear/Terror. Closely linked to distress, among the feelings evoked by
witchcraft, was fear—or outright terror. Witnesses spoke repeatedly of
being "affrighted" by familiars, by strange sights and sounds, by veiled
mutterings or open threats heard from the witch herself. Some of this
testimony described the physical manifestations of fear, in altogether
graphic detail. Betty Brewster "was suspicious of Mrs. Godman, and
spoke to her of it"; the next night she heard "a most dreadful noise which
put her in great fear and trembling, which put her into such a sweat as
she was all on a water."[154] Another of Elizabeth Godman's alleged victims was Mr. Stephen Goodyear, a magistrate in whose house she resided
for a time. Following a petty disagreement between them, "Mrs. Godman
. . . flung out of the room in a discontented way, and cast a fierce look
upon Mr. Goodyear as she went out, and immediately Mr. Goodyear
(though well before) fell into a swoon."[155] There was similar testimony
in the trial of John Godfrey. Goody Holdridge espied a spectral horse

and "immediately [there]after she was taken with extremity of fear and pain, so that she presently fell into a sweat, and I thought she would swoon away; she trembled and shook like a leaf." On another occasion her son Thomas was so "affrighted . . . [that] for the space of two hours [he] was in [such] a sweat that one might have washed hands on his hair."[156]

Anger/Rage. Overwhelmed by their evident fear and distress, the victims appeared as innocent objects of malefic assault. The witch was "wrathful"; they, by contrast, were peaceable, accommodating, ever anxious to please. Such at least was the picture they offered both to themselves and to the local public. Yet there was surely a distortion here—an avoidance, in some part, of important affective reality. And how could it be otherwise? The pain and loss they suffered—seemingly without provocation—must, after all, have ignited some spark of indignation, of resentment, even of anger. They did their best to suppress it, but here and there it showed through plainly enough.

On occasion victims allowed themselves face-to-face outbursts against a witch; significantly, these were most bitter and direct. An instance from the material on John Godfrey bears repeating: "John Carr said, 'What come you hither for, Godfrey, you witching rogue?' . . . And the said Carr immediately ran his fist in the said Godfrey's breast and drove the said Godfrey up against the chimney stock . . . [and] said he would turn the said Godfrey out of doors and kick him down the hill . . . and called the said Godfrey many bad names."[157] In another case a young man confronted the accused (Mercy Disborough) "and bade her come and unbewitch his uncle Grumman's child, or else he would tear her heart out."[158] Additional, presumably similar, episodes were remembered incompletely ("I heard Goody Morse and my dame Wells a-talking together—very loud, and I heard my dame Wells call Goody Morse 'witch'") or with a single summary phrase ("many hard words passed . . . between us").[159] Most prosecution witnesses wished to forget their own part in such openly personal hostilities.

Perhaps if we could hear from the witches directly, we would learn more about anger felt—and expressed—by victims. Unfortunately, such evidence is limited to a very few petitions and rebuttals, themselves worded most carefully. William Morse asserted, in defense of his wife, that certain of the witnesses in her trial had long been "uncharitable" or "through weakness [had] acted uncivilly" toward her.[160] And Katherine Harrison countered the charges of her accusers by alleging their "great prejudice" against her.[161] Indeed, in the latter case animosity toward the witch had found quite tangible (if indirect) expression.

Coincident with the start of her trial for witchcraft Goody Harrison sent to the county court a complaint of "many injuries" she had suffered from the vandalism, presumably, of neighbors. Her oxen had been "spoiled . . . with blows upon the back and side"; a heifer was "stuck with a knife . . . and wounded to death"; a sow had "one of her hind legs cut off"; her hops were "cut and spoiled," her corn "much damnified"—and so on. The list of these "injuries" was very long, and even allowing for the possibility of some exaggeration by the complainant it implied a notably hostile disposition in her neighbors.[162]

The anger of the victims was also revealed in their encounters with the various familiars. What they dared not express to the witch's face they vented in full measure against her imps. They struck, they kicked, they freely cursed these infernal creatures and sometimes even succeeded in injuring or killing them. They would lash out in similar ways at "shapes," "specters," and other "apparitions" of the witch.[163] In all these situations there was, of course, an element of self-defense; but the strength of the response suggests an attacking motive as well.

Consider, finally, the evidence of the fits, where rageful affect became transparently clear. Elizabeth Kelley of Hartford, plunged into "great extremity of misery" by witchcraft, "cried out with great violence" against Goody Ayers. "Oh, father," she demanded again and again, "set on the great furnace and scald her! Get the broad ax and cut off her head!"[164] Rebecca Stearns of Cambridge believed herself afflicted by two neighbors, widow Winifred Holman and daughter Mary. During her many "raging fits" she not only demanded vengeance on the Holmans but also was "carried with rage against her parents and her brothers and sisters . . . so [much] so that we were fain to tie her hands."[165] Katherine Branch of Fairfield, Connecticut, invited the shape of Goody Clawson to "have a turn, heels over head . . . if you will not, I'll beat your head and the wall together."[166] Mercy Short addressed her spectral "tormentor" with terms such as these: "you horrid wretch"; "you devil"; "you beast"; "your poor fool."[167] It is reasonable to speculate that these uninhibited displays spoke to—indeed spoke *for*—many onlookers who were not themselves subject to fits. Officially, the onlookers deplored the "actings" of fits; yet their solicitude for the afflicted implied interest, even encouragement to continue. Officially, they were shocked by the violence of the affect involved; yet they noticed and remembered (and relished?) its every quiver. Thus did their own rage find a suitably vicarious means of expression.

Disgust/Contempt, Shame/Humiliation, Surprise/Startle. Another trio of affects were occasionally, but much less importantly, associated with witchcraft. A measure of disgust/contempt seems frequently to have mixed with fear/terror. The suckling of imps, for instance, evoked both reactions together; likewise the oddities in certain witches' behavior. (Goody Morse was often seen "crabbing the ground with the end of a staff"; widow Holman went "picking about the common"; Elizabeth Godman "gnashed and grinned her teeth in a strange manner"; Elizabeth Seager "came to [a neighbor] . . . and shaked her hand and said, 'How do you? How do you? Mrs. Mygatt.' ")[168] Sometimes disgust appeared in sharper, more unmixed forms. Thus the Hampton couple whose oven Goody Cole had allegedly enchanted was troubled with a "loathsome stink." Another case of witchcraft involved a persistent "strong smell of something like musk [of which] the sick man [i.e. the supposed victim] as well as others complained." And still another found a victim, "in her fits . . . [with] eyes out of her head in a ghastly manner, . . . tongue flaring out of her mouth, . . . and such a smell with her breath that none in the room were able to abide the steam. . . . The hideousness thereof he [i.e. the witness] is not able to express."[169]

Shame/humiliation was evoked by certain of the *effects* attributed to witchcraft. The men who experienced sudden failure in "fowling" or fruit-growing and the women whose spinning or baking was plagued with unwonted difficulty would feel an unavoidable embarrassment. And a single moment's frustration might produce the same result as well. A Springfield victim (of Hugh Parsons) inexplicably lost, then quickly refound, three house-knives—"which made me blush."[170] Another witness in the same case was unable to loosen the tap on a barrel of beer, though he tried with all his strength "till the blood started in my hand." Thereupon the mistress of the house "laughed" at his difficulty, declared she could "fetch it out with [her] little finger," and proceeded to do just that; the witness believed "it could not have been so except it were bewitched."[171]

Clear instances also of surprise/startle are scattered through the records. The victim who encountered a familiar or a spectral shape professed himself "astonished" or "amazed"; likewise one whose livestock or chickens fell suddenly ill. Usually this feeling was admixed with, and subordinate to, other affects (distress, fear, shame). Still, insofar as the suddenness of given occurrences helped to justify their attribution to witchcraft, surprise, too, rates a mention here.

In summary, all the "primary affects," save one, are documented in the witchcraft materials. (The exception is enjoyment/joy; neither the victims nor the accused could take much direct pleasure from their respective situations.) Four of these affects—interest/excitement, distress/anguish, fear/terror, anger/rage—were repeatedly and powerfully enlisted in witchcraft proceedings. The other three—disgust/contempt, shame/humiliation, startle/surprise—played a somewhat lesser part. But this account has more than a descriptive importance. For affects were not merely *effects* (of witchcraft); they operated also as *causes*. Again and again they helped to shape specific behavior, including many of the "symptoms" discussed in the preceding pages.

For example, almost any conversation between principals in witchcraft proceedings was subject to distortion—to misunderstanding, mishearing, and various forms of selective "editing"—under the pressure of strong affect. The "threatening speeches" so widely attributed to supposed witches made an obvious case in point. What the victim heard (and remembered) as a specific threat might, from the witch's standpoint, have been merely an idle comment tossed off in irritation or even in jest. Hugh Parsons wished to withdraw from a bargain he had previously made with the Rev. Moxon about bricks for a chimney in the minister's house, but Moxon insisted on going ahead with it. Witnesses testified that Parsons had said, "I will be even with him . . . he shall get nothing by it." Parsons denied speaking so, but admitted that "this I said: if he would hold me to my bargain, I could pussle him in the bargain." Moxon himself remembered Hugh saying only "that . . . I could not in strictness hold him to the bargain." What, then, were Hugh Parsons's actual words? (And to whom were they spoken, and on what occasions?) The question had an urgent context, for Moxon's two daughters were "taken ill with . . . fits . . . the same week that [he] spoke to Hugh Parsons about his bricks."[172] The witnesses were deeply gripped by the unfolding sequence, and their perceptions (and/or memories) may have been influenced accordingly. Of course, such distortion might well come from the witch as well, but the cases are too numerous and varied to be explained entirely in that way.

To the vagaries of mishearing were added comparable possibilities for mis-seeing. Thomas Bracey "suspected Katherine Harrison of witchcraft," and feared becoming one of her victims. Then one day he saw an astonishing spectacle: "a cart coming to . . . Harrison's house loaded with hay [and] on the top . . . a full calf's head, the ears standing pert up." As he watched, "the calf vanished"—its place taken by Goody Harrison who "appeared not to Thomas before."[173] Was this an instance of spectral transformation, as Bracey himself clearly believed? Goody Harrison's rejoinder suggested otherwise: "whereas he sayeth he saw a calf's head on the cart, I conclude it was possible he might see or hear of a pig's head on the cart, for we brought a pig out of the meadow upon a cart-load of corn or hay about that time."[174]

Edward Jessup, a prosecution witness against Mercy Disborough, had undergone multiple experiences of the same sort; his testimony merits quotation at some length:

> Being at Thomas Disborough's house sometime in the beginning of last winter . . . he asked me to tarry and sup with him. And there I saw a pig roasting that looked very well, but when it came to the table (where we had a very good light) it seemed to me to have no skin upon it, and looked very strangely, but when the said Disborough began to cut it the skin (to my apprehension) seemed again upon it . . . at which strange alteration of the pig I was much concerned. However, fearing to displease his wife by refusing to eat, I did eat some of the pig. . . . [Presently Goody Disborough and another guest argued about a passage in the Scriptures, and] she brought a Bible (that was of very large print) to read the particular scripture, but though I had a good light and looked earnestly upon the book I could not see one letter.

Later the same night, on his way home, the deponent came to a stream which seemed at first "very low," but then "very high." He found a canoe but could not budge it from its place on the bank. ("Ordinarily I could have shoved it into the creek with ease.") He decided next to ride round the stream by a route where he "had often been and knew . . . well." However, he became lost, and his "old cart horse" kept plunging off the road "into the bushes." As a result, "I was the greatest part of the night wandering before I got home, although it was not much more than two miles."[175]

This little odyssey of perceptual distortion, confusion, and plain mischance epitomizes the role of affect in witchcraft proceedings. Goody Disborough was widely rumored to be a witch. Edward Jessup certainly feared her on this account—and perhaps at some level he hated her as well. Overwhelmed with anxiety as he "supped" at her table, he simply could not function in an "ordinary" way. He then interpreted his difficulties as *caused* by the witch. In short, (1) his initial suspicions of her (2) produced the affect, which (3) interfered with his perceptual and mental capacity, thereby (4) confirming his original suspicions. The power of this process lay precisely in its patent circularity: from the standpoint of the accused there was no escape.

But if the process seems relatively clear, the interplay of specific affects is quite another matter. Occasionally a single affect appears to predominate. Thus when John Godfrey approached Daniel Ela one evening "and shaked him by the hands," Ela immediately felt afraid and "thought if the said Godfrey were a witch, he might bewitch his hands . . . and by the by he had much pain in his hands." (Painful sensation "suggested" by fear.)[176] Similarly, when Jonathan Haines could not remember to bring Goody Morse her malt, his mare took sick; and Haines, drawing the inevitable conclusion, vowed never to do her errand, even though he might "lose all that [he] had." (Memory "blocked" by anger.)[177] More often, affects appeared in combination; for example, fear *and* anger made an especially likely pair. But such mixtures are most difficult to analyze, given the usual limitations of the documents. It seems likely that fear was the most widespread of all the affective accompaniments to witchcraft. But anger, distress, and interest were also strongly present—and were also efficacious in their own right.

The *results* are easier to categorize. Perceptual distortions, of the type reported by Edward Jessup, were common not only in the victim-group but also among onlookers and witnesses. Thus, as Margaret Rule "fell into her fits," a crowd of her neighbors watched in evident fascination; and at one point "we perceived something stir upon her pillow at a little distance from her."[178] Again, when Katherine Branch was similarly afflicted, there was one moment which a bystander named Joseph Garnsy would particularly remember: "She shrieked out, 'now . . . I see him . . . there he is'; [and] just at this time to my appearance there seemed to dart in at the west window a sudden light across the room, which did startle and amaze me." In this instance Katherine claimed to see the Devil approaching her, while Joseph saw only his "sudden light." And there was, of course, a difference. The victim, overcome by severe (and chronic) inner conflict, produced a full-blown hallucination, whereas the witness, under the influence of an intense (but temporary) affective stimulus, had a relatively simple form of illusory experience.[179]

Accidents made another category of behavior attributable to powerful affect. Thus, a group of "workmen" gathering timber in the woods one day near Springfield stopped for dinner, and one of them (Thomas Miller) made light of another (Hugh Parsons, the suspected witch). Third parties were "much troubled in . . . mind because [he] . . . spake so plainly, lest some ill event should follow." Minutes afterward, when the group had resumed its labor, Thomas Miller cut his leg.[180] Failures in work can be understood in a similar way: failures in spinning, in baking, in tailoring, of the sort already mentioned. These, too, were "accidents," where accustomed modes of performance became suddenly disorganized.

There was one more affect-related affliction—the most dramatic and dangerous of all. Stated bluntly: some victims of witchcraft were made ill, at least in part, by their own anxiety. Anthropologists have long remarked on this phenomenon in studies of premodern cultures all around the world.[181] A man (or woman) who believes him(her)self to be the target of witches may sicken—may even die—under circumstances that defy medical explanation. There is no disease entity, and no ingestion of poisonous substance. Of course, the culture's explanation—witchcraft—then seems all the more plausible. But, in fact, biological science does support an alternative view. Intense affect—especially "great fear" and "great rage"—is frequently "associated with profound physiological disturbances, widespread through the organism."[182] Adrenal production, the activity of the musculature, the nervous system, heart rate, and blood circulation are all significantly involved. These effects are functional in the short term (e.g. in mobilizing the system to meet an immediate and extreme challenge), but profoundly *dys*functional when continued over a period of many hours or days. The key factor is a gradual decline in blood pressure, with resultant damage to the nerve centers, the heart, and other vital organs. Unless the condition can be somehow reversed the entire organism is progressively weakened. The process retains in all phases its connection to affective stress—to melancholy foreboding, to anxiety, to outright terror. Indeed, in fatal cases death can be attributed to a "true state of shock."[183]

Any sure diagnosis of this type would require close observation of the victim over an extended period of time; and it cannot be forced on admittedly fragmentary materials from centuries ago. Most likely, in many instances, specific disease organisms were the initial and primary cause of bodily affliction. But when the link had been made—in the mind of the victim—to the idea of witchcraft, medical illness might easily be compounded by a disabling charge of affect. Again, the evidence in particular cases is usually insufficient; but here and there we glimpse a victim so desperate about witchcraft, so preoccupied with the matter of affliction, as to justify at least a provisional interpretation along these lines. Recall, for example, the plight of Goody Chandler, repeatedly "affrighted" by shapes and specters and searching through the course of a long illness for some means to prevent witches from entering her house. ("With her staff she made a shift to get to the door and nailed on a horseshoe as well as she could.")[184] Consider the Hadley magistrate Philip Smith, fatally stricken soon after being threatened by "a wretched woman in the town." (He had immediately "declared himself apprehensive of receiving mischief at her hands," and "in his distresses . . . exclaimed very much upon the woman." He seemed quite certain of his impending death; even "the standers-by could in him see one ripening apace for another world.")[185] Note the insistence of Goodwife Rebecca Stearns, as she lay mortally ill, on discussing her alleged tormentor. ("Thus she lay, talking on against Mrs. Holman and Mary to all that came to her, [saying] that they were witches and must be hanged, and so she told them to their faces, and could not be stilled. . . . And she cried out with a loud voice all night to the Lord for help . . . and ever and anon she called out of Mrs. Holman and would have her sent for. . . .")[186] Note, too, that John Chase suffered an attack of "bloody flux," beginning on the "very day" he agreed to testify against Goody Morse and ending "at the very instant . . . I came to court and charged her with it." (Here the chronology of affect—presumably a surge of anxiety as to possible retaliation—and physical complaint corresponded perfectly. It seems that an appearance in court served to relieve the pressure of the affective stimulus.)[187] The list of such episodes could be considerably lengthened, but the common thread is already clear. Witchcraft cases repeatedly suggest the malignant power of fear itself.

Defenses

Unbearable affects and unacceptable wishes evoke, in a quite automatic way, the processes of intrapsychic "defense." Thus is conflict tempered, tension lowered, pain reduced—at least temporarily. According to clinical theory the most common defenses are the following: denial, projection, introjection, repression, reaction formation, undoing, isolation, and regression.[188]

One could probably find in the witchcraft materials individual examples of each entry on this list. Thus "reaction formation" has been identified above as belonging to the afflictive syndrome of one victim-group in particular (the adolescent girls).[189] Similarly, some victims show unmistakable signs of "repression" (the unconsciously purposeful forgetting of internal impulses) and "regression" (a return to the psychological positions of early childhood). But instead of trying to cover the entire spectrum, we shall concentrate on two defenses that seem especially important to this investigation: denial and projection.

Simple denial was the most widely employed means of combatting the painful affect associated with witchcraft. Two separate conversations between victims and their spectral assailants will show the process at work. Mary Hale of Wethersfield was one of those who believed herself tormented by Katherine Harrison. For some weeks she experienced "blows" and "pains" at the hands of unseen shapes; then one night a voice addressed her from the darkness, "saying, . . . 'are you not afraid of me?' Mary said, 'no!' The voice replied, 'I will make you afraid before I have done with you.'" Whereupon Mary was "crushed and oppressed very much." Still she "replied [that] she feared her not, because God had kept her and would keep her still."[190]

Isabel Holdridge testified to quite similar experiences, in the trial of John Godfrey. Her troubles began with an argument over an unpaid debt, in the course of which she had said to Godfrey, "I fear thee not, nor all the devils in Hell." A few nights later, she was plagued with strange "apparitions"—in particular, the shape of a "bear . . . which ground the teeth and shook the claw." The bear referred at once to the previous altercation with Godfrey: "Thou sayest thou art not afraid; then thinkest thou that [this] house will save thee?" Isabel answered, "I hope that Lord Jesus Christ will save me." Upon which the bear "spake" once more: "Thou sayest thou art not afraid of all the devils in Hell, but I will have thy heart blood within a few hours."[191] In both these cases the issue of fear was directly articulated; in both it was met with a vigorous denial. With Hale the defense was successful (at least by her own account); that is, fear did not break her composure. With Holdridge it was apparently unsuccessful: another witness reported that "immediately after she was taken with extremity of fear."[*][192]

If denial was the chief defense raised against fear, then projection played a similar part with respect to the affect anger and the accompanying wish to attack. Indeed, witchcraft encompassed projection at its very core. Again and again the documentary record presents the variant forms of what was, at bottom, a single sequence: (1) Witch and Victim contend over some matter of mutual concern; (2) Victim perceives anger in Witch and fears attack; (3) Victim suffers hurt of one sort or another, and accuses Witch. What this account does not include is any reference to angry feelings in the victim him(her)self—yet it requires no long leap of psychiatric inference to put such elements squarely into the middle of the sequence. Considered from the standpoint of (the victim's)

---

* Occasionally the same defense was raised against incipient anger. When, for example, a victim made specific accusations, her family and friends might express an official skepticism. ("We had not the least suspicion that way. . . . We reproved her [the victim] and urged her not to say so.") Yet other evidence would reveal long-standing enmity between these persons and the supposed witch, which made their protestations seem rather doubtful. In addition, they would freely cooperate with the victim in her afflictions (thus supplying a covert form of encouragement); and their participation in trial proceedings was the final and definitive measure of their real disposition.[193]

inner experience, the steps should read as follows: (1) contention with Witch leaves Victim feeling angered and wishing to attack; (2) Victim cannot tolerate such feelings and unconsciously assigns them to Witch; (3) Victim accuses Witch—in effect saying, "I am not angry, *you* are; I do not wish to attack, *you* do." This is the essence of projection: the attribution to others of inner states which are unacceptable to, and in, oneself. And yet there is one more twist. In making an accusation Victim does in fact attack, with consequences that may be very damaging, even fatal, for Witch. In a sense, therefore, projection allows Victim to have it both ways: the intolerable affect and the inadmissible wish are disowned and indulged at the same time.

To be sure, not all the angers of victims were subject to this defense. In at least a few instances bitter feeling was directly vented at the supposed witch.[194] And in many more instances such feeling was gradually brought to the surface once the accusations had begun to take hold. Openly hostile expression was thought permissible—even laudable—toward those whose status as witches was well established. It was fine to be angry with a figure of anger itself.[195]

Properly understood, projection is a defense against particular wishes (or "drives") and affects. As such, it is related to, yet distinct from, the broader process of "externalization."[196] What externalization most especially denotes is the (unconscious) effort to attribute whole aspects of the self to outside sources.* This, too, is evident in the witchcraft materials. Numerous persons who never saw themselves as primary targets of witchcraft would nonetheless feel considerably invested in particular "suspects." And feeling so, they would actively contribute to the process of accusation. They became the bit-players in the gradually unfolding drama: as producers and consumers of local gossip, as "attendants" to the main victims, or simply as "bystanders." From such participation they derived a kind of vicarious gain—a chance to disclaim and discharge those parts of themselves which seemed most inconsistent with their inner ideals. The composite fantasy of witches, examined previously, was in considerable measure a product of their "externalization." The witch as attacker, as intruder, as envier: this was their "negative identity"—a whole dark underside of early New England character.

---

* The difference can be further expressed as follows. Projection centers on specific feelings toward immediately pertinent objects. Thus the starting-point may be "I feel angry at you"; and the result, "you feel angry at me." Externalization involves more general elements of character, without necessary reference to any particular objects. In paradigmatic form: "I am an angry person" becomes "He [i.e. anyone "available"] is an angry person."

But to put it so is to raise once again the difficult question of the actual conduct of supposed witches. Did they, in fact, utter the "threatening speeches" so frequently attributed to them? And were they, in reality, especially angry persons? The evidence in any given instance is unlikely to provide a sure answer: usually we hear only one side, or, at best, conflicting accounts. Yet an earlier chapter has suggested that many witches were—relative to their peers—rather free in the expression of hostile affect.[197] And there is confirmation of a sort in the clinical literature on projection. "Usually," writes one theorist, "projections . . . are not performed at random but are directed toward some point in reality where they are met halfway. The person [who projects] is sensitized, as it were, to perceive the unconscious of others wherever this perception can be utilized to rationalize his own tendency toward projection."[198]

The same point can be made about externalization: there, too, psychological process and behavioral reality often "meet halfway." In short, the victims who struggled to disclaim unacceptable wishes and affects, and the others who sought to repudiate negative aspects of self—all by way of witchcraft accusations—found suspects whose own conduct allowed (or invited?) such projections and externalizations. In this respect (among others) the principals on all sides in witch trials were joined by deep, though unacknowledged, bonds of psychic complicity.

Psychodynamic Structure

Most of the inquiry so far has been analytic in the literal sense. Major strands in the psychology of witchcraft have been sorted and separated, in order to present the clearest possible view of each one. But now it becomes necessary to turn completely about and adopt a synthetic approach, to see how things connected, overlapped, fitted together, in terms of the underlying "psychic organization." This objective implies significant changes in the substance and manner of inquiry. It points more directly toward the murky domain of "depth psychology," of inner life and unconscious process. And it raises questions of "genetic" or "developmental" context; in short, going *in* (to the unconscious) also means going *back* (to early, even "infantile," modes of experience). In each respect the route leads away from what is sometimes called the "experience-near" and toward the "experience-distant."[199] Increasingly, therefore, theory is needed to help in charting the way.

The organizing structures of inner life have little to do with logic, proportion, balance, and the like; seemingly disparate elements are frequently joined on the basis of symbolic or experiential association. And there is one thematic cluster in the witchcraft materials that vividly exemplifies this point. The main ingredients, described at length in the preceding pages, can be summarized as follows. (1) Infants seemed to make an especially likely, and vulnerable, target for witchcraft; among all the fatalities explained in this way there was clearly disproportionate representation for the very young. (2) Many witches were believed to have an inordinate, and envious, interest in infants and small children. (Some were, in fact, childless.) (3) A number of witches were accused of interfering in the process of infant "nursing." (They would cause soreness or ulcers in the breast; they would make the milk dry up.) (4) Another notorious target of witchcraft was livestock, including (and especially?) milk cows. (5) Witches themselves were thought to "give suck" to their imps and familiars. (6) Courts, local officials, and private citizens would search the bodies of suspected witches for the preternatural "teats" that marked them as the Devil's own.

There is a central preoccupation here with maternal function, especially in regard to infants and small children, which invites further study. Of course, infants of this time and place were very much at risk, relative to other age-groups in the population.[200] Moreover, the forms of their morbidity and mortality may have seemed especially perplexing. (Infant illness was often sudden and dramatic; and communication—in particular, verbal communication—between patient and caretaker was limited or nil.) In short, there was good reason to be anxious about the care of the very young, and it hardly seems surprising that witchcraft belief should have picked up this anxiety. But something else was involved as well. The figure of the witch suckling her imps conveyed a scornful reflection on maternity itself: what has been termed above the witch-as-nurse displayed, in the unconscious, a reverse face—the nurse-as-witch. Here one senses the viewpoint of an aggrieved and angry child, caught up in an archaic form of "sibling rivalry": "I hate my mother who has so unfairly shifted her love from (all-deserving) me to her other (wicked and undeserving) children." Hence the aforementioned cluster of witch-related beliefs seems to have expressed, more or less simultaneously, a parent's fear that infant children may sicken and die, and a child's wish that infant siblings would suffer precisely that fate.

Here once again is the issue of attack-aggression-rage, which looms so large throughout the witchcraft material. Its importance in the psychology of victims, accusers, bystanders (and even the accused themselves) can scarcely be overemphasized: this was what witchcraft most chiefly concerned. Yet infantile sibling rivalry will not alone suffice as explanation; it needs some larger framework of understanding. The succeeding paragraphs propose such a framework—and, by a very roundabout route, return eventually to the subject of aggression.

Recall, for a start, the figure of the witch-as-intruder: this, too, embraced a very large theme. It was as if the witch and her victim were battling back and forth across a vital territory where *boundaries* had assumed the greatest possible significance. On the manifest level the victim and his supporters would labor strenuously to keep the witch at a distance, while she, for her part, was forever "thrusting in." Counter-magical strategies were designed to establish clear and impermeable boundaries (for example, the placement of bay leaves or horseshoes, usually near the threshold of the victim's house). At the level of fantasy, as well, the same theme was powerfully evident. Time and again a spectral witch attacked her victim at home and in bed (coming "through the window" or "in at the keyhole"); there was no way to prevent a "shape" from gaining whatever access she desired. Her favorite targets included the victim's children, his livestock, his personal effects; in short, no part of his household was beyond reach. His private conversation, indeed his very thoughts, might be known to her—also embarrassing events in his past, and important prospects in his future. Of course, the most dramatic of all forms of victimization was outright "possession" by the Devil, a process in which the center of personality was invaded from outside. Here was a total failure of boundary-maintenance.

But concern for boundaries was inseparable from the matter of *control*. The intrusions of the witch were meant to demonstrate, and to enlarge, her power over important aspects of the victim's experience. This issue was articulated with special clarity in the course of fits and the various "spectral" encounters. Could the witch force others to do her bidding (that is, to sign the Devil's book)? Could she manipulate their feelings? (Said one shape, "I will make you afraid before I have done with you.")[201] Could she dictate the details of their behavior? (Said one victim, "*They* say I must not speak it [God's name]. . . . They say I must not go in. . . . They say I shall not eat it . . ." etc. And an afflicted girl, under the watchful care of Cotton Mather, asked her tormentors simply, "Is my life in your hands?")[202] Affliction itself was a direct manifestation of the power of the witch. She attacked in places, and by methods, of her own choosing—and the results corresponded in detail to her plan. Her touch, her look, her words could be instantly efficacious. Occasionally she reduced her victims to small images—to "puppets," in both the literal and the figurative meanings of that term. On the other hand, the witch herself could sometimes be manipulated; a careful application of countermagic might simply reverse the roles of puppet and puppeteer.

Considered from an explicitly psychological standpoint, these elements denote a distinctive mode of "object relations." Subject and object, self and non-self, are poorly distinguished—or, at best, are separated only by brittle, easily movable borders. Connections across (or through) such borders are fluid, dense, more or less continuous. Control is indeed a lively issue here—along with its obverse, autonomy. Important sectors of experience are compressed into the two categories of pleasure and pain; and motives are reduced to love and hate (expressed as succor and attack). To all this is added a heavy reliance on the "defense mechanism" of projection.

But to put matters thus is to raise further questions of cause, of source, of origins. Where, in short, did such patterns come from? The prominence throughout the witchcraft material of projective process offers an important clue. Projection (along with introjection) belongs with the most "archaic" of the defenses; its roots lie buried in the earliest phase of life. Freud himself identified the key link: "The original pleasure ego wants to introject into itself everything that is good and to eject from itself everything that is bad. . . . Expressed in the language of the oldest —the oral—instinctual impulses, the judgement is: 'I should like to eat this,' or 'I should like to spit this out.' "[203] Amidst the turmoil of infant sensation, projection and introjection provide a modicum of order. At best they serve the long-term goal of "structure building" (sorting and connecting constituent parts within the early self); at the least, they help to sharpen the boundaries between self and non-self (since their operation depends on boundaries of some sort).[204]

They remain, forever afterwards, associated with a cluster of "unconscious ego activities."[205] And they carry an implicit reference to the most primitive perceptual experiences of the very young child, who regards his "primary object" (caretaker) as a virtual appendage bound to perform his entire bidding. When this expectation runs afoul of reality, rage is the certain result. Expressed subjectively, the initial impression "She will not do as I want" quickly becomes "She does not love me," which is further elaborated into "She hates me and seeks to hurt me." In later life sudden reversals—such as illness or other misfortune— may recall the feelings of helplessness and frustration of infancy. And these, in turn, may reactivate the characteristically infantile modes of perception. Then—and again later—the sense of being well seems to depend on the care, the loving compliance, of others. Conversely, being unwell has the subjective meaning of being unloved and unprotected, or even of being hated.

These processes can be directly related to the development of the "self-system." They belong to that very early and formative period which Freud designated by the term "primary narcissism" but left for later psychoanalytic theorists—most especially Heinz Kohut—to explore in detail.[206] The building of the "nuclear self" is indeed a central theme here. From the diffuse and disorganized experiences of the newborn infant a core of personality gradually evolves. This core has increasing qualities of cohesiveness (in its internal composition), of boundedness (vis-à-vis the external world), and of continuity (over time). Objects (internal representations of other people) are distinguished with growing clarity, but from an inherently "narcissistic" viewpoint. The budding self conceives a "grandiose fantasy," encompassing power, knowledge, beauty, perfection—and looks for confirmation in all this from the available objects. At the same time the self invests the objects with a perfection of their own—in which it may then share by way of an enduring attachment. (This is, in brief, a matter of "idealization," of primitive hero-worship.) Encounters with reality, and a growing appreciation of intrinsic limitations, bring about the gradual modification of these early narcissistic structures. Infantile grandiosity is rescaled and reworked into "healthy ambition," and infantile idealization yields a stable system of (internalized) values. Meanwhile the nuclear self becomes an effective center for the myriad experiences of later life and the locus of a continuing "esteem" (especially *self*-esteem).[207]

This is but a schematic outline based on *optimal* development, and of course the particulars of individual experience are never so tidy or so happily successful. Indeed, the chief concern here is the negative side— the failures, the deficits, the distortions in the self-system. For witchcraft expressed such things, was rooted in them, to a quite unmistakable degree. The implicit concern with boundary-maintenance was itself a diagnostic sign. Victims were thought to be attached to witches, invaded by witches, overcome by witches—notions that suggest a certain fragility in the nuclear self. The presence of so much angry affect points in a similar direction. However, anger is an insufficiently strong description of the attitudes expressed toward—or, more frequently, projected into— the figure of the witch. There was something raw, uncompromising, altogether "primitive" about these attitudes—a quality readily associated with the clinical category "narcissistic rage."[208] Behind narcissistic rage there usually lies an experience of "narcissistic injury" or insult. And this, in turn, calls attention to the numerous situations of conflict with which accusations of witchcraft were typically bound up. Slighting remarks, threats, petty aspersions on character or behavior often evoked a strong response. There was a prickly side to the early New Englanders which shows through in many sectors of their experience, not least in their concern with witches.[209] Consider, too, the matter of display, the claims of "specialness" implicit in attack by witchcraft. Such claims were most vividly dramatized in full-blown "fits," but, in a lesser measure, they may be imputed to all self-described victims: "The forces of evil have chosen *me* as their target. And you—the standers-by—must attend to me in my hour of affliction."

This discussion has alluded more than once to infantile "ties" with a "primary object." But such terminology may seem excessively abstract, even obfuscating. *Who ordinarily was—and is—the actual, flesh-and-blood "primary object"?* And what is the lasting significance of the "ties" involved here? To raise these questions is to return to a most important problem. Recall the conclusion of Chapter 3 that accused witches were predominantly adult women; recall, too, the difficulty of understanding *why*. Social conditions—the (partially) inferior status of New England women vis-à-vis men—seemed to "fit" with the witch/woman equation, but hardly to explain it.[210] The transcultural aspect of this phenomenon —the common tendency in otherwise disparate societies to define witches as *female*—suggested that interpretive effort might need to reach beyond the particular circumstances of a single time and place. The involvement of both sexes—women no less than men—in prosecuting witches implied another set of parameters. But sociological inquiry yielded no clear line of interpretation, no answers, satisfying these general specifications.

Now, as the problem of gender appears once again, there is a more promising outlook. For the theory of early object relations does furnish some answers (which is to say that the problem itself belongs more to the psychology than to the sociology of witchcraft). The key point is what Dorothy Dinnerstein has called the "female monopoly of early child care," the fact that "for virtually every human the central infant-parent relationship, in which we form our earliest, intense and wordless, feelings toward existence, is a relationship with a woman."[211] Beneath the manifold forms of this relationship (across different cultures, and for different individuals within the same culture), there are certain fundamental regularities.

Infants are, in the first place, entirely dependent on their mothers: for food, for warmth, for nurturance, for entertainment, for virtually all the "good" they know. A mother's power to supply these needs, or not to supply them (depending on her own wishes and resources), lies at the center of infantile experience. She seems, from the infant's own standpoint, "omnipotent and responsible for every blessing and curse of existence."[212] For the blessings she is gratefully loved—but for the curses she is angrily blamed. And every child, no matter how well cared for, knows some discomfort, some disappointment, some moments of loss and separation. These are, moreover, experienced with an immediacy and intensity unmatched in any subsequent phase of life.

But there is more to the infant-mother relationship than helplessness and dependence on the one side and (seemingly) limitless powers on the other. For the mother is critically implicated in the infant's evolving experience of its own center, its own will, its own subjectivity. She is the "non-self" from which self is progressively distinguished; she plays "it" to the infantile "I." She is "the overwhelming, external will"—again the words are Dinnerstein's—"in the face of which the child first learns the necessity for submission." She disposes a vital power "to foster or forbid, to humble or respect, our first steps toward autonomous activity."[213]

As an overall result, "female sentience . . . carries permanently for most of us the atmosphere of that unbounded, shadowy presence toward which all our needs were originally directed." And, also as a result, we attribute to "female intentionality" a menacing aspect of

> the rampant and limitless, the alien and unknowable. It is an intentionality that needs to be . . . corralled and subjugated if we . . . are to feel at all safe in its presence. It needs to be corralled . . . not only because its boundaries are unclear, but also because its wrath is all-potent and the riches it can offer or refuse us [are] bottomless.[214]

These images—to repeat—arise and flourish in all "mother-raised children," that is, in women as well as men. Their lasting power derives from their very early provenance. Their association with "pre-verbal" development is, in fact, of the greatest importance; for since they are "formed entirely without words," they continue thereafter to have a "subterranean life of their own, unmodified by that limited part of human sensibility which we call intelligence."[215] Their force and their distinctiveness are highlighted when they are set alongside the comparable imagery of men. "Male sentience" and "male intentionality" have—within the same context of innerlife experience—a much clearer shape, a far more even coloration. Men appear to stand for reason, for logic, for balance, for whatever is most "cleanly human." This, in turn, reflects developmental circumstance. Men (fathers) are not ordinarily much of a factor in infantile experience. And when (later on) men do begin significantly to impinge on the child's life, they enter an "object world" which is in all ways more developed. The child has some capacity to appreciate their separate "subjectivity"—they are more "you" than "it"—and to take their measure as creatures of human, although still quite outsized, dimensions. Fathers, in short, seem far less "magically formidable" than mothers, from the standpoint of the child.[216]

The "magically formidable" qualities of mothers—enlarged to embrace women in general—are, of course, of the greatest importance here. Indeed, the term would serve nicely to describe witches, as perceived by their victims and accusers. Other elements in the figure of the witch have an equally clear reference to infantile experience: the (seeming) malevolence, the intrusiveness, the capacity to inflict all-consuming hurt and harm. To be sure, impressions received *after* infancy must also be credited: most especially, castration anxiety (in its two different, gender-related forms), and the (awesome, mysterious) role of women as bearers of new life.* But these serve, by and large, to elaborate on themes rooted in the earliest object-world.

There is little doubt, finally, that New England was populated by "mother-raised children."† Childbirth itself was entirely in the hands of women (midwives, and female kin and friends of the mother); it seems, indeed, that men and all younger children were effectively excluded

---

* The link between castration anxiety and more generalized fears of women has been summarized as follows by Karen Horney: "It [castration anxiety] is an anxiety of psychogenic origin that goes back to feelings of guilt and old childhood fears. Its anatomical-psychological nucleus lies in the fact that during intercourse the male has to entrust his genitals to the female body, that he presents her with his semen and interprets this as a surrender of vital strength to the woman, similar to his experiencing the subsiding of erection after intercourse as evidence of having been weakened by the woman." Woman's biological role in bearing children elicits both fear and jealousy. On the one hand, there is the [preconscious] idea that a person who gives life is also capable of taking it away. (Thus, as Simone de Beauvoir has written, "From the day of his birth man begins to die: this is the truth incarnated in the Mother.") On the other hand, child-bearing seems awesome, wonderful, enviable. There is a considerable scientific literature on these issues, and on their relation to misogynous feeling at large.[217] Their presence among the psychological forces that generated witchcraft belief can scarcely be doubted. However, they reflect a specifically *male* viewpoint, and could apply, at most, to the men within the victim-group. And since the *animus* toward witches so clearly embraced persons of both sexes, other factors (e.g. the residues of "early object relations") have greater explanatory power in the present context.

† The implicit reference of the term "raised" continues, for these purposes, to be very *early* childhood.

from such occasions.[218] Breast-feeding—which continued, in the average case, for about one year—would establish a special bond between the mother and her newborn.[219] And this bond seems to have been maintained also in other areas of infant care (judging from scattered notations in personal and local records).[220] By contrast, fathers do not appear in any significant relationship to children until the latter are at least two or three years old. Of course, this division of responsibility for infant nurture is characteristic of virtually every known culture, past and present. It fosters, in turn, a virtually universal "antagonism to women," a misogynous substrate of transcultural dimensions. Its visible outgrowths were—and are—extremely varied, even within a single social setting. But among all such outgrowths none has been more compelling than the figure of the witch. Here was something that the New Englanders shared with countless other specimens of humankind.

There is one additional way to consider this material, involving a shift of reference from the self system and early object relations to what Erik Erikson has called "psychosocial adaptation."[221] Erikson's well-known schedule of developmental stages posits an unfolding of specific "ego qualities" (each encompassing positive and negative "potentialities"). And among such qualities the one associated with the second stage invites particular attention. The issue in this period (roughly the second and third years of life) is defined as "autonomy vs. shame and doubt." If all goes well, boundaries are defined, and "limits" are set, around a "vital perimeter of personal space." Within this space the child seeks "a gradual and well-guided experience of the autonomy of free choice." And the legacy to later life—again, given a favorable result—is "a sense of self-control without loss of self-esteem," accompanied by "a lasting sense of good will and pride." But often, of course, the result is not so favorable, and the "negative potentialities" come into play. Thus an inordinate propensity to shame is usually grounded in the experience of this developmental stage. But it is "doubt" which seems especially pertinent here. Erikson writes,

> Doubt is the brother of shame. Where shame is dependent on the consciousness of being upright and exposed, doubt . . . has much to do with a consciousness of having a front and a back . . . and especially a "behind." For the reverse area of the body . . . cannot be seen by the child, and yet it can be dominated by the will of others. The "behind" is the small being's dark continent, an area of the body which can be magically dominated and effectively invaded by those who would attack one's power of autonomy. . . .

This basic sense of doubt . . . finds its adult expression in para-
noiac fears concerning hidden persecutors and secret persecutions
threatening from behind.*[222]

Genetic Factors

This *potpourri* of interpretive deduction yields some common implications about development—about source-points of the stresses and conflicts
that found outward expression in witchcraft belief. To recapitulate: (1)
"Projection" was everywhere central to witchcraft accusations. And projection, with its "oral" foundation, rates as one of the earliest of all the
psychological "defenses." (2) Witchcraft belief displayed important elements of "magical thinking," especially with respect to implicit stereotypes of women. And these have their roots in the "preverbal" substrate
of infantile experience. (3) The symptoms and fantasies associated with
witchcraft suggest a certain vulnerability in the "self system." Here, too,
the genetic line leads far back toward infancy. (4) The same evidence,
considered from the standpoint of "ego qualities," underscores the issue
of "autonomy" (and its negative correlate "doubt"). And this issue is
said to belong especially to the "second stage" of psychosocial adaptation,
encompassing roughly the second and third years of life. (5) The extreme
symptoms of one particular victim-group, the "afflicted girls," denote
unresolved conflicts in relation to "maternal objects." And the cast of
those conflicts seems largely "pre-oedipal."

Of course, no such interpretations can be made to yield a precise set
of chronological markings, for individual development necessarily sets
something of its own pace. Yet the convergent emphasis on *very early*
experience seems impressive. Terms like "preverbal" and "pre-oedipal"
imply an upper bound of about age three. On the other hand, these
tasks and concerns do not belong to the condition of neonates. They

---

* The passage, as quoted, implies a biological reference for the psychosocial
"potentialities" of the second stage. In short, Erikson links specifically "anal"
concerns to the child's struggle for autonomy and his corresponding vulnerability
to shame and doubt. However, the strength of this link presumably varies, depending on the personal (and cultural) reinforcement in any given case. In
settings where much is made of "toilet training," the anal reference is likely to
be central and obvious. But in a different context—i.e. where such matters are
downplayed—it may have only minimal importance. For an anthropological example of a culture in which the developmental attainment of autonomy is not much
joined to anal preoccupation, see Jean L. Briggs, "The Issues of Autonomy and
Aggression in the Three-year-old: The Utku Eskimo Case," in *Seminars in Psychiatry,* IV (1972), 317–29. In this respect, Puritan child-rearing was more like
the "Eskimo case" than, e.g., the usual pattern of our own time.

require some glimmerings of psychic structure, or at least some movement in that direction; hence age one seems plausible as an approximate
lower bound.

Do these numbers find explicit confirmation in the witchcraft materials
themselves? There is one documentary fragment which deserves at least
a mention: an allegation, from the Salem trials, that one of the accused
witches "appeared [i.e. in her spectral shape] as little as a child of two
years old."[223] In general, however, the records are devoid of developmental reference—hence the need to revert once again to procedures of
inference. What is known generally about the experience of early childhood in seventeenth-century New England? And can this experience be
plausibly connected with the themes explored above in relation to
witchcraft?

There are, in fact, grounds for thinking that age two was an especially
important—and difficult—time in the life of a Puritan child. It was about
then that he was most likely to face the arrival of a younger sibling,
since in most New England families pregnancies were spaced at intervals
of twenty to thirty months.[224] This would mean, in turn, the loss of his
mother's special attention: no longer was he the littlest, and most vulnerable, member of the family. But beyond such intimations from
demography lie important and explicit prescriptions of Puritan child-
rearing. The central task for parents, as defined by the leading exemplars
of New England culture, was "training the will" of their young. Indeed,
their phrase "training the will" was regularly equated with "breaking
the will." Every child was thought to come into the world with inherent
tendencies to "stubbornness and stoutness of mind": these must be
"beaten down" at all costs.[225] One aspect of such tendencies was the
wilful expression of *anger*—and anger was, by Puritan reckoning, the
most dangerous and damnable of human affects.[226] Children must therefore be trained to compliance, to submission, to "peace." To effect such
training, drastic means were sometimes needed. Puritan parents were
not inclined to spare the rod; but more important than physical coercion
was the regular resort to shaming.[227] (Here lies another line of connection to the vital "second stage" in Erikson's formulation, defined as it is
around the polarity of "autonomy vs. shame and doubt.")

Published statements about child-rearing from the period emphasize
that this regime must start early, in order to be fully effective. And while
they are not additionally specific, they do direct attention to the second
and third years of life. For these are the years when much of development seems to center on the expression of personal "will." The child
stands, and walks, and moves more or less freely about; he achieves great

progress in the coordination of hand and eye; he begins consciously to control important bodily processes (e.g. the eliminative ones). Much of cognition remains preverbal; yet he gains at least the rudiments of speech (e.g. those which permit him to give or withhold his assent—"yes" and, above all, "no"). Most two-year-old children are eager to test their new-found capacities in relation to other people. And such testing inevitably yields a quotient of frustration and anger, even where it contributes most directly to the growth of "autonomy."

Now imagine how all this might seem against a backdrop of Puritan values. Wilfulness, self-assertion, competitive struggle, surges of infantile grandiosity, sudden outbursts of anger: thus the markings of "original sin," displayed in unvarnished form. To allow such traits room for growth was to open a way for the Devil, whose own character was defined in virtually the same terms. There could be little doubt where parental and social obligation lay.

Conclusion

This chapter has explored a convergence of evidentiary and theoretical materials which reflect suggestively on the psychology of witchcraft. Developmental theory and clinical data from our own time; seventeenth-century notions of child-rearing; Puritan values in a larger sense; and the particulars of witchcraft proceedings: such are the ingredients of our interpretive model. The model does not constitute "proof" in the traditional manner of historical research, for the connections between one element and the next lie, in part, beyond a scholar's sight-range. Yet there is a sense of fit about the whole, which carries its own persuasiveness.

Some cautions and disclaimers are needed, by way of conclusion. It would be unwise to assign an exclusive "causal" significance to specifically traumatic events forced on New England children in the first few years of life. Any such "reductionist" argument misleads—on at least two counts. For one, it underestimates the importance of manifest cultural tradition. Witchcraft, in all its rich detail, was a subject of *explicit communication*, between persons, communities, and whole generations. Expressed differently: witchcraft was a matter of conscious belief no less than inward (and unconscious) propensity. In addition, the earliest developmental impressions must not be overemphasized at the expense of all succeeding ones. The present investigation has been pressed to the level of roots and sources, but there is no doubting the importance of subsequent reinforcement. Indeed, such reinforcement can be virtually

assumed: if New England children encountered in earliest life a strenuous resistance to their deepest autonomous strivings, they must surely
have had similar experiences in later childhood. The value-system which
supported all this made no intrinsic distinctions as to age. Older children
and "youths" would hear from all sides the Puritan message of "peace,"
of "harmony," of submission—with its corollary warnings against anger
and the open assertion of self. Presumably the same message was received, without words, in countless personal transactions.

These psychological inferences must not, finally, be construed as a
diagnosis of outright pathology. The great majority of the New Englanders who believed in witchcraft were in no meaningful sense "sick" or
otherwise "disturbed." Most of them, like most of us, fell within some
normal range of mental and emotional adaptation. On the other hand,
most of them—again, like most of us—knew certain areas of inner conflict and vulnerability. And—perhaps to a greater degree for them than
is true for us—such areas obtained similar shape and substance among
otherwise different individuals; for theirs was a more unified, less hetero-
geneous culture.

To be sure, some few among them showed in their attitudes toward
witchcraft a vulnerability that ran very deep and proved ultimately disabling. For these few—and the "afflicted girls" come first to mind—the
language of sickness does indeed apply. Their troubles bear direct comparison to clinical experience today; their fits and related behavior were
the outward signs of a disturbance at the center of personality. Though
little is known of their individual histories prior to their involvement in
witchcraft proceedings, one many reasonably infer psychic "lesions" of
a large, and long-standing, kind.

And yet pathology is always a matter of *relative*, not absolute, distinctions. Hence even the most extreme instances of affliction would remain
in some sense comprehensible to the whole community of New Englanders. A girl "in her fits," an older person attributing specific misfortune
to the malefic power of his neighbor, the legion of ordinary folk who
maintained a general belief in the reality and power of witchcraft: all
were joined by strong bonds of inner preoccupation. The difference and
distance between them embraced quantity, not quality; as individuals
they represented a variety of points along a single psychological spectrum.
Every attack by witchcraft summoned deeply responsive echoes in a host
of "bystanders," for the victim was acting out—although (sometimes)
to an "extremity"—pressure-points and vulnerabilities that were widely
shared.

Two points deserve a final restatement. Strong, purposeful, effective as they undeniably were, many of the New Englanders seem to have felt persistently vulnerable in their core sense of self. Tremors of uncertainty plagued their struggle to grow and endure as free-standing individuals; they could not feel confident of maintaining the existential boundaries of their lives. And, in ways examined above at great length, such feelings were evoked with particular intensity by the figure of the witch.

By a separate but parallel route she evoked other feelings as well. The intrusive, demanding traits so widely attributed to her are best viewed as projections. Her victims were presumably uncomfortable about similar tendencies in themselves, about their own wishes to intrude, to encroach, to dominate, to attack—their whole assertive side. As frequently happens in such situations, they dealt with their conflict by externalizing it. Not they, but rather their neighbor—the "witch"—possessed the traits they so deeply despised.

THREE
Sociology

"There are but few towns, if any, but at one time or other have not had one or more in suspicion for witchcraft, as if the place were not complete in its inhabitants without some well-versed in that occupation."

The Rev. Josiah Cotton (1733)

7

"The Mind of Our Town"

It is a winter's day in the year 1658. The village of Easthampton, on Long Island, stirs under a blanket of new snow. A young man, Samuel Parsons, approaches the house of his friend Arthur Howell. Howell is not at home, but his wife, Elizabeth, invites Samuel inside. The two of them sit by the fire. Elizabeth has recently borne her first child; she looks well enough, but complains to Samuel of headache. She thinks she has caught a chill in the current spell of hard weather.*

Samuel chats with her for a while, does a brief errand elsewhere, and returns to find her feeling worse. She binds a cloth around her head and moans with pain. Presently her husband comes in, accompanied by another friend, William Russell. Elizabeth huddles by the fire and says to Arthur: "Love, I am very ill of my head, and fear I shall have the fever."

Arthur urges her to go to bed, but she demurs, saying she cannot rest comfortably there. Eventually she gives in, and the two of them lie down together. Arthur holds her gently in his arms, but her pain worsens and she tosses fitfully.

"Lord, have mercy upon me," she sobs at intervals; and again, "friends, pray for me." As night falls, she turns suddenly to her husband and cries, "I pray God it may not be with me as it was

* This reconstruction of the events surrounding Elizabeth Howell's illness is based on depositions presented at the trial of Goodwife Garlick in 1658.[1] And the words attributed to the principals are taken *verbatim* from those depositions.

with you when you were at your mother Howell's and were senseless! I pray God I may have my senses!"

Shortly thereafter Elizabeth suckles her baby. "Ah, my poor child," she says, "it pities me more for thee than for myself; for if I be ill, to be sure thou wilt be ill too." The baby finishes and is carried from her by Samuel Parsons.

Elizabeth begins to sing the words of a psalm, then stops and shrieks wildly: "A witch! A witch! Now you are come to torture me because I spoke two or three words against you! In the morning you will come fawning. . . ." Her voice trails off and she lapses into a kind of swoon. Her husband, and the others in the room, recoil in alarm.

"The Lord be merciful to her," exclaims Samuel Parsons to William Russell. "I will all be well. It is well if she be not bewitched." The group converses in hushed tones, deciding at length to summon Elizabeth's father.

The father is Mr. Lion Gardiner, a person of much local eminence; his house is just across the street. Gardiner is not yet asleep, for his own wife has been ill and requires his special care. His arrival at the Howells' brings no abatement in Elizabeth's sufferings.

"A witch! A witch!" she shrieks once again, her eyes fixed on the end of the bed.

"What do you see?" her father asks.

"A black thing at the bed's feet," she sobs in reply.

Suddenly she rises to a sitting position and begins to flail at the bedclothes; she is fighting an unseen adversary. Her husband tries forcibly to restrain her, fearing that she may injure herself. He pins her arms to her sides and pulls backward, but this serves only to increase her frenzy. It is several minutes before she will give up the struggle.

Her father returns briefly to his own house. Mrs. Gardiner looks up from her sickbed. "How is Betty?" she ask anxiously.

"She has a fever," he says quietly. Elizabeth has begged him not to acquaint her mother with the details of the case, and to this point he complies.

But next morning, after a second visit across the street, he is more truthful. "Betty is doing very badly," he admits—and Mrs. Gardiner knows that she too must go to her daughter.

"What shall I do, for I cannot rise?" she asks. She struggles awkwardly to her feet, only to sink back on the bed. She rests, tries again, and eventually succeeds. Leaning on a neighbor for support, she shuffles slowly across the space between the two houses.

She reaches Elizabeth's bedside. Weeping, the two women embrace. Arthur and the others leave the room.

"Oh, mother," Elizabeth cries, "oh, mother, I am bewitched."

Mrs. Gardiner draws back momentarily. "No," she says in an uneven voice; "no, you are asleep or dreaming."

But her daughter insists: "I am not asleep. I am not dreaming. Truly, I am bewitched."

The older woman waits, hesitant about the question she will ask next. "Whom?" she finally says. "Whom do you see?"

Elizabeth hesitates, too, before answering; then—in a shriek— "Goody Garlick! Goody Garlick! I see her at the far corner of the bed, and a black thing of hers at the other corner."

More crying. Renewed gestures of attack. A sharp reproof from Mrs. Gardiner.

"Hush, child," she says in her sternest voice. "This is a terrible thing you say. You must never say it again, not to your husband, not to any living soul. For your husband, if he heard you speak so, would surely tell. . . ."

Soon Mrs. Gardiner is obliged to return to her own house and bed. Her place beside Elizabeth is taken by other women of the neighborhood.

But the "affliction" seems to intensify as the day wears on. Incoherent for long stretches, Elizabeth suddenly finds words to speak her mind: "She is a double-tongued woman. . . . She pricks me with pins. . . . Oh, she torments me. . . ." And on and on.

"Whom do you mean?" ask Goody Birdsall and Goody Edwards. "Who torments you so? Tell us, and we would send for her."

For a time Elizabeth will not reply to such questions directly; but later she blurts out a name. "Ah, Garlick, you jeered me when I came to your house to call my husband home. You laughed and jeered me, and I went crying away. Oh, you are a pretty one."

"Garlick?" ask the other women, drawing close; "what of Garlick?"

"Yes," cries Elizabeth, "send for Garlick and his wife."

"But what would you do with her?"

"I would tear her in pieces and leave the birds to pick her bones."

"But why would you do so?"

"Did you not see her last night stand by the bedside, ready to pull me in pieces? She pricked me with pins, and she brought a black thing to the foot of the bed."

Suddenly Elizabeth begins to gag and choke; she clutches her throat; her eyes roll in pain. Goody Edwards comes to her and forces her mouth wide open with the handle of a table knife. But there is nothing to see.

Elizabeth takes some oil and sugar to ease her pain, and is briefly better; then, more coughing—and a pin seems to fall from her mouth to the bed.

With great excitement the other women converge, jostling one another for a better view. Goody Simons holds the pin to the light; she is sure there was no such thing in the house before now.

Darkness comes; some of the women go off to their own houses. Goody Simons will stay and lie with Elizabeth through the night. Meanwhile, Arthur, his friend William Russell, and a slave named Boose prepare to stand guard near the bed. Elizabeth subsides at last into fitful sleep.

Past midnight the men doze off. Suddenly Arthur stiffens; there is a strange sound at the far side of the bed.

"Hark," he says, rousing the other two, "do ye not hear the noise, as if something were scratching there by Betty?"

William and Boose nod their agreement—slowly, fearfully, uncertainly. The men search the bed and its immediate vicinity.

"See," says Arthur, "how the women sleep, close beside each other, their hands down in the bed. The noise comes not from them."

Mystified, the men sit down again. Later, there is new sound— a rumbling and grating on the inside of the fireplace.

"What noise is that?" asks William of his friend.

"None that I know," says Arthur. "To my hearing it's like a great rock were thrown down on a heap of stones, but found no place to rest."

The appearance of the fireplace is normal. The noise is gone. Deeply frightened, the men await the dawn.

The next day is the Sabbath. Families throughout the village prepare for worship. However, the Gardiners and Arthur Howell will stay behind, for Elizabeth's condition is worsening.

She thrashes wildly in the bed, clutching her head and throat. She is very feverish. Her voice, her cough, her sobs roll together. Occasionally, there is an intelligible word or phrase—"Mother . . . Garlick . . . double-tongued . . . ugly thing . . . pins"—the rest is delirium.

The family keeps vigil by her bedside; neighbors come and go. The pastor arrives to lead prayers for her soul. Gradually Elizabeth quiets, and toward evening death brings an end to her struggles.

There is a short funeral, and burial, the following day. The household of the deceased is rearranged: her husband returns to the home of his own parents; her baby—a girl, also called Elizabeth—is put out to nurse. Otherwise the routine of life in the village continues as before.

The events of the preceding week have, however, left a residue of suspicion and fear. Arthur Howell and his friends are certain that Elizabeth has died by "unnatural means." The pin in her mouth, the noises around her bed, the extreme pains that accompained her sickness: these are convergent signs. The victim, moreover, believed herself bewitched, and reduced her belief to a specific accusation.

In fact, this accusation is for many of the villagers immediately persuasive. Goodwife Garlick (another Elizabeth) is a woman of dubious reputation, personally associated by local gossip with witchcraft and diabolism. Now, following Elizabeth Howell's death, memories of prior trouble quicken with new life. Soon they will be joined to a formal proceeding in court.

Indeed, within the week witnesses are offering sworn depositions on Goody Garlick's "witchcraft." The trail leads back several years into the past.

Goody Bishop and Goody Birdsall recall a time when Goody Simons "had her fits." Bishop went to Garlick for "dockweeds" (an herb believed to have curative properties), but Simons refused to use them: "she said she would have them burnt; she did not know what might follow." Whereupon the sick woman and another friend, Goody Davis, threw the weeds into the fire. Simons remarked at the time that "there was one [who] came into a house

at Lynn in like manner, and there came something in after."
Earlier, in the midst of a particularly sharp fit, "Goody Simons
said that there came a black thing into the house, and somebody
of the house inquired who had a black cat; and somebody said
Goody Garlick." Moreover, "Goody Simons . . . said that she
would not have Goody Garlick nor Goody Edwards come near
her." If the details of these episodes seem somewhat obscure, their
thematic import is transparently clear.[2]

Elizabeth Howell died soon after bearing a child; and infants
also figure in other suspicions of the accused. Goody Edwards
recalls some peculiar circumstances surrounding the death of a
grandchild: "Goody Garlick . . . sent to her [Edwards's] daughter
for a little breast milk, and she had some. Presently [there]after
her daughter's milk went away. . . . and . . . the child sickened
about that time." (Another woman who lived nearby had mentioned a similar episode from her own child-bearing experience—
again associated with a request from Garlick "for breast milk.")[3]

Goody Birdsall testified to a story she had heard from her
friend Goody Davis. The two of them were "dressing flax" together when Davis recalled how "she had dressed her child in
clean linen at the Island, and Goody Garlick came in and said
'how pretty the child doth look.' And so soon as she had spoken,
Goody Garlick said 'the child is not well, for it groaneth.' And
Goody Davis said her heart did rise, and . . . when she took the
child from Goody Garlick . . . she saw death on the face of it.
And her child sickened presently, . . . and lay five days and five
nights, and never opened the eyes, nor cried, till it died."[4]

There were other episodes, more briefly remembered: "Goody
Davis [said] . . . upon some difference between Mr. Gardiner or
some of his family and Goodman Garlick, Goodman Garlick gave
out some threatening speeches and suddenly after Mr. Gardiner
had an ox-leg broke upon Ram Island." In addition, a "neger
child . . . was taken away . . . in a strange manner"; "a man . . .
was dead quickly"; "a sow was fat and lusty, and went to pig, and
pigs and pig-bag came out altogether and so died." (In the latter
instance "they did burn the sow's tail, and presently Goody
Garlick did come in"—a suggestive use of counter-magic.)[5]

These testimonies are gathered over a three-week period, and
duly recorded before three town officers. Meanwhile Elizabeth
Garlick and her husband Joshua ponder their defense. Eventually
they decide to lodge a counter-suit: "Joshua Garlick in the behalf

of his wife have entered an action of defamation upon the case against the wife of Falk Davis."[6]

Goody Davis is, in fact, the single most prolific source of the stories linking Goody Garlick with witchcraft. And her own reputation in the village is not the best.

New depositions are taken in order to establish precisely what Goody Davis has alleged, and when, and to whom. Thomas Talmage recalls a visit to her house when there was "reference in her speech concerning Goody Garlick as if she were a witch." But since it happened "long since, he cannot affirm that she did positively say that she was a witch if there were any in New England, or whether she was . . . persuaded she was a witch if there were any in New England."[7]

Similarly, Richard Stratton "heard Goody Davis say that her child died strangely at the Island, and she thought it was bewitched, and she said she did not know of anyone on the Island that could do it unless it were Goody Garlick."[8]

On the latter story a highly skeptical opinion is attributed to Lion Gardiner. According to his tenant, Gardiner believed "that Goody Davis had taken an Indian child to nurse, and for the lucre of a little wampum had merely starved her own child."[9]

Still another witness remembers discussing Goody Garlick with Goody Davis several years previously; Davis had "said Goody Garlick was naught" and had accused her freely of practicing witchcraft. Subsequently, the same witness asked Davis "how she dared to be so familiar with Goody Garlick as she was, since you have spoken so of her. Her answer was, she brought many things to me . . . and is very kind to me, and . . . she said she were as good please the Devil as anger him."[10]

Goody Davis does seem an erratic, unreliable sort; and if hers were the only accusations on hand, the case against Elizabeth Garlick would likely collapse. However, there is too much other evidence for that—and the people of Easthampton press on.

The file of depositions is completed, and the town decides "by a major[ity] vote of the inhabitants" to present Goodwife Garlick for trial by the highest court in their colony.[11]

There, two months later, she is formally indicted: "that not having the fear of God before thine eyes thou hast entertained familiarity with Satan, the Great enemy of God and mankind, and by his help since the year 1650 hath done works above the course of nature to the loss of lives of several persons (with several other sorceries), and in particular the wife of Arthur Howell . . . for which, according to the laws of God and the established law of this Commonwealth, thou deservest to die."[12]

The jurymen consider the evidence, and return their finding: not guilty. Joshua Garlick gives bond for his wife's "good behavior" in the coming months, and the two of them return home.[13]

Meanwhile the magistrates of the high court prepare a letter to the people of Easthampton.[14] "Gentle and Loving Friends" is the opening salutation. Brief comments follow on various points of official business. And then: "we did take that case which was presented from you into serious consideration; and there hath passed a legal trial thereupon. Whereupon, though there did not appear sufficient evidence to prove her guilty, yet we cannot but well approve and commend the Christian care and prudence of those in authority with you, in searching into the case, according to such just suspicion as appeared."

The letter from the magistrates continues: "Also we think good to certify that it is desired and expected by this court that you should carry it neighborly and peaceably, without just offense to Joshua Garlick and his wife, and that they should do the like to you."

Finally, there is the matter of expenses incident to the case. The magistrates propose a division of these between the defendant's husband, the town of Easthampton, and the court itself.

Eleven weeks have passed since Elizabeth Howell's death, and eight years since the first strong suspicions were formed against Goody Garlick. But now the case is closed—at least in an official sense.

Easthampton, though today a part of New York State, had in its beginnings another geographical orientation. The first settlers arrived in the spring of 1649, occupying land that had recently been purchased on their behalf from the local Montauk Indians.[15] These "founders" came largely from the neighboring town of Southampton, which itself had been started only a few years before. Of the latter event John Winthrop made the following note in his journal: "Diverse of the inhabitants of Lynn [Massachusetts], finding themselves straitened, looked out for a new plantation; and going to Long Island, they agreed with the Lord Sterling's agent there, one Mr. Forrett, for a parcel of the isle near the east end, and agreed with the Indians for their right."[16]

In their early years both Southampton and Easthampton sent representatives across Long Island Sound and upriver to Hartford, to affiliate with the colony of Connecticut. Later, following a series of colonial wars and the cession of "New Netherland" from Dutch to English rule, Long Island was joined to the royal province of New York. The people of the eastern towns objected strenuously—but to no avail. For many years thereafter they continued to identify themselves with their neighbors to the north. In 1687 Thomas Dongan, then governor of New York, complained that "most of the people of [Long] Island . . . are of the same stamp as those of New England." And a local historian, writing near the end of the last century, described early Easthampton as "a fragment of New England."[17]

So indeed it was—hence the justification for including this town, and these events, in the present study. In fact, the case of Elizabeth Garlick offers unusually promising materials for social analysis. Town records have been fully preserved. Land deeds are available in substantial numbers. There are three extant tax-lists dating from the early history of the community. And at least a few personal documents have survived. In addition, genealogists have done extensive work on the families of seventeenth-century Easthampton, much of it available in published form.[18]

From these varied materials an effort is made in the following pages to reconstruct the context within which the Garlick trial went forward. The discussion falls into two parts. The first involves the overall shape of life in Easthampton in the late 1650s—a profile of the village in terms of its geography, economy, demography, governance, and social structure. The second attempts a sorting of the local population in relation to these "structural" elements and to the witchcraft proceeding itself.

Easthampton was, and is, a town of peculiar shape. Embracing the extreme eastern tip of Long Island, it is elongated, irregular, and notably varied in its internal topography. Its length (west to east) is nearly twenty miles; its width (north to south) ranges from about five miles to a few hundred yards. It is bounded on three sides by water. To the south it faces the Atlantic across broad beaches. To the east it throws out a desolate but wildly beautiful promontory of rock and sand (Montauk Point). To the north it opens on Long Island Sound, along a shore heavily indented with salt-water inlets, grassy dunes, and rugged beach-cliffs. To the west it fronts Southampton across its only man-made border. Within these bounds lies a territory of rolling plains and woodland. At some points, especially near the perimeter, there are small creeks and ponds.

Within a scant decade the settlers of Easthampton imposed a pattern on the land that would endure for generations. The village center was established at a point less than a mile from the Atlantic beaches and roughly midway between the western border and the "neck" leading toward Montauk Point. A double line of home-lots fronted the main street, which ran roughly north to south. The lots were long and narrow, in the New England manner, and ranged in size from six to twelve acres.[19] These holdings conferred, in turn, proprietary rights to the other lands of the town. By the late 1650s three large "meadows" and two "plains" had been apportioned among the settlers. Some of these sections sustained two or three "divisions" (with every family receiving its own allotment each time). There were also grants of woodland and some "additions" to the home-lots themselves.[20] The result by 1658 was a local geography both complex and far-flung. The settlers had constructed a good dozen "highways" and "cartways" connecting the various parts of their town. There were two small harbors along the northern shoreline, and a number of coastal "landings" as well. Long lines of wooden fencing served to "bound" and protect each of the major land sections.[21]

Although the village center was located toward the south, the life of the place faced north and west. A road led off to Southampton, some ten miles away. And there was at least occasional commerce, across the waters of Long Island Sound, with the towns of the Connecticut coast. More important, especially in the present context, were the various islands of the Sound: Gardiner's Island, Shelter Island, and (farther east) Block Island. The first of these would eventually become a part of Easthampton; but at mid-century it was the personal fief of Lion Gardiner. Situated barely three miles to the north, Gardiner's Island was a little universe in itself. There were lakes and ponds, woodlands and meadows, cliffs of clay and sandy beaches. There was a substantial house for the proprietor and several smaller ones for his "farmers" (tenants); there was also a blacksmith's shop and (probably) a wind-driven mill. Gardiner's Island was clearly a special place, and an aura of mystery gathered around it from the start. It was well known by the end of the seventeenth century as a pirate hide-out. (At least a part of the famous "treasure" of Captain William Kidd was landed and buried there.) And in the 1650s it was a seedbed of the witchcraft accusations against the unfortunate Goodwife Garlick. There will be more to say about this island later on.[22]

To the place that became Easthampton must be added the people— English and Native American. The latter were Montauks, members of the largest and most powerful tribe in eastern Long Island. Their chief at mid-century was one Wyandance, apparently a prudent and generous man—and certainly a good friend to the newly arrived "settlers." In separate transactions of 1648 and 1661 the Montauks sold their proprietary claims to the land of Easthampton, while retaining the right to live on their ancient site at Montauk Point, to hunt in the adjacent woodlands, and to fish in the waters offshore. Though their numbers were steadily depleted by illness and by warfare with other Indians, they remained an active presence in and around Easthampton well into the eighteenth century. They are mentioned again and again in the records of the town, and it seems safe to assume that they were known on a routine basis to most of the Englishmen there.[23]

The settler population itself can be reconstructed with considerable precision. Using 1658—the year of the Garlick prosecution—as a baseline, the summary figures are as follows: 32 households, comprising 178 persons overall, plus 5 young men (recently arrived and unmarried) whose domestic arrangements cannot now be discovered. The population was divided by sex into 105 males and 78 females; indeed, the males predominated in all age-groups. Well over half of these persons (106) were younger than twenty years old. The adult contingent comprised three roughly equal groups in their twenties, thirties, and forties; only a small number were older than fifty.[24]

Additional conclusions of some interest derive from the study of household *heads*. Fourteen of these (44 percent of the total) had lived previously in Southampton—from where, as noted above, the Easthampton settlement was planned. Twenty (or 63 percent) had lived still earlier in the Massachusetts towns of Lynn and Salem. The English origins of 12 were in county Kent (principally around the town of Maidstone); 10 came from other places; and 10 cannot be traced across the Atlantic. Thus it is possible to chart a current of geographical movement running from Kent in Old England, through Essex County in Massachusetts and Southampton on Long Island, with its terminus in Easthampton itself. But the people involved were not consistently the same. Considering Kent, Essex County, and Southampton as the principal "stops" preceding arrival in Easthampton, only 5 (of 32) householders can be associated with all three. Conversely, only 4 had avoided this route entirely. The vast majority (23) had made one (16) or two (7) of the prior stops. It appears, then, that most Easthampton settlers had shared some prior experiences with at least a few other members of the group. It is possible, even probable, that this sharing had involved personal acquaintance— but there is no way now to be sure.

It is equally probable that the settlers consisted predominantly of farmers. A few can be identified as craftsmen—a blacksmith, a weaver, a carpenter—but the major part were keyed by both experience and inclination to agriculture. Certainly they bent their efforts strongly in that direction once they reached Easthampton—a trend which seems all the more impressive given the character of the setting. Surrounded on three sides by water, and strategically located for inter-colonial commerce, they remained nonetheless people of the land.

The records they have left us bespeak this commitment to agriculture on every page. There are elaborate procedures for "dividing" the meadows and plains, rules for restraining pigs and goats, innumerable orders about fencing, provisions for herdsmen and millers and meatpackers. When the town decided to purchase a new store of ammunition, payments were ordered from all householders in "wheat, butter, or cheese." When a witness in a court case was asked about the date of a controversial business transaction, he testified as follows: "touching the time when this was done, it was to my best rememberance when I went either to mowing or making of hay." When defendants were scheduled for a specific date in court, their cattle might serve as bond: e.g. "To the constable of Easthampton—you are by virtue hereof to attach three cows, three calves, and one two-yearling and a steer of Daniel Howe's Senior in an action of trespass on the case . . . to be tried at the next court holden the first Tuesday in April. . . ." When a trial jury brought in a verdict, this too might directly involve farm products: "The jury finds for the plaintiff, 20 bushels [of] Indian corn and the court charges."[25]

The records supply much incidental information about the field-crops grown in Easthampton. Corn is mentioned most often; there is also reference to rye, wheat, turnips, and peas. Presumably these crops constituted the principal yield of the local "arable." The fields were owned in severalty, and there were no fences to separate individual holdings. Each man was required simply to "set sufficient landmarks to bound" his own acreage. Apparently the proprietors planted the same crop all across a given "division" (following, in this respect, an old tradition of open-field agriculture). Town orders occasionally regulated specific details of planting: e.g. "no man, woman, or child shall plant any Indian corn within 8 feet of any outside fence." Quite likely, there was some joint labor across the "bounds" of the individual plots, though on this point no direct evidence survives. Tools are listed in estate inventories: e.g. "2 broad hoes, one spade . . . 2 iron wedges . . . 2 scythes . . . 3 stubbing hoes . . . one cart and wheels and boxes . . . one draught yoke . . . one plow with irons belonging to the same."[26]

Still more conspicuous in the surviving records is the presence—and importance—of domestic animals. Cows, hogs, sheep, goats, and horses are all there—the first most especially. It appears that virtually every householder owned at least a few of these animals, and some had a good many. The pages in the town book devoted simply to "cattle-marks" are voluminous. An inventory from 1657 includes 2 cows, 3 oxen, 2 yearlings, 1 calf, 4 goats, 7 swine, and 6½ loads of hay. Another inventory made two years later shows 4 oxen, 3 cows, 1 steer, 2 calves, and 6 swine. A tax-list from later still (a generation after the Garlick case) presents a full accounting of farm animals owned by residents of Easthampton. The totals of cows and of sheep run well over a thousand, of swine and of horses about two hundred. (Considered from the standpoint of individual households, the medians are: 13 cows, 12 sheep, 2 pigs, and 2 horses.) As early as 1657 the town meeting took steps "for the preventing of our common . . . being overlaid with cattle." Only milk cows and "oxen . . . for present . . . labor" would be allowed there; the rest of the herd must be grazed elsewhere, at a distance from the village center.[27] Some of the flavor of this activity is captured in a young man's deposition to the local court:

> Stephen Hedges declareth that he being at Georgica akeeping goats and hearing somebody adriving cattle as he supposed, he went to see who it was. And finding there Thomas Burnet adriving cattle and . . . seeing . . . one pied-red heifer which he knew to be Goodman Meacham's and . . . three cows more of his . . . [he] said unto Thomas Burnet, "these cattle are none of yours." Saith Thomas Burnet unto me, "take them away" whereupon Richard Bennett and I did drive those cattle from him. Then there was one more black heifer which was not willing to be driven along by . . . Thomas Burnet . . . but came back from him to the other cattle that I and Richard Bennett had taken from him. And then I knew her to be Goodman Meacham's by her ear mark. And Richard Bennett . . . with Stephen Hedges . . . both declare that these cattle were unwilling to be driven by Thomas Burnet and that he was forced to run from one side to the other to drive them along.[28]

This generally agricultural orientation admitted of one exception, deriving from the abundance near outer Long Island of Atlantic sperm whales. Periodically, as ocean storms passed over the area, whales were washed up on the beaches; and the value of the carcasses was not lost upon the people of Easthampton, land-folk though they were. Almost from the beginning of settlement, provision was made to exploit this opportunity. Dead whales were considered public property: each householder was to "do his part of the work about cutting of them out," and to have his fair share of the results. In addition, a rotation of "lookouts" was established at strategic points on the southern shoreline, so that prompt notice might be given whenever a carcass should appear.[29] (The system may have extended a bit farther if, as some authorities believe, the townspeople occasionally set out in small boats in pursuit of live whales which happened to pass near the shore. But evidence on this point is not conclusive, at least for the early period.)

The collaborative procedures adopted with respect to whales epitomized the whole spirit of town governance. For Easthampton, like its Puritan progenitors to the north, was a "commonwealth" in the literal sense of the term. The activities of individual persons and households were carefully adjusted to the interests of the group. The town supervised, in the first place, the recruitment of its own inhabitants: "whosoever shall take up a lot in town shall live upon it himself, and . . . no man shall sell his allotment or any part thereof unless it be to such as the town shall approve of." (Conversely: "no man shall go forth of the town to work or stay in [any] other town or place without acquainting two of the three [select]men at the least, and have liberty from them.") A host of detailed regulations framed routine aspects of local (and domestic) experience. Felled trees must not be left by the roadways, rams must be "aproned," houses must be fitted out with ladders to protect against fire, bitches in heat must not be turned loose, fences must be kept in good repair—to cite only a few of the more obvious instances.[30]

But there was more to all this than restriction and restraint. "Cutting out" whales brought tangible gain to the whole community, and the same could be said of other group-projects noted in the town records. Was new fencing needed in one of the common fields? The proprietors would "view" and "divide" it together. Was it difficult to cross the swamp between the village center and "the eastern plain"? Then the townspeople together would build a "highway"—the work to begin "the 26 of October next . . . and whosoever shall neglect coming shall pay 1 [shilling] 6 [pence] and do his work beside." Did the town's cattle lack a suitable watering-pond? Then one must be "digged at the spring eastward . . . [on] the next second day . . . and Ralph Dayton and Thomas Baker are to oversee the work and see that men bring good, sufficient tools to work with, and all that have cows are to appear at the beat of the drum." Was the danger from wolves increasing? Then "every man shall go tomorrow, if the drum do beat, to the swamp to see if the wolves can be killed, and he that absents himself shall pay 4 shillings."[31]

Some tasks called for individual performance on a rotating basis. One instance, the whaling lookouts, has already been mentioned—and there were others. The town's "dry herd" must be driven to its feeding-ground each day, "and this to be done by turns . . . and Goodman Osbourne to begin, and he that drives them one day is to warn his next neighbor." The responsibilities of village patrol—"watch" by night, "ward" by day —were shared in a similar way. (Moreover, "if any man neglect to warn his neighbors to ward, he shall ward himself the day following.")[32]

Government itself was a shared responsibility. Not only would all householders "make appearance according to the time appointed" at town meetings; they must, in addition, take an active part. ("Every man shall vote by holding up his hands, either with or against, in all matters upon penalty of paying 6d., the thing being before deliberately debated.") Moreover, there was a legal obligation to accept public office, "being chosen"; any that "shall refuse to serve and not give a sufficient reason" were subject to a stiff scale of fines (depending on the office in question).[33]

The spirit of commonwealth was manifest, too, in various provisions for the sharing of good—and bad—fortune. Thus: "whosoever shall find any wrecked goods by the seaside within our bounds, if it be under the value of 10 shillings, it shall remain to him or her that findeth it; but if the thing so found be worth more than 10 shillings, . . . then the overplus shall remain to the town's use." Conversely, if the town's wolf-traps caused "any hurt . . . to any man by having any cattle destroyed . . . then the loss shall be borne by the town, every man to have his part according to his land." And "whatsoever damage shall be done to our cattle by the Indians shall be borne by the whole town."[34]

But this system, while based on reciprocity and sharing, was hardly egalitarian. Much depended on the leadership of a small group of men whose superior qualifications were consistently recognized. The structure of local governance followed the customary New England pattern. The highest office, that of "townsman" (selectman), was filled by three men annually. In some years this trio was joined by four others, and all seven undertook "the careful and comfortable carrying on of the affairs of this town." Another official of considerable importance was the "recorder" or "secretary." In addition, there were constables (and sometimes an assistant constable), fence-viewers, highway overseers, and a supervisor of whaling lookouts. The local militia was led by one, sometimes two, officers. Finally, there were numerous *ad hoc* committees appointed to deal with particular needs and problems as they arose: division of the town's lands, road construction, negotiation of disputes with neighboring communities, special missions to the General Court at Hartford.[35]

Because Easthampton was so remote from the center of authority, its leaders exercised particularly broad powers. The townsmen doubled as "magistrates," presiding over a variety of judicial actions; they also had the "power to marry." Indeed, the town meeting frequently referred to itself as a "general court," in implicit recognition of its unusual situation of autonomy.[36] Not until the 1670s, when all of Long Island was permanently annexed to New York, would Easthampton begin to feel a counterweight of higher authority. The earlier tie to Connecticut was more nominal than real.

Office-holding at the local level was, then, a matter of real power and responsibility—and as such it was not for every man. During the entire decade of the 1650s only eight persons served in the position of "townsman," and most of these did so several times. (The same pool of leaders regularly supplied the membership of important town committees.) Another eight men served at least once in some lesser office. But the remaining householders in the town—fully half of the total—held no public position of any kind. They were the choosers, not the chosen; it was their lot to confer power on others, but not to exercise it directly as individuals.[37]

The very regularity of these patterns of incumbency implies a hierarchy of social prestige. Easthampton—again, like its sister communities to the north—was stratified by rank and status. Just here lies an important challenge to historical reconstruction. What was the range of social difference among the people of the town? To what extent, and in what ways, did the experience of individual townspeople express their particular status-positions?

The criteria of status are nowhere described in the local records. However, it seems possible to infer them from the larger tradition to which Easthampton initially belonged. "Office," "estate," "dignity of descent," "pious disposition": these were the points most often cited as defining social position in early New England.[38] With the exception of the last, they can be reduced to substantive properties and directly applied to the Easthampton data. Individual householders can then be "scored" and ranked in relation to one another. "Office" is revealed in each case by study of the annual elections as listed in the town records. "Estate" (i.e. wealth) can be measured from land records and tax-lists. "Dignity of descent" refers to pedigree, and can be assessed (in most cases) by careful genealogical checking. (An additional rating can be made, in at least some cases, for the spouse's social position.) Allowance must be made for age and length of residence in Easthampton (since both factors would affect the chances of holding office and obtaining wealth). Finally, special provision is needed for occasional and idiosyncratic circumstances, such as a long criminal record (on the negative side) or a clerygman's vocation (on the positive one).

The numerical mechanics of this "scoring system" are presented else-where (see Note following this chapter, p. 242); the results must be summarized here. The Easthampton population, as of 1658, can be divided into three broad status-groups of roughly equal size. This tri-partite scheme is admittedly somewhat arbitrary—though there are hints of a "break," at both of the dividing-points, in the materials them-selves. The "high" and "low" groups each comprise eleven men; the "middle" has ten. Women are not rated separately; they are assumed to have taken the status of their husbands and/or fathers. Several single men are not included because they had arrived too recently for definitive placement in the social system.

The members of the "high" group lead the rest on each of the chief measures. They—and they alone—filled the important offices. Their economic position was consistently advantageous; their land-grants, in particular, were far above the average.[39] They accounted for most local cases of distinguished family background. Seven of them are regularly called "Mr." in the town records (whereas no single member of the other two groups is so designated).

The persons described here as "low" status stand in marked contrast to the above group. With a single minor exception, no one of them exer-cised any public responsibilities at Easthampton during the decade of the 1650s. By and large, they received the smallest allotments of land and possessed the least personal property. Their backgrounds (where ascertainable) were modest in the extreme. At least a few of them were frequently in court, charged with offenses both civil and criminal.

The "middle" group includes—appropriately and obviously—people who occupied intermediate positions on each of the various indices. Most served once or twice in some local office, but they were not "townsmen," "recorders," leaders of the militia, or members of the most powerful com-mittees. Two of them (brothers) came from a family of lesser gentry; the rest seem to have had quite average origins. Their lands and other property were distinctly in the middle range.

It is worth exploring some further points of comparison among the three groups—points which do not bear directly on social rank. For example, did their different levels of accomplishment (and wealth) chiefly reflect a difference of age? In fact, mean age seems quite similar across the board, and what difference there is runs counter to expecta-tion. As of 1658, the members of the first group ("high") averaged forty-two years old, while the comparable figure for groups II ("middle") and III ("low") were forty and forty-four. But perhaps, instead of age, length of residence in Easthampton was a differentiating factor? Again, the figures do not appear significant. Proceeding from group I downwards, average length of residence was 7.1, 7.0, and 6.2 years respectively.

The matter of geographical background also bears scrutiny in this connection—and here the data are somewhat more suggestive. A majority (seven) of the "high" group had originated in Kent and/or made prior stops in Essex County, Massachusetts, and Southampton, Long Island. The remaining four had missed all of the earlier stops; they were, in fact, the only Easthamptonites who had no prior association with others in the settler population. Evidently, strangers did not join in founding the community unless they brought with them quite special—and visible—social credentials.[40] Conversely, they seem to have been welcomed (invited? induced to come?) when they possessed such credentials; more, they were quickly absorbed into the local elite and given commensurate civic responsibilities.

The low-status group embraced a rather different range of geographical movement. Only two of them are traceable to points of origin in Kent, and only one had stopped at Southampton. And all but one moved to Long Island directly from the Essex County towns of Lynn and Salem. The "middle" group was, in this respect, more randomly distributed than either of the other two. Half of them had been born in Kent, half had stopped in Essex County, and half had moved to Easthampton from the neighboring environs of Southampton. (The halves were not, of course, composed of the same people, though there was a degree of overlap.)

It remains to ask how much, and in what ways, social experience within the town was influenced by considerations of status. Here, admittedly, the evidence is rather thin—a motley assortment of fragments, gleaned from several different directions. But, taken cumulatively, it suggests at least the outline of a consistent pattern.

One set of pertinent materials concerns marriage-making. There is record of fifteen marriages between Easthamptonites during the period 1650–1670. In six cases the principals came from families of the same status-level, while in nine they stood one level apart. Significantly, there were no marriages between persons representing the "high" and the "low" groups (two levels apart).[41]

Court actions provide another sort of index. There were some twenty civil suits tried before the Easthampton magistrates in the 1650s. The principals—plaintiffs and defendants—have been analyzed in terms of their social position, with the following overall result. Half of all the plaintiffs (12 out of 23) were "high" status, while more than 80 percent of the defendants belonged to the "low" group. (The "middle" level was underrepresented in both categories.) The same data can be used to determine status-discrepancy in particular cases (i.e. whether those who came to court as adversaries represented the same, or different, status-levels). In only 4 of 26 instances were the principals of similar rank; and in fully 15 they were two levels apart.[42]

In three of the court cases the record supplies not only a summary of results but depositional evidence as well. Witnesses are identified as "plaintiff's witnesses" or "defendant's witnesses"—a procedure which throws some light on *supportive* relationships. Among the twenty witnesses in these cases, fourteen belonged to the same status-group as the principal for whom they testified. In four instances there was a difference of one status-level, and, in the remaining pair, a two-level difference.[43] To conclude with the legal evidence, then: it appears that adversary contact went disproportionately *across* status-lines, whereas supportive contact remained largely *within* such lines.

There is one further matter of some interest in this connection: the spatial arrangement of the town. The original home-lots, as noted earlier, were laid out from north to south along a single street. Land records afford a (mostly) clear picture of their relative position one to another, and suggest a carefully developed pattern. The upper third of the town was almost exclusively the province of low-status families: eight of the nine northernmost lots can be so identified. By contrast, the center of town belonged to the local elite: on one side four out of five adjacent lots were owned by persons in the "high" group, while across the street the sequence was unbroken—five in five. At the extreme south, property reverted to members of the "low" group (three of five original lots). Middle-status householders were somewhat more randomly distributed, although they tended to appear in zones that divided the other two groups (particularly at center-south).[44]

In fact, the street broadened at its center, enclosing a small green on which the first meetinghouse and the burial ground were situated. Directly opposite, on the east side, were the homes of two men whose rank among all the townspeople was quite beyond doubt: the Reverend Thomas James and Captain Lion Gardiner. James was the first pastor of Easthampton; his service would last for nearly half a century. Gardiner was the largest landowner on all of Long Island, a leader in both civic and military affairs, a friend and correspondent of Winthrops, Dudleys, Willises, and their like.[45] To the west of the green lived others only slightly less eminent, including Mr. Thomas Baker, Mr. Robert Bond, and Mr. John Mulford, the three men most often chosen as townsmen. The symbolic importance of all this was hard to miss: the local universe had a single center, spatially and socially. Conversely, the margins were also unified—in both senses.[46]

Grouped as they largely were by residential location, persons of similar status were also grouped in the performance of civic responsibilities. In part, this derived from the spatial factor: some duties were expressly assigned to specific sections of the town. Thus in 1658 "it was ordered that . . . the doing of the general fences . . . shall be done by the two divisions . . . the south end for the south side, and the north end for the north side." At first, the "cutting out of whales" was managed on pre- cisely the same basis; then the two parts were reorganized as three (south, middle, and north). The latter arrangement followed status-lines almost as clearly as geographical ones: the north "company" would henceforth consist of persons of low status, and the middle of men ranked "high." (The south, to be sure, had a more mixed character.)[47]

Other tasks were portioned out as need arose—and, again, with im- plicit (or explicit?) consideration of rank. When plans were made for building the meetinghouse, five men were appointed "to get [make] six loads of thatch within these [next] fourteen days." Three other men would then "fetch [transport] the thatch . . . upon 2 days warning." The former group was uniformly low-status. The latter consisted of two men ranked "high" and one from the "middle." Meanwhile the towns- men for that year would "set out the place for the meetinghouse"; and they, as usual, were "high."[48] For obvious reasons civic performance had its greatest impact on persons near the top of the social hierarchy. Time after time, a relatively few men found themselves working together in important civic projects. They could hardly avoid identifying with one another, or with the status which conferred such responsibilities.

These pages have reviewed a diverse and detailed body of materials on early Easthampton, and two broad themes need final underscoring. All things considered, the life of the town was *corporate* to a remarkable degree. The citizens were indeed a body, each one an integrated part of the larger whole. Experience came to them in, and by, and through the group; literally and figuratively, they lived in each other's presence. Their houses lay huddled together along a single street. Their field-lots were scattered in every direction—two acres here, four acres there, but always among a bevy of neighbors. They accepted common tasks, and they shared both good and bad fortune. They worked together, wor- shipped together, governed together. One can still catch the echo of this densely collective existence in the measured phrases of the town-meeting records: "It is ordered by joint consent of the town. . . ." "The assembly coming together, they chose and appointed. . . ." "It is agreed by us the inhabitants of this town. . . ." "It is the mind of our town. . . ."[49]

But the parts of the body were never equal or interchangeable. Virtually from the start the townspeople sorted themselves by rank. However much they shared, their behavior traced important social boundaries. More likely than not, people of the same rank would intermarry, would live in close proximity, would undertake the same forms of civic responsibility, and would support one another in situations of conflict. Each of these probabilities was reversed when referred to persons of *differing* status; moreover, such persons were far more likely to become adversaries, at least within the framework of the legal system.

Thus were two principles blended in the settlement of Easthampton: corporatism and hierarchy. This was, of course, the very epitome of "the New England way."

Such was the community in which Elizabeth Garlick was first suspected, then formally charged, with the practice of witchcraft. It remains to identify as fully as possible the principals in this proceeding, beginning with the defendant herself.

Goody Garlick was, in the first place, a wife, a mother, a woman of roughly middle age. Her husband is variously mentioned in the records as either "Joshua" or "Joseph." Her children were only two: a son, Joshua, Jr., and a daughter named Remember. They seem, at the time of their mother's trial, to have been not less than twenty years old and not more than thirty. They were as yet unmarried, and probably were living at home. Elizabeth's own age is especially hard to establish but a range from (not younger than) forty-five to (not older than) fifty-five seems plausible.[50]

There are intriguing, though somewhat indefinite, clues to her background and origins. Some years earlier a Boston tailor named William Blanchard had died, leaving small bequests to his "sister Garlick's children." Blanchard was the son of an early immigrant to New England who, in turn, is thought to have come from Normandy of Huguenot parentage. (The name may once have been "Blanchet.") If this was indeed the family of Elizabeth [Blanchard?] Garlick, then she may have been conspicuous on ethnic grounds alone.[51]

There is, however, no other sign of distinctiveness in her familial background. Her (putative) father was evidently a humble sort who had died in 1637; her mother lived on for another twenty-five years, mainly as a resident of Marblehead. Her husband was an ordinary "yeoman" whose first recorded appearance was at Lynn, Massachusetts, in 1639. In that year the Essex County Court had "Joseph Garlick" arrested on a charge of drunkenness (among other "misdemeanors"). Subsequently an indictment for debt was added, and the upshot was an order that Garlick do personal service for one of his creditors over a twelve-month term. A few months later he was again "presented," in a case of slander; but the court eventually discharged him. His associates in these various misadventures were servants like himself—another hint of his humble rank.[52]

There is a twelve-year gap between these court cases and the next recorded reference to Goodman Garlick. Did he remain in Essex County for some while longer? We simply cannot be sure. In 1652 his name finally reappears, in two separate letters from Lion Gardiner to John Winthrop, Jr. "If you have any corn," wrote Gardiner in the first instance, "I desire you to fill my bags, and send [them] by Joseph Garlick." And again: "Whereas you formerly spoke to me to get some shells, I have sent you now by Goodman Garlick 1200, and also 32 shillings in good wampum." Gardiner was writing from his island home, and Winthrop was across the Sound at Saybrook. The letters suggest that Joseph Garlick belonged at this time to the little retinue of "farmers" and "servants" directly in Gardiner's employ.[53]

Indeed the witchcraft documents themselves confirm the Garlicks' presence on Gardiner's Island, probably by 1650 and quite possibly still earlier. But it is also clear that they had left the island by 1653 to take up residence in Easthampton itself. In July of that year the name of Goodman Garlick was included among the recipients of a newly alloted Easthampton meadow—and it recurs quite regularly in the records of the town thereafter.[54]

The year 1653 seems to have divided Garlick's experience in other ways as well. The earlier references make him out a servant to others; but henceforth he was an independent householder and town proprietor. His landholdings were accumulated over a period of many years, in part from regular town grants and in part by purchase or exchange. Eventually he would own some fifteen different plots, comprising a total of nearly a hundred acres. This was about average for long-time residents of Easthampton. Garlick also owned cattle (for which he registered a "cattle mark"), horses, swine, and sheep—again, it seems, in moderate numbers. The earliest extant rate-list (1653) places him in the lowest tax classification; other lists, made two and three decades later, show him roughly in the middle. (In 1675 his taxable estate ranked 25 among a total of 57; in 1683 he came 35 out of 71.)[55]

Once (in 1679) he joined a small "company" of Easthamptonites in a local whaling venture; otherwise his business dealings consisted of occasional sales of land and animals. His son was apparently a miller, and his grandson (another namesake) a weaver; but there is no evidence that Joshua himself was anything more than a simple farmer. For a year or so in the 1650s he had a manservant—one Daniel Fairfield, who was noted in town records as a sexual offender. In 1664 the Garlicks took into their household the son of another Easthampton yeoman "for the term of sixteen years . . . to do for him . . . as for his own." Later still they raised one of their grandsons.[56]

Most of the references to Joshua Garlick in the records of Easthampton involve land allotments, cattle marks, and the like. In 1654, however, he and his wife were cited in separate court actions for having "uttered scandalous speeches" against the wife of one of the town's leading citizens. On another occasion in the same year Joshua Garlick was embroiled in controversy with Captain Gardiner, but the matter was settled by mutual agreement. Garlick never appears as a local office-holder, even on the lowest level, though he was of prime age for such responsibilities during the town's founding years. His only recorded performance of some public duty dates from the year 1689, when the town acknowledged a debt to him of four shillings for "driving rams." Since Garlick was then well into his eighties, this is at least a testament to his sturdy constitution.[57]

Indeed, life and health long maintained were distinctive achievements in both Joshua and Elizabeth Garlick: "reputation says that one lived to be 105 and the other 110." These estimates, reported in a local "account book" some while after the fact, are probably exaggerated by about ten years. The town records noted Joshua's death as follows: "March 7, 1700: Goodman Garlick [deceased], about 100 years old." Elizabeth's passing is not mentioned.[58]

If the Garlicks were people of humble rank and limited accomplishment, so, too, were most of those who came forward as witnesses to Elizabeth's witchcraft in the trial of 1659. But this group deserves full scrutiny on its own terms.

The prosecution witnesses—we might as well call them "accusers"—were nine in number. All but one were currently resident at Easthampton. The information on their geographical origins is too scattered to be useful; however, at least six had stopped previously in Essex

County, Massachusetts, and at least three had lived for a time on Gardiner's Island. Six were women: all married, all with children, and mostly of middle age. (Mary Gardiner, at fifty-seven, was the eldest of this group; the youngest was about thirty.) Three men also enlisted as accusers—each of them relatively young, two of them as yet unmarried.

The position of these accusers in the local status hierarchy is of particular interest. Six of them belonged to the third (and lowest) of the status-groups previously identified, as did the Garlicks themselves. A seventh—the lone witness from outside Easthampton—was of similar rank in his own community. The remaining pair, however, represented the *opposite* end of the social spectrum. This juxtaposition of "high" and "low" appears to have considerable interpretive significance (more fully explained below).

Among the low-status accusers two were especially persistent in their charges against Elizabeth Garlick. And, perhaps not coincidentally, these same two had led especially problematic lives during (and before?) their time at Easthampton. Goody Davis was the object of the counter-suit—for defamation—lodged by the Garlicks as the witchcraft prosecution went forward. Her husband, Falk Davis, had been an early associate of Lion Gardiner, and had lived for some years on Gardiner's Island. He had also lived, in the early 1640s, at Southampton, and in 1651 he was granted a home-lot and other lands in Easthampton. His receipts in these early divisions of town property were substantial—very much on a par with the allotments of men of "high" standing. His marital connections also imply some elevation of rank. Yet he was never a town office-holder at any level; and in 1654 he was involved, along with one of his sons, in a particularly disgraceful criminal proceeding. (The charge was "masturbation," and Davis was punished with both the pillory and a public whipping.) In the 1660s he and his family were found at three different Long Island locations (Southampton, Brookhaven, and Jamaica). By this time his economic position was also reduced; a tax-list from Brookhaven shows Davis, his five sons, and one son-in-law with properties all below the local average.[59] Considered overall, then, his career followed an erratic—essentially downward—course.

Another leading accuser in the witchcraft case was Goodwife Ann Edwards. Her husband, William, was a cooper who had arrived in Easthampton from Lynn, Massachusetts, in 1650. Like Falk Davis he had received above average land allotments from the town; unlike Davis he had also performed some civic responsibilities (constable in 1654, fence-viewer in 1659). But Edwards was evidently a contentious sort—

judging from his record as a litigant at court—and his wife was more so still. As early as 1643, at Lynn, Goody Edwards was convicted of striking and "scoffing" at one of her neighbors. (The bill that "presented" her to the court added this apparently gratuitous comment: "she is conceived to be a very ignorant, selfish, and imperious woman.") In 1652 she was charged with contempt of the court at Easthampton ("desiring the [court's] warrant, that she may burn it"); found guilty, she was either to pay £3 or "have her tongue in a cleft stick." On another occasion she resisted arrest by a local constable, saying "she would . . . kill whosoever should lay hold of her," and "kicked a man [the constable's assistant] and broke his shin." Her local reputation was fashioned accordingly. When a neighbor called her "a base lying woman," her husband filed suit for slander; but most of the witnesses in the case sought to sustain the neighbor's opinion. It seems, finally, that Goody Edwards was herself an occasional object of witchcraft suspicion. According to testimony given at the Garlick trial, one local woman troubled with fits some years earlier had said "that she would not have Goody Garlick nor Goody Edwards come near her."[60]

The victim on that previous occasion was Goodwife Simons, another of the deponents in the 1659 trial. She and her husband, William, were among the most lowly of all Easthampton residents. Apart from an occasional misdemeanor—for example, defamation of Lion Gardiner by Goody Simons, "provoking speeches to the three men in authority" by William—they do not appear in the records in any public context.[61] The same was true of two other witnesses against Garlick: Goody Birdsall and Goody Bishop. Both were wives of ordinary yeoman, of limited property and no evident public distinction.[62]

Two of the male accusers seem to have been particular friends of Arthur and Elizabeth Howell. Samuel Parsons was visiting with Elizabeth on the afternoon when her "affliction" began. Parsons was a bachelor in his late twenties and the owner of a small home-lot at the north end of town. William Russell was a resident of Southampton (where, presumably, he had come to know Arthur). Like Parsons he was young, unmarried, and apparently undistinguished.[63]

From the original list of nine accusers there now remain but two: Arthur Howell and Mrs. Mary Gardiner. To this pair should perhaps be added Elizabeth Howell herself, though she did not live to testify personally against Goody Garlick in court. Elizabeth, of course, was Mary (and Lion) Gardiner's daughter; as a result her social position was quite beyond doubt. Her father was the one man in the present account whose name and fame extended well beyond local bounds.

Indeed, his achievements had spanned the ocean. His origins in England are not known, but as a young man he had gone to Holland to fight in the army of the Prince of Orange against the might of imperial Spain. He spent at least ten years in the Dutch wars, becoming by his own description an "engineer and master of works of fortification." He also married a Dutchwoman. (It is curious that both the witch in this case and her most prominent victim appear to have had one non-English parent.) In 1635 Gardiner emigrated to America, hired by the Connecticut Company of London to supervise the building of a fort at Saybrook. He completed his assignment within two years, and once again tasted war, this time as a leader of the New England forces against the Pequot and Narragansett Indians. In 1639 he obtained the island which would later take his name, and went there with his family and assorted retainers. Fourteen years later he moved into Easthampton; he continued, however, to own and manage his island estate. He died in 1664, but not before setting down the high points of his extraordinary life in a pithy memoir preserved ever since by his descendents.[64]

If Elizabeth Gardiner's social standing was beyond question, so also was Arthur Howell's; in effect, their marriage had joined the first families of two communities. Arthur was the eldest son of Edward Howell of Southampton. Edward, in turn, was heir to a substantial manor in Buckinghamshire in Old England; however, his Puritan sympathies had induced him to join the early migration to New England. He had settled first at Lynn (where his land allotment was a full five hundred acres), and then had led in the founding of Southampton. His property and his manifold public services identify him as a man of the greatest local importance. Most of his sons—though, curiously, not Arthur himself—would later follow in his tracks, holding property and office to a highly conspicuous degree.[65]

From the accusers of Goodwife Garlick, attention moves naturally to other individuals and categories. Six additional people participated either in the trial itself or in the counter-suit against Goody Davis. But their testimony was neutral, or even favorable, from Garlick's standpoint. Four were men, two were women. Three must be classified as high-status, one as "middle," two as "low."

There was also a large pool of Easthamptonites who played no direct role whatsoever in the witchcraft trial. Among these nonparticipants there was clearly disproportionate representation from the "middle" and "high" rank-groups; 9 of 10 in the "middle" group, 7 of 11 in the "high." Conversely, only 2 of 11 people in the "low" group remained wholly outside the proceedings.

Finally, there were Goodwife Garlick's "victims." The roster, briefly summarized, included five persons who had died under suspicious circumstances: a married woman (Elizabeth Howell), an unidentified man, a "neger child," and two infants. In addition, another woman of the town (Goody Simons) had experienced "fits"; an ox had suffered a broken leg; and a litter of piglets had died very strangely. These were the events to which the indictment referred in charging Goody Garlick with "works above the course of nature, to the loss of lives of several persons (with several other sorceries)." They made an imposing list.

The materials canvassed in the preceding pages yield four general conclusions of some sociological import. (1) The prosecution of Goodwife Garlick was an intensely local affair. With two exceptions (and those readily understandable) the participants were all firmly settled residents of Easthampton. They were neighbors; they were trading partners; they were colleagues in various forms of civic enterprise. Together they had shared in the dense and many-sided life of the community. (2) The participants were predominantly married women of childbearing or child-rearing age. (3) Much of the harm attributed to Goodwife Garlick's "sorceries" involved the very young. Two babies still at the breast, another child, a woman who had just given birth (and who suckled her child even as her fits came on), a litter of piglets: such were the leading victims. (4) Most of the accusers were persons of lowly rank —as was the accused herself. There were, however, a few conspicuous exceptions: two accusers and one victim were members by blood or marriage of the town's most eminent family.

These conclusions suggest, in turn, a plot-line for the entire proceeding. At last we can make out elements of sequence and structure in the events which led up to the trial of 1658.

The sequence begins—so far as we can tell—on Gardiner's Island in about the year 1650. The island has a resident population of perhaps half a dozen families: the proprietor, his "farmers," their respective spouses and children. The farmers are modest folk indeed. Most of them have entered Gardiner's employ from irregular careers in agricultural labor or personal service; now, presumably, they are hoping to better themselves.

Life under these circumstances is necessarily confining. Contact beyond the island is difficult for all except the proprietor; experience within the group is correspondingly intense. The women, no less than the men, share with each other the work, the leisure, the lore and gossip which give shape to their lives. But one of them—the wife of Joshua Garlick—stands out. She is different from the others in ways both obvious (her Huguenot extraction) and indefinable. Gradually, difference acquires a sinister connotation. Increasingly, rumor declares that Goody Garlick is in league with the Devil. The others continue to deal with her—they could hardly do otherwise—but when accidents occur, when children or animals grow strangely ill, they suspect their neighbor's *maleficium*.

Inevitably, these suspicions reach the big house where the proprietor lives with his own family. Lion Gardiner remains skeptical, or at least indifferent; but his children are young, interested, and impressionable. David Gardiner (age fourteen), Mary (twelve), and Elizabeth (nine) are often in touch with— and sometimes in the care of—the women of the island. They know Goody Garlick well, they sense her strangeness, they absorb the gossip about her witchcraft.

A few years later the scene shifts. Lion Gardiner moves his household across the bay to the village of Easthampton. Several of his farmers also resettle there, including Joshua Garlick. Goody Garlick's reputation follows her, and soon the people of Easthampton are fully acquainted with the stories of her "witchcraft." However, they react in varying ways. The center of concern is a gossip-group of women who inhabit the north end of the village; the "witch" herself lives among them. The group includes several former residents of Gardiner's Island, though there are also new recruits. The stories have not changed significantly. Goody Garlick is thought to be especially envious of— and active against—young children. (Perhaps she is herself infertile. She has, after all, only two children, and these are now almost full-grown. She and her husband have already hired a servant—a notoriously bad sort at that—to fill out their household.)

But this gossip does not by itself generate organized public action. The substance is commonplace enough; similar stories circulate all the time through dozens of New England communities. Moreover, the people involved are without prestige or influence. The opinions of women like Goody Davis, Goody Edwards, and Goody Simons carry little weight with the men who manage the public life of the town.

Meanwhile the children of Lion Gardiner are growing up. In

1656 Elizabeth turns fifteen, and already she has a suitor. Presently she is betrothed to Arthur Howell, son and heir of the leading man in the next village. They marry in the autumn of 1657. Soon Elizabeth is pregnant, and in the last months of 1658 she gives birth to a daughter.

She is extremely young, by the standards of her time, for the responsibilities of marriage and parenthood. And, following her *accouchement*, she grows anxious, then ill. Somehow the idea of witchcraft suggests itself—and with witchcraft the figure of Goody Garlick. The gossip she heard as a child on Gardiner's Island has stayed with her ever since. Moreover, some recent encounters with the Garlicks have left her feeling both angry and fearful.

When Elizabeth dies, Goody Garlick's witchcraft becomes a crisis demanding response; for now the matter has touched the town's most eminent family. Lion Gardiner remains doubtful, but his wife and son-in-law are ready to prosecute. Thus are the suspicions, the spite, the petty resentments of many years' standing hitched at last to the power-center of the community.

The case will go speedily to court. And the defendant will barely escape with her life.

NOTE

*Social Stratification
in Seventeenth-Century Easthampton*

The line of interpretation advanced in Chapter 7 rests on assessments of the social rank of participants in the proceedings against Elizabeth Garlick. Some readers may wish to have a full description of the method used in making such assessements (especially since the same method has been drawn into other parts of the research for this volume).

It was assumed, first of all, that rank in communities like Easthampton could only be a *relative* measure (i.e. one individual's position in relation to others)—hence the need to study an entire local population. It was further assumed that adult men served as the leading carriers of social rank, and that women derived their own rank (first) from fathers and (later) from husbands. With these assumptions in place, an effort was begun to gauge the social position of every household head in Easthampton, at approximately the time of the Garlick trial (1658). A numerical "scoring system" was created, with appropriate categories and uniform rules and guidelines. The details follow.

Category I: Public Service: Each individual head was scored for his record (if any) of local office-holding. Points were given for each office held (normally, for a one-year term); for example,

3 points {
  town representative to colony authorities, other towns, etc.
  townsman (selectman)
}

2 points {
  town secretary
  member, town committee on land distribution
  assistant townsman
}

1 point {
  constable
  fence-viewer
  highway overseer
  militia officer
  member, other town committee(s)
}

Category II: Personal Background: Each individual head was scored for distinction (or lack thereof) in birth and background; the range was from $+5$ to -5 points. (For example, the son of a "gentleman" or known community leader was given 5 points; conversely, a man of "base" birth would lose 5 points from his total.)

Category III: Marital Connections: Marriage to a woman of distinguished (or base) background was scored on a similar basis (+5 to −5).

Category IV: Property-holding: Economic position was measured from the earliest extant tax-list for the town (1653)—which, in turn, was based on land allotments. (The land allotments were themselves made by reference to rank: the higher the rank, the more the land.) One point was scored for every acre of land taxed. The range was from 13 to 28 acres (and points). In a few individual cases, the figures on the original list were slightly modified to reflect other information in the land records; and several additions were made, for individuals who arrived in Easthampton after 1653.

Further adjustments: Some contingent circumstances required special consideration. (1) A downward adjustment was made to deal with the effects of age and length of residence in Easthampton. (Presumably, older men, and those who were longtime residents, had a greater chance than others to obtain the perquisites of rank—and thus to gain points in the scoring system.) The scores of men over the age of fifty were reduced by 5 points—and those of men between the ages of forty and fifty, by 3 points. Similarly, a 5-point reduction was made for residents of (at least) 7 years' standing, and a 3-point reduction for 4 to 6 year residents. (2) In a few cases, a special increment or decrement was included to account for clearly idiosyncratic circumstances. (For example: the town minister was given an "extra" 10 points, while the score of a man frequently charged with criminal offenses was reduced by 3.)

Finally, the points for each head were summed, and the heads arranged in order of their scores. The resultant list, or "ladder," was divided into three parts of virtually equal size, which stand as the rank-groups used in the chapter-discussion. (See Table 1.) The largest part of the material used in this process of scoring comes from the *Records of the Town of Easthampton, Long Island, Suffolk County, N.Y.* (Sag Harbor, N.Y., 1887–92), 5 vols., *passim.* However, useful additional information has been gleaned from a host of other works in local history and genealogy.

The ladder does not include a few very recent arrivals in Easthampton—young and unmarried men—for whom the available data were too scanty to permit a scoring. (These men did not, in any case, participate in the witch trial.)

No claim of validity is made for the specific order of individuals on the ladder. For example: there is little doubt that Thomas Baker, Lion Gardiner, and John Hand belong in the "high" rank-group; but their position in relation to each other is open to question. (Indeed it seems likely that Gardiner, not Baker, ranked highest of all in the opinions of their fellow-villagers.) Inevitably, social rank includes important but intangible elements which no

Table 1.   Easthampton rank-groups

Group I: High			Group II: Middle		
	Thomas Baker	58 pts.		Charles Barnes	20 pts.
(A)(N)	Lion Gardiner	48		Jeremiah Conkling	20
(N)	John Hand	42		John Stratton	19
	Thomas James	37		Thom. Osbourne, Jr.	19
	John Mulford	36		Thomas Thomson	16
	Thomas Chatfield	34		Jeremiah Meacham	13
	Ralph Dayton	34		William Mulford	13
	Robert Bond	32		Thom. Osbourne, Sr.	12
(A)	Arthur Howell	28		William Barnes	12
	Benjamin Price	26	(N)	Richard Stratton	12
(N)	Thomas Talmage	24			

Group III: Low

(N)	Jeremiah Vaile	10 pts.
(A)	Nathaniel Bishop	10
(A)	Falk Davis	9
(A)	Samuel Parsons	8
	William Fithian	8
	William Hedges	8
(A)	William Edwards	5
(N)	Richard Brooks	5
	Joshua Garlick	2
(A)	Nathan Birdsall	2
(A)	William Simons	2

Note: The symbol (A) designates a household containing one or more accusers of Elizabeth Garlick. The symbol (N) designates a household containing one or more participants in her trial whose testimony was either neutral or favorable to her side.

"scoring system" can fully capture. Moreover, the extant information is much less complete for some individuals than for others—hence some further openings to misrepresentation. But as a *general picture* of local stratification the ladder seems real enough—and useful for social analysis. The high degree of intercorrelation, in the scores obtained for *different* categories, is especially persuasive in this regard. And simple "impressionism"—that is, intuitive reading of the large qualitative record of town life—is additionally supportive.

As noted in the text of this chapter, the experience of the town and of its individual residents does seem to have been strongly influenced by its stratification system. This influence was evident, for example, in patterns of marriage-making and court litigation—as witness the following three tables:

Table 2. Marriages in early Easthampton

		Husband's Rank-Group		
		I	II	III
Wife's	I	3	4	0
Rank-	II	3	1	2
Group	III	0	0	2

Table 3. Adversarial Actions at Court, in Early Easthampton

		Plaintiff's Rank-Group		
		I	II	III
Defendant's	I	0	0	2
Rank-	II	1	1	1
Group	III	13	5	3

Table 4. Supportive Actions at Court, in Early Easthampton

		Principal's Rank-Group		
		I	II	III
Witness's	I	8	0	1
Rank-	II	1	0	3
Group	III	1	0	6

8

"Hard Thoughts and Jealousies"

The story of witchcraft in early New England spotlights very sharply the power of local gossip. Behind the court proceedings—the formal "presentments," the gathering of depositions, the trials themselves—one invariably finds a thick trail of *talk*. Of course, the ultimate source for all this lay in the minds and hearts of the people involved, but the outlet was words—for the most part, spoken words. The fear of supernatural evil sustained a vocabulary both rich and compelling.

This vocabulary was used in many different settings, some of them quite mundane and limited. Thomas Cooper, while arguing with Goodwife Phillips, called her "a blare-eyed witch."[1] Goodwife Holman was presented at court for making "opprobrious speeches" against Elizabeth Hooper; the speeches included such terms as "spiteful old witch" and "base old whore."[2] Mathew Farrington was charged with saying of Thomas Wheeler that "he was the Devil's packhorse, to do the Devil's drudgery."[3] Francis Urselton, in the midst of a lengthy quarrel, "railed on Goodwife Clark, saying she was a devilish woman, and the devil was in her and would have her."[4] Sarah Allen, presented for "keeping company" with her sweetheart on the Sabbath, "wished that the devil had the heart blood of all that spoke against it."[5] John Fosket came to blows with his neighbors, the Mousalls; to Goodwife Mousall he said "that she was a liar . . . and when she was going to the magistrate . . . the devil was at her left hand"—and to her husband "that all that he had was the devil's, for he stood by his bedside and caused his members to rise."[6]

John Pinder was notorious for bitter threats and curses; one witness deposed that "I have heard him use the devil in his mouth often times."[7]

To use the Devil in one's mouth was clearly wrong; but the circumstances were not always those of conflict, and the motive was sometimes other than insult. Occasionally such talk had the look of simple bravado. Thus John Long, a "boy" from Cambridge, was brought to court in the summer of 1668 on various counts of "untoward carriage." For example, "Seeing a mare drinking a long time near Benjamin Switzer's house, [he] swore 'by God, I think the devil is in the mare.'" And "upon the hill, going to play, [he said] I will camp the ball to the devil." And "being asked . . . whether he would go home, he replied, 'what should I go home for, the devil is threshing barley in the cellar.'"[8] Words like these made a near approach to blasphemy; in other instances they crossed the line. Goodwife Hannah Hackleton pleaded guilty to a charge of "uttering direct, express, presumptuous, high-handed blasphemy" and confessed "that she had said there was as much mercy in the devil as in God."[9] In still other cases the Devil's name was invoked as a way of gaining influence in some personal or domestic situation. Thus a servant to the Rev. John Hale of Beverly was accused of threatening another "maid" as follows: "She said she had a book in which she could read and call the devil to kill Sarah." (She also "said if Sarah would do what she bade her, the devil should not catch her.")[10]

"Opprobrious speeches" were serious enough, and blasphemy was (in theory at least) a capital crime. But full-fledged slander made an important category of offenses all of its own. Like the inhabitants of small, premodern communities almost everywhere, the New Englanders were vitally concerned with matters of reputation. Whenever their good name was threatened, they were quick to seek legal recourse; actions for slander and defamation appear all through their court records. And among the many imaginable forms of slander those that touched on witchcraft seemed especially bad.

However, the slander cases involving witchcraft were themselves quite various. Some of them seem, on balance, the direct extension of personal controversy. Thus, in the county court at Hartford in 1678, Edward Messenger filed suit against Edward Bartlett "for defamation . . . for saying that the said Messenger's wife was an old witch or whore or words to the same purpose"; at the same court Messenger also sued Bartlett for debt "to the value of thirty-four shillings."[11] And at Kittery, Maine, in 1660, a peculiar case unfolded around a preacher named Thorp. It seems that the Rev. Thorp had been boarding in the house of a certain Jonas Bailey, when his fondness for drink aroused the indignation of his landlady. Goodwife Bailey "gravely told him his way was contrary to the Gospel of Christ, and desired him to reform his life or leave her house." Eventually "he departed from the house, . . . turned her enemy," and sought to have her "questioned for a witch"—whereupon the Baileys filed suit for slander.[12] According to subsequent testimony, Thorp had frequently declared that Goody Bailey "was a witch . . . a rotten, damned witch as ever held bread . . . a stinking, rotten witch," and the like.[13]

Katherine Messenger and Goodwife Bailey may have been marked as suspect by more than a lone antagonist, but if so the evidence has not survived. There were other slander cases which involved small cliques of neighbors, and at least a few where suspicions ran very wide. The latter produced, by way of trial proceedings, material quite similar to that which supported the prosecution of witchcraft itself. The defendant might wish to "justify" the purported slander by showing (in the words of one court) "that [the plaintiff's] carriage doth . . . render her suspicious of witchcraft."[14] The plaintiff, on the other hand, sought to present the same material in another light. It was her aim to play down the elements of menace and mystery, and to play *up* the gossip which had prompted her suit in the first place.

Either way, the depositional record ran a familiar gamut from odd behavior and sayings, through the petty details of personal dispute, to unexplained (and seemingly occult) forms of mischance. When the widow Marshfield complained against one of her Springfield neighbors "for reporting her to be suspected for a witch," witnesses came forward with the particulars. The defendant's child had died, and also her cow —"and I am persuaded, said she, that they were bewitched." The same person had lost a pound of wool—"and she said she could not tell except the witch had witched it away." Moreover, "she said . . . that there were diverse, strong lights seen of late in the meadow that were never seen before the widow Marshfield came to town . . . and that it was publicly known that the devil followed her house in Windsor [where the widow had earlier resided]."[15]

Stories of this kind often circulated on a second- or third-hand basis. The nub of an early slander case in Essex County, Massachusetts, was as follows: "John Caldwell testifies that being in Goodman Bridges' shop, Goodman [Marshall] being present, he heard him say that a woman and her daughter, gathering berries, saw four women . . . [sitting] upon the ground, but when they came near the women vanished."[16] In another case suit was brought not by the supposed "witch" herself, but by the man to whom such supposition had been attributed: "Thomas Crawley, plaintiff, against Robert Hall, defendant, in an action of slander for saying that he called Robert Sayward's wife witch."[17] Along with the gossip went a certain amount of prying and spying: for example, "Mistress Godman charged Hannah Lamberton . . . [with saying] she lay for somewhat to suck her . . . Hannah said she and her sister Elizabeth went up into the garret above her room, and looked down, and said 'look how she lies, she lies as if somebody was sucking her.' "[18]

A few particular unfortunates were obliged to rebut such charges again and again. Thus Jane James of Marblehead filed three suits for slander over a period of almost twenty years. The first was against Peter Pitford, who had declared "that Goodwife James was a witch and that he saw her in a boat at sea in the likeness of a cat." The second identified Goodwife Gatchell as the source of a similar rumor, "that she [Goody James] was seen going . . . on the water to Boston when she was at the same time in her yard at home." The third charged Richard Rowland with saying that the spectre of Goody James "came in at a hole in the window in Rowland's house and took him by the throat and almost choked him as he lay in his bed."[19]

In many such cases, the plaintiff had motives beyond the desire to clear her name. She knew that local sentiment was building against her, and she feared that she might herself become the target of criminal proceedings. An action for slander was, then, a tactic of forestalling, which allowed the supposed witch to confront her accusers before they were ready to bring their own complaint to court. However, the tactic was not without risk. If the case for the defense seemed credible, the court's interest might abruptly reverse itself—with the plaintiff moving over to the prisoner's dock.[20] The decision to file for slander must, therefore, have been a difficult one. The strategic advantage of seizing the initiative was balanced by the danger of bringing into full view problems that might otherwise resolve themselves.

The immediate outcome of these actions was usually favorable to the plaintiff: the court would (with rare exceptions) sustain the charge of slander, and require from the defendant some suitable form of redress.[21] But the long-range effects were mixed. Local suspicion could not be dissipated by legal *fiat*, and at least a few successful plaintiffs were subsequently tried for witchcraft anyway. A notable case in point was one Mary Parsons of Northampton, Massachusetts. By a relatively early age Goody Parsons had acquired the reputation of witch among certain of her neighbors and peers; and try as she might, over many years, she could never entirely shake it. Indeed, it hung on long enough to touch the lives even of her children and grandchildren. But this is a story which merits retelling—and study—in all of its considerable detail.

On the docket of the Middlesex County Court, for its session of October 7, 1656, is found the following entry: "Joseph Parsons, plaintiff, against Sarah, the wife of James Bridgman, defendant, in an action of the case for slandering her [Parsons' wife] in her name. This action, by consent of both parties, was referred to the judgement of the Honored Bench of Magistrates." A separate document records the magistrates' finding in favor of the plaintiff and their order that the defendant make "public acknowledgement" of the wrong she had done. The acknowledgment was to be a dual performance—once in the town of Northampton, and again at Springfield. Failure to fulfill either part of this requirement would result in a fine of £10.[22]

These few lines do not even hint at the substantive nature of the case. The penalty invoked was moderate, and quite standard for slander suits. The "consent of both parties" on the procedural question implies a spirit of accommodation—even, perhaps, a shared wish to have done with the matter. Yet the file papers from the same court convey a different impression.[23] Numerous and detailed as they are, they show very clearly that Parsons vs. Bridgman was no routine case. The issue at hand was witchcraft, or rather the supposition of witchcraft. The proceedings antecedent to the court hearing were long in duration and complex in structure. The level of feeling, on both sides, was high.

The depositions included in the file papers come to 33 overall. They comprise the testimony of 24 different witnesses. (Some deposed more than once.) Thirteen additional persons are mentioned at one point or another in the papers, yielding a grand total of 37 who had some connection with the case. The 37, in turn, represented 22 different households. Fifteen of the households belonged to the town of Northampton (whose total complement of households at the time was only 32), the remaining 7 to Springfield. These figures suggest a very considerable degree of local interest and involvement.

Taken individually, the depositions seem puzzling—or even, at some points, contradictory. But when sorted in reference to time and place (that is, when and where given) they acquire an unmistakable meaning. In effect, they group themselves into four major sets, corresponding to distinct phases in the slander case itself. They reveal, moreover, the taut lines of a power struggle with effects reaching well beyond the interests of the two principals.

The first set of testimonies was recorded at Northampton on or about the 20th of June, with two of the local selectmen officially in charge. For example:

> Robert Bartlett testifieth that George Langdon told him the last winter that Goody Bridgman and Goody Branch were speaking about Mary Parsons concerning her being a witch. And the said George told to the said Robert that my [Langdon's] wife being there said she could not think so—which the said Goody Bridgman seemed to be distasted with. As also [according to Langdon] they had hard thoughts of the wife of the said Robert [Bartlett] because she was intimate with the said Mary Parsons.[24]

The other depositions in this early group enlarged on the gossip theme. The same Hannah Langdon mentioned in Bartlett's statement testified that "Sarah Bridgman . . . told her that her boy when his knee was sore cried out of the wife of Joseph Parsons." Bridgman had also alleged widespread "jealousies that the wife of Joseph Parsons was not right." For a time Langdon herself had entertained suspicions of Mary Parsons, but recently "it hath pleased God to help her over them, . . . and [she] is sorry she should have [had] hard thoughts of her upon no better grounds." Bridgman had also talked with Margaret Bliss, the mother of Mary Parsons, saying "she had heard there was some discontent between the blind man at Springfield and her daughter . . . and then the child of the blind man had a sounding [?] fit." Hannah Broughton remembered a time when Bridgman had quoted Mr. Pynchon as saying that "if that were true which he had heard, Goody Parsons could not be right." And so on. These depositions converged on the issue of what Goody Bridgman had *said*. As such, they constituted an opening salvo in the effort to prove her a slanderer. At the same time they implied a spirit of antagonism toward Mary Parsons which ran wider than any single person.[25]

The second major group of papers in the case carries a date several weeks later. They were taken before a different official, and probably in a different place (Springfield). And they expressed a different viewpoint, as the recorder noted at the top of the opening page: "Testimonies Taken on Behalf of Sarah, the wife of James Bridgman, the 11th day of August, 1656." There are six separate depositions here, and five more which can probably (though not certainly) be associated with the same occasion.

The Bridgmans themselves supplied lengthy testimony on the events which had caused them to suspect Goody Parsons. The previous summer their eleven-year-old son had suffered a bizarre injury while tending their cows: "In a swamp there came something and gave him a great blow on the head . . . and going a little further he . . . stumbled . . . and put his knee out of joint." Subsequently, the knee was "set," but it would not heal properly—and "he was in grievous torture about a month." Then the boy discovered the cause of his sufferings: "He cried out [that] Goody Parsons would pull off his knee, [saying] 'there she sits on the shelf.' . . . I and my husband labored to quiet him, but could hardly hold him in bed for he was very fierce. We told him there was nobody. . . . 'Yea,' says he, 'there she is; do you not see her? There she runs away and a black mouse follows her.' And this he said many times and with great violence . . . and he was like to die in our apprehension."

At about the same time the Bridgmans had also lost an infant son:

> I [Sarah] being brought to bed, about three days after as I was sitting up, having the child in my lap, there was something that gave a great blow on the door. And that very instant, as I apprehended, my child changed. And I thought with myself and told my girl that I was afraid my child would die. . . . Presently . . . I looking towards the door, through a hole . . . I saw . . . two women pass by the door, with white clothes on their heads; then I concluded my child would die indeed. And I sent my girl out to see who they were, but she could see nobody, and this made me think there is wickedness in the place.[26]

The Bridgmans were joined by other witnesses giving parallel forms of testimony. A couple named Hannum had also suffered grievously—so they thought—at the hands of Goody Parsons. Honor Hannum had "this past winter . . . spun for the said Mary Parsons," and her yarn had invariably proved defective. Parsons had complained, and Hannum had "spun some more . . . to recompense this defect"—but with the same result. This seemed perplexing since Hannum had successfully performed similar work for many others. In the meantime the Hannums rebuffed a request from Goody Parsons to hire one of their daughters as a maidservant. ("Considering what rumors went about of her, . . . I told my daughter she should not go thither to dwell if she might have ten pounds a year.") A few days thereafter the same daughter, "though formerly healthy," became "very sickly"; she had remained so, "and very unhelpful to me," through much of the current summer.[27]

William Hannum had his own part in these dealings. He had argued one evening with Goody Parsons about his wife's spinning—"and the next morning one cow lay in my yard, ready to die, as I thought." (In fact, the cow died some days later.) On another occasion he was chided by Mary Parsons for "abusing her brother's oxen." Hannum rejected the charge, "and she went away in anger"—and shortly thereafter one of his own oxen was fatally bitten by a rattlesnake. Yet a third time he had incurred her anger, by "jesting" with neighbors at Mary's expense. And "she dealt with me about it, showing her offense"; a day later his sow died suddenly. "These things," Hannum concluded, "do something run in my mind, [so] that I cannot have my mind from this woman, that if she be not right this way she may be a cause of these things, though I desire to look at the overarching hand of God in all."[28]

Several other Northampton residents offered testimony designed to show Goodwife Parsons not as a witch but as a liar. ("Goodwife Wright saith that . . . Goody Parsons . . . told her that Goodwife Holton said she would make her candles for her." But "Goodwife Holton was spoken to about this business . . . and denied it.") There were also some revealing allegations about pressure exerted by supporters of Goody Parsons to block the testimony against her. Goodman Elmore, a local official responsible for "swearing some witnesses" in the case, "urged them . . . and [told] them what they should say . . . and did jostle the meaning of the words and writ down what he thought good." Moreover, he "said . . . that he stood for them and would stand for them, meaning Goodwife Parsons."[29]

Finally, two witnesses from Springfield opened up a new line of testimony, bearing on Goody Parsons's *past.* She was herself a former resident of Springfield, having arrived there at least as early as 1646. Even then she was a controversial figure. There were reports, for example, that she had walked on water "and was not wet." Her own husband had gossiped about her extraordinary intuitive powers. ("He said, . . . 'whenever I hide the key of my door, my wife will find it.' ") And "old Mr. Pynchon"—the founder and leading magistrate at Springfield—was said to have "wondered" when these stories were brought to his attention.[30]

The depositions of August 11 were designed ostensibly to defend Sarah Bridgman; but in fact they went far toward indicting Mary Parsons. They carried the threat, implicit in most such slander suits, of reversing the positions of the principals. As such they were bound to call forth a vigorous response from the plaintiff and her supporters. And within a scant few days that response had entered the official record.

Eleven new depositions comprised the third major set, taken at Northampton from August 15 to 18. Several were intended as direct rebuttal to the evidence presented for the other side. Was there any strong ground for suspecting that Goody Bridgman's baby had died from witchcraft? Three women who had attended the birth were skeptical: "The child . . . was sick as soon as it was born," and the mother herself "thought it had taken cold," and suffered from "looseness . . . at the first." (So much, then, for her story of a child born healthy and subsequently "changed" by a sudden "clap on the door" as two mysterious figures passed by outside.) Was there anything strange about the death of William Hannum's ox? Several other men "were present when the ox . . . was stung with the rattlesnake, and they did conceive nothing but what might come to pass in an ordinary way." The same was true for Hannum's cow: a neighbor who had skinned it "found a great quantity of water in the belly of the cow." (Moreover, upon observing this, "William Hannum called to his wife and told her they need not fear, but the cow died of the water." Two witnesses recalled the Hannums saying quite specifically "that they had nothing against Mary Parsons.")[31]

The Hannums themselves now joined in the plaintiff's case. Apparently reversing their stance of the week before, they charged James Bridgman with pressuring them to testify against Mary Parsons. Still another witness described Sarah Bridgman's insistent "jealousies and suspicion." ("She said . . . she could not be satisfied unless . . . Mary was searched by women three times.") And two more recalled how she had turned aside a request that her son's injured knee be subjected to impartial examination.[32]

There was one final group of depositions, taken at Springfield in late September. Three of them, clearly by Bridgman supporters, were designed to discredit Mary Parsons by deepening the shadows in her Springfield past. In 1652 Springfield had been the site of a separate prosecution for witchcraft. The children of the local minister, the Rev. George Moxon, had succumbed to fits, as had "others"—including Mary Parsons. An eyewitness remembered that "as Mr. Moxon's children acted, so did Mary Parsons—just all one." Indeed, she and they were together "carried out of the meeting, it being the Sabbath day." But there were some aspects of Parsons's fits that raised special doubts and suspicions. It was then that "she went over the water and . . . was not wet." She was, moreover, a grown woman, and this by itself set her experience apart from that of the afflicted children.[33]

The relation of Mary Parsons and her husband, during their Springfield years, formed yet another subject of testimony. One man, "being at Joseph Parsons' house, making barrels," had observed a quarrel between the two of them:

He said to his wife that she was led by an evil spirit. Thereupon she said he was the cause of it by locking her into the cellar and leaving her. . . . She said also that when her husband locked her into the cellar, the cellar was full of spirits, and she threw the bedstaff at them and the bedclothes and her pillow, and yet they would not be gone. And from this time, she told me, it was that she fell ill into her fits some few days after. She . . . said . . . the spirits appeared to her like poppets, as she was washing her clothes at the brook, and then she fell into her fits.[34]

But the author of this last deposition (John Mathews) soon had second thoughts about it. In fact, within days he offered another statement, disavowing any "jealousy from himself of Mary Parsons," and declaring that his first testimony "was [given] upon the earnest importunity of James Bridgman and his brother." At the same time magistrate John Pynchon repudiated a comment attributed to him months earlier by Sarah Bridgman herself (see above, p. 251): "Being requested by Goodwife Parsons to declare whether I said . . . [she] could not be right, I accordingly declare that to my remembrance I never said any such word, neither do I remember any reports that I have heard which have given me occasion to speak any such words of Goodwife Parsons."[35]

With this the file papers in Parsons vs. Bridgman were complete. (At least no others have survived.) The date of the final depositions was September 30. One week later the magistrates of Middlesex County rendered their decision, as previously noted. The gathering of evidence had taken an entire summer, but this was, after all, hardly a random process. Each of the first three sets of testimony expressed a unified purpose; only the last was of a mixed character. One set followed another, thrust and counter-thrust, as each side sought to gain the upper hand. In a sense both Bridgman and Parsons were on trial—the former officially so, as a slanderer, the latter by implication, as a witch.

The records afford at least a glimpse of intense maneuvering behind the scenes—of pressures and pleadings that certainly shaped the development of the case and may well have decided its outcome. Goodman Elmore, a Northampton selectman, had openly declared his allegiance to the plaintiff and had tried to alter the testimonies accordingly. (Or so one witness alleged.) The names of two Springfield magistrates (the Pynchons, father and son) were invoked on the side of the defendant; but Mary Parsons herself "requested" John Pynchon to repudiate this connection—and he obliged. John Mathews, apparently regretting his first line of testimony, declared that it was given "upon the earnest importunity" of the defendant's husband and brother. William and

Honor Hannum, while executing a similar change of position, also mentioned pressures from James Bridgman.

The shifting allegiance of the witnesses bears particular consideration. Of the 24 persons who deposed in the case, 11 were associated (initially) with the plaintiff's side and 13 with that of the defendant. However, in 5 instances (2 and 3 respectively) this reflected a family link, making a shift most unlikely. Of the remaining 19 witnesses, 9 for the plaintiff and 10 for the defendant, 5 seem to have changed sides. And all of these 5 moved in the same direction, from defendant to plaintiff; thus a 9–10 split was converted to 14–5. (There was, in addition, one witness for the plaintiff who admitted having had "hard thoughts" of her during a period *before* the trial.)[36]

Geography was also a factor here. With minor exceptions the depositions for the plaintiff were taken entirely in Northampton itself, and those for the defendant at Springfield. Moreover, five of the (ten) defendant's witnesses were residents of Springfield at the time of the trial, and of the remaining five (i.e. those who lived at Northampton) four subsequently switched to the plaintiff. As a result the final alignment of witnesses expressed a marked Springfield vs. Northampton division.

From all this the plaintiff derived an increasingly strong position. Her support was solidly based in Northampton, the home of both principals and the official center of the proceedings. The local leadership seems to have sided with her—and even to have obstructed the efforts of her opponent. By contrast, the defendant's case was made entirely at Springfield, where half of her witnesses were officially resident. As events went forward, all but one of her Northampton supporters went over to the other side. The movement of these witnesses served, in turn, to forecast the ultimate result. Of course, we cannot discover just how and why the county magistrates decided as they did, and it may be that the plaintiff's evidence seemed compelling on its face. But the evidence itself reflected a summer-long contest for strategic advantage. And by the autumn of the year that contest had clearly tipped in favor of Mary Parsons.

From the outcome of Parsons vs. Bridgman, and the struggle which immediately preceded that outcome, inquiry moves backward to the matter of origins. What was there about Mary Parsons to invite "hard thoughts" in the first place? Why might the gossip which connected her with witchcraft seem plausible to at least some of her local peers? And what can be said about the peers themselves? Why, in particular, did Sarah Bridgman assume a leading role here?

The evidence from the slander trial supplies at least part of the answer to such questions. Mary Parsons had experienced "fits" in a witchcraft case at Springfield some five years earlier, and this was unusual in persons fully adult. Moreover, some of her "actings" in this condition had elicited suspicion rather than sympathy: perhaps she was less a victim than a perpetrator of magic. Her own husband had lent credence to these suspicions, in conversations with their Springfield neighbors. Indeed, Mary herself (according to one informant) had spoken of confronting "spirits" on various occasions.

There were other things to be said against her as well. She and her husband were frequently and notoriously at odds with one another. During part of their time at Springfield he had sought to confine her to their house. (Otherwise, he said, she "would go out in the night and . . . when she went out a woman went out with her and came in with her.") When this tactic failed, he locked her in the basement. (It was then, she claimed later on, that she had first encountered her "spirits.") There was at least one quite public episode—again at Springfield—which amounted to a family free-for-all. Joseph was "beating one of his little children, for losing its shoe," when Mary came running "to save it, because she had beaten it before as she said." Whereupon Joseph "thrust her away," and the two of them continued to struggle until he "had in a sort beaten [her]."[37] It was also alleged that Mary Parsons paid little heed to truth. (Several of the trial depositions were designed to catch her in a "made lie.") And her manner could be harsh, or openly accusatory. ("Mary Parsons came and challenged me about the yarn I spun for her." . . . "Mary Parsons came to me and did chide with me for abusing her brother's oxen.")[38]

These events, this reputation, invited unfriendly gossip. But would they by themselves have prompted the very special antagonism—the hatred, the envy, the fear—that was usually implicit in an accusation of witchcraft? Just here there are other factors to consider, involving the entire shape of Mary Parsons's career.

She was born in England in about the year 1628.[39] Her parents were Thomas and Margaret Bliss; she was, probably, their first child. However, Margaret seems to have been Thomas's second wife, and there were at least three older children (presumably from her father's previous marriage). There would, in addition, be seven younger ones (after Mary) born to her mother.[40]

The particulars of this family's arrival in New England are not known —though tradition has preserved a date of 1635.[41] Evidently they lived first at Mount Wollaston (then a part of Boston, now belonging to

Braintree).[42] Quite soon, however, they removed to Hartford, where in 1640 their lands were officially recorded.[43] Hartford would remain their home until the death of Thomas Bliss roughly a decade later, but they made little impression on the public life of the place. Thomas held no public office (though belonging at the time of his arrival to the age-group most liable to civic responsibilities). He had not been among the first comers, and hence held no regular rights of proprietorship.[44] He pleaded but one minor court case, and was himself presented once only—"for not training."[45] The amount of his lands was slightly below the local median.[46] The inventory of his estate, taken in February 1651, depicts the household of (at most) an average yeoman. (For example: "his house and a lot belonging to it . . . meadow and upland . . . 2 cows and 2 year-old calves . . . one bedstead . . . a trundle bed . . . a flock bed . . . one loom . . . 2 axes and 4 old hoes . . . 2 brass pots, 1 iron pot, 2 kettles, 1 skillet . . . 2 old bibles.") The total value of his property was £86, another modest figure.[47] The estate passed to the widow "for her use and [for] the education of her children." In making this arrangement the court followed Thomas's own wish, expressed "as he lay on his death-bed." (His daughter Mary was recorded as being "ready to testify" to the same.)[48]

The New England experience of this man appears, in sum, undistinguished. However, his earlier life may well have been very different. Such at least is the burden of a remarkable story of the Bliss family during the years just prior to their departure from Old England. Unfortunately, the story comes to us without firm documentation: it stands therefore as a provisional *addendum* to the main threads of the current chapter.[49]

Thomas Bliss, the emigrant, was by this account the son and name-sake of a well-to-do, locally influential citizen in the village of Belstone, county Devon. In the opening decades of the seventeenth century the father had become a determined advocate of the Puritan cause and had participated with like-minded neighbors in acts of protest against religious "oppression." On one particular occasion he and three of his sons (George, Jonathan, and Thomas, Jr.) had accompanied a party, led by the local member of parliament, in riding up to London to engage both king and archbishop in direct confrontation. The upshot was their imprisonment and the levying of heavy fines (said to have been in excess of £1000) in lieu of their freedom. Payment of the fines required the virtual liquidation of the family estate, and even then there was not enough money to free all four Blisses. Thus one of the sons—Jonathan

—remained in jail some while longer, was severely whipped in the public square at Exeter, and never thereafter recovered his health.

Impoverished and broken in his own health, Thomas, Sr., subsequently returned to Belstone and lived in the household of his daughter, Lady Elizabeth Calcliffe. She was the wife of a knighted "gentleman" who had remained a regular communicant of the Anglican church (thus avoiding persecution). As the crisis of the realm deepened, the father summoned his sons, divided among them what patrimony he still retained, and advised them to remove to New England. Thomas, Jr., and George left soon thereafter; Jonathan was too ill to join them, but sent at least one of his sons in their care. During the years that followed, Lady Calcliffe sought to temper the privations of her relatives across the sea by sending them periodic shipments of clothing and food. And it was in her personal correspondence—regrettably, long since lost—that this part of the Bliss family history was remembered for succeeding generations.

Assuming the reality of all (or most) of this, we must try to imagine its effect on Mary [Bliss] Parsons. She would have been only a small child when the fortunes of her family hit their lowest point—father and grandfather in prison, the rest brought near to poverty. She was perhaps eight years old when her parents took her off to the New World. She was eleven or twelve when they decided on still another move, to the rude little settlement at Hartford. There for a time life stabilized, and Mary grew to womanhood as an average member of an ordinary New England community. But in 1646 she married Joseph Parsons and went to live in Springfield. And this was another turning-point. Henceforth her life would be increasingly set apart from the average.

Joseph Parsons had been born in about the year 1619; like his bride he seems to have come originally from Devonshire.[50] His first appearance in any extant records dates from the summer of 1636, when he witnessed a deed transferring Indian lands near Springfield to William Pynchon and two other men.[51] Joseph was unusually young to have an official part in such an important transaction, and this circumstance (among others) has caused genealogists to infer familial ties between the Parsonses and the Pynchons. There is no sure evidence to prove such ties, but they remain a real—and intriguing—possibility.[52] William Pynchon, and later his son John, were truly preeminent figures in the early history of the Connecticut Valley. And Joseph Parsons was for many years their business associate, their friend, and perhaps their kin.

The earliest references to Joseph in the Pynchon family account books

include credits for various small services: "a day's work in hay-time,"
[more] "work in hay-time," and "bringing up my goods" (transport from
one location to another).[53] So perhaps he began as a simple farmer, who
(like many of his local peers) was at least occasionally in the employ
of others. However, there are hints—on the debit side of the Pynchon
ledger—of a second, more distinctive, orientation. When Joseph purchased rugs, iron, and wampum, it may have been for the purpose of
entering the Indian trade.[54]

In any case, by the time of his marriage to Mary Bliss, Joseph was
already launched on the road to prosperity. A tax-list showed him in the
top third of local property-holders, while still two or three years away
from his thirtieth birthday.[55] He began to hold local offices: highway
overseer in 1645 and 1646, fence-viewer in 1650, and then selectman
in 1651 and 1652.[56] In 1654 Joseph moved his family to Northampton
(while retaining, however, most of his holdings at Springfield). He assumed at once a position of leadership in the new settlement. He served
on numerous town committees, including the one which arranged the
building of the first meeting-house. He was selectman three years running (1657–59) and again at intervals thereafter. (In 1656, wishing to
concentrate all his energies on his personal affairs, he asked to be "freed
from any office . . . for this year" and offered to pay the town 20 shillings
for such exemption; his terms were accepted and the request granted.)
He became "clerk" of the local "trainband" and later "cornet" (lieutenant and standard-bearer) of the Hampshire County militia.[57]

But it was as a merchant that Joseph made his greatest mark. In about
1654 he obtained from the Pynchons a share in their chartered monopoly
of the Connecticut Valley fur trade. This was without doubt a highly
profitable activity for him—just how profitable can be seen, once again,
in the pages of the Pynchon account books. In 1655 Joseph purchased
from the Pynchons some £25 worth of "trading cloth"; by the 1660s his
line for that item had multiplied by four or five times. Meanwhile he
was bringing out, and selling to the Pynchons, furs in commensurate
quantities (e.g. "331 lbs [and] ½ of winter beaver . . . 19 lb. of beaver
. . . 5 otters . . . and raccoon skins . . . 2 moose skins").[58] One incidental
result of the trade was a growing familiarity with Indian ways and
customs. Often thereafter the settlers would call on Joseph to take the
lead in official dealings with the native population.[59]

From furs he moved on to other forms of commerce. He seems to
have maintained a retail store in Northampton, supplied at least in part
by the Pynchons' own business in Springfield. He sold and shipped

large quantities of wheat, peas, butter, and cheese; and the range of his enterprise extended through all the Connecticut River towns, and eastward to Boston. He was part owner of the first gristmill in Northampton, and sole owner of its first sawmill. He was licensed, beginning in 1661, to "keep an ordinary" and also to "sell wines or strong liquors, as need shall require." He bought and sold lands through the whole length of the valley, becoming, among other things, the largest property-holder in the town of Northfield—even though he never lived there. In 1675 he bought a warehouse and ships' wharf in Boston, and gained the privileges of a merchant of that city. When he died in 1683 he owned land and other properties in six different towns, and his total worth was well over £2000. Moreover, he had by that time provided several of his older children with handsome "settlements" of their own.[60]

Like other successful merchants of this era, Joseph Parsons was often in court—usually as a plaintiff, but at least occasionally as a defendant. Civil actions filed by or against him—for debt, for "unlawful distraint," for "nonperformance of covenant," and the like—are scattered through the records of several different courts. At least a few of the charges involving Joseph were more serious. In 1664, for example, he was presented and "admonished" in court for his "lascivious carriage to some women of Northampton." A few months later he was fined £5 for his "high contempt of authority" in resisting a constable's efforts to attach some of his property in another case. (Witnesses reported some "scuffling in the business, whereby blood was drawn between them." Joseph publicly acknowledged his offence, and the court abated part of his fine.) A year later Joseph was fined again "for contemptuous behavior toward the Northampton commissioners and toward the selectmen, and for disorderly carriage when the company were about the choice of military officers." These cases suggest something of his character and personal style. Defined by his own achievements as a man of authority, Joseph did not easily brook the authority of others. Energetic, shrewd, resourceful as he evidently was, he displayed a rough edge in dealings with others. He was, on all these grounds, a figure to be reckoned with.[61]

Measured from start to finish, the career of Joseph Parsons was a success story more commensurate with the milieu of the nineteenth than of the seventeenth century. His estate was the largest one probated before 1700 in all of Hampshire County. Yet there were always some reminders of his modest beginnings. For example, no public record ever identifies him with the honorific "Mr." And his two brothers, also migrants to New England, remained firmly in the ranks of average folk.

Thomas Parsons was a long-time resident of Windsor, Connecticut; while Benjamin—like Joseph himself—lived first at Springfield and then at Northampton. Both were farmers, both achieved positions of respect but not preeminence in their local communities, both held property in the middle range.[62]

Of course, Mary Parsons shared the fruits of her husband's extraordinary career. Its precise effect on her cannot be discovered from any evidence now extant; however, local tradition has remembered her as being "possessed of great beauty and talents, but . . . not very amiable. . . . exclusive in the choice of her associates, and . . . of haughty manners."[63] This tradition may well reflect the antagonism of her detractors as much as the reality of her own disposition. But there are, as noted, some hints of a parallel sort in the trial testimonies themselves. And when, years later, there were renewed charges against her, Mary responded with remarkable vigor and directness. (Of this, more below.)

She was not, moreover, the only strong woman in the family: her mother, the widow Margaret Bliss, also deserves notice here. When Thomas Bliss died (in 1650), Margaret was left with the sole care of seven children still in their minority. She promptly sold her home at Hartford and moved upriver to Springfield, where daughter Mary and a grown stepson, Nathaniel, were already resident. Margaret's widowhood would last for another three decades. Her resources at the outset were relatively meagre, but she managed—*more* than managed—with what she had. She made particularly effective use of the courts. She filed, and won, lawsuits on a variety of counts and charges: for example, "for detaining her cow wrongfully"; "for damage done in her Indian corn by [the defendant's] swine"; "for [defects in] ditching and quick-setting a hedge in her meadow"; "[for] debt to the value of 35 shillings"; and (this one against the town of Springfield) "for the annoyance she receives by the passage of the water to the mill."[64] She served as guardian to at least two of her grandsons (and sometimes went into court to protect *their* interests). Her estate, when probated in 1684, came to £278—an increase of more than three-fold over her husband's inventory.[65] It made an unusual record by any standards—and, for a widow, perhaps a unique one.

It seems possible, moreover, that Margaret Bliss and Mary [Bliss] Parsons were specially identified with one another. When Thomas had died intestate, it was Mary who could testify to his deathbed wish that the widow receive his estate. When the widow herself died, Mary received a personal bequest from her of "wearing clothes, bedding, and household stuff." And when Mary was first accused of practicing witchcraft, her mother undertook a direct role of support. (She may indeed have sought out the principal accuser, Sarah Bridgman, in a spirit of face-to-face challenge.)[66]

There is one additional record to consider from Mary Parsons's life—the record of her own motherhood. Here, too, her achievements were noteworthy. She bore the first of her children within a year of her marriage, and the last some twenty-five years later when she was already a grandmother. She had two sets of twins, no one of whom survived infancy, but nine of her remaining ten children reached adulthood. And so the totals read: 12 pregnancies, 14 babies delivered (and named), 9 children raised to maturity; two and one-half decades of child-bearing, and four and one-half of child-rearing. No other woman in seventeenth-century Northampton could match these figures overall.[67]

The experience of Mary Parsons bears comparison with that of one other Northamptonite, in particular. Sarah Bridgman was the sole object of Mary's slander suit—and clearly was at the center of the suspicions, the rumors, the gossip which had associated Mary with witchcraft. The personal histories of these two women exhibit both parallels and contrasts, which reflect suggestively on their confrontation of 1655–56.

Sarah [Lyman] Bridgman was born in the parish of High Ongar, county Essex; the record of her baptism, on February 8, 1620, is still preserved there. She was the sixth of nine children of Richard and Sarah [Osborne] Lyman. (However, three of her older siblings had died young, before she was born.)[68] In 1629 her father sold his properties in Essex, evidently having decided to emigrate from England.[69] The family did not actually leave until the summer of 1631, when they joined a group of "about sixty" passengers on the ship Lyon bound from London to Massachusetts Bay. This was, from the New England standpoint, a very important sailing. The ship carried Mrs. Margaret Winthrop, John Winthrop, Jr. (wife and son of the Massachusetts governor), and the Rev. John Eliot (subsequently famed as the "Apostle to the Indians")—among other notables. Its arrival in Boston occasioned salutes, celebrations, and general thanksgiving.[70] Like many of their fellow-passengers the Lymans settled first in Roxbury, where Eliot was soon installed as pastor. In 1635 Richard was recorded a freeman of the Bay Colony. However, just a few weeks later he joined one of the earliest settlement parties to Connecticut. And in 1636 he was listed as a proprietor of the town of Hartford.[71]

The social position of the Lymans seems, at least initially, to have been rather high. Genealogists have attempted to give them an elaborate aristocratic pedigree; and while much of the evidence is too thin to be convincing, one impressive link—to Sir John Leman, knight, merchant, and in 1616 Lord Mayor of London—has been established by extant correspondence.[72] Tradition asserts that Richard Lyman came to New England "with considerable estate, keeping two servants." The terms of his Hartford proprietorship provide more solid evidence on this point. His share in the "undivided lands" was fixed at thirty acres, which placed him in the top quarter of all local householders. (Thomas Bliss, by contrast, was down for six acres, a bottom-quarter figure.)[73]

Yet his several changes of place and circumstance took a toll on Richard Lyman. The Rev. Eliot composed a record of early members of the Roxbury church, which included the following:

> Richard Lyman . . . came to New England in the 9th month, 1631. He brought children: Phyllis, Richard, Sarah, ——, John. He was an ancient Christian, but weak; yet after some time of trial and quickening he joined the church. When the great removal was made to Connecticut he also went, and underwent much affliction; for going toward winter, his cattle were lost in driving, and some of them never found again. And the winter being cold, and [the settlers] ill-provided, he was sick and melancholy. Yet after[ward] he had some revivings through God's mercy and died in the year 1640.[74]

Elsewhere in Eliot's list are found the names of Lyman's wife and his eldest daughter Phyllis. There was special adversity in the life of the daughter as well: "God wrought upon her heart in this land [and] she grew deaf—which disease increasing, was a great affliction to her."[75]

As Eliot noted, Richard Lyman died in 1640. His wife died about a year later—initiating for their children a period of domestic reorganization. Phyllis had already left the Lyman household in order to marry another Hartford yeoman. Before her death the widow Lyman had prepared a "note" directing that Richard, Jr. (at twenty-three, the eldest surviving son) "perform her husband's will" and take charge of his two younger brothers, John (age eighteen) and Robert (twelve).[76] Precisely how these events affected Sarah (now about twenty-one) is not clear, but her marriage to James Bridgman occurred in about 1642. Bridgman first appears in the Hartford records as the purchaser, in 1640 or 1641, of a small home-lot on the south side of town. Significantly, the land of Richard Lyman was only one lot away.[77]

The Bridgmans did not long remain at Hartford. The year 1644 found them resettled in Springfield; there they would live for an even decade. James Bridgman filled several local offices at Springfield: fence-viewer, highway overseer, constable, "presenter." Twice he was punished for small "breaches of town orders."[78] His work was divided between farming and the occasional practice of carpentry.[79] A tax-list of 1646 displays him as an average sort of property-holder—as does the record of his lands.[80]

In 1654 the Bridgmans moved once again, to join the fledgling community at Northampton. The outward manifestations of their life seem to have continued much as before: minor offices for James (constable, fence-viewer, sealer of weights and measures), scattered appearances in court (twice for debt, once for "contempt of authority" in obstructing the county marshals), a middle position in the local wealth hierarchy.[81] Meanwhile there was the usual brood of children, though with a quotient of early mortality that was higher than usual for New England families. The records of Springfield and Northampton mention eight Bridgman births, spanning the years 1643 to 1658. But only four of these children (three girls and one boy) survived infancy; the others (three boys and one girl) died at ages of two weeks, four weeks, six weeks, and nine months, respectively. Sarah Bridgman herself died at the age of about forty-seven, in 1668. A few years later James was freed from training obligations with the local militia, because of "weakness of body," and death claimed him in 1676. When his estate was probated, the inventory yielded a total value of £114.[82]

There are other threads to follows in the story of this family. In marrying James Bridgman and moving to Springfield, Sarah had separated herself from her three Lyman brothers (as well as her older sister). The brothers remained in Connecticut, leaving only modest traces in the public record, until 1655; then they removed, evidently together, to Northampton. Two of them, Richard and John, were married by this time—and well married, too. Their wives had come from substantial Connecticut families; their fathers-in-law were recognized local leaders. Richard and John Lyman would themselves assume leadership roles in Northampton. Both became selectmen, and were frequently chosen to important town committees. Both became wealthy, at least by village standards. Richard died somewhat prematurely in 1662, leaving an estate worth some £500. John lived on until 1690, when his wealth amounted to more than £900.[83]

However, the life of Robert Lyman, the youngest of the three brothers, made a strikingly different story. As a young man, Robert was frequently in court: for debt (several times), for living alone (contrary to law), for breaking into the "common pound" at Hartford. On one occasion he was indicted, convicted, and heavily fined for "gross, lascivious carriage and misdemeanor": he had tried to lure another man's wife into an adulterous relation. Eventually he married—his wife was from a Northampton family of little distinction—and fathered nine children. He continued right along to be a frequent litigant (both as plaintiff and as defendant); once he sued for slander, citing gossip that had linked him with the Devil. Robert was remembered later as a restless sort—a man unwilling to settle into regular occupations. He enjoyed hunting and fishing, and his chief contribution to the local economy was the discovery of a lead mine. He moved for a time to New Jersey, then returned to Northampton. In 1680 three of his children were taken from him by court order and placed in other families, on account of his "very low condition." Still later he was described as being in a "state of distemperature" and unable to manage his affairs. His end was not recorded; but according to family lore he froze to death on a winter's day, having wandered deep into the woods on one of his custmory "rambles."[84]

Considered overall, the experience of the Lyman family presents a number of interesting variations on a theme. The theme was profound social and geographic dislocation; the variations were expressed in the eventual destinies of the individual family members. The career of Richard Lyman, the father, seems after his arrival in New England to have spiralled downward into misfortune, shrunken resources, and "melancholy." Presumably his children shared in this descent, at least for a time. Soon before and just after Richard's death his two daughters had taken husbands of very average social credentials; and their lives thereafter were generally undistinguished. Two of Richard's sons—Richard, Jr., and John—found a direct route back to wealth and local prominence. But the third son, Robert, followed a roundabout, and troubled, and essentially descending course of his own making. It was as if the older pair had reclaimed the social elevation to which the Lymans were previously accustomed, while the youngest extended the slide of the father's last years. The daughters—to pursue the metaphor—had simply moved sideways.

The sequence must be further considered from the standpoint of the one Lyman who particularly concerns us here. When Sarah was nine, her parents gave up the familial home in county Essex, and when she was eleven they set sail for New England. When she was fifteen they moved, once again, to Connecticut. From this wilderness journey the family emerged with damage both to their property and to their morale (at least to the father's morale). When Sarah was twenty her father died; and a year later her mother was gone as well. She married at about twenty-two, and soon removed with her husband to Springfield. As a woman of thirty-four she made her fifth (and final) move, to Northampton.

We should remember at this point that the lifeline of Mary [Bliss] Parsons was also quite discontinuous. Like Sarah, Mary had (probably) experienced severe dislocation as a child.[85] Like Sarah, she was moved about repeatedly once her family had arrived in the New World. And also like Sarah, Mary had lived through a time when the family fortunes were much diminished and its prestige reduced. But *unlike* Sarah, Mary had effectively recovered and recouped—by marrying Joseph, and sharing in the fruits of his remarkable rise to wealth and power. It is interesting, in this connection, that local remembrance of the Parsons case has emphasized the factor of *envy*: Mary Parsons is said to have "excited jealousy" by reason of her social position, her beauty, and her "haughty" manner.[86] If jealousy is founded in embittered comparisons of self and other, then Sarah Bridgman was uniquely situated to make such comparisons—and to feel their full sting. Despite all the similarities in the early lives of these two women, their ultimate destinies were radically different. And the advantages—at least from Sarah's viewpoint —must have seemed to fall entirely on one side.

Of course, it took many years for the social distance between the Parsonses and the Bridgmans to widen to its full extent, but the trend was abundantly clear by at least 1656. Joseph Parsons was already marked as a town leader—so much so that he paid a fee in that year to avoid office and concentrate on his business affairs. And he was already prosperous, thanks in no small part to an alliance formed with the region's most eminent family, the Pynchons.

There were other points of comparison as well. On May 1, 1655 Mary Parsons gave birth to a son, Ebenezer—who was in fact the first English child born in Northampton. On the thirtieth day of the same month Sarah Bridgman also bore a son, and named him James after his father. But James Bridgman, junior, died two weeks later—under circumstances that were fully remembered in the subsequent witchcraft/slander trial. Moreover, in that same summer the Bridgmans' only surviving son (John) was stricken with a mysterious ailment of the knee. (And this, too, would be drawn into the trial proceeding.) Meanwhile Ebenezer Parsons survived and would eventually grow to adulthood—as did the three older Parsons boys.[87]

The concurrent arrival in Northampton of Sarah Bridgman's brothers —Richard, John, and Robert Lyman—should also be noticed here. Their presence might well have affected her, but in two rather different ways. On the one hand, they added familial support and strength of a sort which had been missing from her life hitherto. Perhaps at some level this made her feel emboldened to act on her suspicions of Mary Parsons. On the other hand, the evident prosperity and distinction of the two eldest brothers may also have called attention to Sarah's far more humble circumstances. They were in the process of reclaiming the Lyman birthright, but what of *her*?

The birthright issue can hardly have applied in the case of the other trial participants. There was no one else, among all the Northampton settlers, whose experience of social dislocation approached that of Sarah Bridgman, her Lyman brothers, and Mary and Joseph Parsons.[88] Hence, it would be misleading to construe the entire episode from this standpoint. Each side in the dispute had its own cast of supporting players, and they, too, merit some consideration.

As noted earlier, the trial proceedings expressed a sharp contest for advantage lasting through the summer of 1656. At the outset the two sides were almost evenly matched; by the end the plaintiff had pulled well ahead. But to say this is to deal only with numbers; what, in addition, can be learned about the distribution of social quality, about rank and prestige? Twelve persons joined initially with Sarah Bridgman, and when studied in relation to a social profile of the entire citizenry they divide as follows: nine came from the lowest status-group (bottom third), and three from the middle (second third); there were none at all from the top (first third).[89] The pattern for Mary Parsons's supporters was notably different. The largest number—five of nine—represented the topmost group; there was also one from the middle and three from the bottom.[90] As the proceedings developed, five of those who had initially witnessed for Bridgman switched to Parsons; and all five were bottom-third. An important element of social process is thus quite clearly suggested. The weight of rank was on the side of the plaintiff from the beginning. And it may have tipped the balance for several lesser participants.

We must consider, secondly, the special role of women on the defendant's side. Honor Hannum, Joanna Branch, and Hannah Langdon had all for a time supported Sarah in her suspicions of the "witch": together they formed the gossip-group from which particular allegations moved out to the larger community. As noted, Sarah Bridgman's concern with witchcraft ran strongly to illness and death in children, hence the parental status of her allies is also of some interest. In 1656 Honor Hannum was a woman in her early or middle forties, married, and the mother of five children (the youngest being about five years old). Hannah Langdon was approximately the same age, and had at least five children of her own (the youngest being about four). Joanna Branch was in her late thirties, married—and childless.[91] In short, each of these women had reason to be preoccupied with the matter of child-bearing. In two cases child-bearing had recently ended; in the third it had never materialized at all. There was the basis here for some personal resonance to the claims and charges that Sarah Bridgman would ultimately bring forward.

We should reemphasize, finally, the ambivalent setting of these events in a geographic sense. Both the plaintiff and the defendant had come to Northampton after several years' residence in Springfield. Six of the defendant's supporters still lived in Springfield, and two others had done so previously. By contrast, all but one of those on the plaintiff's side were Northampton residents, and all but that same one had come to Northampton from towns and villages in Connecticut. (The exception was John Pynchon, friend and business partner of Joseph Parsons.) The Springfield connections of this entire case seem, therefore, abundantly clear.

In fact, Springfield had experienced a protracted period of agitation about witchcraft going back at least seven years. The apparent start was a slander case in 1649, mentioned briefly earlier in this chapter: the widow Marshfield vs. Mary Parsons (no kin to the Northampton "witch"), "for reporting her to be suspected for a witch."[92] Two years later the court heard formal charges of witchcraft against this same Mary Parsons and against her husband Hugh.[93] It seems, moreover, that there were additional suspects whose identity can no longer be discovered. The contemporary chronicler, Edward Johnson, included in his *Wonder-Working Providence* the following note about Springfield: "There hath of late been more than one or two in this town greatly suspected of witchcraft, yet they have used much diligence, both for the finding them out, and for the Lord's assisting them against their witchery: yet they have, as is supposed, bewitched not a few persons, among whom [are] two of the reverend elder's children."[94] And a correspondent "from Natick in New England," writing for a London newspaper in 1651, described "sad frowns of the Lord upon us, chiefly in regard of fascinations and witchcraft. . . . Four in Springfield were detected, whereof one was executed for murder of her own child, and was doubtless a witch; another is condemned, a third under trial, a fourth under suspicion."[95]

Mary [Bliss] Parsons was herself deeply affected by these proceedings.

She suffered fits (though beyond the usual age for such experiences); she roamed about in a distracted manner; she talked of encounters with evil "spirits." This was, assuredly, a difficult period in her life. She had borne twin sons in the summer of 1649 and seen both of them die soon thereafter. Her father, Thomas Bliss, had also died, apparently during the succeeding winter. Her relation to her husband was somewhat troubled. And her neighbors—judging from their later testimony—regarded her with a certain wariness. The records do not reveal Sarah Bridgman's impressions of all this, but presumably she followed it with interest. And she did not forget it upon moving to Northampton.

Mary Parsons was successful in the trial of 1656, but the animus which had prompted this proceeding would not go away. Her name was cleared, but only from the legal standpoint. In the years that followed, her husband prospered ever more greatly, her children grew in number and (mostly) flourished, her mother and brothers sank the Bliss family roots deep into the Connecticut Valley. But her reputation for witchcraft hung on.

In 1674 the whole matter was renewed in court—with the important difference that now Mary Parsons was cast as defendant. Unfortunately, most of the evidence from this later case has disappeared. All that survives is the summary material from the dockets of the two courts involved. Still, it is possible to reconstruct the sequence of events in at least a skeletal form—and to discover some important lines of connection to the witchcraft/slander action of eighteen years previous.[96]

In August 1674 a young woman of Northampton, Mary Bartlett, had died rather suddenly. She was twenty-two, the wife of Samual Bartlett, and the mother of an infant son. More important in the present connection was her family of origin: she was a daughter of James and Sarah [Lyman] Bridgman. Her husband and father jointly believed, as they later testified in court, that "she came to her end by some unlawful and unnatural means, . . . viz. by means of some evil instrument." And they had distinct ideas about the *person* most likely to have used such means.

On September 29 the Hampshire County Court received "diverse testimonies" on the matter. Samuel Bartlett came forward "to show the grounds of his fears and suspicion." James Bridgman sent a statement "entreating that diligent inquisition may be made concerning the death of . . . his daughter." And Mary Parsons was also there—on her own initiative: "She having intimation that such things were bruited abroad, and that she should be called in question . . . she voluntarily made her appearance in court, desiring to clear herself of such an execrable crime." The court examined her, considered all the evidence, and deferred further action to its next meeting in November. There followed a second deferral "for special reasons" (about which the court did not elaborate).

On January 5, 1675, the county magistrates conducted their most extended hearing of the case. The previous depositions were reviewed, and (apparently) some new ones were taken. Both Samuel Bartlett and Mary Parsons were present in person once again. Mary was "called to speak for herself, [and] she did assert her own innocency, often mentioning . . . how clear she was of such a crime, and that the righteous God knew her innocency—with whom she had left her cause." Bartlett, meanwhile, produced testimonies both "many and various, some of them being demonstrations of witchcraft, and others sorely reflecting upon Mary Parsons as being guilty that way." The magistrates decided that final jurisdiction in such matters belonged not to them but to the Court of Assistants in Boston. Still, considering "the season" and "the remoteness" (i.e. of their own court from Boston) and "the difficulties, if not incapabilities, of persons there to appear," they determined to do their utmost "in inquiring into the case." Among other things, they appointed a committee of "soberdized, chaste women" to conduct a body-search on Mary Parsons, to see "whether any marks of witchcraft might appear." (The result was "an account" which the court did not disclose.) Eventually, all the documents were gathered and forwarded to Boston, with a covering letter from "the worshipful Major Pynchon to the governor." Joseph Parsons was ordered to pay bond "for his wife's appearance . . . if required . . . before the governor or magistrates or Court of Assistants."[97]

At the same court, and apparently as part of the same proceeding, "some testimony" was offered "reflecting on John Parsons." John was Mary's second son; he was twenty-four at the time, and as yet unmarried. How and why he should have been implicated in the charges against his mother cannot now be discovered; but the evidence was in any case unpersuasive. The court did "not find . . . any such weight whereby he should be prosecuted on suspicion of witchcraft" and discharged him accordingly.[98]

Meanwhile the case against Mary Parsons moved toward its final round. On March 2, Mary was taken to Boston, "presented" at the Court of Assistants, and formally indicted by the grand jury. Thereupon the court ordered her commitment to prison until "her further trial." The trial came some ten weeks later (May 13, 1675). An imposing roster of Assistants lined the bench: the governor, the deputy-governor, and a dozen magistrates (including her husband's old associate, John Pynchon). However, her fate rested with "the jury of trials for life and death"—twelve men, of no particular distinction, from Boston and the surrounding towns. The indictment was read one last time: "Mary Parsons, the wife of Joseph Parsons . . . being instigated by the Devil, hath . . . entered into familiarity with the Devil, and committed several acts of witchcraft on the person or persons of one or more." The evidence in the case was also read. And "the prisoner at the bar, holding up her hand and pleading not guilty, . . . [put] herself on her trial."

The tension of this moment must have been very great, but it does not come through in the final, spare notation of the court recorder: "The jury brought in their verdict. They found her not guilty. And so she was discharged."[99]

The social underpinnings of this later trial are largely obscured, since the depositional evidence is gone. We do know of the key roles played by James Bridgman and Mary [Bridgman] Bartlett, and this by itself establishes an unmistakable connection with the proceedings of two decades previous. The participation of Samuel Bartlett is on its face more difficult to explain. Samuel's father, Robert, had helped in the earlier case to *defend* Mary Parsons. On the other hand, there is evidence of conflict between the two families in the interim; and Samuel's "great grief" over the loss of his wife must have exerted an influence all of its own.[100]

Otherwise we can simply update our picture of the "witch" herself. She was now, for one thing, a woman in her middle years. She had borne her last child (two years previously), and her eldest had already reached maturity. She had thus joined the age-group most frequently associated with witchcraft. Her social and economic rank was, of course, fully established: there was no longer the aspect of rapidly increasing advantage. In wealth alone the Parsonses stood far above all their Northampton neighbors. Indeed, the magistrates who presided in Mary's trial were no more than her peers. Some of them knew her personally, and the rest would surely have known *of* her. To see such a figure held for many weeks in prison, and then standing "at the bar" as defendant, must have been highly affecting.

And yet, perhaps there remained some doubt about her qualifications for high rank. She was still the daughter of Thomas Bliss, erstwhile "inhabitant" of Hartford, Connecticut. She was still Goodwife—not Mrs.—Mary Parsons.[101] She seems to have been illiterate, or at least unable to write (even her name).[102] She was not a member of the Northampton church. (By contrast, her husband Joseph had been admitted to membership when the church was founded in 1661. So, too, had most of her antagonists in the 1656 trial—not excluding Sarah Bridgman.)[103] And was there also some lingering antipathy to her on more personal grounds? Her impulse, for example, to confront her accusers directly and "voluntarily" in the 1674 trial seems courageous in retrospect; but it may have left a different impression among her own peers. Perhaps, *in context*, this was a woman too assertive for her own good.

Of Mary's life subsequent to 1674 there is little direct information. She and her husband would eventually give up their home in Northampton and move (back) to Springfield. Joseph Parsons would die in 1683, and Mary—like her own mother—would enter a very long widowhood. She remained thereafter in Springfield, completed the rearing of her numerous progeny, and saw her sons—and then her grandsons—assume positions of prominence in several Connecticut Valley towns. Death claimed her in January 1712, when she was about eighty-five years old.[104]

She was not again tried for witchcraft, but neither was she free from local suspicion. Some writers have surmised that she was blamed for the death, under mysterious circumstances, of a Northampton neighbor in 1678. (The court investigated this death but returned no indictments.)[105] And there is one last, indirect—but telling—sign of her vulnerability to gossip of witchcraft. It comes from the record of the local court for a session held on January 9, 1702:

> Mr. Peletiah Glover complaining against Betty Negro for bad language striking his son Peletiah, who came and was present— charging Betty that she told him that his grandmother had killed two persons over the river, and had killed Mrs. Pynchon and half-killed the Colonel, and that his mother was half a witch. To which Richard White and Tom Negro gave in evidence that she said on Monday night, the fifth of this instant January, when then Betty owned it [that] she had so said, etc.
>
> We find her very culpable for her base tongue and words as aforesaid . . . We sentence said Betty to be well whipped on the naked body by the constable with ten lashes well laid on: which was performed accordingly by constable Thomas Bliss. . . .
>
> Present: John Pynchon, Justice [of the] Peace; [Joseph] Parsons, Justice [of the] Peace.[106]

There are some familiar names here. The first of the justices was the same John Pynchon who had joined Joseph Parsons in many business ventures—and who had participated directly in both of the trial proceedings around Mary Parsons's witchcraft. The other justice was the first Joseph Parsons's son and namesake—and a man of great prominence in the affairs of Northampton during the opening decades of the eighteenth century.[107] The constable, Thomas Bliss, was the grandson of the emigrant Thomas; he was also, therefore, Mary Parsons's nephew.

But who were the Peletiah Glovers, father and son? And who was the grandmother alleged to have "killed two persons over the river"? The answer is easily discovered—and, at this point, is hardly surprising. Mr. Peletiah Glover was a Springfield merchant of much wealth and prominence; his son, Peletiah, junior, was a boy of fourteen. The wife and mother in this family was Mrs. Hannah Glover—*née* Hannah *Parsons*.[108] And she, in turn, was the daughter of (the first) Joseph Parsons. It was Hannah's maternal inheritance that made her, in Betty Negro's words, "half a witch." By this reckoning Mary Parsons still counted as a full-blooded specimen.

9

Communities:
The Social Matrix
of Witchcraft

Recent scholarship in early American history declares, as one of its central presumptions, the primacy of local experience. The "little community" appears as the single most apposite unit of study. Within narrow and wholly familiar bounds—so the argument goes—did the vast majority of colonial Americans encounter the forces which shaped their lives. Decisions of state, made in the king's court an ocean away, concerned them rarely and remotely, or not at all. Enactments by provincial governors and assemblies came closer in their effects—but not (by and large) very close. More important by far were the activities of local institutions, the informal structures of neighborhoods, the whole dense fabric of face-to-face exchange.[1]

This viewpoint finds powerful support in the present study. Witchcraft belonged, first and last, to the life of the little community. Indeed, scores of New England communities created their own individual histories of witchcraft, no two entirely alike. Suspicion and gossip, charge and counter-charge, the resort to private magic and/or formal proceedings in court: all were geared to local conditions. To be sure, the *lore* of witchcraft was common to the region, indeed to the entire English-speaking world. And reports of particular episodes were easily carried from one locale to another. But the episodes themselves—their human shape and substance—reflected a progression of village events.

The same has been true of other witchcraft, outside New England, and before and after the seventeenth century. The local frame stands clear in the present (or recent) experience of Cewa tribesmen in central

Africa, of Dobu islanders in the Pacific, of Navajo Indians in the American Southwest, and also in the premodern experience of peasants in southern Germany and of mountain folk along the French-Swiss border.[2] Cultural anthropologists have seen in this a special opportunity: witchcraft as a pathway to the inner structures of community life. Thus witchcraft has obtained an important place in anthropological studies generally. Articles and monographs proliferate, and few ethnographies seem complete without some pages (or chapters) on the subject. The roster of contributing scholars includes some very honored names: E. E. Evans-Pritchard, Bronislaw Malinowski, Claude Levi-Strauss, Clyde Kluckhohn—to mention only a few.[3]

Of course, historians no less than anthropologists are drawn to comparative research; and in this topical area they are fortunate to have such sharply drawn markers to guide their way. In fact, several historians have travelled the route already. Keith Thomas and Alan Macfarlane made extensive use of anthropological literature in carrying out their own research on witchcraft in sixteenth- and seventeenth-century England. William Monter and Erik Midelfort canvassed the same literature, and "applied" it somewhat more cautiously, in studying other parts of premodern Europe.[4]

The anthropology of witchcraft is, in its present state, a rich and complex structure—difficult to summarize in a few paragraphs or pages. Still, there are certain recurrent themes which can be outlined here as a way of introducing subsequent parts of the discussion. In the first place, anthropological study presents witchcraft as an index of fundamental human relationships—as a signpost to "weak points" in an overall social "system." Witchcraft charges, by this account, follow lines of intrinsic tension and hostility. Their sources are not so much personal as "structural"; typically, they express conflicts of role, of status, of formal situation. Chronic strains in the relation of "affines," rivalry between claimants to a single office or position, struggles for access to valued resources: such are the common breeding-grounds of witchcraft. To be sure, some conflicts are themselves mediated by structural arrangements (e.g. courts, arbitration procedures), while others may be harmlessly diverted toward "outlets" in ritual expression. Witchcraft, in short, most often occurs where there is *both* unusual tension *and* a lack of appropriate outlets (and/or means of resolution). As such it provides what M. G. Marwick has called a "social strain gauge."[5]

But this is just one view of the matter, in effect an academic view. The metaphor of the "gauge" reflects an investigator's need for methods and concepts suited to the analysis of cultural materials. What of witchcraft in relation to the needs of the culture itself—and of its constituent members? Here, too, anthropologists have fashioned sharp guidelines, even "models." Their leading construct is the powerful, though admittedly controversial, idea of "functionalism." Witchcraft beliefs (and accusations) are thought to perform functions, confer advantages, impart strength and resiliency to the social fabric as a whole. For example, witchcraft serves to define and epitomize evil. It belongs therefore to "moral philosophy"; it marks the boundaries of culturally acceptable action. Moreover, it directly and constructively *influences* action, since individual actors are inclined to respect prevailing norms lest (otherwise) they be considered witches. Hence witchcraft is an aspect of "social control," and its effects are profoundly "conservative."[6]

Should this seem too benign a picture, some theorists are quick to stress another, evidently darker, side. "Witchcraft is a force in social relations," writes Philip Mayer. "It is something that can break up a friendship, or a marriage, or a community; it is a banner under which people hate, denounce, and kill one another." Yet even here a "function" may be served, an advantage gained. Witchcraft charges "bring to a head the tensions and strains of [a difficult] relationship." They furnish "a pretext for quarreling," which in turn may yield a new balance of social forces—a measure indeed of "conflict resolution."[7] Such quarreling, however personal on its face, sometimes carries deep and dynamic social meaning. In one well-known study, sorcery charges are construed as "catalysts to the normal process of [clan] segmentation"; they are "a means by which redunant, insupportable relationships, which through being close and personal cannot be quietly contracted out of, are dramatically blasted away." Here (and in other cases as well) witchcraft acts "as an instrument for breaking off relations."[8]

To be sure, the functionalist approach has its limits, its problems— and its critics. The anthropologist Mary Douglas argues cogently that "if the believers themselves regard [witchcraft] as an unmitigated scourge, this too is a datum to be fitted into the analysis. Witchcraft is not merely a brutal midwife delivering new forms to society, though it may be this; it is also an aggravator of all hostilities and fears, an obstacle to peaceful cooperation."[9] And the historian Erik Midelfort concludes from his study of witchcraft in sixteenth-century Germany that "the largest . . . trials . . . served no valid social function and were indeed dysfunctional. Society was not made stronger and more cohesive by such trials, but weaker and more torn by suspicion and resentment."[10] This vein of criticism runs especially to the explicit rigidities, and implicit tautologies, built into functionalism—and to its foundation in "a homeostatic model of society." Especially disconcerting from a historian's standpoint is the inelasticity of such a model in the face of *change*.

Yet if functional*ism* seems suspect (i.e. as scientific dogma), functions themselves are not so easily dismissed. Human societies do have parts which fit together (more or less) and express a variety of reciprocal interests. And witchcraft makes no exception. Midelfort avers that "small witch trials" (as contrasted with "major panics") in southern Germany did "reinforce social boundaries and traditional morals."[11] Macfarlane affirms the value of "function" concepts freed from implicit links to "conservative forces." In his English data, witchcraft beliefs and accusations appear as "a neutral weapon," which served in some instances to express "older social sanctions" and in others "to generate the energy for the creation of *new* 'moral laws.' "[12] Finally, Mary Douglas, for all her strictures and criticisms (noted above), also believes

> that the possibilities of functional analysis have not been exhausted. Take away the rigidity and crudity of the homeostatic control model and it still provides an explanatory framework based on the idea of a communication system. People are trying to control one another, albeit with small success. The idea of the witch is used to whip their own consciences or those of their friends. The witch image is as effective as the idea of the community is strong.[13]

The resonance of this summary with early New England materials is immediately, and intuitively, persuasive. It can well serve as text for the discussion to follow.

Witchcraft as "Strain Gauge": Social Relationships

The association of witchcraft with "weak points in the social structure" suggests two research questions of large importance. First, what was the predominant pattern of *relationship* between the parties chiefly involved? Second, what *situations* most frequently yielded witchcraft suspicions— and accusations? Each question deserves careful and extended consideration. And together they lead right to the center of our subject.

In some cultures the relationships expressed by witchcraft have a three-way aspect: witch, accuser, and victim appear as distinct agents, each one of whom contributes to the sum of relevant events. Witch-victim relationships may then be viewed as representing prevailing *estimates of interpersonal tension*, and witch-accuser relationships as *actual expressions of such tension*. Victim-accuser relationships, by contrast, are patently and profoundly *affiliative*. In fact, the New England case cannot easily be fitted to this triangular model, since victim and accuser were so often the same person. Their two positions were effectively collapsed into one, with the main lines of interaction simplified accordingly. Such simplification is itself worth noticing: here, evidently, the estimates and the realities of tension roughly coincided. To be sure, certain of the victims did not (sometimes could not) make substantive accusations. Infants supposed to have been made ill or killed by witchcraft are an obvious case in point; there it was left to parents to identify a culprit. Yet the parents would be victims, too—in the worry and feelings of loss that such experiences inevitably brought to them. In still other instances the accusers included some who were (at the same time) victims and some who were not. Typically, the latter played secondary (i.e. supporting) roles and were themselves sufferers by virtue of their personal connection —family or friendship—to the principal victim.

From this there follows an obvious and important adaptation of strategy. To reconstruct the social context of New England witchcraft is to spotlight a set of *bi*polar relationships—between the accused witches, on the one side, and the accuser/victims, on the other. A witchcraft accusation was, in a sense, just one aspect of a long and continually unfolding connection between two people. There was much that came before, and, in some instances at least, there would be much to come afterward. Ideally, the *entire* sequence should be examined, beginning, middle, and end; however, the extant materials cannot be stretched that far. In some cases a record of accusation is all that survives. In others there are suggestive fragments from earlier and later. Occasionally (as, for example, with Mary [Bliss] Parsons and Sarah [Lyman] Bridgman)[14] it is possible to plot the lines of intersecting lives and *infer* the development through time of a gathering tension. Yet the sum of these possibilities is limited at best. By and large, the developmental aspect of witch and accuser/victim relationships is beyond recovery. The evidence itself directs attention elsewhere—toward the "structural" dimension of such relationships, the circumstances which shaped and defined them irrespective of time.

Geography, for example, had deep bearing on witchcraft. It is apparent, on the very surface of things, that the accused and their accuser/victims would ordinarily belong to the same village-community. What is not so apparent on the surface—and thus deserves the most careful attention— is the spatial aspect of these relationships within the community. Were the chief parties to witchcraft cases likely to belong to the same neighborhood? Were they often, in fact, *next-door* neighbors? The documentary record contains many hints, and some quite explicit indications, on this question. Goody Glover, accused at Boston in 1688, lived "in the neighborhood" of her alleged victims (the children of John Goodwin).[15] Hannah Jones was suspected of causing the "lithobolia" that plagued "her neighbor" (George Walton) in New Hampshire.[16] Jane James of Marblehead was accused by one Peter Pitford, who "said that his garden fruits and such things [as] he had did never prosper so long as he lived near that woman."[17] When Goodwife Morse was suspected at Newbury, "one of the neighbors" (and then "another") tried counter-magic— "upon which they say their houses were much disturbed."[18] When widow Holman was charged at Cambridge with bewitching Rebecca Stearns, the evidence given in court assumed proximity of residence: "she [Stearns] looked out of her window and saw Mary Holman running about . . . and presently she was taken sick, almost struck dead as she thought."[19]

The impressions gained from these glancing references can be amplified by spatial models developed for the most fully documented cases. Three such are presented below.

The first describes the residential geography of Easthampton, Long Island, at the time of Elizabeth Garlick's trial for witchcraft. The accused lived at the northern end of the village. Four of her leading accusers lived just across the street. Her next-door neighbors also gave evidence (of a somewhat ambiguous sort). Several other accusers and/or deponents lived further south—but the overall "tilt" of involvement seems clear. A similar, and even clearer, pattern is evident for Springfield, Massachusetts during the trials of Mary and Hugh Parsons. (See the second of the accompanying models.) The two "witches" lived at the lower (southern) end of the village; their leading accusers and victims were concentrated in the immediate neighborhood. Indeed, each of the southernmost households was represented by one or more deponents in these trials (at "high" or "medium" levels of participation). "Low"-level participants and non-participants filled out the central and northern sectors of the town. Finally, there is the case of Jane James of Marblehead. (See the third model.) Goodwife James and all of her known accusers lived in one small enclave to the southwest of the main community. So far as the records reveal, other local residents had no part whatsoever in the accusations voiced against her.

Jane James was never actually indicted for witchcraft; her accusers were relatively few, and next-door neighbors (and perhaps of dubious reputation themselves). Elizabeth Garlick and the Parsonses, by contrast, *were* subject to formal prosecution; their accusers were far more

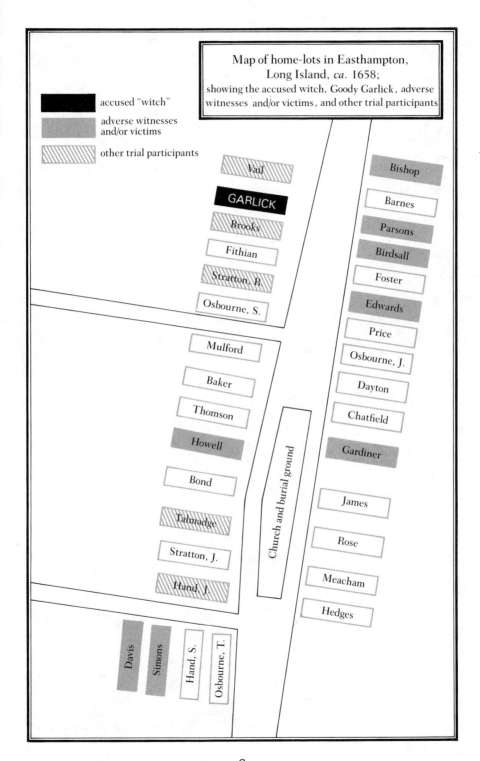

Map of home-lots in Easthampton,
Long Island, *ca.* 1658;
showing the accused witch, Goody Garlick, adverse
witnesses and/or victims, and other trial participants

accused "witch"

adverse witnesses
and/or victims

other trial participants

Vail

GARLICK

Brooks

Fithian

Stratton, R.

Osbourne, S.

Bishop

Barnes

Parsons

Birdsall

Foster

Edwards

Price

Osbourne, J.

Dayton

Chatfield

Mulford

Baker

Thomson

Howell

Bond

Talmadge

Stratton, J.

Hand, J.

Church and burial ground

Gardiner

James

Rose

Meacham

Hedges

Davis

Simons

Hand, S.

Osbourne, T.

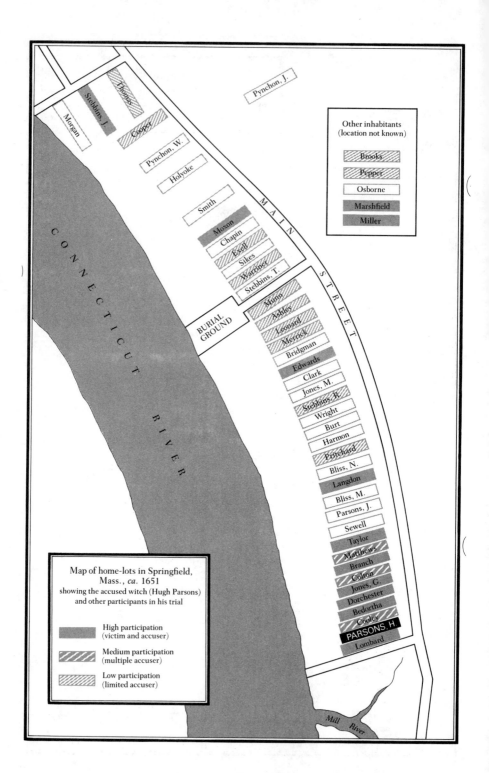

Map of home-lots in Springfield, Mass., ca. 1651
showing the accused witch (Hugh Parsons) and other participants in his trial

High participation (victim and accuser)

Medium participation (multiple accuser)

Low participation (limited accuser)

Other inhabitants (location not known)

Brooks

Pepper

Osborne

Marshfield

Miller

CONNECTICUT RIVER

MAIN STREET

BURIAL GROUND

Mill River

Morgan
Stebbins, J.
Thomas
Cooper
Pynchon, W.
Holyoke
Smith
Moxon
Chapin
Excell
Sikes
Warriner
Stebbins, T.
Pynchon, J.
Munn
Ashley
Leonard
Merrick
Bridgman
Edwards
Clark
Jones, M.
Stebbins, B.
Wright
Burt
Harmon
Pritchard
Bliss, N.
Langdon
Bliss, M.
Parsons, J.
Sewell
Taylor
Matthews
Branch
Colton
Jones, G.
Dorchester
Bedortha
Cooley
PARSONS, H.
Lombard

282

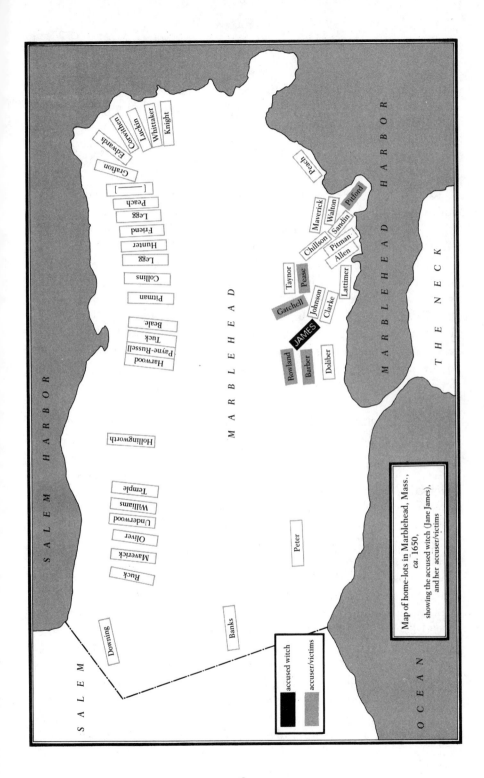

Map of home-lots in Marblehead, Mass., *ca.* 1650, showing the accused witch (Jane James), and her accuser/victims

SALEM HARBOR

MARBLEHEAD HARBOR

MARBLEHEAD

THE NECK

SALEM

OCEAN

accused witch

accuser/victims

Cornwillen
Luckin
Whittaker
Knight
Edwards
Grafton
Peach
Legg
Friend
Hunter
Legg
Collins
Pitman
Beale
Tuck
Payne-Russell
Harwood

Peach
Maverick
Walton
Piford
Sandin
Chillson
Pitman
Allen
Taynor
Pease
Gatchell
Johnson
Clarke
Lattimer
JAMES
Rowland
Barber
Doliber

Hollingworth

Temple
Williams
Underwood
Oliver
Maverick
Ruck

Peter

Downing

Banks

numerous, and more nearly representative of a full village community. These cases can be taken to represent two stages—earlier and later—in the development of witchcraft proceedings. The first was severely limited in its spatial aspect—a matter of gossip for a handful of adjacent households. The second was much broader in scope, and thus more worthy of official attention. Yet even then the neighborhood focus remained evident. In sum, among the various determinants of concern with witches and their *maleficium,* simple proximity of residence ranked high.

Kinship is another possible determinant. In some cultures today witchcraft accusations appear with special force and frequency among co-wives in polygamous unions, among in-laws, among members of the same clan or lineage. Was there any comparable pattern in early New England? Were the participants in witchcraft cases—so often linked as neighbors—also linked by ties of blood or marriage? Currently available evidence yields the following: Two women charged their husbands with witchcraft. (However, both had themselves been previously charged, and were under sentence of death. And one—Mary Parsons of Springfield—was closer to outright insanity than any other suspect.)[20] One man seems to have actively encouraged charges against his wife. (But he, too, looks deranged.) And two others entertained at least private suspicions of their wives (but within a broad context of marital discord).[21] A woman accused her own father (again as part of a long-standing family quarrel), and a man apparently joined in proceedings against his "cousin" (but himself disputed the nature of their connection).[22] The sum of this material does not seem large. Accusations of witchcraft almost never followed blood-lines. Their correlation with marriage was a little stronger, but usually implicated other, plainly idiosyncratic circumstances. There are no grounds here for associating witchcraft with rooted—and "structural"—tensions in the lives of families or kin.

The matter of *formal relationships* suggests a different range of interpretive possibility. Perhaps accused and accuser were linked in some contractual and/or instrumental way. Again the evidence is less than impressive overall. In several instances the accuser was concurrently employed by the accused.[23] One alleged witch was a lodger in the household of her accusers, another was landlord (with her alleged victim as renter/boarder).[24] But these arrangements were generally *ad hoc,* and short-term, and quite personal in their defining circumstances.

Indeed, it is the personal element that stands out in all the materials. The relationships of witches and accuser/victims were not defined by, or limited to, any single strand of experience. On the contrary, such relationships were typically complex, many-sided, and altogether *dense.*

Nowhere does the surviving evidence afford a full view of all particulars; nonetheless their basic shape and tenor does quite frequently come clear. The trial of Winifred and Mary Holman furnishes a good example. The chief accusers, a neighbor-family named Gibson, recalled numerous small encounters with each or both of the suspects. Mary would frequently drop by to "borrow a skillet," to caress an infant as it lay "asleep in the cradle," to "get fire" for her own household. (Indeed, the latter errand brought her to the Gibsons "every morning, and sometimes twice in the day.") Winifred might come (uninvited) to ask "how do your daughter"—and she offered more than once "to prescribe some herbs for her." The Gibsons, for their part, "put a pair of stockings" (for mending?) with the Holmans Since their houses were so close each party could follow the comings and goings of the other. Thus the suspects were observed "hoeing," "gleaning," "stripping off corn," "carrying sand," "digging a hole in the common," "turning round . . . at the oak," "running about," "sitting . . . at a hole of water," "going towards [a] neighbor's house," and "going out towards night into swamps and byways." (The widow Holman's dress was particularly remembered. She appeared "sometimes in one sort of apparel and sometimes in another"; once on a rainy Sabbath she went out "without any hat on her head.") Proximity led to chance meetings between members of the two families ("by the stile" or "at the rails") and occasions for enmity and misunderstanding. (John Gibson was "afflicted with Mrs. Holman's hens . . . I could not keep them out of my barn, from destroying my corn.")[25]

In other cases the evidence speaks more briefly, but to much the same effect. William Branch (accuser/victim) had wished that Hugh Parsons (accused witch) would not make "so many errands to my house for several things"; still he "could not tell how to deny him what he desired."[26] Goody Davis (accuser/victim), when asked why she was "so familiar" with Elizabeth Garlick (witch), answered that "she brought me many things [such] as mault . . . and is very kind to me."[27] Such material reveals an expectation that contact with witches be reduced and qualified; but this was not an easy thing to achieve. Residential proximity, established habit and custom, all the arrangements of village life served to sustain—not limit—social density.

There is, finally, the matter of *social position*—of "standing" (their term) or "status" (ours) in the total village community. Can witches, on the one side, and accuser/victims, on the other, be grouped in this respect as well? It has been shown already that the accused were predominantly of humble rank (with one group of interesting and not unimportant exceptions).[28] Moreover, the court papers yield scattered, but suggestive comments by individual trial-participants. Goody Clawson accosted her neighbor (and accuser) Abigail Westcott thus: "What? Are you proud of your fine clothes? You love to be mistress, but you never shall be. . . ."[29] And there was a revealing exchange between Eunice Cole and *her* neighbor Hopestill Austin (when Austin barred the way to an upstairs room where a third woman was giving birth to a child): "Goody Cole said, 'Is there gentle folk above?' This deponent said, 'Gentle or simple, ye shall not go up!' "[30]

Here and there, observers from the period touched directly on the same theme. The Rev. Josiah Cotton of Massachusetts remarked that witchcraft charges seemed to fall disproportionately on "the poor"—and "when it comes to the better sort the prosecution commonly ceases."[31] And William Hubbard underscored the influence in trial proceedings of the "vox populi." Often, he wrote, suspects "are condemned . . . by the common people . . . upon very slight grounds."[32] The latter comment was linked to a short description of the trial of Mrs. Ann Hibbens. "The jury found her guilty," Hubbard noted, "but the magistrates consented not, so the matter came to the General Court, where she was condemned by the Deputies . . . and executed."[33] Evidently the jury had expressed the "vox populi," while the magistrates represented another viewpoint—perhaps reflecting their higher social position. It was left to the deputies to decide the issue once and for all.

Elements of the same sequence appeared elsewhere as well. Hugh Parsons, like Mrs. Hibbens, was convicted by the jury and reprieved by the magistrates; but in his case the deputies voted an acquittal.[34] Elizabeth Seager of Hartford was found "guilty of familiarity with Satan" by a Hartford court in 1665; a year later the Court of Assistants overturned her conviction on an apparent technicality and ordered her "set . . . free from further suffering and imprisonment."[35] The same court ordered a similar reversal following the conviction of Katherine Harrison of Wethersfield a few years later.[36] The case of Elizabeth Morse was summarized many years after the fact by her pastor, the Rev. John Hale: "the jury brought her in guilty; yet the governor, Simon Bradstreet, Esq., and some of the magistrates reprieved her, being unsatisfied in the verdict." Eventually she was freed from jail (though not without considerable opposition from the colony's General Court) and "carried to her own house." There "her husband . . . desired some neighbor ministers to meet together and discourse [with] his wife." The ministers found her conversation to be "very Christian," and as to the question of her guilt in witchcraft they "inclined to the more charitable side."[37]

This pattern of alignment—juries *versus* magistrates and ministers—

is particularly evident in the trial of Mercy Disborough of Fairfield, Connecticut. Indeed, records from the Disborough case show distinct differences of beliefs and values—behind competing judgments on the matter at hand. The jury was at first unable to reach a verdict; at a subsequent court, however, they found the defendant guilty. The magistrates were evidently not persuaded and "sent [the jury] forth upon a second consideration"—a most unusual proceeding. But the jurymen "returned that they saw no reason to alter their verdict." The court temporarily "approved" this result, but soon afterward appointed a special committee of magistrates to review the entire case. Meanwhile, too, "advice" was sought from local ministers. The ministers responded first: their judgment "as to the evidence left to our consideration" was cautiously but clearly skeptical. The key prosecution witness evoked for them "a suspicion of counterfeiting," and other material introduced as evidence seemed no more convincing. "The endeavor of conviction of witchcraft by swimming" was "unlawful and sinful." (On this point the ministers noted their "concurrence with the generality of divines.") "Unusual excrescences" found upon the bodies of the accused proved little unless certified by "able physicians." And "as to . . . strange accidents . . . [like] the dying of cattle, etc.," they made "very slender and uncertain grounds" for trial proceedings.[38] Swimming tests, body-marks, strange accidents: all these "proofs" were well established in the popular lore of witchcraft. Yet the ministers would not—*could* not—credit them.

The report of the magistrates' committee, received some months later, was similar in substance and much sharper in tone. There were, to begin with, certain technical irregularities in the court's actions, which alone would suffice to "reprieve" the defendant. There was no confession, and no clear testimony "proving . . . acts done . . . which could not be but by the help of the Devil." Instead there were "the common things of spectral evidence, ill events after quarrels or threats, teats, water trials, and the like, with suspicious words—all of which are discarded, and some of them abominated, by the most judicious as to be convictive of witchcraft." In conclusion, the magistrates wrote: "Those that will make witchcraft of such things will make hanging work apace."[39]

These materials from the Disborough trial are worth examining in detail because they reveal so clearly an important line of social difference as to conceptions of witchcraft. But the same line can be inferred in other cases as well. On one side stood the "common people" (as William Hubbard described them), with their concern for "the common things," their simple credulity, their readiness to accuse witches upon "slight" or "slender" or "uncertain" grounds. On the other side stood "the most

judicious"—magistrates and ministers, for example—who, while ac-
knowledging the *general* reality of witchcraft, held a much narrower
view of its specific manifestations.

From differences of belief emerged differences in behavior—visible
not only in the overruling of juries by magistrates, but also in forms and
degrees of participation through all stages of witchcraft proceedings.
Some of our case-studies merit review and reconsideration from this
perspective.

> *Parsons vs. Bridgman* (Northampton, Massachusetts, 1656):
> In this case—where the issue was slander, that is, the making of
> false accusations about witchcraft—lines of rank and "standing"
> were clearly drawn from the outset. The plaintiff herself was a
> member of the local elite; the defendant was placed far down
> the social scale. The plantiff's supporters—in short, those who
> resisted the gossip that cast her as a witch—were largely her
> social peers. (As part of the research on this case Northampton
> families were sorted by various measures into three status-cate-
> gories of roughly equal size. The results showed that five of nine
> initial deponents for Mary Parsons belonged to the highest cate-
> gory.) Meanwhile the defendant's supporters—those most ready
> to credit suspicion of the alleged witch—were predominantly
> low-status. (Nine of twelve were rated in the bottom group, and
> none in the top.)[40]
>
> *Elizabeth Garlick* (tried for witchcraft, Easthampton, Long
> Island, 1658): Rumors and gossip against this defendant circu-
> lated for a long time—first among her fellow-residents on
> Gardiner's Island; later in the village of Easthampton (to which
> Garlick had removed about two years before her trial). At the
> center of this activity was a group of perhaps half a dozen women
> who, like Garlick herself, were distinctly humble folk. (Indeed,
> every one of them can safely be ranked in the lowest of three
> Easthampton status-groups.) As long as the gossip was confined
> to this group, it *remained* gossip—no more and no less. But then
> came a turning-point: Goody Garlick was linked to the death of
> a young woman in the town's leading family. The "victim," on
> her deathbed, named Garlick in very definite terms, and soon
> thereafter the bereaved husband joined the list of "accusers." The
> result was a full-blown court case, in which the defendant barely
> escaped conviction. This sequence seems to imply a decisive im-
> portance for social rank and influence. Without the added weight

of accusation from within the ranks of the local elite, the case against Goody Garlick might never have reached the trial stage.[41]

Jane James (long-time suspect, Marblehead, Massachusetts, 1650s–60s): The case against Goodwife James never did reach the trial stage. Indeed, it is known to us only as a result of several actions for slander filed by James herself over a period of almost two decades. The defendants were all persons of little property and no visible distinction. (Moreover, as noted previously, they resided in one territorial enclave somewhat removed from the main part of the Marblehead community.) The suspicions they harbored against Goody James were of the usual sort: she had appeared "at sea in the likeness of a cat"; she "came in at a hole in the window" and assaulted (that is, "almost choked") an unwitting victim. Had these suspicions circulated beyond her immediate neighbors and peers, they might well have sustained a prosecution in court. But here (in direct contrast to the Garlick case) there was no enlargement of the accuser/victim group toward persons of leadership status.[42]

Hugh Parsons (tried for witchcraft, Springfield, Massachusetts, 1652): The records of early Springfield, and the depositional files from Hugh Parsons's trial, are remarkably full; as such they afford fine opportunities for social analysis. The 42 families resident at Springfield in 1652 can be rated both for social rank and for participation in the witchcraft proceedings. The measures used here have three parts: for rank, top third, middle third, and bottom third, and for participation levels, high, moderate, and none. The resultant correlations can be expressed in a simple table:

Table 1.   Participation levels

		High	Moderate	None	Total
	Top	2	5	7	14
Rank	Middle	2	6	6	14
	Bottom	7	4	3	14
	Total	11	15	16	42

Clearly, bottom-third families made the largest contribution to the trial proceedings, at least in quantitative terms. Top- and middle-third participation was roughly similar—and was weighted on the negative side. The differences implied here can be sharp-

ened by comparing smaller groups from opposite ends of the
social ladder. Of the six families ranked topmost for the whole
town five took no part whatsoever in the Parsons trial. The lone
exception—the family of Rev. George Moxon, Springfield's first
pastor—was deeply involved: two daughters were victims ("taken
ill with fits"), and Moxon himself came forward as an accuser.
The six bottom-ranked families yield a very different profile. Of
this group five participated in the trial, three at a "high" level.
The exception here was the family of one Thomas Sewell—and
it does not seem hard to explain. Bessie Sewell, Thomas's wife,
was herself a suspected witch, directly implicated by some of the
testimony against Hugh Parsons. The Parsons trial, viewed *in
toto,* looks strikingly similar to the case of Goody Garlick. Suspicion was well entrenched among Springfield's humblest citizens: they would constitute a broad base of support for action
(that is, legal proceedings) against the alleged witch. But another
element was needed, too—a measure of social "quality" to sup-
plement their "quantity"—and this is what the Moxons supplied.
As one of Springfield's largest property-holders, as a graduate of
Cambridge, as an erstwhile representative to the General Court,
George Moxon qualified as "gentleman" several times over. As
pastor, he would always find a respectful, receptive hearing for
his ideas and opinions. When persons of his standing joined in
witchcraft accusations there were bound to be significant effects.[43]

Katherine Harrison (tried for witchcraft, Wethersfield, Connecticut, 1668): The Harrison case, described at length in a
subsequent chapter, was so long in unfolding and so complex in
its episodic structure as to imperil all efforts of analytic summary.
The problem is made harder still by incomplete and occasionally
confusing evidence. Nonetheless certain underlying elements of
social process do come clear. Suspicion of widow Harrison began
in about the year 1650 within a group of servants in a single
household at Hartford (of which she was herself a part). It
festered, and gradually deepened, among various families in the
town of Wethersfield (to which she moved in about 1653). Her
chief antagonists in this pre-trial stage included six women of
middle age and "low" social status, two younger women of relatively "high" status, and two young men of "middle" status. In
1668 the ranks of her accusers were significantly augmented.
Illness and death in three different families—two of high, one
of middle, status—were newly ascribed to Harrison's witchcraft.

The upshot was a complicated series of legal proceedings: three separate trials, two ending in a hung jury, the third in a conviction; a reversal of this verdict by the magistrates (1669); and Harrison's removal—in effect, her banishment—from the colony (1670). A petition to protest her (temporary) freedom from custody in 1669 reveals the forces arrayed against her in the final stages: the signers were disproportionately of high status. In sum, the development of the case over time can be correlated with rising levels of social participation—rising both in a numerical sense and in terms of social quality.[44]

Eunice Cole (tried for witchcraft, Hampton, New Hampshire, 1656): More than any other case the trial of Goody Cole presents a picture of unified effort right across the social spectrum. When Hampton's population is sorted by reference to status differentials, prosecution witnesses are found in each of three constituent groups (high, middle, and low). The high group furnishes the largest number (seven witnesses), but low is nearly as well represented (six), and middle is only somewhat farther behind (four). Unfortunately about half of the actual depositions have been lost, and of those that do survive some are too brief or vague to be informative. Thus it is impossible to correlate social position with particular forms of accusation or with the progress of events over time. In effect, the records offer only a snapshot of accuser/victims at the time the case went to trial.[45]

It seems clear, in sum, that persons of every rank participated in witchcraft proceedings. But it is also clear that such participation differed —in form, in degree, and in overall effect—among the various status-levels. Perhaps most typically, ideas about particular suspects developed first among people of little or no distinction. In some (many?) instances suspicion did not spread much further, and hence did not yield action of a formal sort (i.e. in court). In other cases, however, persons of higher rank and larger influence joined the fray. And when that happened, legal measures became far more likely. Full-blown jury-trials invariably displayed alliances spanning a broad social range; *some* representation at high status-levels was requisite to move witchcraft charges into the courts. At the same time the weight of social distinction might go the opposite way. Magistrates and ministers were more cautious about believing (and acting on) specific charges than average folk. At least occasionally they used positions of official responsibility to discourage, or even to countermand, the prosecution of witchcraft.

Considered together, these findings serve to underscore the importance of status-difference in the lives, and minds, and actions of the early New Englanders. Of course, there is nothing especially new or startling here; students of the period have long noticed a deep concern with "rank," an instinct (almost) of "deference." Still, such attitudes were so deep and so instinctive that they are liable now to fall through the scholarly cracks. Their expression, for example, in sumptuary laws, in terms of address, in seating-plans for local meeting-houses is well and widely known, but not perhaps sufficiently appreciated. They need continued study and added emphasis—attitudes *about* rank, informing the actions of individuals identified *by* rank (among other criteria), in particular times and places. Civic duty, the legal process, religious devotion, friendship, courtship and marriage, the exchange of neighborly aid and courtesies: all these, and more, were potential areas of impact. Witchcraft was just an instance, and a special one at that. But surely there were comparable effects right across the spectrum of social behavior.

Witchcraft as "Strain Gauge":
Social Situations

The "strain" intrinsic to witchcraft cases extended in two different directions. In addition to tense *relationships* there was the matter of problematic *situations*. Individual agents, however smoothly (or painfully) related to one another, would respond also to innumerable contact-experiences. Many of these would go easily enough; some might prove difficult but ultimately manageable; still others might leave lasting residues of bitterness; and at least a few would directly energize witchcraft proceedings. Can it be shown that certain forms of contact and interaction belonged, to a disproportionate extent, to the last of these categories? Were there, in short, some experiences that carried a special potential for witchcraft—a risk, on one side, of falling victim to *maleficium*, and, on the other, of standing accused as malefactor?

Fragments of an answer to such questions are scattered through the case materials. Especially valuable are the depositional records which reveal direct antecedents to witchcraft charges:

> Mr. Moxon . . . saith, the same week that I spake to Hugh Parsons about the bricks, and to his wife about another business, my daughter was taken ill with her fits.[46]

> Rebecca Smith . . . testifieth . . . that . . . Goodwife Gilbert had a black cap which she had lent to Katherine Harrison, and Katherine

Harrison desired to have the said cap, but Goody Gilbert refused to sell it to Katherine. After[ward] Goodwife Gilbert wore the said cap; and when she had the said cap on her head, her head and shoulders was much afflicted.[47]

Susannah Trimmings [testified that] at night, going home . . . she heard a rustling in the woods . . . and presently after there did appear to her a woman whom she apprehended to be old Goodwife Walford. She [that is, Walford] asked me where my consort was. I answered, I had none. She said, "thy consort is at home by this time; lend me a pound of cotton." I told her I had but two pounds in the house, and I would not spare any to my mother. She said I had better have done it, that my sorrow was great already and it should be greater. . . . She then left me, and I was struck as with a clap of fire on the back. . . . She [Trimmings] continued that night and day very ill, and is still bad of her limbs, and complains still daily of it.[48]

Nicholas Disborough of Hartford in New England was strangely molested by stones, pieces of earth, cobs of Indian corn, etc. falling upon and about him. . . . This molestation began soon after a controversy arose between Disborough and another person about a chest of clothes.[49]

The most obvious aspect of these episodes is their association with conflict. And, indeed, the same association could be shown again and again from the extant records. Sometimes it appears in more generalized form. Thus a court petition urging formal charges against John Godfrey began: "Whereas diverse [persons] of esteem with us, and as we hear in other places also, have suffered losses in their estates and some affliction on their bodies . . . which, as they suppose, doth . . . arise . . . upon differences had betwixt themselves and one John Godfrey . . ."[50] Thus, too, a magistrates' summary of "grounds for examination" of a witch included the following: "if after quarreling or threatening, a personal mischief doth follow . . ."[51] And there is some behavioral confirmation of the same point in the skepticism (noted previously) of those Connecticut jurists who reversed the conviction of Mercy Disborough; among the "common things" which they refused to credit as "convictive of witchcraft" was the matter of "ill events, after quarrels or threats."[52]

But the bare fact of conflict offers at most a limited insight into the varied situations that appear to have fostered charges of witchcraft. One needs to ask what *manner* of conflict, what *objects* of conflict, and what *roles* in conflict for the parties directly concerned. To answer these questions nearly one hundred depositions (from two dozen separate cases) have been sorted and grouped in the following set of tables.

Table 2 confirms the overall presence of conflict in the materials, but also notices some exceptions. In five cases the alleged witchcraft accompanied encounters of an ostensibly friendly sort. ("As I was going to cut the tobacco, Hugh Parsons came in and said, 'Where is the man? Are you ready to go to the meeting?' I said, 'By the by; as soon as I have taken a pipe of tobacco.' So he stayed and took some with me.")[53] In three other cases there was "neutral" contact—that is, apparently without affective content. ("Allen Ball informed the court that one time Elizabeth Godman . . . came into his yard. His wife asked what she came for. She said to see her calf.")[54] And in three more there was no antecedent encounter at all—so far as the extant records reveal. Of course, the vagaries of record-keeping (and of record-survival) must be clearly recognized here. It is possible, perhaps probable, that unrecorded conflict contributed to at least some of these apparently atypical cases. It also seems clear that any contact with previously suspected witches was liable to sinister interpretation. A motive to conflict was assumed in such persons, and surface appearances might well be misleading.

The predominant setting for conflict, antecedent to witchcraft, was the transfer of goods, services, and information. One party—usually the alleged witch—approached the other in order to obtain some quite specific resource. Typically, the approach was rebuffed. And this, in turn, evoked a "threatening" or "cursing" response—and left a residue of

Table 2. Forms of contact antecedent to witchcraft

		Total	Accused initiates	Victim initiates	Initiative unknown
Contact with conflict	Transfer goods/services/ information	54	44	5	5
	Personal confrontation	12	4	8	—
	Unspecified quarreling	12	—	—	12
	Miscellaneous and other	7	1	5	1
Contact without conflict	Social overture	5	5	—	—
	Neutral contact	3	3	—	—
No contact indicated		3	—	—	3
	Total episodes	96	57	18	21

Table 3. Forms of exchange antecedent to witchcraft

	Total	Accused initiates	Victim initiates	Initiative unknown
Buy	9	9	—	—
Borrow	5	4	1	—
Ask	21	19	2	—
Take	1	—	1	—
Reclaim	5	5	—	—
Complain/change bargain	9	6	1	2
Unclear	4	1	—	3
Total episodes	54	44	5	5

bitterness on both sides. The terms of these exchanges were highly variable from one instance to the next. Sometimes there was an offer to buy. ("Goodwife Thorp complained that Mrs. Godman came to her house to buy some chickens; she said she had none to sell.")[55] Occasionally there was a request to borrow. ("Thomas Bracey . . . testifieth . . . that formerly James Wakeley would have borrowed a saddle of the said Thomas Bracey, which the said Thomas Bracey denied to lend to him.")[56] In other cases the issue was a claim for debt. ("Isabel Holdred deposed that John Godfrey came . . . and demanded a debt of her husband and . . . demanded if we would not pay him [and] the deponent

Table 4. Objects of exchange

Property		28
	Money	0
	Food/drink	9
	Produce	3
	Land	2
	Cattle/fowl	2
	Other	12
Service		10
Employment		5
Information		2
Debt		4
Access		3
Shelter		—
Unclear		2
Total		54

answered 'yes, tonight or tomorrow, if we had it.' ")[57] Or resentment about an agreement previously made. ("Hugh Parsons saith . . . 'If he would hold me to my bargain I could pussle him in the bargain.' ")[58]

But the most common element in this whole range of cases was a simple request—in effect, the asking of a favor. ("Goody Harrison's daughter came for some emptyings; I told her I had none. . . ."[59] "Mary [Parsons] desired me to let her have one of my daughters to dwell with her, and I, considering what rumors went about of her, was loath to let her go there to dwell. . . ."[60] "She [Eunice Cole] desired me to flea this cow, and presently after she charged me with killing it. . . ."[61] "Goody Garlick sent to her for breast milk, and presently after her milk dried away. . . .")[62] Surely such requests were made and received on countless occasions in every New England village. Presumably, too, some were refused for good and sufficient reasons—and without repercussions. Yet where witches were involved, simple things became, inevitably, more complicated.

It is worth noting, and emphasizing, that the initiative in these transactions normally belonged to the witch. Yet the role of the victim was hardly a passive one. He (or she) must respond to the dealings proposed —most often to reject them. And this might entail a substantial declaration of *self*-interest. (George Langdon rebuffed a request from Hugh Parsons "to buy some hay . . . for he had already sold more . . . than he could spare, and said he should now want himself.")[63] Occasionally there was a special note of peremptory, even angry, dismissal. (One woman, after refusing a request from Elizabeth Godman, had "bid her begone, she cared not for her company."[64] Another, in rebuffing Elizabeth Garlick, "spoke two or three words against her.")[65] It seems likely, moreover, that these accounts underrepresented the feelings actually expressed— in view of their usual source.

In one form of contact-experience (identified in Table 2 as "personal confrontation") victims frequently took the lead. Here was no transfer of goods or services, but rather a heated discussion of some mutually resonant theme. The most common theme in such cases was witchcraft itself—specifically, the suspect's own activity that way. Thus Elizabeth Titcomb engaged in "discourse" with Goody Morse "of the report that went of her as touching her name for witchcraft, and endeavoring to convince her of the wickedness of it."[66] Similarly, Mr. Stephen Goodyear (deputy governor of the New Haven Colony) "fell into a swoon . . . after he had spoken something one night in the exposition of the chapter"—something that his lodger, Elizabeth Godman, "liked not, but said it was against her."[67] Other confrontations involved efforts to exclude a suspect from one setting or another (a prayer meeting, a neighbor's childbed).[68] However different in detail—and in the expressed intentions of the participants—these initiatives conveyed a sharp accusatory thrust. Predictably, there was a price to pay in residual guilt and fear, and in the "afflictions" which might directly ensue.

The *objects* of conflict between witches and victims also deserve attention. But Table 4 presents a rather scattered, inconclusive picture. Just over half the cases analyzed here involved some form of property: food and drink, produce, land, cattle, or "other" (the largest single category). The remainder included service ("errands," "a small piece of work"), opportunities for employment ("to plow," "to keep the cows"), and privileged information of one sort or another (especially about court proceedings). It is perhaps worth noticing what does *not* appear; money, clothing, housing, domestic furnishings, civic honors and perquisites, religious or devotional preferment. Some of these things were not much present in village life generally (money, for instance); others had great, and controversial, importance, but remained separate in their social consequences from witchcraft.

Of course, there were many controversies, quarrels, "contentions" that had no connection with witchcraft whatsoever. One has only to dip into court records to appreciate the ubiquity of conflict in early New England life. And one is then bound to ask what *sorts* of conflict were especially liable to breed suspicions of witchcraft. Or, to frame the question in the broadest terms, where did witchcraft "fit" within a whole variegated spectrum of inducement and response to conflict? Recall the anthropologist's *dictum* that witchcraft most often appears in situations which combine high levels of tension with an absence of "outlets" or ready means of resolution.

In fact, New England society maintained several ways to resolve or reduce conflict. The legal system was the most formal of these, and evidently the most compelling.[69] Adjacent to the civil and criminal courts stood the churches with their own forms of ecclesiastical jurisprudence.[70] Related to these, but clearly important in their own right, were the various mechanisms of arbitration. And still further in the background (at least from *our* viewpoint) were innumerable third-party efforts of dispute settlement.[71] Finally, there was physical combat or "club law," which might in relatively rare instances serve as its own form of settlement.[72]

Taken altogether this made an impressive array—quite sufficient, one might think, to deal with the tensions of simple village-communities. Moreover, its substantive operations seem flexible, well-integrated, and (for the most part) efficient. Debt, trespass, breach of contract, property disputes of all kinds, were the stuff of court proceedings throughout New England. Some cases were put to arbitration, especially where there were several points of controversy and a "package" settlement seemed desirable. And, where feelings had been elevated and harsh words exchanged, additional efforts of peacemaking might develop either informally (with interested third-parties acting as mediators) or under the auspices of the church. Assault was normally reserved for the civil courts —though here, too, church congregations might undertake to deal with residues of ill will. Episodes of slander and defamation might go through several stages of resolution: challenges to fight, neighborhood mediation, inquiries by the local church-meeting, and regular lawsuits.

But this review does not quite cover the full range of source-points for personal tension and "controversy." When, indeed, it is measured against our profile of "situations" associated with witchcraft some striking differences emerge. When requests for food or drink were spurned, when loans of household property were denied, when cooperation in farmwork was refused, ill feeling on one or both sides was the likely result. Yet there were no grounds here for a court case, for an appeal to the church —let alone for a resort to personal violence. As Keith Thomas has written of comparable materials from premodern England, the principals "existed in a state of concealed hostility, for which society provided no legitimate outlet."[73]

Thomas and his colleague Macfarlane have developed a compelling model of interpretation that might well be applicable to New—no less than Old—English witchcraft. The key element is an "essential conflict between neighborliness and individualism." Viewed in *historical* context this conflict belonged to a long-term process of change—"the breakdown of the tradition of mutual help upon which many English village communities were based." The change was hardest on the "dependent members" of such communities—on widows, the poor, the elderly, the incompetent, and others whose subsistence had been underwritten by local charity. But there were strains and difficulties at all levels. More fortunate persons—who constituted the traditional source of charity— were caught between the old values and the new. They were more likely now to resent and refuse a neighbor's appeal for help, yet they could not feel comfortable with such refusals. "The ensuing guilt," Thomas concludes, "was fertile ground for witchcraft accusations, since subsequent misfortune could be seen as retaliation on the part of the witch."[74]

The latter part of this analysis seems somewhat doubtful in relation to the materials of the present study. Charity (in the strict sense) was less often an issue in the English colonies than in the mother country. Land was plentiful; hence the means of subsistence were generally available. Since life expectation was unusually long, widowhood was relatively uncommon. (Moreover, widows found abundant opportunities for remarriage, given a widespread imbalance in the sex-ratio.)[75] Of course, every community included at least a small group of "dependents" whose maintenance was occasionally problematic. A few such persons were indeed charged as witches. (Rachel Clinton and Eunice Cole make two rather conspicious examples; see Chapters 1 and 10.) However, most witches were *not* indigent or otherwise "dependent"; and most "dependents" were never accused of practicing witchcraft. Without a better fit in the actual membership of these two groups, there are insufficient grounds for inferring an important "structural" connection.

But if dependency as such does not figure largely in the history of New England witchcraft, the broader issue of "neighborliness" *versus* "individualism" seems powerfully resonant. Indeed, it could be argued that this issue was dramatized in early New England as nowhere else. On the one side, ancient traditions of community—or of "commonwealth," as the Puritans themselves would have said—were fixed at the heart of the New England way. Harmony, unity, cooperation, brotherhood: these were the values most widely expressed, and most profoundly honored, in the culture at large. John Winthrop set the standard for his companions and followers in a famous sermon on "Christian charity" delivered aboard the emigrant ship *Arbella* enroute to the New World. "We must be knit together," he declared, "as one man . . . and . . . must delight in each other, make others' condition our own, rejoice together, mourn together, labor and suffer together, always having before our eyes our commission and community in the work."[76] These precepts would in short order be translated into specific institutions and procedures in organized communities all across the region.

Yet the New World environment played an ironic trick on the Puritans. The uprooting itself, the "wilderness," the abundance of land, the fragility of all (transplanted) institutions, the spreading incentives to move and change and grow: all this worked to *undermine* community— or, at the least, to establish an alternative standard which was no less powerful for remaining unexpressed.[77] Actually the new standard *was* expressed, though not (for the most part) in so many words. Its outline can be traced, and its strength measured, in the elaborately detailed account-books of village merchants, in the spare diaries of yeoman farmers, and in the files of local courts.[78] Such materials display in bold relief the ingredients of a newly emergent pattern: land changing hands at a remarkable rate, contracts drawn (and remembered) with great precision, debts recorded in minute detail, inheritances challenged, boundaries rearranged, common fields reduced to private holdings, timberlands despoiled, and through it all particular men and women maneuvering vigorously for personal advantage. Here was the "individualism," the "self-help," of Thomas and Macfarlane—with a vengeance.

Eventually, the one standard would overwhelm the other (without entirely destroying it); but that is another story. The point here is the conflict between the two, and the fact that for generations they remained roughly counterbalanced. Both displayed powerful cultural supports. Both reached deep into the minds and hearts of average folk. Both informed action.

It is, in sum, hardly surprising that the transfer (or sharing) of personal resources should have proved especially problematic for such people. "We must . . . make others' condition our own," counselled Winthrop in his *Arbella* sermon. "I told her I had but two pounds [of cotton] in my house, and I would not spare any to my mother," said Susannah Trimmings in rebuffing an appeal from her neighbor, the suspected witch Goody Walford. Trimmings could not, however, square this behavior with her own conscience, where the values of "Christian charity" waxed strong—hence the exaggerated terms of her response; hence, too, her subsequent sense of being "struck as with a clap of fire on the back." In effect, what she experienced was a somatic "conversion" rooted in her own guilt—and ultimately in the divided values of the culture at large.

The "Functions" of Witchcraft

There remains, at the last, the important and difficult issue of witchcraft "functions." The current debate among anthropologists should serve to warn against reduction to merely mechanical formulas.[79] One cannot expect to find any single set of functions that would cover all cases; moreover, it should not be surprising if certain cases seem effectively *dys*functional overall. Indeed, in every case there were some negative aspects: for instance, a diversion of energy from regular social activity, and attitudes of bitterness that might considerably outlast a trial proceeding.

Midelfort's distinction between "major panics" and "small trials" provides an opening for discussion. The Salem "hysteria" of 1692–93 surely qualifies for the former category where the dysfunctional elements predominate. The trauma of that time would linger for decades, would indeed forge a chain of reactive and remedial actions (lawsuits, ecclesiastical disputes, family vendettas). Scant months after the last of the trials New Englanders began to rethink and regret the whole affair: some, like Samuel Sewall, accepted public "blame and shame" for their personal participation.[80] And if contemporaries reached such profoundly negative conclusions about Salem, we—their posterity—can hardly think otherwise.

But Salem appears to have been unique in this respect. So far as the records reveal, no other case prompted any considerable aftermath of soul-searching and regret. In general, individuals and communities involved in witchcraft cases accepted their necessity, and—at least sometimes—applauded their results. By their own lights, of course, such cases were eminently "functional." Who among them would question the goal of opposing evil in this, its most insidious guise?

And what of "functions" in a different—more objective—sense? The matter of *aftermath* presents an interesting clue. Reduced to their simplest terms, witchcraft trials might end in three ways: (1) the conviction and execution of the suspect; (2) the acquittal and removal of the suspect from her (his) community; (3) the acquittal and return of the suspect to her pre-trial situation. The third seems to have been the most common result; the second was apparently least common; the first came somewhere between. Each alternative bears further consideration.

The execution of a witch was evidently a drastic recourse, and there is no sign that accusers, or juries, or judges viewed it otherwise. Scattered notations in the extant records suggest that such events were long and widely remembered. (Margaret Jones, for example, was hanged at Boston in 1648; fifty years later John Hale vividly recalled the day, and a visit he had made to the convict "in the company of some neighbors" as a boy of twelve.)[81] A witchcraft conviction amounted to a violent excision from the community: a person, hated or feared but altogether familiar, was simply destroyed. Usually, it seems, the surviving kin would make haste to leave; sometimes they disappear from (our) view. Alice Young, New England's first known convict for witchcraft, was hanged at Windsor, Connecticut in 1647. Immediately thereafter her husband John sold his land and moved away—but *where* he went is not known. (A female Young—probably a daughter—turns up later in Springfield.)[82] The process of dispersal is a little easier to follow for the family of Alice Lake, convicted and executed at Dorchester in about 1650. Her husband Henry moved away at once; his name appears regularly in the records of Portsmouth, Rhode Island, beginning in April 1651. Meanwhile the four Lake children, all less than ten years old, remained in Dorchester. One, probably the youngest, was "bound out" by the town meeting to a local family for a "consideration" of £26—and was dead within two years. The other three were also placed in (separate) Dorchester households. At this point their trail becomes badly obscured. (One was living as a servant to an uncle—still in Dorchester—in 1659.) Later, having reached adulthood, the same three were found in Rhode Island—and then in Plymouth Colony, where their father had removed by 1673. It appears, therefore, that the family was eventually reunited, some two decades after the event that had broken it apart.[83]

To have lost a wife or a mother in this fashion must have seemed catastrophic; one can imagine a mix of feelings (grief, anger, shame, fear) so sharp and so incongruous as to defy ordinary processes of adaptation. But what were the effects of an execution on other members of the community? Did they feel "cleansed" in some sense? Were they newly inclined to scrutinize their own lives for signs of moral or behavioral shortcoming? The answer to both questions is probably—but not provably—affirmative. An anthropologist with extensive experience of African cultures notes the cathartic effect of having publicly condemned and executed a witch. Those involved feel "purged," for they have "found the enemy who made things go wrong for all of them; they have destroyed him; they can all breathe more easily."[84] One imagines the same reaction, following similar events, among the early New Englanders. They, too, would experience an end to stress and worry—or at least to one source thereof.

There were, of course, other ways to achieve this result. As noted above, some trials effectively removed the suspect from the scene of difficulty without ending her (his) life. Hugh Parsons abandoned his home in Springfield immediately following his trial, and acquittal, on charges of witchcraft. A year later he was writing from Boston to settle accounts with old creditors; and later still he appeared in Rhode Island.[85] Katherine Harrison of Wethersfield gained an acquittal from the charges against her but agreed to go elsewhere as soon as the trial was over. (The court records, in noting this arrangement, imply her voluntary consent; but it looks in retrospect like a form of banishment.)[86] Other suspects fled their homes before trials could be started (for example, several from Hartford who, in the early 1660s, surreptitiously decamped to Rhode Island).[87] At least a few managed to escape even after indictment and conviction. Nicholas Jennings of Saybrook, Connecticut, was found guilty on a witchcraft charge in 1661; his wife Margaret was acquitted but "strongly suspected." Sometime later they turned up on Long Island.

Apparently they had left without their children, two of whom were "bound out" to Saybrook families by local courts.[88]

One can readily understand the impulse of these people to flee the scene of their difficulties. To remain, after all, would leave them vulnerable to renewed charges and proceedings, and there was always the risk that next time the verdict would go against them. What seems surprising—and extremely suggestive in the present context—is the fact that so many *other* accused witches elected to stay on in their homes, surrounded by the very people who most strongly suspected them. The case-materials display this pattern repeatedly: for example, Rachel Clinton—holding fast in Ipswich in the face of two separate witchcraft trials and other tribulations;[89] and John Godfrey—continuing to circulate through several Essex County towns where his reputation (for witchcraft, among other things) was notorious;[90] and Elizabeth Garlick—returning to Easthampton after acquittal by the Court of Assistants at Hartford, and living on there for another half-century . . .[91] In the Garlick case the court advised the people of Easthampton that they should "carry it neighborly and peaceably" with the accused—implicitly recognizing the possibility of trouble.[92] In other cases there is no record of any official concern. Indeed, the Godfrey case produced the remarkable spectacle of a suspect living as a lodger in the household of his erstwhile accusers just a short while after going to trial.

To understand all this is a difficult but important task. For a start, decisions to "remove" would sometimes carry a severe price. Widow Harrison, for example, left substantial properties behind, and the Jenningses left their children. Moreover, there might be difficulty in gaining admittance as a certified "inhabitant" in another place, especially if the applicant's reputation for witchcraft had accompanied her.[93] There was also the advantage of familiarity (in one's home village) and the risk of the unknown (elsewhere). Perhaps a suspect felt safer where she knew the situation out of long experience, knew the people, knew what to expect—however bad.

And yet the issue cannot be entirely settled this way. The fact that some witches did pick up and leave, the fact that the dangers in staying ran to life itself, the fact that countless ordinary New Englanders contrived to change their place of residence (sometimes more than once): all this suggests additional—and less practical—circumstances coming strongly into play. Perhaps, beyond those considerations that weighed against a separation of witch-suspects and their accusers, there were some elements actually pulling them together. Perhaps, indeed, the two sides were joined by covert needs, or attraction, or affinity.[94] The suspect, for her part, obtained some advantage from her notoriety. She had become, if nothing else, a figure to be reckoned with—an object not just of hatred but of fear and even (in one sense) of respect. Her words and deeds commanded attention through a broad circle of her peers.*

And what of the accusers—and of other community-members? Was the presence of a suspect in some ways gratifying, or at least useful, to them as well? One point immediately suggests itself: witches could be *blamed* for a good deal of trouble and difficulty. In this respect the belief in witchcraft was very useful indeed. To discover an unseen hand at work in one's life was to dispel mystery, to explain misfortune, to excuse incompetence. Of course, the situation was somewhat ambiguous in its results: certain forms of stress were reduced or avoided, while others (in relation to the witch herself) were accepted, even heightened. In effect this was a shift, not a final resolution, but it seems on balance to have been preferable for the people most directly concerned. And there is one further, related consideration. Witches, in being *blamed*, served as legitimate targets for angry feeling. Resentments originating in various far-flung corners of experience might find an outlet here. In general, Puritan values condemned the expression of anger most severely, but witchcraft made an exception. It seems plausible, therefore, that the belief in witchcraft should have helped to maintain both personal and social equilibrium.

But even as witchcraft opened exceptions to established moral boundaries, it served to sharpen those same boundaries—and ultimately to strengthen them. For here was a vivid composite of traits and motives emphatically defined as evil. "There is in witchcraft," wrote Cotton Mather, "a most explicit renouncing of all that is holy and just and good." And again: "Witchcraft—what shall I say of it! It is the furthest effort of our original sin; and all that can make any practice or persons odious is here in the exalt[at]ion of it."[95] Moreover, witchcraft was exemplified, was personified, in the witch herself—"sin incarnate," as more than one writer put it. In effect, witches advertised the nature and the wages of sin in their all-too-corporeal presence. In this connection it is well to recall the substantive attributes of witches, as experienced (or imagined) by the populace at large. Angry motive, contentious behavior, a rough and grasping style: these qualities stood out in the persons

---

* Perhaps, too, some of the accused witches specifically welcomed negative, or hostile, attention. If so, they conformed to a well-known character type, in which one can sense a virtual compulsion to elicit hostility. The roots of this pattern may lie in unconscious guilt—and a consequent need for expressions of "punishment." Or, alternatively, there may be a paranoid dynamic at work, which hostile encounters both feed and confirm.

actually accused.[96] Meanwhile, fantasy produced the same picture, but in stronger, more lurid colors—the witch as "attacker," with all that such a figure implied.[97]

Directly opposite the witch—across the same moral boundary—stood the figure of the good man, the man most likely to have been "elected" by God for "salvation." Cotton Mather paused, amidst a long discussion of witchcraft, to describe his qualities: "Let us more generally agree to maintain a kind opinion one of another. That charity, without which even our giving our bodies to be burned would profit nothing, uses to proceed by this rule: it is kind, it is not easily provoked, it thinks no evil, it believes all things, hopes all things."[98] Kindliness vs. malignity, charity vs. self-concern, harmony vs. conflict, the witches vs. the sainted ones: here is an absolutely central line of meaning for the present study. It appears, and reappears, throughout; indeed it joins the biographical, the psychological, and now the sociological parts of our task.

To reaffirm these vital norms and commitments was, moreover, to renew the inner bonds of community. Witchcraft proceedings declared a moral *and* social opposition. The lines drawn divided not only right from wrong, but also allies from foes, in-group from out-group, "us" from "them."[99] Said one minister, addressing himself directly to witches wherever found: "All mankind is now . . . set against you. You have proclaimed yourselves mortal enemies to all men, and they cannot but mortally hate and abominate you."[100] Said another, with particular reference to the Salem affair:

> The Devil . . . has decoyed a fearful knot of proud, forward, igno-rant, envious, and malicious creatures, to list themselves in his horrid service, by entering their names in a book by him tendered unto them. These witches, whereof above a score have now con-fessed . . . have met in hellish rendezvous, wherein the confessors do say they have had their diabolical sacraments, imitating the baptism and the supper of our Lord. In these hellish meetings these monsters have associated themselves to do no less a thing than to destroy the Kingdom of our Lord Jesus Christ in these parts of the world. . . .[101]

In short, the witches themselves made a community which reversed the principles, and mocked the ritual practices, of truly God-fearing souls. And as the one category was identified for all to see, so would the other show—in deeper, fuller measure—its own intrinsic qualities.

That witchcraft might serve to unify "us" by lopping off one of "them" is evident throughout the case materials. Gossip itself was a binding force. In the months preceding the trial of Hugh Parsons his Springfield,

Massachusetts neighbors became increasingly "agitated" on the subject of witchcraft. Women meeting "in the street" or "at home," men at work "in the woods," swapped stories of "strange doings in the town." Their mood was one of shared anticipation. Parsons himself felt isolated and extruded by all this: he "would not speak anything about these things," he "held down his head," he "sat dumb," he ate his dinner (after a morning's labor in company with others) "on a bough . . . [apart from] the rest."[102]

Often, of course, there was a particular victim to center the group's excitement. When Elizabeth Howell lay ill under suspicious circumstances in the winter of 1658 her Easthampton, Long Island, friends hovered around searching for clues to her "affliction." Together they prodded Elizabeth for names ("Garlick? What of Garlick?"). Together they studied the peculiarities of the case (for instance, a large pin that seemed to "fall from her mouth"). Together they circulated reports of their findings among the townspeople at large.[103] When Elizabeth Knapp was "in her fits" at Groton, Massachusetts, in 1671, she was repeatedly observed by "a large company." Her efforts to fix blame on a particular witch did not succeed, and ultimately her troubles were diagnosed as "demonic possession." But public interest remained high throughout. Indeed, in one climactic scene her neighbors, singly and jointly, exchanged taunts with a Devil "speaking vocally" from inside her.[104]

Where local suspicion and gossip led on to legal proceedings, there was another kind of focus. The summoning of witnesses, the actual taking of depositions, the "examination" of defendants—accusers, victims, and sympathetic "bystanders" bringing a "child of Satan" to justice—this was nothing if not a *joint* enterprise.[105] And when a trial was concluded, and a verdict rendered, the same group-pressures would continue to operate. Executions were, of course, public events of great moment. Ministers and magistrates, seeking to extract last-minute confessions and/or repentance from the convict, furnished a lead to "crowds" of fascinated onlookers.[106] Sometimes the excitement would continue after the event itself—witness the macabre scene (noted above) around the body of the Fairfield witch, Goodwife Knapp.[107] Presumably, too, the weeks and months following such events would bring special sermons, additional gossip, official dealings with the family and estate of the convict. "There is a voice in it to the whole land, but in a more special manner to poor Groton," said Samuel Willard to his pastoral flock after the extraordinary times of Elizabeth Knapp's possession. "It is not a judgement afar off, but it is near us, yea, among us. God hath in His wisdom singled out this poor town . . . of all the others in this wilderness."[108] One can imagine the effect of these words on the Rev. Willard's auditors—the worry, the excitement, even the pride, at having been thus "singled out." Indelibly they were marked by shared experience.

But the meanings of witchcraft ran well beyond (what one anthropologist has called) "moral philosophy." From defining and personifying the boundaries between good and evil, and from renewing an active sense of group identity, there followed in implicit sequence the "function" of *control*. The ministers themselves saw this clearly enough—and sought to make the most of it on their own terms. Their projects of recording and publishing "illustrious providences" (including witchcraft) were carefully designed to bolster traditional religious values. Acquaintance with such "amazing" and frightening events might serve to "confute . . . atheism and Sadducism," and to "reprove the madness of ungodly men."[109] In the long run the strengthening of belief in witchcraft might constructively influence behavior.

The writings of the ministers also afford insight into the workings of this process in personal terms. They warned, first of all, that immoral or antisocial conduct would directly invite the Devil's attention and give him a chance to find new recruits. Thus the Rev. Deodat Lawson declared, in a famous sermon on the Salem trials: "By giving way unto sinful and unruly passions such as envy, malice, or hatred of our neighbors and brethren, . . . [we] do endanger the letting in [of] Satan and his temptations."[110] Cotton Mather wrote to a friend, at about the same time: "When a sinful child of man distempers himself with some exorbitant motions in his mind, . . . a Devil then soon presents himself unto him, and he demands, 'are you willing that I should go do this or that for you?' [And] if the man once comply, the Devil hath him now in a most horrid snare."[111]

Moreover, some of the Devil's "snares" did not require willing compliance from the man (or woman) involved. Religious folk would recognize that ostensibly innocent persons might sometimes be "represented" in the shape of witch-like tormentors. Perhaps, though, they were not actually so innocent; Cotton Mather posed these questions:

> Who can certainly say what other degrees or methods of sinning, besides that of a diabolical compact, may give the Devils advantage to act in the shape of them that have miscarried? . . . May not some that have been ready upon feeble grounds uncharitably to censure and reproach other people be punished for it by *spectres* for a while exposing *them* to censure and reproach?[112]

Even to be a victim of witchcraft was to face some painful questions. For neither Satan nor individual witches could launch an attack without God's implied assent. Thus, when John Goodwin saw his own children grievously "afflicted" and "tormented" (at Boston, in 1688), he felt impelled "to look into my own heart and life, and see how matters did there stand between God and my own soul, and see wherefore the Lord was thus contending with me. And upon inquiry I found cause to judge myself, and to justify the Lord."[113]

And victims suffered not only *self*-blame, but also the "censure" of others. When Elizabeth Knapp was afflicted at Groton, her neighbors reasoned thus: "Surely, there is some special reason, some more than ordinary provocation—why else is God come out upon that family, rather than upon any other family?" Samuel Willard, who reported this "common" reaction, was himself of two minds about it. He did not wish "to make those whom the judgement nextly concerns to be regardless of God's hand upon them." At the same time, he urged others to be cautious in this matter of judging, and to remember that they too were sinners who "might have been chosen in the room of this person to have been hung up as a sign, and a wonder, and an astonishment, for others with sad hearts to have looked upon."[114]

Viewed in sum and in sociological perspective, these beliefs displayed considerable power to control and constrain behavior. An individual tempted to action at variance with community standards might anticipate one of several possibilities. (1) He (or she) might himself be suspected as a witch—with all the peril that such suspicion implied. (2) He might open himself to spectral "representation" by the Devil—and thus to "censure and reproach" from his peers. (3) He, or members of his family, might become victims of witchcraft—and be "hung up as a sign . . . for others with sad hearts to [look] upon." In each case, group sanctions, or pressures, or attitudes, would apply the decisive element of constraint. Witchcraft served, then, as a kind of fulcrum enabling the community to exert leverage on potentially or actually recalcitrant individuals. Its effectiveness cannot now be measured, since effectiveness in this sense would amount to (mis)deeds prevented. What the evidence largely presents is a roster of cases where the leverage had failed, where particular men and women—the accused witches—were thought to have defied group standards and gone their own way. Unfortunately, we can make no comparable studies of other instances in which the system "worked." There is no way to search the hearts and minds of average New Englanders for motives to "sin" that may ultimately have been held in check by consideration of witchcraft. But the human probabilities seem clear. We confront here a *schema* of such unmistakable lines—from motive, to perception, to fear, to (self-)restraint—that we can scarcely doubt its salience for behavior. There were, of course, other checks on behavior, deriving from both social and psychological sources. Few persons could have worried about witchcraft on a continuous basis. But compared to most alternative "controls" witchcraft carried a special charge of meaning. On at least some occasions, perhaps quite often, it entered strongly into the elaborate calculus which shaped the conduct of individual New Englanders.

Witchcraft and Community: A Summing-up

This discussion has explored the manifold connections between witchcraft as a matter of belief for individual men and women, and personal behavior based on such belief, and the ordering of entire communities. Witchcraft cases exposed particular stress-points in group experience; at the same time they exemplified patterns of social constraint around which village and neighborhood groups were organized. In a sense, therefore, the study of witchcraft affords some uniquely diagnostic views —of the parts of New England society, but also of the whole.

The association of witchcraft and community—one might well say, the embeddedness of witchcraft *in* community—is hardly in itself a novel finding. The same association (broadly conceived) appears in many different cultural settings, past and present, around the world. Yet its force and direction, its meaning, its consequences, its operative "function": all this is variable and highly dependent on other circumstances of the particular community in view. Most commonly, witchcraft beliefs (and accusations) serve to protect group life, but at least occasionally they mark its disintegration. And there is a range of intermediate possibilities.

What, then, can one conclude about New England witchcraft and New England communities as distinctive historical specimens? First, that their linkage was *especially* tight and telling—because community itself was such a key value for the Puritans. Second, that witchcraft operated primarily as a "conservative," cohesive force (though not without some counter-potential, that is, for enhancing group conflict). Third, that witchcraft laid bare—and, in a sense, controlled—a critical point of tension in New England society: cooperative values *versus* individualistic ones, giving and sharing *versus* taking and accumulating—describe it as one may.

There is a final and plainly critical issue to mention. Witchcraft seems to have held a larger importance in early New England than in other, contemporaneous settings. Precise comparison is impossible, but this much can be said. In Old England and in most parts of continental Europe witchcraft faded dramatically after the middle of the seventeenth century—faded, that is, as a matter of serious belief, widely held and widely influential for behavior. Similarly, in other parts of the American colonies witchcraft belief was present but not potent, and actions based on such belief were scattered and inconsequential. Yet in New England, to repeat, the case was very much otherwise. And why?

Two factors look, in retrospect, particularly decisive. One was organized religion. As legions of scholars have agreed, and as every school-child knows, life in early New England was fitted to religious imperatives in ways quite extraordinary even by the standards of the premodern world. The case can be overstated, and sometimes is, but in this respect the Puritans deserve the reputation that history has given them. Simply put: their religious experience was distinctive in its intensity—and in some qualitative aspects as well. They regarded themselves as participants in a cosmic struggle between the forces of God and of Satan for control of the universe. History was, by their lights, a theater of unceasing warfare—grand in scale, terrifying in character, and fraught with the gravest consequences for all concerned.

This was the context within which Puritans sought to understand witchcraft; but if it did indeed afford understanding, it also raised the stakes all around. Clergymen repeatedly emphasized, in their sermons and published writings, the dangers posed by Satan's "incarnate legions." Witches were viewed as shock-troops in "an horrible plot against all mankind."[115] Moreover, the plot might plausibly be imagined to have singled out New England as a special target. "If ever there were witches, . . ." wrote Samuel Parris of Salem, "here are multitudes in New England."[116] And Cotton Mather explained why: "If any are scandalized that New England, a place of as serious piety as any I can hear of under Heaven, should be troubled so much with witches, I think 'tis no wonder: where will the Devil show the most malice but where he is hated, and hateth, most?"[117]

Such pronouncements cannot be made to stand for all New Englanders in all respects. Popular attitudes toward witchcraft and the views of the ministers were not of a piece: the latter were more fully and explicitly theological; the former were flavored by folk-traditions of magic, fortune-telling, healing, and the like.[118] But with that difference understood, one can still impute wide *influence* to clerical opinion. Indeed, in those scattered passages where the record offers a glimpse of average persons encountering witchcraft, their own theocentric stance is quite evident. When threatened with harm by spectral "shapes" they answered (in one case), "I hope that Lord Jesus Christ will save me," or (in another) "she feared not because God had kept her and would keep her still."[119] (A third victim was more resigned: "I thought, let God do what He will.")[120] When confronted with the Devil "speaking through" a demoniac, "one told him [that] God had him in chains," and another taunted that "God is stronger than thou."[121]

Witches—Satan—God's overarching "providence"—the warfare of opposing spiritual kingdoms—New England as an especially important battlefield: key strands, all, in a tightly stretched and broadly shared web of associations. Thus was witchcraft infused, underscored, *amplified* at virtually every point by "Puritan" religion.

And alongside the cognitive web—in effect, supporting it—lay the web of social experience. We who live in a world of huge metropolitan populations, infinitely complex social and economic structures, and highly "differentiated"—sometimes anonymous—modes of experience cannot easily appreciate the *personal* quality of life in a premodern village. But we should try. The spatial dimensions are narrow enough: go a few hundred yards in any direction from the town center (or "green"), and habitation stops, fields and forest begin. Within this little circumference lies a main street; a few side-roads; home lots laid one against the next without intermission; houses drawn up close to the street, and facing the street and each other. The human dimensions are no less confined: perhaps a hundred families (in the average case), comprising a total of five or six hundred souls. Each individual resident knows, and is known to, all the others. More, each individual sees all the others on multiple occasions and in widely different contexts: Imagine:

> The brickmaker who rebuilds your chimney is also the constable who brings you a summons to court, an occupant of the next bench in the meetinghouse, the owner of a share adjacent to one of yours in the "upland" meadow, a rival for water-rights to the stream that flows behind that meadow, a fellow-member of the local "train band" (i.e. militia), an occasional companion at the local "ordinary," a creditor (from services performed for you the previous summer but not as yet paid for), a potential customer for wool from the sheep you have begun to raise, the father of a child who is currently a bond-servant in your house, a colleague

on a town committee to repair and improve the public roadways.
... And so on. Do the two of you enjoy your shared experiences?
Not necessarily. Do you know each other well? Most certainly.

Of course, not all village relationships would have quite this same
density, but none would lack it altogether. Each and every social transaction was personal in the fullest sense. The rewards one sought and
sometimes found, the losses sustained, the hopes raised, the disappointments suffered: all this depended on other, entirely familiar human
beings. With us today—to draw the contrast very baldly—the comparable
range of activity passes through and around institutions. Moreover, our
institutions are many in number and various in operation; and we deal
with them separately, one for this reason, another for that. Of course,
they confront us with people—but people who are performing "roles,"
and who are otherwise unknown to us. In the usual course of events
such dealings are decidedly *impersonal*.

How different the premodern village! There personal influence was,
or seemed to be, all-powerful. In that context witchcraft made sense, and
was almost a logical necessity. For witchcraft coupled one important
category of events—sudden misfortune, loss, suffering—with some notably personal referents.

We call this pattern "premodern" in a general way, and so it was.
Early New England made a case in point, and an unusually vivid one.
Village life seems to have been *more* dense there than in most other
parts of the contemporaneous world. And the sense of personal influence
on experience was correspondingly greater.

We conclude, then, that life in early New England expressed a double
concern of extraordinary intensity—with things unseen and supernatural,
but also with things most tangible and personal. For a time at least, the
one reinforced the other. And, along the seam of their convergence,
witchcraft would continue to root, to rise, even to flourish.

FOUR
History

"I believe there never was a poor plantation more pursued . . . than our New England . . . First, the Indian *powwaws* . . . Then *seducing spirits* . . . After this, a continual *blast* upon some of our principal grains . . . Herewithal, wasting *sicknesses* . . . Next, many adversaries of our own language . . . Desolating *fires* also . . . And *losses* by sea . . . Besides all which . . . the devils are come down upon us with such a wrath as is justly . . . the astonishment of the world."

The Rev. Cotton Mather (1693)

10

"From Generation to Generation"

A trial for witchcraft was invariably a powerful *event*, a moment of intense drama in the lives of all those who supported the proceedings, or sought desperately to defend against them, or merely stood by and watched. But such trials were just the high points on a variable "curve" of personal and communal anxieties. The survival in quantity of court records, and the relative paucity of material on everyday circumstance, may lead us into errors of emphasis. We must periodically remind ourselves that witchcraft—or a concern therewith—was a *persistent* feature of life in early New England.

The history of Hampton (until 1679 a part of the province of Massachusetts Bay, but belonging thereafter to New Hampshire) seems especially well suited for making this point. For more than twenty years the people of Hampton worried and gossiped about the dubious character of their neighbor, Goodwife Eunice Cole. On at least three occasions they brought her to court for conduct indicating "familiarity with the Devil." She became, in truth, a local celebrity, familiar not only to Hamptonites but also to residents of neighboring towns and to passing boatmen who traded along the New England coast. From a variety of local records it is possible to grasp the long-term continuity in the experience of this alleged witch, and in the town's dealings with her. One can even trace lines of personal contact along which her reputation passed through time and across generations, adding new recruits to the legion of her accusers and victims.

Goody Cole was the first and most notorious witch at Hampton, but

she was not the last. As she grew older, attention shifted to other women.
New arrests were made, testimony taken, bonds filed—although, in the
end, matters were resolved short of actual convictions. After 1680 there
were no further legal actions of this sort, but witchcraft remained a part
of the popular consciousness. Well into the eighteenth century, Hamptonites sensed the Devil at work around them.

New towns were stitched together from a dense fabric of personal
experience—the multiform biographies of all the individuals in the
founding group. Inevitably, of course, the strength and substance of
individual contributions was highly variable. In Hampton the single
most powerful influence during the founding period was the Rev.
Stephen Bachiller.

The thread of Bachiller's personal history reached far back into the
sixteenth century. Born somewhere in the south of England in about
1560, he was graduated from Oxford in 1586, ordained a minister of
the Anglican Church, and appointed vicar of Wherwhell in county
Hampshire. By the turn of the century he was deeply involved in the
Puritan movement—for which cause he was deprived, in 1605, of his
ministerial living. His movements during the following twenty-five years
are difficult to trace, but it seems that he preached sporadically to non-
conforming groups in various parts of England (and perhaps in Holland). In 1632, when he was already past seventy years old, the Rev.
Bachiller sailed for New England, accompanied by a number of relatives, friends, and ecclesiastical followers.[1]

Accepting a call to preach at Saugus (later Lynn) in the Bay Colony,
he became at once a center of contention there. Perhaps his views were
somewhat "antinomian"; in any case, his preaching was suspended by
order of the General Court "for his contempt of authority." Moving
temporarily to Ipswich with his little retinue, Bachiller now sought a
new locus farther from the seat of government. He considered, then
abandoned, a proposal to settle at Yarmouth on Cape Cod. (Governor
Winthrop noted, with evident admiration, that Bachiller, "though about
seventy-six years of age . . . went thither [to Yarmouth] on foot in a
very hard season"—the distance from Ipswich being about a hundred
miles.) Soon the Bachiller party was found at Newbury; it was from
there that they planned the settlement of Hampton.[2]

In the autumn of 1638 the General Court granted their petition "to
begin a plantation at Winnacunnet" (the Indian name for the site).[3]
There were fifteen signers, and Stephen Bachiller's name headed the
list.[4] The hard, physical work of "foundation" began almost immedi-

ately, and by the next spring a little village was alive and flourishing there, ready for legal incorporation.[5] Meanwhile a tide of additional settlers flowed rapidly in.[6] By the end of the year there were some sixty families on the site—a total that held, with only minor fluctuations, for several decades. The usual administrative procedures were established, around the focal point of the town meeting. Officers were elected: selectmen, constables, herdsmen (right from the start the town was much involved with cattle-raising),[7] woodwards, haywards, surveyors. Land was parcelled out, according to a complicated (and somewhat obscure) set of criteria. As a result, most settlers received modest, but adequate acreage (in a range from 10 to 30), while ten obtained much larger holdings (80–150 acres), and five were granted "farms" (250–300 acres).[8] Such inequities were characteristic of all New England towns —though in this case the scale of difference seems exceptionally large.

On other fronts trouble loomed, virtually from the start. Roughly concurrent with the settlement of Hampton, another group had founded the town of Exeter, several miles to the west.[9] Led by John Wheelright —recently exiled from Massachusetts for his role in the Hutchinson controversy—and largely sympathetic to "antinomian" views, these people had chosen a site hitherto beyond the borders of the Bay Colony. Their territorial claims were based on a purchase from the local Indians. However, the terms of this purchase embraced parts of Hampton as well; hence there ensued a sharp struggle between the two fledgling communities. A short while later Hampton's boundaries were questioned by her *southern* neighbor, the town of Salisbury. The dispute with Exeter was gradually resolved—but not so the other one. Indeed, Hampton and Salisbury engaged in repeated controversy over their common border for another two hundred fifty years! (The line between two colonies—later states—was also at issue.)[10]

But far more serious, in the short run, was the growth of conflict within the population of Hampton itself. Some of the particulars are no longer discoverable, but the level of feeling seems clear. Winthrop noted, among his journal entries for 1644, that "the contentions at Hampton were grown to a great height."[11] Once again Stephen Bachiller was found in the eye of the storm. Incredibly—for he was now an octogenarian—he stood accused of "soliciting the chastity of his neighbor's wife." As a result, he was removed from his ministry (a familiar experience), and formally excommunicated. His supporters tried strenuously, but unsuccessfully, to reverse these actions by appealing to the General Court; they were, it seems, considerably outnumbered within the church congregation.[12] By the late 1640s Bachiller had moved off to Portsmouth,

from where he launched a series of lawsuits against his former parishioners at Hampton, claiming "wages" still due for his services.[13] In 1654
he recrossed the ocean, and in 1660 died near London "in the one
hundredth year of his age."[14]

Behind the "scandals" laid at the minister's door lurked problems of
another sort. Almost certainly, the membership of the Hampton church
was divided over *ecclesiastical* issues, with Bachiller propounding one
viewpoint, and his pastoral colleague—the Rev. Timothy Dalton—the
other. It has been surmised that Bachiller was too "independent" by the
standards of his community, even that the Massachusetts leadership
connived at his ouster; but evidence on these points is lacking.[15] What
seems clearer is a difference in English origins, between the members
of the opposing groups. Careful study of signatures on rival petitions,
and of ancestral lines to England, shows that most of Bachiller's followers
had come from the southern counties, while the Dalton faction was
predominantly East Anglian.[16] Bachiller himself noted these differences,
in a bitter letter addressed to the elders of the church at Boston. Dalton,
he charged, had "been the cause of all the dishonor that accrued . . . to
myself . . . by his irregular proceedings, and abuse of the power of the
church in his hands, by the major part cleaving to him, being his country-
men and acquaintances in old England."[17]

Strenuous efforts were made to heal this breach in the years 1643 and
1644. "Diverse meetings . . . [with] magistrates and elders" might temporarily dampen the controversy, but—as Winthrop noted—then it
"brake out presently again, each side being apt to take fire upon any
provocation." After this point the record thins out, and questions remain
about the process leading to a final resolution. No doubt the decision of
the Rev. Bachiller to "voluntarily remove [from Hampton] for peace sake"
constitutes at least a part of the answer.[18]

With Bachiller gone, conflict swirled away from religion and morality,
toward issues of property and politics. In 1646 the town held special
meetings to decide the ownership of a vast tract of previously ungranted
lands, known as the "cow commons." The upshot was a carefully cali-
brated plan dividing the lands into 147 shares, and in turn assigning
these shares to the established residents. As before, the distribution was
an unequal one, with individual householders receiving one, two, or
three shares, depending on size of family—and of tax-rate. Objections
were raised by some who felt short-changed in these assignments, and
so Hampton was obliged once more to turn to outside arbitration. The
usual remonstrances to the General Court brought the usual response,
the appointment of a select committee "to search and examine all differ-

ences at Hampton."[19] There was a weary sense of *déjà vu*: in the words of one petition, "our differences have been so long and tedious, as that they even make our spirits to droop under them."[20] Eventually, the original order about the commons was allowed to stand, with only minor modifications.

It would be tedious, and unnecessary, to present further details of town conflict in these years, but two general conclusions are worth mentioning. First, substantive issues, as they arose, regularly threatened to immerse the town in new controversy—so raw were sensitivities on all sides.[21] But, second, the overall *level* of conflict diminished perceptibly with the passage of time. Indeed, after the early 1650s Hampton seems to have achieved a *modus vivendi*, with which most, it not all, of her citizens were reasonably comfortable. When new troubles developed, they were effectively contained by procedures internal to the community.

The formal history of witchcraft in Hampton begins with the year 1656. That there was an *informal* history, extending some time farther back, seems likely—but not provable from extant materials.[22] In any case, by the spring of 1656 Hamptonites were giving evidence on a wide scale, directed toward the prosecution of Goodwife Eunice Cole. An initial brace of depositions was taken by magistrates in Essex County that April, and was forwarded to Boston for use in a trial before the General Court the following September. The court solicited further testimony of its own, so that some two dozen witnesses eventually took part.[23] Nine manuscript depositions survive today, and provide at least a sampling of the charges against Goody Cole. Two of these imputed illness (a grown man) and death (an infant girl) to her *maleficium*; three others alleged acts of destruction against domestic animals. The same materials noted a variety of suspicious and seemingly occult phenomena: strange scrapings against houses, fierce cats appearing suddenly and then disappearing, a private conversation that was somehow known to the accused.[24]

But who was Goody Cole? What can be learned of her character? And what was the pattern of her relations with others? The trial testimonies themselves yield some parts of the answer to such questions. She was, first of all, a woman given to threats and curses against those she perceived as antagonists. ("Goodwife Cole said that if this deponent's calves . . . did eat any of her grass, she wished it might poison or choke them.")[25] She was herself quite ready to proclaim the influence of witchery. ("Goodwife Cole said that she was sure there was a witch in

the town, . . . and that thirteen years ago she knew one bewitched as
Goodwife Marston's child was.")[26] She was not reluctant to confront
established authority. ("At a meeting with the selectmen, Eunice Cole
came in . . . and demanded help of the selectmen for wood or other
things; and the selectmen told her she had an estate of her own, and
needed no help of the town.")[27]

These scattered glimpses of Eunice Cole interacting with her accusers
can be supplemented by evidence of other kinds. She had arrived in
New England some two decades before, together with her husband, a
carpenter named William. A bill from November 1637 noted the manner of their coming: "William Cole . . . to pay unto Matthew Craddock
of London, merchant, the sum of ten pounds of current money . . . for
his and his wife's passage, and so to be free of their service to Mr.
Craddock."[28] (Twenty years later Craddock took the Coles to court over
this debt, "to this day never satisfied.") There was no reference, here or
elsewhere, to any younger Coles, and it seems safe to assume that the
couple was childless.

It is evident, too, that the Coles were quite poor. Recently freed from
service to an English merchant, they assumed a modest position in the
little community of Mount Wollaston (later Braintree) just to the south
of Boston.[29] Mount Wollaston was the initial base of the controversial
"antinomian" preacher, John Wheelwright; it was from there that he
and his followers set out to found the town of Exeter. Because they
moved beyond the reach of any provincial authority, the Exeter group
drew up special articles of "combination" as a basis for self-government.
All of the first-comers set their hands to these articles, promising thereby
to "submit ourselves . . . to Godly and Christian laws." Included in the
list is the name of William Cole, undersigned with a crude personal
mark.[30]

The Coles spent five uneventful years in Exeter. A land division
among early householders, with the usual pattern of unequal shares,
finds William near the middle of the list.[31] Twice he went to court in
minor actions—once as plaintiff, once as defendant.[32] In 1643 he served
as fence-viewer, the only civil office he ever held in New England.[33]

It is not known why the Coles moved to Hampton in 1644, but this
change marked a sharp downward turn in their fortunes.[34] In remarkably short order they incurred the enmity of their new neighbors. In
1645 Eunice was charged at Salisbury Court with having made "slander-
ous speeches" against other Hampton women.[35] Two years later the
Coles were sued for the recovery of several pigs which plaintiff alleged
they had wrongfully withheld. The court decided against them, and

when the constable went to execute the verdict, a violent ruckus ensued. Witnesses reported that Eunice cried "murder, murder," while William ranted about "thieves in the town"; together they bit the constable's hands, knocked him down, and "pulled the swine from him."[36] From this sequence the authorities developed additional, and more serious, charges—whose resolution is not recorded. In 1651 Eunice was admonished at court for new "misdemeanors," and in 1654 she was "presented" to still another jury.[37] There were, moreover, additional trials for which records are now lost.

If the Coles, and especially Eunice, were increasingly marked as deviant from a legal standpoint, they also gravitated quickly toward the bottom of the local status hierarchy. Hampton tax-lists from 1647 to 1653 show William Cole "rated" fifty-first among sixty householders in the former instance, and dead last out of seventy-two in the latter.[38] A floor plan for the meeting-house, dated 1650, finds William seated near the rear (among men far younger than himself), and Eunice consigned to the back bench of a gallery that was yet to be constructed![39]

But what of the community in which the Coles found themselves so invidiously placed? Careful demographic reconstruction, focused on the year 1656, has yielded a reasonably clear profile.[40] The total population was a little more than 350, the number of households approximately 65, the average size of household 5.6. The age-structure was heavily skewed toward youth (62 percent of the inhabitants were under twenty years old); among people fully adult there were nearly equal numbers in brackets of thirty to thirty-nine, forty to forty-nine, and over fifty years. Among heads of household and their wives, fully half had lived in Hampton since the time of its founding; two-thirds had been there for at least ten years, and all but a handful for at least five. Of those whose place of origin in England can be traced, some 70 percent came from the eastern counties of Norfolk, Suffolk, and Essex. (It was to the influence of this majority that Stephen Bachiller ascribed his own downfall.) Before settling in Hampton, nearly all had stopped at least briefly in some other New England community—Watertown and Exeter, most especially; also Salem, Newbury, Ipswich, and Dedham.

The spatial arrangement of Hampton was relatively simple. Most of the population lived in a central, nucleated village, clustered on all sides of the "meeting-house green." Several families, however, had home-lots along the roadways that connected the village with the ocean shore (two miles east), or with a ships' "landing" just to the south on Taylor's River.[41] The social structure of Hampton embraced a familiar range of ranks and statuses. Year after year a cadre of perhaps a dozen families filled most of the major town offices, paid the highest taxes (because they controlled the most property), and occupied the coveted front-row seats in the meeting-house.[42]

Here, then, was Hampton on the eve of its first witchcraft trial: a community no longer new, increasingly stable, self-contained, and self-sufficient—a fully-formed social organism, by the standards of its own time and culture. The prosecution of Eunice Cole itself affirms this impression of integrated structure, for the people who testified against her represented a notably broad spectrum of local townsfolk; no single descriptive category will suffice to characterize them. For example, their spatial disposition within the town was almost random. Three sides of the village green produced witnesses for the trial; so, too, did the settlements along the outlying roads.[43] Nor was place of origin a significant determinant of trial participation; East Anglians predominated, but not disproportionately to their numbers in the town—and other regions of Old England were represented as well.[44] A strong majority of the witnesses belonged to the families of "firstcomers," but several had arrived only within the previous decade.[45] The sexes were evenly represented (eleven apiece); and, with the exception of three young persons and one elderly widower, all the witnesses were married. Only the categories of age and social position yield anything like an uneven distribution. The age-group thirty to thirty-nine was somewhat more heavily represented (relative to its overall size) than other ten-year brackets.[46] And the status-group classified "high," as against "middle" and "low," was also distinctly preponderant. (The "low" group produced its fair share of witnesses, while the "middle" was somewhat underrepresented.)[47]

In sum, this analysis of the witnesses to Eunice Cole's "witchcraft" reveals a general movement against her, led by people of recognized standing in the community. Her prospects must, then, have seemed rather bleak, in the summer of 1656, as her case headed for trial before the Court of Assistants.

Unfortunately, the verdict in this case is nowhere recorded. All previous writers on Hampton have assumed a conviction—and a punishment by whippings and long imprisonment.[48] However, there is reason to conclude otherwise. Witchcraft was a capital crime in Massachusetts Bay, and a judgment of guilt invariably brought the death sentence. Yet Goody Cole was certainly *not* executed. Indeed she was back in Hampton by at least 1658, creating new difficulties for herself and her neighbors.[49]

The sequence of her life in these, and succeeding, years is extremely difficult to follow, for only some parts are documented. In 1660 she was prosecuted for "unseemly speeches . . . in saying to Huldah Hussey [a young neighbor], 'where is your mother Mingay, that whore? . . . She is abed with your father, that whore-master.' "[50] A short while later she was in jail at Boston, petitioning the court "for her liberty." (With considerable pathos, she pleaded her own "condition" as an "aged and weak woman," and the special needs of her husband—"he being 88 years of age, and troubled often with swellings and aches in his body . . . at which times I do take such pains with him as none but a wife would do.")[51] In October 1662 the court granted her request, upon certain conditions, and she evidently returned to Hampton before the end of the year.[52]

Her husband, however, had died that summer, and local authorities were already in the process of settling his estate. William Cole had written a will in May 1662, leaving Eunice only her "clothes which she left with me," and giving the rest of his property to a neighbor named Thomas Webster "upon condition of his keeping of me comfortably during the term of my natural life."[53] Eunice could hardly have been pleased with this plan, but the records do not show her own part in the probate arrangements. Subsequently, the court elected to modify William Cole's will, dividing the estate evenly between Webster and the unfortunate widow. After various debts had been paid Eunice's share came to a mere £8, and this, in turn, was ordered withheld from her "to be improved" by the selectmen "for her necessity."[54] Almost certainly, these proceedings left a residue of bitter feeling, sufficient to energize still another charge of witchcraft—ten years later.[55]

Meanwhile Eunice Cole continued to bounce back and forth between Hampton and the Boston jail. The spring of 1665 found her approaching the General Court with a new petition for release from imprisonment —which was granted "upon her [giving] security to depart from, and abide out of, this jurisdiction."[56] It does not appear that she accepted these terms: how, after all, would an elderly, improverished widow start over in an entirely new setting? Perhaps, then, she remained a prisoner for some years longer;[57] there is no further trace of her at Hampton until about 1670.

Whatever the legal troubles of Goody Cole in the decade of the 1660s, witchcraft was not among them. Other crimes (such as "unseemly speeches") served to sustain her adversary relationship with the townspeople of Hampton. But there is no reason to think that her reputation for witchcraft had been dissipated; on the contrary, it flourished as vigorously as ever. One episode, recalled much later, will serve to illustrate. The setting was Hampton, on an evening near the end of the year 1662; a selectmen named Abraham Perkins was approaching her house on an errand, when:

> I heard a discoursing . . . and, harkening, I heard the voice of Eunice Cole and a great hollow voice answer her, and the said Eunice seemed to be discontented with something, finding fault, and the said hollow voice spake to her again in a strange and un-worldly [?] manner . . . as if one had spoken out of the earth or in some hollow vessel. . . . And I being much amazed to hear that voice, I went and called Abraham Drake and Alexander Denham, and we three went to her house and harkened, and heard the said Eunice Cole speak and the said strange voice answer her diverse times, and the said Eunice Cole went up and down in the house and clattered the door to and again, and spake as she went, and the said voice made her answer in a strange manner . . . and there was a shimmering of a red color in the chimney corner.[58]

This exchange, so patently terrifying to the men who watched and listened, would eventually sustain a formal indictment, charging that "Eunice Cole of Hampton, widow, . . . not having the fear of God before her eyes, and being instigated by the Devil, did on the 24th of November in the year 1662 . . . enter into covenant with the Devil. . . ."[59] Significantly, however, the indictment was not returned until 1673. Doubtless, in the interim there was much local gossip about the "shimmering" presence which had visited widow Cole on that fateful November evening; but for ten years it remained gossip—and nothing more.

This sequence raises obvious questions of *timing*, and invites further investigation of the history of Hampton during the intervening years. Why did the community wait so long before renewing its legal battle against witchcraft? As mentioned previously, Eunice Cole may have spent much of this period in prison at Boston; if so, the incentive for a new prosecution would have been somewhat diminished. However, that is not the whole story. For during the decade of the 1660s Hamptonites were increasingly preoccupied with *external* risks and dangers. The problem which faced them was not new, but now—as never before —it threatened their property, their political rights, and the integrity of their community.

In order to understand this situation, it is necessary to trace the history of the so-called "Mason patent" for northern New England.[60] Deriving from grants by King Charles I to a minor courtier and colonial adventurer named Captain John Mason, the patent remained until mid-century largely undeveloped. Meanwhile, settlers arrived in the designated region, establishing new towns (including Hampton) under the administrative oversight of Massachusetts Bay. In 1650 John Mason's grandson and principal heir obtained in England a judgment favorable to the family claim—which, however, was immediately contested by the Bay Colony. Out of favor with the Cromwell regime, the Masons had no quick opportunity to break this impasse.

But their prospects brightened considerably following the restoration of the monarchy in 1660. The new king's attorney general reaffirmed that "Robert Mason . . . had a good and legal title to the Province of New Hampshire."[61] And the royal "commission" sent to New England in 1664–65 sharpened the issue by making it for the first time immediate and *personal*. Among other things, the commissioners challenged the jurisdiction of Massachusetts over the New Hampshire towns; indeed, at Portsmouth they appointed new officials directly responsible to the king. The whole region experienced, as a result, an extreme public agitation.[62] The political status of the various towns seemed suddenly unclear, and their territorial rights insecure; moreover, detached from Massachusetts, they would be far more vulnerable to the designs of Robert Mason.

As one of the communities directly involved, Hampton shared in the general excitement. During the summer of 1665 the town held special meetings to consider various avenues of response. Eventually a committee was appointed to "remonstrate" with the commissioners, and to "make answer to any claims or objections" that might be made against the rights of the local citizenry.[63] Subsequent meetings declared the strong desire of Hamptonites to retain their connection with Massachusetts. In all this they cooperated closely with their neighbors at Exeter, Portsmouth, and Dover.[64] Toward the end of the year the commissioners returned to England, with the issue still unresolved. The people of New Hampshire obtained thereby a brief period of remission; but Mason continued to press his interests as best he could, and he would find new—and better—openings in the future.

In 1672 the long-festering currents of fear and spite converged to produce the second major witchcraft prosecution at Hampton. Two developments seem to have opened the way. First, the "crisis" of the previous decade had temporarily abated, permitting the reassertion of *internal* concerns. And, second, Eunice Cole had returned home, under circumstances that were bound to create difficulty. The record suggests that she was now wholly a public charge. Apparently she was living in a small hut erected by the town; meanwhile individual householders took turns in supplying her daily needs for food and fuel.[65]

As in her previous trial for witchcraft, the prosecution mounted a large body of testimony against Eunice Cole. Fourteen depositions, taken between October 1672 and April 1673, are still extant;[66] they record the impressions of sixteen different witnesses, about twelve distinct episodes. Once again the *range* of the witness-group seems notable—whether measured in terms of age, sex, social position, or place of residence.

But most striking of all, in this 1673 case, is the blending of old and new material. Several major depositions recall events from a much earlier period: an angry encounter with the defendant "about 16 or 17 years ago";[67] a Sabbath service "many years since" when a "small creature . . . fell out of the bosom of Eunice Cole";[68] the mysterious death of a newborn child to whom Eunice had been denied access, "about ten years ago";[69] her alleged "covenant" with the Devil, made on a November evening in 1662.[70] The court accepted such evidence, "though it speaks of what was done many years since, because it was never brought in against her before."[71]

Of course, there was much new evidence as well. The town constable, whose task it was to deliver to Eunice Cole the maintenance donated by the townspeople, recounted a series of recent misadventures. Eunice, he noted, "would be often finding fault with him about her provision, and complaining that it was not so good as was brought in to him"—whereupon his own bread turned rotten, and for weeks together "we could never make any bread . . . at home but it would stink and prove loathsome." Inevitably, the deponants grew "suspicious that Goody Cole had enchanted our oven."[72] On another occasion Eunice quarreled with a local night-watch, and "the next day [he] fell sick, and lay sick about a fortnight."[73] There were renewed allegations that imps "sucked" on Eunice during Sabbath services.[74] But—most important among the newer charges—she was supposed to have "used means" on a young girl named Ann Smith, "all tending to entice her to live with her."[75]

Four different witnesses gave evidence on this latter point: Ann Smith herself (called "about the age of nine years"), Anna Huggins (age fourteen), Sarah Clifford (age thirty), and Bridget Clifford (age fifty-six).[76] One episode, in particular, exemplified the larger pattern:

> Bridget Clifford . . . saith [that] the last summer . . . she sent Ann Smith into the cabbage yard, and some [time] after my daughter Sarah said that she heard her cry in the orchard. And . . . when she came crying out of the orchard, I asked her what she ailed, and she said she knew not, but when she came she spake these words:

"she will knock me on the head: she will kill me." And . . . my daughter Sarah took her up and carried her into her house which was near mine. And when she had laid her in the cradle, the child related to us two that when she was in the cabbage yard there came an old woman to her in a blue coat and a blue cap and a blue apron and a white neckcloth, and took her up and carried her under the persimmon tree, and told her that she would live with her. Then, said she, "the old woman struck me on the head with a stone"; and then she turned into a little dog and ran up the tree, and flew away like an eagle.[77]

Among the many intriguing aspects of this testimony, the "enticement" theme commands special attention. Evidently this was not a new accusation against Goody Cole. The court noted that "it was her design formerly to insinuate herself into young ones," and recalled an earlier trial when another local girl had testified "how many ways, and in how many forms, she [Eunice] did appear to her."[78] There is pathos, as well as terror, in these charges. Herself childless through many years of marriage, Eunice Cole may have sought in her widowhood to become a "parent," after all. It would be easy enough to understand her yearnings in this direction, given a culture which consistently affirmed childbearing as a central part of life.

But there are further questions to raise here. Why, for example, was Ann Smith the particular object of the widow's interest? How did this one girl fall under the shadow of those dark fears and pressures which had attached to Goody Cole from a much earlier time? To explore such issues is to commit oneself to some painfully complicated demographic reconstruction; but the outcome will be worth the effort.

Ann Smith's personal history begins with her birth, at Exeter, in the year 1663.[79] She was the second child of one Nicholas Smith; her brother, Nathaniel, was three years older.[80] Her mother died when she was still an infant, and both Ann and Nathaniel were subsequently "placed" in the family of William Godfrey of Hampton. Their natural father remarried within a few years, but evidently made no effort to reclaim the children for his own household. William and Margery Godfrey, henceforth foster-parents for the two young Smiths, were already well along in life.[81] Each had been previously married and widowed; each had children by the former spouse. In addition, they had raised a son and two daughters of their own, who ranged in age from about eighteen to twenty-four when the Smiths came into the household.

William Godfrey died in 1671, and soon thereafter his widow made her third marriage—to a Hampton neighbor named John Marion.[82]

Nathaniel Smith remained with his adoptive mother through these various changes.[83] Ann, however, was by 1672 transferred to still another family, headed by Goodman John Clifford.[84] The Clifford household was itself extremely complex, for John had been married twice previously, and his current wife, Bridget, at least once; moreover, there were children from all of their earlier unions.[85] As of 1672 the Clifford *ménage* comprised the following persons:

	Years
John Clifford	57
Bridget [----] (Huggins) Clifford	56
Hannah Clifford (d. of John and first wife)	23
Bridget Huggins (d. of Bridget and first husband)	21
Israel Clifford (s. of John and first wife)	19
Joseph Richardson (s. of John's second wife and her previous husband)	17
Benjamin Richardson (s. of John's second wife and her previous husband)	15
Elizabeth Clifford (d. of John and second wife)	13
Anna Huggins (d. of Bridget and first husband)	13
Nathaniel Huggins (s. of Bridget and first husband)	12
Esther Clifford (d. of John and second wife)	10
Ann Smith (d. of Nicholas Smith; adoptive d. of William Godfrey)	9
Isaac Clifford (s. of John and second wife)	8

Meanwhile, John Clifford, junior (son of John and his first wife), was living in the next house, with his bride of two years, Sarah [Godfrey] Clifford.[86]

This situation requires summary, from the particular vantage point of Ann Smith. The Cliffords' was the *third* household in which she had lived. She had experienced the loss by death, first of her natural mother, and later of her adoptive father; and, in each case, the surviving parent (natural father, adoptive mother) had acceded in her transfer to a new setting. Her current family was composed of thirteen persons, including eleven children with four different surnames.

To be sure, fosterage was not uncommon in early New England; more than a few families were rearranged by the death of one spouse, and the remarriage of the other. But the complexity of the Clifford household was extreme, and the changes experienced by young Ann Smith were unusually frequent and jarring. Under all these circumstances, Ann might well have felt her new position (among the Cliffords) to be somewhat uncomfortable, even precarious. Where was her real *home*? To whom did she finally *belong*? Was it fanciful to suppose, as life continued to move her about, that she might one day fall into the clutches of a witch-mother?

These data help to explain why Eunice Cole, longing for a child "to live with her," might have fastened her interest on Ann Smith. They also suggest why Ann herself might have been made especially jittery by any overt approach. But there is still more to ask about the circumstances which brought these two together. How had Ann come to learn of the widow's "witchcraft" in the course of her childhood years? To what extent was she prepared, by those around her, for what would happen in the summer of 1672?

It is clear, in the first place, that the Clifford family supported her charges against Eunice Cole; three of them supplied personal testimony for the prosecution. But these three—Bridget Clifford, Sarah Clifford, and Anna Huggins—were themselves recent arrivals in the household; and, in each case, it was *prior* experience that shaped their participation in the 1673 trial. Bridget had served as a witness in the first witchcraft prosecution, seventeen years before.[87] She was then the wife of John Huggins—who, as town constable, had once been responsible for whipping Goody Cole.[88] Anna Huggins was Bridget's daughter by her first husband. And Sarah Clifford was originally Sarah Godfrey, daughter of William; her brother, John, was another of the witnesses at the earlier trial.[89]

The Godfrey connection was important in one final way. William Godfrey's wife, Margery, was the mother by a previous marriage of Thomas Webster—the same man whom William Cole had designated as his principal legatee.[90] This suggests the following possibilities, hypothetical but hardly fanciful. Widow Cole would likely have resented Thomas Webster's claim to property that she regarded as rightfully her own. And Webster, knowing her reputation as a grasping sort, surely *expected* such resentment; more, he anticipated some form of retaliation. These anxieties were freely expressed in the home of his mother—where Ann Smith, young and impressionable, was living as a foster-child. Time and again, she would hear of the spiteful widow in terms that left too little, or too much, to the imagination. (Had Goody Cole muttered a curse, as she passed by the gate this morning? What was she doing beside Thomas Webster's barn on the day his cows took sick?) This much, we can reasonably suppose, Ann Smith carried with her in moving from one foster-family to the next.

To summarize, the lives of Eunice Cole and Ann Smith were joined in a social web of many strands and complicated structure. Smiths, Godfreys, Websters, Cliffords, Hugginses: each of these families contributed something to the sequence that would eventually bring the orphaned girl and the elderly widow into fateful contact. It remains now to characterize the entire *group* of witnesses in the 1673 trial, so as to show their collective relation to the defendant through time and space. Of sixteen deponents, three had also participated in the trial of 1656. Five more were relatives of people who had witnessed on that earlier occasion. Four had moved into Hampton since 1656, and four were from neighboring towns. Among all of these together, at least seven (and perhaps as many as nine) were under the age of thirty-five. The total picture reveals, first, some widening of the defendant's reputation beyond the borders of Hampton proper,[91] and, second, a process of transmission from one generation to the next. Like Sabbath services and barn-raisings, Goody Cole's witchcraft had become a local institution.

Convicted in the minds of her Hampton neighbors, Eunice would still have her day in court at Boston. In April 1673 the Essex County magistrates ordered her committed to jail "in order to her further trial."[92] Her case was called late that summer, and the grand jury approved her indictment.[93] But the final verdict turned in her favor—just barely: "In the case of Eunice Cole, now prisoner at the bar, [we find her] not legally guilty according to indictment, but [there is] just ground of vehement suspicion of her having had familiarity with the Devil."[94] So back she went, to whatever was left of her life in Hampton.

Several years later Hampton undertook its third, and last, prosecution for witchcraft. Interestingly, Eunice Cole was no longer the leading figure; other women had now been pushed to center stage. The case began with the death of a little child—Moses Godfrey, age fifteen months—in July 1680. A jury of inquest found "grounds of suspicion that the said child was murdered by witchcraft."[95] Naming no names, the jurymen nonetheless alluded to "a party suspected," and the following day the court took bond from one John Fuller to guarantee that "Rachel, his wife, shall appear . . . to answer what shall be charged against her in point of witchcraft."[96]

In fact, the suspicious death of the Godfrey child was not the only count against Goodwife Fuller.[97] Various personal testimonies portrayed her as a generally eccentric figure. Often she had played the role of an expert on witchcraft, describing "how those that were witches did go abroad at night." Once she had named "several persons that she reckoned as witches and wizards in this town."[98] (Her list included Eunice Cole.) On another occasion she had told a neighbor of "a great rout at Goodman Roby's . . . when [witches] had pulled Doctor Reed out of the bed, and with an enchanted bridle did intend to lead a jaunt."[99] Moreover, she had specifically advised the Godfrey family to "lay sweet bays under the threshold; it would keep a witch from coming in." As things turned out, this procedure served to implicate Rachel herself:

> One of the girls . . . laid bays under the threshold of the back door all the way, and half way of the breadth of the fore door. And soon after Rachel Fuller came to the house. And she had always formerly come in at the back door, which is next her house, but now she went about to the fore door, and though the door stood open, yet she crowded in on that side the bays lay not, and rubbed her back against the [door]-post so as that she rubbed off her hat. And then she sat down, and made ugly faces, and nestled about. . . . And when she was in the house, she looked under the door where the bays lay.[100]

Rachel Fuller diverged, in one respect, from the usual pattern in these cases; at twenty-five, she was among the *youngest* persons ever to stand trial for witchcraft in colonial New England. Married just three years before, she had two small sons of her own. Her father, John Brabrook, had been an early and prominent settler at Watertown;[101] Rachel, however, did not know him, for he died in the year of her birth.[102] Her mother was left to raise eight small children. As time passed, the family became increasingly dependent on public assistance.[103] (Even before John Brabrook's death, there was a house-fire, which devastated the family properties.)[104] Several Brabrook children were farmed out into foster-households. Rachel lived for some period with an uncle—a *rich* uncle, at that—in Newbury.[105] Her marriage to John Fuller of Hampton came in 1677. Like Rachel, Fuller had been raised by an uncle, and tasted wealth and prestige without really sharing in it.[106] Perhaps these ambiguities, these elements of social and personal dislocation, contributed indirectly to the process from which Rachel emerged as "suspect." Other accused witches came from similarly checkered backgrounds. Surely, however, the immediate source of the feeling against her was her manifest eccentricity—and her strong interest in all things occult. Such a woman, however youthful, could not but alarm her neighbors.

A second person was charged as a witch that summer at Hampton. Isabella Towle by name, she was a woman in her late forties, married, and the mother of nine children.[107] Her husband, Philip, was first a "seaman," and later a "yeoman" of average position in the community. Beyond this the record does not speak. Particularly unfortunate is the lack of any material on the substantive charges against Goodwife Towle. All that survives is a court order, from September 1680, that "Rachel Fuller and Isabel Towle, being apprehended and committed upon suspicion of witchcraft . . . still continue in prison till bond be given for their good behavior of £100 apiece, during the Court's pleasure."[108] Both defendants were discharged in the following year.

But were there *other* defendants, in addition to these two? A single, stray reference supplies a familiar name: "At a quarter court held at Hampton, . . . 7 September 1680, . . . Eunice Cole, of Hampton [was] by authority committed to prison on suspicion of being a witch; and, upon examination of testimonies, the Court vehemently suspects her so to be, but [there is] not full proof. [Defendant] is sentenced and confined to imprisonment, and to be kept in durance until this court take further orders, with a lock to be kept on her leg. In the meantime, the selectmen of Hampton [are] to take care to provide for her as formerly, that she may be retained."[109]

The timing of these events invites further comment. As noted previously, the "Mason patent" had claimed the attention of Hamptonites at intervals since at least mid-century; here, indeed, was the single greatest threat to their life as a community. In the 1650s, when the town produced its first witchcraft prosecution, the Masons could find no good openings to press their case. In the 1660s events turned sharply in their favor, and Hampton, like the other New Hampshire settlements, was preoccupied with questions of political defense; meanwhile there were no indictments for witchcraft.

The same reverse correlation can be posited for the 1670s. In the early part of this decade the threat from outside had temporarily abated, and the years 1672–73 brought new efforts in court to rid the town of its most notorious "witch." But soon thereafter the Masons returned to the attack. In 1675 they gained more legal judgments in their favor.[110] And in 1676 Edward Randolph, the Crown's leading trouble-shooter for colonial affairs, arrived in Boston to press various claims against New England—including that of the Masons.[111] Randolph went to New Hampshire in person, and aroused a flurry of anxious reaction. At Hampton, for example, the minister and other leading men drafted an urgent statement "to clear [the townspeople] from having any hand in damnifying Mr. Mason . . . and for the full vindication of their rights."[112] The upshot was renewed litigation in England—and, finally, a decision to constitute the New Hampshire towns as a separate, *royal* province. A commission from the king in 1679 established new machinery of government, providing considerable scope for the colonists themselves.[113] Once again, the Mason threat seemed to recede—and, once again (in 1680), Hamptonites made witchcraft their central point of concern.

But the Masons were not done yet. Disappointed in their hopes for political control of New Hampshire, they still held claims to ownership of the *land*. In 1681 Robert Mason visited the colony, and sought to persuade (or frighten) individual settlers into accepting leases for their property.[114] These efforts were largely unsuccessful, and so Mason returned to England and mounted a new strategy. In 1682 his friend, Edward Cranfield, received appointment as governor of New Hampshire, under a commission that conferred extraordinarily wide powers.[115] The following years were tumultuous ones for New Hampshire; charges of "rebellion" and "tyranny" flew back and forth between the Cranfield administration and the local citizenry. At Hampton, in fact, plans were laid for armed protest—plans that were frustrated only by prompt intervention from the governor himself. The insurgent leader, one Edward Gove, was arrested, tried for "high treason," convicted, and condemned to death; eventually, however, his sentence was commuted to imprisonment in the Tower of London.[116] So it was that Hampton, and "Gove's Rebellion," have a modest claim to be considered in the story of resistance to imperial oppression.

Meanwhile, the governor had issued a new proclamation, requiring that the people of the colony take leases on their houses and lands from Robert Mason. A spate of lawsuits followed—most of them decided, allegedly by packed juries, in favor of Mason.[117] Inevitably, there were appeals, which prolonged the controversy through the Andros regime of the late 1680s and beyond.

The political history of Hampton need not detain us further, for we have reached a terminus in the sequence of local witchcraft trials. But if the *trials* ended in 1680, the belief in witches—and the fears which attended such belief—continued long thereafter. Here we must leave the relatively firm ground of documentary evidence (contemporaneous with the events described), and enter the uncertain area of folk "tradition." Such material is not susceptible to detailed analysis; but it deserves to be sampled, if only briefly.

The lore of Hampton mentions at least two local "witches" from the eighteenth century. One was a woman named Brown—apparently elderly, widowed, and extremely poor. She lived by herself on an isolated road, and at least some Hamptonites were fearful of passing that way. The only printed reference to her witchcraft notes the mysterious disappearance of some pigs, whose owner had stopped one day to visit with her. While she lived, there must have been many similar stories— circulating by word of mouth among the townspeople, and becoming in time a staple part of everyday gossip.[118]

The second eighteenth-century witch at Hampton cuts a strikingly different figure. "General" Jonathan Moulton carried the name of an old and extremely prominent local family. He served with distinction in various Indian wars and in the Revolution itself.[119] He was frequently a town officer and a deputy to the colonial legislature; he was also elected as a delegate to the convention that drew up the state constitution. He was a businessman of great energy and wide interests. For many years his "store" was the hub of economic life in Hampton; he owned, as well, a number of local mills. After the Revolution he speculated heavily in *lands* all over New Hampshire.[120] From these activities he prospered greatly—some thought too greatly. His reputation was that of a "sharp dealer." On one occasion, at least, his property was vandalized by a "violent, riotous, and tumultuous" mob, which accused him of turning an unfair profit from goods washed up on Hampton beach in a ship-wreck.[121] But this man's reputation reached out in other directions as well. Shrewd and sharp as he was, his great wealth seemed to some Hamptonites inexplicable except by reference to supernatural influence. Rumor declared that Moulton was in league with the Devil.

One incident served to crystallize the full range of these attitudes. Late on a March night in 1769, Jonathan Moulton's house burned to the ground. It was, in truth, a mansion by the standards of the time; and the fire made sensational news, reported in detail as far away as Boston.[122] There was no injury to persons, but the loss in property was estimated at a full £3000. Evidently, there were many in Hampton who felt that Moulton had simply received his due. Indeed—according to later tradi-tion—

> the report was at once spread far and wide that the fire had been set by the Devil, because the General had cheated him in a bar-gain. . . . The "facts" have been stated thus: The Devil was to have the General's soul after a certain number of years, in con-sideration of which, at stated periods he was to fill the General's boot with gold and silver—the boot being hung up in the chimney for that purpose. Whether a bootful at a time was not sufficient to meet his demands for money is not stated; but on a time when [the Devil] came to fill the boot, he found it took a quantity so vast that he descended into the chimney to see what the matter was, and to his surprise he found that the General had cut off the foot of the

boot! And the room below was so full of money that he could not proceed to the door, and was compelled to go back up the chimney again.[123]

This account diverged at many points from the pattern in comparable cases a century earlier. The suspect was a man of the highest social and economic position. His "witchcraft" was entirely a matter of acquisitiveness, not malice and destruction for its own sake. Moreover, there was no obvious victim here—save the Devil himself. Moulton may be viewed as an early capitalist, in a society whose main features were still *pre*-capitalist. His great and distinctive talent was the use of money to create *more* money. This form of enterprise was equated with "cheating" not only because of its prodigious success, but also because it ignored traditional values.

Financial manipulation was, indeed, central to the story of Moulton's transactions with the Devil. A bootful of money can become a roomful —if clever "tricks" are employed. (It is striking, by way of contrast, that seventeenth-century witchcraft rarely seemed to involve money; instead, the property at risk typically comprised land, produce, domestic animals, food, drink, and the like.) But if greed was Moulton's sin, the *envy* of his detractors seems equally evident. There is even a hint of admiration here; how many men, after all, had managed to fool the Devil? Finally, there is humor; then, as now, such a tale would surely evoke amusement. But, again, these attitudinal postures marked a change in the lore of witchcraft. They belonged to the world of eighteenth-century folk culture, where the Devil and his legions displayed a new, less menacing aspect than heretofore.

The burning of his house was only a temporary setback for Jonathan Moulton; quickly he built a new one, more grand than the first. His later years brought additional honors and greater prosperity—but no discernible mellowing of local attitudes toward his person and career. A town historian writes "that news of his death [in 1788] was carried to the haymakers on the marsh; and the cry 'General Moulton is dead!' was passed along from mouth to mouth for miles, in no regretful tones."[124] And there is one more story attached to his death. His body, having been prepared for burial, was suddenly missing from the coffin. The people of Hampton were not surprised. "The Devil," they whispered knowingly to one another, "has got his own at last."[125]

As time passed, new names and new events were added to the lore of Hampton witchcraft; but always, it seems, Eunice Cole retained pride of place. Well down into the nineteenth century the legend of her deeds, and *mis*deeds, was embellished through constant retelling. About 1840 a Hamptonite wrote of Goody Cole as follows: "Whatever may have been the old woman's crimes and misfortunes, still many a mother has been indebted to her for hushing their crying children. The fear of her name would alarm the most courageous, or subdue the worst temper, from generation to generation."[126]

These elements of local tradition go well beyond the documentary record from the various trials of Eunice Cole. Their relation to the historical reality of seventeenth-century Hampton is quite uncertain; but they do reveal much about the place of witchcraft in the minds of *later* generations of Hamptonites. What, then, were the tales which subdued tempers and hushed the cries of children? A few examples will have to suffice.

A carpenter named Peter Johnson, born and raised at Hampton in the settlement years, was one of several young men who dared to "torment" Goody Cole, "playing upon her many a trick." On a particular occasion, while Johnson was framing a house, Goody Cole stood by and taunted him about his work. In a flash of anger the carpenter hurled his axe in her direction. The axe missed its target and stuck in the ground, "the handle upwards"—and Johnson could not pull it free. Eventually, he made apologies and asked Eunice "to give him his axe again"; whereupon she lifted it out "with the greatest ease." On an evening not long thereafter, several "young folks" peeked at Goody Cole's window, "and saw her busily engaged in turning a bowl with something in it, apparently in the shape of a boat; at last she turned it over and exclaimed, 'there, the Devil has got the imps.' That night news came that Peter Johnson, carpenter, and James Philbrick, mariner, were drowned at the same hour in the river near the creek now [*circa* 1840] known as Cole's creek."[127]

Vengeance, of terrible proportions, was always a central theme in the legend of Goody Cole. One special instance caught the attention long afterward of a famous American poet. In the autumn of 1657 a boat had capsized in Hampton harbor with dreadful result, as noted in the town records: "The sad hand of God [came] upon eight persons, going in a vessel by sea from Hampton to Boston, who were all swallowed up in the ocean. . . ."[128] But the "sad hand of God" was not the only way to explain this disaster. A quite different version was preserved in folklore—and then in a poem, "The Wreck of Rivermouth," by John Greenleaf Whittier:

Once in the old colonial days,
Two hundred years ago and more,
A boat sailed through the winding ways
Of Hampton River to that low shore. . . .

"Fie on the witch!" cried a merry girl,
  As they rounded the point where goody Cole
Sat by her door with her wheel atwirl,
  A bent and blear-eyed poor old soul.
"Oho!" she muttered, "ye're brave today!
  But I hear the little waves laugh and say,
'The broth will be cold that waits at home;
  For it's one to go, but another to come!' "

"She's cursed," said the skipper; "speak her fair.
  I'm scary always to see her shake
Her wicked head, with its wild gray hair,
  And nose like a hawk, and eyes like a snake,"
But merrily still, with laugh and shout,
From Hampton River the boat sailed out. . . .

They saw not the shadow that walked beside,
They heard not the feet with silence shed,
But thicker and thicker a hot mist grew,
Shot by the lightnings through and through
And muffled growls, like the growl of a beast,
Ran along the sky from west to east. . . .

Veering and tacking, they backward wore;
And just as a breath from the woods ashore
Blew out to whisper of danger past,
The wrath of the storm came down at last!
The skipper hauled at the heavy sail:
"God be our help," he only cried.
As the roaring gale, like the stroke of a flail,
Smote the boat on its starboard side.

Suddenly seaward swept the squall;
The low sun smote through cloudy rack;
the shoals stood clear in the light, and all
The trend of the coast lay hard and black.

But far and wide as eye could reach,
No life was seen upon wave or beach.
The boat that went out at morning never
Sailed back again into Hampton River.[129]

Goody Cole's own end is not mentioned in the town records; but once again "tradition" has preserved a chilling account. In her last illness she remained alone in her house, with all the windows and doors boarded up save one. Presently the neighbors, seeing no further sign of her, mustered their courage and forced their way in. They found her quite dead. As quickly as they could, they dug a hole in the ground beside the house. They threw the body down, covered it, and then "drove a stake through it, with a horseshoe attached, to prevent her from ever coming up again."[130]

The alleged site of this strange burial is still a point of interest among the people of Hampton. So, too, is the Cole house-lot, with its ancient well. For the latter, special claims are made. It is said that ship-masters used to stop there to fill their casks, in the belief that the water would never become brackish.[131]

In 1938, on the three hundredth anniversary of the founding of Hampton, the town took official action to square accounts with Goody Cole: "*Resolved*, that we, the citizens . . . of Hampton, in the town meeting assembled, do hereby declare that we believe that Eunice (Goody) Cole was unjustly accused of witchcraft and familiarity with the Devil in the 17th century, and we do hereby restore to the said Eunice (Goody) Cole her rightful place as a citizen of the town of Hampton."[132] The resolution was passed by unanimous vote.

In fact, the legend of Goody Cole has become a cherished part of the local culture. A bronze urn in the Town Hall holds some material purported to be her earthly remains. A stone memorial on the village green affirms her twentieth-century rehabilitation. There are exhibits on her life in the museum of the local historical society. There are even some *new* tales in which she plays a ghostly, though harmless, part: an aged figure, in tattered shawl, seen walking late at night along a deserted road, or stopping in the early dawn to peer at gravestones by the edge of the green.[133]

And now an author's postscript. Picture the living room of a comfortable house in Hampton. A stranger has come there, to examine a venerable manuscript, held in this family through many generations. Laboriously, his eyes move across the page, straining to unravel the cramped and irregular script of a bygone era. Two girls, aged nine or ten, arrive home from school; after a brief greeting they move off into an alcove and begin to play. Awash in the sounds of their game, the stranger looks up from his work and listens. "Goody Cole," cries one of the girls, "I'll be Goody Cole!" "Yes," responds the other, "and I'll be the one who gives you a whipping—you mean old witch!"[134]

It is a long way from her time to ours, but Goody Cole has made the whole journey.

11

"Hearts Against Hearts"

There is a fashionable view of early American history which gives to New England the overall designation of "Puritan" but which also asserts the distinctive character of each of its constituent parts. Thus Rhode Island was a bubbling kettle of social and religious experimentation—a haven for Quakers, Gortonists, atheists, land speculators, merchants, and "adventurers" of all sorts. Plymouth was a lazy, "separatist" backwater. Massachusetts was the clear fountainhead of the "New England way"; but, from noble beginnings, the Bay Colony traced a course of "declension," as commerce and worldliness transformed her leading settlements. To the north, in New Hampshire and Maine, society barely maintained a foothold; explorers, trappers, traders, and hardscrabble farmers careened about in a natural—and cultural—wilderness.

In this historical melodrama, Connecticut has typically played the straight man. Here, we are told, was the most stable and tranquil of the New England colonies, and in some ways the most successfully Puritan. Connecticut was a true "congregational commonwealth";[1] a "close-knit, tightly-controlled, homogeneous community";[2] an "isolated . . . agricultural community of steady habits," whose history was "almost entirely without those colorful incidents—conflicts and disorders—that kept other colonies in a more or less continuous state of disturbance."[3]

In actual fact, seventeenth-century Connecticut fits this description only partially. Perhaps it can be argued that the settlers of the colony included a higher proportion of *bona fide* Puritans than was true elsewhere, that religion was more deeply entrenched as the basis of personal and community life, that there was more "inwardness" and greater resistance to alien influences. But to show this is *not* to prove control, harmony, steadiness, the achievement of a "peaceable kingdom." Indeed, the evidence might better support an opposite characterization; what stands out, in the early history of Connecticut, is an extraordinary pattern of trouble and turmoil. Virtually from the start, Indians, floods, and disease took a heavy toll in life and property. To these environmental hazards were added deep pressures from within. In each of the "most ancient" settlements there grew over time a spirit of chronic factionalism.

Here lies a story vital to the understanding of early New England; unfortunately, many of the particulars, and some of the central themes, are now lost from view. For the earliest of the Connecticut disputes (in the 1630s and 40s) detailed evidence is almost completely lacking. However, the situation is somewhat better with respect to the period of greatest conflict, the late 1650s. The struggles of those years were remembered thereafter as the "Hartford controversy"; in fact, they embraced Windsor and Wethersfield as well. All New England watched with alarm as Connecticut plunged into "schism, and sudden censures, and angry removes . . . prayers against prayers, hearts against hearts, tears against tears, tongues against tongues, and fasts against fasts, and horrible prejudices and underminings."[4] The words are Cotton Mather's, and allowance must be made for his usual hyperbole. Still, there is no mistaking the extremity of the situation. Issues were joined in a torrent of petitions and counter-petitions. The General Court contrived elaborate measures to suppress "differences." Councils with leading men from the neighboring colonies repeatedly explored the middle ground between opposing positions. Towns quite literally split apart, with dissident groups moving away *en masse.* Translated into human terms, this meant decisions by hundreds of people to leave their settled homes for new and unknown destinations in the wilderness: here was the ultimate measure of the feelings involved.[5] Similar pressures developed elsewhere in New England, but none quite so severe as these. It is curious how fully scholars have managed to overlook them.

From such fraternal strife it is not a long step to witchcraft—and in this regard, as well, Connecticut set the pace for the rest of New England. Connecticut produced the first known trial for witchcraft anywhere on the North American continent. Connecticut endured the first witchcraft "panic" (defined, for the moment, as a chain of accusations leading from one person to another). And Connecticut appears to have executed more alleged witches than any other colony—if the Salem outbreak alone be excepted.

What follows is an effort to assess the place of witchcraft in the early years of Wethersfield, one of the three original Connecticut towns. Four times inhabitants of Wethersfield were summoned to court on charges of witchcraft.[6] The sum of the results was one certain, and two probable, executions, one banishment, and one successful flight from criminal prosecution. These events were played out against the backdrop of some four decades of Wethersfield history. Three of the witchcraft cases can be studied only briefly—scanty records will permit no more. But in the fourth and final instance the possibilities are much fuller. The largest part of this chapter is focused there—on the troubles and trials of an unlucky widow named Katherine Harrison, her leading accusers, and, indeed, the entire range of her Wethersfield contemporaries.

Wethersfield has a good claim to be the oldest permanent settlement in Connecticut. According to the best available evidence, its founding occurred in the late summer or early fall of 1634, when a group of perhaps a dozen "planters" arrived from Watertown in Massachusetts Bay.[7] Their number was considerably augmented the following year by another twenty or more migrants with their respective families. In all this the town benefited from a general migration out of the Bay Colony, which also spawned the settlements at Hartford and Windsor, and (farther north) at Springfield. Though Massachusetts was itself but a few years old, there had arisen in some quarters a sense of contracting opportunities, of "straitness for want of land."[8] In addition, there were conflicts of religious leadership. William Hubbard, author of the first general history of New England, noted that "two such eminent stars, as were Mr. Cotton and Mr. Hooker, both of the same magnitude though of differing influence, could not well continue in one and the same orb [in Massachusetts Bay]."[9] It was, of course, Hooker who led in the founding of Hartford; his new "orb" would soon embrace the other river settlements as well.

The earliest arrivals at Wethersfield were entirely from Watertown, and at first their political and religious life was adjunct to their mother-community. (Indeed, the settlement was called Watertown for eighteen months or so.) However, in 1636 the town received its own name, its first civil officers, and the right to form a separate church. Its territorial basis was established through negotiations with the local Indians, and efforts were made to specify its exact boundaries.[10] A central "village" began to develop west of the Connecticut River (and below the Hartford line),[11] but the town lands stretched across the river for several miles to the east. Rapidly the settlers addressed the problem of dividing these lands, within general categories of home-lots, meadows, "plains," and "fields." Specific allotments were linked to size of family and social status. The process was effectively completed by 1639; for the next three decades there would be no more "general divisions," though the town made special grants to a good many individuals.[12]

The lands adjacent to the river seem to have been quite fertile, at least by New England standards, and the economic basis of Wethersfield's growth was chiefly agricultural. Nonetheless there was from the start a certain amount of trading activity—in hemp, and furs, and cattle —which connected the town with its neighbors to the north, and ultimately with the wider world of transatlantic commerce. There was a good harbor just above the village, and the records refer to some early "warehouses."[13]

But if, in some ways, Wethersfield opened an inviting prospect to its founders, there were also grounds for deep concern. Relations to the nearby Indians were especially problematic. Trade with Indians could be highly profitable but was marred by repeated incidents of violence and death. Several English traders lost their lives at the hands of Connecticut tribesmen—including John Oldham, one of the very first settlers at Wethersfield—and the toll was higher still on the other side.[14] These personal hostilities led quite rapidly to the so-called Pequot War, which opened in April 1637 with a "massacre" at Wethersfield. A raiding-party of Pequot warriors approached from the south, camped on an island in the middle of the river, and attacked as the townspeople went to work in their fields near the bank. The result, according to John Winthrop's journal, was nine English dead, two "maids" taken captive, and a slaughter of the town's cattle.[15] Immediately thereafter, the General Court laid plans for an "offensive war," and at the end of May sent a force of some one hundred twenty men downriver toward the major Pequot encampment. This time the Indians were caught unawares— and were cut down by the hundreds. But although the war ended in complete victory for the English, it was not soon forgotten. At Wethersfield, the scars must have been particularly deep.

These matters deserve emphasis because they are so easily missed in historical retrospect. *Fear* was an elemental part of life in all of the new settlements. The situation at Wethersfield was vividly recalled, years later, by the son of the town's first "settled" pastor:

> The meeting-house was solid made, to withstand the wicked assaults of the redskins. Its foundations was laid in the fear of the Lord, but its walls was truly laid in the fear of the Indians, for many and great was the terrors of 'em. I do mind me that all the able-bodied

men did work thereat, and the old and feeble did watch in turns
to espy if any savages was in hiding near, and every man kept his
musket nigh to his hand. I do not myself remember any of the
attacks made by large bodies of Indians whilst we did remain in
Wethersfield, but did oftentimes hear of 'em. Several families which
did live back a ways from the river was either murdered or capti-
vated in my boyhood, and we all did live in constant fear of the
like. . . . After the redskins the great terror of our lives at Wethersfield . . . was the wolves. Catamounts were bad enough, and so
was the bears, but it was the wolves that was the worst. The noise
of their howlings was enough to curdle the blood of the stoutest,
and I have never seen the man that did not shiver at the sound of
a pack of 'em. What with the way we hated 'em, and the good
money that was offered for their heads, we do not hear 'em now
so much, but when I do I feel again the young hatred rising in my
blood, and it is not a sin because God made 'em to be hated. My
mother and sister did each of 'em kill more than one of the gray
howlers, and once my oldest sister shot a bear that came too near
the house.[16]

Statements like this one remind us that New England was once a
frontier in the fullest sense. Wolves, bears, and Indians belonged equally
to the experience of colonial "settlers" and to that of later generations of
western "pioneers."

The Pequot War was barely over when Wethersfield experienced
another sort of difficulty: a profound "rent" within its own citizenry.
Winthrop's journal reports that "the church . . . itself was not only
divided from the rest of the town, etc., but, of those seven which were
the church, four fell off, so as it was conceived that thereby the church
was dissolved."[17] Outside mediation proved unavailing, and it appeared
that "one party must remove to some other place." The problem was to
decide *which* party—and so the struggle simmered along. Still, the next
few years witnessed a massive exodus from Wethersfield, in response
almost certainly to the pervasive mood of "contention and alienation."
In the fall of 1639 a dozen families moved off to the new settlement of
Milford. Others left soon thereafter for New Haven, Guilford, Stratford,
and Saybrook. In the summer of 1641 came the biggest removal of all; it
was indeed a virtual "secession." Some thirty-five Wethersfield householders took part, led by the Rev. Richard Denton. Leaving Connecticut
altogether, they moved to a new site within the boundaries of the
fledgling New Haven Colony. The town they founded was known
henceforth by the name of Stamford.[18]

To this point in the history of Wethersfield the dominant theme was instability. A substantial majority of the early settlers had by 1641 moved on to other places. The original leadership of the town was badly fragmented; three ministers had come and gone, as had several important "gentlemen." (Of the twelve men who represented Wethersfield in the General Court between 1636–40 eight were no longer present in 1641, and two more left in 1644.) The church was so badly decimated that its very existence was briefly in doubt: according to local tradition, its records had accompanied the bulk of its memership to Stamford.[19]

Meanwhile, however, newcomers were entering Wethersfield nearly as fast as the emigrants left, so there was no arrest in overall growth. Most of these newcomers would remain for many years—some for the rest of their lives. In the records of the early and middle 1640s there appear for the first time several names that would henceforth loom large in the town: Boreman, Hale, Hitchcock, Hollister, Latimer, Riley, and Welles. From such people was formed a new, and lasting, leadership cadre. The church remained an arena of conflict for some while longer, even with a new man—the Rev. Henry Smith—in the pastorate.[20] In 1643 the differences within the membership became once again "exceeding great." The pastor himself was the central issue, and the General Court advised, after "sad and serious consideration," that "the best way for recovering and preserving the public peace is that Mr. Smith lay down his place."[21] At least a dozen families left Wethersfield at about this time to found the new settlement of Branford.[22] Eventually, the trouble was resolved (or at least scaled down), and Smith stayed on as minister until his death several years later. By the middle of the decade Wethersfield was moving gradually toward a more settled existence.

The first of the Wethersfield witchcraft cases occurred in 1648. There is a single, sparse notation in the court records: "The jury finds the bill of indictment against Mary Johnson, that by her own confession she is guilty of familiarity with the Devil."[23] Luckily, certain additional particulars appear in a later writing by Cotton Mather:

> She said her first familiarity with the Devil came through *discontent*, and wishing the Devil to take this and that, and the Devil to do that and t'other thing; whereupon a Devil appeared unto her, *tendering* her what services might best *content* her. A Devil accordingly did for her many services. Her master blamed her for not carrying out the ashes, and a devil afterwards would clear the hearth of ashes for her. Her master sending her to drive out the hogs that sometimes broke into their field, a devil would scour the hogs away, and make her laugh to see how he fazed them. She con-

fessed that she had murdered a child, and committed uncleanness both with *men* and with *devils*. In the time of her imprisonment, the famous Mr. Stone was at great pains to promote her conversion from the Devil to God; and she was by the best observers judged very penitent, both before her execution and at it. . . . And she died in a frame extremely to the satisfaction of them that were spectators of it.[24]

Once before, Mary Johnson had been in court—in the summer of 1646, when charged with "thievery." (She was convicted, and sentenced to be whipped.)[25] Otherwise she is a historical phantom, impossible to study, or portray, in three-dimensional detail.

The limited evidence available suggests, at a minimum, that this was an atypical case. The element of confession, of self-conviction, was something that appeared in witchcraft proceedings only a few times before Salem. Moreover, it is not clear that anyone in Wethersfield felt *attacked* by Mary Johnson's witchcraft. The indictment mentioned only "familiarity with the Devil," and her own statement emphasized the same theme. The reference to having "murdered a child" seems rather vague; if such acts had been widely suspected, they would surely have taken priority in her trial. Also, the allusion to sexual misconduct is quite unusual in context. Finally, the accused was a domestic servant—and as such was probably unmarried and relatively young (under thirty?). These things, too, set her apart from the majority of New England witches.

Although this earliest case of witchcraft cannot be directly related to other activities and other people in Wethersfield, there was one concurrent *event* that bears consideration. The years 1647 and 1648 brought to New England a heavy siege of "epidemical sickness." Winthrop's Journal reported forty to fifty deaths each, in Massachusetts Bay and in Connecticut, and these figures may be considerably underestimated.[26] Among the Connecticut towns the fullest vital records for this period came from Windsor. The appended graph of mortality in Windsor makes an obvious and telling point: fifty-two deaths recorded in the two epidemic years (twenty were children), a level not reached again until near the end of the century.[27] At about this same time Windsor made its own beginning with witchcraft trials. Winthrop's Journal for the spring of 1647 contains this tantalizing entry: "One ——— of Windsor arraigned and executed for a witch."[28] The blank is filled in the notes of the local town clerk: "May 26. 47 Alse Young was hanged." This was, indeed, the earliest of all New England witchcraft trials, preceding Mary Johnson's by more than a year.[29] Meanwhile, Massachusetts was about

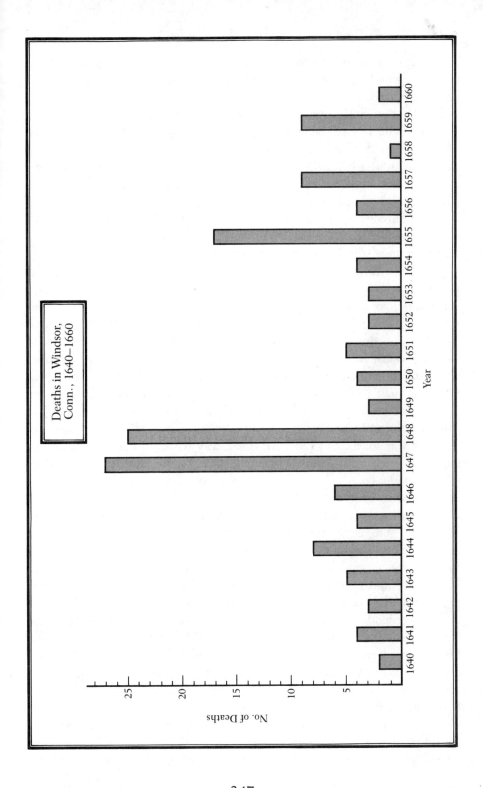

Deaths in Windsor, Conn., 1640–1660

No. of Deaths

Year

to become similarly involved. There, too, the first full-fledged prosecutions coincided with, or immediately followed, the "epidemical sickness." (See Appendix.)

For Wethersfield, unfortunately, the early records are too sketchy to permit a careful, chronological analysis of mortality levels, but a number of individual deaths can be documented. Two of the town's foremost men died in 1648: the Rev. Henry Smith, the pastor mentioned earlier, and Mr. Leonard Chester, a certified "gentleman" and one of the original planters. (The same year saw the passing, at Hartford, of the Rev. Thomas Hooker—spiritual leader of the entire Connecticut colony.) Was it merely coincidence that 1648 also brought the first "proven" intervention of the Devil in the affairs of Wethersfield?

Less than three years after the trial of Mary Johnson, Wethersfield produced a second witchcraft case. The accused were a married couple, John and Joan Carrington by name. Charged with having "entertained familiarity with Satan, the great enemy of God and mankind, and by his help . . . done works above the course of nature," the Carringtons were convicted in March 1651 and sentenced to death.[30] In the absence of explicit documentation, their execution cannot be proven—but seems highly probable all the same. In March 1653 probate was filed on John Carrington's estate. The inventory came to £23.11s., and debts reduced this total almost by half.[31]

As in the Johnson case, there is no way to recover a picture of the supposed "victims"—if any. However, John Carrington did leave a thin trail of evidence which permits partial reconstruction of his earlier life. He arrived in Boston, from England, aboard a ship called the *Susan and Ellen*, during the summer of 1635; he was accompanied by a wife named Mary.[32] There is no trace of his movements between that time and August 1643, when a deed of sale locates him in Wethersfield.[33] In June 1644 he was defendant in a civil action before the "particular Court" at Hartford,[34] and in 1650 the same court fined him ten pounds for bartering a gun with an Indian.[35] Meanwhile he was active in a modest way at Wethersfield, buying land by private transaction in 1647, and receiving a small grant from the town in 1649.[36] The legal records identify him as a carpenter.[37] In December 1645 another resident of Wethersfield, one Edward Veir, took sick and died, leaving a will which made several references to John Carrington and a third party named Thomas Kirkham. Apparently Carrington, Kirkham, and Veir had recently completed a deal for "peas and wheat," and they may have been growing corn together as well. Veir was concerned that his friends not "lose anything" as a result of his death; he also asked that they be paid for making his coffin.[38] Veir was unmarried, and his properties were relatively few; Kirkham appears (from other sources) to have stayed poor throughout a long residence in Wethersfield;[39] and Carrington's own inventory was among the smallest in the whole range of early Connecticut probates. Hence the picture suggested here is one of close collaboration among three of the most humble members of the community.

At the time of their arrival in Boston John and Mary Carrington were both recorded as being thirty-three years old. No children were listed as traveling with them. However, there is reason to believe that they subsequently produced at least one son—namely, a second John Carrington, later of Farmington, Connecticut. No specific birth-date can be assigned to this child, though 1640 seems a reasonable (if approximate) supposition.[40] It is clear, in any event, that Mary Carrington died at some point in this sequence, and that her husband was remarried to a woman variously called Joan or Joanna. For it was Joan Carrington who stood indicted with John in 1651. In sum, the "witches" in this case were a married couple of roughly middle age. (John was forty-nine at the time of his trial; his wife, most likely, was also in her forties.) John was in his second marriage (and possibly Joan was, too). John had been resident in Wethersfield for at least eight years, certainly long enough to establish a "reputation." His economic position was quite lowly—likewise, no doubt, his social status. (He never held any offices in Wethersfield.) Perhaps his only distinction was his alleged ability to "do works above the course of nature." And that was an unlucky distinction indeed.

After the trial of the Carringtons Wethersfield remained free of witchcraft, or at least of witchcraft *proceedings*, for more than a decade. In the meantime, however, the town was increasingly overtaken by other forms of conflict, some of them internal and some in response to pressures from outside. This sequence was enormously complicated, and cannot be understood apart from parallel events in Hartford.

The background to the infamous "Hartford controversy" is virtually impossible to reconstruct. We know in a general way that religion was centrally at issue, but there is a lamentable dearth of hard detail.[41] Even Cotton Mather, so much closer than we to the time and spirit of all this, confessed that its "true original" seemed "almost as obscure as the rise of the Connecticut River."[42]

However begun, the battle was fully joined and gaining momentum by the mid-1650s. The Hartford pastor, the Rev. Samuel Stone, sought to introduce certain new departures in religious doctrine and discipline. More specifically, Stone was identified with the so-called "halfway covenant" and with a "presbyterian" scheme of church polity. Though a majority of the membership supported him, there was also strong opposition from a group subsequently called the "strict congregational- ists." Representatives of neighboring churches attempted in 1654 and 1655 to restore harmony, but without effect. In 1656 and again in 1657 there were councils with the churches of Massachusetts Bay, leading to a formal "pacification." But this agreement fell apart within months, and the two factions became more embittered and alienated than before.[43]

Now, the trouble spilled over the boundaries of Hartford proper. The dissident group proposed to withdraw completely from Stone's congre- gation, and to join instead with the church at Wethersfield.[44] There were complicated negotiations among the various parties during the last months of 1657. However, in February 1658 the General Court put a stop to all this "until the matters in controversy between the church of Hartford and the brethren that have withdrawn be brought to an issue in that way that the court shall determine."[45]

Meanwhile the church at Wethersfield was itself moving toward con- flict and division. The roots of the trouble there, as at Hartford, cannot be discovered, but the immediate issue was an effort within the mem- bership to remove the minister, the Rev. John Russell. The records make reference to an earlier occasion—a court proceeding—when Mr. Russell had acted in a way that his critics found "ambiguous, rash, and sinful." Apparently he gave testimony that reflected adversely on "Lieut." John Hollister, a leading man in town (indeed, a deputy from Wethers- field to the General Court).[46] Hollister's name headed a list of some fifty signers on a public "petition" against Russell of August 1658.[47] As usual, the magistrates responded with proposals for compromise. They declared, on the one hand, that the petition had "strained" truth and was therefore "blameable," and, on the other, that Mr. Russell's "oath" was indeed "ambiguous." They rejected for the time being the petitioners' charge that the pastor was "altogether unfit" for his position, and exhorted both sides to "walk lovingly together."[48] But these soothing gestures did little to reverse the drift of events. Shortly thereafter Mr. Russell had engineered a vote of excommunication against Hollister, under circumstances which returned the whole affair to the courts the next winter.[49] And there were new combatants on both sides. A spate of slander charges expressed the rising level of feeling.[50]

While the magistrates searched vainly for middle ground, there were growing portents of a permanent separation. The Hartford "withdrawers" had already made overtures to the General Court of Massachusetts Bay, and gained approval for a new settlement in the western part of that colony.[51] The Russell faction at Wethersfield proposed to join them. There were further delays: in the summer of 1659 the Rev. Russell was still in Wethersfield,[52] and the following autumn a final council with churchmen from Massachusetts produced yet another "reconciliation" among the various factions at Hartford.[53] But this was a purely symbolic achievement. Already the dissident vanguard had left Connecticut and was breaking ground at a site upriver soon to be christened Hadley.[54] Some twenty-two families from Wethersfield, led by the Rev. Russell, joined with thirty-six from Hartford (the group opposed to Stone) in founding the new settlement.[55] Once again these Connecticut Puritans had arrived at their final solution to the problem of social conflict: outright, and permanent, "division."

In its immediate impact the departure of the Hadley group must have been profoundly disorganizing. Land and other properties were reshuffled at a rapid rate. The church was temporarily paralyzed, since Russell's followers included the largest part of the regular membership. (According to one account, there remained "but five [members] under censure and one who was silent.")[56] For a time there were doubts about the legitimacy of such a body; but in 1661, after the congregation had undergone a process of internal "regathering," the General Court declared "that the said church is the true and undoubted church of Wethersfield."[57] It was not easy to find, and hold, a new pastor for the town—presumably because of the tumultuous events of the preceding years. Five different men preached at Wethersfield in the early 1660s— and quickly moved on to other places.[58] Only with the arrival of the Rev. Gershom Bulkeley, in 1666, did the town resolve this problem of "temporary supplies" to its pulpit. There was less disruption in the realm of civil affairs. In the years before the final break the anti-Russell faction had established control of local government, for (although outnumbered in church) they formed a clear majority of the total populace. By and large, the same men who had filled town offices before 1660 continued to lead Wethersfield in the following decade.

Witchcraft, so conspicuously absent from Connecticut life during the period of the Hartford controversy, reappeared soon thereafter. In 1661 there was a full-scale trial at Saybrook; a couple named Jennings were accused, indicted, and narrowly acquitted.[59] The following year brought to the Connecticut Valley the most extended and complex set of witchcraft proceedings anywhere in New England before 1692. The death of an eight-year-old child, the fits and delusions of an adolescent girl, the confession of a middle-aged woman: so the sequence unfolded.

Accusations began to surface in the spring of 1662, and evidence was
still being heard three years later. In the meantime, there were some
fourteen indictments, against eleven different persons; still others were
implicated, though not, it appears, brought to trial. Four of the accused
were found guilty, and almost certainly were executed; five fled the
colony at some point during their prosecution; one was imprisoned and
then freed owing to outside intercession; and, in the remaining case, the
jury could not agree on a verdict. It made, all in all, a forbidding total.[60]

Hartford was the undoubted center of these proceedings, but Wethersfield was also considerably involved. Two of the peripheral figures—
Elizabeth and John Blackleach—were residents of the town; suspicions
were voiced against both, but did not lead to formal charges.[61] Rebecca
Greensmith, whose confession was pivotal in the larger development of
the affair, had previously lived in Wethersfield as the wife of a man
named Abraham Elsen.[62] Following Elsen's death she had moved to
Hartford to marry one Jarvis Mudge; widowed yet again, she married
Nathaniel Greensmith—who shared her fate in the witchcraft trials.
(Nathaniel himself owned land in Wethersfield, and may have lived
there at an earlier time.)[63] In testifying about her own witchcraft,
Rebecca Greensmith implicated two current residents of Wethersfield:
"There was a meeting [of witches] under a tree in the green . . . and
there we danced and had a bottle of sack"; among those present were
"James Wakeley . . . and Henry Palmer's wife of Wethersfield."[64]

Katherine Palmer had been an object of local suspicion some years
previously. In 1659 and 1660 the family of Mr. John Robbins, an early
and esteemed settler of Wethersfield, had sustained a bitter siege of
illness and death; Mrs. Robbins, a son named Samuel, and then Mr.
Robbins himself succumbed at intervals of a few months.[65] Before her
death, according to later evidence, Mrs. Robbins "very much complained
against Goody Palmer as one that caused her afflictions, and cried out
that she saw her, and . . . Mr. Robbins two or three times forewarned the
said Palmer not to come to his house, yet nevertheless the said Palmer
would thrust herself into the company."[66] The outcome of these accusations is not immediately clear, for there is no formal indictment in any
extant court papers.

Henry and Katherine Palmer had lived in Wethersfield since at least
1642. Four children were subsequently noted as born to them there.
They were people of modest means; Henry was apparently a carpenter
by trade, and he held but one, minor town office.[67] Interestingly enough,
the Palmers do not appear after 1663 in either local (Wethersfield) or
colony (Connecticut) records—which may indicate a removal from their

home of twenty years. Did they perhaps flee, in order to avoid an impending prosecution for witchcraft and the risk of death on the gallows? This line of speculation leads naturally to Rhode Island—the favorite place of refuge for others who had been similarly accused.[68] In fact, a man named Henry Palmer does appear in Rhode Island records from the late 1660s onward (and not before).[69] A resident of Newport, he was occasionally in court over property matters—and once in a case of defamation. The record of the latter proceeding is clearly of present interest: "Stephen Sebeere shall acknowledge unto Henry Palmer . . . [that he hath] done wrong unto him and his wife in saying that his wife is a witch."[70] Here is strong, if not totally decisive, evidence linking the Wethersfield Palmers and the Newport Palmers as one and the same. In colonial New England, as in many other times and places, a reputation was hard to shake. It appears that Katherine Palmer had indeed left Wethersfield for reasons of self-protection—although, from time to time, her neighbors would still call her witch.

Another suspected witch who chose flight, in preference to the workings of legal process, was James Wakeley—also of Wethersfield. Wakeley's long and tortuous career in New England is worth at least a brief retelling. His earliest appearances in land records place him at Hartford by, or before, 1643.[71] He seems to have been a man of considerable wealth and entrepreneurial bent; he was frequently involved in mercantile activities, though later evidence identifies him as a weaver.[72] Most striking of all was his extensive involvement in litigation. From 1643 to 1663 James Wakeley went to court no less than thirty-seven times (twenty-one as plaintiff, and sixteen as defendant).[73] This total was matched by few of his Connecticut contemporaries; it provides a quantitative basis (though unfortunately without qualitative support) for characterizing Wakeley as an extremely contentious man.

Apart from a brother named Henry, James Wakeley seems to have arrived in Connecticut without family. In 1652, however, he married Alice Boosey of Wethersfield, under somewhat peculiar and controversial circumstances. Their courtship was long and fractured. In the fall of 1650 Wakeley filed a legal action against Alice Boosey for "breach of covenants." The court found no evidence of a final "contract of marriage" between them, but "sufficient to evince some engagement or promise"; hence the defendant's "proceeding with another before a clear disengagement [from Wakeley] . . . was at least disorderly."[74] As a wealthy widow, Alice Boosey was a prize matrimonial prospect,[75] and so Wakeley, having won his legal suit, continued his romantic one. This, too, ended successfully—though not for another couple of years.[76] Even then some questions were raised, for the General Court felt obliged to declare "the . . . marrying [of] James Wakeley and the widow Boosey to be legal."[77]

At about the time he married the widow Boosey, James Wakeley moved from Hartford to Wethersfield. He purchased the house of his wife's former husband, and became stepfather to her several children.[78] Interestingly, there was a temporary decline in the pace of his activities at court (only three cases in the next seven years); perhaps family life mellowed, or at least distracted, him. In all, he had approximately a decade of uninterrupted residence in Wethersfield; then, in the latter part of 1662, the witchhunt fetched him up.

The record of James Wakeley's experience as an accused witch is regrettably incomplete. Most clear are his various comings and goings in relation to anticipated charges; least so is the nature of those charges, and their source. In January 1663 the court noted that he had "lately fled" and ordered that his estate "be secured and kept safe" while the town selectmen made inventory of its contents.[79] In March "the sequestration laid on James Wakeley's estate [was] . . . continued until the Court take it off, though his wife might "pay and receive debts."[80] By July he had returned to Wethersfield: "James Wakeley . . . being present . . . the magistrates . . . do hereby take off the sequestration . . . upon [his] . . . estate."[81] Perhaps he remained nearby during the next two years, for, in the summer of 1665, he posted a large personal bond for his appearance before a forthcoming session of the court.[82] In fact, he soon fled once more, and this time it was for good. The court responded by "destraining" his bond, and later ordered the sale of some "housing and land" of Wakeley's "for the benefit of the country."[83]

By then Wakeley was fully resettled in Providence, Rhode Island.[84] From time to time he sent petitions to the Connecticut General Court for an "abatement" of his forfeiture—which the magistrates routinely denied, "having with much patience waited long to see whether the petitioner would appear before them to make answer to what was objected against him."[85] In 1676 he asked the court "to have his wife Alice Wakeley sent to him by order of authority to Rhode Island, or to grant a bill of divorce from the said Alice." She, for her part, protested that "James Wakeley before marriage . . . [had promised] that he would not remove her from Wethersfield, her then and present dwelling place, without her consent"—a claim which the court accepted.[86] In 1680 both husband and wife filed pleas for divorce, based on the fact that James had been living in Rhode Island for the past "fourteen or fifteen years" —ever since he left Connecticut to escape prosecution for "a capital crime." Again the magistrates demurred, but they changed their position in one significant respect: "James Wakeley's coming to live in Wethersfield shall be of no offense to them, neither shall they call him to account for any former matters, provided there be no renewed complaining of the same nature which may necessarily cause the Court to reflect upon these former matters."[87] This rather doubtful olive branch was not sufficient to bring Wakeley back. Alice died three years later, leaving properties that were unusually extensive for a woman.[88] The last extant trace of James is still another petition from Rhode Island, dated 1690: he was vainly pleading for a portion of his late wife's estate.[89]

This sequence suggests that James Wakeley was prosecuted, or threatened with prosecution, on two different occasions—first, in the latter months of 1662, and again in the summer of 1665. (Apparently there was a period between these dates when the charges were withdrawn, permitting his temporary return to Wethersfield.) Unfortunately, there is but one surviving deposition that reveals any of the substantive allegations against Wakeley. Dated August 1668 (well after Wakeley's departure for Rhode Island), it attempts to link Wakeley with Katherine Harrison as confederates in witchcraft. The deponent, a young man named Thomas Bracey, recalled various misfortunes that befell him following a quarrel with Wakeley. Indeed, the culmination had been a spectral assault, with Wakeley and Harrison appearing at night "by the bedside" and "afflicting and pinching [Bracey] as if his flesh had been pulled from his bones."[90] It was a famiilar—but always frightening—story.

Once feeling had been aroused to this point, and charges pressed, and court and community mobilized against him, Wakeley was understandably reluctant to return to Wethersfield. Even many years later there could be no absolute guarantee against "renewed complaining of the same nature" from his erstwhile accusers—witchcraft reputations being what they were. And so James Wakeley stayed put, in Rhode Island— apparently much poorer in a material sense, but protected from the enmities that had threatened his life.[91]

The troubles of Katherine Palmer and James Wakeley have led naturally to the last of the Wethersfield "witches"—the intriguing personage of Katherine Harrison, whose indictment, conviction, and eventual banishment greatly preoccupied the town in the years 1668–70. As mentioned above, the only extant depositions against Palmer and Wakeley come from the same period, and seem directly related to the Harrison trial. Perhaps this testimony was meant to impute guilt by association with two persons already discredited by their flight from prosecution.

But if so, it was a minor flourish, for Katherine Harrison had become in her own right a lively, and conspicuous, and deeply feared influence on the life of Wethersfield.

Any biographical picture of this woman is necessarily truncated; only a portion of her life—perhaps the middle third—can be effectively studied. The earliest specific datum is one that she herself provided, while testifying at a court inquiry of 1670: "She saith that she hath lived at Wethersfield 19 years, and came from England thither."[92] When checked against other material, this statement needs correction in one particular. Katherine came out of England in 1651—this much can be accepted—but she did *not* go directly to Wethersfield. Instead, for perhaps two years (1651–53) she lived and worked in Hartford as servant to a merchant named "Captain" John Cullick.[93]

The Cullick household was, in fact, the point of origin for the suspicions that would eventually overwhelm her. Her fellow-servants, family members, and neighbors retained from this period vivid memories of Katherine's eccentric and provocative behavior, memories which poured out in court testimony years later. She had been, by various accounts, a "notorious liar," a "sabbath breaker"—perhaps even a prostitute ("one that followed the army in England").[94] She had performed feats of strength and dexterity that seemed impossible "without some unlawful help."[95] (For example, she "did often spin so great a quantity of fine linen yarn as the said [deponent] did never know, nor heard of any other woman that could spin so much.")[96] All this was telling enough; but far more decisive, among the impressions she left, was her interest in telling fortunes. Time and again she flaunted her knowledge of "many matters that were in future time to be accomplished."[97] She claimed for herself a particular sophistication, based on "great familiarity" with the noted English astrologer William Lilly. Some witnesses recalled her saying that "she had read Mr. Lilly's book in England"; others inferred a more personal tutelage.[98]

These talents were exercised chiefly on the younger members of the Cullick household (including the "master's daughters");[99] one instance will serve to convey their characteristic tenor. Elizabeth Bateman, a fellow maidservant, had as her suitor a young man named William Chapman. Their courtship was long and serious, but Captain Cullick did not approve. Hence complaint was made to the local magistrates, and Chapman was prosecuted for violating a law that forbade dependent persons from making "any motion or suit by way of marriage" without the consent of "parents, master, or guardian." Still, the couple persevered, and Elizabeth herself "thought that she should have been married to

William Chapman" eventually. Enter the fortune-teller: "Katherine Harrison affirmed that she [Elizabeth] should not be married to William . . . but to one named Simon." The sequence thereafter is obscure, but when Elizabeth came forward to testify in the Harrison trial of 1668 she identified herself as "the wife of Simon Smith."[100]

Perhaps such successes gratified Katherine's pride, but they also marked her in ways that would prove damaging later on. To predict the future was to tread the narrow borders of legitimacy, as then defined. In some contexts this could be dismissed as idle pastime, but much depended on the people involved. A group of ministers, approached by the court for advice in the Harrison trial, pronounced a harsh judgment on fortune-telling when practiced by "vicious persons":

> Those things, whether past, present, or to come, which are indeed secret—that is, [which] cannot be known by human skill in arts, or strength of reason arguing from the course of nature—nor are made known by divine revelation . . . must needs be known (if at all) by information from the Devil. . . . [Hence] communication of such things, in way of divination . . . seems to us to argue familiarity with the Devil.[101]

The above picture of Katherine Harrison during her time as a maid-servant was presented in court testimony years after the fact, and was contradicted (in a formal "petition") by Katherine herself. Yet it derived from several different sources, and there was complete agreement on details. Moreover, Katherine's rejoinder seemed conspicuously weak and non-specific. To the matter of fortune-telling, and the other imputations of bad character, she responded simply "I know nothing of it."[102] Instead she concentrated on the single issue of her departure from Captain Cullick's service. According to various deponents, she had been "turned out" because of her "evil conversation in word and deed."[103] But Katherine alleged "that the reason why my master could not keep me was . . . some disagreement between me and the widow that was then [also] Captain Cullick's servant." She pointed to "Captain Cullick's coming to visit me at Wethersfield" as evidence of a friendly disposition on his part.[104]

Whatever the truth of all this, Katherine appeared in Wethersfield by May 1653, and married a local "inhabitant" named John Harrison.[105] (Her maiden name, incidentally, is nowhere indicated.) With this her life entered a new and somewhat more routine phase. In short order she bore three daughters,[106] and for some years thereafter her life compassed a familiar round of domestic responsibilities. In one respect alone is there

evidence from these years that distinguishes Katherine from the average
Connecticut goodwife. She had special skills in medicine, and was frequently involved in the treatment of local people who fell sick. There
are various references to this in the materials from the witchcraft trial.
A widow deposed that when her late husband came home from a trip
upriver "he was ill, and Goodwife Harrison did help him with diet,
drink, and plasters."[107] (The treatment was not satisfactory, and so the
patient turned elsewhere—to another local "physician"—for assistance.)
A man's toe became infected, and Katherine "dressed" it. (This infection
may have been fatal, in the long run; the testimony is ambiguous.)[108]
A baby sickened and died, in spite of Katherine's ministrations. ("I can
say . . . that I was no ways prejudicial to the health of the child.")[109]
The exact nature of this doctoring is unclear. Seventeenth-century
medicine was part science, part folklore, part superstition, and, at the
lower end of the spectrum, it merged with distinctly questionable activities—like fortune-telling. Katherine's personal interest in "things to
come" is less well attested for the period of her marriage than before,
but does not seem to have ended entirely.[110] And, in the minds of others,
her dual role—as healer and fortune-teller—may well have formed a
continuum.

Katherine's husband, John, seems a strangely elusive figure in the
annals of Wethersfield. There is fragmentary evidence to indicate his
arrival there in the late 1640s.[111] His lands are recorded in the usual
fashion, and one source gives his occupation as "merchant."[112] At his
death he left a large estate—more than £900—which is consistent with
a mercantile orientation.[113] On the other hand, there is only one reference to John Harrison in any court records, and he was hardly more
conspicuous in town affairs.[114] He was elected to minor office from time
to time (town crier, fence-viewer, surveyor, and constable), but overall
his public service was much below the norm for men of wealth.

There are questions here which the available evidence does not resolve.
But one line of interpretation forcefully suggests itself. Assume that John
Harrison came to Wethersfield as a man of no distinction and few (economic) resources; that he married a woman of equally common background (a former maidservant); that by virtue of cleverness and sheer
luck they prospered as few of their peers ever could; and that such
unusual "mobility" gave rise to instinctive resentment elsewhere in the
community. This resentment against the Harrisons as a *family*, and the
dubious reputation of Katherine as an *individual*, then locked together
in an attitudinal matrix—from which suspicions of witchcraft almost
predictably emerged. (For people accustomed to firm status lines and a

stable pattern of economic relationships, rapid changes of fortune seemed inherently "remarkable"—hence particularly susceptible to supernatural explanation.) For a time these suspicions remained at the level of rumor and gossip, but in 1666 the death of John Harrison left his widow suddenly unprotected—and vulnerable. Within two years the case against her became open and official; the rest is in the public record.

This reconstruction, conjectural in some parts, can be amply documented in others. Thus the trial testimony of 1668 does indeed reflect long-standing suspicion of Katherine in the community at large. Stories of her various misdeeds had passed from mouth to mouth, in tones of breathless excitement:

> The said Philip [Smith] parted from the said Joseph [Dickenson], and a small time after Joseph met Philip again, and then the said Philip affirmed. . . . The said Joseph went homeward, and met Samuel Belden riding. . . . Samuel Belden asked Joseph whether he had seen. . . . Then Joseph asked Samuel whether he had seen. . . . The said Samuel told Joseph aforesaid that he saw . . . Etcetera.[115]

Much of this testimony recounted events from many years previous; in fact, some of it was taken at Hadley from people who had left Wethersfield in the great schism of 1659–60. It appears that in certain quarters Katherine had been considered a witch virtually from the time of her arrival in Wethersfield.[116]

In the months following John Harrison's death Katherine's relations with her fellow-townspeople rapidly deteriorated. The upshot was a series of court cases in the fall of 1668. There were three suits over conflicting claims to property—all of them decided against Katherine.[117] But perhaps more important, and certainly more revealing, was her involvement in two slander cases begun by her neighbors Michael and Ann Griswold. In the first instance, Katherine had reportedly said that "Michael Griswold would hang her though he damned a thousand souls, and as for his own soul it was damned long ago"; in the second, that Griswold's wife was "a savage whore, with other expressions of the like nature." The jury voted to convict on both counts, with fines totalling £40.[118] Katherine appealed straightaway to the Court of Assistants, and sent a long "declaration" in her defense. She admitted uttering some "hasty, unadvised, and passionate expressions" about the Griswolds, but had subsequently offered a "full and free confession of my fault . . . to repair the wound that I had given to their names by a plaster as broad as the sore." This should have sufficed to resolve the matter—or so it seemed to Katherine—but the plaintiffs evidently preferred a "full purse" to "my repentance." In concluding her plea to the magistrates, Katherine asked for special forbearance, "being a distressed widow, a female, a weaker vessel subject to passion, meeting with overbearing exercises by evil instruments. . . ."[119]

The "overbearing exercises" mentioned herein were the subject of still another petition from Katherine Harrison. Delivered to the court in October 1668, this document described "many injuries . . . [which] have happened since my husband's death." The list was long, the details full, the mood deeply resentful:

> In the first place . . . we had a yoke of oxen, one of which [was] spoiled, at our stile before our door, with blows upon the back and side. . . . About a fortnight or three weeks after the former we had a cow spoiled, her back broke and two of her ribs. . . . Nextly, I had a cow at the side of my yard, her jaw bone broke and one of her hoofs, and a hole bored in her side. . . . Nextly I had a three-year-old heifer in the meadow stuck with a knife. . . . More, I had a matter of 30 poles of hops cut and spoiled. . . .[120]

This is merely a sampling of Katherine's "grievances"—which, as listed, involved thirteen separate episodes. Even allowing for some exaggeration, there is more than enough here to declare the extremity of Katherine's plight. A woman of much property—and this, too, her petition declares—she was now hopelessly at odds with her neighbors. Events had reached such an *impasse* as to defy all but the most drastic forms of resolution. In a sense that is just what her trial for witchcraft would finally accomplish.

The prosecution of Katherine Harrison was a protracted affair, encompassing two full years from beginning to end. Careful study of the documentary record reveals significant elements of pattern and structure in the movement of events over time. Social, geographic, and evidentiary factors were joined in a gathering drama with several distinct phases.

A beginning was made in the months of May and June 1668. Four of the extant depositions date from that spring, and there is reason to think that another five, now lost but mentioned elsewhere, were given at roughly the same time.[121] All nine of the witnesses were resident in Wethersfield, all but one were persons of average or less than average social position, and all but two were adult women. Their testimony reduced to legal form the staple currency of local gossip during ten or more preceding years. A poor goodwife had seen the shape of Katherine Harrison ("and her black dog") hovering near a sick friend.[122] Another woman had faced a similar "apparition" late one night, just before her infant son fell mortally ill. ("I said, 'the Lord bless me and my child; here is Goody Harrison. . . .' ")[123] A teen-aged boy was temporarily paralyzed when he spied Katherine Harrison milking a cow "that was none of her own."[124] All of these testimonies converged in charging outright *maleficium*: episodes of injury and illness, sometimes deadly in result, attributed by the victims to Katherine's witchcraft.

Although such *maleficium* formed the core of every serious witchcraft prosecution, other evidence might help to strengthen the case. Accordingly, in August 1668 efforts were made to obtain new testimony against Katherine Harrison on two quite different fronts. It was then that several witnesses from Hartford set down their memories of the accused during her time of service in the household of Captain Cullick. This was essentially "character evidence" (her fortune-telling and other questionable behavior), designed to portray her, even long before, as a sort of proto-witch.[125] Still another group of important depositions was gathered from among the ex-Wethersfield settlers at Hadley, and sent downriver to the court in Connecticut. These people, too, retained a vivid picture of Katherine, though eight eventful years of their lives had passed by in the meantime. Four witnesses, all men, recalled various manifestations of supernatural power (though not, for the most part, of *maleficium*) in which their erstwhile neighbor had been significantly involved. The Harrisons' bee-swarm flew "over the great river" and immediately returned; their cattle were lost and found under peculiar circumstances; a calf's head, with "the ears standing pert up," appeared atop their hay-cart, and suddenly changed to a human form; another man's oxen loosened a tether "of [their] own accord" and ran wildly about.[126]

The clustering of the testimony into three distinct categories is itself a revealing datum. The Hartford evidence—Katherine as servant—has the earliest point of reference. Next come the Hadley depositions, presenting Katherine as she seemed to her fellow-townspeople in about the year 1660. Finally, there are the witnesses from Wethersfield itself, most of them with evidence from the period between 1660 and 1668. These materials, so readily arranged in chronological sequence, can also be sorted by way of *content*. The character portrayal of the first group gives way to the (relatively harmless) magic and mystery of the second, and moves finally to the baleful *maleficium* of the third. Though harder to trace in other cases of witchcraft, this was a fairly typical progression.

Another issue concurrently presents itself. The geographic dispersion of the many deponents against Katherine Harrison, and the substantive range of their testimony, suggest that the prosecution may have been centrally organized. It is even possible to read the timing and venue of the various depositions as tracks of a single individual—moving plan-fully from south to north along the Connecticut River (Wethersfield, to Hartford, to Hadley), and building the case, piece by piece, as he went. Of course, possible does not mean provable, but Katherine had her own suspicions in the matter. Recall her slandering Michael Griswold, "saying [he] would hang her, though he damned a thousand souls."[127] This comment, uttered late in the summer of 1668, seems to admit of only one reference; how else might Griswold hang her—except through a conviction for witchcraft? And whose souls could he have damned—save those of the numerous witnesses induced to give what Katherine regarded as false testimony?

Whatever the degree of Michael Griswold's initiative in all this,[128] there was by early autumn much testimony against Katherine. It is a plausible assumption that she went to trial soon thereafter, and if so, she was evidently acquitted. (Local tradition recalls a hung jury.)[129] Just here lies an unfortunate *lacuna* in the court summary; the deposi-tions themselves, however, contain the special notation "sworn in Court" —in some instances, "exhibited in Court"—on October 29, 1668. Almost certainly this was the date of a first indictment.

The autumn proceeding was only a preliminary skirmish. Suspicions festered through the ensuing winter,[130] and in May 1669 Katherine was newly summoned to appear before the Court of Assistants. In this in-stance the full indictment survives: "Katherine Harrison . . . thou hast had familiarity with Satan . . . and by his help hast acted things beyond and beside the ordinary course of nature, and hast thereby hurt the bodies of diverse of the subjects of our sovereign lord, the King."[131] Katherine pleaded not guilty, and a jury trial followed. Most of the earlier depositions were presented again, but there was also new evidence dealing with Katherine's activities in the meanwhile. The jurymen, "finding difficulty in the matter, [could] not as yet agree," whereupon the magistrates ordered them to continue deliberating and "to give in a verdict" at the October session of the court.[132]

Katherine Harrison was to remain in custody at Hartford, pending the final resolution of her case. But she managed somehow to obtain her release, and returned that summer to Wethersfield. Her neighbors were indignant and afraid; soon a petition was circulating through the town. Eventually signed by thirty-eight men, and forwarded to the authorities in Hartford, this document urged that Katherine be forthwith remanded to jail.[133] It also noted some recent developments in the case. Since the day of Katherine's release, "very evil, hurtful, and dangerous effects" had been visited on several of her Wethersfield neighbors. (Eight were mentioned by name—some of them "oppressed," some "afflicted," and some "affrighted.") This had served to create a new pool of witnesses against her, who offered either to supply written testimony or to "declare themselves" in person at court. John Blackleach (previously mentioned),[134] whose wife was among Katherine's most recent "victims," would take the lead henceforth in "the opening and clearing [of] the whole case."

The response of Katherine herself to these latest charges was decidely ambiguous. On the one hand, she composed and sent to court a personal statement of rebuttal.[135] She also offered to submit to an ancient "test" of witches, by "trying whether she could sink or swim in the water." (Only the guilty would float—buoyed up, presumably, by the Devil.) On the other hand, she rapidly "disposed of the great part of her estate to others in trust," which caused her neighbors to suspect "that she intendeth to be gone."[136]

Whether the aforementioned petition achieved its objective is not recorded. But Katherine was returned to court the following October—and the jury, at long last, voted to convict her.[137] Sentencing was apparently deferred while the magistrates conducted their own review. In May 1670 they decided to set aside the jury's verdict: "This court cannot concur with them so as to sentence her to death." Instead, they directed her "to mind the fulfillment of removing from Wethersfield, which is what will lend most to her own safety and the contentment of the people who are her neighbors."[138] This was, in short, a decree of banishment; but the wording implies that Katherine had already agreed to leave.

A scant few weeks later she appeared in the town of Westchester, New York. However, her reputation had accompanied (or preceded) her, and her wish to settle there was immediately opposed. New litigation began, and dragged on through the summer. The outcome served, for once, to vindicate Katherine; in October she was cleared of "suspicion" and granted liberty "to remain in the town of Westchester, where she now resides, or anywhere else in the government during her pleasure."[139]

After this her trail rapidly peters out. It appears that she left Westchester sometime in 1671, perhaps *en route* to Long Island.[140] In 1672 she filed, at the Hartford county court, no less than *eleven* concurrent legal suits against her former associates in Wethersfield, and the record indicates that she was there in person.[141] Just possibly there were further efforts to convict her of witchcraft, in New York, at late as 1673; but no firm evidence survives.[142] *Exit* Katherine Harrison—her role on this particular stage apparently ended.

. . .

As the foregoing narrative has shown, there was broad public support at Wethersfield for the proceedings against Katherine Harrison. Nonetheless, individuals participated in varying ways and degrees—and there were some who took no part at all. Were there underlying factors that might help to explain such variance? The question must be asked, even though the extant data will supply only scattered fragments of an answer.

It is possible to divide the families of Wethersfield into four categories based on the extent of their personal involvement in the Harrison trials —and termed, in what follows, "major," "intermediate," "minor" and "none."[143] These groups can then be compared with reference to specific indices of social and demographic position. Four such comparisons yield *no* significant result: age of family head, presence of small children in the household, ancestral place of origin in England, and overall litigiousness. Members of the different "participation" categories were distributed randomly for each of these measures.

Three additional measures deserve a closer look. One shows a modest difference between "participants" and "non-participants" in length of residence at Wethersfield. The latter included a higher proportion of recent arrivals in the town; however, long-time inhabitants were divided almost evenly among the respective categories.[144] Analysis of socioeconomic position does not, at first sight, seem productive; people of "high," "middle," and "low" status are substantially represented in each of the participation groups.[145] Yet, as noted earlier in the chapter, there are strong signs of a pattern when the Harrison proceedings are considered *over time*.[146] The first of the witnesses to come forward with adverse testimony were mostly women of average or less than average status. Persons of higher rank tended to dominate the later phase; they were, for example, disproportionately represented among the signers of the petition submitted in the summer of 1669.[147]

A final point of interest is the possibility of linkage between the witchcraft case of the late 1660s and prior events in the history of Wethersfield—particularly the bitter struggles that had split the town apart a decade before. Recall that the town had divided, on that earlier occasion, into partisans and opponents of the pastor, the Rev. John Russell. Many —but not all—of the partisan group had left Wethersfield to found the new settlement at Hadley. The opposition was led by Lieut. John Hollister; its membership can be inferred from the list of names on a petition criticizing Russell's ministry in 1658.[148] This document presents an opportunity for still another sorting of the various participants in the prosecution of Katherine Harrison. Broadly summarized, the results are as follows: individuals with "major" and "intermediate" participation levels are somewhat *less* likely to be found among the anti-Russell group than their counterparts in the "minor" and "none" categories.[149] John Harrison, late husband of the accused, was himself a signer of the petition. Meanwhile the prosecution witnesses from Hadley were identified —historically, if not personally—with the side that favored Russell; perhaps their readiness to testify, from such a distance, reflected the troubled past.

To be sure, these correlations are very irregular and imperfect. A granddaughter of Lieut. Hollister was among the alleged *victims* of Katherine's witchcraft, and at least a few of her *accusers* had associated with Hollister in the earlier struggle. Hence it would be wrong to impute a dynamic relationship between these two episodes. Rather, the "Hartford controversy" (in its Wethersfield extension) was part of the backdrop which influenced, but hardly energized, the course of the witchcraft trials. In general, the lines that had divided the town ten years before were still visible—but in some *individual* cases, current and pressing circumstances had submerged former patterns of allegiance. What this analysis shows, therefore, is an old social fissure in the process of closing.

The trial of Katherine Harrison was a terminal point in the history of witchcraft at Wethersfield. No formal prosecutions associated with residents of the town are noted for the period after 1670. This does not mean that witchcraft *suspicions* died out entirely—here the record is mute—but never again would such suspicions lead to the courts. It is not possible to understand fully the implications, or the causes, of a change like this one. Even with a time machine, and the chance to visit colonial Wethersfield at first hand, such understanding would come hard. But certain themes and trends in the life of the town, during the closing decades of the seventeenth century, deserve at least a summary review.

One is struck, first of all, by the absence of severe internal conflict; there was nothing to match the troubles that plagued Wethersfield during its earliest years and again in the 1650s.[150] Perhaps as a consequence of this relative tranquillity, there was a low and mostly stable rate of residential turnover. Newcomers appeared occasionally, and from time to time persons born in Wethersfield moved away; but considered overall, such comings and goings did not amount to much. The significant turnover in Wethersfield, after 1670, was wrought by the passage of generations—the replacement of older people by their maturing sons and daughters.

There was also an important shift in the local leadership cadre. A group of men who had dominated town government in the 1650s and 60s died, or were otherwise "retired." A new and younger group came to the fore, and remained there until nearly the end of the century.[151] In addition to this change of personnel, there was some further enhancement of leadership *stability*. The pool of men from which leaders were chosen gradually contracted; the same few individuals served the town, in various official capacities, year after year.[152]

There were salutary developments in the relation of Wethersfield to her neighbors, both Indian and colonial. Rankling uncertainties had lingered for many years over some of the deeds and treaties between the founders of the town and the local Wongunk tribesmen. In 1671 leaders from both sides negotiated an agreement which seemed definitive, and mutually satisfactory.[153] The senior Wongunk chieftain, one Tarramagus, proved still more obliging in the period immediately thereafter. He began by authorizing new grants of land to several private individuals, and concluded by approving a vast sale of territories on the east side of the Connecticut River to the town as a whole. The latter transaction, variously known as the "Five-Mile Extension" or "Great Indian Purchase," was financed by a general tax on all householders in January 1674.[154]

This expansion was corporate and communal, but it must have been felt by individuals as well. In 1670 the town had voted its first "general division" of common lands in more than three decades. Seventy-seven householders benefited, as a large area to the west of the main village was carved up into private holdings.[155] The same trend was manifest through the next fifteen years, in numerous grants to individuals made by order of the town meeting.[156]

At about the same time Wethersfield addressed territorial issues involving the adjacent English communities. In 1670 she settled her western boundary, by agreement with the people of Farmington. In the following year there was comparable success with both the northern and southern lines (fronting Hartford and Middletown, respectively).[157] From all this activity the town achieved a territorial basis more secure, and far more ample, than ever before. Stretching a full fourteen miles from east to west, and roughly six miles from north to south, Wethersfield had now reached her maximum size.

With growth came dispersion. The first tentative outreach away from the center, toward the east, had begun sometime in the 1650s. By 1670 there were perhaps a dozen families living on scattered sites across the river; by 1690 there were three dozen; shortly thereafter the entire section was split off from its Wethersfield "parent" and incorporated as the town of Glastonbury.[158] To the south, another little hamlet was gradually germinating; known informally as Rocky Hill,[159] its builders were chiefly matured sons from established families in Wethersfield proper. Meanwhile, yet a third settlement developed during the 1680s, within the newly divided section near the western line; much later it would become the town of Newington.[160] In some parts of New England this centrifugal process brought overt tension and conflict—but not, it appears, at Wethersfield.[161] Perhaps because the interests and tone of the different sections remained roughly similar, perhaps because they were all bound by ties of family and friendship, dispersion was accepted —even, in some instances, encouraged.[162]

There was concurrent development and diversification in the economic life of Wethersfield. Gristmills, sawmills, warehouses, landings, and shipyards—most of them begun after 1670—marked the direction of change.[163] Production for export seems to have increased, at least modestly. Pipestaves, horses, tobacco, salted meat, and cornmeal moved out of Wethersfield toward destinations as far away as the West Indies. To be sure, most of the population continued to be small-scale farmers, but for at least some of them there were attractive openings into a commercial and inter-colonial market.

The closing decades of the century were not entirely tranquil—as witness King Philip's War and the process of imperial reorganization that produced the Dominion of New England. Yet in places like Wethersfield these difficulties were experienced as deriving from exterior sources. They remained, in their effects, at some distance from the spatial, and political, core of town life. Indeed, by directing popular energies outward they may even have diminished certain forms of intramural tension.

Here, then, is an overview of Wethersfield in the period immediately following the last of her witchcraft cases. Reduced levels of factional conflict; a high rate of residential persistence; new, and stable, leadership; the resolution of differences with Indian and colonial neighbors; marked territorial growth; gradual dispersion of settlement; economic and occupational diversification; occasional, but intense, involvement in "outside" events and processes—these were the salient features. In most respects the pace of change was quite modest; but, taken cumulatively, the effect was substantial. In a word, there was more variety, more openness, more *space* in every sense; the press of inner strains and conflicts was modified correspondingly. From all this, Wethersfield became by the end of the century a perceptibly different place. And—for eccentrics, for deviants, even for suspected witches—most probably a *better* place.

12

Communities:
Witchcraft over Time

At both Hampton and Wethersfield, the history of witchcraft was threaded into the fabric of local experience. The timing and outcome of witchcraft episodes reflected a zig-zag progression of village events. Of course, the particulars differed from one place to the next. Yet beneath this surface variety there were important regularities of rhythm and context.

It is clear, first of all, that witchcraft was a continuous presence in the life of local communities. At least the *belief* in witchcraft was continuous—and, from all available signs, was widely dispersed among the general population. A rich lore of occultism arrived with the first settlers of New England, and was passed along through generations of their descendants. On the other hand, specific forms of *action*—toward and about witchcraft—would vary markedly over time. The range of action embraced personal (sometimes private) comment at one end, and formal trial proceedings at the other. Trials were usually preceded by months or years of preparation, during which suspicion intensified and spread, gossip flourished, relations between accused and accusers gradually deteriorated.

But these "peaks" in witchcraft history, and their corresponding "valleys," cannot be fully understood in terms of individual personalities. For they reflected as well the life of the group—of entire communities. There were broad configurations of circumstance that served at some points in time to encourage proceedings against witchcraft, and in other periods to inhibit them. The materials from our case-studies display the importance of one factor above all others: the presence, or absence, of social conflict. In technical language, this was a matter of "reverse correlation." Witchcraft proceedings and episodes of conflict did not appear together, in the same time and place; instead they waxed and waned, in alternating sequence.

The history of Hampton, for example, opened with great inner struggle (divisions in the church, disputes over the control of property). There was also some external "controversy" (over boundaries with neighboring townships). In time (after 1650) the town achieved a more stable condition; then, and only then, did it make its formal beginning with witchcraft. The decade of the 1660s brought new experiences of conflict (the struggle to preserve the town's autonomy against a proprietary claimant backed by Crown officials); meanwhile there were no witchcraft trails. The early 1670s temporarily reversed this equation (another witchcraft case, a reduction of conflict), and the later 1670s reversed it yet again (no witchcraft, renewed conflict). A similar pair of changes marked the 1680s.

The history of Wethersfield can be fitted to the same track. An early phase of conflict (Indian wars, religious controversy) yielded after 1645 to quieter conditions—which, in turn, brought witchcraft to the town for the first time. The "Hartford controversy," with its Wethersfield extension, dominated the middle and later years of the following decade —years without witchcraft trials. The controversy was finally settled in about 1660—just before the start of an unusually complicated and prolonged set of witchcraft proceedings.

Of course, generalization based on two cases is hazardous. Ideally, dozens of "community studies" would be needed, each one informed by similar methods and questions. That is plainly impossible, but some additional fragments of local history do imply support for the main finding. Springfield, Massachusetts, for example, was riven with conflict in the decade of the 1640s. The issues were religious ones: the town's founder, William Pynchon, and its pastor, Rev. George Moxon, were charged with supporting "heresy." (Both men would subsequently return to England.) In 1651, just as the trouble was reaching a conclusion, Springfield was overtaken by witchcraft. (Several children, including two of the Rev. Moxon's, became "afflicted"; three adults went to trial, and others were "suspected.")[1] Or—to take another example—Newbury, Massachusetts, was a town notorious for controversy during the middle of the century. Again, the root of the problem was religious doctrine and practice—specifically, the supposed "Presbyterianism" of the local minister, the Rev. Nathaniel Parker. The townsfolk divided into pro- and anti-Parker factions, and for a good two decades their differences engaged the attention of ecclesiastical councils, of the county courts, and even of the highest provincial authorities. The climax of this long and bitter struggle was reached in the early 1670s; soon thereafter the town achieved a settlement—and, in 1678, plunged into witchcraft proceedings (the trials of Caleb Powell and Elizabeth Morse).[2] There are hints of the same sequence from still other town histories (Hartford, Windsor, and Fairfield, in Connecticut; Cambridge and Northampton, in Massachusetts Bay; Portsmouth, in New Hampshire).[3] There is the opposite case of a town like Dedham, Massachusetts—which saw no witchcraft trials, and which, according to its most recent historian, maintained a remarkable inner harmony through most of the seventeenth century.[4] There is also some convergent evidence bearing on New England as a whole.

Here, in sum, is the outline—if not the full proof—of an important relationship. Witchcraft and conflict exclude one another at any given point in time, yet when viewed *through* time they appear to be joined. The question is how—and why? Two forms of response suggest themselves. Perhaps, in the first place, there was a factor of limited social (and personal) resources, a single center of local preoccupation. Caught in the roils of controversy, a community would not (could not?) simultaneously sponsor witchcraft proceedings. The energies which sustained both kinds of experience were, by this account, the same—and were not readily divisible. Yet perhaps, too, there was a deeper element of reciprocity. And if so, the progression *from* conflict *toward* witchcraft should probably be assigned a critical importance. Conflict was inherently problematic, not to say calamitous, when set in the scale of New England values. It called invariably for explanation, and sometimes for scapegoats. "Faction," "schism," "controversy": whatever the nomenclature, the cause was thought to be some combination of human sinfulness and Satanic guile. In short, episodes of conflict would leave the people involved with an edge of inner tension. The impulse to search out witchcraft may, under such circumstances, have been markedly strengthened. ＼ New Englanders viewed conflict not simply as an invitation to God's wrath but also as an *expression* of it. God was already angered—else He would not have allowed the social "peace" to be thus disturbed. And He showed other marks of divine disfavor. There appears, in the material on Wethersfield, a possible link between outbreaks of epidemic illness and the start of witchcraft proceedings. Illness was typically experienced as a "providence" and thus would prompt both personal and collective soul-searching. Presumably, the same pattern of response obtained for other forms of sudden misfortune. This pattern will shortly require further consideration—in the context of regional, rather than local, evidence.

But before turning away from single communities, it may be worth speculating somewhat more broadly about implicit elements of chronological sequence. Perhaps, indeed, such speculation might yield a composite profile of local history in direct relation to witchcraft. Note that witch-trials were generally absent from the earliest phase of town experience. It was as if the exigencies of settling a new place conferred some temporary immunity. Settlement deserves, in fact, more systematic study from scholars than it has yet received; some of its main features seem both regular and recurrent. Often there was great instability: factionalism, trouble with neighboring communities (both English and Indian), and high population turnover.[5] This situation—in effect, an initial "shakedown"—was not conducive to the development of full-blown witchcraft proceedings, which required time and a certain constancy of social relations.

So it was, in most communities, that witchcraft appeared a decade or more after the date of founding. There followed a period (perhaps two generations) when witchcraft was likely to make its greatest impression. Private doubts and gossip, around one or more suspects, might then have a regular place in the local culture. From all this would come occasional intervals of extreme anxiety—and actual trial cases. Such cases expressed an intricate blend of personal and group pressures, among which, as already noted, conflict seems to have been especially important. Eventually witchcraft would disappear as a matter of formal proceedings. This last part of the sequence is extremely hard to analyze from a distance of three centuries; perhaps, however, one key factor was a certain loosening of the social tissues themselves. The Wethersfield example is at least suggestive. The growth and dispersion of the local populace, a somewhat broadened range of economic activity, an increasingly firm system of social stratification: these interlocking trends seem gradually to have modified the tensions amid which witchcraft had flourished.[6]

Our modal profile of witchcraft history has, then, three parts or stages: beginning, middle, and end. We will, in due course, have more to say about the third stage; but first we must try to refine our view of the middle. And this requires a change in our line of vision. In effect, we must alter our focus so as to see much larger sections of the landscape before us.

Although a single community remains the primary unit for understanding witchcraft cases, it does not embrace every contributing factor.

Local populations did not—*could* not—live in isolation from one another; indeed, there were important elements of experience they effectively shared. Central threads in their individual histories ran together, influenced by events and trends of broader dimensions. Ecology, culture, politics, and history itself joined them in various ways. Each community struck its own balance between satisfaction and distress, but at least some of the ingredients were the same.

It is, once again, the distress that most concerns us, since witchcraft was associated so clearly with experiences of misfortune. We must inquire about particular situations and distinct periods of time when levels of human distress—in New England as a whole—were significantly elevated. What was their relation to the *regional* incidence of witchcraft cases from one year or decade to the next? We use the term "distress" in an admittedly imprecise way, extending it to cover all forms of actual or anticipated suffering. We must deal, moreover, in "correlations" pure and simple; we cannot show explicit lines of influence or causation. Still, the task posed here demands a serious response. We are obliged to connect our subject, however tentatively, with the larger history of early New England.

But that history, for these purposes, cannot be fully read from the available *corpus* of scholarship. For we are seeking to enter the minds and attitudes of the New Englanders themselves. What seemed to them important and meaningful (and, in some instances, stressful) may or may not strike historians the same way. But here it is *their own* view that matters most. Comets, weather, and epidemic disease—to cite a few obvious examples—have little or no place in current scholarship on colonial America; yet each would figure significantly in accounts from the period. Hence, in attempting to measure felt levels of "distress" in this corner of history, we must rely as directly as possible on the record left to us by the historical actors themselves. Diaries, personal correspondence, ceremonial observances, and (not least) their own historical writings provide us with most of what we wish to know.

The following pages offer a survey of distinct events, all of which seem to have created some anxiety, stress, or outright suffering among substantial numbers of the New Englanders. The events are grouped under three broad headings: what we shall call "harms," "signs," and "controversies." Since the aim of all this, and at least some of the materials, may seem unorthodox, we proceed initially by way of a narrative. A subsequent discussion explores analytic connections to the ebb and flow of witchcraft proceedings.

Harms

Among the most dreaded and socially disruptive forms of suffering visited upon the New Englanders were those associated with epidemic disease. It is hard now even to conceive the enormity of the scourges which repeatedly overwhelmed premodern populations in all parts of the world. Recent studies have demonstrated that relative to most such populations early New England was quite fortunate: the average expectation of life was greater, and the overall rate of mortality lower, than was the case, for example, in the "mother country."[7] However, New England knew all the principal illnesses of the Old World; her advantage was a matter of degree. It is significant, too, that this advantage appears to have gone quite unnoticed at the time.[8]

After the well-known mortality of the earliest years—the "starving times" experienced at both Plymouth and Massachusetts Bay—the first general outbreak of illness seems to have come in 1647–48. Its beginnings were observed in the coastal towns of Massachusetts, but eventually it spread "throughout the country"; modern study of contemporaneous accounts yields a tentative diagnosis of influenza.[9] A similar, and equally "general," outbreak followed in 1655,[10] while lesser episodes occurred in 1650–51 (in and around Boston),[11] in 1658,[12] in 1661 ("in many parts of the country"),[13] and in the summer of 1668 (especially in Connecticut).[14] Smallpox, mercifully absent during the settlement phase of New England history, made a first appearance (largely confined to Boston) in 1649,[15] returned in 1666–67,[16] and struck again on a massive and devastating scale in 1677–78.[17] The decade of the 1670s was especially notable for morbidity: dysentery was widespread in its opening years, with "several [other] diseases" following immediately thereafter.[18] Influenza-like episodes recurred in Massachusetts in 1676 and 1679,[19] and in both the Bay Colony and Connecticut during 1682–83.[20] A severe (sometimes fatal) outbreak of measles "prevailed exceedingly in this land" in 1688–89.[21] A fourth smallpox epidemic, even worse than its predecessors, began in the closing months of 1689 and continued through most of the next year.[22] The last serious outbreak of disabling illness in the seventeenth century—apparently more influenza—occurred in 1697–98.[23]

Weather made a second category of significant harm. Like agricultural folk everywhere, the New Englanders were obliged to attend closely to the day-by-day sequence of rain and sun and wind, of warmth and cold; it is no accident that diaries from the period are filled with meteorological observation. What concerns us here is the matter of weather *extremes*—particular episodes or seasons of unusual hardship. In certain years, for example, there were great autumnal storms, which we can recognize as Atlantic hurricanes. (The settlers themselves could not have encountered this particular type of storm prior to their arrival in New England.) John Winthrop's journal notes a dreadful "tempest" of August 1635, which "blew down many hundreds of trees, . . . overthrew some houses, and drove the ships from their anchors," with considerable loss of life (especially at sea).[24] Spring storms, with their massive runoff from melting snows, could be equally damaging. Extensive floods occurred, especially in the Connecticut River Valley, during the early months of 1642 and again in both 1645 and 1646.[25] The latter two episodes bracketed an entire year of unusually harsh weather, including another hurricane (in October) and "the earliest and sharpest winter [according to Winthrop] we had since we came here."[26] Devastating springtime floods occurred again in 1661 and 1692.[27] The worst of all seventeenth-century hurricanes seem to have been those of August 1675 and September 1683.[28] And the two winters of 1696–97 and 1697–98 were notable both for length and for severity.[29]

Tightly linked to the vagaries of the weather was the success—or failure—of village agriculture. Two consecutive summers, 1641 and 1642, were so generally rainy as to cause a sharp reduction in overall crop yields;[30] similar conditions prevailed in 1658 and 1698.[31] Conversely, some summers were characterized by drought (1665, 1666, 1670, 1681) with no less adverse results.[32] But the heaviest blow to early New England agriculture came not from weather but from a spreading blight —first on wheat, and then on "all sorts of grain."[33] The problem appeared in some parts of Massachusetts as early as 1663,[34] worsened in 1664 ("this year it pleased God to smite the fruits of the earth . . . with blasting and mildew, whereby most of it was utterly spoiled"),[35] and in 1665 moved south and west to Connecticut, Plymouth, and New Haven.[36] The effects were manifest each summer for the rest of the decade, with "greater scarcity having not been known," according to one diarist, "for very many years."[37] Eventually New England farmers made appropriate adjustments, reducing or abandoning their efforts at grain cultivation; but the shock and worry of those first blight years left a deep impression.[38]

There were other threats to agriculture besides poor weather and crop disease. In July 1646, wrote the Rev. John Eliot, "we had a very strange hand of God upon us, that upon a sudden, innumerable armies of caterpillars filled the country all over all the English plantations [and] devoured some whole meadows of grass, . . . barley, . . . tender corn, . . . wheat, . . . [and] oats."[39] Additional, though apparently less severe, infestations of caterpillars were noted in the summers of 1649, 1658, 1665, and 1666.[40] And in midsummer 1648 tiny flies "filled the woods from Connecticut to Sudbury," eating "the young sprouts of the trees" and causing considerable spoilage to orchards.[41]

Housefires made a special (and dreaded) category of harm; local though they were in their immediate effects, they would often draw notice throughout a wide region. To understand this is to credit the difficulties faced by premodern populations in controlling and extinguishing fire. There was always a strong chance that flames would spread from their original source to adjacent properties and structures; whole neighborhoods might thus be imperiled. The roster of major fires in seventeenth-century New England begins with the winter of 1643–44, when Winthrop reported "very many houses . . . burned down" in Boston, with greater losses of property "than in 14 years before."[42] There were two "great fires" within a week in April 1645—one at Boston (involving an explosion of local gunpowder stores), the other at Salem.[43] Boston, as the region's largest community, continued in the years that followed to have the worst of these experiences. One fire in November 1676 reportedly destroyed forty to fifty different properties (including the "north church"),[44] another in August 1679 "consumed some hundreds of houses and warehouses,"[45] and still another in October 1683 devastated large sectors of the waterfront.[46] Three major "conflagrations" (and numerous smaller ones) within seven years put the entire town on edge, and fostered intense suspicions of arson. Additional fires of substantial proportions occurred—again at Boston—in August 1690 and July 1692.[47]

Fires can be associated with a larger category of accidental mishap—which might also include drownings, the destruction of life or property by lightning bolts, unintended shootings, and ships lost at sea. Many such incidents are noted by diarists from the period;[48] but most involved just one or two people, and made only a local impression. Shipwrecks could, and did, command wider notice (because the loss was greater). Thus Winthrop noted two particularly unfortunate shipping accidents within a few months of one another in 1635–36.[49] But much the worst incidents of this kind occurred, in untimely convergence, during the middle of the following decade. In December 1645 a large vessel called the *Seafort*, newly built at Boston and laden with goods and passengers, was wrecked near the coast of Spain.[50] The next winter a ship from

Roxbury was lost ("and many cast away in her"),[51] and soon after that another from New Haven disappeared with "about seventy persons" on board (including magistrates, church leaders, and others "of very precious account").[52] There was a concurrent series of losses in trading vessels—all of which prompted Edward Johnson to write as follows: "The Lord was pleased to command the wind and seas to give us a jog on the elbow by sinking the very chief of our shipping in the deep, and splitting them in shivers against the shores."[53]

One final category of harm that also deserves notice is material hardship of a general kind. The economy of early New England was subject to at least occasional fluctuations, in relation to weather, crop yields, and the vagaries of overseas politics. Within the seventeenth century the period of greatest difficulty seems to have been the opening part of the fifth decade.[54] The root cause, as those affected clearly realized, was the outbreak of civil war in England—and the attendant drop in New World trade and immigration. Marketing patterns throughout the empire were disrupted, and New England experienced what one scholar has called its "first depression."[55] The value of all properties—but especially of land and cattle—declined precipitously. (For example, "cows . . . fell of a sudden in one week from £22 the cow to 6, 7, or £8 the cow at most.")[56] The initial deflation occurred in 1640; two years later conditions were but slightly improved, and, according to Winthrop, "many . . . concluded there would be no subsisting here, and . . . began to hasten away."[57] A full recovery seems to have come only in the mid-1640s.

Subsequent hard times—similar to, but perhaps less severe than, that earlier period—came in the mid-1660s and again in the late 1690s. The former was associated with the wheat blight and a disturbing series of adjustments in imperial relations. The low point seems to have occurred in 1665, when the Boston merchant John Hull summarized matters as follows: "All employments [have] a smite upon them . . . all men are rather going backward than increasing their estates."[58] The hardships of the century's last years derived quite directly from the adversities of weather. A fast-day proclamation in March 1698 specifically noted "the sharpness and long continuance of the winter season, whereby the cattle and stock of the country is much wasted."[59] Governor Wolcott of Connecticut wrote that "the year 1697 was a year of great scarcity. The summer was cool and cloudy—not a month without a frost in it—the winter very long and severe. . . . There was a great cry for bread—the cattle famishing in the yards for want—the sickness very distressing and mortal."[60]

Signs

The "harms" described in the preceding section were experienced as punishments from "providence." They expressed in tangible and painful form God's recurrent displeasure with the doings of wayward mankind. The "signs" considered next were warnings of punishment to come; hence they, too, might generate much public anxiety.

Celestial phenomena of various kinds made an obvious case in point: comets, eclipses, meteors, aurora, even rainbows. Here, it seemed, were messages flashed directly from the heavens "to awake the secure world."[61] As such, they were carefully noted by diarists and other record-keepers of the time. "By the testimony of the sacred scriptures and the common histories of former ages," wrote one man, "comets do usually precede and portend great calamities and notable changes."[62] There were some current examples. Thus on the night of December 9, 1652, a "star [comet] appeared . . . great for compass, with long blaze . . . to the east";[63] according to the records of the First Church of Boston, "every night it was less and less till the 22nd of the same month, and then it did no more appear, it being the night before our reverend teacher Mr. John Cotton died, the greatest star in the churches of Christ."[64] In 1664 another "great blazing star appeared . . . which continued some months."[65] A Connecticut clergyman located its principal "effects" across the ocean (e.g. "a great and dreadful plague that followed the next summer, . . . a dreadful war by sea with the Dutch, and the burning of London the second year following"), but there were concurrent worries for New England.[66] And when a second comet appeared a few months later the General Court of Massachusetts Bay decreed a public fast, citing "the alarm from Heaven given us in the awful appearance of the comets, both this and the last year, warning us to be watchful."[67] The spring of 1668 brought still another "appearance" of the same sort. Several of New England's leading clergymen died soon thereafter, moving one diarist to comment: "Possibly the death of these precious servants of Christ might be the last thing signified by the blaze or beam appearing the last February."[68] The final two comets of the century appeared in November 1680 ("a great blazing star . . . terrible and awful")[69] and August 1682 ("a great star but a small stream," which—noted a young Harvard tutor—"I sat up on purpose to see . . . [until] about half an hour past one of the clock.")[70]

Eclipses were less noticed—and less feared—than comets; they were also, of course, more common. Yet at least occasionally they, too, might "precede and portend" some "notable event." Thus on July 2, 1684, a

Massachusetts clergyman made this entry in his diary: "We had a great eclipse of the sun . . . almost total. This day Mr. Rogers, President of Harvard College, died about the time of the sun's going out of the eclipse."[71] Even rainbows might carry special meaning. One particularly dramatic instance was described by Samuel Sewall, writing in his diary on January 18, 1687: "People were gazing at it from one end of the town to t'other." (At church on the following lecture-day the preacher "spake of the inverted rainbow, God shooting at somebody.")[72]

Signs of God's "awful providence" came from the earth no less than the sky. As Nathaniel Morton wrote in his *New England's Memorial*, earthquakes were "great and terrible works of God, and . . . usually ominous to some strokes and visitations of His hand unto places and people where they are." Sometimes, indeed, earthquakes constituted "strokes" in themselves, bringing death and destruction on "the children of men, to their great overthrow and confusion."[73] In other (less violent) instances they simply delivered a warning.

Seventeenth-century New England experienced at least ten earthquakes powerful enough to elicit written comment. The worst occurred during the afternoon of June 1, 1638, when (according to one account) the ground suddenly rose "up and down like the waves of the sea."[74] There was some damage to property (but apparently not to people), and alarm was manifest throughout the region. ("Diverse men, . . . being at work in the fields . . . cast down their working-tools, and ran with ghostly, terrified looks, to the next company they could meet withal.")[75] Ministers were quick to discern "a sign from the Lord . . . that He was purposed to shake the kingdoms of Europe's earth"—and, of course, subsequent events proved them right.[76] Lesser earthquakes were felt in January 1639,[77] March 1644,[78] January 1661,[79] January 1663,[80] April and December 1668,[81] February 1685,[82] November 1690,[83] and January 1694.[84] Little is known of their particulars, but they can hardly have caused much damage.

In addition to comets, eclipses, and earthquakes New Englanders noticed a variety of puzzling—and apparently providential—happenstance. There were strange nocturnal lights ("sometimes they shot out flames and sometimes sparkles");[85] sudden, inexplicable noises ("a mighty report heard in the air . . . bigger than the report of any cannon");[86] spectral ships ("with three masts . . . tackling and sails, and . . . upon . . . the poop, a man standing with one hand akimbo; then arose a great smoke . . . and in that smoke she vanished away");[87] and anomalies of human and animal reproduction ("a calf brought forth with one head and three mouths, three noses, and six eyes—what these prodigies portended the Lord only knows, which in His due time He will manifest").[88] Such "prodigies" made a powerful impression on all who witnessed them first-hand and prompted intense speculation as to providential meanings. However, in most cases they were held to a local context, and their impact was correspondingly limited.

It is important to recognize, in addition, that many of the "harms" discussed previously also carried the force of "signs." Diseases, storms, fires, and the rest: these were *both* injurious in themselves and indicative of divine displeasure—"chastening strokes" from God and "portents" of more (perhaps worse) to come. Like other "signs" they served to heighten anxiety for the future.

Controversies

Seventeenth-century usage made "controversy" a general term for human conflict. Disputes, rivalries, even violence and warfare were joined here in a single category—which brings into focus a third major source of stress and anxiety among the New Englanders.

The roster of actual controversies in early New England yields a simple organizing typology. Some were essentially internal affairs—local disputes of the sort noticed in the case-study chapters, and also the somewhat wider conflicts involving whole communities or regions. A second type was geographically external, but involved other Englishmen: for example, disputes with the "mother country" (or her official representatives) or with colonies elsewhere in North America. A third type was external in a cultural sense but not in a geographic one; conflict with Indians was its most obvious and important form. A fourth type was external in both the geographic and the cultural sense: e.g. problems with Dutch or French settlements elsewhere in North America. The events embraced by these sub-categories are well known to early American historians; indeed they are the stuff of conventional "political history." As such they need only the briefest review here.

Type I: The first wide-scale division within the population of early New England was prompted by the "antinomian controversy" of 1636–37. The charismatic personality and "heretic" opinions of Anne Hutchinson were its principal source, and Boston was its geographical center; but the effects were felt throughout Massachusetts Bay.[89] A second wave of conflict overtook Massachusetts in the early and middle years of the following decade. Prolonged dispute over the form of government itself reached a peak with the famous "remonstrance" of Robert Child and his associates in 1646; there were also religious challenges from Baptists and followers of the Rhode Island sectarian Samuel Gorton. The sum of all this was nothing less than a "severe constitutional crisis."[90] In the 1650s the spirit of controversy subsided in Massachusetts, but flared powerfully in Connecticut. A split in the Hartford church spread to Windsor and Wethersfield as well; four years and incalculable effort were needed to achieve its resolution.[91] The decade of the 60s brought renewed confrontations with "heresy" (Quakers in 1660–61, Anabaptists in 1665–68), though apparently without substantial public involvement.[92] A more serious problem for religious orthodoxy was the struggle of the late 1660s, within many individual congregations, over Presbyterianism, the Halfway Covenant, and a host of related issues.[93] But this was the last of the major internal conflicts of the century; henceforth the dangers to New England came, in one sense or another, from outside.

Type II: Two periods stand out as being especially difficult—and distressing—because of conflict with other Englishmen. The restoration of the Stuart monarchy in 1660 implied, for "Puritan" colonists, a distinct threat of political and religious coercion. Their anxiety mounted during the succeeding months and years, especially when the king dispatched a team of investigatory "commissioners" to New England in 1664–65.[94] The threat lessened soon thereafter, but was massively revived in the 1680s. The revocation of the Massachusetts charter in 1684 was followed by the establishment of a new imperial government, the so-called Dominion of New England, in 1686; the encroachment on the long-cherished "liberties" of New Englanders, and even on their lands, was now very keenly felt. It took a new dynastic upheaval—the Glorious Revolution of 1689—to restore (at least partially) their former condition.[95]

Type III: It would be hard to overestimate the anxiety, not to say the hatred and terror, generated by conflict with local Indians. The danger was immediate and palpable; no man (or woman) was exempt. King Philip's War (1675–77) claims pride of place among *all* the sufferings visited on early New England; no other event was so intensely painful for such a broad spectrum of the population.[96] But other wars, and rumors of war, must also be mentioned. The Pequot War (1636–37) was certainly alarming, though localized and limited in terms of actual hostilities.[97] In 1642–43 and again in 1653–54 conflict with Indians was widely expected—and feared.[98] (The first of these scares led to the founding of the United Colonies of New England, a formal association of Massachusetts Bay, Connecticut, and Plymouth for common defense; the second prompted extensive military preparations and even an armed expedition to deal with the supposed "conspirators.") Finally, the last dozen years of the century brought repeated conflict with Indians all along the northern and western borders of settlement: isolated killings, wholesale "massacres"—one might well say, chronic "guerilla warfare." These events were somewhat removed from the major centers of population; yet they were noticed with alarm throughout New England.[99]

Type IV: To a large degree sheer distance protected the New Englanders against conflict with people from continental Europe. But this protection was not total, since at least two European states had established settlements within the same general region of North America. France claimed "Acadia" (New Brunswick and Nova Scotia), and for a period in 1643–44 there was much fear of trouble from that quarter.[100] The Dutch, meanwhile, colonized New Netherland (New York), surrendered sovereignty to the English in 1664, and then briefly regained it in 1673; the latter change caused a sharp flurry of concern in New England.[101] In 1690 French Canada loomed as an adversary once again. Indeed, New England mounted a large military expedition against Quebec, which ended that autumn in ignominious defeat.[102]

Throughout the period New England was, of course, apprised of political developments overseas. Hence the Puritan Revolution in the mother country, and the inter-European wars of the 1660s, sparked both interest and some anxiety.[103] Nevertheless the sum total of such concern was limited. The dynastic and imperial struggles of Europe seemed largely external to New England throughout the seventeenth century. However much they might affect the region in the long run, attention would center on events that were visibly closer to home.

Connections with Witchcraft

To make this motley assortment of experiences yield any sort of pattern is plainly a difficult task. Yet one can recognize, for a start, some differential effects as *between* the three categories of distress. The case-study chapters have already suggested that "harms" and "signs" should be construed as predisposing elements for witchcraft, and "controversies" as inhibiting ones. Yet this formulation needs refinement in at least one respect. Distress must be measured for duration as well as intensity; the emotional state can, and often does, outlast its initial stimulus. Thus particular "harms" and "signs" are likely to have left a *residuum* of anxiety for a year or two after the fact. The same consideration applies to conflict (i.e. "controversies") as well. For if conflict was inhibiting to witchcraft in the time of its actual occurrence, its aftermath may have reversed this effect. Again, the case studies are suggestive: at both

Hampton and Wethersfield witchcraft seems to have *followed* periods of local dispute. As noted above, New Englanders put a deeply negative cast on "controversy" of all kinds—hence their distress upon finding themselves directly involved in (responsible for?) such events. Bluntly stated, conflict was likely to produce that particular form of distress we call guilt. This tendency must have been strongest when the context was wholly internal (e.g. factional or personal rivalry), and weakest when there was clearly an outside source (e.g. Indians).

It is time at last for the attempt to align "harms," "signs," and "controversies" with the chronology of witchcraft. The fit is less than perfect, but much beyond what random association would predict. Consider the following:

There were very few proceedings against witchcraft in the earliest period of New England history. Presumably, the work of settlement was itself an absorbing process. Events soon yielded cause for distress: "harms" such as the hurricane of 1635, and "signs" like the earthquake of 1638. But these were more than counterbalanced by the inhibiting effect of conflict: local struggles attendant on the founding of many new towns, an internal crisis of larger scope (the Antinomian controversy), and an external one (the Pequot War). At least one witch was accused in 1638 (the earthquake year, the aftermath of Antinomianism), but this was followed by nearly a decade free of such proceedings. Beginning in 1640 the rebellion in the mother country raised both hopes and fears among the New Englanders—and contributed as well to much economic hardship. Once again, however, there was a counterweight of controversy—the "constitutional crisis" of 1642–46 in Massachusetts, and the Indian scares of 1642–43.

Witchcraft cases began in earnest during the late 1640s, and a high rate of incidence was maintained in both Massachusetts and Connecticut until the middle of the following decade. In fact, the balance of predisposing and inhibiting factors had shifted dramatically. The great shipwrecks of 1645–46, the caterpillar infestation and severe weather of 1646, and most especially the disease outbreaks of 1647–48 and 1650–51: these were "harms" of the first magnitude. There was also (in Massachusetts) some residual stress from the conflicts of the years immediately preceding, and at least one alarming "sign" (the comet of 1652). During this same period, moreover, New England experienced relatively little new conflict of either the internal or the external kind.

The years from 1656 to 1660 presented a mixed picture. The incidence of witchcraft fell off sharply in Connecticut—consumed, as that colony was, by the "Hartford controversy." But witchcraft cases continued in Massachusetts—where there was much in the way of "harm" (epidemic disease, a new caterpillar infestation, and more severe weather), but little conflict.

The next decade reversed these positions. Massachusetts dropped down, in terms of witchcraft cases, while Connecticut surged to a new high. And what was the balance of presumably related influences? A large comet (1664), along with other, lesser "signs"; "fevers" (1661); the smallpox epidemic of 1666–67; and, most especially, the annual crop blights (after 1662): these events must all be counted as conducive to witchcraft. In Connecticut there were some additional predisposing elements: devastating floods (in 1661), and an "aftermath effect" from the now-concluded Hartford controversy. The Stuart Restoration of 1660 was a source of worry to both colonies—but far *more* so to Massachusetts. There the threat to political charters was keenly felt, and was rendered palpable with the arrival of the King's commissioners (1664–65); the resultant preoccupation would serve to inhibit witchcraft. To this "external conflict" were added "internal" ones—the religious disputes of the late 1660s, of which the most sensational result was a permanent split in the first church of Boston.

There followed still another period of reversal: five years (1669–1674) during which prosecutions for witchcraft increased markedly in Massachusetts and declined virtually to nil in Connecticut. In Connecticut religious controversy continued into the 1670s, with formal "divisions" occurring in the congregations at Hartford, Windsor, and elsewhere. In Massachusetts, by contrast, the crisis was passed, and the early 70s became a time of "aftermath." Meanwhile the crop blight deepened, and was complicated by adverse weather (drought in 1670, drought followed by severe storms in 1672). Illness was also rife (dysentery and "fevers"). And, in Massachusetts, there was perhaps a special source of distress—the deaths, in remarkable convergence, of a whole cadre of ecclesiastical leaders. (Wrote one contemporary, shortly after the fact: "Hitherto it had pleased the Father of Light to bless the New England churches with the continuance of many worthy and eminent divines . . . but about this time they were bereft of a great number of them, within the compass of a few years.")[104]

The period from 1675 through 1678 represented a low point in the half-century "curve" of witchcraft cases; indeed, in both Massachusetts and Connecticut there were no prosecutions at all during these years. Of "harms" there were plenty, especially in Massachusetts: the hurricane of 1675; the Boston fire of 1676; epidemic sickness, also in 1676; and the smallpox outbreak of 1677–78. But against such normally predisposing influences stood one massive counter-force: the desperate absorption of the entire region in King Philip's War. For the time being danger from the invisible world was superseded by combat with a host of quite present and visible Indian enemies.

The period after the war's end brought a marked renewal of witch-craft proceedings, fully a dozen cases within five years (1679–83) in Massachusetts alone. There were new "harms" (the influenza outbreaks of 1679 and 1682–83, the devastating Boston fire of 1679, and a number of smaller fires attributed to arson) and at least two distinct "signs" (the comets of 1680 and 1682). Doubtless, too, there was a residue of jittery feeling from the extreme troubles so lately concluded. Meanwhile, there were no new conflicts, internal or external, to divert social energies into other courses. It must be said that Connecticut seems *not* to have been much involved with witchcraft during these years, although the balance of circumstantial influences was roughly similar.

Between 1684 and 1691 witchcraft prosecutions became once again infrequent in both colonies. The effect of some very considerable "harms" (especially the measles and smallpox epidemics of the late 1680s) was outweighed by renewed experiences of conflict. The long-festering crisis of imperial authority climaxed in a series of jolting events (the revocation of the charter of Massachusetts Bay; the establishment, and then the demise, of the Dominion of New England). In addition, there were new hostilities with Indian tribes and with French Canada.

This chronology now reaches the single greatest peak in the curve of activity against witchcraft: the notorious Salem trials of 1692–93 (which in fact encompassed much of eastern Massachusetts), and a less-known but still important sequence of prosecutions in Connecticut. The im-perial crisis was partially eased—Massachusetts had just received a new charter—yet much uncertainty remained. The troubles and tensions of the preceding years found release in a terrible spasm of witch-hunting.

There is insufficient space here to launch a careful discussion of the Salem affair, but a few brief observations may be offered. Why, in particular, did this one episode attain such massive proportions—i.e. in the sheer *quantity* of persons involved? The early 1690s seem, in the first place, to have been a time of extreme and pervasive anxiety in New England. The difficulties experienced during the preceding fifteen years had added up to an almost intolerable sum: the wars were more devastating, the epidemic illnesses more prevalent and "mortal," the constitutional changes more unsettling, than in any earlier period of the region's history. It was not hard to see in all this a *general* movement of Divine Providence against New England.[105] Meanwhile, too, there were powerful undercurrents of social change—old enough in their origins, but newly visible in some of their effects. The growth of commerce, the signs in some quarters of a more cosmopolitan spirit, the increasing strength of a merchant class: these were key elements in a process of transformation "from Puritan to Yankee" (a favorite phrase of New England historians).[106] The twin themes of providence *and* change particularly informed religious discourse—hence the "jeremiad," that distinctive artifact of early New England worship.[107] New Englanders, high and low, near and far, could scarcely escape feeling that a crisis was at hand.[108]

The strains that fostered this sense of crisis were powerfully evident at Salem, perhaps more so than in any other New England community. For Salem was a place split down the middle—was, in fact, two places of markedly different spatial, economic, and cultural orientations. On the one side (near the coast) stood Salem Town, a flourishing center of commerce, cosmopolitan in outlook and urban in style, dominated by an increasingly affluent cadre of merchants and tradesmen. On the other side (in the interior) lay Salem Village, an agricultural hamlet of limited resources, provincial, homogeneous, wedded to traditional ways and values. So it was that the history of Salem in the closing decades of the seventeenth century expressed a deep clash of interests. Both civil and religious experience were infected by chronic "faction"—and, as another study has brilliantly demonstrated, the witchcraft trials of the 1690s were simply the climactic act in a long drama of local discord. Almost without exception it was the Villagers who played the roles of "accuser" and/or "victim," and the Townspeople who were cast as "witches."[109]

To conclude this brief digression: the Salem witch-hunt reached epidemic proportions for two reasons specific to one time and place. First, concern with witchcraft was there directly joined to internal factionalism; thus one accusation quickly suggested others in an irresistible process of guilt by association. (In other instances, witchcraft trials and factional conflict were *alternated*; their relation to one another was complementary rather than concurrent.) Second, the social climate of New England as a whole was then unusually strained, anxious, ambivalent. As a result, the "infection" spread well beyond Salem, and adjacent communities produced responsive accusations of their own.

The last years of the century (1694–99) produced little by way of witchcraft proceedings, in either Massachusetts or Connecticut. The extraordinary winters of 1696–97 and 1697–98 should perhaps be counted as "harms"; likewise the associated "scarcity" of the intervening months. (The only two indictments for witchcraft during this entire period occurred in 1697.) Meanwhile warfare with Indians was painfully renewed, though at some distance from the major centers of settlement. There was no significant "internal conflict" (beyond the scale of local communities). But the Salem outbreak generated a reaction which may well have served to restrain new activity against witchcraft. A sense that events had spun out of control troubled many New Englanders after Salem. The wholesale assault on reputation, property, and life itself seemed in retrospect tragically unjustified; henceforth, in such matters, much greater caution would be exercised.[110]

The foregoing survey has traced the extent of witchcraft prosecutions over time in seventeenth-century New England. There was, in fact, no single pattern for the entire region; and for analytic purposes it has been necessary to distinguish between the two major areas of settlement, Massachusetts (including New Hampshire and Plymouth) and Connecticut (including the New Haven Colony). At both the beginning and the end of this chronology (1630–54; 1684–99) we find the two areas moving together; but during a long middle period (1655–83) they were largely out of phase.

Of greater interest are the general relationships, suggested by all the materials, between witchcraft proceedings and specific elements in the historical environment. These relationships can now be restated and summarized as follows. *Predisposing factors* (i.e. favorable to witchcraft proceedings): (1) a combination of "harms" in a given year and/or the year immediately preceding; (2) a major "sign" during the given year and/or the year immediately preceding; (3) a major internal "controversy," concluded one to three years previously. *Inhibiting factors* (unfavorable to witchcraft proceedings): (4) a major internal "controversy" during the given year; (5) a major external "controversy" during the given year.

No one of these factors correlates with all the changes in witchcraft incidence. It is only when they are considered together that a pattern of fit seems to emerge. Admittedly, this pattern is rough and incomplete along several of its edges, and its inner meaning is far from clear. We cannot safely use the language of cause and effect for our various "factors"; "correlation" remains the more accurate term. Nonetheless one important issue seems resolved. Witchcraft was no meandering sideshow, isolated from the larger history of early New England. On the contrary: it belonged to—and in—that history virtually from beginning to end.

After the Seventeenth Century

The *official* record of witchcraft in New England belongs entirely to the seventeenth century. The greatest and most destructive of the trial proceedings was also virtually the last. The formal machinery of the law would never thereafter be trained against witches. There would be no more executions, no convictions, indeed no actual indictments on any such charge.

However, it would be wrong to infer—from the absence after 1700 of legal proceedings—an end to the history we have been trying to understand. In all its *unofficial* aspects that history would long continue. As a matter of individual and collective preoccupation, and even of informal *action*, witchcraft was part of New England life well into the nineteenth century. Its vestigial remnants could almost certainly be discovered not far from our own time.

The evidence for these later parts of the story is quite scattered and fragmentary, but the fragments do come together. There are some contemporary references—from diaries, personal papers, and the like. A Protestant minister, on a "missionary" tour through eastern Maine in the autumn of 1800, wrote as follows of his visit to the town of Fayette: "Lodged with Dr. Hall. Here . . . was *witchcraft* in plenty. A man had been troubled six months, and it was thought he must die. He is emaciated and often horribly distressed. A Mr. Billings, a Baptist teacher, soon to be ordained, has lost his milk for some time. The end of a cheese would come and go, and boil off from the fire, and finally come to nothing, etc. etc."[111] Another clergyman, writing in the middle of the eighteenth century, offered this more general observation: "There are but few towns, if any, but at one time or other have not had one or more in suspicion for witchcraft, as if the place were not complete in its inhabitants without some well-versed in that occupation."[112] The minister himself did not much credit "that occupation"; most charges of witchcraft seemed to him poorly founded or downright false. Still, he recognized the existence of some "Scripture witches" (persons who actively oppose God and "use unlawful means to cure diseases, or to discover events past or to come"), and he urged severity in dealing with them.[113] This type of ambivalence seems to have become a characteristic posture after the early eighteenth century. Witchcraft was hard to square with "enlightened" standards and values, yet it could not be dismissed entirely. Thus a farmer from Long Island, writing in 1799, averred that "it is contrary to my senses and my reason, and ridiculous for me to believe in witchcraft, and was it not for what has happened to me and fallen in the way of my observation, I should despise the very idea of spirits having power to act or operate on the minds or bodies of creatures. . . ." This disclaimer served to preface a long account of "strange occurrences . . . in the course of my life"—many of them attributed to a local "gang of witches."[114]

Similar accounts are preserved in dozens of town histories from all across New England. As written, they have the unmistakable flavor of local folklore; yet they deal with actual people and real situations. As before, the objects of suspicion are generally women of at least middle age, while their opponents (and supposed victims) represent a broad spectrum of age and gender. Experiences of conflict still constitute the visible source of suspicion: the rub of discordant personalities, petty jealousies, refusals of cooperation or charity, and all manner of neighborhood squabbling. At least occasionally there is some approach to, or by, higher authority—if not the courts, then the clergy and other leaders of the local church.

For example, in eighteenth-century Hopkinton, New Hampshire:

> there were at least two great witches in town. They were "witch Webber" and "witch Burbank." . . . It were impossible to tell how much harm might have resulted from witchcraft in Hopkinton, had it not been for the Rev. Elijah Fletcher. He was minister of the town from 1773 to 1786. When "witchcraft" threatened the community, he referred the matter to Rev. Timothy Walker of Concord. The Rev. Mr. Walker told the people that "the most they had to fear from witches was from talking about them; that if they would cease talking about them and let them alone they would soon disappear."[115]

Again, in Bristol, Connecticut, during the period 1800–1810:

> witchcraft caused much excitement . . . and greatly frightened some of the good people. One young girl, Norton by name, . . . declared that she was bewitched by her aunt, who, she said, had often put a bridle upon her and driven her through the air to Albany, where great witch-meetings were held. Elder Wildman became interested in this girl, and had her brought to his own house that he might exorcise her. She stayed overnight, and after midnight the Elder, thoroughly frightened by the awful sights and sounds which had appeared to him, begged some of the neighbors to come and stay with him. One bold unbeliever, who offered to go with him, was frightened into convulsions by what he saw and heard, and was sick a long time in consequence. Deacon

Dutton, of the Baptist Church, incurred the enmity of the witches, and an ox which he was driving one day was suddenly torn apart by some invisible power. Other people were tormented by unseen hands pinching them, sticking red hot pins into their flesh, and bringing strange maladies upon them.[116]

One additional episode of alleged witchcraft is worth summarizing here, if only because its particulars were recorded by a contemporary in great detail. The setting was Littleton, Massachusetts; the year, 1720; a girl of eleven, Elizabeth Blanchard by name, began to act "after a very strange manner." From time to time she "fell into trances . . . and visions. . . . She would drop down as one thunderstruck. . . . She would frequently tear her clothes, and disfigure herself, bite her attendants, and spit upon them and her visitors too. . . . She did frequently complain of wounds and pinches and prickings, which she said she had received by invisible hands." Soon her two younger sisters were behaving in a similar fashion, and presently all three joined in accusing "a certain woman of the town for afflicting them." The parents were greatly alarmed and "treated them with all imaginable tenderness. They sent for physicians to find what was amiss in their bodies, and for the elders to pray . . . over them; and the credulous neighbors came often to visit and pity them." There were indeed "many conjectures" as to the cause of their troubles. "Some thought they labored of bodily maladies; others that their minds were disordered. . . . Others . . . thought them to be underwitted; others that they were perverse and wicked children. But the greater number thought and said they were under an evil hand, or possessed by Satan. This was the general cry of the town." As the "general cry" intensified, the supposed witch fell ill, "took to her chamber, and died within a few weeks"—whereupon the Blanchard children were returned to a normal condition. There was continued discussion of the case for some while afterward. "Some of the good neighbors suspected . . . falsehood, [but] the children persisted in it, that they offered nothing but the truth throughout . . . their supposed trials and afflictions." Eventually, however, "their consciences contradicted them." Elizabeth Blanchard, grown to womanhood, confessed to her pastor that she and her sisters had concocted the whole affair, led by "folly and pride" into a course of outright "deceit."[117]

Although the witchcraft of the eighteenth and nineteenth centuries seems in certain respects quite similar to the pattern of the settlement era, there were also important elements of change. Broadly speaking, the change involved a gradual reduction of both *affect* and *imagery*. The figure of the witch was effectively scaled down, so as to shrink the elements of death-dealing power, and to emphasize those of sheer eccentricity. The motif of physical "affliction" grew increasingly rare and attenuated. (The Blanchard children of Littleton, in 1720, can be viewed as direct legatees of the afflicted girls at Salem; by contrast, the Norton girl at Bristol, in about 1800, seems a kind of sport.) The harm attributed to witchcraft was confined more and more to routine domestic mishap (the butter that would not come), nightmares (of being "ridden"), and simple "mischief" (moments of embarrassment and confusion). Such elements had always been part of the witch's *maleficium*, but now they were virtually the whole of it.

Indeed, the harm done *by* the witch seems, in this later lore, far less impressive than what was done *to* her. Here, again, one finds a significant enlargement of an old theme. The witch had always been considered vulnerable to skillfully applied counter-magic; at least occasionally she was herself a victim. By the nineteenth century, however, she was likely to be the *chief* victim—the biggest loser—in the overall exchange of hostilities. Here are a few more examples:

> A cat scampers across a road in the village of Exeter, Rhode Island, startling the horse-team of a farmer who is carting lumber to market. At once a suspicion forms in the farmer's mind: the culprit is actually a woman of the neighborhood, whose "witchcraft" has allowed her to assume the shape of a cat. Quickly he shoots the cat with a silver bullet (the most effective known ammunition in such cases). At about the same time, in another part of the village, the suspected "witch" has a bad fall and breaks her hip.[118]

> A resident of Salem, New Hampshire, finds his cow "looking strangely" and attributes the problem to sorcery by a neighbor. Adopting a time-honored strategy of counter-magic, he cuts the ears and tail off his cow and burns them; soon thereafter the "witch" turns up dead in a housefire.[119]

> Some women of Wentworth, New Hampshire, are trying without success to churn a store of butter. One of them thrusts a hot poker into the churn. At once there is a loud scream from somewhere outdoors—and the butter comes. Soon afterward a long-suspected neighbor is found to have suffered a bad burn on her legs.[120]

> A farmer in West Newbury, Vermont, is frightened by a bevy of spectral shapes dancing in his fireplace late at night. He blames

a woman of the town, and carefully fashions her image from tallow and beeswax. He then punctures the image with thorns and melts it in the fire; meanwhile the woman in question trips on some stairs in her own house and breaks her neck.[121]

The details of these exchanges cannot be verified as fact; but, for present purposes, fact is less important than the total gestalt. The witches of nineteenth-century New England are portrayed, again and again, as suffering terrible hurt. Indeed, local tradition tends to linger over their suffering, to an extent that now seems gratuitous—or downright cruel. It is as if witches had come to serve less as implicit scapegoats (objects of blame) and more as explicit targets (objects of attack). To be sure, suspected witches were no longer prosecuted in the courts, imprisoned, and executed; from such dangers they were henceforth protected. Yet this change, too, reflected a shift in the larger balance of forces. When the witches' *maleficium* was limited to routine mishap and mischief, and when their own vulnerability to counter-magic had become so great, there was little need to confront them with the organized might of the community.

The figure of the witch, as conceived by seventeenth-century New Englanders, was powerful, dangerous, an altogether formidable adversary. But there developed subsequently a different image that is with us still—the witch as *hag*. Thus, for instance, did the poet Whittier describe Moll Pitcher, a celebrated "witch" and fortune-teller of eighteenth-century Lynn, Massachusetts:

> She stood upon a bare, tall crag
> Which overlooked her rugged cot—
> A wasted, gray, and meagre hag,
> In features evil as her lot.
> She had the crooked nose of a witch,
> And a crooked back and chin;
> And in her gait she had a hitch,
> And in her hand she carried a switch,
> To aid her work of sin. . . .[122]

The picture has a hundred variations, but there is a nucleus of central features which appear everywhere. The hag-witch is characteristically *old*—and on that account *decrepit*. She is also *ugly* in a physical sense. She is, in many versions, *eccentric*—disorganized, confused, a trifle "dotty." Finally, she is *an isolate*: she lives alone and enjoys no supportive human contact.

It is not possible, given the extant data, to measure this composite portrait against the actual circumstances of supposed witches in the eighteenth and nineteenth centuries. Yet the portrait itself bears consideration. Its highly pejorative nature is obvious—and significant in its details. The connotations of age, for instance, were increasingly unfavorable: to be old in the midst of "Young America" was to be weak, incompetent, out of touch.[123] To be physically unattractive was also a marked disadvantage; personal appearance—the whole matter of "good looks"—seems to have become a considerable preoccupation during the nineteenth century.[124] Moreover, eccentricity and isolation had long been shaded on the down side. But the fact of negative coloration would not by itself distinguish this imagery from social evaluations of witchcraft in other times and places. The important issue is: negative *in what ways* and *to what effect*? The hag-witch is, in sum, a figure of weakness —or at least of profound vulnerabilities. She retains power in one sort, and to this extent she may still inspire fear. Yet she is also a fit target for contempt, for mockery, for mischief at the hands of her peers and neighbors. As such she marks for us the last—declining—phase in the history of a once-mighty tradition. When witches had come to seem pathetic, their final demise as cultural referents could not be far off.

Many questions remain to be asked about the process of decline and demise. And the questions, once asked, do not yield ready answers. Clearly this topic lies well beyond the reach of the present study, yet it seems worth offering a few general statements or hypotheses now—if only to suggest lines of further research.

In the first place, the growth of skeptical attitudes toward witchcraft was a very gradual, incremental process. Initially, doubts ran only to specific accusations. There was no strong reason to question the existence of witchcraft itself—only the ability of fallible mortals to distinguish the genuine article from fraudulent "delusions." Indeed, many writers on the subject were careful to make precisely this point. The Rev. John Hale, whose *Modest Inquiry* was one of the first revisionist accounts of Salem, cautioned against being "driven . . . into that which is indeed an extreme on the other hand . . . viz. to deny [that] any such persons . . . by the Devil's aid discover secrets, or do work wonders."[125] The book contained a prefatory endorsement by Hale's colleague, the Rev. John Higginson, urging "fuller and fuller inquiry into the matter of witchcraft, especially into the positive part: How witches may be so discovered that innocent persons may be preserved, and none but the guilty may suffer."[126] Of course, the example of Salem served to underscore the difficulty attending all such discovery. As Higginson noted, "it left on the minds of men a sad remembrance"; almost immediately some began to speak of "mistakes," "errors," "failings," and "the guilt of innocent blood."[127] There followed, over the next two decades, a long chain of personal recantations (a judge, Samuel Sewall; an accuser, Anne Putnam; an entire corps of jurymen) and collective penance (official days of fasting and prayer).[128] The terrible events of 1692–93 left to succeeding generations of New Englanders a legacy of doubt about all "particular accusations" of witchcraft.

One of the people who embraced this legacy was the Rev. Ebenezer Turrell, author in 1728 of the "discourse" (mentioned earlier) on the troubles of the Blanchard children of Littleton. "Although I . . . firmly believe [in] the existence of spirits, an invisible world, and particularly the agency of Satan and his instruments in afflicting the children of men," wrote Turrell, "yet I fear the world has been wretchedly imposed upon by relations of such matters. . . . Many things have been dubbed witchcraft, and called the works of the devil, which were nothing more than the contrivance of the children of men. . . ."[129] By the end of the eighteenth century these distinctions were becoming increasingly blurred. Thus Goodman Smith of Long Island seemed almost embarrassed to report those "strange occurrences" which had "fallen in the way of my observation"—and but for which "I should despise the very idea [of witchcraft]."[130] Smith, in effect, reversed the earlier balance of opinion, by crediting particular instances of witchcraft even as he doubted the larger phenomenon. Here was tacit reflection of a new and deeper skepticism, which would eventually sweep all before it.

The decline of witchcraft did not proceed evenly or equally through all of the major social ranks. Persons of more than average education and wealth composed an advance guard of skeptics—in some individual cases as early as the Salem trials,[131] and in ever larger numbers by the second half of the eighteenth century. Conversely, it was among humbler folk that the old beliefs hung on. These contrasting viewpoints reflected, no doubt, different levels of access to the advanced learning of the day. Keith Thomas has explored with great subtlety the complex relations between the decline of English witchcraft on the one hand, and the growth of modern "scientific" attitudes on the other.[132] Comparable studies do not exist for eighteenth- and nineteenth-century North America; but the same *general* pattern can be safely assumed. The spreading assumption of an orderly universe; a strengthened belief in the natural (and ultimately discoverable) causation of human events; the rise of "mechanical philosophy"; and—building on all these trends—what

Thomas has called "a new faith in the potentialities of human initiative": such influences served, on both sides of the ocean, to undermine the traditional world-view of which witchcraft was a part. And, again on both sides, their impact was greatest among people who stood at or near the top of the social pyramid.

The abrupt halt in witchcraft *proceedings* at the end of the seventeenth century in New England can now be more fully understood. To summarize: There was a new climate of caution and skepticism about the possibility of proving the identity of particular witches—and, of course, proof was the essence of legal proceedings. (The lesson of Salem seemed especially instructive on this point.) Moreover, skepticism advanced particularly among the most powerful and privileged elements of society—in short, among those elements which controlled the machinery of justice. The influence of community leaders had, during the previous century, often been crucial in moving witchcraft accusations into the courts; after 1700 their influence was exerted in the opposite direction.

But to understand the (much slower) decline in *accusations* themselves, we must look below the visible surface of events. Indeed, we must return to the informing strategy of this entire study. Biography, psychology, sociology, and history: each of the four categories discloses long-term change, bearing in one way or another on the question of decline. Let us consider them briefly, and in sequence.

Biography

The association of witchcraft with a certain biographical type was dependent on traditional values, which were themselves more and more discounted after the middle of the eighteenth century. The rootlessness of a John Godfrey, the provocative style of a Rachel Clinton or a Eunice Cole, the social climbing of a Mary Parsons: each of these traits, or characters, would eventually lose much of its negative coloration. To be rootless, or at least "restless," became virtually a norm for Americans of the nineteenth century.[133] Indeed, there was an increasingly positive valuation here—as witness, for example, the figure of the pioneer. By the same token, self-assertion and aggressiveness were assimilated to a new ethic of individualism and entrepreneurship—to what contemporaries would (approvingly) call "the go-ahead spirit."[134]

Moreover, this same ethic conveyed some direct affirmation of social mobility: to go ahead meant also to go *up* in the status hierarchy. Individuals would henceforth measure their achievements, if not their very lives and selves, by the distance traveled from their specific points of origin. "From rags to riches," "from a log cabin to the White House": thus the popular clichés. To be sure, there was much fond remembrance of an earlier, simpler, and more stable social order.[135] Emotionally freighted images of pastoral landscapes and tidy villages—enclosing at their center the "sanctified precincts of Home"—expressed an enduring attachment to all that was left behind.[136] But the requirements of the time pointed forward: to change, to movement, to a massively gathering tide of creative ferment. And ferment meant friction in human relations. A certain abrasiveness seemed unavoidable in those who would seriously pursue the grail of "success."[137] Here, too, there was widespread apprehension about change; etiquette books, for example, continued to elaborate conventional models of "polite style." But in the world of "practical affairs" such considerations no longer applied. Style counted for less than morals—and even the latter seemed imperiled.

All this is to suggest how the witch, as traditionally conceived, became increasingly an anachronism. And there is more to say in the same connection, with specific reference to women. A developing cluster of ideas and attitudes about gender produced a new cultural figure of wide influence, the so-called "True Woman," whose pure nature was itself proof against motions of direct assault.[138] But, considered overall, the new standard worked to diminish *actual* women. For one thing, it literally domesticated them, by confining them to the "home sphere"; for another, it deprived them of "standing in the world." It severed their intrinsic associations with the power and mystery of Nature, by defining them (among other ways) as "passionless."[139] It even depreciated their biological function as bearers of children, by construing pregnancy as "a delicate [and embarrassing] condition," and by supporting a strictly "medical" approach to childbirth.[140] (Not coincidentally, women were excluded from their own traditional role as doctors and healers to others.) In a word, nineteenth-century women were left substantially *disempowered*. But here lay a final irony. From powerlessness women gained a measure of protection against ancient forms of misogyny. Women's power had been, after all, *key* to witchcraft, and now that key was gone.

Psychology

If the fear of witchcraft expressed, in effect, a conflict over inner promptings to assertiveness and aggression, then the decline of such fear must also be related to a shift in dynamic psychology. Either the conflict was handled in a new way (e.g. a shift from one defensive style to another), or its level and salience were greatly reduced. In fact, the latter seems the more plausible line of interpretation. As noted already, the evolving culture of nineteenth-century America sponsored a more accepting attitude toward human aggression—at least in some circumstances. Anger in a righteous cause (e.g. social and moral reform), competitive striving for success, the physical violence of organized sports and the frontier: all this was permissible, even encouraged, for large sectors of the population.[141] No doubt there were many other circumstances where aggression seemed inappropriate, if not immoral; and the central Puritan virtue of "peaceableness" was still officially honored. Yet the total balance had shifted unmistakably. Deeds and decisions expressing the "natural force" of individuals were more and more widely approved—and seemed, in any case, essential to "going ahead."[142]

These changes were rooted in new modes of child-rearing. The old emphasis on "breaking the will," the old preoccupation with early manifestations of "original sin," had faded considerably by the mid-nineteenth century. Infants were seen as morally neutral (or, better still, as "innocent"); with the right sort of encouragement they might even show "inborn inclinations" to good.[143] To rear children under such conditions was more a matter of "nurture" (a new and resonant term) than of repression and conquest—which is to say, in the language of modern theory, that the developing "self" evoked an increasingly affirmative range of response.[144] There was less and less ground here for the formation of those anxious attitudes—that sense of permeable boundaries, that lack of inner autonomy—amid which the fear of witchcraft had previously flourished.

The results were felt most forcibly in one particular category of (hitherto) prime "victims"—that of young adult men. From an early age American boys were encouraged to think of ever-widening opportunity. ("You can be what you like.") The premodern pattern of development, with its lasting familial entanglements and its implicit hostility to *self*-determination, was very nearly reversed. Young men now attained maturity by growing away from parents and kin, by making independent choices (of occupation, of residence, of values; of spouse, of associates, of friends).[145] Of course, this process carried its own psychological price —but a different price from the earlier one.

A second category of erstwhile victims—women in midlife—also seems to have been less tightly positioned. Disempowered though they fundamentally were, nineteenth-century women obtained a measure of autonomy within their prescribed "sphere." Home was preeminently *their* ground, domesticity uniquely *their* vocation. Along with domesticity came a burgeoning spirit of "sisterhood"—which, in turn, offered valuable aid and comfort in moments of particular distress.[146] Moreover, the menopausal "change of life" cannot have been so marked, and painful, as formerly. Child-bearing was ended—by design—for more and more women, at earlier and earlier ages.[147] Indeed, child-bearing yielded to child-*rearing* at the center of women's experience.[148] Maternity, not fecundity, became the touchstone of their gender—and maternity, unlike fecundity, might be extended far into later life.*

Adolescent girls had once played a notoriously important part in witchcraft cases, but their situation too was changing. Numerous different reflections of women's experience in the nineteenth century yield a notably favorable picture of the pre-adult years. Evidently, these years brought a special freedom of movement (and behavior?) in comparison with other parts of the female life-course. Tocqueville himself rendered the now-famous judgment that "nowhere [else] are young women surrendered so early or so completely to their own guidance"—and other foreign visitors agreed.[149] Girls within the age-range of (roughly) fifteen to twenty would circulate quite extensively outside their homes—with friends and beaux, to balls and "bees" and even (in some cases) income-producing work. To be sure, adolescence brought *inner* burdens, but these were felt more by boys than by girls. And there were mitigating circumstances as well: the outlet provided by religious conversion (ever more powerfully linked with the pre-adult years), the creation of "semi-dependent" settings for this age-group, the growing recognition of adolescence as a separate "stage of life" with its own requirements and vulnerabilities.[150]

In sum, the argument from "psychology" emphasizes the experience of three groups. Each had once played a central role in witch-hunting, reflecting particular circumstances of pressure and difficulty. When in time those circumstances altered, the motive to believe (and act on) charges of witchcraft was diminished. This process corresponded to still

---

* A comparison of the *different* parts of the female life-cycle may help to sharpen this point. Young women (e.g. twenty to thirty years old) in nineteenth-century America experienced what has been called a "marriage trauma"—a period of crisis around the tightly linked issues of separation from parents and community of origin, of commitment to a spouse, of responsibility for a new home. Elderly women (those past sixty) were subject to a painful isolation—as the maternal "nest" became finally empty. By contrast, the situation of women in midlife looks at least moderately favorable.

broader changes—in values, in child-rearing, in character formation—affecting the population as a whole. Thus those *interior* sources, which had so strongly fed the larger current of belief and behavior, gradually went dry.

Sociology

Several broad lines of change served to rearrange the social underpinnings of witchcraft. For one, the sheer density of early New England life was steadily reduced with the passage of the generations. The original form of the nucleated village disintegrated after the end of the seventeenth century. Dispersed settlement became the norm—not only on the frontier, but also through vast sections of the agricultural heartland and in parts of New England as well.[151] Social no less than spatial relationships were powerfully affected. The notion of an "organic" community gave way to "pluralism": in such circumstances "deviance," or simple eccentricity, would seem less and less menacing.[152] The growing size of many communities was also a factor here. Witchcraft belief had flourished within small units of population, where social relationships were typically multi-faceted and personalized. In seventeenth-century New England any two men might be neighbors, co-workers, fellow-worshippers in church, fellow-citizens and/or office-holders in local government, and partners in the exchange of countless everyday goods and services. In a sense it was not unreasonable that a disturbance in one part of the relationship should affect other parts as well. Conversely, witchcraft belief *waned* wherever population units grew large, social relationships became limited and "segmented," and many elements of experience seemed, in effect, impersonal. There it would be much harder to find, within one's human surround, specific targets of blame for personal misfortune and suffering. It was no accident that witchcraft never appeared in cities, or that it survived longest in villages well removed from urban influence.

The enlarged scale of community life also implicated the "functions" that witchcraft had traditionally performed. Social boundaries could no longer be set, and internal loyalties affirmed, in the old way. Of course, all groups need to define themselves by one means or another; but the targeting of individual "witches" (known on a personal basis) hardly served once a community had attained a certain size and complexity. Moreover, the issues and values—even the value-*conflicts*—identified by the figure of the witch were less and less salient after the middle of the eighteenth century. Witchcraft cases had, in the early period, exemplified a profound social tension—between "neighborliness" on the one hand and "individualism" on the other, between the ancient standard of "commonwealth" and the pursuit of personal interest. But the course of American development eventually resolved this tension (or greatly scaled it down) by subordinating the first set of values to the second. A new belief took hold—that the welfare of *all* was best served where each individual sought his own gain.

History

As "individualism" and "pluralism" transformed the American value-system, conflict itself would no longer seem an unmitigated evil. The rhythm of experience *around* conflict—so integral to witchcraft in the early period—began to flatten out in the eighteenth century; in the nineteenth it could hardly be discovered at all. Indeed, the health of any community was seen to require the open expression of divergent viewpoints and interests. Competition, struggle, challenge, and response: thus a dominant strain in the emergent ethos of "modernization."[153] Fewer and fewer people would agonize over factional and personal strife, or seek to connect such experiences with providential "chastening."

And the change went deeper still. A whole way of experiencing history was gradually superseded. The idea of "providence" itself faded, at least in relation to everyday events. Moreover, the larger notion of the connectedness of events was considerably relaxed. The early New Englanders had been disposed to see every particular "happening" as inwardly linked to many others—with the whole forming a densely interwoven tapestry of historical experience. In that context the strenuous study of "harms" and "signs"—the effort, in short, to understand such linkages—made eminently good sense. And witchcraft, as part of the context, also made sense. But later generations were more inclined to take events one at a time, without looking backward or forward (or *inward*) for special meaning. In a sense, Americans were becoming a-historical.

The burden of this concluding argument has been to emphasize the weakening of those ideational, social, and psychological structures which had traditionally supported the belief in witchcraft. Where such belief was once largely "functional," it became with the passage of time simply irrelevant. Put crudely, Americans of the modern period had less *need* to credit the existence, and malign activity, of witches.

And yet the matter will not quite rest there. For, as witches disappeared from view, other figures were obliged to take their place. Blacks, Indians, immigrants of various kinds; Jews, Catholics, Mormons, atheists; Masons, anarchists, Communists: around these new targets "witch-hunting" has been repeatedly revived all through American history. The long and continuing life of the *metaphor* itself bespeaks an underlying connection. Consideration of "need" and motive must, then, be construed in two ways—the one highly specific and circumstantial, the other, broad, generic, even trans-historical.

Witchcraft, literally understood, is a story of particular times and places, and of richly idiosyncratic human situations. But it is also part of another story—much larger, still current, ever painful.

A scholar who has lived for many years with the first kind of story ends by feeling acutely aware of the second. And he yields the last word to a poet from another time:

> Witchcraft was hung, in History,
> But History and I
> Find all the Witchcraft that we need
> Around us, every Day—
> > *Emily Dickinson* (c. 1883)

Appendix

List of Known Witchcraft Cases

in Seventeenth-Century New England

This list includes all known accusations of witchcraft within the designated period, except those of the Salem trials. (For a comparable list for Salem, see Paul Boyer and Stephen Nissenbaum, eds., *Salem Village Witchcraft: A Documentary Record of Local Conflict in Colonial New England* [Belmont, California: Wadsworth Publishing Co., 1972], pp. 376–78.)

Column I (*Accusation*) includes cases for which there is evidence of witchcraft accusation or suspicion but without recorded action taken in the courts. Column II (*Complaint*) indicates some formal step toward prosecution of the accused (e.g. petitioning, deposing about particular circumstances). Column III (*Presentment/Indictment*) shows appearance before the courts by the accused, preliminary to a *Trial* (Column IV). Columns V (*Acquittal*) and VI (*Conviction*) show the outcomes of trials, where known, and Column VII (*Confession*) designates those among the accused who accepted guilt in the charges against them. Column VIII (*Execution*) shows cases from which capital sentence resulted. Column IX (*Slander*) lists the cases in which legal action was initiated by the suspected witch, not the supposed victim. Column X (*Repeater*) notes cases in which the suspected witch had been previously in court on similar charges.

Parentheses, (X), indicate probable, but not certain, inclusion in the specified category. Cases listed without inter-line spacing were connected as parts of a cluster of accusations and/or legal proceedings.

The notations (f) and (m), in the column *Given Name*, designate the gender of the accused (female and male, respectively) in certain instances where the name itself is not known.

Year	Surname	Given name	Colony	Town	Accusation	Complaint	Presentment/ Indictment	Trial	Acquittal	Conviction	Confession	Execution	Slander	Repeater
1638	Hawkins	Jane	Mass.	Boston		X	X							
1640	Hutchinson	Anne	R.I.	Aquiday	X									
1640	Collins	(m)	R.I.	Aquiday	X									
1640	Hales	(m)	R.I.	Aquiday	X									
1647	Young	Alice	Conn.	Windsor		X	X	X		X		X		
1647(?)	Kendall	Elizabeth	Mass.	Cambridge		X	X	X		X		X		
1648	Jones	Margaret	Mass.	Charlestown		X	X	X		X		X		
1648	Jones	Thomas	Mass.	Charlestown		X	X							
1648	Johnson	Mary	Conn.	Wethersfield		X	X	X		X	X	X		
1649	Marshfield	(f)	Mass.	Springfield									X	
1650	Stratton	Alice	Mass.	Watertown									X	
1650	James	Jane	Mass.	Marblehead									X	
1651	James	Jane	Mass.	Marblehead									X	X
1651	Carrington	Joan	Conn.	Wethersfield		X	X	X		X		X		
1651	Carrington	John	Conn.	Wethersfield		X	X	X		X		X		
1651	Parsons	Mary	Mass.	Springfield		X	X	X	X					
1651	Parsons	Hugh	Mass.	Springfield		X	X	X		X verdict reversed				

Year	Surname	Given	Colony	Town	1	2	3	4	5	6	7	8
1651	Merrick	Sarah	Mass.	Springfield	X	?						
1651	Sewell	Bessie	Mass.	Springfield	X	?						
1651(?)	Lake	Alice	Mass.	Dorchester		X	X	X		X	X	
1651	Bassett	(f)	Conn.	Fairfield		X	X	X	X	X	X	
1652	Stratton	Alice	Mass.	Watertown		X	X					X
1652	Bradstreet	John	Mass.	Rowley		X	X	X				
1653(?)	Knapp	(f)	Conn.	Fairfield		X	X	X		X		
1653	Collins	Jane	Mass.	Lynn		X	X					
1653	Evans	Agnes	Mass.	Gloucester							X	
1653	Dutch	Grace	Mass.	Gloucester							X	
1653	Perkins	Elizabeth	Mass.	Gloucester							X	
1653	Vinson	Sarah	Mass.	Gloucester							X	
1653	Godman	Elizabeth	New Haven	New Haven		X	X	X			X	
1654	Gilbert	Lydia	Conn.	Windsor		X	X	X	(X)		X	
1654	Staples	Mary	New Haven	New Haven		X					X	
1655	Godman	Elizabeth	New Haven	New Haven		X	X	X		X		X
1655	Bailey	(f)	New Haven	New Haven		X	X	X		X		
1655	Bailey	Nicholas	New Haven	New Haven		X	X	X		X		
1655	Batchelor	(f)	Mass.	Ipswich		X						
1656	Walford	Jane	Mass.	Portsmouth[a]		X	X	(X)				
1656	Evans	(f)	Mass.	Portsmouth[a]	X							

Year	Surname	Given name	Colony	Town	Accusation	Complaint	Presentment/ Indictment	Trial	Acquittal	Conviction	Confession	Execution	Slander	Repeater
1656	Cole	Eunice	Mass.	Hampton[a]		X	X	X	X					
1656	Hibbens	Ann	Mass.	Boston		X	X	X		X		X		
1656	Parsons	Mary	Mass.	Northampton									X	
1657	Brown	William	Mass.	Gloucester		X	(X)							
1657	Meaker	William	New Haven	New Haven									X	
1658	Garlick	Elizabeth	Conn.	Easthampton[b]		X	X	X	X					
1659	Godfrey	John	Mass.	Andover		X	X	X	X					
1659	Godfrey	John	Mass.	Andover									X	X
1659	—	—	Conn.	Saybrook		X	X							
1659	Holman	Winifred	Mass.	Cambridge		X	X	X	(X)					
1659	Holman	Mary	Mass.	Cambridge		X	X	X	(X)					
1659	Bailey	Elizabeth	Mass.	York[c]		X	X	X	X					
1660	Holman	Winifred	Mass.	Cambridge									X	X
1660	Holman	Winifred	Mass.	Cambridge		X	X							
1660	Holmes	(f)	Plymouth	Scituate									X	X
1660	Palmer	Katherine	Conn.	Wethersfield		X								

Date	Surname	Given name	Colony	Town	1	2	3	4	5	6	7
1661	Jennings	Margaret	Conn.	Saybrook	X	X	X	X			
1661	Jennings	Nicholas	Conn.	Saybrook	X	X	X	X			
1662	Godfrey	John	Mass.	Haverhill	X			X			X
1662	Godfrey	John	Mass.	Haverhill	X					X	X
1662–3	Evans	(f)	Mass.	Portsmouth[a]	X	(X)	(X)				X
1662	Varlet	Judith	Conn.	Hartford	X	X	(X)			(X)	
1662	Sanford	Mary	Conn.	Hartford	X	X	X	X		(X)	
1662	Sanford	Andrew	Conn.	Hartford	X	X	X	X			
1662	Ayers	(f)	Conn.	Hartford	X	X	X	X		escaped	
1662–3	Blackleach	Elizabeth	Conn.	Wethersfield	X	X	X				
1662–3	Blackleach	John	Conn.	Wethersfield	X	X	X				
1662–3	Wakeley	James	Conn.	Hartford	X	X	X			escaped	
1662–3	Greensmith	Rebecca	Conn.	Hartford	X	X	X		X	X	X
1662–3	Greensmith	Nathaniel	Conn.	Hartford	X	X	X		X	X	X
1663	Barnes	Mary	Conn.	Farmington	X	X	X		X		X
1663 (Jan)	Seager	Elizabeth	Conn.	Hartford	X	X	X	X			
1663 (Jul)	Seager	Elizabeth	Conn.	Hartford	X	X	X	X			
1664	Hall	Mary	Conn.	Setauket[b]	X	X	X	X			
1665	Godfrey	John	Mass.	Haverhill	X	X	X		X		X
1665	Seager	Elizabeth	Conn.	Hartford	X	X	X		X verdict reversed		X
1665	Wakeley	James	Conn.	Hartford	X	X			escaped		X
1665	Hall	Mary	Conn.	Setauket[b]	X	X	X	X			X
1665	Hall	Ralph	Conn.	Setauket[b]	X	X	X	X			X
1665	Gleason	(f)	Mass.	Cambridge	X	X	X				

Year	Surname	Given name	Colony	Town	Accusation	Complaint	Presentment/ Indictment	Trial	Acquittal	Conviction	Confession	Execution	Slander	Repeater
1667	James	Jane	Mass.	Marblehead									X	X
1667	Crawford	Edith	Mass.	Salem									X	X
1667	Griswold	Hannah	Conn.	Saybrook									X	
1667	Graves	William	Conn.	Stamford		X	(X)							
1668	Harrison	Katherine	Conn.	Wethersfield		X	X	X	X					
1669	Wells	Thomas	Mass.	Ipswich		X								
1669	Walford	Jane	Mass.	Portsmouth^a		X	(X)							X
1669	Williams	Robert	Mass.	Hadley		X	X	X	X					
1669	Dibble	Sarah	Conn.	Stamford	X									
1669	Martin	Susannah	Mass.	Amesbury		X	X	(X)	(X)					
1670(?)	Burt	Ann	Mass.	Lynn		X	X	(X)	(X)					
1671	—	(f)	Mass.	Groton	X									
1672	Palmer	Katherine	R.I.	Newport		X							X	X
1673	Cole	Eunice	Mass.	Hampton^a		X	X	X	X					X
1673	Edmunds	Anna	Mass.	Lynn		X	X	X	X					

	Name	Given	Colony	Town							
1673	Messenger	(f)	Conn.	Windsor							X
1674–5	Parsons	Mary	Mass.	Northampton	X	X	X	X			X
1676	Ingham	Mary	Plymouth	Scituate	X	X					
1677	Beamon	Alice	Mass.	Springfield							X
1678	Burr	(f)	Conn.	Wethersfield							X
1679	—	(f)	Mass.	Northampton	X						
1679	Powell	Caleb	Mass.	Newbury	X	X	X				
1679	Morse	Elizabeth	Mass.	Newbury	X	X	X			X verdict reversed	
1680	Fuller	Rachel	New Hamp.	Hampton	X	X	X				
1680	Towle	Isabella	New Hamp.	Hampton	X	X	X				
1680	Cole	Eunice	New Hamp.	Hampton	X	X	X				X
1680	Oliver	Bridget	Mass.	Salem	X	X	(X)	(X)			
1680	Gifford	Margaret	Mass.	Lynn	X	X	X				
1681	Hale	Mary	Mass.	Boston	X	X	X				
1682	Jones	Hannah	New Hamp.	Portsmouth	X	X					
1682	—	—	Conn.	Hartford					X		
1682	—	(f)	Mass.	Kittery^e					X		
1683	Fuller	James	Mass.	Springfield	X	X	X				
1683	Travally	(f)	New York	Southampton^d							X

Year	Surname	Given name	Colony	Town	Accusation	Complaint	Presentment/ Indictment	Trial	Acquittal	Conviction	Confession	Execution	Slander	Repeater
1683	Webster	Mary	Mass.	Hadley		X	X	X	X					
1685	Webster	Mary	Mass.	Hadley			X	X					X	X
1687(?)	Clinton	Rachel	Mass.	Ipswich		X								
1688	Glover	(f)	Mass.	Boston		X	X	X		X	X	X		
1688	—	(f)	Mass.	Boston		X	X				X			
1688	—	(f)	Mass.	Boston	X									
1688	—	(f)	Mass.	Boston	X									
1689	—	(f)	Mass.	Boston	X									X
1689	Bowden	(f)	Conn.	New Haven									X	
1691	Hale	Mary	Mass.	Boston		X	X							X
1691	Randall	Mary	Mass.	Northampton		X	X							
1692	Disborough	Mercy	Conn.	Fairfield		X	X	X		X reprieved				
1692	Clawson	Elizabeth	Conn.	Stamford		X	X	X	X					
1692	Staples	Mary	Conn.	Fairfield		X	X							X
1692	Harvey	Mary	Conn.	Fairfield		X	X							
1692	Harvey	Hannah	Conn.	Fairfield		X	X							
1692	Miller	(f)	Conn.	Fairfield	X									
1692	Benham	Winifred	Conn.	Wallingford		X	X							

408

	Croasia	Hugh	Conn.	Stratford				
1692						X	X	X
1693	—	(f)	Mass.	Boston	X		X	
1693	—	(f)	Mass.	Boston	X		X	
1697	Benham	Winifred	Conn.	Wallingford		X	X	X
1697	Benham	Winifred, Jr.	Conn.	Wallingford		X	X	X
1680s(?)	—	(f)	Mass.	Salem(?)	X			
1680s(?)	—	(f)	Mass.	Salem(?)	X			
1680s(?)	—	(f)	Mass.	Salem(?)	X			
1680s(?)	—	(f)	Mass.	?	X			

[a] This town, which today belongs to New Hampshire, was initially part of the Massachusetts Bay Colony.
[b] This Long Island town, which today belongs to New York, was initially within the jurisdiction of the Connecticut Colony.
[c] This town, which today belongs to the state of Maine, was initially part of the Massachusetts Bay Colony.
[d] This town, though by 1683 attached to New York, had previously belonged to Connecticut and was still within the cultural ambit of New England.

Notes

The following sources are cited with particular frequency throughout the text. Full citations are given here; a briefer form is used in individual notes. In all other instances, full citation is given for first usage within a given chapter and a shorter form thereafter (in the same chapter).

Manuscript Sources

County Court, Ipswich: Records, 1645–1663. (Essex County Courthouse; Salem, Mass.)

County Court, Ipswich: Records, 1664–1674. (Essex County Courthouse; Salem, Mass.)

County Court, Ipswich: Records, 1666–1682. (Essex County Courthouse; Salem, Mass.)

County Court, Norfolk: Records, 1648–1678. (Essex County Courthouse; Salem, Mass.)

County Court, Salem: Records, 1667–1679. (Essex County Courthouse; Salem, Mass.)

Essex County Court Papers: Original Depositions and Other Materials from the Proceedings of the Quarterly Courts of Essex County, Mass. (Essex County Courthouse; Salem, Mass.)

Massachusetts Archives. (Statehouse; Boston, Mass.)

Middlesex Court Files: Original Depositions and Other Materials from the Proceedings of the Quarterly Courts of Middesex County, Mass. (Middlesex County Courthouse; East Cambridge, Mass.)

Samuel Willys Collection: Records of Trials for Witchcraft in Connecticut. (Connecticut State Library; Hartford, Conn.)

Suffolk Court Files: Original Depositions and Other Materials from the Proceedings of the Quarterly Courts of Suffolk County, Mass. (Suffolk County Courthouse; Boston, Mass.)

Willys Papers: Records of Trials for Witchcraft in Connecticut. (Ann Mary Brown Memorial, Brown University Library; Providence, Rhode Island.)

Printed Sources

Bouton, Nathaniel, ed., *Documents and Records Relating to the Province of New Hampshire*, 5 vols. (Concord, N.H., 1867–80).

Boyer, Paul, and Stephen Nissenbaum, eds., *Salem Village Witchcraft: A Documentary Record of Local Conflict in Colonial New England* (Belmont, Calif., 1972).

Burr, Charles Lincoln, ed., *Narratives of the Witchcraft Cases* (repr. New York, 1968).

Dexter, Franklin B., ed., *New Haven Town Records, 1649–1662* (New Haven, Conn., 1917).

Drake, Samuel G., *Annals of Witchcraft in New England* (New York, 1869).

Hoadly, Charles J., ed., *Records of the Colony or Jurisdiction of New Haven*, 2 vols. (New Haven, Conn., 1857–58).

Hosmer, J. K., ed., *Winthrop's Journal*, 2 vols. (New York, 1908).

The Mather Papers, in Massachusetts Historical Society, *Collections*, 4th ser., VIII.

Noble, John, and John F. Cronin, eds., *Records of the Court of Assistants of the Colony of Massachusetts Bay, 1630–1692*, 3 vols. (Boston, 1901–1928).

Probate Records of Essex County, Massachusetts, 3 vols. (Salem, Mass., 1916–20).

Records and Files of the Quarterly Courts of Essex County, Massachusetts, 9 vols. (Salem, Mass., 1911–78).

Records of the Particular Court of Connecticut, 1639–1663, in Connecticut Historical Society, *Collections*, XXII.

Shurtleff, Nathaniel B., ed., *Records of the Governor and Company of Massachusetts Bay, in New England*, 5 vols. (Boston, 1853–54).

Shurtleff, Nathaniel B., and David Pulsifer, eds., *Records of the Colony of New Plymouth, in New England*, 12 vols. (Boston, 1855–61).

Trumbull, J. Hammond, and Charles J. Hoadly, eds., *The Public Records of the Colony of Connecticut*, 15 vols. (Hartford, Conn., 1850–90).

Notes to Introduction

1. John Higginson, "An Epistle to the Reader," in John Hale, "A Modest Enquiry into the Nature of Witchcraft," reprinted in Burr, ed., *Narratives*, 400.

2. Perry Miller—to cite only one example—declared of the Salem affair that

"the intellectual history of New England can be written as though no such thing ever happened. It had no effect on the ecclesiastical or political situation, it does not figure in the institutional or ideological development." See Miller, *The New England Mind: From Colony to Province* (Boston, 1961), 191.

3. Higginson had, for example, furnished ideas and materials for Increase Mather's treatise on witchcraft, "An Essay for the Recording of Illustrious Providences." See his letter in *The Mather Papers*, 282–87.

4. Higginson, "Epistle," in Burr, ed., *Narratives*, 400.

5. *Records of the Particular Court of Connecticut, 1639–1663*, 106–7.

6. *Ibid.*, 131.

7. Thomas Gilbert (husband of Lydia) rendered an "account of debts due" to and from Henry Stiles, when the latter's estate was being probated. This document is reprinted in full in Homer Worthington Brainard, Harold Simeon Gilbert, and Clarence Almon Torrey, *The Gilbert Family* (New Haven, Conn., priv. printed, 1953), 15–17.

8. *Records of the Particular Court of Connecticut, 1639–1663*, 131.

9. This undocumented reconstruction is based on such actual instances of ministers' response to witchcraft cases as Deodat Lawson, "Christ's Fidelity the Only Shield Against Satan's Malignity . . ." (2nd ed., London, 1704), and Samuel Willard, "Useful Instructions for a Professing People in Times of Great Security and Degeneracy" (Cambridge, Mass., 1673).

10. For a full account of this case, see Cotton Mather, "Memorable Providences Relating to Witchcrafts and Possessions," in Burr, ed., *Narratives*, 99–131.

11. On the specific issue of the victim's belief in his own "affliction," and the effects of such belief, see below, Chapter 6.

12. On the evolution of English law with respect to witchcraft, see Wallace Notestein, *A History of Witchcraft in England* (repr. New York, 1968), ch. 1.

13. The Plymouth statute of 1636 was the earliest one in any of the British colonies. See Drake, *Annals of Witchcraft*, 56. The "laws of judgement" of Southampton, Long Island, were drawn up in 1641; they have been reprinted in George R. Howell, *The Early History of Southampton, L.I., New York* (Albany, N.Y., 1887), 464ff.

14. At least there was no torture of a direct sort (e.g. beating, stretching on a rack, etc.). To be sure, some suspects may have been deprived of sleep, as part of a regime of "watching" them for possible connection with satanic imps. And a few were "ducked" in water, in accordance with an ancient test for witchcraft. (To float was to increase suspicion of diabolical "familiarity"; to sink was to deflect it.) There were also, of course, deep psychological pressures and torments for those who stood formally accused. Vivid examples of the latter can be found in a famous

"statement" submitted by several women of Andover, Massachusetts, in recanting confessions which they had previously made during the trials at Salem. See Burr, ed., *Narratives*, 374–75.

15. See below, Chapter 9.
16. See Appendix B for a complete list of these cases.
17. See the "List of All Persons Accused of Witchcraft in 1692," in Boyer and Nissenbaum, eds., *Salem Village Witchcraft*, 376–78.
18. A. D. J. Macfarlane, *Witchcraft in Tudor and Stuart England* (New York, 1970), 57, 60.
19. C. L. Ewen, *Witch-Hunting and Witch Trials* (London, 1929), 112.
20. Macfarlane, *Witchcraft*, 62. For another discussion of the total of accused witches, see Keith Thomas, *Religion and the Decline of Magic* (New York, 1971), 450–51.
21. For an excellent study presenting quantitative data on one part of this comparison, see H. C. Erik Midelfort, *Witch Hunting in Southwestern Germany, 1562–1684: The Social and Intellectual Foundations* (Stanford, Calif., 1972).
22. A summary of these intra-European differences, with references to specific branches of monographic research, is found in Norman Cohn, *Europe's Inner Demons: An Enquiry Inspired by the Great Witch-Hunt* (New York, 1975), 253–55.
23. On witchcraft elsewhere in the British colonies of North America, see Lawrence J. Spagnola, "The Witchcraft Cases of Maryland and Virginia, 1626–1712," honors thesis, History Department, Harvard College (1977); Richard Beale Davis, "The Devil in Virginia in the Seventeenth Century," *Virginia Magazine of History and Biography*, LXV (1957), 131–49; F. N. Parke, "Witchcraft in Maryland," *Maryland Historical Magazine*, XXXI (December 1936), 271–98; "Witchcraft in New York," New York Historical Society, *Collections* (1869), 273–76; Tom Pete Cross, "Witchcraft in North Carolina," *Studies in Philology*, XVI (July 1919), 217–87. For a sampling of non-New England case materials, see Burr, ed., *Narratives*, 39–52, 79–88, 433–42.
24. On the distinction between psychological and sociological approaches to witchcraft study, see M. G. Marwick, "The Social Context of Cewa Witch Beliefs," in *Africa*, XXII (1952), 120–22. For an excellent instance of an integrated "psycho-social" method, see Robert Levine, *Culture, Behavior and Personality* (Chicago, 1973), ch. 17.

Notes to Chapter 1

1. Manuscript depositions in Suffolk Court Files, no. 2660.
2. Manuscript holdings, Cornell University Library, Ithaca, N.Y. The heading on this document, "Witchcraft 1687," is in a separate hand and was probably added at some later time. The date 1687 corresponds fairly

well with evidence internal to the document itself. But there are no other extant records with which to join this deposition, and so we cannot be sure of its legal import. That it belonged to some effort to bring Rachel before a quarterly court in Essex County is only an assumption—though a reasonable one.

3. See *The New England Historical and Genealogical Register*, XIV (1860), 307. The certificate also mentions four additional persons, with surnames other than Haffield. There is an implication that Richard Haffield was in some way responsible for these passengers as well: Were they, possibly, his servants? They do not, however, appear in connection with Haffield, or members of his family, in any subsequent document.

4. Manuscript deposition by Alice Tilly, March 27, 1668. See Suffolk Court Files, no. 931. It is apparent, from other evidence, that the above mentioned son of Richard and Judith Haffield had died before the family migrated to New England. See *Probate Records of Essex County, Massachusetts*, II, 118–19.

5. See p. 25.

6. Richard Haffield's will is printed in *The New England Historical and Genealogical Register*, III (1849), 156.

7. Deposition by Symon Thompson, April 4, 1668. See *Probate Records of Essex County, Massachusetts*, II, 117.

8. Petition to the General Court, of Josiah Cobbett, Mary Cobbett, John Ilsley, Sarah Ilsley. See *ibid.*, II, 119.

9. The original grant to Richard Haffield, made in 1635, was a house-lot, six acres of "planting land," twenty acres of "meadow," and one hundred acres of (unspecified) "land." See "Records of the Town of Ipswich from 1634 to 1674," manuscript copy by Nathaniel Farley (1894), 16 (Town Clerk's Office, Ipswich, Mass.).

10. See *ibid.*, 98, 199; Essex County Court Papers, VI, leaf 56. The Haffields' tenant for a good many years was one Richard Brabrook. The court records show occasional difficulties with this man over the payment of rent.

11. *Records and Files of the Quarterly Courts of Essex County, Massachusetts*, I, 278. According to the sumptuary laws then in force throughout Massachusetts Bay, members of families with an aggregate wealth of over £200 were entitled to wear "silks, . . . gold and silver lace," and the like. See Shurtleff, ed., *Records of the Governor and Company of Massachusetts Bay*, III, 243–44.

12. On this point, see John Demos, *A Little Commonwealth: Family Life in Plymouth Colony* (New York, 1970), 66–67.

13. For the presentment, see Essex County Court Papers, I, leaf 74; for the sentence, County Court, Ipswich: Records, 1645–1663, leaf 8.

14. See "Records of the Town of Ipswich from 1634 to 1674," 193.

15. County Court, Ipswich: Records, 1664–1674, leaf 92 (reverse).

16. *Ibid.*, leaf 94 (reverse).

17. The suit is noted in *Records and Files of the Quarterly Courts of Essex County, Massachusetts*, III, 371. (Manuscript volume could not be located.) There are sixteen manuscript papers from the case in Essex County Court Papers, XII, leaves 22–25.

18. The first direct note of Lawrence Clinton's presence in Ipswich was the record of his marriage in December 1665. (*Vital Records of the Town of Ipswich, Mass.*, II, 104.) On March 27, 1666, he appeared in court for the first time, "upon presentment for lying, and for cozzening and cheating." He was found guilty and sentenced to be whipped—or, alternatively, to pay a fine of 40 shillings plus court costs. (See County Court, Ipswich: Records, 1664–1674, leaf 93.) Was this, possibly, in reference to the arrangements for purchasing his "freedom" from Robert Cross? If so, it can be viewed as a preliminary skirmish before the big battle occasioned by the suits brought by Thomas White. The latter could not begin, of course, until White had obtained full guardianship over Martha Haffield and her property—i.e. some six months after Clinton's initial presentment.

19. The marriage is noted in *Vital Records of the Town of Ipswich, Mass.*, II, 104. Clinton's approximate age is calculated from later depositional statements; for example, on November 26, 1667, he testified, "aged 24 years." (See Essex County Court Papers, XIII, leaf 11.)

20. Deposition by Lawrence Clinton, November 29, 1666. See Essex County Court Papers, XII, leaf 22.

21. Deposition by Samuel Graves, November 23, 1666; *ibid.*, XII, leaf 25.

22. Deposition by William Durgi, November 26, 1666; *ibid.*, XII, leaf 23. See also deposition by Shoreborn Wilson, November 23, 1666; *ibid.*, XII, leaf 25.

23. Deposition by Richard Brabook, November 26, 1666; *ibid.*, XII, leaf 24. A similar point was made in testimony by Jonathan Whipple, Jr., November 23, 1666; *ibid.*, XIII, leaf 25.

24. Deposition by Jeremiah Belcher, November 23, 1666; *ibid.*, XII, leaf 25.

25. Deposition by William Nelson, November 26, 1666; *ibid.*, XII, leaf 24. This testimony was corroborated by Harlackenden Symonds, November 26, 1666; *ibid.*, XII, leaf 24.

26. Depositions by Thomas Fiske, November 28, 1666 and November 29, 1666; *ibid.*, XII, leaves 23, 25.

27. See *Records and Files of the Quarterly Courts of Essex County, Massachusetts*, III, 371. (Manuscript record could not be located.)

28. See *ibid.*, III, 456.

29. Depositions by Ruth White, November 26, 1667; Essex County Court Papers, XIII, leaves 10, 12. Corroborating testimony came from Richard Brabrook (deposition, June 20, 1667; *ibid.*, XIII, leaf 11) and James Ford

(deposition, November 23, 1667; *ibid.*, XIII, leaf 11). As to Robert Cross being "the leading man" in this affair, there was interesting testimony from Joanna Fiske: "She heard Lawrence Clinton say that his master Cross and he had agreed for his time for less. But the said Cross got him into the parlor, and there [they] drank to each other . . . he saying 'I drink to you, master'; and Cross said, 'I thank you, man.' And then he put his hand into his pocket and pulled out more money and gave [it to] him." (Deposition, November 26, 1667; *ibid.*, XIII, leaf 11.)

30. Deposition by Rachel Clinton, November 27, 1667; *ibid.*, XIII, leaf 11.

31. See the records of the General Court for May 27, 1669; Shurtleff, ed., *Records of the Governor and Company of Massachusetts Bay*, IV, part two, 226.

32. Petition of Rachel Clinton to the quarterly court of Essex County, Mass., no date given; Essex County Court Papers, XIII, leaf 29. This petition is included in a section of court papers headed "Miscellaneous Papers 1667"—a date which finds confirmation in some internal references. Most likely, it was filed between December 1667 and February 1668.

33. See *Records and Files of the Quarterly Courts of Essex County, Massachusetts*, III, 468.

34. Inventory of the estate of Martha Haffield, March 30, 1668; in *Probate Records of Essex County, Massachusetts*, II, 115–16.

35. See *ibid.*, II, 117–18.

36. Martha Haffield's will, dated June 11, 1662, is printed in *ibid.*, II, 116–118.

37. In the course of this litigation, there was testimony that Richard Haffield had stated *verbally* a wish for an equal division among all his children of property beyond the total value of the portions. See deposition by Symon Thompson, April 4, 1668; *ibid.*, II, 117.

38. A petition to the General Court from the Cobbetts and Ilsleys, dated April 29, 1668, is printed in *Probate Records of Essex County, Massachusetts*, II, 118–19. The court ruled that the petitioners should pursue their case through "the ordinary course of law." This they did—in fact, twice —in quarterly courts at Salem (June 30, 1668, and November 24, 1668). Thomas White was defendant both times (presumably in his role as Martha Haffield's executor). The first suit was withdrawn. The second ended as follows: "The jury finds for the defendant, costs of court, if the will of Richard Haffield were legal; if otherwise, we then find [that] it belongs to the Honorable Bench to make an equal division of Haffield's estate. The Court finds the will to be legal." See County Court, Salem: Records, 1667–1679, leaf 9 (reverse) and leaf 16. The verdict was appealed to the Court of Assistants—where it was, however, sustained. A final petition, to the General Court, dated May 19, 1669, was also turned aside. See Massachusetts Archives, vol. XV-B, 114, 116. The

plaintiffs' case would not stand up because Haffield's will made no reference to property beyond the total necessary for the specified portions. This decision was left, by default, to the executor.

39. Abstracts of these probates are printed in *Probate Records of Essex County, Massachusetts*, II, 119–20.

40. Rachel alleged that her £30 portion "which she had by her father's last will and testament . . . was first put into the hands of her brother[-in-law] White, where it hath been detained [for] the space of thirteen years. . . . And she can by no means recover out of his hands any part of the interest and principal." (Petition to the Quarterly Court of Essex County, no date given; Essex County Court Papers, XIII, leaf 29.) But it does seem that Rachel received some family monies—else she could not have paid for the "freedom" of her husband Lawrence. The Haffields' tenant, Richard Brabrook, believed that at some point "her mother gave her [Rachel] one or two and thirty pieces of gold; and her mother's reason was . . . because her brothers-in-law had her portion in their hands, and she doubted whether she should get it or no." (Deposition, November 26, 1666; *ibid.*, XII, leaf 24.) Another witness, Jeremiah Belcher, corroborated this story. (Deposition, November 23, 1666; *ibid.*, XII, leaf 25.)

41. Petition of Rachel Clinton to the Quarterly Court of Essex County, no date given; Essex County Court Papers, XIII, leaf 29.

42. See County Court, Ipswich: Records, 1664–1674, leaf 97 (reverse). The John Clarke mentioned in this case was a resident of Wenham at the time. Twice more in 1667 Clarke was involved in court actions over alleged indecencies with local women. He firmly denied all charges, and the courts apparently acquitted him. But clearly he had a reputation for such things, and perhaps there was some reality behind it. See *Records and Files of the Quarterly Courts of Essex County, Massachusetts*, III, 438, 469. Manuscript depositions in these cases are in Essex County Court Papers, XII, leaf 25, and XIII, leaf 25.

43. County Court, Ipswich: Records, 1666–1682, leaf 61.

44. County Court, Salem: Records, 1667–1679, leaf 34.

45. County Court, Ipswich: Records, 1666–1682, leaf 97.

46. Essex County Court Papers, XVIII, leaf 91.

47. *Ibid.*, XVIII, leaf 91. See also County Court, Ipswich: Records, 1666–1682, leaf 169.

48. See County Court, Ipswich: Records, 1664–1674, leaf 132 (reverse), and Essex County Court Papers, XXI, leaf 53.

49. County Court, Ipswich: Records, 1666–1682, leaf 279.

50. See Essex County Court Papers, XXV, leaf 125; also County Court, Ipswich: Records, 1666–1682, leaf 283. Strangely, the extant records do not show that Lawrence was presented for the same offense.

51. Manuscript depositions in this case (by Elizabeth Abbott, Margaret Boreman, and Elizabeth Boreman) are in Essex County Court Papers,

XX, leaf 144. There is also a "bill of charges" from Arthur Abbott, "for Mary Greeley's lying in," in *ibid.*, XX, leaf 148. Abbott was obliged to sue for payment of these charges, and in the end the court ordered Clinton to become a servant to Abbott until the entire sum was worked off. See *Records and Files of the Quarterly Courts of Essex County, Massachusetts*, VII, 110, 181.

52. Ipswich Town Records: Births, Marriages, and Deaths (Town Clerk's Office, Ipswich, Mass.).
53. County Court, Ipswich: Records, 1666–1682, leaf 293.
54. *Ibid.*, leaf 297.
55. See *Records and Files of the Quarterly Courts of Essex County, Massachusetts*, VI, 344.
56. *Ibid.*, VI, 374–75.
57. *Ibid.*, VIII, 17.
58. Petition to the General Court, October 12, 1681; Massachusetts Archives, IX, leaf 104.
59. "Records of the Town of Ipswich from 1634 to 1674," 352.
60. See *Records and Files of the Quarterly Courts of Essex County, Massachusetts*, VII, 157.
61. Essex County Court Papers, XVI, leaf 125; XVIII, leaf 91. County Court, Ipswich: Records, 1666–1682, leaves 169, 223, 280; *Records and Files of the Quarterly Courts of Essex County, Massachusetts*, VII, 353.
62. (Mrs.) E. J. Clinton, "The Clinton Family of Connecticut," in *The New England Historical and Genealogical Register*, LXIX (1915), 50.
63. *Ibid.*, 50ff.
64. *Ibid.*, 51.
65. "Records of the Town of Ipswich from 1674 to 1696," manuscript copy by Nathaniel Farley (1894), 208, 220, 221, 222, 224, 229, 252, 273 (Town Clerk's Office, Ipswich, Mass.).
66. *Ibid.*, 208.
67. (Mrs.) E. J. Clinton, "The Clinton Family of Connecticut," 51.

Notes to Chapter 2

1. On the distribution of the accused by *gender*, and on the particular situation of male witches, see pp. 60–64.
2. This deposition is printed in full in *Records and Files of the Quarterly Courts of Essex County, Massachusetts*, II, 160. In 1666, at a later trial for witchcraft, William Howard of Hampton, N.H., gave testimony which partially corroborates the Osgood deposition. Howard recalled an incident "about 26 years ago," when he met a person "like John Godfrey" ("and as I suppose he did then name himself by that name") who was "following of cattle . . . on Newbury plain." The man had identified himself as "Mr. Spencer's apprentice" and had offered to serve Howard

when "his time was . . . out." See Noble and Cronin, eds., *Records of the Court of Assistants of the Colony of Massachusetts Bay*, III, 159.

3. *Records and Files of the Quarterly Courts of Essex County, Massachusetts*, I, 250; II, 288.

4. There is no published study of the interesting question of age-consciousness among early New Englanders (or, indeed, in other English-speaking populations of the same era). However, limited samplings of depositional records made for the present investigation suggest that discrepancies of 1 to 3 years (i.e. between age-reports given by the same individual on different occasions) were relatively common.

5. See *The New England Historical and Genealogical Register*, IX (1885), 267.

6. These identifications with place of origin have been developed largely by reference to Charles E. Banks, *Topographical Dictionary of 2885 English Emigrants to New England, 1620–1650* (Philadelphia, 1937).

7. There is one detail about this beginning that may deserve mention. The original John Spencer—presumably Godfrey's master—had a brief and unhappy career in New England. A founder of the town of Newbury, he was quickly a leading citizen there; he became indeed a magistrate and representative to the General Court of the Massachusetts Bay Colony. However, he was implicated in the "Antinomian heresy" of 1637, and returned to England the following year. His estate was left to a nephew and namesake. (It was the younger "Mr. Spencer" for whom Godfrey was working as herdsman at the time of the episode described in William Osgood's deposition.) One wonders about the effect of this outcome—high rank and esteem, followed by deviation and disgrace—on a young and perhaps impressionable member of Spencer's *entourage*.

8. *Records and Files of the Quarterly Courts of Essex County, Massachusetts*, I, 43, 53, 164.

9. *Ibid.*, I, 142, 162, 168, 179.

10. *Ibid.*, II, 39, 159.

11. *Ibid.*, II, 65, 66, 143, 157, 158, 160.

12. *Ibid.*, II, 157–58.

13. The basis for this conclusion is as follows. In June 1659 Godfrey was "bound" by the county court for an appearance at the General Court in Boston. Witchcraft, as a capital crime, could *only* be tried in the General Court; and no other court actions in which Godfrey was then involved were sufficiently serious to warrant this procedure. (See *ibid.*, II, 166.) Moreover, there is independent evidence that Godfrey was imprisoned during some part of this year—e.g. the testimony, in a later court case, that he had engaged to work for Francis Urselton of Topsfield when "he came out of Ipswich jail" in the summer of 1659. (See Urselton vs. Godfrey, in *ibid.*, II, 175.)

14. *Ibid.*, II, 157.

15. Some of these depositions are printed in *ibid.*, II, 157–62. Other testimony, in manuscript, is in the Suffolk Court Files, II, no. 322.
16. Haverhill, Andover, Rowley, Amesbury, Ipswich, Salisbury.
17. Deposition in Suffolk Court Files, II, no. 322.
18. Deposition, in *ibid.*, II, no. 322.
19. See p. 36.
20. See the depositions by Tyler and members of his family, in Suffolk Court Files, II, no. 322. The statement attributed to Godfrey that the bird "came to suck [Tyler's] wife" itself carried an imputation of witchcraft. For, according to traditional lore, witches were attended by "familiars"—animals or birds given to sucking on preternatural "teats."
21. Deposition by Charles Browne, *ibid.*
22. Deposition by Elizabeth Ayres, *ibid.*
23. Deposition by Elizabeth Ayres, *ibid.*
24. Deposition by Thomas Fowler, *ibid.* Godfrey's relation to cattle calls to mind a child's attachment to favorite pets—where tenderness is usually based on some form of "identification" (with "alter ego" qualities). Perhaps this singular man, seemingly so tough in his *interpersonal* life, showed a softer, more emphatic side in his care of domestic animals.
25. See *Records and Files of the Quarterly Courts of Essex County, Massachusetts*, II, 175.
26. See *ibid.*, II, 185, 209, 212, 216, 222, 250, 274, 277, 279, 297, 299, 301, 327, 328, 343, 353, 366, 367, 376, 377, 385, 408, 409, 412, 430, 437, 438.
27. See *ibid.*, II, 328, 343, 353, 366.
28. See *ibid.*, III, 10, 27, 29.
29. *Ibid.*, III, 74, 120ff.
30. The evidential difficulty here is the fragmentary nature of the records of the General Court, where, alone, capital crimes like witchcraft could be tried. Slander, by contrast, was a matter for the county courts, from which excellent records survive. Two things suggest that Godfrey was (at least) indicted. First, the Singletary deposition on his experience in Ipswich jail (see text) was copied from the original in Salem and filed with various Boston records at the Suffolk court. (Such material would not ordinarily be needed in Boston, except in connection with a capital case.) Second, Singletary's alleged comment—"is this witch on this side [of] Boston gallows yet?"—strongly implies a trial proceeding (again the reference to Boston is indicative). See Suffolk Court Files, II, leaf 543.
31. *Records and Files of the Quarterly Courts of Essex County, Massachusetts*, III, 120.
32. *Ibid.*, III, 121–22.
33. See Noble and Cronin, eds., *Records of the Court of Assistants of the Colony of Massachusetts Bay*, III, 151–52, 158–61.
34. *Ibid.*, III, 151–52.
35. There is a deposition by John Remington in Suffolk Court Files, II, leaf

322. Depositions by his wife, Abigail, and son, John Remington, Jr., are printed in Noble and Cronin, eds., *Records of the Court of Assistants of the Colony of Massachusetts Bay*, III, 160–61.

36. *Ibid.*, III, 160.

37. Deposition in Suffolk Court Files, II, no. 322.

38. The range of John Godfrey's legal entanglements extended at least as far as Plymouth Colony, where in 1666 he appeared before the General Court as plaintiff in a probate case. See Nathaniel B. Shurtleff and David Pulsifer, eds. *Records of the Colony of New Plymouth, in New England*, II, 130–31.

39. Deposition by Elizabeth Gott, March 31, 1668, in the case of Mr. Antipas Newman vs. Thomas White. See *Records and Files of the Quarterly Courts of Essex County, Massachusetts*, IV, 9.

40. Deposition by Thomas Wells, November 24, 1668, in the prosecution of Stephen Cross; *ibid.*, IV, 78. The reference to Godfrey's appearance is singular, and most intriguing. As litigant, as "usuror"—and perhaps as "witch"—he evidently looked the part.

41. Deposition by Thomas Chandler, June 24, 1662, in *ibid.*, II, 410.

42. Godfrey vs. Salter, *ibid.*, III, 423. For other cases in which verdicts against Godfrey were not accepted, see Godfrey vs. Whitaker, *ibid.*, III, 454; Godfrey vs. Whitaker, *ibid.*, IV, 28; Godfrey vs. Button, *ibid.*, IV, 29; Todd vs. Godfrey, *ibid.*, IV, 71; Godfrey vs. Button, *ibid.*, IV, 152; Ela vs. Godfrey, *ibid.*, IV, 181.

43. Godfrey vs. Whitaker, *ibid.*, III, 421ff. For other instances in which (apparently) Godfrey's interests were abused by officers of the Court, see Godfrey vs. Ela, *ibid.*, IV, 178; Godfrey vs. Skerry, *ibid.*, IV, 372; Godfrey vs. Clark, *ibid.*, V, 182. Parallel evidence on Godfrey's difficulties with the court came from several witnesses in the case of Godfrey vs. Ela (for defamation) in 1669. James Ordway testified that he had intended to post bond on Godfrey's behalf, "but the matter was made so odious by the Court . . . [that] he would not. . . . The Judge of the Court said he did believe that no man will have the face to appear in this case to be bound for him." Abiel Somerby quoted the same judge as saying, "We shall not take a thousand pounds bond in this case [and] then the voice of the people that stood by was that there should be no bond taken for him, which did discourage those that was intended to be bound for him." See Noble and Cronin, eds., *Records of the Court of Assistants of the Colony of Massachusetts Bay*, III, 155.

44. See *Records and Files of the Quarterly Courts of Essex County, Massachusetts*, IV, 130, 185, 186, 372–73.

45. *Ibid.*, IV, 130, 153. These prosecutions for theft involved incidents in Boston, and were tried in Suffolk County Court. See Noble and Cronin, eds., *Records of the Court of Assistants of the Colony of Massachusetts Bay*, III, 154–55.

46. *Records and Files of the Quarterly Courts of Essex County, Massachusetts*, IV, 132. Similar charges were made against Godfrey—but apparently not prosecuted—a few years later. See *ibid.*, IV, 372–73.

47. *Ibid.*, III, 251, 352; IV, 119.

48. *Ibid.*, III, 352.

49. *Ibid.*, IV, 119.

50. *Ibid.*, IV, 187, 239.

51. *Ibid.*, IV, 152.

52. Depositions from this case are printed in Noble and Cronin, eds., *Records of the Court of Assistants of the Colony of Massachusetts Bay*, III, 154–58.

53. See *ibid.*, III, 155–56.

54. There is, however, an intriguing notation in an almanac belonging to Samuel Sewall of Boston: "1675: July 27, 3. John Godfrey" (see Massachusetts Historical Society, *Collections*, 5th ser., V, 9). Sewall's connection with Godfrey is otherwise undocumented; however, it is tempting to interpret this as a reference to Godfrey's death (or perhaps his burial).

55. There was a prior "indenture" between Godfrey and "Benjamin Thompson of Boston . . . schoolmaster" which spelled out certain particulars. Dated July 3, 1670, this deed granted to Thompson all of Godfrey's estate ("as well this side as beyond seas"), to take effect "immediately after the said Godfrey's decease." The original copy of this document cannot be located, but it is quoted in Sara Loring Bailey, *Historical Sketches of Andover* (Boston, 1880), 54.

56. *Records and Files of the Quarterly Courts of Essex County, Massachusetts*, V, 71, 88, 248ff.

57. Peter Godfrey was born in England in about 1631, came to Massachusetts as a boy, married Mary Browne (daughter of Thomas), spent his entire adult life in the town of Newbury, and died in 1697. He was a "yeoman" of average means. (His estate was inventoried at £252, after his death.) None of these personal data would appear to tilt the case for, or against, the possibility of a blood-relation to John Godfrey. There is, however, one intriguing piece of evidence, which connects the two men in *some* fashion—in the file bearing on the administration of John Godfrey's estate. The court took testimony from Peter and his wife, to the effect that John had been at their house a month before he died and had discussed with them certain particulars of the estate. Peter seems to have initiated the conversation: "Said I to him, 'you may die and leave your things to you know not who.'" Was Peter angling for a legacy—*perhaps* on the basis of kinship? If so, he must have been quite disappointed by the eventual settlement. (See *Records and Files of the Quarterly Courts of Essex County, Massachusetts*, V, 71.) It should be said that this is the only datum showing *close* contact between John and Peter Godfrey; otherwise the evidence is fragmentary and indirect. There is no warrant

whatsoever for inferring a continuous pattern of interaction between the two men; on a day-to-day basis John Godfrey was much more deeply involved with many other people.

58. Of course, there is no way to "prove" such a hypothesis by reference to the usual canons of historical scholarship; certainly there is nothing in the records to suggest that John Godfrey had any overtly homosexual relationships. But, from a *clinical* standpoint, the picture as a whole is indicative. I am indebted to Virginia Demos for suggesting this interpretation, and to Ernest S. Wolf for confirming its plausibility on the basis of long experience in psychoanalytic practice.

59. See *ibid.*, II, 366ff.; IV, 186; IV, 132; V, 88ff.

60. See p. 39.

61. *Records and Files of the Quarterly Courts of Essex County, Massachusetts,* IV, 187, 239.

62. See the deposition by Elizabeth Whitaker, quoted on p. 40. See also the deposition by John Carr and Moses Tyler, November 26, 1661: "John Godfrey came to the house of Job Tyler on a Sabbath day, after afternoon meeting, and demanded a reckoning of said Tyler. The latter said he thought it strange that he should be so earnest, not being a convenient time, and that he would reckon with him in the morning. Whereupon the said Godfrey was in a rage, and said he would take a sudden course," etc. *Ibid.*, II, 328.

63. Deposition by Jonathan Singletary, Suffolk Court Files, V, no. 543.

64. *Records and Files of the Quarterly Courts of Essex County, Massachusetts,* III, 121–22.

65. More than one hundred years ago, the historian Charles W. Upham noted Godfrey's extraordinary contentiousness: "he had more lawsuits, it is probable, than any other man in the colony." See C. W. Upham, *Salem Witchcraft,* 2 vols. (Boston, 1867), I, 436. This judgment is impossible to verify in terms of broad statistical samples; but four of Godfrey's Essex County neighbors have been studied as to the extent of their own activity at court. The results are as follows. Job Tyler appeared in 17 cases overall (7 as plaintiff, 10 as defendant); John Remington, in 7 cases (1 as plaintiff, 6 as defendant); Abraham Whitaker, in 29 cases (6 as plaintiff, 23 as defendant); and William Holdridge, in 3 cases (2 as plaintiff, 1 as defendant). These figures, crude and limited as they are, strongly support the notion that John Godfrey was litigious far beyond prevailing norms.

66. However, at least a few of the female "witches" were similarly detached —as widows, childless women, or whatever. See pp. 74–75.

67. See pp. 86–90, and also pp. 174–77.

68. On this boundary-setting function, see pp. 304–7.

69. The overall scope and predominant forms of geographic mobility in early New England is a subject of some dispute among historians.

Studies such as Darrett Rutman, *Winthrop's Boston* (Chapel Hill, N.C., 1965), John Demos, *A Little Commonwealth* (New York, 1970), Kenneth Lockridge, *A New England Town* (New York, 1970), Philip Greven, *Four Generations* (Ithaca, N.Y., 1970), and Linda Auwers Bissell, "From Generation to Generation," *William and Mary Quarterly,* 3rd ser. XXXI (1974), 79–110, seem in this regard to reach rather different conclusions. My own (revised) impression—based on incomplete studies of towns such as Springfield and Northampton, Massachusetts, and Hampton and Exeter, New Hampshire—is that mobility was extremely high among the settler generation, but dropped off markedly among their descendants. All studies to date agree on one point: namely, the value placed on stable residence, and the normative opposition to moving about.

70. For an excellent study of factional strife in one particular town, see Paul Boyer and Stephen Nissenbaum, *Salem Possessed: The Social Origins of Witchcraft* (Cambridge, Mass., 1974). The relation of such experiences to witchcraft cases is explored at length, below, in Part Four.

Notes to Chapter 3

1. A complete list of these cases, and of the suspects themselves, is presented in Appendix B.
2. *Records of the Particular Court of Connecticut, 1639–1663,* 70.
3. James Fitch to Increase Mather, July 1, 1684, in *The Mather Papers,* 475–76.
4. Cotton Mather, "Another Brand Plucked Out of the Burning, or, More Wonders of the Invisible World," in Burr, ed., *Narratives,* 321.
5. Diary of Noahdiah Russell, in *The New England Historical and Genealogical Register,* VII, 59.
6. See Paul Boyer and Stephen Nissenbaum, *Salem Possessed: The Social Origins of Witchcraft* (Cambridge, Mass., 1974).
7. Boyer and Nissenbaum, eds., *The Salem Witchcraft Papers,* III, 816.
8. *Ibid.,* II, 401.
9. *Ibid.,* I, 122.
10. Note that comparison between different groups of the witches who *are* known (e.g. those who were convicted and executed, those who were tried but acquitted, those who were merely "presented," and those who were suspected but never subject to prosecution at court) reveals no significant difference in most areas of biographical experience.
11. It is not widely understood that the term "witch" could (and did) apply, in premodern times, to men as well as women. This was a matter of language only; it has no bearing on the empirical fact that most actual suspects were women.
12. Among the "grounds for examination of a witch" (as formulated by magistrates in Connecticut) was the following: "If the party suspected

be the son or daughter, the servant or familiar friend, near neighbor or old companion of a known or convicted witch, this [is] also a presumption; for witchcraft is an art that may be learned and conveyed from man to man, and oft it falleth out that a witch dying leaveth some of the aforesaid heirs of her witchcraft." An early copy of this statement (undated) is in the Willys Papers, W-38.

13. Mary Parsons of Springfield, Massachusetts, joined in the prosecution of her husband Hugh; likewise Rebecca Greensmith (of Hartford, Connecticut) with her husband Nathaniel.

14. *Records and Files of the Quarterly Courts of Essex County, Massachusetts,* VII, 357.

15. Noble and Cronin, eds., *Records of the Court of Assistants of the Colony of Massachusetts Bay,* I, 228–29.

16. Connecticut Archives: Crimes and Misdemeanors, 1st ser. (1662–1789), I, part one, leaves 185–86 (Connecticut State Library, Hartford, Conn.).

17. *Records and Files of the Quarterly Courts of Essex County, Massachusetts,* I, 265.

18. The only surviving record of this case is found in the Hampshire County Probate Records, I, leaf 114 (Registry of Probate, Northampton, Mass.).

19. Numerous depositions in this case are in the Willys Papers, W-8, W-9.

20. *Records and Files of the Quarterly Courts of Essex County, Massachusetts,* II, 36–38. The manuscript documents in this case—of which the printed record affords a much condensed version—are in the Essex County Court Papers, III, leaves 108–13.

21. Hoadly, ed., *Records of the Colony or Jurisdiction of New Haven,* II, 224–25; and Dexter, ed., *New Haven Town Records, 1649–1662,* 317–318.

22. *Records and Files of the Quarterly Courts of Essex County, Massachusetts,* IV, 78, 99.

23. On Godfrey, see above, Chapter 2. On Wakeley, see below, Chapter 11.

24. See, e.g., A. D. J. Macfarlane, *Witchcraft in Tudor and Stuart England* (London, 1970); H. C. Erik Midelfort, *Witch Hunting in Southwestern Germany: The Social and Intellectual Foundations* (Stanford, Calif., 1972); E. William Monter, *Witchcraft in France and Switzerland: The Borderlands During the Reformation* (Ithaca, N.Y., 1976).

25. On these "structural" aspects of domestic life in early New England, see John Demos, *A Little Commonwealth* (New York, 1970), ch. 5. See also Richard B. Morris, *Studies in the History of American Law* (New York, 1930), ch. 3.

26. The fullest account of the Hutchinson controversy is found in Emery Battis, *Saints and Sectaries: Anne Hutchinson and the Antinomian Controversy* (Chapel Hill, N.C., 1962).

27. "Proceedings of Excommunication Against Mistress Anne Hibbens of Boston (1640)," in John Demos, ed., *Remarkable Providences: The American Culture, 1600–1760* (New York, 1972), 229. The printed document is a shortened version of a virtual transcript included in a manuscript volume of "Notes on John Cotton's Sermons" by Robert Keayne. The original is in the Massachusetts Historical Society (Boston).

28. Examples of these behaviors can be found scattered through the records of every New England court. See, e.g., *Records and Files of the Quarterly Courts of Essex County Massachusetts*, II, 444; III, 460.

29. *Ibid.*, II, 344, 433.

30. *Ibid.*, VIII, 102–3, 293; Shurtleff and Pulsifer, eds., *Records of the Colony of New Plymouth, in New England*, III, 75; V, 29.

31. As an admittedly extreme example of attacking behavior by women toward men, consider the following case from the records of a court held at Wethersfield, Connecticut, March 2, 1670: "Mary, the wife of John Coultman, and Abigail, the wife of John Betts, being convicted before the court for notorious, lascivious practices, in offering violence to Edward Hall, in pulling down his breeches, and in taking up of his shirt before and behind, and pinning it over his shoulders, and with their hands clapping him on the naked back and on the naked belly, and for pulling down John Lattimore his breeches and drawers, and pulling of him up and down the room by his shirt, and taking up his shirt behind and striking him, and for their lascivious carriages toward Sigismund Ricketts when he was in bed, and their threatening to deal with Andrew Pinson as they did with John Lattimore and Edward Hall, with several lascivious expressions that passed from them in these actions, the court considering these things as they are circumstanced (together with the desire of the General Court that such seasonable and exemplary punishment be inflicted upon such offenders that others may hear and fear) do judge the said Mary Coultman and Abigail Betts forthwith severely punished by whipping on the naked body." Connecticut Colonial Probate Records, III: County Court, 1663–1677, leaf 106 (Connecticut State Library, Hartford, Conn.).

32. See John Demos, "Old Age in Early New England," in Demos and Sarane Boocock, eds., *Turning Points: Historical and Sociological Essays on the Family* (Chicago, 1978), 248–87.

33. Cf. Cotton Mather, *Addresses to Old Men and Young Men and Little Children* (Boston, 1690).

34. See Anne Bradstreet, "The Four Ages of Man," in Jeannine Hensley, ed., *The Works of Anne Bradstreet* (Cambridge, Mass., 1967), 51–63. This poem is one of a very few writings from early America in which "middle age" is mentioned as such.

35. These themes are more fully explored in John Demos, "The Changing

Shape of the Life Cycle in American History," unpublished paper prepared for the Smithsonian Institution's Sixth International Symposium,
"Kin and Communities: The Peopling of America" (1977).

36. Cotton Mather, "A Brand Plucked Out of the Burning," in Burr, ed.,
    Narratives, 270.

37. See pp. 155–56.

38. See pp. 73 and 170–71.

39. Boyer and Nissenbaum, eds., *The Salem Witchcraft Papers*, II, 615,
    617.

40. Deposition by Samuel Clark, in *Provincial Records and Court Papers of
    New Hampshire*, New Hampshire Historical Society, *Collections*, VIII,
    100.

41. Documents from this case are found in the Middlesex Court Files, fold-
    ers 22, 25, papers 1468–1480.

42. See G. C. Bancroft and G. M. Curtis, *A Century of Meriden* (Meriden,
    Conn., 1906), part one, 254–59; and *New Haven Genealogical Maga-
    zine*, IV, 955–58.

43. See court documents in the Willys Papers, W-21, W-22, W-37, W-39.

44. For example, the apparent connection between the convicted witch
    Alice Young (of Windsor, Connecticut) and Alice [Young] Beamon
    (of Springfield, Massachusetts) explored below in Chapter 11, n. 29;
    and the link between Mary [Bliss] Parsons and Peletiah Glover, also
    discussed in Chapter 8, pp. 273–74.

45. On the sons of Lydia Gilbert and their careers subsequent to her trial,
    see Homer Worthington Brainard, Harold Simeon Gilbert, and Clarence
    Almon Torrey, *The Gilbert Family* (New Haven, Conn., 1953), 25ff.

46. On the career of David Lake, see *The American Genealogist*, XII, 20–22.

47. On the career of Erasmus James, Jr., see Winifred L. Holman, "The
    James Family of Marblehead, Massachusetts," unpublished essay
    (1932), in the holdings of the New England Historic Genealogical
    Society (Boston), 7–8.

48. On the children of Mary [Bliss] Parsons, see Albert Ross Parsons, "Par-
    sons Genealogies," in Henry M. Burt, *Cornet Joseph Parsons: One of
    the Founders of Springfield and Northampton, Massachusetts* (Garden
    City, N.Y., 1898), 107ff.

49. Judith Varlet was one of the first persons caught up in the chain of
    witch trials at Hartford, Connecticut in 1662–63. She was strongly im-
    plicated in the "fits" of Ann Cole (the victim who carried on in Dutch),
    and she was also accused by the confessing witch Rebecca Greensmith.
    A letter on her behalf from Gov. Stuyvesant to Gov. John Winthrop, Jr.,
    of Connecticut has been preserved in the Robert C. Winthrop Collec-
    tion, I, no. 1 (Connecticut State Library, Hartford). On other aspects
    of her case, see a letter from John Whiting to Increase Mather, Decem-

ber 4, 1662, in *The Mather Papers*, 466–69; and testimony by Rebecca Greensmith in the Samuel Willys Collection, no. 1.

50. Cotton Mather, "Memorable Providences, Relating to Witchcrafts and Possessions," in Burr, ed., *Narratives*, 103–4.

51. See p. 233.

52. Her first marriage, and the courtship which would lead to her second, were discussed in a letter from William Pynchon to John Winthrop, September 15, 1645. See *The Winthrop Papers*, Massachusetts Historical Society, *Collections*, 4th ser., V, 45–46.

53. For example: John and Elizabeth Blackleach (of Wethersfield, Connecticut) and Margaret Gifford (of Lynn, Massachusetts). Goodwife Batchelor (a suspect, during the 1650s, at Ipswich, Massachusetts) was apparently a Baptist or Quaker.

54. One scholar has concluded that "the English assumed that the devil behind Indian culture was a different and weaker devil than their own." (William Simmons, "Puritan Witchcraft: An Anthropologist's View," unpublished paper, Anthropological Society of Washington [1975], 8.) Cotton Mather once performed an intriguing linguistic experiment while addressing a group of demons which had possessed a woman of his neighborhood. He spoke successively in Latin, Greek, and Hebrew, and was apparently understood each time; but when he tried Natick (the language of a local Indian tribe) "the Daemons did seem as if they did not understand it." (Quoted in *ibid.*, 8.)

55. Rachel Clinton of Ipswich, Massachusetts. (See pp. 31–32.) Mary Parsons of Springfield had been divorced from her first husband, but was remarried at the time of her witchcraft trial.

56. *Records and Files of the Quarterly Courts of Essex County, Massachusetts*, I, 274.

57. *Ibid.*, IV, 90. Further evidence of trouble in the Olivers' marriage is found in *ibid.*, VI, 386.

58. See "Hugh Parsons' Examination," in Drake, *Annals of Witchcraft*, 236, 237, 234.

59. Several depositions on the Dibbles are in the Connecticut Archives: Crimes, Misdemeanors, Divorces, 1st ser., III, leaves 211–13. See also Records of the Colony of Connecticut, LIII, leaf 11 (Connecticut State Library, Hartford).

60. Evidence of disharmony in the marriages of various Salem witches can be found scattered through Boyer and Nissenbaum, eds., *The Salem Witchcraft Papers*. See, e.g., the material on Mary Bradbury (I, 124), George Burroughs (I, 162–63), Sarah Cole (I, 233), Mary Parker (II, 632), and John Willard (III, 842, 844).

61. County Court, Salem: Records, 1667–1679, leaf 13; Essex County Court Papers, XIII, leaf 72; *ibid.*, XV, leaves 102–3.

62. Willys Papers, W–8, W–9.
63. See County Court, Norfolk: Records, 1648–1678, leaf 111 (reverse).
64. See John Demos, *A Little Commonwealth*, 49–50, 137–38.
65. "Declaration of Anne Butler," in *The New England Historical and Genealogical Register*, LXXII, 192.
66. Hoadly, ed., *Records of the Colony or Jurisdiction of New Haven*, II, 29–36, 151–52; Dexter, ed., *New Haven Town Records*, 249–52, 256–257.
67. Middlesex Court Files, folders 22, 25, papers 1468–80.
68. Noble and Cronin, eds., *Records of the Court of Assistants of the Colony of Massachusetts Bay*, I, 188–89; Suffolk Court Files, XXIII, leaf 1958, and XXIV, leaf 1972.
69. Cotton Mather, "Memorable Providences Relating to Witchcrafts and Possessions," in Burr, ed., *Narratives*, 100ff.
70. "Proceedings of Excommunication," in Demos, ed., *Remarkable Providences*, 222–39; Shurtleff, ed., *Records of the Governor and Company of Massachusetts Bay*, IV, part one, 269. Notice of the death of William Hibbens ("one of our honored magistrates," and "a man very serviceable in his place," etc.) is found in the diary of the Boston merchant John Hull; see American Antiquarian Society, *Transactions and Collections*, III, 176.
71. Hampton, New Hampshire, and Wethersfield, Connecticut.
72. *Records and Files of the Quarterly Courts of Essex County, Massachusetts*, I, 75–184; III, 21–227. *Records of the Suffolk County Court*, in Colonial Society of Massachusetts, *Collections*, XXIX, 31–194. *Records of the Particular Court of Connecticut, 1639–1663*, 77–159. Joseph H. Smith, ed., *Colonial Justice in Western Massachusetts, 1639–1702: The Pynchon Court Record* (Cambridge, Mass., 1961), 221–310.
73. The culprit was Mrs. Hibbens. See "Proceedings of Excommunication," in Demos, ed., *Remarkable Providences*, 234.
74. Barbara Ehrenreich and Deirdre English, "Witches, Midwives, and Nurses: A History of Women Healers" (Glass Mountain Pamphlets, Oyster Bay, N.Y., n.d.); Mary Nelson, "Why Witches Were Women," in Jo Freeman, ed., *Women: A Feminist Perspective* (Palo Alto, Calif., 1975), 335–50; Thomas R. Forbes, *The Midwife and the Witch* (New Haven, Conn., 1966).
75. Jane Hawkins of Boston and Hannah Jones of Portsmouth.
76. Depositions by Hopestill Austin and Elizabeth Pearson, in Suffolk Court Files, XIII, leaf 1228.
77. For example, Winifred Holman (of Cambridge) and Elizabeth Garlick (of Easthampton). See Middlesex Court Files, folders 22, 25, papers 1468–1480; and *Records of the Town of Easthampton, Long Island, Suffolk County, N.Y.*, 5 vols. (Sag Harbor, N.Y., 1887–92), I, 134–35.

78. Testimony by Mrs. Jane Sewall, in the trial of Elizabeth Morse; see Drake, *Annals of Witchcraft*, 281.

79. Keith Thomas, *Religion and the Decline of Magic* (New York, 1971), chs. 7–8; A. D. J. Macfarlane, *Witchcraft in Tudor and Stuart England* (London, 1970), ch. 8.

80. Deposition by Margaret Mirack, in the trial of Elizabeth Morse; see Drake, *Annals of Witchcraft*, 287. Research for the present study has uncovered only one other instance when the term was used (also as a kind of epithet): "Mrs. Turner, questioning him about [a dispute between neighbors over property], he told her she was a cunning woman." See Hoadly, ed., *Records of the Colony or Jurisdiction of New Haven*, II, 258.

81. See her testimony in an Essex County court case of 1680; *Records and Files of the Quarterly Courts of Essex County, Massachusetts*, VII, 395.

82. *Ibid.*, II, 226–28, 231; V, 55; VI, 180.

83. *Ibid.*, II, 227.

84. Depositions by Goody Bishop and Goody Birdsall, in *Records of the Town of Easthampton*, I, 134–35.

85. Deposition by "the wife of Jacob Johnson," in the trial of Katherine Harrison; Willys Papers, W-16.

86. Cotton Mather, "Another Brand Plucked Out of the Burning," in Burr, ed., *Narratives*, 311.

87. "A Relation of the Passages Between Mrs. Holman and Her Daughter Mary and the Wife of Charles Stearns," in Middlesex Court Files, folder 25, paper 1477.

88. Deposition by Hannah Weacome, in the trial of Mary Hale; Suffolk Court Files, XXIV, no. 1972.

89. Deposition by Mary Godfrey, in the trial of Rachel Fuller; see Bouton, ed., *Documents and Records Relating to the Province of New Hampshire*, I, 416. The same episode was described by John Godfrey (Mary's husband) in a separate deposition; *ibid.*, I, 418.

90. See Hosmer, ed., *Winthrop's Journal*, II, 344–45.

91. On the Burts' arrival in New England, see Charles E. Banks, *The Planters of the Commonwealth* (repr. Baltimore, Md., 1972), 164. Details of their subsequent career can be found scattered through *Records and Files of the Quarterly Courts of Essex County, Massachusetts*; see, e.g., I, 9, 10, 12, 14, 56, 64, 81, 101, 135, 172, 209, 284; II, 124, 250, 269, 270, 282, 329–30, 387, 401. Ann Burt's will and inventory is in *ibid.*, V, 203–4.

92. Deposition by Madeleine Pearson, in Essex County Court Papers, XV, leaf 63; depositions by Jacob Knight and Bethiah Carter, in *Records and Files of the Quarterly Courts of Essex County, Massachusetts*, IV, 207–8.

93. Two recent discussions of this pattern are T. H. Breen and Stephen

Foster, "Moving to the New World: The Character of Early Massachusetts Immigration," in *William and Mary Quarterly*, 3rd ser., XXX, 189–222; and David Grayson Allen, *In English Ways: The Movement of Societies and the Transferal of English Local Law and Custom to Massachusetts Bay in the Seventeenth Century* (Chapel Hill, N.C., 1981), ch. 6.

94. Records of litigation involving Wakeley are in *Records of the Particular Court of Connecticut, 1639–1663, passim.*

95. See *ibid., passim.*

96. Connecticut Colonial Probate Records, III: County Court, 1663–1677, leaves 78–81, 118 (Connecticut State Library, Hartford).

97. *Records and Files of the Quarterly Courts of Essex County, Massachusetts*, IV, 31, 37; V, 19, 43, 398, 423; VI, 10, 16; XII, 339–40; VIII, 113.

98. "Proceedings of Excommunication," in Demos, ed., *Remarkable Providences*, 222–39.

99. William Hubbard, *A General History of New England* (repr. Boston, 1848), 574.

100. Testimony by Elizabeth Bennett, at the examination of Mercy Disborough; Willys Papers, W-33.

101. Testimony by Blanche Bedortha, at the examination of Hugh Parsons; Drake, *Annals of Witchcraft*, 224.

102. Complaint by Susannah Trimmings, in the trial of Jane Walford; see Bouton, ed., *Documents and Records Relating to the Province of New Hampshire*, I, 217.

103. Testimony by Goody Thorp, in the trial of Elizabeth Godman; see Dexter, ed., *New Haven Town Records*, 250.

104. Testimony by Thomas Bennett, at the examination of Mercy Disborough; Willys Papers, W-33.

105. Testimony by Samuel Marshfield, at the examination of Hugh Parsons; Drake, *Annals of Witchcraft*, 250.

106. Deposition by Thomas Philbrick, in the trial of Eunice Cole; see Massachusetts Archives, CXXXV, no. 2.

107. Testimony by Goodwife Prince, in the trial of William Browne; Essex County Court Papers, III, leaf 110.

108. Testimony by Abigail Westcott, in the trial of Elizabeth Clawson; Willys Papers, W-29.

109. Testimony by Mr. Hooke, at the examination of Elizabeth Godman, in Hoadley, ed., *Records of the Colony or Jurisdiction of New Haven*, II, 31; testimony by David Wheeler, in the trial of Elizabeth Morse, in Drake, *Annals of Witchcraft*, 286; deposition by Hannah Weacome, in the trial of Mary Hale, Suffolk Court Files, XXIV, no. 1972.

110. See Cotton Mather, *Magnalia Christi Americana*, 2 vols. (2nd ed., Hartford, Conn., 1853), II, 456.

111. "The Declaration of Katharine Harrison, in Her Appeal to the Court of Assistants," in Connecticut Archives: Crimes and Misdemeanors, 1st ser. (1662–1789), I, part one, no. 34–a.
112. Statement by Hugh Parsons, at his examination, in Drake, *Annals of Witchcraft*, 234.
113. Deposition by Charles Browne, in the trial of John Godfrey; Suffolk Court Files, II, no. 322.
114. Deposition by Thomas Cooper, in the trial of Hugh Parsons; Drake, *Annals of Witchcraft*, 245.
115. *Records and Files of the Quarterly Courts of Essex County, Massachusetts*, IV, 99.
116. Deposition by Goodwife Garrett, in the trial of Elizabeth Seager; Willys Papers, W-4.
117. Testimony by Mr. Hooke, at the examination of Elizabeth Godman, in Hoadly, ed., *Records of the Colony or Jurisdiction of New Haven*, II, 31.
118. Testimony by Mrs. Goodyear; *ibid.*, II, 34.
119. Testimony by Mary Parsons, at the examination of Hugh Parsons; Drake, *Annals of Witchcraft*, 233–34.
120. Deposition by Mary Dunkin, in the trial of Alice Stratton (for slander), Middlesex Court Files, folder 2; report of the jury, in the trial of Elizabeth Seager, Willys Papers, W–2; depositions by Rebecca Hill, Deborah Lockwood, and Bethiah Brundish, in the case of Ludlow vs. Staples (defamation), in Hoadly, ed., *Records of the Colony or Jurisdiction of New Haven*, II, 83.
121. See, for example, the will of John Smith of Martha's Vineyard (Massachusetts), in Charles E. Banks, *The History of Martha's Vineyard*, 2 vols. (Boston, 1911), II, 112; and also the will of John Thorndike of Beverly (Massachusetts), in *Probate Records of Essex County, Massachusetts*, II, 206–7.
122. For example, the case of Alice and John Eaton of Dedham, Massachusetts, 1684, in Massachusetts Archives, IX, leaf 106; and also that of John and Frances Hutchinson of Haverhill, Massachusetts, 1685, in *ibid.*, IX, leaf 116.
123. Deposition by John Osgood of Andover, Massachusetts, in *Records and Files of the Quarterly Courts of Essex County, Massachusetts*, VI, 229. There are similar cases in Middlesex Court Files, folder 33, paper 2187; Hoadly, ed., *Records of the Colony or Jurisdiction of New Haven*, II, 300; and County Court, Norfolk: Records, 1648–1678, leaf 70.
124. County Court Records, New Haven County, I, leaf 148 (Connecticut State Library, Hartford, Conn.).
125. County Court, Norfolk: Records, 1648–1678, leaf 86 (reverse).
126. If there is any exception to this general statement, it is found in the case of Mary Parsons of Springfield (Massachusetts). Goodwife Parsons

does seem to have experienced extreme depression, and some "distraction," over the deaths of her two infant children. She was, in fact, charged with causing one of those deaths. But her criminal conviction was for murder; she was simultaneously acquitted of practicing witchcraft. See the various testimonies, by and about her, included as part of her husband's examination, in Drake, *Annals of Witchcraft*, 219–58.

127. Deposition by David Wheeler, in the trial of Elizabeth Morse; Drake, *Annals of Witchcraft*, 261.

128. See above, Chapter 2.

129. "Proceedings of Excommunication," in Demos, ed., *Remarkable Providences*, 222–39.

130. See above, n. 96.

131. See Hampshire County Probate Records, I, leaves 158–60.

132. Willys Papers, W-19.

133. *Ibid.*, W-19.

134. John Hale, "A Modest Enquiry into the Nature of Witchcraft," in Burr, ed., *Narratives*, 408; Hosmer, ed., *Winthrop's Journal*, II, 345.

135. Deposition by Mary Dunkin, in the trial of Alice Stratton (for slander); Middlesex Court Files, folder 2.

136. See the depositions in Staples vs. Ludlow; Hoadly, ed., *Records of the Colony or Jurisdiction of New Haven*, II, 84–88.

Notes to Chapter 4

1. For a case in point, see Cotton Mather's "treatment" of Martha Goodwin, as described in his "Memorable Providences, Relating to Witchcrafts and Possessions," reprinted in Burr, ed., *Narratives*, 110ff.

2. See, for example, John Whiting, "An Account of a Remarkable Passage of Divine Providence that Happened in Hartford, in the Year of our Lord 1662," in *The Mather Papers*, 466–69; and letter from John Russell to Increase Mather, August 2, 1683, in *ibid.*, 86–88.

3. Increase Mather, "An Essay for the Recording of Illustrious Providences," partially reprinted in Burr, ed., *Narratives*, 8–38.

4. This document was first published in *The Mather Papers*, 555–70. It has been twice reprinted: in Samuel A. Green, *Groton in the Witchcraft Times* (Groton, Mass., 1883), 7–21; and in John Demos, ed., *Remarkable Providences* (New York, 1972), 358–71. The original manuscript is currently in the Boston Public Library, Boston, Mass.

5. See Burr, ed., *Narratives*, 21–23.

6. The case is cited in Cotton Mather's famous work of the early eighteenth century, *Magnalia Christi Americana* 2 vols. (2nd ed., Hartford, Conn., 1853), II, 449–50.

7. See Demos, ed., *Remarkable Providences*, 358.

8. In describing Elizabeth's first severe fits (November 1–2) Willard made

reference to "those few weeks that she had dwelt with us." See *ibid.*, 360.

9. *Ibid.*, 358.
10. *Ibid.*, 364.
11. *Ibid.*, 359.
12. *Ibid.*, 362.
13. *Ibid.*, 367.
14. *Ibid.*, 367.
15. *Ibid.*, 359.
16. *Ibid.*, 359.
17. *Ibid.*, 361, 367.
18. *Ibid.*, 370.
19. *Ibid.*, 359.
20. *Ibid.*, 361.
21. *Ibid.*, 362.
22. *Ibid.*, 362.
23. *Ibid.*, 364
24. *Ibid.*, 361.
25. See pp. 108–9.
26. Demos, ed., *Remarkable Providences*, 362.
27. *Ibid.*, 361, 363–64.
28. *Ibid.*, 363.
29. *Ibid.*, 361.
30. *Ibid.*, 366.
31. *Ibid.*, 367.
32. *Ibid.*, 360.
33. *Ibid.*, 360.
34. *Ibid.*, 359.
35. *Ibid.*, 363.
36. *Ibid.*, 363.
37. *Ibid.*, 363.
38. *Ibid.*, 361.
39. *Ibid.*, 360.
40. *Ibid.*, 360.
41. *Ibid.*, 360.
42. *Ibid.*, 361.
43. *Ibid.*, 359.
44. See p. 107.
45. Demos, ed., *Remarkable Providences*, 359–60.
46. *Ibid.*, 361.
47. *Ibid.*, 361.
48. *Ibid.*, 362.
49. *Ibid.*, 362.
50. *Ibid.*, 362–63.

51. *Ibid.*, 365.
52. *Ibid.*, 363. Elizabeth described this episode as having occurred "when she lived at Lancaster"—which was also the home (after about 1665) of Major Simon Willard (Samuel's father). It seems a reasonable inference that she was at the time a servant in the elder Willard's household.
53. *Ibid.*, 364.
54. *Ibid.*, 366.
55. *Ibid.*, 365.
56. *Ibid.*, 365–66.
57. *Ibid.*, 366–67.
58. *Ibid.*, 367.
59. *Ibid.*, 368.
60. *Ibid.*, 368–69.
61. *Ibid.*, 369.
62. *Ibid.*, 369.
63. *Ibid.*, 369–70.
64. The fullest account of William Knapp's life is found in a set of typescript materials compiled by Alfred Averill Knapp, "William Knapp and Some of His Descendants: A Genealogy," currently in the possession of the New England Historic Genealogical Society, Boston, Mass. This compilation is not, however, altogether trustworthy as to details, and should be checked against primary records wherever possible. On William Knapp's children, insofar as they are known, see chart in the text, "Knapp-Warren Genealogy."
65. *Watertown Records,* 5 vols. (Watertown, Mass., 1894–1907), I, part one, 24, 25, 29, 30.
66. Order of the Court of Assistants, held at Boston, December 5, 1643, as noted in Noble and Cronin, eds., *Records of the Court of Assistants of the Colony of Massachusetts Bay,* II, 136.
67. The estate of William Knapp, inventoried on August 31, 1658, was assessed to a total value of £129. The manuscript inventory is in Probate Records of Middlesex County, I, 227–28 (Registry of Probates and Deeds, Middlesex County, East Cambridge, Mass.).
68. Shurtleff, ed., *Records of the Governor and Company of Massachusetts Bay,* I, 133, 199, 318. These offenses were all tried before the General Court of the Bay Colony. On a later occasion Knapp was convicted, by the quarterly court of Middlesex County, for "unseemly speeches," and made to sit in the town stocks as punishment. A few still extant depositions suggest that Knapp's personal style was particularly rough and abrasive. For example, he had belittled the local schoolmaster for want of discipline in the classroom, saying "he had no more power over his scholars than a dog." (With specific reference to *one* scholar, Knapp averred that "if he were in the [master's] room, he would whip the asshole of the boy.") Similarly, he had on numerous occasions called a

neighbor "a base slave and lying slave," and said "he would hew down his fence." According to the court, William Knapp, "acknowledged the substance" of all this. (See Records of the Middlesex County Court, I [1649–1663], leaf 8, and depositions by Richard Norcross and Robert Daniel, in Middlesex Court Files, folder 3; Clerk's Office, Middlesex County Court, East Cambridge, Mass.)

69. See Alfred Averill Knapp, "William Knapp and Some of His Descendants." William Knapp's estate was the object of repeated attention in the courts for at least five years after his death. The official "division" of his property was made on April 15, 1660, but the administrators were changed both before and after that date. Certain of the court orders hint at conflict among his heirs; for example, on October 5, 1658 the constable of Watertown was ordered to deliver to widow Knapp "her chest . . . and other necessary household utensils which John Knapp by attachment hath detained from her." (John Knapp was one of William's sons.) On these matters, see Records of the Middlesex County Court, I, leaves 139, 140, 149, 151, 153, 231.

70. See Alfred Averill Knapp, "William Knapp and Some of His Descendants."

71. Records of the Middlesex County Court, I, leaf 225.

72. Court session of June 19, 1656, as noted in *ibid.*, I, leaf 84.

73. The problems raised by the birth of this child are noted, first, in the records of the General Court (May 14, 1656), and subsequently in the town records of Watertown. Since the child was an orphan, special arrangements were made for his/her care by foster-parents; in fact, four different arrangements were required within the space of a year and a half. See Shurtleff, ed., *Records of the Governor and Company of Massachusetts Bay*, III, 403–4; and IV, part one, 262–63; *Watertown Records*, I, part one, 46, 47, 48, 51, 53, 54. Of Mary Davis herself, the following biographical data has been gleaned from New England source materials. She was born Mary Spring, in about the year 1623. She was the eldest child of John and Elinor Spring, who were settled in Watertown by 1634. She married one John Davis in about 1642, and bore a daughter—also named Mary—on March 20, 1643. She probably had a son, John Davis, Jr. (whose presence in Watertown is noted as late as 1679), though in this case a definite relationship cannot be established. Her husband apparently died within a few years of their marriage. Her illegitimate child was born at some point in the spring of 1656; the vital records do not supply the exact date. The daughter Mary was sent, after 1656, to live as a maidservant in the household of her uncle Henry Spring. (She herself bore an out-of-wedlock child in 1665—who, in turn, was raised by foster-parents.) On these various points, see Henry Bond, *Genealogies of the Families and Descendants of the Early Settlers of Watertown, Massachusetts* (2nd ed., Boston, 1860), 197, 441,

752; *Watertown Records*, I, part one, 87, 129; and Davis vs. Phillips, manuscript depositions (September 3, 1666) in Middlesex Court Files, folder 42. The most intriguing question, from the standpoint of the present study, involves the later disposition of the child born to widow Davis in 1656 (and allegedly fathered by James Knapp). Was he/she (the sex is nowhere indicated) raised at Watertown, during the same period when Elizabeth Knapp was growing up there? Unfortunately, the extant data do not provide an answer.

74. At its hearing on June 19, 1656 the court ordered a bond of £40 taken from James Knapp, to guarantee "his appearance at the next County Court to be held at Cambridge in October next." (See Records of the Middlesex County Court, I, leaf 84.) The records from the October session, however, make no mention of the case. The fact of indictment —and, possibly, a trial—at the county level is itself puzzling; as a capital crime, adultery would normally fall within the jurisdiction of the Court of Assistants (the highest judicial authority in the colony). It seems safe to assume that Knapp was *not* convicted, since otherwise he would have incurred some form of disabling penalty (if not death itself). Perhaps his case was set aside for lack of sufficient evidence, short of a full-fledged prosecution. Or perhaps he was tried and acquitted before the Court of Assistants (from which records, covering this period, have largely been lost).

75. Court session of April 7, 1657; see Records of the Middlesex County Court, I, leaf 106.

76. More specifically, James Knapp was fined for inadequate restraint of hogs, by town order, April 9, 1657, see *Watertown Records*, I, part one, 53.

77. No less than seven separate acts of theft were charged against John Knapp. See court session of April 7, 1657; Records of the Middlesex County Court, I, leaf 103. Depositions in this case are in Middlesex Court Files, folder 18.

78. Court order of December 30, 1656, as noted in Records of the Middlesex County Court, I, leaf 98.

79. *Watertown Records*, I, part one, 73. This transaction suggests that James Knapp may have followed his father's trade of carpentry—implying, as it does, that he constructed (or repaired) the local stocks.

80. On a list of "acre rights" accruing to the original settlers, James Knapp is down for 15 acres. This places him near the middle of the entire group (51 persons). The tax-rate of 1681 shows the names of 73 householders—24 of whom are assessed higher than Knapp, and 48 lower. See Samuel A. Green, ed., *The Early Records of Groton, Massachusetts, 1662–1707* (Groton, Mass., 1880), 50, 65.

81. *Ibid.*, 14, 17 23, 27, 30, 40, 42, 47, 49, 53, 57, 58, 64, and *passim*.

82. *Ibid.*, 10, 12, 16, 20, 30, 31, 38, 39, 40, 41, 42, 45, 46, 49, 51, 53, 59, 64.

83. *Ibid.*, 46, 64.
84. Her baptism on July 21, 1629 is recorded in the parish register of Nayland, county Suffolk; see *New England Historical and Genealogical Register*, LXIV (1908), 353.
85. The will of John Warren's father and the baptismal records of his children are printed in *ibid.*, LXIV (1908), 348–50, 353ff. His prosecution for religious non-conformity is mentioned in J. Gardner Bartlett, *Gregory Stone Genealogy* (Boston, 1918), 43.
86. John Warren's lands are listed in *Watertown Records*, I, second part, 100. By the end of his life Warren's wealth had apparently shrunk somewhat; his estate was inventoried at a relatively modest level of £177. Manuscript copies of his will and inventory are in Probate Records of Middlesex County, no. 23682 (Registry of Probates and Deeds, Middlesex County, East Cambridge, Mass.).
87. Warren was selectman of Watertown in 1636, and again in 1640. In 1635 he and Abraham Brown (another leader among the settler-group) were appointed to lay out all the highways in the town. See *Watertown Records*, I, part one, 2, 5, 6, 12, 14.
88. In October 1651 Warren was convicted of offenses against the laws concerning baptism. In April 1653, and again in June 1654, he was fined for frequent absences from public worship. In March 1659 he was to be warned for further neglect of public worship, but the constable reported that "old Warren is not to be found in town." See Records of the Middlesex County Court, I, leaves 26, 37, 38; also Bond, *Genealogies of the Families and Descendants of the Early Settlers of Watertown, Mass.*, 619.
89. In May 1661 Warren's was one of two Watertown houses ordered searched for Quakers; see *ibid.*, 619.
90. *Watertown Records*, I, part three, 17.
91. See the diary of John Hull, as printed in American Antiquarian Society, *Transactions and Collections*, III, 192.
92. There were three other adult women of this surname in eastern Massachusetts during the period in question: Elizabeth [Warren] Knapp's mother-in-law and two of her sisters-in-law. But all three seem to have been in good possession of their faculties. The preoccupation of Hull's "troublesome . . . woman" with Quakers also seems suggestive—since John Warren (Elizabeth's father) was a known Quaker sympathizer, and had attracted the attention of local authorities on that account. There is, moreover, an interesting bequest in Warren's will (of some ten years later): "I give to my . . . daughter Elizabeth [Knapp] a book called The Plain Man's Pathway to Heaven." See Probate Records of Middlesex County, no. 23682.
93. See above, nn. 8 and 52.
94. Demos, ed., *Remarkable Providences*, 360.

95. See Lucius R. Paige, *History of Cambridge, Massachusetts, 1630–1877* (Boston, 1877), 652.

96. Green, ed., *The Early Records of Groton, Massachusetts, 1662–1707*, 43.

97. *Ibid.*, 66. Samuel Scripture's name follows that of James Knapp, on the rate-list of 1681. This suggests that the two lived on adjoining lots—perhaps Knapp had given some of his own land to his son-in-law—or (less likely) that they shared a single household.

98. *Ibid.*, 65, 82, 96, 114, 118.

99. Scripture's name is included on a list of soldiers in the war, published in *New England Historical and Genealogical Register*, XLI (1885), 409. See also *ibid.*, XLIII (1887), 277.

100. *Vital Records of Groton, Massachusetts* (Salem, Mass., 1916), I, 212–213.

101. *Ibid.*, I, 212–13.

102. This biographical summary draws heavily on material in Seymour Van Dyken, *Samuel Willard, 1640–1707: Preacher of Orthodoxy in an Era of Change* (Grand Rapids, Mich., 1972).

103. As a result, there is a useful description of Willard's life and career in John Langdon Sibley, *Biographical Sketches of the Graduates of Harvard University*, II (Cambridge, Mass., 1881), 13–36.

104. Van Dyken, *Samuel Willard, 1640–1707*, 26–27.

105. Abigail [Sherman] Willard was a daughter of the Rev. John Sherman, pastor at Watertown. After her death in 1676 Willard married Eunice Tyng, the daughter of a leading Boston merchant and magistrate. He had six children by his first wife, and fourteen by his second. Names and birth-dates of Willard children can be found in Charles H. Pope, *Willard Genealogy*, I (Boston, 1915).

106. See Van Dyken, *Samuel Willard, 1640–1707*, 33–37.

107. The Third Church had its beginning, in 1669, as the result of a secession by a "liberal" faction within the First Church of Boston. On this point, see Richard Simmons, "The Founding of the Third Church in Boston," *William and Mary Quarterly*, 3rd ser., XXVI (1969), 241–52. In 1679 Samuel Willard was a leader in the so-called "reforming synod" of New England clergymen; see Van Dyken, 38–39 and *passim*. The rivalry between Increase Mather and Willard—"the one puristically inclined, the other leaning toward moderation"—is explored in David D. Hall, *The Faithful Shepherd: A History of the New England Ministry in the Seventeenth Century* (Chapel Hill, N.C., 1972), 195ff.

108. Ebenezer Pemberton, *A Funeral Sermon on the Death of that Learned and Excellent Divine, The Reverend Mr. Samuel Willard* (Boston, 1707), 63.

109. Demos, ed., *Remarkable Providences*, 370–71.

110. In technical language: "The essence of conversion is the shifting or

displacement of psychic energy from the cathexis of mental processes to that of somatic innervations in order for the latter to express in a distorted way the derivatives of repressed forbidden wishes." (Leo Rangell, "The Nature of Conversion," *Journal of the American Psychoanalytic Association*, VII [1959], 636). Conversion was an organizing concept of major importance in the development of modern psychiatry. Many of the classic cases studied by Charcot, Janet, and Freud featured conversion symptoms of one sort or another, and almost invariably such symptoms were associated with the nosological category of "hysterias." However, recent studies have questioned this association, in the face of much evidence that non-hysteric patients are also subject to conversion experiences. (See, for example, Paul Chodoff and Henry Lyons, "Hysteria, the Hysterical Personality, and 'Hysterical' Conversion," in *American Journal of Psychiatry*, CXIV [1958], 734–40.) There is the additional problem that the term "hysteria" has been so widely and loosely applied that its meaning is now quite elastic—not to say, confused. Thus the discussion in this chapter avoids the term altogether. Nonetheless some of the earlier writings on hysteria do have a certain resonance to the material at hand. Consider the following summary of major elements in the "hysterical character" as presented in the work of Wilhelm Reich: "a compulsive need to be loved and admired; intense feelings of inadequacy, which may be conscious or unconscious; a strong dependency on the approval of others for self-esteem; a powerful capacity for dramatization and somatic compliance; and a tendency to repress aggressive feelings or attitudes, or to act them out in concealed ways." (Judd Marmor, "Orality in the Hysterical Personality," *Journal of the American Psychoanalytic Association*, I [1953], 657–58.) There are clear points of contact between this general overview and the symptomatic picture evinced in the case of Elizabeth Knapp.

111. Although this account of the dynamic process in conversion survives in recent and revisionist work, there are changed views as to the range of underlying impulse and affect. It was formerly thought that conversion derives exclusively from sexual conflicts; now, however, most writers accord equal consideration to the role of repressed aggression. See, for example, Paul Chodoff, "A Re-examination of Some Aspects of Conversion Hysteria," in *Psychiatry*, XVII (1954), 75–81; Rangell, "The Nature of Conversion," 655ff.; and Samuel Silverman, "The Role of the Aggressive Drives in the Conversion Process," in Felix Deutsch, ed., *On the Mysterious Leap from the Mind to the Body: A Workshop Study on the Theory of Conversion* (New York, 1959), 110–30.

112. Here, too, one encounters the marked impact of recent revisionism. According to classical psychoanalytic theory, "hysterical conversion" is invariably associated with fixations in the "genital" stage. But opinions have changed to such an extent that one writer can now state flatly:

"All conversion is . . . pre-genital by nature." (Melitta Sperling, "Conversion Hysteria and Conversion Symptoms: A Revision of Classification and Concepts," *Journal of the American Psychoanalytic Association,* XXI [1973], 769.) On the profoundly "regressive" nature of the conversion process, see Rangell, "The Nature of Conversion," 652–53. Marmor's important article, published in 1953, argues the special significance of oral conflicts in the genesis of conversion symptoms. In his view the developmental history of most patients with such symptoms reveals either "intense frustration of oral-receptive needs as a consequence of defection or rejection by one or both parent figures, or excessive gratification of these needs . . ." (Marmor, "Orality in the Hysterical Personality," 662).

113. The developmental significance of projection and introjection has been presented most fully in the work of the "English school" of child analysis. See, for example, Paula Heimann, "A Combination of Defense Mechanisms in Paranoid States"; Hans A. Thorner, "Three Defenses Against Inner Persecution"; and Joan Riviere, "The Unconscious Phantasy of an Inner World Reflected in Examples From Literature," in Melanie Klein *et al., New Directions in Psychoanalysis* (London, 1955), 240–65, 282–306, 346–69. Also: Paula Heimann, "Certain Functions of Introjection and Projection in Early Infancy," in Melanie Klein *et al., Developments in Psychoanalysis* (London, 1952), 122–68. For a slightly different view of these matters, see Anna Freud, *The Ego and the Mechanisms of Defense* (rev. ed., New York, 1966), 43–44, 51–52, 113–23.

114. See John C. Whitehorn, "The Concept of 'Meaning' and 'Cause' in Psychodynamics," *American Journal of Psychiatry,* CIV (1947), 289–292.

115. Demos, ed., *Remarkable Providences,* 369.

116. The standard psychoanalytic view of "secondary gains" is presented in Otto Fenichel, *The Psychoanalytic Theory of Neurosis* (New York, 1945), 126ff., 461ff.

117. On this point, see Frederick J. Ziegler, John B. Imboden, and Eugene Meyer, "Contemporary Conversion Reactions: A Clinical Study," in *American Journal of Psychiatry,* CXVI (1960), 901–9. Ziegler and his co-authors note that the most common conversion symptom simulating organic illness is simple pain. They argue, further, that present-day patients who evince "the classical symptoms of 'loss of function' or 'hystero-epilepsy' . . . are apt to come from comparatively backward rural areas, where there is cultural acceptance of these symptoms," while more "sophisticated" patients (also subject to conversion) "expertly simulate complicated disease entities." Thus they conclude that "symptom patterns change with changing medical knowledge of the patient and of his cultural milieu."

118. This denial (or shifting) of responsibility is, in fact, an aspect of most "conversion" symptomatology. Ziegler *et al.* make the following argument: "Phenomenologically, conversion reactions in general enable the patient to avoid or reduce affective distress by substituting fantasy-endowed and symbolically expressive somatic distress or dysfunction. In this way, an intolerable affective problem may apparently be 'converted' into a face-saving physical-medical one, in which the patient shifts the responsibility for remedial action from himself to others, including the physician" (*ibid.*, 905).

119. See, for example, Josef Breuer and Sigmund Freud, *Studies in Hysteria* (1895), in James Strachey, ed., *The Standard Edition of the Complete Psychological Works of Sigmund Freud*, 24 vols. (London, 1953–74), II; and Sigmund Freud, "Fragment of an Analysis of a Case of Hysteria" (1905), in *ibid.*, V, 7–122. There is a useful essay by Felix Deutsch and Elvin V. Semrad, "Survey of Freud's Writings on the Conversion Symptom," in Deutsch, ed., *On the Mysterious Leap from the Mind to the Body*, 27–46.

120. On the traditional psychoanalytic view of "anxiety hysteria," see Fenichel, *The Psychoanalytic Theory of Neurosis*, 193–215.

121. Consumers of recent clinical and theoretical writings in psychoanalysis will recognize a heavy indebtedness, throughout the discussion of this case, to the work of Heinz Kohut and his colleagues at The Institute for Psychoanalysis in Chicago. On the distinction between libidinal and narcissistic transferences, see Kohut, *The Analysis of the Self* (New York, 1971), 18–24ff. and *passim*.

122. Viewed from a developmental perspective, the sequence is roughly as follows. The infant "self" (once it has achieved some degree of cohesion and stability) is, at first, inherently "grandiose"; it presumes its own monopoly of power, beauty, and all imaginable "good." Other persons within its social field are experienced as extensions of self, and expected to perform a simple "mirroring" function. Gradually, however, reality intervenes and the self is obliged to relinquish this narrow view of its own grandeur. It accepts and accommodates this disappointment by investing the same qualities of omnipotence, omniscience, and the like in an "object" figure (usually the representation of a parent)—to which it claims an intrinsic connection. It must be emphasized that even in the latter case there is no true "object relationship" (i.e. where the other is perceived as an independent source of initiative, and "cathected" with emotional interest); thus the narcissistically significant others are designated "self-objects." See Kohut, *ibid.*, 32ff. and *passim*.

123. Demos, ed., *Remarkable Providences*, 371. There is a case-report in Sperling, "Conversion Hysteria and Conversion Symptoms" (see especially p. 755), which bears comparison with this feature of the data on Elizabeth Knapp. In the transference the patient (called "Mrs. A")

displayed "deep resentment and distrust of her mother . . . which had been covered up by an attitude of idealization and overattachment." Moreover, Sperling notes that "feelings of loneliness, [of] emptiness, of impending doom . . . and fears of giving in to self-destructive impulses . . . were prominent in the analysis." These latter feelings seem analogous to the experience of Elizabeth Knapp during her periods of intermission.

124. There are at least intimations of sexual feeling in the episode when the Devil spoke from inside Elizabeth. Having blackened Willard ("you black rogue," etc.), she—or, rather, her Devil—said, "I am a pretty black boy [and] this is my pretty girl"; and also, "you had better love me." See p. 109.

125. See Kohut, *The Analysis of the Self*, 67, 97–98.

126. Again Sperling's patient, "Mrs. A.", makes an interesting point of comparison ("Conversion Hysteria and Conversion Symptoms," 757). The technical name for this symptom is aphonia; it was part of the clinical picture reported by Freud in the famous case of "Dora." (Sigmund Freud, "Fragment of an Analysis of a Case Hysteria," in Strachey, ed., *The Standard Edition of the Complete Psychological Works of Sigmund Freud*, V, 22–24, 39–41.) Freud, as Sperling remarks, "only pointed to the libidinal aspects of this symptom," yet "the destructive aspects" are often of even greater significance. Returning once more to Elizabeth Knapp, we should note her feeling "when she was taken speechless . . . as if a string was tied about the roots of her tongue, and reached down into her vitals." (See p. 101.) This metaphor implies a belief that her powers of speech were directly linked to the "badness" deep inside her—and thus must be restrained at all costs. Recall, too, that words *did* come forth from Elizabeth—and with no apparent difficulty—when the Devil had "possessed" her directly.

127. Dogs have long played a distinctive and lively role in the human unconscious. For all their reputation as "man's best friend," they serve as well to represent some deeply *unfriendly* tendencies. Many children, for example, pass through a stage of being much afraid of dogs, and the significance of this barking, biting animal as a projection of their own (repressed) anger is a psychological commonplace. Elizabeth Knapp does not show fear of dogs; instead, she becomes a dog—just as she would later become (temporarily) a Devil. Note that her dog-like behavior is alternated with imitations of another, quite different animal, i.e. "bleating like a calf." The latter, perhaps, is a representation of her dependent-receptive wish—the desire to take in sustenance (milk) from a maternal source. (Cows, of course, were supremely significant, as givers of milk, in the rural culture of colonial New England.) To summarize: we infer that Elizabeth frequently could not speak because the receptive wish and the destructive aim were too closely joined—in her

mouth. But when she reverted to simulating animal-behavior, the two elements were driven apart; then she was able, alternately, to bleat *and* to bark.

128. The writings of the Kleinian analysts are replete with resonant parallels to the "projection" behavior of Elizabeth Knapp. Thus, for example, Hans Thorner describes "a case of hysteria" in which the patient experienced irresistible aggressive impulses "which appeared as something foreign in herself, which did not come from her, *but from another person in her.*" (Italics added. See Thorner, "Three Defenses Against Inner Persecution," in Klein *et al., New Directions in Psychoanalysis,* 302ff.) And Joan Riviere summarizes the Kleinian view of malevolent "inner objects" in the following terms: "In our earliest days, but later in life too, when the self feels full of ruthless egoism or hate, . . . intense anxiety arises, both for ourselves and for the endangered objects; the violence of the fierce greed and hate raging within . . . is unutterably terrifying. It is then omnipotently denied and dissociated from the self, but is attributed instead to the persons inside who are the objects of the hate or greed, and are then felt to have provoked hate by their hate. It is they who are felt as bad: envious, robbing, ruthless, murderous. Thus it happens that a good helping person, or part of a person, changes shape and turns into a terrifying and dangerous enemy inside one; *one is felt to be 'possessed of a devil' inside.*" (Italics added. See Riviere, "The Unconscious Phantasy of an Inner World Reflected in Examples from Literature," in *ibid.,* 364–65.)

129. See Heinz Kohut, "Thoughts on Narcissism and Narcissistic Rage," in *The Psychoanalytic Study of the Child,* XXVII (1972), 360–400.

130. Heinz Kohut, *The Analysis of the Self,* 5, 13–14, 97, 118–21, 128, and *passim.*

132. Kohut's patient, "Miss F.," is a case in point; *ibid.,* 283–84. For more general comments on "depletion" states, see *ibid.,* 16–17, 227.

133. This point is developed at some length in John Demos, *A Little Commonwealth* (New York, 1970), 134–39. See also Demos, "Developmental Perspectives on the History of Childhood," *The Journal of Interdisciplinary History,* II (1971), 315–27.

134. Figures are not currently available to substantiate this assertion. However, in the author's personal experience of "reconstituting" thousands of early New England families from local and genealogical records, only two other such cases have appeared. (That is to say: only two other families in which husband and wife lived at least to age forty, while rearing but a single child.)

135. See pp. 111–13.

136. One striking piece of *non*-evidence should be noted: Elizabeth Knapp's mother is mentioned scarcely at all in the documentary materials on which this discussion is based. Presumably, however, she was a living

presence throughout the period, for Willard's "Brief Account" refers to "her [Elizabeth's] parents." (Moreover, John Warren's will, written in 1667, directs specific bequests to "my daughter Elizabeth Knapp"; see Probate Records of Middlesex County, no. 23682.) If, then, she remained uninvolved in the manifold troubles experienced by her daughter, the question becomes *why?* Was she perhaps a woman chronically depressed—and thus perceived by others as incapable of offering meaningful help?

137. See, for example, Edmund Morgan, *The Puritan Family* (New York, 1966), 75–79, 108–32; and Demos, *A Little Commonwealth*, 71–75, 107–17.

138. On the laws relating to "excess" in clothing, see, Shurtleff, ed., *Records of the Governor and Company of Massachusetts Bay*, I, 126 and III, 243–44.

139. An analyst experienced in the treatment of patients with narcissistic personality disorders has noted certain "common patterns" of personal and family history associated with such disorders. One of the most common is described thus: "a withdrawn, preoccupied, non-reactive, depressive type of mother, with a formal, correct father." See Max Forman, "The Case for a Clear-cut Clinical Distinction Between the Narcissistic Personality Disorders and the Oedipal Fixations" (unpublished essay, 1974).

140. Demos, ed., *Remarkable Providences*, 362.

141. *Ibid.*, 359, 360, 361, 363, 364.

142. *Ibid.*, 371.

143. *Ibid.*, 367–68.

144. Samuel Willard, *Useful Instructions for a Professing People in Times of Great Security and Degeneracy* (Cambridge, Mass., 1673), 32.

145. *Ibid.*, 32.

146. *Ibid.*, 30.

Notes to Chapter 5

1. The single most extended account of this phenomenon, in early New England, is found in an essay by Richard Chamberlain, "Lithobolia: or, the Stone-Throwing Devil" (1698); see Burr, ed., *Narratives*, 58–77.

2. Deposition by William and Elizabeth Morse, in the trial of Caleb Powell; see, *Records and Files of the Quarterly Courts of Essex County, Massachusetts*, VII, 355, 356, 358. The printed record is a slightly edited version of original documents in the Essex County Court Papers, XXXII, leaves 130–33. A further account and summary of the entire case against Caleb Powell is found in Increase Mather, "An Essay for the Recording of Illustrious Providences," in Burr, ed., *Narratives*, 23–32. Mather's essay

includes some details not found in the extant depositions, especially as to the progress of events after the court hearing of December 8.

3. Deposition by William and Elizabeth Morse, in *Records and Files of the Quarterly Courts of Essex County, Massachusetts*, VII, 355, 357. There was additional testimony, from other sources, about Powell's claims to occult knowledge: for example, "John Badger affirmeth that, being at William Morse his house, I heard Caleb Powell say that he thought by astrology, and I think he said by astronomy, and with it he could find out whether or no there were diabolical means used about the said Morse," etc. See Essex County Court Papers, XXXII, leaf 131.

4. Deposition by Elizabeth Titcomb and deposition by Sarah Hale and Joseph Mirack, in the trial of Caleb Powell; *Records and Files of the Quarterly Courts of Essex County, Massachusetts*, VIII, 357, 355.

5. Deposition by William and Elizabeth Morse; *ibid.*, VII, 357.

6. *Ibid.*, VII, 358.

7. Deposition by John Emerson, in the trial of Caleb Powell; *ibid.*, VII, 357.

8. The Morses' "complaint" against Powell is in *ibid.*, VII, 355. See also Essex County Court Papers, XXXII, leaves 130–33.

9. Deposition by William and Elizabeth Morse; *Records and Files of the Quarterly Courts of Essex County, Massachusetts*, VII, 357.

10. The details of John Stiles's "fits" are presented in Mather, "An Essay for the Recording of Illustrious Providences"; see Burr, ed., *Narratives*, 27–30.

11. Most of these depositions are printed in Drake, *Annals of Witchcraft*, 258–68.

12. The indictment of Elizabeth Morse is found in Noble and Cronin, eds., *Records of the Court of Assistants of the Colony of Massachusetts Bay*, I, 159. The order for her arrest is in Drake, *Annals of Witchcraft*, 269–70.

13. See "the humble petition of William Morse . . . to the honoured General Court," as printed in Joshua Coffin, *A Sketch of the History of Newbury, Newburyport, and West Newbury* (Boston, 1845), 127–29.

14. The original depositions are in the Essex County Court Papers, XXXII, leaves 130–33.

15. A manuscript copy of this verdict is in *ibid.*, XXXII, leaf 133. See also John J. Currier, *History of Newbury, Mass., 1635–1902* (Boston, 1902), 186.

16. See Drake, *Annals of Witchcraft*, 275–87.

17. The "summons" to the witnesses is in *ibid.*, 270–71. Subsequent claims for their "costs" (i.e. expenses in going to Boston to testify) are in *ibid.*, 287–92, 294–96.

18. The original copy of this court order is in the Suffolk Court Files, XXII, no. 1870. The women appointed would subsequently return to the court a finding of "teats . . . in her privates" and other unusual "appearances"

which seemed to weigh on the side of her guilt. The original of their report is also in *ibid.*, XXII, leaf 1870.

19. Noble and Cronin, eds., *Records of the Court of Assistants of the Colony of Massachusetts Bay*, I, 159; Massachusetts Archives, CXXXV, no. 18. These results are also printed in Coffin, *A Sketch of the History of Newbury*, 126–27.
20. *Ibid.*, 127.
21. *Ibid.*, 127.
22. See Drake, *Annals of Witchcraft*, 147.
23. See Coffin, *A Sketch of the History of Newbury*, 127–29.
24. Massachusetts Archives, CXXXV, no. 19. See also Currier, *History of Newbury*, 188.
25. Noble and Cronin, eds., *Records of the Court of Assistants of the Colony of Massachusetts Bay*, I, 189–90.
26. William Morse's will, dated August 6, 1683, is printed in Asa P. Morse, *Memorial of the Family of Morse* (Cambridgeport, Mass., 1896), part one, 96.
27. John Hale, "A Modest Enquiry into the Nature of Witchcraft," in Burr, ed., *Narratives*, 412.
28. Deposition by David Wheeler, in the trial of Elizabeth Morse, in Drake, *Annals of Witchcraft*, 261.
29. Deposition by John Mighell, *ibid.*, 268; deposition by Mrs. Jane Sewall, *ibid.*, 281; deposition by Elizabeth Titcomb, *ibid.*, 278; deposition by Margaret Mirack, *ibid.*, 287.
30. Deposition by Esther Wilson, *ibid.*, 275–76.
31. Deposition by John Chase, *ibid.*, 280; deposition by Elizabeth Titcomb, *ibid.*, 277–78.
32. Deposition by Ann Ordway; manuscript document in Suffolk Court Files, XXII, leaf 1870.
33. Deposition by David Wheeler, in Drake, *Annals of Witchcraft,* 286.
34. Deposition by Zachariah Davis; manuscript document in Massachusetts Archives, CXXXV, no. 14.
35. Deposition by John Mighell, in Drake, *Annals of Witchcraft,* 268; deposition by Jonathan Haines, manuscript document in Suffolk Court Files, XXII, leaf 1870; deposition by Joshua Richardson, in Drake, *Annals of Witchcraft,* 263.
36. See the reference to testimony by John Chase, in the "humble petition of William Morse," etc., as printed in Coffin, *A Sketch of the History of Newbury*, 128; and deposition by Elizabeth Titcomb, in Drake, *Annals of Witchcraft*, 258–59.
37. Deposition by Lydia Titcomb, *ibid.*, 278–79.
38. Deposition by Jonathan Woodman, *ibid.*, 259–60.
39. Deposition by Robert Earle, *ibid.*, 269.
40. Deposition by John March, *ibid.*, 283.

41. Deposition by Margaret Mirack, *ibid.*, 287; deposition by Robert Earle, *ibid.*, 269; deposition by James Brown, *ibid.*, 284.

42. Deposition by James Brown, *ibid.*, 284.

43. Deposition by Caleb Moody, *ibid.*, 265.

44. Deposition by Caleb Moody, *ibid.*, 263.

45. See the reference to William Fanning, in the deposition by Caleb Moody, *ibid.*, 265.

46. Deposition by Joshua Richardson, *ibid.*, 262.

47. Deposition by Caleb Moody, *ibid.*, 263.

48. Deposition by John Mighell, *ibid.*, 267.

49. Deposition by David Wheeler, *ibid.*, 286.

50. Deposition by Zachariah Davis, Massachusetts Archives, CXXXV, no. 14.

51. Deposition by Jonathan Haines, Suffolk Court Files, XXII, leaf 1870.

52. Deposition by John Chase, in Drake, *Annals of Witchcraft*, 280.

53. Deposition by Elizabeth Titcomb, *ibid.*, 277; and deposition by Susannah Titcomb, *ibid.*, 279.

54. Deposition by William Fanning, *ibid.*, 265–66.

55. Deposition by Zachariah Davis, Massachusetts Archives, CXXXV, no. 14.

56. Deposition by Jonathan Haines, Suffolk Court Files, XXII, leaf 1870.

57. Note that quite frequently the age of a victim at the time of "affliction" was different from his/her age at the time of deposing in court. The difference means that average age-of-victims computes to significantly less (i.e. younger) than average age-of-witnesses—and the *former* is the chief consideration here.

58. For some further discussion of "middle age" in early America, see pp. 67–68. In calling these victims "peers" of Goodwife Morse (who was sixty-five years old at the time of her trial), we take note of the fact that the charges against her dated from long before. She was herself a woman in her forties when initially suspected.

59. Deposition by Ann Ordway, in Suffolk Court Files, XXII, leaf 1870; deposition by Elizabeth Titcomb, in Drake, *Annals of Witchcraft*, 277–278; deposition by Susannah Tappin, *ibid.*, 279; deposition by Esther Wilson, *ibid.*, 275–76; deposition by John March (about Elizabeth Morse and Goodwife Wells), *ibid.*, 282–83.

60. Deposition by Elizabeth Titcomb, *ibid.*, 278.

61. Deposition by Ann Ordway, in Suffolk Court Files, XXII, leaf 1870; reference to testimony by widow Goodwin, in "the humble petition of William Morse," in Coffin, *A Sketch of the History of Newbury*, 128.

62. Deposition by Elizabeth Titcomb, with "affirming" statements by Lydia Titcomb and Peniel Titcomb, in Drake, *Annals of Witchcraft*, 258–59.

63. Deposition by Mrs. Jane Sewall, *ibid.*, 281.

64. Deposition by Esther Wilson, *ibid.*, 275–77; deposition by John Chase, *ibid.*, 280.

65. For further discussion of "menopausal" experience in relation to witch-craft accusations, see pp. 155–56.

66. A long list of names given to cows can be compiled by consulting almost any file of early New England wills and estate inventories. Strikingly, such names seem not to have been given to other domestic animals. Thus, for example, the same will mentioned cows named "Velvet," "Cherry," "Colley," "Gentle," "young Whiteface," "Butter," "Gallant," and "Gold-ing"— and "the horse I had of Nehemiah Grover," "my two mares," "the brown yearling," and "my sheep." (See the estate of Roger Haskell, of Beverly, Mass., in *The Probate Records of Essex County, Massachusetts*, II, 87–88.) This difference in naming patterns is taken to reflect a dif-ference in emotional investment as well: in short, cows were the *most* precious of all livestock properties for the early New Englanders.

67. Darrett B. Rutman, *Husbandmen of Plymouth: Farms and Villages in the Old Colony* (Boston, 1967), 48.

68. Deposition by Esther Wilson, in Drake, *Annals of Witchcraft*, 275–77.

69. Deposition by William Fanning, *ibid.*, 266.

70. Deposition by Margaret Mirack, *ibid.*, 287.

71. Deposition by James Brown, *ibid.*, 284.

72. Deposition by Mary Tucker, in the trial of Caleb Powell; manuscript document in the Essex County Court Papers, XXXII, leaf 132.

73. Mather, "An Essay for the Recording of Illustrious Providences," in Burr, ed., *Narratives*, 29.

74. Deposition by William and Elizabeth Morse, *Records and Files of the Quarterly Courts of Essex County, Massachusetts*, VII, 357, 358.

75. *Ibid.*, 358.

76. Presentment of John Stiles, May 3, 1680; Essex County Court Papers, XXXIII, leaf 26.

77. Deposition by Israel Webster, deposition by Thomas Titcomb, January 7, 1679; *ibid.*, XXXIII, leaf 26.

78. Deposition by William Fanning, in Drake, *Annals of Witchcraft*, 265–66.

79. Robert Stiles of Rowley, Mass., and Robert Stiles of Dorchester, Mass.; see Henry R. Stiles, *The Stiles Family in America* (Jersey City, N.J., 1895).

80. "The Last Will and Testament of William Morse of Newbury, Mass.," in Morse, *Memorial of the Family of Morse*, part one, 96–97.

81. Details of this liaison, and its *sequellae*, can be found in *Records and Files of the Quarterly Courts of Essex County, Massachusetts*, VI, 206, 256, 426; VII, 97.

82. "The Last Will and Testament of William Morse of Newbury, Mass.," in Morse, *Memorial of the Family of Morse*, part one, 96–97.

83. See *ibid.*, part two, 3ff., and also J. Howard Morse and Emily W. Leavitt, *Morse Genealogy* (New York, 1903), 2–3.

84. "The humble petition of William Morse", in Coffin, *A Sketch of the History of Newbury*, 129.

Notes to Chapter 6

1. "The Determinants of Personality Formation," in Clyde Kluckohn and Henry A. Murrays, eds., *Personality in Nature, Society, and Culture*, 2nd ed. (New York, 1953), 53.
2. See pp. 144–45.
3. See John Demos, *A Little Commonwealth* (New York, 1970), 68–69.
4. In one sample of seventeenth-century New England women, 65 percent had their last child after the age of forty. See Patricia Trainor O'Malley, "Rowley, Massachusetts, 1639–1730: Dissent, Division and Delimitation in a Colonial Town" (unpublished Ph.D. diss., Boston College, 1975), 211.
5. See, for example, B. L. Neugarten, V. Wood, R. J. Kraines, and B. Loomis, "Women's Attitudes toward Menopause," in B. L. Neugarten, ed., *Middle Age and Aging* (Chicago, 1968), 195–200; K. Stern and M. Prados, "Personality Studies in Menopausal Women," *American Journal of Psychiatry*, CIII (1946), 358–67; and P. Weideger, *Menstruation and Menopause* (New York, 1976). For a survey of the literature on this subject see S. M. McKinlay and J. B. McKinlay, "Selected Studies of the Menopause: An Annotated Bibliography," in *Journal of Biosocial Science*, V (1973), 533–55.
6. For an especially interesting discussion of this phenomenon see David Gutmann, "The Cross-Cultural Perspective: Notes toward a Comparative Psychology of Aging," in J. E. Birren and K. W. Schaie, eds., *Handbook of the Psychology of Aging* (New York, 1977), 302–26.
7. See Sacvan Bercovitch, *The Puritan Origins of the American Self* (New Haven, Conn., 1975), ch. 1; Richard L. Bushman, *From Puritan to Yankee: Character and the Social Order in Connecticut, 1690–1765* (New York, 1967), ch. 1; Philip J. Greven, Jr., *The Protestant Temperament: Patterns of Child-Rearing, Religious Experience, and the Self in Early America* (New York, 1977); and Emory B. Elliott, *Power and the Pulpit in Puritan New England* (Princeton, N.J., 1975), chs. 1–2.
8. Demos, *A Little Commonwealth*, ch. 10.
9. Philip J. Greven, Jr., "Family Structure in Seventeenth-Century Andover, Massachusetts," *William and Mary Quarterly*, 3rd ser., XXIII (1966), 234–56.
10. There are scattered references to the everyday activities of adolescent girls in court records from early New England. On average age at marriage, see Demos, *A Little Commonwealth*, 151, and Philip J. Greven,

Jr., *Four Generations: Population, Land, and Family in Colonial Andover, Massachusetts* (Ithaca, N.Y., 1970), 121. On age at menarche see Peter Laslett, "Age at Menarche in Europe Since the Eighteenth Century," in Theodore K. Rabb and Robert I. Rotberg, eds., *The Family in History: Interdisciplinary Essays* (New York, 1976), 28–47.

11. These issues are discussed at some length in Demos, *A Little Commonwealth*, 145–50. For a different line of interpretation, see Ross Beales, "In Search of the Historical Child: Miniature Adulthood and Youth in Colonial New England," in *American Quarterly*, XXVII (1975), 379–398.

12. The reference is to Martha Goodwin, a girl of thirteen who experienced severe fits in and around her home at Boston in the year 1688. A long account of this case was published by Cotton Mather in his "Memorable Providences, Relating to Witchcrafts and Possessions," and reprinted in Burr, ed., *Narratives*, 111.

13. *Ibid.*, 109.

14. *Ibid.*, 119.

15. *Ibid.*, 107.

16. The experience of Elizabeth Knapp makes an obvious case in point. But no less was true of the Goodwin children of Boston (see *ibid.*, 99–131), Ann Cole of Hartford (*ibid.*, 18–21), and of course the various "afflicted children" at the Salem trials in 1692–93.

17. Joan Riviere, "On the Genesis of Psychical Conflict in Earliest Infancy," in M. Klein, P. Heimann, S. Isaacs, and J. Riviere, *Developments in Psychoanalysis* (London, 1952), 50.

18. Joan Riviere, "The Unconscious Phantasy of an Inner World Reflected in Examples from Literature," in M. Klein *et al.*, *New Directions in Psychoanalysis* (London, 1955), 364–65.

19. The overall view of adolescence presented here draws heavily on the work of Peter Blos—especially his book *On Adolescence: A Psychoanalytic Interpretation* (New York, 1962). See also his essays "Character Formation in Adolescence," in *The Psychoanalytic Study of the Child*, XXIII (1968), 245–63, and "The Second Individuation Process of Adolescence," in *ibid.*, XXV (1970), 162–86.

20. Blos, *On Adolescence*, 11; Blos, "Character Formation in Adolescence," 253.

21. Blos, *On Adolescence*, 68.

22. *Ibid.*, 28ff.

23. Examination of Mercy Disborough and Elizabeth Clawson (Stamford, Connecticut, May 27–28, 1692), manuscript paper in the Willys Papers, W-19.

24. The words are those of Mercy Short, as quoted by Cotton Mather; see Burr, ed., *Narratives*, 268.

25. Anna Freud, "Adolescence," in *The Psychoanalytic Study of the Child*, XIII (1958), 270–71.

26. On adolescence and the development of the self, see E. Wolf, J. Gedo, and D. Terman, "On the Adolescent Process as a Transformation of the Self," in *Journal of Youth and Adolescence*, I (1972), 257, 272, and Philip C. Gradolph, "Developmental Vicissitudes of the Self and the Ego-Ideal during Adolescence" (unpublished paper, presented at the Central States Conference of the American Society for Adolescent Psychiatry, October 1976).

27. Among the victims of witchcraft who experienced this particular form of affliction were Mercy Short (see Burr, ed., *Narratives*, 266ff.), Margaret Rule (see *ibid.*, 312ff.), and Winifred Holman (see Middlesex Court Files, folder 25). The comment by Cotton Mather is included in his treatise "A Brand Plucked Out of the Burning," as reprinted in Burr, ed., *Narratives*, 266.

28. Hilda Bruch, *Eating Disorders: Obesity, Anorexia Nervosa, and the Person Within* (New York, 1973), 85, 250. The work of Bruch and her colleagues has generally been regarded as definitive for *anorexia*; however, see also a recent study by Salvador Minuchin, Lester Baker, and Bernice Rosman, *Psychosomatic Families: Anorexia Nervosa in Context* (Cambridge, Mass., 1978).

29. Bruch, *Eating Disorders*, 82ff.

30. Some sufferers from *anorexia* seem, as children, to have been powerfully encouraged to "perform" in various public settings (e.g. family gatherings); the parents in one instance declared pride in their daughter for being a "complete exhibitionist." The element of narcissistic enhancement seems patent here; however, it must be set alongside the equally obvious tendency to narcissistic insult (deflation). Presumably it is the stop-and-go combination of enhancement and deflation which so distorts the experience of archaic "grandiosity." On these and related points see *ibid.*, 329ff.

31. *Ibid.*, 254.

32. Numerous materials from the trials of Mary and Hugh Parsons are printed in Drake, *Annals of Witchcraft*, app. 1. For the deposition by William Branch, see p. 256.

33. *Ibid.*, 279.

34. Cotton Mather, "Memorable Providences, Relating to Witchcrafts and Possessions," in Burr, ed., *Narratives*, 132.

35. Deposition by Susannah Trimmings, in the trial of Jane Walford; see New Hampshire Historical Society, *Collections*, I, 255.

36. Cotton Mather, "Memorable Providences, Relating to Witchcrafts and Possessions," in Burr, ed., *Narratives*, 140.

37. The Diaries of John Hull, in American Antiquarian Society, *Transac-

tions and Collections, III (1857), 181; *Records and Files of the Quarterly Courts of Essex County, Massachusetts*, VI, 229; *Probate Records of Essex County, Massachusetts*, II, 206; Hoadly, ed., *Records of the Colony or Jurisdiction of New Haven*, II, 300.

38. See, for example, the various cases cited in the Medical Journal of John Winthrop, Jr. (manuscript volume, Massachusetts Historical Society, Boston), *passim*. See also *Records and Files of the Quarterly Courts of Essex County, Massachusetts*, VII, 304; and Hampton (N.H.) Church Records (manuscript volume, New England Historic Genealogical Society, Boston), 3–4 and *passim*.

39. "Diary of Samuel Sewall," Massachusetts Historical Society, *Collections*, 5th ser., V, 15–16.

40. Essex County Court Papers, XXVI, leaf 131.

41. Hampton (N.H.) Church Records, 3–4.

42. *Ibid.*, 3–4; Medical Journal of John Winthrop, Jr., 25; Letter of John Haynes to John Winthrop, Jr., August 7, 1651, in *The Winthrop Papers*, Massachusetts Historical Society, *Collections*, 4th ser., VII, 453; Diaries of John Hull, 182; *ibid.*, 191.

43. See p. 116.

44. Letter from Thomas Walley to John Cotton, undated (probably 1677), in American Antiquarian Society, *Proceedings*, LVIII, 261–62. At least occasionally, behavior that approximated "fits" or "possession" was attributed to "fantasy"—i.e. the victim's imagination. (See, in this connection, the testimony of Eliza Barton in the case of Jane Walford, New Hampshire Historical Society, *Collections*, I, 256; and also that of Hannah Robbins in the case of Katherine Palmer, Willys Papers, W-7.) There was also the possibility of outright "dissembling"—that is, a calculated effort to fake the symptons of possession. (See, for example, the opinions noted in the testimony of Joseph Garnsy about the experience of Katherine Branch, in the trial of Mercy Disborough and Elizabeth Clawson, Samuel Willys Collection, no. 30.)

45. See pp. 239–41.

46. Deposition by John Gammon, Sr., in the trial of Mercy Disborough and Elizabeth Clawson; Willys Papers, W-33.

47. Deposition by Rebecca Smith, in the trial of Katherine Harrison; Samuel Willys Collection, no. 10.

48. Deposition by George Colton, in the trial of Hugh Parsons; see Drake, *Annals of Witchcraft*, 236.

49. Testimony given in "the Examination of Elizabeth Godman," printed in Hoadly, ed., *Records of the Colony or Jurisdiction of New Haven*, II, 31.

50. Deposition by Esther Wilson, in the trial of Elizabeth Morse; see Drake, *Annals of Witchcraft*, 267.

51. Deposition by John Finch, in the trial of Mercy Disborough and Elizabeth Clawson; Willys Papers, W-32.

52. Deposition by Alice Wakely, in the trial of Katherine Harrison; Samuel Willys Collection, no. 17.

53. Testimony entitled "Mr. Rossiter's and Mr. Pitkin's Observation about Kelly's Child," in the trial of Goodwife [————] Ayres; Willys Papers, W-5.

54. Deposition by Hannah Robbins, in the trial of Katherine Palmer; Willys Papers, W-7.

55. Testimony of John Matthews, in the Pynchon Court Record; Joseph H. Smith, ed., *Colonial Justice in Western Massachusetts* (Cambridge, Mass., 1961), 219.

56. Letter of Nathaniel Mather to Increase Mather, quoted in Burr, ed., *Narratives*, 408–9, n.4. There was a similar aspect to the trial of Mary Parsons; according to John Hale, she "said the occasion of her familiarity with Satan was this: She had lost a child and was exceedingly discontented at it and longed—oh, that she might see her child again. And at last the Devil in likeness of her child came to her bedside and talked to her . . ." (John Hale, "A Modest Enquiry into the Nature of Witchcraft," in *ibid.*, 410).

57. Deposition by Joan Francis, in the trial of Katherine Harrison; Willys Papers, W-15.

58. Deposition by John Godfrey, in the trial of Rachel Fuller; see Bouton, ed., *Documents and Records Relating to the Province of New Hampshire*, I, 418.

59. Manuscript paper, entitled "In the Case of Eunice Cole," undated, in Massachusetts Archives, CXXXV, no. 13.

60. On the extent of childlessness among accused witches, see pp. 72–73. On Eunice Cole, see below, Chapter 11.

61. Deposition by David Wheeler, in the trial of Elizabeth Morse; see Drake, *Annals of Witchcraft*, 286.

62. Deposition by Henry Pease, in the court action of Erasmus James, plaintiff, and Peter Pitford, defendant; Essex County Court Papers, I, leaf 71.

63. Deposition by Thomas Bracey, in the trial of Katherine Harrison; Willys Papers, W-10.

64. Testimony by John Gibson, in the trial of Winifred Holman; Middlesex Court Files, folder 25.

65. Deposition by Joan Francis, in the trial of Katherine Harrison (Willys Papers, W-15); deposition by Ann Godfrey, in the trial of Mercy Disborough and Elizabeth Clawson (*ibid.*, W-33); deposition by Margaret Garrett, in the trial of Elizabeth Seager (*ibid.*, W-4); deposition by Robert Smith, in the trial of Eunice Cole (Massachusetts Archives, CXXXV, no. 11).

66. Deposition by Zachariah Davis, in the trial of Elizabeth Morse; *ibid.*, no. 14.

67. Deposition by John Gibson, in the trial of Winifred Holman; Middlesex Court Files, folder 25.

68. Deposition by Mary Newman, in the trial of Mercy Disborough and Elizabeth Clawson; Samuel Willys Collection, no. 20.

69. Deposition by Goodwife [―――] Thorp, in Hoadly, ed., *Records of the Colony or Jurisdiction of New Haven,* II, 35.

70. Deposition by Mary Coleman, in the trial of Eunice Cole; Massachusetts Archives, CXXXV, no. 2.

71. See above, Chapter 5.

72. See, for example, Norman Cohn, *Europe's Inner Demons* (New York, 1975); A. D. J. Macfarlane, *Witchcraft in Tudor and Stuart England* (London, 1970); and Keith Thomas, *Religion and the Decline of Magic* (New York, 1971).

73. Deodat Lawson, *Christ's Fidelity the Only Shield Against Satan's Malignity,* 2nd ed. (London, 1714), 15, 10, 2.

74. Cotton Mather, *The Wonders of the Invisible World,* John Russell Smith, ed. (London, 1862), 12–13.

75. Deposition by Joseph Garnsy, in the trial of Mercy Disborough and Elizabeth Clawson (Samuel Willys Collection, no. 30); Samuel Willard, "A Brief Account of a Strange and Unusual Providence of God Befallen to Elizabeth Knapp of Groton," in Demos, ed., *Remarkable Providences,* 367; Cotton Mather, "A Brand Plucked Out of the Burning," in Burr, ed., *Narratives,* 261.

76. Deposition by Goodwife [―――] Burr and Samuel Burr, in the trial of Goodwife [―――] Ayres; Samuel Willys Collection, no. 3.

77. Testimony of Rebecca Greensmith; Samuel Willys Collection, no. 1.

78. Deposition by Thomas Cooper, in the trial of Hugh Parsons; see Drake, *Annals of Witchcraft,* 245.

79. See "A Bill against Conjuration, Witchcraft, and Dealing with Evil and Wicked Spirits" (1692), in Massachusetts Archives, CXXXV, nos. 68–69.

80. Records of the Suffolk County Court, 1671–1680, in Colonial Society of Massachusetts, *Publications,* XXIX (1933), 485–86.

81. John Hale, "A Modest Enquiry into the Nature of Witchcraft," in Burr, ed., *Narratives,* 431.

82. Hosmer, ed., *Winthrop's Journal,* II, 344.

83. See, for example, the deposition by Daniel Ela, in the trial of John Godfrey (Suffolk Court Files, II, no. 322), and the deposition by Elizabeth Titcomb, in the trial of Elizabeth Morse (printed in Drake, *Annals of Witchcraft,* 277). *Touch* figured prominently in other cases—and not always as a malignant influence. There was, for example, a kind of "experiment" applied in some instances, whereby accused witches were

"discovered" through their touch. Thus a particular suspect was brought to Elizabeth Knapp—and Elizabeth "knew her very touch from any other." (See p. 105.) Goodwife Ayres, suspected of bewitching Elizabeth Kelly to death, was made to view the corpse and then "to handle it"; as a result a "great spot" appeared on the child's face, which "was not seen before." (Samuel Willys Collection, no. 5.) On the other hand, one suspect was reportedly induced (by neighborhood threats) to "unbewitch" an afflicted child: "she came over to the child, and stroked it, and said [that] God forbade that she should hurt the child, and soon after the child was well." (Deposition by John Gammon, Sr., in the trial of Mercy Disborough and Elizabeth Clawson; Willys Papers, W-33.) And, in the Salem trials, the fits of several victims were stopped (temporarily) when the accused touched them.

84. Examination of Mercy Disborough and Elizabeth Clawson (Stamford, Connecticut, May 27–28, 1692); Willys Papers, W-19. Depositions by Abraham Finch, Jr., and David Selleck; Willys Papers, W-25, W-27.

85. Note, for example, the following points in the depositional material against John Godfrey. "Charles Browne . . . deposed that . . . said Godfrey spoke that if witches . . . looked steadfastly upon any creature it would die." And also: "Isabel Holdridge deposed that [she saw the shape of] a beast . . . and it came toward them, and . . . her heart began to ache, for it seemed to have great eyes" (*Records and Files of the Quarterly Courts of Essex County, Massachusetts*, II, 160, 158). The trial of Winifred Holman produced testimony as to the suffering of a sick child "upon Mrs. Holman's looking on it" (Middlesex Court Files, folder 25).

86. From the trial of Goodwife [———] Glover, as reported in Cotton Mather, "Memorable Providences, Relating to Witchcrafts and Possessions"; see Burr, ed., *Narratives*, 104.

87. See, for example, Cotton Mather's account of the affliction of Margaret Rule, included in Robert Calef, "More Wonders of the Invisible World" (Burr, ed., *Narratives*, 318).

88. *Ibid.*, 104, 318.

89. Deposition by David Wheeler, in the trial of Elizabeth Morse; see Drake, *Annals of Witchcraft*, 286.

90. Deposition by Daniel Westcott, in the trial of Mercy Disborough and Elizabeth Clawson; Willys Papers, W-28.

91. Deposition by Eleazer Slawson, in the trial of Mercy Disborough and Elizabeth Clawson; Samuel Willys Collection, no. 19.

92. Testimony of Goodwife [———] Larremore, in the court action of Mrs. Elizabeth Godman, plaintiff, and Goodwife [———] Larremore, defendant; see Hoadly, ed., *Records of the Colony or Jurisdiction of New Haven*, II, 29.

93. Cotton Mather, "Memorable Providences, Relating to Witchcrafts and Possessions," in Burr, ed., *Narratives,* 136.

94. See p. 102.

95. Deodat Lawson, *Christ's Fidelity the Only Shield,* 70–71. For a very similar statement, see Samuel Willard, *Useful Instructions for a Professing People* (Cambridge, Mass., 1673), 34.

96. Cotton Mather, *The Wonders of the Invisible World,* 97.

97. *Ibid.,* 89.

98. *Ibid.,* 90, 51; Lawson, *Christ's Fidelity the Only Shield,* 24.

99. Cotton Mather, *The Wonders of the Invisible World,* 46.

100. *Ibid.,* 84. See also Samuel Willard, *Useful Instructions for a Professing People,* 32. Willard referred, obliquely, to the issue of God's "allowing" Satanic activity, when discussing the possession of Elizabeth Knapp: "It is not usual for God to give Satan such liberty and power, so to rack and torture . . . poor creatures. . . ."

101. Deposition by Thomas Coleman and Abraham Drake, in the trial of Eunice Cole; see manuscript collection entitled "Trials for Witchcraft in New England," Houghton Library, Harvard University, Cambridge, Mass.

102. Deposition by Anthony Dorchester, in the trial of Hugh Parsons; see Drake, *Annals of Witchcraft,* 230–31.

103. Samuel Willard, "A Brief Account of a Strange and Unusual Providence of God Befallen to Elizabeth Knapp of Groton," in Demos, ed., *Remarkable Providences,* 359; deposition by Hester Ward, in the court action of Thomas Staples, plaintiff, and Roger Ludlow, defendant, in Hoadly, ed., *Records of the Colony or Jurisdiction of New Haven,* II, 80; Cotton Mather, "Memorable Providences, Relating to Witchcrafts and Possessions," in Burr, ed., *Narratives,* 138; examination of Mercy Disborough and Elizabeth Clawson (Stamford, Conn., May 27–28, 1692), Willys Papers, W-19; Cotton Mather, "A Brand Plucked Out of the Burning," in Burr, ed., *Narratives,* 268.

104. Cotton Mather, *The Wonders of the Invisible World,* 176.

105. Deposition by Hannah Robbins, in the trial of Katherine Palmer; Willys Papers, W-7.

106. Deposition by Esther Wilson, in the trial of Elizabeth Morse; see Drake, *Annals of Witchcraft,* 276.

107. Deposition by Hannah Manning, in the trial of Mary Hale; Suffolk Court Files, XXIV, no. 1972.

108. Deposition by Jonathan Thing, in the trial of Eunice Cole; Suffolk Court Files, XIII, no. 1228.

109. Testimony of Mrs. [———] Mygatt, in the trial of Elizabeth Seager; Willys Papers, W-3.

110. Order of the Court, in the action of Mrs. Elizabeth Godman, plaintiff,

and Goodwife [———] Larremore, defendant; Hoadly, ed., *Records of the Colony or Jurisdiction of New Haven*, II, 30–31.

111. Deposition by Mary Perkins, in the trial of Eunice Cole; Massachusetts Archives, CXXXV, no. 7.

112. Deposition by Elizabeth Shaw, in the trial of Eunice Cole; Suffolk Court Files, XIII, no. 1228.

113. Deposition by Robert Earle, in the trial of Elizabeth Morse; see Drake, *Annals of Witchcraft*, 269.

114. Deposition by David Selleck, in the trial of Mercy Disborough and Elizabeth Clawson; Willys Papers, W-27.

115. Hosmer, ed., *Winthrop's Journal*, II, 344.

116. *Ibid.*, II, 344.

117. The quoted words are from the charge to a committee appointed in the case of Mercy Disborough and Elizabeth Clawson. (See Examination of Mercy Disborough and Elizabeth Clawson, Stamford, Conn., May 27–28, 1692; Willys Papers, W-19.) On the appointment of similar committees in other cases, see, for example, the order of the court, in the case of Mary Parsons (1673), as printed in James Hammond Trumbull, *The History of Northampton, Mass.* (Northampton, Mass., 1898), 231; and also the deposition of Mary Perkins, in the trial of Eunice Cole (Massachusetts Archives, CXXXV, no. 7).

118. Examination of Mercy Disborough and Elizabeth Clawson (Stamford, Conn., May 27–28, 1692); Willys Papers, W-19.

119. Deposition by Mary Perkins, in the trial of Eunice Cole; Massachusetts Archives, CXXXV, no. 7. See also *ibid.*, CXXXV, no. 13.

120. Report of a committee to search the bodies of Mercy Disborough and Elizabeth Clawson; Connecticut Archives, Crimes and Misdemeanors, ser. 1 (1662–1789), 1, part one, leaf 187.

121. Deposition by Richard Ormsby, in the trial of Eunice Cole; Massachusetts Archives, CXXXV, no. 3.

122. Deposition by Charles Browne, in the trial of John Godfrey; Suffolk Court Files, II, no. 322. See also the deposition of John How (in *ibid.*, II, no. 322) on local gossip that Godfrey "hath the marks of a witch."

123. Deposition by Mrs. Sarah Bates, in the trial of Mercy Disborough and Elizabeth Clawson; Willys Papers, W-31. Other witnesses against Goodwife Clawson mentioned a long-standing "report amongst some in the town" about her physical peculiarities. (See the deposition by Richard Holmes; Samuel Willys Collection, no. 24.) On the same matter, see also the depositions by Sarah Finch, Mary Ambler, Bethiah Weld, and Martha Holmes, in the trial of Mercy Disborough and Elizabeth Clawson; Willys Papers, W-31.

124. Deposition by Richard Ormsby, in the trial of Eunice Cole; Massachusetts Archives, CXXXV, no. 3.

125. Deposition by Goodwife [————] Duncan, in the trial of Alice Stratton; Middlesex Court Files, folder 2.

126. Court Action of Thomas Staples, plaintiff, and Roger Ludlow, defendant; see Hoadly, ed., *Records of the Colony or Jurisdiction of New Haven*, II, 80–84.

127. Deposition by Mary Hambleton, in the trial of Mary Hale; Suffolk Court Files, XXIII, no. 1958.

128. Deposition by Ann Edwards, in the trial of Elizabeth Garlick; see *Records of the Town of Easthampton, Long Island, Suffolk County, N.Y.* 5 vols. (Sag Harbor, N.Y., 1887–92), I, 134.

129. See John Hale, "A Modest Enquiry into the Nature of Witchcraft," in Burr, ed., *Narratives*, 411, and Cotton Mather, "Memorable Providences, Relating to Witchcrafts and Possessions," in *ibid.*, 102–3, 128–29. For an example of non-clerical opposition to counter-magic, see the deposition by Esther Wilson, in the trial of Elizabeth Morse (Drake, *Annals of Witchcraft*, 276).

130. Cotton Mather, "Memorable Providences, Relating to Witchcrafts and Possessions," in Burr, ed., *Narratives*, 128, 102.

131. See pp. 138–39.

132. Deposition by Esther Wilson, in the trial of Elizabeth Morse; see Drake, *Annals of Witchcraft*, 276.

133. Depositions by George Langdon, Hannah Langdon, and John Lombard, in the trial of Hugh Parsons; see *ibid.*, 219–222.

134. Deposition by Mary Godfrey, in the trial of Rachael Fuller; see Bouton, ed., *Documents and Records Relating to the Province of New Hampshire*, I, 416.

135. Hoadly, ed., *Records of the Colony or Jurisdiction of New Haven*, II, 224; depositions by Elizabeth Bennett, Sr., and Elizabeth Bennett, Jr., in the trial of Mercy Disborough and Elizabeth Clawson (Willys Papers, W-33); deposition by Daniel Westcott in the trial of Mercy Disborough and Elizabeth Clawson (Willys Papers, W-28); deposition by Rebecca Smith, in the trial of Katherine Harrison (Samuel Willys Collection, no. 10); deposition by Elizabeth Titcomb, in the trial of Elizabeth Morse (Drake, *Annals of Witchcraft*, 258).

136. Depositions by Hannah Weacome and Elizabeth Bent, in the trial of Mary Hale; Suffolk Court Files, XXIV, no. 1972.

137. Depositions by Elizabeth Bennett, Sr., Elizabeth Bennett, Jr., and Ann Godfrey, in the trial of Mercy Disborough and Elizabeth Clawson; Willys Papers, W-33.

138. Deposition by Jonathan Woodman, in the trial of Elizabeth Morse; see Drake, *Annals of Witchcraft*, 259–60. William Morse replied to this charge (among others), contending that his wife's injury had come from "the fall of a piece [when she was] reaching down [for] some bacon in our chimney." (Note: "piece" was a period term for firearms.)

See Josiah Coffin, *A Sketch of the History of Newbury, Newburyport, and West Newbury* (Boston, 1845), 129.

139. Deposition by Margaret Garrett, in the trial of Elizabeth Seager; Willys Papers, W-4.

140. The following section relies heavily on the work of the psychologist Silvan Tomkins. For Tomkins has produced the most comprehensive —and persuasive—account of affective experience in the currently available academic literature. Long neglected by psychologists, affect is now a subject of increasing interest and systematic study. Tomkins's theory is set forth in his two-volume work *Affect, Imagery, Consciousness,* 2 vols. (New York, 1962, 1963). Other valuable studies in this field include: Magda B. Arnold, *Emotion and Personality* (New York, 1960); Magda B. Arnold, ed., *Feelings and Emotions* (New York, 1970); Carroll E. Izard, *The Face of Emotion* (New York, 1971); Peter Knapp, *Expression of the Emotions in Man* (New York, 1963); James Hillman, *Emotion: A Comprehensive Phenomenology of Theories and Their Meanings for Therapy* (Evanston, Ill., 1963); Paul Ekman, *Darwin and Facial Expression: A Century of Research in Review* (New York, 1973); Stanley Schachter, *Emotion, Obesity, and Crime* (New York, 1971); George Mandler, *Mind and Emotion* (New York, 1975). For personal guidance and tutelage in the study of affect, I am especially grateful to Virginia Demos—whose own research will shortly be added to the above list.

141. Deposition by Henry Gray, in the trial of Mercy Disborough and Elizabeth Clawson; Willys Papers, W-33.

142. Deposition by Thomas Burnham, in the trial of Hugh Parsons; see Drake, *Annals of Witchcraft,* 223.

143. See p. 109.

144. See pp. 92–93.

145. Deposition by Thomas Bracey, in the trial of Katherine Harrison; Willys Papers, W-10.

146. Deposition by Joanna Sleeper, in the trial of Eunice Cole; Suffolk Court Files, I, no. 256a.

147. Deposition by Mrs. Mary Gardiner, in the trial of Elizabeth Garlick; see *Records of the Town of Easthampton, Long Island, Suffolk County, N.Y.,* I, 133.

148. Deposition by Hannah Robbins, in the trial of Katherine Palmer; Willys Papers, W-7.

149. Deposition by William Hannum, in the trial of Mary Parsons; Middlesex Court Files, folder 16, no. 665.

150. Deposition by John Lovejoy, in the trial of John Godfrey (Suffolk Court Files, II, no. 322); testimony given at "the examination of Elizabeth Godman" (Hoadly, ed., *Records of the Colony or Jurisdiction of New Haven,* II, 31).

151. Deposition by Margaret Garrett, in the trial of Elizabeth Seager; Willys Papers, W-4.
152. Deposition by Goodwife [————] Duncan, in the trial of Alice Stratton; Middlesex Court Files, folder 2.
153. Deposition by Elizabeth Titcomb, in the trial of Elizabeth Morse; see Drake, *Annals of Witchcraft*, 278.
154. Testimony given at "the examination of Elizabeth Godman"; see Hoadly, ed., *Records of the Colony or Jurisdiction of New Haven*, II, 33.
155. *Ibid.*, 30.
156. Depositions by Thomas Haynes and Isabel Holdridge, in the trial of John Godfrey; see *Records and Files of the Quarterly Courts of Essex County, Massachusetts*, II, 158–59.
157. Deposition by Thomas Chandler, in the action of John Godfrey, plaintiff, and John Carr, defendant; see *Records and Files of the Quarterly Courts of Essex County, Massachusetts*, II, 410.
158. Deposition by Thomas Bennett, Jr., in the trial of Mercy Disborough and Elizabeth Clawson; Willys Papers, W-33.
159. Deposition by John March, in the trial of Elizabeth Morse (Drake, *Annals of Witchcraft*, 283); deposition by Henry Gray, in the trial of Mercy Disborough and Elizabeth Clawson (Willys Papers, W-33).
160. See Coffin, *A Sketch of the History of Newbury*, 127–29.
161. Petition of Katherine Harrison, to the General Court of Connecticut; Winthrop Papers, XIV, 8 (Massachusetts Historical Society, Boston, Mass.).
162. Petition entitled "Widow Harrison's Grievances"; Willys Papers, W–12.
163. See, for example, the depositions by Thomas Haynes and Isabel Holdridge, in the trial of John Godfrey (*Records and Files of the Quarterly Courts of Essex County, Massachusetts*, II, 158–59); and Cotton Mather's account of the affliction of the Goodwin children, in his "Memorable Providences, Relating to Witchcrafts and Possessions," in Burr, ed., *Narratives*, 107.
164. Deposition by John and Bethiah Kelly, in the trial of Goodwife [————] Ayres; Willys Papers, W-6.
165. Deposition by John Gibson, in the trial of Winifred Holman; Middlesex Court Files, folder 25.
166. Examination of Mercy Disborough and Elizabeth Clawson (Stamford, Conn., May 27–28, 1692); Willys Papers, W-10.
167. Cotton Mather, "A Brand Plucked Out of the Burning," in Burr, ed., *Narratives*, 268–71.
168. Deposition by David Wheeler, in the trial of Elizabeth Morse (Drake, *Annals of Witchcraft*, 261); deposition by Rebecca Gibson and John Gibson, Jr., in the trial of Winifred Holman (Middlesex Court Files, folder 25); testimony given by Goodwife Thorp (Dexter, ed., *New*

Haven Town Records, 251); deposition of Mrs. [————] Mygatt, in the trial of Elizabeth Seager (Willys Papers, W-3).

169. Deposition by Robert and Susannah Smith, in the trial of Eunice Cole (Massachuetts Archives, CXXXV, no. 11); Cotton Mather, "Memorable Providences, Relating to Witchcrafts and Possessions," in Burr, ed., *Narratives*, 133.

170. Deposition by Griffin Jones, in the trial of Hugh Parsons; see Drake, *Annals of Witchcraft*, 233.

171. Deposition by Jonathan Taylor, in the trial of Hugh Parsons; see *ibid.*, 246.

172. Depositions by John Matthews and George Moxon, testimony by Mary Parsons, and "answers" by Hugh Parsons; see *ibid.*, 227–29.

173. Deposition by Thomas Bracey, in the trial of Katherine Harrison; Willys Papers, W-10.

174. Petition of Katherine Harrison, to the General Court of Connecticut; Winthrop Papers, XIV, 8.

175. Deposition by Edward Jessup, in the trial of Mercy Disborough and Elizabeth Clawson; Willys Papers, W-35.

176. Deposition by Daniel Ela, in the trial of John Godfrey; Suffolk Court Files, II, no. 322.

177. Deposition by Jonathan Haines, in the trial of Elizabeth Morse; Suffolk Court Files, XXII, no. 1870.

178. Cotton Mather, "The Afflictions of Margaret Rule," in Robert Calef, "More Wonders of the Invisible World"; see Burr, ed., *Narratives*, 315.

179. Deposition by Joseph Garnsy, in the trial of Mercy Disborough and Elizabeth Clawson; Samuel Willys Collection, no. 30.

180. Depositions by Thomas Miller, Thomas Cooper, and Mary Parsons, in the trial of Hugh Parsons; see Drake, *Annals of Witchcraft*, 222–23.

181. See the references in Walter B. Cannon, " 'Voodoo' Death," *American Anthropologist*, XLIV (1942), 169–81. See also: Edward Norbeck, *Religion in Primitive Society* (New York, 1961), and Hutton Webster, *Taboo: A Sociological Study* (Stanford, California, 1942).

182. Cannon, " 'Voodoo' Death," 172. See also Walter B. Cannon, *Bodily Changes in Pain, Anger, Fear, and Rage* (New York, 1929).

183. Cannon, " 'Voodoo' Death," 176.

184. Deposition by Esther Wilson, in the trial of Elizabeth Morse; see Drake, *Annals of Witchcraft*, 275.

185. Cotton Mather, "Memorable Providences, Relating to Witchcrafts and Possessions," in Burr, ed., *Narratives*, 132.

186. Deposition by John Gibson, in the trial of Winifred Holman; Middlesex Court Files, folder 25.

187. Deposition by John Chase, in the trial of Elizabeth Morse; see Drake, *Annals of Witchcraft*, 280.

188. For a good, short summary of the psychoanalytic theory of defenses, see Otto Fenichel, *The Psychoanalytic Theory of Neurosis* (New York, 1945), ch. 9. The foremost work in this area is Anna Freud, *The Ego and the Mechanisms of Defense*, rev. ed. (New York, 1966).

189. See p. 163.

190. Deposition by Mary Hale, in the trial of Katherine Harrison; Willys Papers, W-17.

191. Deposition by Isabel Holdridge, in the trial of John Godfrey; see *Records and Files of the Quarterly Courts of Essex County, Massachusetts*, II, 158–59.

192. Deposition by Thomas Haynes, in the trial of John Godfrey; see *ibid.*, II, 158.

193. See, for example, the lengthy depositions by the family of Rebecca [Gibson] Stearns, in the trial of Winifred Holman; Middlesex Court Files, folder 25.

194. See pp. 187–88.

195. This pattern is quite clearly exemplified in the cases of John Godfrey, Hugh Parsons, and Mercy Disborough and Elizabeth Clawson. On Godfrey, see above, Chapter 2; on Hugh Parsons, see Drake, *Annals of Witchcraft*, app. 1; on Disborough and Clawson, see manuscript documents in the Willys Papers and the Samuel Willys Collection.

196. See Jack Novick and Kerry Kelly, "Projection and Externalization," in *The Psychoanalytic Study of the Child*, XXV (1970), 69–95.

197. See above, Chapter 3.

198. Fenichel, *The Psychoanalytic Theory of Neurosis*, 141.

199. The terms are familiar ones in recent psychoanalytic writing. See, for example, Heinz Kohut, *The Analysis of the Self* (New York, 1971).

200. Maris A. Vinovskis, "Mortality Rates and Trends in Massachusetts before 1830," *Journal of Economic History*, XXXII (1972), 195–201; David E. Stannard, *The Puritan Way of Death*, 54–55; Demos, *A Little Commonwealth*, 131–32; Kenneth A. Lockridge, "The Popula- of Dedham, Massachusetts, 1636–1736," in *Economic History Review*, 2nd ser., XIX (1966), 329; James K. Somerville, "A Demographic Profile of the Salem Family 1660–1700," unpublished paper presented at the conference on social history, Stony Brook, N.Y. (1969).

201. Deposition by Mary Hale, in the trial of Katherine Harrison; Willys Papers, W-17.

202. Cotton Mather, "Memorable Providences, Relating to Witchcrafts and Possessions," in Burr, ed., *Narratives*, 112, 116, 111; Cotton Mather, "A Brand Plucked Out of the Burning," in *ibid.*, 269.

203. Sigmund Freud, "Negation," in Strachey, ed., *The Standard Edition of the Complete Psychological Works of Sigmund Freud*, XIX, 237.

204. Anna Freud, *The Ego and the Mechanisms of Defense*, 51–53.

205. The term—and the main elements of the argument presented in this

paragraph—are taken from the work of Abraham Kardiner. See his *The Individual and His Society* (New York, 1939), 305–10.

206. Sigmund Freud, "On Narcissism," in Strachey, ed., *The Standard Edition of the Complete Psychological Works of Sigmund Freud*, XIV, 69–102, and "An Outline of Psychoanalysis," in *ibid.*, XXIII, 150ff. Kohut's work is most fully presented in his two books, *The Analysis of the Self* (New York, 1971) and *The Restoration of the Self* (New York, 1977). See also Otto Kernberg, *Borderline Conditions and Pathological Narcissism* (New York, 1975).

207. For an excellent summary of recent work by Kohut and his colleagues, see Ernest S. Wolf, "Recent Advances in the Psychology of the Self: An Outline of Basic Concepts," in *Comprehensive Psychiatry*, XVII (1976), 37–46.

208. Heinz Kohut, "Thoughts on Narcissism and Narcissistic Rage," in *The Psychoanalytic Study of the Child*, XXVII (1972), 360–400; see also Kohut, *The Restoration of the Self*, 116ff.

209. Demos, *A Little Commonwealth*, 49–51; Bushman, *From Puritan to Yankee*, ch. 1.

210. See pp. 63–64.

211. Dorothy Dinnerstein, *The Mermaid and the Minotaur: Sexual Arrangements and Human Malaise* (New York, 1976), 33. Dinnerstein's extraordinary book—easily the best of all studies on the psychological underpinnings of misogyny—provides the basis for this discussion of the woman/witch equation.

212. *Ibid.*, 108.

213. *Ibid.*, 28–29, 165.

214. *Ibid.*, 164.

215. *Ibid.*, 84.

216. *Ibid.*, 175–76.

217. Karen Horney, *Feminine Psychology*, Harold Kelman, ed. (New York, 1967); see especially "The Distrust Between the Sexes," 107–18. Wolfgang Lederer, *The Fear of Women* (New York, 1968). H. R. Hays, *The Dangerous Sex* (New York, 1964). Joseph Rheingold, *The Fear of Being a Woman* (New York, 1964). Bruno Bettelheim, *Symbolic Wounds* (New York, 1954). Marjorie C. Barnett, " 'I Can't' versus 'He Won't,' " in *Journal of the American Psychoanalytic Association*, XVI (1968), 588–600. Edith Jacobson, "Development of the Wish for a Child in Boys," in *The Psychoanalytic Study of the Child*, V (1950), 139–52. Daniel S. Jaffe, "The Masculine Envy of Woman's Procreative Function," in *Journal of the American Psychoanalytic Association*, XVI (1968), 121–48. Kato van Leeuwen, "Pregnancy Envy in the Male," in *International Journal of Psychoanalysis*, XLVII (1966), 319–24. Robert C. Bak, "The Phallic Woman," in *The Psychoanalytic Study of the Child*, XXIII (1968), 15–36.

218. This, at any rate, is the strong impression gained from personal and legal records dealing with episodes of childbirth, and from manuals of midwifery. See the brief account of colonial practice in Richard W. Wertz and Dorothy C. Wertz, *Lying In: A History of Childbirth in America* (New York, 1977).

219. Demos, *A Little Commonwealth*, 133.

220. Whenever infants are mentioned in records from the period, their mothers are invariably found with them.

221. See Erik H. Erikson, *Childhood and Society*, 2nd ed. (New York, 1963), ch. 7, "Eight Ages of Man."

222. *Ibid.*, 253–54.

223. Testimony by Hannah Post, printed in Massachusetts Historical Society, *Collections*, III, 224.

224. Demos, *A Little Commonwealth*, 68.

225. Robert Ashton, ed., *The Works of John Robinson*, 2 vols. (Boston, 1851), I, 245–47.

226. *Ibid.*, I, 226.

227. See, for example, the opinions of Cotton Mather on discipline of the young in his little treatise "Some Special Points Relating to the Education of My Children," reprinted in Perry Miller and Thomas A. Johnson, eds., *The Puritans*, 2 vols. (New York, 1963), II, 724–27. See also the words which Mather attributed (elsewhere) to his clerical colleague, Nathaniel Ward: "Of young persons he would himself give this advice: 'Whatever you do, be sure to maintain shame in them,' for if that once be gone, there is no hope that they'll ever come to good"; *Magnalia Christi Americana* (Hartford, 1853), I, 522.

Notes to Chapter 7

1. The deponents (and the dates of their testimony) were as follows: Samuel Parsons (February 19, 1658), William Russell (February 19, 1658), Goodwife Simons (February 24, 1658), Mrs. Gardiner (February 24, 1658), Goody Brooks (February 27, 1658), Goody Birdsall (March 11, 1658), Goody Edwards (March 11, 1658). These materials are published in *Records of the Town of Easthampton, Long Island, Suffolk County, N.Y.*, 5 vols. (Sag Harbor, N.Y., 1887–92), I, 128–30, 132–33, 139–40.

2. Depositions by Goody Bishop (February 27, 1658) and Goody Birdsall (February 27, 1658), in *ibid.*, I, 134–35.

3. Deposition by Goody Edwards (February 27, 1658), in *ibid.*, I, 134.

4. Deposition by Goody Birdsall (February 27, 1658), in *ibid.*, I, 135.

5. Deposition by Goody Hand (February 27, 1658), in *ibid.*, I, 134–35.

6. See *ibid.*, I, 140.

7. Deposition by Thomas Talmage (March 1, 1658), in *ibid.*, I, 152–53.

8. Deposition by Richard Stratton (March 8, 1658), in *ibid.*, I, 154–55.
9. Deposition by Goodman Vaile (February 27, 1658), in *ibid.*, I, 136.
10. Deposition by Goody Hand (February 27, 1658), in *ibid.*, I, 134–35.
11. *Ibid.*, I, 140.
12. *Records of the Particular Court of Connecticut, 1639–1663*, 188.
13. *Ibid.*, 188–89.
14. This letter is reprinted in Trumbull and Hoadly, eds., *The Public Records of the Colony of Connecticut*, I, 572–73.
15. On the founding and early history of Easthampton consult the following: Jeanette Edwards Rattray, *East Hampton History* (East Hampton, N.Y., 1953); John Lyon Gardiner, "Notes and Observations on the Town of East Hampton, L.I.," in E. B. O'Callaghan, ed., *The Documentary History of the State of New York*, 4 vols., (Albany, N.Y., 1849–57), I, 674–86; Martha B. Flint, *Early Long Island: A Colonial Study* (New York, 1896); Gabriel Furman, *Antiquities of Long Island* (New York, 1875); Benjamin F. Thompson, *The History of Long Island*, 2nd ed. (New York, 1843), vol. I; Nathaniel S. Prime, *History of Long Island* (New York, 1845); Silas Wood, *A Sketch of the First Settlement of the Several Towns of Long Island* (Brooklyn, N.Y., 1828).
16. John Winthrop, *The History of New England from 1630–1649*, James Savage, ed., 2 vols. (Boston, Mass., 1838), II, 5. On the founding of Southampton, see James Truslow Adams, *History of the Town of Southampton* (Bridgehampton, L.I., 1918); also Thompson, Prime, and Wood, as cited in preceding note.
17. H. P. Hedges, "Introduction," in *Records of the Town of Easthampton*, I, 12. The comment by Gov. Dongan is quoted in Flint, *Early Long Island*, 222.
18. Records of the town meeting and of the local court are printed in *Records of the Town of Easthampton*, I. The same volume contains much information about land ownership. Tax-lists can be found in *ibid.*, 66, and in O'Callaghan, ed., *The Documentary History of the State of New York*, II, 441–42, 539–42. The best single compilation of genealogical materials is in Rattray, *East Hampton History*; there are also various genealogies of particular families associated with the town.
19. A map showing the homelots of the early settlers is published in Arthur W. Talmage, *The Talmadge, Tallmadge, and Talmage Genealogy* (New York, 1909).
20. The various divisions of town lands are carefully described in *Records of the Town of Easthampton*, I, *passim*.
21. Provisions for fencing—a public matter—are noted in *ibid.*, I, *passim*.
22. For a full and richly evocative account of the history of Gardiner's Island, see Robert Payne, *The Island* (New York, 1958). See also Robert D. L. Gardiner, "Gardiner's Island," in *New York History*, XIV, 53–60, and David Gardiner, "The Gardiner Family and the Lordship and Manor of

Gardiner's Island," in *The New York Genealogical and Biographical Record,* XXIII, 159–90.

23. See, for example, *Records of the Town of Easthampton,* I, 8, 11, 21, 30, 31, and *passim.*

24. See Appendix A, Table 1. The roster of inhabitants, on which this summary is based, has been compiled from all available source materials on early Easthampton. (See the various citations in notes 15 and 18 above.) Some imprecision in individual cases seems unavoidable (e.g. as to exact age), but this should not substantially affect the group totals.

25. *Records of the Town of Easthampton,* I, 31, 77, 29, 119.

26. *Ibid.,* I, 27, 37, 44, 257, 103, 179.

27. *Ibid.,* I, 112, 179, 110. The tax-list with detailed information on domestic animals was made in the year 1683 and is printed in O'Callaghan, ed., *The Documentary History of the State of New York,* II, 539–42.

28. *Records of the Town of Easthampton,* I, 100–101.

29. *Ibid.,* I, 8, 18, 29, 54, 171. For an account of early whaling enterprise, with some reference to Easthampton, see Everett J. Edwards and Jeanette Edwards Rattray, *"Whale Off!" The Story of American Shore Whaling* (New York, 1956).

30. *Records of the Town of Easthampton,* I, 7, 32, 20, 14, 17, 11, 13, 15.

31. *Ibid.,* I, 20, 27, 36, 55.

32. *Ibid.,* I, 44, 31. For additional examples of the rotation of civic responsibilities, see *ibid.,* I, 171, 185, 192, 218.

33. *Ibid.,* I, 7, 28–29, 100. The manuscript original of the town records apparently contained passages of notes and other abbreviated material, in which there was reference to particular violations of these orders, viz. the names of some men who were "wanting at the meeting," or simply "not voting." (There was also an occasion when several "withdrew from the meeting, when we were about the meadow.") See *ibid.,* I, 85–87, 141–44.

34. *Ibid.,* I, 14, 10, 203.

35. The standard oaths of office for townsman, recorder, and constable are in *ibid.,* I, 6–7. The powers attaching to the office of townsman are described at intervals throughout the town records; see, for example, I, 7, 17, 18, 20. On other offices, and on the special committees, see *ibid.,* I, *passim.*

36. See, for example, *ibid.,* I, 7, 10, 12, 17.

37. Most town offices were filled on an annual basis, at a meeting held in early October. The names of incumbents were then duly noted in the town records.

38. These categories are the ones most frequently applied by New England villages when "seating the meetinghouse." On the latter practice, see Robert J. Dinkin, "Provincial Massachusetts: A Deferential or a Democratic Society," unpub. Ph.D. diss., Columbia University (1968). Dinkin's study also throws light on general questions of social stratifica-

tion in early New England—as does another unpublished dissertation, by Linda Auwers Bissell, "Family, Friends, and Neighbors: Social Interaction in Seventeenth-Century Windsor, Connecticut," Brandeis University (1973). There is also some useful material in Gary B. Nash, *Class and Society in Early America* (Englewood Cliffs, N.J., 1970).

39. The average of land-allotments by rank-groups was as follows. Group I (high), 20.7 acres; Group II (middle), 16.1 acres; Group III (low), 14.7 acres.

40. The householders who arrived in Easthampton without apparent connections to Kent, the Essex County towns in Massachusetts, or Southampton were Lion Gardiner, Thomas James, Thomas Chatfield, and Benjamin Price. All four can be firmly identified with the topmost status-group.

41. See Note on Social Stratification, Table 2, p. 245.

42. See Note on Social Stratification, Table 3, p. 245.

43. See Note on Social Stratification, Table 4, p. 245.

44. A map of early home-lots in the town appears in Chapter 9. See p. 281.

45. For a fuller description of Lion Gardiner's life and accomplishments, see p. 238. The singular eminence of Gardiner and the Rev. James is illustrated by certain provisions noted in the town records. The Rev. James, for example, was to "have liberty to grind [corn] on the second day of the week when he cometh [to the mill], and he shall not be letted [i.e. delayed] by any men, but shall take place before any other that shall tend there before his team cometh." Similarly, all householders were required to join in "cutting out" whales—except that "Mr. James and Mr. Gardiner shall give a quart of liquor apiece to the cutters of every whale and be free from cutting." *Records of the Town of Easthampton*, I, 273, 199.

46. It is not known how many towns in early New England presented the same correlation of spatial and social patterning. (But see also Bissell, "Family, Friends, and Neighbors.") We do know that New Englanders typically arranged other forms of space so as to express differences in rank—"seating the meetinghouse" being the most obvious case in point. Unfortunately, there is no extant seating list for the Easthampton church. It should be noted, finally, that field allotments at Easthampton reflected status in quantitative terms (i.e. size of grant) but not geographical ones (proximity to others). Apparently the fact of residence gave a singular importance to the way home-lots were distributed.

47. *Records of the Town of Easthampton*, I, 154, 199.

48. *Ibid.*, I, 19–20.

49. *Ibid.*, I, 12, 16, 13, 224.

50. These ages must be estimated from a rather roundabout set of calculations. It is known that Joshua Garlick, junior, married Elizabeth Hardie in about the year 1664. The couple had five children (born between 1665

and 1677), but Joshua, Jr., died in 1677. His widow was remarried in 1679, and had one child by her second husband (John Parsons) in 1680. This suggests a birth date for Elizabeth not much before 1640 (i.e. making her not much over forty when her last child was born). The assumption that Joshua Garlick, Jr., was perhaps one to five years older than his wife makes his birth date fall between the years 1630 and 1640. Remember Garlick (daughter of Joshua, Sr., and Elizabeth) was married to Richard Shaw in about 1660. (In November of that year Joshua, Sr., deeded lands to "my son-in-law Richard Shaw".) She had seven children, born between about 1661 and 1672. This suggests that her own birth occurred no earlier than 1630 and no later than 1640. In sum, *both* of Elizabeth Garlick's children seem to have been born during the decade of the 1630s. The mother, in turn, cannot easily have been born after 1615 and it is unlikely that she was born earlier than 1605 (which, from other evidence, seems about the year when her husband was born). On the families of Joshua Garlick, Jr., and Remember Garlick, see Norman H. Vanaman, "The Account Book of John Parsons," in *The Cape May County, New Jersey Magazine of History and Genealogy*, II (1943), 167–170. On the family of Elizabeth [Hardie] Garlick, see John E. Stilwell, *Historical and Genealogical Miscellany: Data Relating to the Settlement and Settlers of New York and New Jersey*, III (New York, 1914), and *The American Genealogist*, XXI, 119. There is also pertinent information scattered through the pages of the *Records of the Town of Easthampton*.

51. That William Blanchard's "sister Garlick" was indeed Elizabeth (wife of Joshua) cannot be finally proved. However, exhaustive research in archival materials from early New England has uncovered no other persons carrying the same surname. The fact that Goody Ann Blanchard, and apparently also William himself, lived in Essex County (like the Garlicks) during the 1640s, serves to strengthen the case. On the latter point, see the various Blanchard references in *Records and Files of the Quarterly Courts of Essex County, Massachusetts*, I, 45, 57, 79. For a careful genealogical study of the Blanchard family, see *New England Historical and Genealogical Register*, XCIII, 162–70.

52. *Records and Files of the Quarterly Courts of Essex County, Massachusetts*, I, 13, 16, 19, 23. The original notations of these court appearances by Joseph Garlick are in a manuscript volume, Essex County Court, 1638–1648, leaves 44, 54, 62, 73 (Essex County Courthouse, Salem, Mass.).

53. Letters of Lion Gardiner to John Winthrop, Jr., February 28, 1652 and undated (but probably January 1652), in *The Winthrop Papers*, Massachusetts Historical Society, *Collections*, 4th ser., VII, 62–63.

54. See the list of allotments in the "northwest meadow," dated July 5, 1653, in *Records of the Town of Easthampton*, I, 37. That the Garlicks had

previously resided on Gardiner's Island is established by several of the depositions charging Elizabeth with witchcraft. (Thus, for example, Goody Hand recalled Goody Davis's comment when the Garlicks were moving to Easthampton "that the town would repent it as well as they had done at the island"; *ibid.*, I, 135.) Note also the accusation, mentioned in Garlick's indictment before the court at Hartford, that she had performed her witchcraft "since the year 1650." (*Records of the Particular Court of Connecticut, 1639–1663*, 188.)

55. Garlick's lands are listed, apparently in full, in *Records of the Town of Easthampton*, I, 488. His cattle-mark is noted in *ibid.*, I, 236. The early tax-lists are in *ibid.*, I, 66, and in O'Callaghan, ed., *The Documentary History of the State of New York*, II, 441–42, 539–42.

56. The whaling enterprise is noted in *Records of the Town of Easthampton*, I, 430. Daniel Fairfield was called "servant of Joshua Garlick" in May 1654; at the time Fairfield was being prosecuted with several others, for "masturbation" (see *ibid.*, I, 57). It is tempting to connect this man with the most notorious sexual offender in the early history of New England —the Daniel Fairfield of Salem, Mass., who in 1641 was convicted of "wanton dalliance" with three young daughters of a local magistrate; however, firm evidence to make such a connection is lacking. A summary of the Salem Fairfield's misdeeds may be found in Edwin Powers, *Crime and Punishment in Early Massachusettes, 1620–1692* (Boston, 1966), 265–66. The deed of indenture, binding Caleb Dayton to the Garlicks "for the term of sixteen years," is in *Records of the Town of Easthampton*, I, 224. Another deed, from 1693, documents the presence of John Shaw in the Garlick household ("whereas I, John Shaw . . . was brought up by my grandfather Joshua Garlick as his child"); see *ibid.*, II, 290–91.

57. *Ibid.*, I, 58; II, 250.

58. The figures attributed to local "reputation" are quoted in Norman H. Vanaman, "The Account Book of John Parsons," *The Cape May County, New Jersey Magazine of History and Genealogy*, II, 167–70. The notation of Joshua Garlick's death is in *Records of the Town of Easthampton*, V, 554. There is some evidence that the Garlicks spent their last years with their grandchild Richard Shaw. This presumably was the reason behind two deeds to Shaw, in 1692 and 1693, conveying the Garlick's entire estate. See *ibid.*, II, 279, 292.

59. Falk Davis was one of two co-signers, with Lion Gardiner, of the deed establishing the latter's proprietorship of Gardiner's Island in 1639. (See *Records of the Town of Easthampton*, I, 2.) Before moving to Gardiner's Island, Davis lived briefly at Hartford, Connecticut; in 1639 he sold his house and lands there. (See Hartford Town Votes, in Connecticut Historical Society, *Collections*, VI, [Hartford, 1897], 15.) Davis's Easthampton land portion is noted in *Records of the Town of Easthampton*, I, 66. After his first wife had died, in about 1659, Davis was remarried to

Mary [——————] (Haines) Dayton, a two-time widow whose previous husbands were quite prominent townsmen. His trial for masturbation is
noted in *ibid.*, I, 57. For other traces of his career see the town records
of Southhampton, Brookhaven, and Jamaica, N.Y.—in addition to those
of Easthampton itself.

60. William Edwards's land portion is noted in the rate-list for 1653, in
Records of the Town of Easthampton, I, 66. His appearances at court
in the early 1650s are recorded in *ibid.*, I, 20, 21, 33. (There was also a
slander suit, and then a counter-suit, involving Edwards and a resident
of Southampton; see *Southampton Town Records*, II, 31. On his involvement, still earlier, in Essex County Court cases, see *Records and Files of
the Quarterly Courts of Essex County, Massachusetts*, I, 29, 32, 42, 156,
162, 172.) On the various court proceedings against his wife Ann, see
ibid., I, 58, and *Records of the Town of Easthampton*, I, 21, 32–33, 314.
The remark linking Ann Edwards to Goody Garlick (and witchcraft)
is reported in the deposition by Goody Bishop in *ibid.*, I, 134. For
genealogical information on the Edwards family see *New York Genealogical and Biographical Record*, LXXXII, 5ff.

61. William Simons seems to have lived alternately at Easthampton and on
Gardiner's Island. (When Lion Gardiner died in 1663, the inventory of
his estate included a house on the island that "Goodman Simons lives
in." *Southampton Town Records*, II, 47.) Simons's land portion at Easthampton was in the lowest category. (*Records of the Town of Easthampton*, I, 66.) On the court cases involving Simons and his wife, see *ibid.*,
I, 58, 67, 87.

62. On Nathan Birdsall: see his landholdings, listed in *Records of the Town
of Easthampton*, I, 442; his father Henry's inventory in *Records and
Files of the Quarterly Courts of Essex County, Massachusetts*, I, 246;
records of his various misdemeanors at New Haven (where he lived in
the 1640s), in Hoadly, ed., *Records of the Colony and Plantation of
New Haven*, I, 109, 120, 152; records of his trial (with his wife) for
defamation of the minister, at Easthampton, in *Records of the Town of
Easthampton*, I, 181; and notice of his subsequent doings in local records
from Southhold and Hempstead, Long Island. See also George A.
Birdsall, *The Birdsall Family* (priv. printed, 1964). On Nathaniel
Bishop, see his landholdings in *Records of the Town of Easthampton*,
I, 440; his will in New York Historical Society, *Collections*, XXV, 472;
numerous references to the doings of his father and brothers in *Records
and Files of the Quarterly Courts of Essex County, Massachusetts*, I,
passim.

63. William Russell's presence at Southampton is noted in local records from
the year 1657 and thereafter. He had one of the lowest rights of "commonage" of all the town's residents. His death by drowning in 1678

prompted an inquest—on which, see New York Historical Society, *Collections*, XXV, 113. On other aspects of his career, see Adams, *History of the Town of Southampton, passim.*

64. The best single account of Lion Gardiner and his immediate family is found in David Gardiner, "The Gardiner Family and the Lordship and Manor of Gardiner's Island," in *New York Genealogical and Biographical Record*, XXIII, 159–90. See also Payne, *The Island.*

65. On the early history of the Howell family, see *New York Genealogical and Biographical Record*, XXVIII, 51ff., and Emma Howell Ross, *Descendants of Edward Howell* (priv. printed, 1968).

Notes to Chapter 8

1. Essex County Court Papers, XXVII, leaf 128.
2. *Ibid.*, XXVII, leaf 121.
3. *Records and Files of the Quarterly Courts of Essex County, Massachusetts*, II, 157.
4. *Ibid.*, II, 246.
5. New London County Court Records, III, leaf 38 (Connecticut State Library, Hartford).
6. Middlesex Court Files, folder 34, paper 2300.
7. Essex County Court Papers, VI, leaf 33.
8. Middlesex Court Files, folder 45, paper not numbered.
9. Connecticut Colonial Probate Records, III (County Court, 1663–1677), paper 35. For additional materials in this case see Connecticut Archives: Crimes and Misdemeanors, Series 1 (1662–1789), I, part one, papers 8, 9 (Connecticut State Library, Hartford).
10. *Records and Files of the Quarterly Courts of Essex County, Massachusetts*, VII, 46, 49.
11. Connecticut Colonial Probate Records, III (County Court, 1663–1677), paper 128.
12. See Charles Thornton Libby, ed., *Province and Court Records of Maine*, 4 vols. (Portland, Maine, 1929–58), II, 86.
13. James Phinney Baxter, ed., *Documentary History of the State of Maine*, 2nd ser., IV, 168–69.
14. Mrs. Elizabeth Godman vs. Mr. Stephen Goodyear *et al.* (August 4, 1653); Hoadly, ed., *Records of the Colony or Jurisdiction of New Haven*, II, 30.
15. Noted in the Pynchon Court Record; see Joseph H. Smith, ed., *Colonial Justice in Western Massachusetts* (Cambridge, Mass., 1961), 219–20.
16. *Records and Files of the Quarterly Courts of Essex County, Massachusetts*, I, 301, 325.
17. County Court, Norfolk: Records, 1648–78, leaf 22.

18. Hoadly, ed., *Records of the Colony or Jurisdiction of New Haven*, II, 34.

19. County Court, Salem: Records, 1648–55; leaves 28, 33; Essex County Court Papers, I, leaf 71; *ibid.*, XII, leaves 86–87.

20. See, for example, Godman vs. Goodyear *et al.*, in Hoadly, ed., *Records of the Colony or Jurisdiction of New Haven*, II, 30. Another such case occurred in Cambridge, Massachusetts, in 1659–60, in connection with widow Winifred Holman. (See Middlesex County Court Records, I, 165; Middlesex Court Files, folder 25, papers 1468–1480).

21. Twenty-six cases of witchcraft/slander are noted in records still extant from early New England. Six were terminated short of a verdict ("non-suited"). Fifteen were decided in favor of the plaintiff. And the remaining five were decided for the defendant.

22. Middlesex County Court Records, I, 91, 92.

23. Middlesex Court Files, folder 16, papers 626, 646–74.

24. *Ibid.*, paper 658.

25. *Ibid.*, papers 666, 662, 672.

26. *Ibid.*, paper 665.

27. *Ibid.*, paper 665.

28. *Ibid.*, paper 665.

29. *Ibid.*, paper 664.

30. *Ibid.*, paper 665.

31. *Ibid.*, papers 673, 659, 661, 660, 668.

32. *Ibid.*, papers 669, 673, 663.

33. Deposition by Simon Beamon, September 19, 1656 (Autograph File, Houghton Library, Harvard University, Cambridge, Mass.); Middlesex Court Files, folder 16, paper 674.

34. *Ibid.*, paper 674.

35. *Ibid.*, papers 646, 672.

36. The reference here is to Hannah Langdon; see *ibid.*, paper 666.

37. *Ibid.*, papers 665, 674.

38. *Ibid.*, paper 665.

39. There is no extant document which directly establishes a birth date for Mary Parsons. However, the medical journal of John Winthrop, Jr., in a reference from the year 1666, calls her "about 40." (See the extracts from the journal printed in *The American Genealogist*, XXIV, 45.) This estimate is consistent also with the year of her marriage (1646) and the year of the birth of her last child (1672).

40. The most recent genealogical account of the Bliss family is found in *The American Genealogist*, LII (1976), 193–97. For earlier accounts (also useful) see Mary Lovering Holman, *Ancestry of Colonel John Harrington Stevens and His Wife Frances Helen Miller* (Concord, N.H., 1948), 345–47; Mary Walton Ferris, *Dawes-Gates Ancestral*

Lines, 2 vols. (place not given, 1931), II, 123–27; and John Homer Bliss, *Genealogy of the Bliss Family in America* (Boston, 1881).

41. See *ibid.*, 22.

42. In February 1640 "Thomas Blysse" of Mount Wollaston was granted lands in proportion to his family of "9 heads." (See *Second Report of the Record Commissioners of the City of Boston, Containing the Boston Records, 1634–1660, and the Book of Possessions* [Boston, 1881], 50.) Some genealogists have been disposed to regard this as referring to a second Thomas Bliss, who was subsequently settled at Rehoboth. However, the date and the indicated family size seem to make a better fit with our Thomas (the father of Mary).

43. Connecticut Historical Society, *Collections*, XIV, 256–58.

44. The names of Thomas Bliss, Sr., and Thomas Bliss, Jr., were included in a list of "such inhabitants as were granted lots to have only at the town's courtesy, with liberty to fetch wood and keep swine or cows by proportion on the common." This list was entered in the Hartford Book of Distributions, immediately after the names of the regular proprietors ("such inhabitants as have rights in undivided lands"). See *ibid.*, VI, 16–20. There is reason to think that members of the non-proprietary group were subsequently accorded some rights in undivided lands, for their names appear on a list of grantees receiving "lots" on the east side of the Connecticut River in 1641. (See *ibid.*, VI, 49–53.) There was also a special grant to Thomas Bliss, Sr., made in March 1641 (*ibid.*, VI, 48).

45. The court case is noted in the records of the Particular Court for May 21, 1647: "In the action of Bliss, plaintiff, against Lyman and Arnold, the defendants are to pay 20 shillings and costs of court." (See *Records of the Particular Court of Connecticut, 1639–1663*, 46.) The defendants are not further identified, but the Lyman name is of obvious interest here. At a minimum, this case shows direct (and adversary) involvement between members of the Bliss and Lyman families almost a decade before Mary [Bliss] Parsons opposed Sarah [Lyman] Bridgman in the witchcraft/slander trial at Northampton. On the prosecution of Thomas Bliss for failure to attend military training, see *ibid.*, 45.

46. The lands of Thomas Bliss are listed in full in Connecticut Historical Society, *Collections*, VI, 256–58. His share in the special division of lots on the east side of the town was 6 acres. He was, in fact, one of 24 persons to receive a 6-acre portion. There were 110 other Hartford inhabitants who received lots larger than this, and only 12 with smaller portions. (See *ibid.*, VI 49–53.)

47. For the inventory of Thomas Bliss's estate, and the actions of the court in dealing with it, see Colonial Records of Connecticut, LV, 28 (Connecticut State Library, Hartford, Conn.).

48. Mary [Bliss] Parsons was by this time living at Springfield. Apparently she had returned to visit her parents during her father's last illness. See *ibid.*, LV, 28.

49. This story is fully recounted in Bliss, *Geneology of the Bliss Family in America,* 16–20—where it is described as belonging to "the ancient traditions of the Bliss family." Genealogists have not been willing to accept it without some documentary confirmation; indeed they have advanced at least two alternative theories of the Bliss origins. One of these links the family with the parish of Daventry in Northampton-shire; however, the Thomas Bliss found there was almost certainly the Rehoboth—rather than the Hartford—settler. A more recent study proposes a connection to the village of Redborough in Gloucestershire —yet here, too, there are difficulties. (On these points, see Charles Arthur Hoppin, *The Bliss Book* [Boston, 1913]; and Myrtle Stevens Hyde, "Thomas and Margaret Hulins Bliss of Hartford Connecticut," in *The American Genealogist*, LII, 193–97.) The case for holding to the "traditional" account (preserved by succeeding Bliss generations) depends on the very richness and intricacy of that account; it is hard to imagine so much information having been put together so elaborately with no historical foundation at all. (On the other hand, it is equally hard to feel confident about particular details.) There is the additional, and intriguing, point that a Belstone link for the Blisses would bring their origins and those of Joseph Parsons into very close proximity. Not only do Belstone and Great Torrington belong to the same county (Devon); they also belong to the same part of that county. It is thus not improbable that Joseph Parsons and Mary Bliss should have formed their relation (at least in part) on a feeling of common origins—and not impossible that their families were previously known to each other in Old England.

50. The basis for this supposition is a letter from a great-nephew of Joseph's, the Rev. Jonathan Parsons, dated October 20, 1769. Addressing his own son, the Rev. Jonathan writes as follows about the family origins: "I will tell you as near as my memory enables me (as I have no record of the matter but what I heard from my parents). I suppose my great-grandfather Parsons came from Great Torrington about 20 or 30 miles from Tiverton and not far from Exeter. He came over and brought my grandfather, Benjamin Parsons, and other children, about 130 years ago, perhaps 140." This letter is published in *The New England Historical and Genealogical Register*, XII (1858), 175. The year of Joseph Parsons's birth is inferred from his testimony in a Northampton court case of 1662. He stated therein that he was about seventeen at the time of witnessing William Pynchon's land purchase of 1636. On this point, see Holman, *Ancestry of Colonel John Harrington Stevens*, 338.

51. On this transaction, see Ferris, *Dawes-Gates Ancestral Lines*, II, 625.

52. The most exhaustive extant study of the Parsons genealogy has established a connection by marriage between an Essex branch of the family and a first cousin of William Pynchon. However, the link between the Essex and the Devonshire Parsonses remains problematic. See Henry M. Burt, *Cornet Joseph Parsons* (Garden City, N.Y., 1898), 93.

53. Pynchon Account Books, I, 100 (Manuscript volume in the Judd Manuscripts, Forbes Library, Northampton, Mass.).

54. *Ibid.*, I, 100.

55. The list is printed in Henry M. Burt, *The First Century in the History of Springfield*, 2 vols. (Springfield, Mass., 1898), I, 190–91.

56. These details of Joseph Parsons's life are more fully explored in Burt, *Cornet Joseph Parsons*, 13–15.

57. On the public life of Joseph Parsons at Northampton, see *ibid.*, 43–44, 49–51, 56–57; and Ferris, *Dawes-Gates Ancestral Lines*, II, 627ff. For original material see the Town Records of Northampton, I, *passim* (manuscript volume at the Town Hall, Northampton, Mass.).

58. Most of the extensive Parsons-Pynchon dealings, as noted in the Pynchon Account Books, have been excerpted and printed in Burt, *Cornet Joseph Parsons*, 18–42.

59. As noted in Burt, *Cornet Joseph Parsons*, 57, and Ferris, *Dawes-Gates Ancestral Lines*, II, 629.

60. The inventory of Joseph Parsons's estate, as presented to a county court on March 25, 1684, is printed in Burt, *Cornet Joseph Parsons*, 66–68. The decedent had left no will, and so the court was asked to ratify an elaborate settlement formulated by his survivors; this, too, is in *ibid.*, 68–71. Of his business activities the fullest record is found in the Pynchon Account Books. His role as proprietor of a "store" at Northampton is evidenced by the scope and bulk of his orders from Pynchon —many of which had nothing to do with the fur trade (e.g. "6 lbs. sugar . . . 1 lb. pepper . . . 3 doz. gr[ea]t silk buttons . . . 1 doz. awl blades . . . 3 inkhorns . . . 3 doz. small scissors . . . 200 of 8d. nails . . ." and an enormous variety of fabric types). The geographical range of his dealings is clear from occasional references, in his account with Pynchon, to other persons and communities (e.g. "Received for what I allow you [Joseph Parsons] for fetching your goods from Hartford"; "Paid for you to Goodman Bissell [of Windsor]"; "Joseph Parsons, debtor: 10 shillings in money at Boston"). On these points, see the extracts from the Pynchon Account Book, in Burt, *Cornet Joseph Parsons*, 18–42. On Parsons's role as ordinary-keeper, mill-owner, and land speculator, see Ferris, *Dawes-Gates Ancestral Lines*, II, 628–30.

61. A number of the court cases involving Joseph Parsons are described in Burt, *Cornet Joseph Parsons*, 51–56. See also the Pynchon Court Record, in Smith, ed., *Colonial Justice in Western Massachusetts*, 221–22, 238, 295; *Records of the Particular Court of Connecticut*,

1639–1663, 79–80; Hampshire County Probate Records, I (manuscript volume in the Town Hall, Northampton, Mass.), 34, 39–40 and *passim*.

62. For brief summaries of the careers of Benjamin and Thomas Parsons, see Burt, *Cornet Joseph Parsons*, 78, 105.

63. See Ferris, *Dawes-Gates Ancestral Lines*, II, 634.

64. Pynchon Court Record, in Smith, ed., *Colonial Justice in Western Massachusetts*, 96, 230, 290, 250.

65. *Ibid.*, 234, 298. The will of Margaret Bliss is printed in Holman, *Ancestry of Colonel John Harrington Stevens*, 346–47. The manuscript copy of her inventory is in Hampshire County Probate Records, II, 22.

66. Colonial Records of Connecticut, LV, 28; Holman, *Ancestry of Colonel John Harrington Stevens*, 346; deposition by Margaret Bliss, June 20, 1656, in Middlesex Court Files, folder 16, paper 662.

67. On the names and birth-dates of Mary Parsons's children, see Ferris, *Dawes-Gates Ancestral Lines*, II, 636. The comparison with other Northampton families is based on a variety of genealogical works, and on family reconstitution carried out by the author.

68. The most concise, and most reliable, source of genealogical information about the Lyman family is Holman, *Ancestry of Colonel John Harrington Stevens*, 383–87.

69. See *ibid.*, 384. The sale of Richard Lyman's properties covered "two messuages, a garden, orchard and diverse lands arable, also a meadow and pasture." At about the same time Richard's brother, Henry Lyman, sold property in a neighboring village; hence it appears that the two of them had decided to emigrate together. But Henry died soon after arriving in New England.

70. A partial list of passengers for this sailing is found in Charles Edward Banks, *The Planters of the Commonwealth* (Baltimore, 1972), 94–95. The ship's arrival was noted in the journal of Governor Winthrop himself. See Hosmer, ed., *Winthrop's Journal*, I, 70.

71. Connecticut Historical Society, *Collections*, VI, 18–19.

72. The most ambitious attempt to provide the Lymans with aristocratic connections is found in Coleman Lyman, *Genealogy of the Lyman Family in Great Britain and America* (Albany, N.Y., 1872), part one. Other genealogists have noted errors in this work which undercut many of its conclusions. (See, for example, L. E. deForest and A. L. deForest, *Moore and Allied Families* [New York, 1938], 348.) However, there are some letters, still extant, in which Elizabeth Lyman, the widow of Henry (and thus a sister-in-law of Richard), addresses Sir John Leman as "kinsman." See Holman, *Ancestry of Colonel John Harrington Stevens*, 383.

73. Lyman, *Genealogy of the Lyman Family*, 36; Connecticut Historical Society, *Collections*, VI, 22–23. There is one other point of comparison between Richard Lyman and Thomas Bliss, with respect to property.

Richard's "home-lot" was three acres large; Thomas's was two roods, i.e. approximately one-half an acre. See *ibid.*, XIV, 256, 271.

74. This passage is quoted in Holman, *Ancestry of Colonel John Harrington Stevens*, 384.

75. *Ibid.*, 384.

76. Richard Lyman's estate yielded a total value of about £83. His will, the inventory of his estate, and the "note" left by his wife before her decrease, are printed in Trumbull and Hoadly, eds., *The Public Records of the Colony of Connecticut*, I, 442–44.

77. The earliest references to Hartford lands belonging to James Bridgman are in Connecticut Historical Society, *Collections*, XIV, 297, 570. The proximity of Bridgman's home-lot to that of the Lymans can be inferred from the descriptions of their respective boundaries; see *ibid.*, XIV, 271, 570.

78. A short summary of this part of James Bridgman's life as reconstructed from scattered references in the town records of Springfield and elsewhere, is found in Burt Nichols Bridgman and Joseph Clark Bridgman, *Genealogy of the Bridgman Family* (Hyde Park, Mass., 1894), 9–12. See also the Pynchon Court Record, in Smith, ed., *Colonial Justice in Western Massachusetts*, 215, 220, 221, 229.

79. Antiquarians and genealogists have long supposed that James Bridgman was by trade a carpenter. This idea finds confirmation in the Pynchon Account Books, where James is credited with services such as "the making of 2 bedsteads"; "sawing planks for the mill"; and "5 days in joiner's work." See Pynchon Account Books, I, 69–71.

80. The tax-list is printed in Burt, *The First Century in the History of Springfield*, I, 190–91. The lands owned by James Bridgman at the time of his death are described in the inventory of his estate, as printed in Bridgman and Bridgman, *Genealogy of the Bridgman Family*, 13–14.

81. *Ibid.*, 11–13. For original materials, see the Town Records of Northampton, I, *passim*, and the Pynchon Court Record, in Smith, ed., *Colonial Justice in Western Massachusetts*, 219, 239, 261. The assessment of James Bridgman's wealth, in relation to that of his fellow-townsmen, is based in part on the list of proprietary holdings in James Hammond Trumbull, *The History of Northampton, Mass.* (Northampton, 1898), 145–47.

82. On these points see Bridgman and Bridgman, *Genealogy of the Bridgman Family, passim*.

83. Scattered material on the experience of the Lyman brothers during the period 1642–56 is found in the *Records of the Particular Court of Connecticut, 1639–1663*, 18, 46, 83, 120, 122, 136, 151, 158, 161. A list of the mill-rates paid by Hartford inhabitants between 1655 and 1657 finds all three Lymans included for the first of these years, but not for the other two. This dates their departure for Northampton in

a definite way. (See Connecticut Historical Society, *Collections*, XIV, 495–97.) On the brothers' marriages see Holman, *Ancestry of Colonel John Harrigton Stevens*, 385–86. On the public careers of Richard and John Lyman at Northampton, see deForest and deForest, *Moore and Allied Families*, 348–54; Lyman, *Genealogy of the Lyman Family*, 35–40; and original materials in the Town Records of Northampton, I, *passim*. For the inventory of Richard Lyman, see Hampshire County Probate Records, I, 14–17; on John Lyman's inventory, see Lyman, *Genealogy of the Lyman Family*, 40–41.

84. Robert Lyman's court cases are noted in *Records of the Particular Court of Connecticut, 1639–1663*, XXII, 136, 211, 256; the Pynchon Court Record, in Smith, ed., *Colonial Justice in Western Massachusetts*, 248; Hampshire County Probate Records, I, 68 and *passim*. There is a good short account of his life in Lyman, *Genealogy of the Lyman Family*, 42–44. Court orders for putting out his children, and ensuring his own subsistence, are found in Hampshire County Probate Records, I.

85. Of course, the early parts of this sequence—as recounted here, from Bliss family "traditions"—lack documentary confirmation. However, even if one sets aside their story of suffering in the face of religious persecution, the themes of "dislocation" for Mary [Bliss] Parsons, and of contrast between her experience and that of Sarah [Lyman] Bridgman, remain intact. There was, in short, sufficient dislocation in her *New* England experience to support the central argument of this chapter.

86. See Trumbull, *The History of Northampton, Mass.*, 51–52; Ferris, *Dawes-Gates Ancestral Lines*, II, 634; Judd Manuscripts (Northampton Volumes), I, 47; II, 170.

87. The sense of ill fate concerning her motherhood may have continued to reverberate in Sarah during the succeeding winter and spring. Her next child, born in January 1657, must have been conceived in April 1656. This implies an interval of some ten months between the death of the one infant and the start of the next pregnancy. Was Sarah, during this period, perhaps doubtful about her prospects of conceiving again—and, if doubtful, then doubly resentful against Mary Parsons? She must, moreover, have discovered her new pregnancy in May or June of 1656—a discovery which could well have excited new anxieties. (Would *this* baby survive any more easily than the previous one?) The summer of 1656 was, of course, the time when the crisis in her relation to Mary Parsons reached its ultimate stage (at least from the legal standpoint).

88. This conclusion is based on extensive work in family reconstitution, covering the entire population of Northampton in the settlement years.

89. These totals, it will be noticed, do not precisely conform to some of the figures presented earlier in the chapter (see p. 256). The discrepancy

reflects a slight shift of viewpoint. The first set of figures embraced actual deponents in the 1656 court case. This second set involves all persons who can be identified as taking one or the other side; it thus includes a few who did not, so far as we know, actually testify in court. Note, too, that *both* sets exclude persons related to the two principals by blood or marriage.

90. The status rankings summarized here are based on a method of analysis more fully described elsewhere in this volume. (See pp. 242–45.) Once again, members of the principals' families are not included.

91. Family reconstitution by the author.

92. See p. 248.

93. There is a useful summary of this earlier Parsons case in Mason A. Green, *Springfield: 1636–1686* (Springfield, Mass., 1888), 101–9. Many original depositions survive, and are found now in the manuscript holdings of the New York Public Library; they are also printed in Drake, *Annals of Witchcraft*, 219–58.

94. Edward Johnson, *Wonder-Working Providence*, William F. Poole, ed. (Andover, Mass., 1867), 199.

95. This letter, published in the *Mercurius Publicus* on September 25, 1651, is quoted in Justin Winsor, *Memorial History of Boston*, 137.

96. Summaries of the hearings held by the county court in this case are found in Hampshire County Probate Records, I, 158–60. A slightly edited version is published in Trumbull, *The History of Northampton, Mass.*, 230–31.

97. See *ibid.*, 231.

98. Hampshire County Probate Records, I, 160.

99. The actions of the Court of Assistants in this case are summarized in Noble and Cronin, eds., *Records of the Court of Assistants of the Colony of Massachusetts Bay*, I, 31, 33.

100. The evidence of conflict between the Bartlett and Parsons families comes from court records for the 1660s and 1670s. In 1664, for example, Joseph Parsons was prosecuted—and convicted—at court on a charge of "opposing and resisting the constable of Northampton in [the] execution of his office and work." The constable in question was Robert Bartlett; and the evidence showed "some scuffling in the business, whereby blood was drawn between them." In the end Bartlett, too, was judged responsible—apparently for being over-zealous in his efforts to subdue Parsons—and both men were ordered to pay fines. For another case, involving an (unspecified) slander, between the two families, see Parsons vs. Bartlett, Hampshire County Court Records, I, 26 (American Antiquarian Society, Worcester, Mass.).

101. There is one extant reference to Mary Parsons which does include the prefix "Mrs."; however, it comes from the very last years of her life—long after the period of her court cases around witchcraft. See the

Pynchon Court Record, in Smith, ed., *Colonial Justice in Western Massachusetts*, 374.

102. The inference of her illiteracy was made by Sylvester Judd, in preparing his detailed notes on Northampton history. See the Judd Manuscripts (Northampton volumes), II, 170. There is apparent confirmation in the Pynchon Court Record, in Smith, ed., *Colonial Justice in Western Massachusetts*, 374.

103. A list of members of the Northampton church is printed in Trumbull, *The History of Northampton, Mass.*, 106–7.

104. The date of her death is given in Holman, *Ancestry of Colonel John Harrington Stevens*, 338.

105. The death in question was that of John Stebbins of Northampton. For the court's action in the matter, see Hampshire County Probate Records, I, 201. An argument that Mary Parsons may have been a suspect in this case as well is made in a short article by Alice Manning, "Witches in the Connecticut Valley: A Historical Perspective," in *The Daily Hampshire Gazette*, December 15, 1976, 35.

106. The Pynchon Court Record, in Smith, ed., *Colonial Justice in Western Massachusetts*, 375. It is interesting to find that the defendant had charged the boy's grandmother with having "killed Mrs. Pynchon and half killed the Colonel." Mrs. Amy [Willys] Pynchon had, in fact, died three years previously. Her husband Colonel John Pynchon would himself die another year hence—and perhaps he already seemed much weakened. (He was at the time more than 80 years old.)

107. On the career of this Joseph Parsons, see Holman, *Ancestry of Colonel John Harrington Stevens*, 340.

108. For information on the family of Mr. Peletiah Glover, see Burt, *The First Century in the History of Springfield*, 110–11.

Notes to Chapter 9

1. Among the numerous "community studies" in early American history, see especially Charles Grant, *Democracy in the Connecticut Frontier Town of Kent* (New York, 1961); Sumner Chilton Powell, *Puritan Village: The Formation of a New England Town* (Middletown, Conn., 1963); Darrett B. Rutman, *Winthrop's Boston: A Portrait of a Puritan Town* (Chapel Hill, N.C., 1965); Kenneth Lockridge, *A New England Town: The First Hundred Years* (New York, 1970); Philip J. Greven, Jr., *Four Generations: Population, Land, and Family in Colonial Andover, Massachusetts* (Ithaca, N.Y., 1970); Michael Zuckerman, *Peaceable Kingdoms: New England Towns in the Eighteenth Century* (New York, 1970); John Demos, *A Little Commonwealth: Family Life in Plymouth Colony* (New York, 1970). For surveys and assessments of this literature, see John Murrin, "Review Essay," *History and*

Theory, XI (1972), 226–75, and David J. Russo, *Families and Communities: A New View of American History* (Nashville, Tenn., 1974). The classic anthropological statement of this approach—and a direct inspiration for many of the aforementioned historical studies—is found in Robert Redfield, *The Little Community* (Chicago, 1956).

2. See M. G. Marwick, *Sorcery in Its Social Setting: A Study of the Northern Rhodesian Cewa* (Manchester, Eng., 1965); R. F. Fortune, *Sorcerers of Dobu: The Social Anthropology of the Dobu Islanders of the Western Pacific* (New York, 1932); Clyde Kluckohn, *Navajo Witchcraft* (Boston, 1967); H. C. E. Midelfort, *Witch Hunting in Southwestern Germany, 1562–1684: The Social and Intellectual Foundations* (Stanford, Calif., 1972); E. William Monter, *Witchcraft in France and Switzerland: The Borderlands during the Reformation* (Ithaca, N.Y., 1976).

3. E. E. Evans-Pritchard, *Witchcraft, Oracles, and Magic among the Azande* (Oxford, Eng., 1937); B. Malinowski, *Magic, Science, and Religion, and Other Essays* (Glencoe, Ill., 1948); Claude Levi-Strauss, "The Sorcerer and His Magic," in his *Structural Anthropology* (New York, 1963); Kluckohn, *Navajo Witchcraft*. A useful selection of anthropological writings on witchcraft can be found in John Middletown, ed., *Magic, Witchcraft, and Curing* (Garden City, N.Y., 1967).

4. Keith Thomas, *Religion and the Decline of Magic* (New York, 1971); A. D. J. Macfarlane, *Witchcraft in Tudor and Stuart England* (London, 1970); Monter, *Witchcraft in France and Switzerland*; Midelfort, *Witch Hunting in Southwestern Germany*.

5. M. G. Marwick, "Witchcraft as a Social Strain-Gauge," in Marwick, ed., *Witchcraft and Sorcery: Selected Readings* (Harmondsworth, Eng., 1970), 280–95. Keith Thomas makes the same point for historians: "Witch beliefs are . . . of interest . . . for the light they throw upon weak points in the social structure." See Thomas, "Anthropology and the Study of English Witchcraft," in Mary Douglas, ed., *Witchcraft Confessions and Accusations* (London, 1970), 68.

6. This viewpoint is presented with particular effectiveness in Max Gluckman, *Custom and Conflict in Africa* (London, 1963), ch. 4.

7. Philip Mayer, "Witches," in Marwick, ed., *Witchcraft and Sorcery*, esp. 54–55.

8. M. G. Marwick, "The Sociology of Sorcery in a Central African Tribe," in Middleton, ed., *Magic, Witchcraft, and Curing*, 113; Mary Douglas, "Introduction," in Douglas, ed., *Witchcraft Confessions and Accusations*, xxi.

9. Mary Douglas, "Techniques of Sorcery Control in Central Africa," in John Middleton and E. H. Winter, eds., *Witchcraft and Sorcery in East Africa* (London, 1963), 141.

10. Midelfort, *Witch Hunting in Southwestern Germany*, 4.

11. *Ibid.*, 4.

12. Macfarlane, *Witchcraft in Tudor and Stuart England*, 248.

13. Douglas, "Introduction," in Douglas, ed., *Witchcraft Confessions and Accusations*, xxv.

14. See above, Chapter 8.

15. Cotton Mather, "Memorable Providences Relating to Witchcrafts and Possessions," in Burr, ed., *Narratives*, 100.

16. Richard Chamberlain, "Lithobilia: or, The Stone-Throwing Devil" (London, 1698), in Burr, ed., *Narratives*, 61.

17. Pitford's accusation is reported in a deposition by Henry Pease, undated, in Essex County Court Papers, I, leaf 71.

18. Increase Mather, "An Essay for the Recording of Illustrious Providences" (Boston, 1684), in Burr, ed., *Narratives*, 31.

19. Deposition by John Gibson, undated, in the trial of Winifred Holman; Middlesex Court Files, folder 25.

20. Mary Parsons accused her husband, Hugh, at Springfield, Mass., 1651. Rebecca Greensmith accused her husband, Nathaniel, at Hartford, Conn., 1662.

21. Zachary Dibble encouraged neighbors to suspect his wife, Sarah, at Stanford, Conn., 1669. William Morse appears to have harbored some private suspicions of his wife, Elizabeth, at Newbury, Mass., 1679; likewise Joseph Parsons of his wife, Mary, at Northampton, Mass., 1656.

22. William Graves was accused by his daughter Abigail [Graves] Debell, at Stamford, Conn., 1667. Among the witnesses against Katherine Harrison was a man she called "cousin," Josiah Gilbert, at Wethersfield, Conn., 1668.

23. John Mighell, one of the accusers of Elizabeth Morse of Newbury (1679), had been hired to work on her house. Jacob Johnson, an alleged victim (and an accuser) of Katherine Harrison of Wethersfield, Conn. (1668), "was employed by Goodman Harrison [Katherine's husband] to go to Windsor with a canoe for meal." (Deposition by "the wife of Jacob Johnson," May 27, 1668, in the trial of Katherine Harrison; Willys Papers, W-16.)

24. Elizabeth Godman, prosecuted at New Haven in 1653, had been a lodger in the house of one of her accusers, Mr. Stephen Goodyear. Lydia Gilbert, convicted of witchcraft at Windsor, Connecticut, in 1654, had "boarded" her alleged victim, Henry Stiles.

25. See depositions by John Gibson, undated, in the trial of Winifred Holman; Middlesex Court Files, folder 25.

26. Deposition by William Branch, March 13, 1651, in the trial of Hugh Parsons, in Drake, *Annals of Witchcraft*, 256.

27. Deposition by Goody Hand, February 27, 1658, in the trial of Elizabeth Garlick, in *Records of the Town of Easthampton, Long Island, Suffolk County, N.Y.*, 5 vols., (Sag Harbor, N.Y., 1887–92), I, 134–35.

28. See pp. 84–86.

29. Deposition by Abigail Westcott, September 12, 1692, in the trial of Elizabeth Clawson; Willys Papers, W-29.

30. Deposition by Hopestill Austin, September 5, 1673, in the trial of Elizabeth Cole; Suffolk Court Files, XIII, no. 1228.

31. Josiah Cotton, "Some Observations Concerning Witches, Spirits, and Apparitions, Collected From Diverse Authors" (1733), manuscript document, in Houghton Library, Harvard University, 53–54.

32. William Hubbard, *A General History of New England* (repr. Boston, 1848), 574.

33. *Ibid.*, 574.

34. Shurtleff, ed., *Records of the Governor and Company of Massachusetts Bay*, III, 273; see also IV, 96. (Manuscript copies of findings by the grand jury and "the jury of life and death," in the trial of Hugh Parsons, are in the New York Public Library, New York, N.Y.)

35. Connecticut Colonial Probate Records, vol. III: County Court 1663–1677 (Connecticut State Library, Hartford, Connecticut), leaves 35–36, 52.

36. Records of the Colony of Connecticut, LIII (Connecticut State Library, Hartford, Connecticut), leaves 5, 7.

37. John Hale, "A Modest Enquiry Into the Nature of Witchcraft," in Burr, ed., *Narratives*, 412.

38. Willys Papers, W-30, W-36, W-39.

39. *Ibid.*, W-36.

40. See above, Chapter 8.

41. See above, Chapter 7.

42. Papers relating to these actions are scattered through the manuscript records of the Essex County Court (Clerk's Office, Essex County Courthouse, Salem, Mass.). See especially "County Court, Ipswich: Records, 1645–1663," leaf 21; "County Court, Salem: Records, 1648–1655," leaves 28, 33; "Essex County Court Papers," I, leaf 71; *ibid.*, XII, leaves 86–87; "County Court, Salem: Records, 1667–1679," leaf 1.

43. Most of the depositions in the trial of Hugh Parsons are published in Drake, *Annals of Witchcraft*, 219–58. (Three additional depositions are in *The New England Historical and Genealogical Register*, XXXV [1881], 152–53.) Estimates of the social position of trial participants are based on research in the early records of Springfield, Mass. and neighboring towns. See also Henry M. Burt, *The First Century in the History of Springfield*, 2 vols. (Springfield, Mass., 1898); Henry A. Wright, *Early Springfield and Longmeadow* (Rutland, Vt., 1940); Mason A. Green, *Springfield: 1636–1886* (Springfield, Mass., 1888); Sylvester Judd, *History of Hadley* (Northampton, Mass., 1863); Joseph H. Smith, ed., *Colonial Justice in Western Massachusetts* (Cambridge, Mass., 1961).

44. See below, Chapter 11.

45. See below, Chapter 10.

46. Testimony given at the "examination of Hugh Parsons," May 18, 1651, printed in Drake, *Annals of Witchcraft*, 228.

47. Deposition by Rebecca Smith, October 12, 1668, in the trial of Katherine Harrison; Samuel Willys Collection, no. 10.

48. Complaint of Susannah Trimmings, April 18, 1656, in the trial of Jane Walford, printed in New Hampshire Historical Society, *Collections*, I, 255.

49. This account is taken from Increase Mather, "An Essay for the Recording of Illustrious Providences," in Burr, ed., *Narratives*, 33–34.

50. *Records and Files of the Quarterly Courts of Essex County, Mass.*, II, 158–59.

51. "Grounds for Examination of a Witch," undated; Willys Papers, W-38.

52. "Reasons of Reprieving Mrs. Mercy Disborough," May 12, 1693; Willys Papers, W-36.

53. Deposition by Griffin Jones, February 25, 1652, in the trial of Hugh Parsons; Drake, *Annals of Witchcraft*, 233.

54. Proceedings of "a court held at New Haven," August 7, 1655; Dexter, ed., *New Haven Town Records, 1649–1662*, 252.

55. Complaint of Goodwife Thorp, at the "examination" of Elizabeth Godman, June 16, 1653; Hoadly, ed., *Records of the Colony or Jurisdiction of New Haven*, II, 35.

56. Deposition by Thomas Bracey, August 13, 1668, in the trial of James Wakeley; Willys Papers, W-10.

57. Deposition by Isabel Holdridge, undated, in the trial of John Godfrey; *Records and Files of the Quarterly Courts of Essex County, Massachusetts*, II, 158.

58. "Answer" by Hugh Parsons, during his examination for witchcraft, May 18, 1651; Drake, *Annals of Witchcraft*, 228.

59. Deposition by Joan Francis, October 29, 1668, in the trial of Katherine Harrison; Willys Papers, W-15.

60. Deposition by Honor Hannum, August 11, 1656, in the case of Parsons vs. Bridgman; Middlesex Court Files, folder 16, paper 665.

61. Deposition by Abraham Drake, September 4, 1656, in the trial of Eunice Cole; Massachusetts Archives, CCCXXXV, no. 3.

62. Deposition by Goody Edwards, February 17, 1658, in the trial of Elizabeth Garlick; *Records of the Town of Easthampton*, I, 134.

63. Testimony given at the "examination" of Hugh Parsons, May 18, 1651; Drake, *Annals of Witchcraft*, 221.

64. Proceedings of "a court held at New Haven," August 7, 1655, printed in Dexter, ed., *New Haven Town Records, 1649–1662*, 252.

65. Deposition by Samuel Parsons, February 19, 1658, in the trial of Elizabeth Garlick; *Records of the Town of Easthampton*, I, 129.

66. Deposition by Elizabeth Titcomb, May 14, 1680, in the trial of Elizabeth Morse; Drake, *Annals of Witchcraft*, 278.

67. Proceedings of a "court of magistrates held at New Haven," August 4, 1653; Hoadly, ed., *Records of the Colony or Jurisdiction of New Haven*, II, 30.

68. Deposition by Hannah Robbins, undated, in the trial of Katherine Palmer (Willys Papers, W-7); deposition by Hopestill Austin, September 5, 1673, in the trial of Eunice Cole (Suffolk Court Files, XIII, no. 1228).

69. On the legal system in seventeenth-century New England, see George L. Haskins, *Law and Authority in Early Massachusetts* (New York, 1960); Smith, *Colonial Justice in Western Massachusetts* (Cambridge, Mass., 1961); and David T. Konig, *Law and Society in Puritan Massachusetts: Essex County, 1629–1692* (Chapel Hill, N.C., 1979).

70. See Emil Oberholzer, *Delinquent Saints: Disciplinary Action in the Early Congregational Churches of Massachusetts* (New York, 1956).

71. We have as yet no considerable study of the use of arbitration (and other informal procedures for dispute settlement) in early New England. But on their importance for one particular community, see Lockridge, *A New England Town*.

72. For occasional instances of disputes leading to physical violence see, e.g., *Records and Files of the Quarterly Courts of Essex County, Massachusetts, passim*.

73. Keith Thomas, "Anthropology and the Study of English Witchcraft," in Douglas, ed., *Witchcraft Confessions and Accusations*, 68.

74. *Ibid.*, 67.

75. On widowhood, remarriage, and the sex-ratio in early New England, see Demos, *A Little Commonwealth*, 67, 151, 194; and Herbert Moller, "Sex Composition and Correlated Culture Patterns of Colonial America," *William and Mary Quarterly*, 3d ser., II (1945), 115–17.

76. John Winthrop, "A Model of Christian Charity," in *The Winthrop Papers*, II, 294–95. This aspect of Puritan values is fully, and persuasively, explored in Stephen Foster, *Their Solitary Way: The Puritan Ethic in the First Century of Settlement in New England* (New Haven, Conn., 1971), 41–64.

77. For a fuller statement of this theme, see John Demos, "Character and the Social Order in Puritan New England," in Howard H. Quint, Milton Cantor, and Dean Albertson, eds., *Main Problems in American History*, 4th ed., 2 vols. (Homewood, Ill., 1978), I, 1–20. See also Rutman, *Winthrop's Boston*.

78. See, for example, the account books of William and John Pynchon, Connecticut Valley Historical Museum, Springfield, Mass.; Sidney H. Miner and George D. Stanton, Jr., eds., *The Diary of Thomas Minor, Stonington, Connecticut, 1653–1684* (New London, Conn., 1899);

Records and Files of the Quarterly Courts of Essex County, Mass., passim.

79. See pp. 277–78.

80. Sewall describes this event in a diary entry written on January 15, 1697. See M. Halsey Thomas, ed., *The Diary of Samuel Sewall, 1674–1729*, 2 vols. (New York, 1973), I, 366–67.

81. John Hale, "A Modest Enquiry Into the Nature of Witchcraft," in Burr, ed., *Narratives*, 408.

82. On this case and its sequellae, see below, Chapter 11, note 29.

83. There are two references to the case of Goodwife Lake in seventeenth-century materials (though both date from some years after the actual fact). One is found in John Hale, "A Modest Enquiry Into the Nature of Witchcraft," in Burr, ed., *Narratives*, 408–9; the other is in a letter from Nathaniel Mather to Increase Mather, December 31, 1684, printed in *The Mather Papers*. The arrangements for the placement and care of the Lake children, following their mother's death, are noted in *Dorchester Town Records: Fourth Report of the Record Commissioners* (Boston, 1880), 306–8, 310–11; and there are other Lake references in the same source, *passim*. For additional information on the family's history, and especially on its second-generation members, see G. Andrews Moriarty, "The Early Rhode Island Lakes," in *The American Genealogist*, XII, 17–24.

84. Philip Mayer, "Witches," in Marwick, ed., *Witchcraft and Sorcery*, 57.

85. Records of dealings with Hugh Parsons, following his removal to Boston, are found in the account books of William and John Pynchon, Connecticut Valley Historical Society, Springfield, Mass., volume I. His later career in Rhode Island can be traced through *The Early Records of the Town of Portsmouth, Rhode Island* (Providence, 1901).

86. See p. 363.

87. See pp. 352–53.

88. See Chapter 11, note 59.

89. See Chapter 1.

90. See Chapter 2.

91. See Chapter 7.

92. Trumbull and Hoadly, eds., *The Public Records of the Colony of Connecticut*, I, 573.

93. As happened, for example, to Katherine Harrison of Wethersfield, Conn., when she attempted to resettle in Westchester, New York. See documents reprinted in Burr, ed., *Narratives*, 48–52.

94. This theme is explored quite fully in the case of John Godfrey, above (Chapter 2).

95. Cotton Mather, "Memorable Providences, Relating to Witchcrafts and Possessions" (Boston, 1689), as printed in David Levin, ed., *What Happened in Salem?* 2nd ed. (New York, 1960), 98, 99.

96. See above, Chapter 3.

97. See above, Chapter 6.

98. Cotton Mather, *The Wonders of the Invisible World*, John Russell Smith, ed. (Boston, 1862), 23.

99. Mayer, "Witches," in Marwick, ed., *Witchcraft and Sorcery*, 58.

100. Deodat Lawson, "Christ's Fidelity the Only Shield Against Satan's Malignity . . ." (2nd ed., London, 1704), 66.

101. Cotton Mather, *The Wonders of the Invisible World*, 80–81.

102. See Drake, *Annals of Witchcraft*, 219–56.

103. See above, Chapter 7.

104. See above, Chapter 4.

105. Court proceedings against John Godfrey, for example, began with a "petition" signed by eleven Essex County residents. (See *Records and Files of the Quarterly Courts of Essex County, Massachusetts*, II, 157–58.) When Katherine Harrison was released from prison, with witchcraft charges still pending against her, no less than 38 of her Wethersfield neighbors signed and submitted a formal complaint. (Carolyn S. Langdon, "A Complaint Against Katherine Harrison, 1669," *Bulletin of the Connecticut Historical Society*, XXXIV, 18–25.)

106. For brief descriptions of events leading up to the execution of witches, see Cotton Mather, "Memorable Providences, Relating to Witchcrafts and Possessions," in Burr, ed., *Narratives*, 106 (case of Goodwife Glover), and John Hale, "A Modest Enquiry into the Nature of Witchcraft," in *ibid.*, 408 (case of Margaret Jones) and 409 (case of Alice Lake).

107. See p. 181.

108. Samuel Willard, "Useful Instructions for a Professing People in Times of Great Security and Degeneracy" (Cambridge, Mass., 1673), 32.

109. Cotton Mather, "Memorable Providences, Relating to Witchcrafts and Possessions," in Burr, ed., *Narratives*, 98.

110. Deodat Lawson, "Christ's Fidelity the Only Shield Against Satan's Malignity . . . ," 70.

111. Letter from Cotton Mather to John Richards, May 31, 1692, in *The Mather Papers*, 396.

112. Cotton Mather, *The Wonders of the Invisible World*, 19.

113. John Goodwin, "Mantissa," in Cotton Mather, "Memorable Providences, Relating to Witchcrafts and Possessions," in Burr, ed., *Narratives*, 127.

114. Samuel Willard, "Useful Instructions for a Professing People in Times of Great Security and Degeneracy," 30–31.

115. See, for example, Cotton Mather, *The Wonders of the Invisible World*, 12–13.

116. Samuel Parris, "These Shall Make War With the Lamb" (a sermon preached at Salem, September 11, 1692), printed in Boyer and Nissenbaum, eds., *Salem-Village Witchcraft*, 134.

117. Cotton Mather, *The Wonders of the Invisible World*, 10.
118. See p. 173.
119. Deposition by Isabel Holdridge, undated, in the trial of John Godfrey; *Records and Files of the Quarterly Courts of Essex County, Massachusetts*, II, 158–59. Deposition by Mary Hale, in the trial of Katherine Harrison; Willys Papers, W-17.
120. Deposition by Jonathan Taylor, April 7, 1651, in the trial of Hugh Parsons; Drake, *Annals of Witchcraft*, 247.
121. Samuel Willard, "A Brief Account of a Strange and Unusual Providence of God Befallen to Elizabeth Knapp of Groton," in John Demos, ed., *Remarkable Providences: The American Culture, 1600–1760* (New York, 1972), 368–69.

Notes to Chapter 10

1. On Bachiller's life, see *The New England Historical and Genealogical Register*, XXXXVI (1892), 58–64, 157–61, 246–51, 345–50; and Sybil Noyes, Charles Thornton Libby, and Walter Goodwin Davis, *Genealogical Dictionary of Maine and New Hampshire* (repr. Baltimore, Md., 1972), 81–82.
2. See Hosmer, ed., *Winthrop's Journal*, I, 266.
3. Petition to the General Court, September 6, 1638, in Noble and Cronin, eds., *Records of the Court of Assistants of the Colony of Massachusetts Bay*, I, 236. A memorandum noting approval of the petition is in Suffolk Court Files, no. 26.
4. For an excellent study of the settler-group, see V. C. Sanborn, "The Grantees and Settlement of Hampton, N.H.," in *Essex Institute Historical Collections*, LIII (1917), 228–49.
5. See letter of Stephen Bachiller to John Winthrop, Jr., October 9, 1638, in *The Winthrop Papers*, IV, 69.
6. See Joseph Dow, *History of the Town of Hampton, New Hampshire*, 2 vols., (Salem, Mass., 1893), I, ch. 1. This work, one of the finest of all New England local histories, is an indispensable reference.
7. The contemporary chronicler of New England life, Edward Johnson, wrote as follows about Hampton: "The great store of salt marsh did entice this people to set down their habitation there, for as yet cows and cattle of that kind were not come to the great downfall in their price, of which they have about 450 head." See J. Franklin Jameson, ed., *Johnson's Wonder-Working Providence, 1628–1651* (New York, 1910), 188–89.
8. See Dow, *History of the Town of Hampton, N.H.*, I, 17–19. Another list, composed in June 1640 and noting houselot sizes only, may be found in the Town Book of Hampton, I, 41–45. (Manuscript volume, Town Offices, Hampton, N.H.)

9. The standard work on Exeter is Charles H. Bell, *History of the Town of Exeter, New Hampshire* (Exeter, N.H., 1888). See especially pp. 8, 18, 23, 44.

10. Dow, *History of the Town of Hampton, N.H.*, I, ch. 7.

11. Hosmer, ed., *Winthrop's Journal*, II, 179.

12. Dow, *History of the Town of Hampton, N.H.*, I, 346–47. See also William Hubbard, *A General History of New England*, 2nd ed. (Boston, 1848), 420–21; and Hosmer, ed., *Winthrop's Journal*, II, 45–46. Hubbard reports that Bachiller had at first denied the charges against him, but "was forced soon after, by the terror of his conscience, to confess it openly in the church." Apparently this was an especially bad period in Bachiller's life, for (again, according to Hubbard) "his house, and near all his substance, was consumed by fire."

13. Dow, *History of the Town of Hampton, N.H.*, I, 348.

14. See *The New England Historical and Genealogical Register*, XII (1858), 272.

15. Dow, *History of the Town of Hampton, N.H.*, I, 346.

16. On the settler-group, see Sanborn, "Grantees and Settlement of Hampton, N.H." Petitions and other material relating to this controversy are in the Massachusetts Archives. The origins of many early Hamptonites are noted in Charles E. Banks, *Topographical Dictionary of 2885 English Emigrants to New England, 1620–1650* (Philadelphia, 1937), and in various family genealogies.

17. Letter from Stephen Bachiller, to John Winthrop and the elders of the church at Boston, February 26, 1644, in *The Winthrop Papers*, IV, 446–49. Writing in his journal, Winthrop placed some blame on both parties to the struggle, though he attributed special importance to Stephen Bachiller's contentious personality: viz. "Mr. Bachiller had been in three places . . . and through his means, as was supposed, the churches fell to such divisions, as no peace could be till he was removed." Hosmer, ed., *Winthrop's Journal*, II, 179.

18. *Ibid.*, II, 179.

19. This controversy is described in Dow, *History of the Town of Hampton, N.H.*, I, 31–34. A "true and perfect list of the Shares of the Common" is printed on p. 33. Petitions, and other material pertaining to the resolution of the case by the General Court, are in Shurtleff, ed., *Records of the Governor and Company of Massachusetts Bay*, III, 66ff.

20. Petition, signed by William Howard on behalf of the town, quoted in Dow, *History of the Town of Hampton, N.H.*, I, 32.

21. In 1649 there was controversy over the ownership of the town "ox-common." Significantly, the matter was resolved by a local committee of leading men—without recourse to outside arbitration. See *ibid.*, I, 39–40. In 1651 new conflict was created by Stephen Bachiller's efforts to collect back-"wages." (It appears that two residents of the town,

serving as the minister's agents, had succeeded in distraining the "goods and lands" of several others.) See Shurtleff, ed., *Records of the Governor and Company of Massachusetts Bay*, III, 253.

22. For example, the following testimony from the trial of Eunice Cole in 1656: "Goody Marston and Goodwife Susannah Palmer . . . saith that goodwife Cole said that . . . thirteen years ago she knew one bewitched as goodwife Marston's child was, and she was sure that party was bewitched for it told her so . . . and she had prayed [for] this thirteen years that God would discover that witch." (Manuscript deposition, April 8, 1656; Massachusetts Archives, CXXXV, leaf 2.)

23. There is a manuscript list of persons who had "expended time in witnessing against Eunice Cole on trial for witchcraft" in Suffolk Court Files, no. 26203. The list contains eighteen names. Six more persons can be identified, from other materials, as having joined in this prosecution.

24. See Massachusetts Archives, CXXXV, nos. 2–3, depositions by Goody Marston and Goodwife Susannah Palmer (April 8, 1656), Thomas Philbrick (undated), Sobriety Moulton and Goodwife Sleeper (April 10, 1656), Mary Coleman (undated), Richard Ormsby and Ensign Goddard (April 12, 1656), Abraham Perkins and John Redman (September 4, 1656), Abraham Drake (September 4, 1656); Suffolk Court Files, no. 256a, deposition by Joanna Sleeper (September 4, 1656); *Trials for Witchcraft in New England*, Houghton Library, Harvard University, Cambridge, Mass., deposition by Thomas Coleman and Abraham Drake (September 5, 1656).

25. Deposition by Thomas Philbrick (undated), in Massachusetts Archives, CXXXV, no. 2.

26. Deposition by Goody Marston and Susannah Palmer (April 8, 1656), *ibid.*, CXXXV, no. 2.

27. Deposition by Thomas Coleman and Abraham Drake (September 5, 1656), in *Trials for Witchcraft in New England*. There was a suspicious aftermath to this incident. Denied the assistance she sought, Eunice Cole allegedly complained to the selectmen that "they could help goodman Robie, being a lusty man, and [yet] she could have none." The man she referred to, one Henry Robie, "lost a cow and a sheep very strangely . . . two or three days after this."

28. See Middlesex Court Files, no. 1219. There are also copies of a claim filed by Craddock's "agent" on June 26, 1657 for payment of this bill, and of the court's decision in the case.

29. A small grant of land to William Cole was noted in the town records of Boston, February 20, 1637. See *Second Report of the Record Commissioners of the City of Boston* (Boston, 1877), 15.

30. This document is reprinted in John Demos, ed., *Remarkable Providences: The American Culture, 1600–1760* (New York, 1972), 192–93.

Three other manuscript documents bear the name of William Cole with an accompanying signature-mark. (See his bill to Matthew Craddock, November 16, 1637, in Middlesex Court Files, no. 1219; petition from Exeter, to the General Court of Massachusetts Bay, 1643, in Massachusetts Archives, CXII, no. 9; and the petition from Hampton on behalf of Lieut. Robert Pike, 1654, in *ibid.*, X, nos. 299–300.) This evidence makes it seem probable—though not certain—that Cole was illiterate. His wife also used a signature-mark. (See her petition to the Governor and General Court of Massachusetts Bay, undated, in *ibid.*, X, no. 281.)

31. The list is printed in Bell, *History of the Town of Exeter, N.H.*, 436.
32. Both actions were decided on September 5, 1643. See *ibid.*, 444, 445.
33. *Ibid.*, 445.
34. The Coles had received land in Hampton, as part of the general "division" of June 30, 1640. (See the Town Book of Hampton, I, leaf 21.) However, it is clear that Exeter remained their place of residence for four years thereafter.
35. See *Records and Files of the Quarterly Courts of Essex County, Massachusetts*, I, 88.
36. Presentments to a court held at Ipswich, September 28, 1647, in Essex County Court Papers, I, leaf not numbered; see also County Court, Ipswich: Records, 1645–1663, leaf 12.
37. Norfolk County Court Papers, 1650–1680, leaves 30, 50. (Manuscript volume, Clerk's Office, Essex County Courthouse, Salem, Mass.)
38. See town rate, in the Town Book of Hampton, I, leaf 34. (This list is not dated, but can be attributed from internal evidence to the later months of 1647.) The original record of the rate for 1653 has apparently been lost; however, a copy was included by Edmund Willoughby Toppan, in his Manuscript History of Hampton (unpublished; written about 1850), book two, 187. (The latter volume is currently owned by Mrs. Winslow White, Hampton, N.H.)
39. See the Town Book of Hampton, I, leaves 28–29. The plan is reprinted in Noyes *et al.*, *Genealogical Dictionary of Maine and New Hampshire*, 55.
40. This summary reflects a detailed effort to reconstruct the entire population of Hampton at the time of Eunice Cole's first formal trial for witchcraft. The reconstruction is based primarily on the superbly full and accurate information in Noyes *et al.*, *ibid.*, and on the genealogies in Dow, *History of the Town of Hampton, N.H.*, II. Additional material has been taken from various genealogies of individual families, and from the Town Book and Vital Records. The information as to place of origin, in England, has been drawn chiefly from Banks, *Topographical Dictionary of 2885 English Emigrants to New England, 1620–1650.*

41. For a useful map of Hampton, in the early years, prepared by Lucy E. Dow and A. W. Locke, see Dow, *History of the Town of Hampton, N.H.,* inside back cover. This has been checked against the original land records, in the Town Book of Hampton, II.

42. An effort has been made to construct a "status-ladder" for the various Hampton families, by analyzing the extant tax lists, the meeting-house plan of 1650, wills and inventories and patterns of local office-holding. See the Town Book of Hampton, I, leaf 34; E. W. Toppan, Manuscript History of Hampton, II, 187; *Probate Records of Essex County, Massachusetts;* Noyes, *et al., Genealogical Dictionary of Maine and New Hampshire,* 55; Dow, *History of the Town of Hampton, N.H.,* I, 563–78.

43. Witnesses came from two families living west of the green, four families on the north side, and six on the east. Four more resided in other parts of the town.

44. Among fifteen witnesses whose place of origin can be traced, 9 came from eastern England (among a total of 56 adults associated with that region, in the overall population of Hampton). For other regions, the figures are as follows: *north,* 2 (out of 4); *center and west,* 1 (out of 7); *south,* 3 (out of 12).

45. Among 20 witnesses whose arrival in Hampton can be dated, 13 came in the years 1638–40, 1 in 1641–45, 4 in 1646–50, and 2 in 1651–55.

46. Among 22 witnesses whose ages can be approximately determined, 8 (out of a cohort of 37 in the total population) were between the ages thirty to thirty-nine. Four (of 38) were twenty to twenty-nine; 4 (of 33) were forty to forty-nine; and 4 (of 29) were fifty or over. In addition, there were two witnesses younger than twenty years old.

47. A "scoring system," based on considerations of wealth, office-holding, and seating in the meeting-house, has been used to divide the adult population into three status-groups of roughly equal size. Eleven witnesses against Eunice Cole are thereby classified "high" (out of 46, in the population as a whole); 4 are "middle" (out of 41); and 7 are "low" (out of 41).

48. See, for example, Dow, *History of the Town of Hampton, N.H.,* I, 54–64; and James W. Tucker, "The Witch of Hampton" (pamphlet, privately published, no date given).

49. An obscure, but important, reference in the Town Records seems to establish this point. Under a heading entitled "The accounts of the County of Norfolk for the Court held at Salisbury, the 12th [day] of the 2nd month 1659," there is the following entry: "To Rich. Ormsby, for expense about G. Cole, [16]58: 00.05.00." Ormsby, a local constable, could not have had any responsibilities for Eunice Cole unless she was, at the time designated, physically present in Hampton. (See

the Town Book of Hampton, II, leaf 343.) There is also the evident fact that she was soon thereafter (perhaps 1659?) charged with making "unseemly speeches" about her neighbors. (See text, below.)

50. Norfolk County Court Papers, 1650–1680, leaves 16, 18.

51. "The Humble Petition of Eunice Cole, wife of William Cole of Hampton, Now Prisoner at Boston," in Massachusetts Archives, X, no. 281. The petition is not dated. However, other writers have assigned it to the year 1662, and this appears, from internal evidence, to be accurate.

52. See Shurtleff, ed., *Records of the Governor and Company of Massachusetts Bay*, IV, part two, 70. The evidence on this point is somewhat confusing, for the court made it a "condition" of Eunice Cole's release that she "depart, within one month . . . out of this jurisdiction, and not to return again upon penalty of her former sentence being executed against her." She appears, nonetheless, to have returned to her home in Hampton (still within the "jurisdiction" of Massachusetts Bay), for there, on November 24, 1662, she was observed in conversation with a strange presence alleged to be the Devil. (See p. 324.) Note also that in November 1662 the county court ordered payment to Henry Green of Hampton "for watching one day and one night with Eunice Cole." This procedure is not otherwise explained, but, again, it seems to establish goody Cole's reappearance in the town. See *Records and Files of the Quarterly Courts of Essex County, Massachusetts*, III, 4.

53. A manuscript copy of William Cole's will is in Essex County Probates, no. 6001 (Registry of Probates, Salem, Mass.). There is also an inventory of Cole's estate, taken by Thomas Webster acting as "executor." The estate included a house-lot and housing (valued at £20), an acre of meadowland, two cows, a heifer, a pig, a feather-mattress and other bedding, a Bible, small quantities of yarn and hemp, and a variety of kitchen furnishings (mostly described as "old," and valued low). The total value of these properties was estimated at £53, 19s.

54. See court orders of October 14, 1662, April 14, 1663, and October 13, 1663, in "County Court, Norfolk: Records, 1648–1678," leaves 56 (reverse), 60 (reverse), 65.

55. See p. 329.

56. Court order, May 3, 1665, in Shurtleff, ed., *Records of the Governor and Company of Massachusetts Bay*, IV, part two, 149.

57. According to one source, the prison-keeper at Boston was receiving payment "for keeping goodwife Cole," as late as June 1668. (See Samuel G. Drake, *Annals of Witchcraft*, 101.) However, the documents which support this assertion are not identified by Drake; they may indeed have been lost between his time and ours.

58. Deposition by Abraham Perkins, Sr., April 7, 1673, in Suffolk Court

Files, XIII, no. 1228. The deposition dates this episode to a time "when William Fifield was constable." Fifield was constable of Hampton only once—in the year 1662.

59. See Massachusetts Archives, CXXXV, no. 16.

60. See Charles E. Clark, *The Eastern Frontier: The Settlement of Northern New England* (New York, 1970), 16–18, and *passim*.

61. Quoted in Dow, *History of the Town of Hampton, N.H.*, I, 90.

62. *Ibid.*, I, 91–92.

63. *Ibid.*, I, 91.

64. *Ibid.*, I, 93.

65. This arrangement is mentioned in the deposition by Robert Smith, August 29, 1673, in Massachusetts Archives, CXXXV, no. 11. See also Dow, *History of the Town of Hampton, N.H.*, I, 79–80.

66. See Massachusetts Archives, CXXXV, nos. 4–15, and Suffolk Court Files, XIII, no. 1228.

67. Deposition by Jonathan Thing, September 5, 1673, in Suffolk Court Files, XIII, no. 1228.

68. Deposition by Mary Perkins, April 7, 1673, in Massachusetts Archives, CXXXV, no. 7.

69. Deposition by Hopestill Austin, September 5, 1673, in Suffolk Court Files, XIII, no. 1228.

70. Deposition by Abraham Perkins, April 7, 1673, in *ibid.*, XIII, no. 1228.

71. Paper entitled "In the Case of Eunice Cole," undated, in Massachusetts Archives, CXXXV, no. 13. This document contains decisions handed down by the court with reference to several questions of evidence in the 1673 trial.

72. Deposition by Robert Smith, August 29, 1673, in *ibid.*, CXXXV, no. 11.

73. Deposition by John Mason, April 7, 1673, in Suffolk Court Files, XIII, no. 1228.

74. Deposition by Elizabeth Shaw, April 8, 1673, in *ibid.*, XIII, no. 1228.

75. Paper entitled "In the Case of Eunice Cole," undated, in Massachusetts Archives, CXXXV, no. 13.

76. These depositions are all in *ibid.*, CXXXV, nos. 4, 5, 6, 8.

77. Deposition by Bridget Clifford, April 7, 1673, in *ibid.*, CXXXV, no. 8.

78. Paper, entitled "In the Case of Eunice Cole," undated, in *ibid.*, CXXXV, no. 13.

79. These genealogical reconstructions are based on materials in Noyes, *et al.*, *Genealogical Dictionary of Maine and New Hampshire*, 151, 269, 355–56, 646, 731; in Dow, *History of the Town of Hampton, N.H.*, II; and in the Town Records of Hampton, *passim*.

80. Nicholas Smith, born about 1629 in England, came to Exeter before 1658. The name of his first wife is not known. They had children: Nathaniel (born, September 3, 1660), and Ann (born, February 8,

1663). Nicholas Smith married, second, Mary [Satchell] Dale, about 1666. He died June 22, 1673.

81. William Godfrey was born, probably in one of the eastern counties of England, between 1600 and 1608. He was resident at Watertown, in Massachusetts Bay, by 1639, and moved to Hampton in 1649. He married, first, Sarah [————], about 1630; they had one child, John, born about 1632. He married, second, Margery [————] Webster, in 1638; they had three children, Isaac (born 1639), Sarah (born 1642), and Doborah (born 1645). William Godfrey died March 25, 1671. Margery Webster, born about 1609, was the widow of Thomas Webster (who died in county Norfolk, England, in 1634). By her first husband she had one child, Thomas, born in 1631. She married, third, John Marion, September 14, 1671, and died May 2, 1687.

82. John Marion was born, probably about 1610, in county Essex, England, was briefly at Watertown in Massachusetts Bay (early 1640s), and came to Hampton in 1645. He married, first, Sarah Eddy, before 1640, who died January 26, 1671. They had at least four children, born between 1641 and 1650. John Marion was living as late as 1684; his death is not recorded.

83. Note the following order, by the County Court at Salisbury, April 10, 1677: "Nathaniel Smith, being given to Deacon William Godfrey and his wife Margery as their own, and they having kept him from [the time when he was] a child, [and] Deacon Godfrey being now dead, and his widow having married John Marion, the Court orders that Smith shall continue and abide with the said Marion and [his] wife until he comes to the age of one-and-twenty years, and shall do them faithful service." (Quoted in Dow, *History of the Town of Hampton, N.H.*, II, 978.) On July 31, 1680 Nathaniel Smith was found dead "in a canoe at the landing place, with his face bloody"; an inquest decided that "water was the cause of his death by drowning." (Quoted in *ibid.*, II, 978.)

84. See the grand jury "presentment" of Eunice Cole, October 9, 1672, in Massachusetts Archives, CXXXV, no. 7. This document mentions both Ann Smith and John Clifford, senior, "who hath the charge of her by her father." There is also a separate reference to Clifford and "a child [again, Ann Smith] which was committed to his wife's tuition." (See the paper entitled "In the Case of Eunice Cole," Massachusetts Archives, CXXXV, no. 13.)

85. John Clifford was born, about 1615, in county Nottingham, England. He was an original proprietor of the town of Salisbury, in 1640, and was resident at Hampton by 1642. He married, first, Sarah [————], about 1640; she died about 1655. They had children: John (born about 1640), Hannah (born 1649), Elizabeth (born 1651), Israel (born about 1653). John Clifford married, second, Elizabeth [Wiseman] Richard-

son, September 28, 1658; she died December 1, 1667. They had children: Elizabeth (born 1659), Mahitable (date of birth uncertain, died young), Esther (born 1662), Isaac (born 1664), Mary (born 1666, died 1669). John Clifford married, third, Bridget [————] Huggins, February 6, 1672. He died in 1694. Bridget [————] Huggins was born about 1617 in England. She married, first, John Huggins, about 1638. John Huggins was born in England (perhaps in county Norfolk) about 1609. He was in Dedham by 1638, and came to Hampton in 1639. He and his wife had children: Susannah (born 1640), Esther (born about 1642), John (born about 1646), Elizabeth (born about 1648), Mary (born 1650, perhaps died young), Bridget (born 1651), Martha (born 1654), Anna (born 1659), and Nathaniel (born 1660). Bridget Huggins was living in 1680; her death is not recorded.

86. John Clifford, Jr., married Sarah Godfrey, August 18, 1670. They had eight children, the first of whom (John) was born February 7, 1672.

87. Bridget Huggins's testimony from the earlier case does not survive. However, her name is included on a list of witnesses against Eunice Cole, from the year 1656, in Suffolk Court Files, no. 26203.

88. See deposition by Ephraim Winsley, April 29, 1673, in *ibid.*, no. 1228.

89. The name of John Godfrey is included on a list of witnesses against Eunice Cole in the 1656 trial, in *ibid.*, no. 26203.

90. See p. 323. See also n. 53 above.

91. One episode, recounted as part of the prosecution case, appears to have taken place in Boston. See depositions by Hopestill Austin, September 5, 1673, and Elizabeth Person, September 5, 1673, in Suffolk Court Files, no. 1228.

92. Order of the County court, held at Salisbury, April 29, 1673, in Massachusetts Archives, CXXXV, no. 7.

93. See *ibid.*, CXXXV, no. 16.

94. See *ibid.*, CXXXV, no. 15.

95. See Bouton, ed., *Documents and Records Relating to the Province of New Hampshire*, I, 415.

96. *Ibid.*, I, 415.

97. For some of the depositional evidence on the death of Moses Godfrey, see p. 82.

98. Deposition by Elizabeth Denham and Mary Godfrey, July 14, 1680, in Bouton, ed., *Documents and Records Relating to the Province of New Hampshire*, I, 416–17.

99. Deposition by Nathaniel Smith, July 14, 1680, in *ibid.*, I, 417–18. Curiously, this witness was the elder brother of Ann Smith, whose role in the prosecution of Eunice Cole (1673) has been fully discussed above. Nathaniel died, apparently from drowning, a scant two weeks after giving this testimony. (See n. 83 above.)

100. Deposition of Mary Godfrey, July 14, 1680, in *ibid.*, I, 417.

101. On Brabrook's affairs in Watertown, see *Watertown Records*, 5 vols. (Watertown, Mass., 1894–1907), I, part one, 14, 26, 28, 29, 30, 34, 38, 39, 40, 43, 44, 45, 46, 47, 51, 53, 55, 59, 77, 78, 82, 92, 93, 100; also part second, 122; and part third, 8, 10.

102. The date of John Brabrook's death is not recorded. His name appeared for the last time in the town records on October 14, 1654; by January 1655 his wife was being mentioned as "the widow Brabrook." See *Watertown Records*, I, part one, 38–40, 44.

103. In January 1655 the selectmen of Watertown appointed three men to oversee the affairs of the Brabrook family. For several years thereafter the town made *ad hoc* grants of money to widow Brabrook, and arranged for the "hiring" of her land, cows, and other property. By 1663 the town was forced to provide "for the keeping of widow Brabrook" for one full year at a time. In 1668 the selectmen ordered "Brabrook's house and land (being seized by execution) . . . sold to pay the town's debts." See *ibid.*, I, part one, 44, 77, 78, 82, 100.

104. Town order, December 20, 1651; Brabrook was to be compensated £30, "toward his loss by fire." *Ibid.*, I, part one, 26.

105. On June 28, 1668, Joseph, Sarah, and Rachel Brabrook petitioned the county court "that Henry Short of Newbury and Simon Thompson of Ipswich be appointed their guardians." (*Probate Records of Essex County, Massachusetts*, II, 130.) In September 1669 Rachel Brabrook testified in a court case involving members of Henry Short's family. It appears, moreover, that she was the "ward" in the Short household who experienced some "lewdness" at the hands of a neighboring manservant. (See *Records and Files of the Quarterly Courts of Essex County, Massachusetts*, IV, 179–80.) Henry Short, brother of Rachel's mother, was an early and prominent settler of Newbury; he held many local offices, up to and including that of selectman. After his death, his estate was valued at more than £1800. (See *Probate Records of Essex County, Massachusetts*, II, 345–49.)

106. John Fuller was born in Ipswich in about 1643. (His father, also named John, had come from England in 1635, and had married Elizabeth Emerson, daughter of another Ipswich resident.) When still a boy John, Jr., was sent to live in the household of his uncle, William Fuller, at Hampton; his brother—a second William—went along. William Fuller, senior, had no children of his own, and seems to have treated these nephews more or less as adopted sons. When John Fuller, Sr., died, he made only token bequests to his sons, John, Jr., and William, because "their uncle hath undertaken to give them sufficient portions." William, Sr., paid the highest rate among all Hampton householders in 1647; moreover, his name is found near the top of two subsequent rate lists. He held many local offices, and was twice elected deputy from Hampton to the Massachusetts General Court. But John, Jr.—his

allegedly "sufficient portion" notwithstanding—never approached the same level of wealth and prestige. On a town list of 1680, for example, his "rate" falls among the bottom third of the householders. See William H. Fuller, *Genealogy of Some Descendants of Captain Matthew Fuller* (1914; no place given), 175–76; "John Fuller of Ipswich, Mass., 1634," in *The New England Historical and Genealogical Register*, LIII, 335ff.; *Probate Records of Essex County, Massachusetts*, II, 57–61.

107. This woman was born Isabella Austin, dau. of Francis and Isabella [Bland] Austin, in about the year 1633. Her father, an early resident of Hampton, died in 1642, and her mother was remarried thereafter to Thomas Leavitt. The Bland connection, on the mother's side, was a distinguished one: "Mr." John Bland was an early and prominent settler of Martha's Vineyard. Moreover, Thomas Leavitt was a man of considerable stature within Hampton itself. Isabella Austin married Philip Towle November 19, 1657. Towle's origins are not known, though local tradition makes him out an Irishman. He arrived in Hampton just a short while before his marriage. Philip and Isabella [Austin] Towle had children: Philip (born 1659), Caleb (born 1661, killed by Indians 1677), Joshua (born 1663), Mary (born 1665), Joseph and Benjamin (twins, born 1669). Francis (born 1672), John (born 1674), Caleb (born 1678). Philip Towle died in 1696, aged about eighty; his widow died in 1719. See Noyes, *et al., Genealogical Dictionary of Maine and New Hampshire*, 68–69, 95–96, 425, 689; and the Town Book of Hampton, *passim.*

108. Quoted in Dow, *History of the Town of Hampton, N.H.*, I, 85.

109. From a quarterly court, held at Hampton, September 7, 1680, quoted in D. Hamilton Hurd, *History of Rockingham and Stratford Counties, New Hampshire* (Philadelphia, 1882), 322.

110. See Dow, *History of the Town of Hampton, N.H.*, I, 94.

111. See Michael G. Hall, *Edward Randolph and the American Colonies* (Chapel Hill, N.C., 1960), 36–37, and Dow, *History of the Town of Hampton, N.H.*, II, 94.

112. *Ibid.*, I, 94.

113. See Clark, *The Eastern Frontier*, 56–58, and Dow, *History of the Town of Hampton, N.H.*, I, 95–97. The new framework of government included a president, a council, and an assembly. The latter was to consist of deputies chosen by the various towns. The councillors were appointed from London, but at first these appointments fell entirely to residents of New Hampshire.

114. See *ibid.*, I, 100.

115. *Ibid.*, I, 101–2.

116. Various materials pertaining to this affair are printed in Bouton, ed., *Documents and Records Relating to the Province of New Hampshire,*

I, 458–62. See also Dow, *History of the Town of Hampton, N.H.*, I, 103–5.

117. *Ibid.*, I, 106.

118. Roland D. Sawyer, "History of Earlier Hampton: The Witchcraft Days," manuscript in possession of the Meeting House Green Memorial and Historical Association, Inc., Hampton, N.H.

119. On various particulars of Jonathan Moulton's life, see Dow, *History of the Town of Hampton, N.H.*, I, 209, 212, 215, 249, 251, 255, 262, 264, 268, 270, 271, 273, 278, 287, 399, 403, 404, 406, 536, 550, and II, 870. Moulton was born, the son of Jacob and Sarah [Smith] Moulton, in about 1726. He married, first, Abigail Smith, February 22, 1749. They had children: Joseph (born 1749), Sarah (born 1752), Jonathan (born 1754), Mary (born about 1756, died 1760), Abigail (born 1758), Benning (born 1761), Anne (born 1763), William (born 1766), Elizabeth (born 1768), Jacob (born 1770), Joseph (born 1772). Jonathan Moulton married, second, Sarah Emery, September 11, 1776. They had children: Sally (born 1779), Emery (born 1782), John (born 1783), Nathaniel (born 1787).

120. See Dow, *History of the Town of Hampton, N.H.*, I, 278. The grand scale of his business operations may be illustrated by reference to a circular of 1785, in which Moulton advertised sale of some 80 thousand acres of land (comprising most, or all, of eight separate townships). Apparently, this circular was directed especially to Ireland.

121. See *ibid.*, I, 212–14.

122. Passages from the report of this fire in the *Boston Chronicle*, March 20, 1769, are quoted in Dow, *History of the Town of Hampton, N.H.*, I, 215.

123. This story is quoted from Drake, *Annals of Witchcraft*, 156–57.

124. Dow, *History of the Town of Hampton, N.H.*, I, 278.

125. Drake, *Annals of Witchcraft*, 157.

126. Toppan, Manuscript History of Hampton, III, 45.

127. *Ibid.*, III, 40ff. See also Hurd, *History of Rockingham and Stratford Counties, New Hampshire*, 322.

128. Quoted in Dow, *History of the Town of Hampton, N.H.*, I, 57.

129. John Greenleaf Whittier, *The Complete Poetical Works of John Greenleaf Whittier* (Cambridge, Mass., 1894), 245–46. "The Wreck of Rivermouth" was written in 1864. The verses quoted here are only a part of the entire poem. Whittier wrote a second poem, entitled "The Changeling," in which Eunice Cole again figures as a principal. See *ibid.*, 251.

130. Slightly different versions of this story may be found in Toppan, Manuscript History of Hampton, III, 45 and Hurd, *History of Rockingham and Stratford Counties, New Hampshire*, 322.

131. Local tradition; see manuscript holdings of the Meeting House Green Memorial and Historical Association, Inc., Hampton, N.H.

132. Article 16, Town Meeting, March 8, 1938, quoted in James W. Tucker, "The Witch of Hampton."

133. *Ibid.*

134. Personal observation, November 16, 1971; house of Mrs. Winslow White, Hampton, N.H.

Notes to Chapter 11

1. Mary Jeanne Anderson Jones, *Congregational Commonwealth: Connecticut 1636–1662* (Middletown, Conn., 1968), 3.

2. Richard L. Bushman, *From Puritan to Yankee* (Cambridge, Mass., 1967), ix.

3. Charles M. Andrews, *Our Earliest Colonial Settlements* (New York, 1933), 118.

4. Cotton Mather, *Magnalia Christi Americana*, 2 vols. (2nd ed., Hartford, Conn., 1853), I, 436.

5. Some years later William Hubbard commented, in typically elegant fashion: "Some of the inhabitants chose rather to remove elsewhere and to live in a cottage in a wilderness, than to abide any longer in the fire of contention in a beautiful habitation." See his *A General History of New England* (repr. Boston, 1848), 314.

6. There was, in addition, one recorded accusation of witchcraft, which does not seem to have generated a formal trial. See p. 352, on the suspicions against Goodwife Palmer in relation to several deaths in the family of John Robbins.

7. See "Code of Laws Established by the General Court, May, 1650", in Trumbull and Hoadly, eds., *Public Records of the Colony of Connecticut*, I, 513. Also: Sherman W. Adams and Henry R. Stiles, *The History of Ancient Wethersfield, Connecticut*, 2 vols. (New York, 1904), I, 23; and Charles M. Andrews, *The River Towns of Connecticut*, in the Johns Hopkins University Studies in Historical and Political Science, 7th ser., nos. 7–9 (Baltimore, Maryland, 1889), 13–16. The volumes by Adams and Stiles provide the fullest extant local history of Wethersfield. Andrews's monograph, though nearly a century old, is still the best single account of the settlement phase of the Connecticut colony. As to the identity of the Westhersfield planters, see Adams and Stiles, *The History of Ancient Wethersfield*, I, 24ff.

8. Hosmer, ed., *Winthrop's Journal*, I, 124, 132.

9. Hubbard, *A General History of New England*, 72.

10. There is some indication that these dealings with Indians over land were attended by difficulties—which may well have helped to bring on

the Pequot War. See Adams and Stiles, *History of Ancient Wethers-field*, I, 43–45.

11. A map entitled "The Village of Wethersfield, Conn., 1634 to 1644, Showing the Houselots of Original Settlers," is in *ibid.*, I, facing page 44.

12. On the early land divisions, see *ibid.*, I, 91ff.

13. As noted in *ibid.*, 1, 130.

14. There is a detailed account of the murder of John Oldham—one of the most vivid figures in the settlement period of New England history—in Hosmer, ed., *Winthrop's Journal*, I, 183–85. On the murder of other traders by Indians, see John Underhill, "News From America," in Massachusetts Historical Society, *Collections*, 3rd ser., VI, 7, 15.

15. There are various contemporary accounts of this attack. See John Mason, "A Brief History of the Pequot War," in Massachusetts Historical Society, *Collections*, 2nd ser., VIII, 132; Letter of Thomas Hooker to John Winthrop, undated, in *ibid.*, 4th ser., VI, 388; John Underhill, "News From America," in *ibid.*, 3rd ser., VI, 15. There was a macabre aftermath to this attack, reported by Captain Underhill as follows: "Having finished their action, they suddenly returned again bringing with them two maids [as] captives, having put poles in their boats, as we put masts in our boats, and upon them hung our Englishmen's and women's shirts and smocks, instead of sails, and in way of bravado came along in sight of us as we stood upon Saybrook fort."

16. This passage is part of a letter, dated Jan. 1, 1699, from Samuel Smith (then of Hadley, Mass.) to his son Ichabod Smith (of Suffield, Conn.). The letter is published in Adams and Stiles, *History of Ancient Wethersfield*, I, 153–55.

17. Hosmer, ed., *Winthrop's Journal*, I, 307. See also Hubbard, *A General History of New England*, 313–14.

18. On these early "removals" from Wethersfield, see Adams and Stiles, *History of Ancient Wethersfield*, I, 137–49.

19. See Elijah B. Huntington, *History of Stamford, Connecticut* (Stamford, Conn., 1868), 15.

20. According to his son, Samuel, Henry Smith had come from England to Watertown, in Massachusetts Bay, in 1636 or 1637, and had moved on to Connecticut "after a year or two." Thus he may have been one of several early preachers at Wethersfield, although he was not "settled" in the pulpit there until at least 1641. Smith was involved in controversy almost from his first days at Wethersfield. In the winter of 1640 the court was obliged to mediate "a difference . . . between Mr. Smith and some others of Wethersfield, about the measure of some ground." (See *Records of the Particular Court of Connecticut, 1639–1663*, 9). In November 1643 three men from Wethersfield were fined for "divulging and setting [their] hand to a writing, called a declaration, tend-

ing to the defamation of Mr. Smith," and two others for "proferring a
role of diverse grievances against Mr. Smith, and failing of proof in
the prosecution thereof." (Trumbull and Hoadly, eds., *Public Records
of the Colony of Connecticut,* I, 97.)

21. *Ibid.,* I, 87. This was the recommendation, in April 1643, of a court-
appointed "committee" on the troubles at Wethersfield. Since Smith
declined to leave, controversy continued through the following summer;
in July the magistrates established new *ad hoc* procedures "that the
differences may be ripened, . . . and a final end put thereunto." (*Ibid.,*
I, 90.) As a result "many complaints [were] made wherein Mr. Smith
was accused and judged to lie under much guilt. But upon a full hearing . . . it was found that most of their accusations were mistakes,
wherein Mr. Smith was much wronged, both by false reports and unjust
surmises." Thus, in November, it was ordered that "whosoever . . .
shall hereafter . . . continue or renew any of the former complaints
wherein [Mr. Smith] hath been cleared by this Court . . . shall forfeit
to the country ten pounds for every such offense." (*Ibid.,* I, 98–99.)
For once, in the annals of seventeenth-century Connecticut, a policy of
forcible suppression of conflict seems to have achieved the desired result.

22. On the Branford settlers, see Adams and Stiles, *History of Ancient
Wethersfield,* I, 156–57.

23. Particular Court, December 7, 1648, as noted in *Records of the Particular Court of Connecticut, 1639–1663,* 56.

24. Cotton Mather, *Magnalia Christi Americana,* II, 456. There is another
account by Mather, similar in most details, in his "Memorable Providences, Relating to Witchcrafts and Possessions," in Burr, ed., *Narratives,* 135–36. The case is also mentioned in a letter from Nathaniel
Mather to Increase Mather, March 26, 1684, in Massachusetts Historical Society, *Collections,* 4th ser., VIII, 58, and in John Hale, "A
Modest Enquiry into the Nature of Witchcraft," in Burr, ed., *Narratives,* 410.

25. Particular Court, October 1, 1646, as noted in *Records of the Particular
Court of Connecticut, 1639–1663,* 43.

26. Winthrop described the disease as follows: "It took them like a cold,
and a light fever with it. Such as bled or used cooling drinks died;
those who took comfortable things, for most part recovered, and that
in a few days." (Hosmer, ed., *Winthrop's Journal,* II, 326.) The estimate of forty to fifty deaths each in Massachusetts and Connecticut
hardly comports with the figures for Windsor (see graph). Since the
average mortality per year at Windsor was about five (during the mid-
1640s and early 1650s), and since fifty-two deaths were recorded in the
years 1647–48, it would appear that some forty or more deaths are
attributable to the epidemic in this one town alone.

27. The figures are based on the notes of Matthew Grant, an early town clerk at Windsor, printed in *Some Early Records and Documents of, and Relating to, the Town of Windsor, Connecticut, 1639–1703* (Hartford, 1930). I am grateful to Linda Auwers for calling my attention to these mortality data.

28. Hosmer, ed., *Winthrop's Journal*, II, 323.

29. This case has presented formidable problems for witchcraft scholars. The Alice Young in question is not mentioned elsewhere in the documentary record of early New England. It seems probable that she was the wife of one John Young, whose lands at Windsor were recorded as early as 1640. The same man sold all his holdings in Windsor in 1649 —perhaps as part of a removal from the town, following the execution of his wife. A John Young subsequently appears in the records of Stratford; dying there in 1661, he left a modest estate (including "carpentry tools") and no specific heirs. Very probably, however, he and his wife had raised at least one child—a second Alice Young, recorded as marrying Simon Beamon at Springfield on December 15, 1654. The line of connection to the Windsor "witch" is suggested by the following facts. (1) The children born to Simon Beamon included both a John and an Alice (and it was customary to name children after grandparents). (2) There is no other Young mentioned in any seventeenth-century records at Springfield (implying a place of origin, for Alice [Young] Beamon, outside of the immediate area). (3) Two Beamon children seem, when grown, to have married Windsor residents, and one of them settled there. (4) Years later (1677) Thomas Beamon, son of Alice [Young] Beamon sued another man for slander—specifically, for saying that "his mother was a witch, and he looked like one." (Was not the unsaid presumption here "like mother, like daughter"?) Admitting the speculative nature of these conjectures, a rough profile of the first New England witch can now be sketched. She was a married woman, probably no younger than forty nor older than fifty-five, with at least one child (aged between ten and twenty at the time of the mother's death). Her husband was a humble sort, perhaps a carpenter by trade. They had lived in Windsor for at least seven years before her trial and conviction. On John Young, see Town Records, Windsor, Conn. (manuscript copy, made in 1722–23, at the Connecticut State Library, Hartford), I, 9, 16, 19, 20, 44, 88, 107, 112; Connecticut Probates, file no. 6313 (manuscript record, at the Connecticut State Library, Hartford), *Records of the Particular Court of Connecticut, 1639–1663*, 244–46. On Simon and Alice [Young] Beamon, see Mary Walton Ferris, ed., *Dawes-Gates Ancestral Lines*, 2 vols. (1931, no place given), II, 105ff.; Hampshire County Probate Records, I, leaf 182 (manuscript record at Registry of Probate, Northampton, Mass.);

Hampshire County Court Records, 1677–1696 (manuscript volume at the American Antiquarian Society, Worcester, Mass.), case of Beamon vs. Fisher, March 27, 1677.

30. *Records of the Particular Court of Connecticut, 1639–1663,* 93.

31. *Ibid.,* 116. See also Charles W. Manwaring, *A Digest of the Early Connecticut Probate Records,* 3 vols. (Hartford, 1904), I, 103–4.

32. Passenger list for the *Susan and Ellen,* sailing of May 1635, in Charles E. Banks, *The Planters of the Commonwealth* (Boston, 1930), 133.

33. As noted in Adams and Stiles, *History of Ancient Wethersfield,* I, 257.

34. *Records of the Particular Court of Connecticut, 1639–1663,* 26.

35. *Ibid.,* 78.

36. Wethersfield Town Votes, I (manuscript volume, in Connecticut State Library, Hartford), leaves 111, 210; Adams and Stiles, *History of Ancient Wethersfield,* I, 257.

37. *Records of the Particular Court of Connecticut, 1639–1663,* 93.

38. The will and inventory of Edward Veir are published in Trumbull and Hoadly, eds., *Public Records of the Colony of Connecticut,* I, 463–64.

39. Thomas Kirkham was in Wethersfield by the early 1640s. His wife Mary was hired by the town to sweep the inside of the meeting house in 1648 and 1649; he himself contracted to repair the outside. The records of a court case in 1651 show him to be deeply in debt. (His creditors at this time numbered 21.) A tax-list for the entire town, dated 1674, places Kirkham near the absolute bottom in property-holdings. See: Wethersfield Town Votes, I, leaf 32; *Records of the Particular Court of Connecticut, 1639–1663,* 102, 104, 105; Adams and Stiles, *History of Ancient Wethersfield,* II, 912–14.

40. The name of the younger John Carrington appears in a variety of local records from Farmington in the 1660s and 1670s, though he was deprived of his "proprietorship" there (for unspecified reasons) in 1682. He died before 1690, when inventory was taken on his estate, and he may have spent his last years in Waterbury, Connecticut. Since his wife was deceased at about the same time, the court was obliged to make special provision for his six children (whose names and ages, ranging from three to twenty-three years, are given in the Court Records). The fact that the two eldest children were named John and Mary suggests that their father was indeed a son of the convicted witch. These data also suggest that the second John Carrington was born to the wife listed as arriving in 1635. See: Manwaring, *A Digest of the Early Connecticut Probate Records,* I, 423–24; Mabel S. Hurlbut, *Farmington Town Clerks* (Hartford, Connecticut, 1943), 30; Charles H. S. Davis, *History of Wallingford, Connecticut* (Meriden, Conn., 1870), 666–67; Mary Ethel Tilley, *Carrington: A Brief Historical Sketch of the Name and Family* (Rougemont, N.C., 1943).

41. The controversy has not been adequately studied by historians. There

are brief accounts in Sylvester Judd, *History of Hadley* (Springfield, Mass., 1905), 3–10; J. H. Trumbull, ed., *Memorial History of Hartford County, Connecticut, 1633–1884*, 3 vols. (Hartford, Conn., 1886), I, 280–81; George L. Walker, *History of the First Church in Hartford* (Hartford, Conn., 1884); and Adams and Stiles, *History of Ancient Wethersfield*, I, 159–63. Political and legal aspects of the affair can be traced through public records; see especially Trumbull and Hoadly, eds., *The Public Records of the Colony of Connecticut*, I, 288, 290, 312, 314, 317, 320–33, 339, 343, and *Records of the Particular Court of Connecticut, 1639–1663, passim*. An important collection of documents, now mostly in British archival deposits, is published in the Connecticut Historical Society, *Collections*, II, 52–125.

42. Cotton Mather, *Magnalia Christi Americana*, I, 436.

43. Trumbull and Hoadly, eds., *Public Records of the Colony of Connecticut*, I, 288, 290; Connecticut Historical Society, *Collections*, II, 54ff.

44. The question of "withdrawal" from one congregation, and merger with another, was difficult and unusual—if not unprecedented. The members of the Wethersfield church apparently wondered whether they could legitimately cooperate in such a plan. There is an interesting letter of advice on this subject, from the Rev. John Davenport of New Haven to the Wethersfield church, published in Connecticut Historical Society, *Collections*, II, 88–92.

45. Trumbull and Hoadly, eds., *Public Records of the Colony of Connecticut*, I, 312.

46. It seems plausible to think that issues of religious doctrine and discipline also figured prominently in the Wethersfield conflict—although the records are virtually mute on this score. It *is* clear that Mr. Russell supported the viewpoint later identified as "strict Congregationalist." This placed him on the opposite side from Samuel Stone; this, too, makes comprehensible the desire of the "withdrawers" at Hartford to join the Wethersfield congregation. Note that at a quarterly court, held at Hartford on December 3, 1657, Russell was accused of "reading a paper on the Lord's Day (being the 29th of November last) at Wethersfield, which tended to the defamation of Mr. Stone and the church at Hartford." (Connecticut Historical Society, *Collections*, II, 78.) Russell's position on all this—and especially his rejection of the "halfway covenant"—remained firm, in the years following his removal to Hadley. (See his letter to Increase Mather, March 28, 1681, in *The Mather Papers*, 82–84.) What the evidence does *not* show is the doctrinal viewpoint of Russell's opponents (led by Hollister) in the Wethersfield struggle. It is easy to assume that they were more "presbyterian" in their ideas of church governance, and more liberal on the issue of qualifications for membership; but there is no firm documentation.

47. This petition is published in Adams and Stiles, *History of Ancient Wethersfield*, I, 160.

48. Trumbull and Hoadly, eds., *Public Records of the Colony of Connecticut*, I, 319–20.

49. *Ibid.*, I, 330–31.

50. *Records of the Particular Court of Connecticut, 1639–1663*, 194.

51. Shurtleff, ed., *Records of the Governor and Company of Massachusetts Bay*, IV, part one, 328, 368. For a narrative account of these maneuvers, see Judd, *History of Hadley*, 11ff.

52. Trumbull and Hoadly, eds., *Public Records of the Colony of Connecticut*, I, 342.

53. *Ibid.*, I, 339, 343.

54. See the order of the General Court of Massachusetts Bay, May 28, 1659: "whereas . . . they have begun to remove to Norwottuck, with several families. . . ." (Norwottuck was the original—Indian—name of the Hadley settlement.) In Shurtleff, ed., *Records of the Governor and Company of Massachusetts Bay*, IV, part one, 368.

55. Stiles compiled a list of the Wethersfield families involved in the settlement at Hadley. See Adams and Stiles, *History of Ancient Wethersfield*, I, 164.

56. From the diary of Ezra Stiles, quoted in *ibid.*, I, 164.

57. Trumbull and Hoadly, eds., *Public Records of the Colony of Connecticut*, I, 363.

58. The pastors involved were the following: the Rev. John Cotton, Jr. (served at Wethersfield, 1660–63); the Rev. Joseph Haynes (1663–64); the Rev. Thomas Buckingham (1664); the Rev. Jonathan Willoughby (1664–65); the Rev. Samuel Wakeman (1665–66). See Adams and Stiles, *History of Ancient Wethersfield*, I, 322–23.

59. On September 5, 1661, the Particular Court indicted Nicholas and Margaret [Bedford] Jennings on the following charges: "thou hast entertained familiarity with Satan, the great enemy of God and mankind, and by his help hast done works above the course of nature, to the loss of lives of several persons, and, in particular, the wife of Reynolds Marvin with the child of Balthazar deWolfe, with other sorceries." The jury divided on the verdict—some judging the defendants to be guilty outright, but others finding no more than "strong suspicion of guilt." Several weeks later the court directed that two Jennings children be apprenticed to local families—an action which clearly implies that the accused were no longer present. That they had been executed in the meantime is possible—though not likely, given the ambiguous verdict of the jury. More probably, they had fled, or been banished; for, in the later 1660s, there is record of a man named Nicholas Jennings recently arrived on Long Island. On this case see: *Records of the Particular Court of Connecticut, 1639–1663*, 238, 240,

243; Trumbull and Hoadly, eds., *Public Records of the Colony of Connecticut*, I, 397; Lillie Pauline White, *Jennings, Davidson, and Allied Families* (Seattle, Wash., 1944), 9; Gilman Gates, *Saybrook at the Mouth of the Connecticut* (New Haven, Conn., 1935), 141; Town Records of Newtown, N.Y. (typescript copy, in the library of the New England Historic Genealogical Society, Boston); Records of the Colony of Connecticut, LIII (manuscript volume in Connecticut State Library, Hartford), leaf 17.

60. There are brief, and incomplete, accounts of the Hartford trials of 1662, by Charles J. Hoadly, "A Case of Witchcraft in Hartford," in *The Connecticut Magazine*, V (1899), 557–61; by C. H. Levermore, "Witchcraft in Connecticut," *The New Englander*, XLIV (1885), 806–10; by J. Hammond Trumbull, *Memorial History of Hartford County, Connecticut, 1633–1884*, 3 vols. (Boston, 1886), I, 274; and by John M. Taylor, *The Witchcraft Delusion in Colonial Connecticut* (New York, 1908), 96–100, and *passim*. The source materials are somewhat scattered and fragmentary. Several indictments are included in *Records of the Particular Court of Connecticut, 1639–1663*, 251, 258, 259. There are manuscript depositions and other court papers in the Willys Papers and the Samuel Willys Collection. For the impressions of an eyewitness, written down twenty years after the event, see a letter from John Whiting to Increase Mather, December 4, 1682, published in *The Mather Papers*, 466–69. Mather drew heavily on this letter in comprising his own account for "An Essay for the Recording of Illustrious Providences," in Burr, ed., *Narratives*, 18–21. There is an interesting letter from Gov. Peter Stuyvesant of New Netherland to Gov. John Winthrop, Jr., of Connecticut, on the case of Judith Varlet "imprisoned upon pretend accusation of witchery." (Stuyvesant, a relative of Varlet's by marriage, used his influence to obtain her release. She then left Hartford for New York and married Nicholas Bayard, a leading figure in the subsequent history of that colony.) See manuscript papers in the Robert C. Winthrop Collection (Connecticut State Library, Hartford), I, leaf 1. See also the materials in C. J. Hoadly, "Manuscript Notes on Witchcraft" (Connecticut Historical Society, Hartford).

61. See the manuscript deposition by Mrs. Maria Skreech, in the Willys Papers, W-1. "Mr." John Blackleach was a merchant of some prominence, first at Salem, then at Boston, and later at both Hartford and Wethersfield. His wife, *née* Elizabeth Bacon, was the daughter of an extremely wealthy "mariner" (i.e. ship-owner and trader) in London. His mercantile activities brought John Blackleach quite frequently into court; charges against him included "oppression" (price-gouging) and "contemptuous expressions against several persons in authority in this colony." In the latter instance, the court reduced his punishment "considering some weakness that too evidently appears that he is incident

unto." (It would be most interesting to know the nature of this "weakness.") *Records of the Particular Court of Connecticut, 1639–1663,* 155; Trumbull and Hoadly, eds., *Public Records of the Colony of Connecticut,* I, 376–77. Though not formally indicted in the witchcraft trials of 1662, Blackleach brought several suits for slander and defamation the following winter (content not specified). *Records of the Particular Court of Connecticut, 1639–1663,* 261. Note also the following reference in a letter written many years later (John Lucas to Samuel Willys, 1694): "Mr. Blackleach was my true fortune-teller, though my youth would not let me believe it." (Willys Papers, published in Connecticut Historical Society, *Collections,* XXI, 348.) But if John Blackleach was occasionally suspected of performing witchcraft, he could also take the role of prosecutor. In the witchcraft trial of Katherine Harrison, for example, he was the major force in organizing a petition to urge her imprisonment while court action was pending. His wife was one of those who had allegedly been attacked by Harrison's witchcraft. See p. 363.

62. Abraham Elsen's lands at Wethersfield are listed in manuscript papers in Records of the Colony of Connecticut, XLVII, leaf 57. The births of two children to Abraham and Rebecca Elsen (in 1644 and 1646) are recorded in Wethersfield Land Records, I, leaves 12, 37. (These volumes are in the Connecticut State Library, Hartford.)

63. Nathaniel Greensmith's lands in Wethersfield are noted (as abutting the lands of Samuel Wright) in *ibid.,* I, leaf 34.

64. Rebecca Greensmith's confession, dated January 8, 1662(–63), is in the Samuel Willys Collection, no. 1.

65. Mrs. Robbins was "deceased about middle of September 1659," the son Samuel "about the latter end of November 1659," and Mr. Robbins himself "the 27th day of June 1660." From Wethersfield Land Records, I, leaf 39. The same volume records the birth of four children in this family, between 1641 and 1649. See *ibid.,* leaf 16. Mr. John Robbins was settled in Wethersfield by or before 1638. He held various town offices, including that of selectman, and was four times a deputy from Wethersfield to the General Court. After his death his estate was inventoried at nearly £600—a total that placed him among the wealthiest of the early Wethersfield settlers. His lands are recorded in *ibid.,* leaves 190–92.

66. Manuscript deposition by Hannah Robbins, Willys Papers, W-7. The deponent further noted that her father "had drawn out a writing relating to prove witchcraft occasioning the death of his wife, but now she knoweth not where it is." Moreover, when her sister Mary became mortally ill some years later (about 1667) she, too, "complained of witches as occasioning her sickness." This deposition is undated, but appears from internal evidence to have been given in 1667 or 1668. It is unclear

whether or not there was at this time a formal proceeding against Katherine Palmer—or whether Hannah Robbins's testimony was in some way a part of the trial of Katherine Harrison.

67. Excepting references to his lands, Palmer is mentioned in the town records only twice: in 1651, when he contracted to clapboard the meetinghouse, and in 1662, when he was chosen to serve a year's term as a surveyor. See Wethersfield Town Votes, I, leaves 39, 96. The births of his children are noted in Wethersfield Land Records, I, leaf 16.

68. The letter from John Whiting to Increase Mather, noted above, declared that "most of the other persons [accused at the Hartford trials, but not executed] . . . made their escape into another part of the country." See *The Mather Papers*, 469. Those definitely known to have "made escape" were William and Elizabeth Ayres, Elizabeth Seager, and James Wakeley (see below). There is an interesting reference to this situation in a petition submitted in 1668 by the town of Stonington, Connecticut, to the colony's General Court. Stonington was located near the boundary of Rhode Island, and was then at the center of an inter-colony dispute. Among the complaints which the petitioners alleged against their Rhode Island foes, as evidence of hostile intent, was the following: "they take in newcomers contrary to order, viz. Goodwife Seager, James Wakeley, and the tinker." Trumbull and Hoadly, eds., *Public Records of the Colony of Connecticut*, II, 531.

69. See *The Early Records of the Town of Providence, Rhode Island*, 21 vols. (Providence, R.I., 1892–1915), XV, 128, 143, 148, 197, 199, 202; and *Rhode Island Court Records*, II (Providence, R.I., 1922), 85, 87.

70. *Rhode Island Land Evidences, Abstracts*, I: 1648–1696 (Providence, 1921), 25. To call someone a witch was never a casual matter, and it is fair to say that most statements of this sort reflected a long-standing reputation of the person "slandered." Thus the comment attributed here to Stephen Sebeere is indeed an important link in the chain of evidence that reveals the later whereabouts of the Palmers.

71. Records of the Colony of Connecticut, XLVII, leaf 43.

72. Trumbull and Hoadly, eds., *Public Records of the Colony of Connecticut*, IV, 35–36.

73. *Records of the Particular Court of Connecticut, 1639–1663*, 28, 29, 30, 43, 45, 46, 49, 51, 52, 53, 62, 63, 69, 70, 71, 72, 74, 88, 89, 90, 91, 99, 100, 101, 102, 106, 108, 116, 117, 118, 119, 120, 132, 174, 179, 195, 196, 222, 224, 227, 229, 232, 233, 234, 235, 236, 240, 244.

74. *Ibid.*, 91.

75. Her first husband, James Boosey, had come to Wethersfield in the late 1630s, and died there in 1649. He served in various town offices, and on many local committees, and held the military title of "lieutenant". He was deputy from Wethersfield to the General Court almost continuously from 1639–49. His estate was inventoried at nearly £1000—

one of the largest such valuations in the early history of the colony. (Among his possessions were the tools of a "joiner" and "wheelwright.") See Wethersfield Town Votes, *passim*; Trumbull and Hoadly, eds., *Public Records of the Colony of Connecticut*, I, 30, 42, 47, 60, 69, 125, 238.

76. As noted in the manuscript records: "James Wakeley was married to Alice Boosey, the fifth day of October 1652." (Records of the Colony of Connecticut, XLVII, leaf 121.)

77. Trumbull and Hoadly, eds., *Public Records of the Colony of Connecticut*, I, 238.

78. The lands of James Wakeley, including those formerly owned by James Boosey, are listed in Wethersfield Land Records, I, leaves 76, 77. James and Alice Boosey had at least five children, the eldest born about 1632, the youngest in 1646. There is no record of any children from the marriage of Alice Boosey and James Wakeley.

79. *Records of the Particular Court of Connecticut, 1639–1663*, 260–61.

80. The court directed that in managing the estate Wakeley's wife should consult with two particular gentlemen of the community. *Ibid.*, 266.

81. For his failure to appear in Court the previous winter—which evinced an intolerable "contempt of authority"—the magistrates fined Wakeley £5. This action, and the order which revoked the sequestration of his estate, are in Connecticut Colonial Probate Records, III: County Court, 1663–1677, leaf 5. (Connecticut State Library, Hartford. It may be useful to emphasize, for scholars interested in seventeenth-century Connecticut, that a full file of records from the Hartford county court, during the period 1663–77, is found on the reverse side of the pages of this probate volume. I am grateful to Linda Auwers for calling this to my attention.)

82. Two associates joined Wakeley in this bond, but their liability—after he had fled—was apparently discounted. See Connecticut Colonial Probate Records, III: County Court, 1663–1677, leaf 37.

83. See court orders of May 10, 1666, and May 9, 1667, in Trumbull and Hoadly, eds., *Public Records of the Colony of Connecticut*, II, 34, 59.

84. Wakeley's presence at Providence is noted at various points in *The Early Records of the Town of Providence*, XV. Note the inclusion of Wakeley's name in the complaint of the townspeople of Stonington, Connecticut against their Rhode Island adversaries in 1668. (See note 68, above.)

85. From the Court of Assistants, May 6, 1673, as noted in Records of the Colony of Connecticut, LIII, leaf 14.

86. At the Court of Assistants, October 5, 1676, as noted in Records of the Colony of Connecticut, LIII, leaf 22.

87. The actual divorce petitions are in Connecticut Archives: Crimes and

Misdemeanors, III, leaves 215, 216. The response to these petitions was given at a Court of Assistants, October 7, 1680, as noted in Records of the Colony of Connecticut, LIII, leaf 30 (Manuscript volumes in the Connecticut State Library, Hartford).

88. The inventory of Alice Wakeley's estate came to £318. See Manwaring, ed., *A Digest of the Early Connecticut Probate Records*, II, 224.

89. Trumbull and Hoadly, eds., *Public Records of the Colony of Connecticut*, IV, 35–36, 49.

90. Deposition by Thomas Bracey, August 13, 1668; Willys Papers, W-10.

91. Wakeley's diminished fortunes are apparent in the low figure assigned him in the Providence tax-rate of 1684. See *The Early Records of the Town of Providence*, XV, 47, 51.

92. From evidence taken "at the fort" in New York, July 7, 1670; reprinted in Burr, ed., *Narratives*, 48. Katherine Harrison was at this time newly removed to Westchester, New York, and already the object of formal "complaint." (See p. 363.)

93. There are several different testimonies on her years in the Cullick household. See depositions by Thomas Whaples, William Warren, and Mary Olcott (Samuel Willys Collection, nos. 7, 8, 11); and also the deposition by Elizabeth Smith (Willys Papers, W-11). John Cullick was an early and esteemed resident of Hartford; he would later become a leader of the group opposed to the ministry of Samuel Stone, and he joined the "withdrawers" in the settlement of Hadley.

94. See depositions by Elizabeth Smith (*ibid.*, W-11) and by Alexander Keeney and Samuel Hurlbut (Samuel Willys Collection, no. 15). The statement by Keeney and Hurlbut referred to another man—one Josiah Gilbert—as having first-hand information about Katherine's life in Old England. Her exact relationship to the Gilbert family (there were several branches in Connecticut) is an interesting but unresolved problem in genealogical research. In one instance Katherine herself made written mention of "my cousin Gilbert." (See her petition, undated, in Winthrop Papers, XIV, leaf 8, at the Massachusetts Historical Society, Boston.) However, Josiah Gilbert reportedly said that she "called him cousin, but he knew no such matter." (See the deposition by Keeney and Hurlbut, mentioned above.) The question derives importance from the fact that Lydia Gilbert (mother of Josiah) was tried, convicted, and executed as a witch at Windsor, Connecticut, in 1654. If Katherine was indeed connected in some way to the Gilberts, she may well have aroused suspicion on this very account (among others). There are further grounds for speculation here, in that members of the Gilbert family (1) were appointed guardians of Katherine's children in 1666, (2) were made overseers of her estate in 1670, and (3) were personally familiar with Westchester, New York, where Katherine moved follow-

ing her banishment from Connecticut. On these points, see Homer W. Brainard, Harold S. Gilbert, and Clarence A. Torrey, *The Gilbert Family* (New Haven, Conn., 1953), 10, 11, 64.

95. Deposition by Thomas Whaples; Samuel Willys Collection, no. 7.

96. Deposition by Elizabeth Smith; Willys Papers, W-11.

97. Deposition by Elizabeth Smith; *ibid.*, W-11.

98. Depositions by Elizabeth Smith (*ibid.*, W-11), and by Thomas Whaples and William Warren (Samuel Willys Collection, nos. 7, 12). William Lilly (1602–1681) was born at Diseworth, Leics., but spent his adult life in London. On the possibility that Katherine had known Lilly personally, see *The American Genealogist*, XLIII, 215–16.

99. Deposition by William Warren; Samuel Willys Collection, no. 12.

100. This episode is described in the depositions by Elizabeth Smith (Willys Papers, W-11) and Mary Olcott (Samuel Willys Collection, no. 8). The case against William Chapman is noted in *Records of the Particular Court of Connecticut, 1639–1663*, 124–25. As to the accuracy of Katherine Harrison's prediction, it is possible to see in all this simply her shrewd appreciation of immediate realities. The negative aspect of the prediction—i.e. that Elizabeth would *not* marry Chapman—may have been founded on master Cullick's disapproval of the match. And the positive element—that she *would* marry a man named Simon—was, perhaps, a veiled reference to a fellow-servant at Cullick's named Simon Sackett. (If so, it was a mere coincidence of given names that made the prediction "come true.")

101. See the manuscript document entitled "The Answer of Some Ministers to the Questions Propounded to Them by the Honored Magistrates"; Willys Papers, W-18.

102. See her petition, undated, in Winthrop Papers, XIV, leaf 8, at the Massachusetts Historical Society, Boston.

103. Deposition by Elizabeth Smith; Willys Papers, W-11.

104. Katherine Harrison, petition; Winthrop Papers, XIV, leaf 8.

105. See Wethersfield Land Records, I, leaf 18.

106. Rebecca, born February 10, 1654; Mary, born June 8, 1655; Sarah, born March 9, 1657. See *ibid.*, I, leaf 38.

107. Depositions by "the wife of Jacob Johnson"; Willys Papers, W-16. Very little can be learned about this woman, about Jacob Johnson (her husband at the time of her testimony), or about her former husband (Katherine Harrison's patient). Even the *name* of the latter man is lost.

108. See the reference to Goodwife Towsland's testimony, in Katherine Harrison's petition; Winthrop Papers, XIV, leaf 8. Katherine's patient, in this instance, was John Edwards, an early settler at Wethersfield who had died in 1664. His widow was remarried thereafter, to a Goodman Towsland of Hartford. Evidently she had testified against Kathe-

rine as part of the witchcraft trial of 1669, but the record of her testimony does not survive.

109. See the reference to testimony by Goodman Boreman *et al.*, in Katherine Harrison's petition; Winthrop Papers, XIV, leaf 8. The child in question was a son of Mr. Josiah Willard of Wethersfield.

110. For example: in the spring of 1669, according to sworn testimony, Katherine Harrison said of two Wethersfield residents: "I shall shortly see them gone, both them and theirs." Deposition by Samuel Martin, Sr.; Samuel Willys Collection, no. 13.

111. See Adams and Stiles, *History of Ancient Wethersfield*, I, 273.

112. Wethersfield Land Records, I, leaf 110.

113. Manwaring, ed., *A Digest of the Early Connecticut Probate Records*, I, 206.

114. See the summary of actions of the particular court, May 21, 1653, in *Records of the Particular Court of Connecticut, 1639–1663*, 117, 118; Wethersfield Town Votes, I, *passim*.

115. Deposition by Joseph Dickinson; Willys Papers, W-13.

116. Depositions by Richard Montague (Samuel Willys Collection, no. 9), Joseph Dickinson (Willys Papers, W-13), and John Graves (*ibid.*, W-14). Some references in Katherine Harrison's rebuttal to her accusers imply witchcraft suspicion dating well back into the 1650s. For example, there was testimony in the 1668 trial from Sarah Wickham, about a frightening "apparition" of Katherine. In the course of a complicated response, Katherine noted that this allegation referred to a time long previous—since when Wickham had "put . . . a child to nurse to her." Now Katherine's children were born during the period 1654–57; only then, it appears, could she have served as a wet-nurse. Hence this sequence supplies an approximate date for the "apparition" recalled by Goodwife Wickham: no later than about 1658, and perhaps earlier. See Katherine Harrison's petition, Winthrop Papers, XIV, leaf 8; also the deposition by Mary Kirkham, Willys Papers, W-16.

117. Chester vs. Harrison; Pewamsquin vs. Harrison; Harrison vs. Latimer. County Court, Hartford, September 3 and November 5, 1668. See Connecticut Colonial Probate Records, III, leaves 79, 80, 81.

118. County Court, Hartford, September 3, 1668. See *ibid.*, III, leaves 78, 79, 80.

119. "The Declaration of Katherine Harrison, in her Appeal to the Court of Assistants"; Connecticut Archives: Crimes and Misdemeanors, series one, 1662–1789, I, part one, no. 34-a.

120. "A complaint of several grievances of the widow Harrison," Willys Papers, W-12.

121. The depositions still extant are by Mary Kirkham, Joan Francis, John Welles, and "the wife of Jacob Johnson." The witnesses whose testi-

mony does not survive were Sarah Wickham, Rebecca Smith, Sarah Deming, and Michael and Ann Griswold. Their accusations are noted in Katherine Harrison's petition of rebuttal. (Winthrop Papers, XIV, leaf 8.) The association in time of this entire group of testimonies is inferred from the internal arrangement of the abovementioned petition.

122. Deposition by Mary Kirkham; Willys Papers, W-16.

123. Deposition by Joan Francis; Willys Papers, W-15. The child in question was probably James Francis, born March 1, 1663, died February 14, 1665 (Wethersfield Vital Records, Connecticut State Library, Hartford.)

124. Deposition by John Welles; Samuel Willys Collection, no. 6

125. See pp. 356–57.

126. Depositions by Richard Montague (Samuel Willys Collection, no. 9), Joseph Dickinson (Willys Papers, W-13), Thomas Bracey (*ibid.*, W-10), and John Graves (*ibid.*, W-14).

127. See p. 359.

128. In a later phase of the case, John Blackleach played an organizing role; see the petition against Katherine Harrison (undated, but evidently presented in the summer of 1669; Connecticut Historical Society, Hartford), as noted on page 363. This petition states that Blackleach had "taken much pains in the prosecution of this cause from the beginning," but there is no independent evidence of such "pains" before 1669.

129. Adams and Stiles, *History of Ancient Wethersfield*, I, 682.

130. Testimony given by Mary Hale makes a vivid example of such suspicions. See her deposition; Willys Papers, W-17.

131. Court of Assistants, at Hartford, May 25, 1669. See Records of the Colony of Connecticut, LIII, leaves 1–2.

132. *Ibid.*, LIII, leaf 2.

133. For an interesting piece of analysis, concerned mainly with the petition-signers, see Carolyn S. Langdon, "A Complaint Against Katherine Harrison, 1669," in the *Bulletin of the Connecticut Historical Society*, XXXIV, 18–25.

134. As noted on p. 352, Blackleach had himself been a suspect (of a peripheral sort) in the witchcraft trials of 1662–63. For additional details of his life and career, see note 61, above.

135. See her petition; Winthrop Papers, XIV, leaf 8.

136. See the petition against Katherine Harrison, undated; Connecticut Historical Society, Hartford.

137. Court of Assistants, Hartford, October 12, 1669; see Records of the Colony of Connecticut, LIII, leaf 5.

138. Court of Assistants, Hartford, May 20, 1670; see Records of the Colony of Connecticut, LIII, leaf 7.

139. Documents from these New York proceedings are reprinted in Burr, ed., *Narratives*, 48–52.

140. There are clear indications of difficulty between Katherine Harrison and her new neighbors in Westchester, in legal documents filed with the Court of Assizes in New York, April 1671. The same documents mention efforts by Katherine to remove her property from Westechester; there is also a warrant to assist her in recovering certain missing "goods", directed to "any of the constables or other officers upon Long Island." See *Minutes of the Executive Council of the Province of New York* (Albany, N.Y., 1910), II, 393–95; also Berthold Fernow, ed., *The Records of New Amsterdam* (New York, 1897), VI, 302, 306.

141. At the same court Jonathan Gilbert divested himself of a previous responsibility for "the management of the estate of [Katherine] Harrison," and Katherine herself "in court, declared" her acceptance of this action. See the record of the "special county court," Hartford, January 18, 1672, in Connecticut Colonial Probate Records, III: County Court, 1663–1677, leaf 118.

142. See Drake, *Annals of Witchcraft*, 133–34; C. H. Levermore, "Witchcraft in Connecticut," *The New Englander*, XLIV (1885), 812. Both these nineteenth-century scholars of witchcraft mention unsuccessful prosecutions of Katherine Harrison in 1672 and again in 1673 (when the Dutch had briefly regained control of New York). However, they do not cite evidence for this; and none can be found today.

143. These categories are based on the following set of distinctions. A "major" rating is assigned to those families in which some person (or persons) had allegedly suffered illness, death, or other misfortune, as a result of Katherine Harrison's witchcraft. An "intermediate" rating is given for sworn testimony clearly adverse to Katherine (but without claims of personal harm to the witness). Signatures on the petition for Katherine's imprisonment (summer, 1669) earn a "minor" rating. And "none" denotes the absence of all of the above. In cases of multiple participation (e.g. a petition-signer who also deposed against Katherine), the "highest" of the possible ratings is assigned. Note that all evaluations are made in reference to *families*.

144. A "recent" arrival is defined here as anyone who had moved into the town since 1655. The results, briefly summarized, are as follows. "Major" participation: 3 out of 15 families (20 percent). "Intermediate" participation: 0 out of 11 families (00 percent). "Minor" participation: 4 out of 20 families (20 percent). No participation: 12 out of 33 families (36 percent).

145. Status positions were assigned to all families resident in the town in 1668, so as to yield three groups of "upper" (27 families), "middle" (25 families), and "lower" (25 families) rank. In fact, there is a modest

overall tendency correlating higher participation levels with "upper" and "middle" status, and lesser participation with the "lower" group; but it does not attain statistical significance. Most of this effect derives from the greater number of non-participants in the third category. (Non-participants divide as follows: "upper," 8 out of 27 families; "middle," 8 out of 25 families; "lower," 14 out of 25 families.)

146. See pp. 360–61.

147. Among the 38 men who signed this document, 18 are classified as "upper" status, 9 as "middle" status, and 8 as "lower" status. The three remaining signers seem to have been only briefly resident at Wethersfield, and should be regarded as transients rather than regular inhabitants.

148. See Adams and Stiles, *History of Ancient Wethersfield*, I, 160.

149. Among those with "major" or "intermediate" participation levels, 9 out of 22 had signed Hollister's declaration. In the "minor" and "none" categories, the comparable figures are 22 out of 34. Note that the sample size is less than the sum-total of Wethersfield family-heads in 1668. This is because some of the latter group were either (a) not resident in Wethersfield, or (b) not yet adult, at the time the declaration was circulated. Hence they are considered ineligible for inclusion in the present analysis.

150. The closest approximation to a factional dispute is found in the aftermath of the "Dominion" period. When the Andros regime was overthrown, in 1689, there were some at Wethersfield who opposed a return to "charter" government. Their position was expressed in various broadsides, petitions, and minor acts of resistance. Their ideological leader was Gershom Bulkeley, who had long since abandoned his ministry for a career in trade, land speculation, and government. In his old age Bulkeley had become a kind of "Tory"—a vigorous defender of royal prerogative. (His views on these and other questions are fully laid out in a treatise, entitled *Will and Doom: or the Miseries of Connecticut By and Under An Usurped and Arbitrary Power.* This work has been printed in Connecticut Historical Society, *Collections*, III. For details of Bulkeley's political career, see the introduction to *Will and Doom*, by C. J. Hoadly, in *ibid.*, 71–78; and James M. Poteet, "A Homecoming: The Bulkeley Family in New England," *The New England Quarterly*, XLVII [1974], 30–50.) It should be noted, however, that there was no comparable group at Wethersfield, active on the other side. Certainly the charter government had its supporters in the town, but they did not feel obliged to take a public stand. In short, this was primarily a challenge, by a particular group, to external authority; it was *not* an intramural struggle in the old sense.

151. This change is most readily documented through analysis of the town's representation in the General Court. In the period 1655–70, that repre-

sentation fell most often to Samuel Boreman (b. 1615), John Nott (b. *ca.* 1605–10), and John Deming (b *ca.* 1610–15). In the following fifteen years (1670–85) Samuel Talcott (b. 1635), John Chester (b. 1635), and James Treat (b. 1634) achieved a similar, or even stronger, record of dominance.

152. Some simple arithmetic will help to make the point. Deputies to the General Court were chosen, two per session, at somewhat irregular intervals (two or three sessions each year). The twenty years from 1665 through 1684 can be divided into four five-year periods, in order to analyze stability of representation. Between 1665 and 1669 the office of Deputy, from Wethersfield, was filled 26 times; the two leading holders of this office (John Nott and John Deming) accounted for 16 of the total (62 percent). For succeeding periods the comparable figures (always based on the two men most frequently chosen) are as follows. 1670–74: Samuel Talcott and James Treat, 18 out of 24 cases (75 percent). 1675–79: Samuel Talcott and John Chester, 16 out of 18 cases (89 percent). 1680–84: Samuel Talcott and John Chester, 17 out of 22 cases (77 percent).

153. See Adams and Stiles, *History of Ancient Wethersfield*, I, 43–45.

154. *Ibid.*, I, 104ff.

155. *Ibid.*, I, 102; II, 740.

156. *Ibid.*, I, 102, 103, 110.

157. *Ibid.*, I, 118–30.

158. *Ibid.*, I, 189–95.

159. *Ibid.*, I, 195–99; II, ch. 19.

160. *Ibid.*, II, ch. 19.

161. See, for example, Sumner C. Powell, *Puritan Village* (Middletown, Conn., 1961), and Paul Boyer and Stephen Nissenbaum, *Salem Possessed: The Social Origins of Witchcraft* (Cambridge, Mass., 1974).

162. Note, for example, the actions of the Wethersfield town meeting with respect to the settlement, and eventual incorporation of Glastonbury— as described in Adams and Stiles, *History of Ancient Wethersfield*, I, 194.

163. *Ibid.*, I, 130; II, 540–43, 636–50.

Notes to Chapter 12

1. There is no comprehensive account of this episode in print, though parts of it are treated here and there in the present volume. Many of the relevant primary materials (i.e. court depositions) are found in Drake, *Annals of Witchcraft*, 219–56. For a useful (unpublished) summary of the case, see Stephen Innes, "A Patriarchal Society: Economic Dependency and Social Order in Springfield, Massachusetts, 1636–

1702" (Ph.D. diss., Northwestern University, 1977), ch. 5. I am grateful to Dr. Innes for allowing me to consult his work.

2. See above, Chapter 5.

3. The witchcraft cases of these several towns have not heretofore been studied in detail. And only one of them (the trial of Mary Parsons of Northampton, Mass.) is treated in the present volume. The "hints" referred to in the text are, then, no more than one scholar's impressions based on some acquaintance with primary records from each town.

4. See Kenneth A. Lockridge, *A New England Town: The First Hundred Years* (New York, 1970).

5. These forms of instability were conspicuous in the "settlement" phase of both town histories presented above (Chapters 10 and 11). For evidence of a similar situation in still another town, consult Linda Auwers, "Family, Friends, and Neighbors: Social Interaction in Seventeenth-Century Windsor, Connecticut" (Ph.D. diss., Brandeis University, 1975).

6. See pp. 365–67.

7. Compare, e.g., the picture of life expectation presented in Demos, *A Little Commonwealth: Family Life in Plymouth Colony* (New York, 1970), Philip J. Greven, Jr., *Four Generations: Population, Land, and Family in Colonial Andover, Massachusetts* (Ithaca, N.Y., 1970), and Susan L. Norton, "Population Growth in Colonial America: A Study of Ipswich, Massachusetts," *Population Studies*, XXV, 433–52, with the evidence (for Old England) in E. A. Wrigley, *Population and History* (New York, 1969). On the same point, see also Daniel Scott Smith, "The Demographic History of Colonial New England," *Journal of Economic History*, XXXII, 165–83, and John Demos, "Old Age in Early New England," in John Demos and Sarane Spence Boocock, eds., *Turning Points: Historical and Sociological Essays on the Family* (Chicago, 1978), 248–87.

8. The present author has not encountered a single reference in contemporaneous writings to the extraordinary longevity of the early New Englanders. Indeed, a contrary impression may have prevailed—witness a comment by Cotton Mather that "scarce three in a hundred live to three score and ten." (Mather, *A Good Old Age* [Boston, 1726], 4.) The real figure, as adduced by recent research, would be at least 30 in 100. (See Demos, "Old Age in Early New England," 257.)

9. The fullest general treatment of epidemic disease in early New England is found in John Duffy, *Epidemics in Colonial America* (Baton Rouge, La., 1953). Contemporaneous descriptions of the outbreak of 1647–48 can be found in the diary of John Winthrop and "Rev. John Eliot's Records of the First Church of Roxbury." See Hosmer, ed., *Winthrop's Journal*, II, 326; *New England Historical and Genealogical Register*, XXXIII, 237. The General Court of Massachusetts Bay declared a fast-

day in response to this "visitation" from God; see Shurtleff, ed., *Records of the Governor and Company of Massacuhsetts Bay*, II, 229. On the "diagnosis" of the medical picture presented in these sources, see Ernest Caulfield, "The Pursuit of a Pestilence," in American Antiquarian Society, *Transactions and Proceedings*, LX, 21–50. For some further discussion of the impact on one particular community (Windsor, Connecticut), see pp. 346–47.

10. See William Hubbard, *A General History of New England* (repr. Boston, 1848), 554; Records of the Rev. Samuel Danforth, in *Sixth Report of the Record Commissioners of the City of Boston* (Boston, 1880), 197.

11. See J. Franklin Jameson, ed., *Johnson's Wonder-Working Providence, 1628–1651* (New York, 1910), 254–55; Nathaniel Morton, *New England's Memorial* (repr. Boston, 1869), 161–62.

12. Records of Rev. Samuel Danforth, 198; Diary of John Hull, in American Antiquarian Society, *Transactions and Collections*, III, 184; Isabel M. Calder, ed., *Letters of John Davenport* (New Haven, Conn., 1937), 125–27.

13. Diary of John Hull, 204.

14. Records of Rev. Samuel Danforth, 207; "Bradstreet's Journal," *New England Historical and Genealogical Register*, VIII, 326.

15. Records of Rev. Samuel Danforth, 197.

16. According to John Hull, "between forty and fifty died" at Boston. See Diary of John Hull, 223. Other references to this epidemic are in "Bradstreet's Journal," 325; Morton, *New England's Memorial*, 207; Records of Rev. Samuel Danforth, 205. A fast-day declaration of the General Court of Massachusetts Bay, November 22, 1666, mentioned "the small pox" first on a list of "inflictions [by] . . . the Lord's hand." See Shurtleff, ed., *Records of the Governor and Company of Massachusetts Bay*, IV, part two, 321.

17. One estimate was that "2 or 300 died" in and around Boston alone. See "Bradstreet's Journal," 330–31. Other descriptions of this epidemic are in the Diary of John Hull, 243ff.; "William Adams: His Book," in Massachusetts Historical Society, *Collections*, 4th ser., I, 21; "Diary of Lawrence Hammond," in Massachusetts Historical Society, *Proceedings*, 2nd ser., VII, 168–69.

18. These outbreaks, characterized by "flux and vomiting," seem to have recurred at intervals from 1669 through 1672. The effects were especially grave for the children involved, but adults did not escape. In fact, the period 1669–72 brought to New England a remarkable convergence of deaths of *clergymen*—which must have heightened the overall sense of morbidity. On the latter point, see page 383. For details of the whole sequence, see Diary of John Hull, 230, 233, 234; Records of Rev. Samuel Danforth, 208, 210, 211; "Bradstreet's Journal,"

327. Fast-days, taking special account of "the frowns of God towards many in unusual sicknesses and diseases," were declared in Massachusetts Bay and Connecticut. See Shurtleff, ed., *Records of the Governor and Company of Massacuhsetts Bay*, IV, part one, 534; and Trumbull and Hoadly, eds., *Public Records of the Colony of Connecticut*, II, 124–25.

19. Diary of John Hull, 241; "Bradstreet's Journal," 330; "Rev. John Eliot's Records," 415; Shurtleff, ed., *Records of the Governor and Company of Massachusetts Bay*, V, 221.

20. "Diary of Noahdiah Russell," *New England Historical and Genealogical Register*, VII, 59; "Bradstreet's Journal," 333. See also fast-day proclamations in Shurtleff, ed., *Records of the Governor and Company of Massachusetts Bay*, V, 388, and Trumbull and Hoadly, eds., *Public Records of the Colony of Connecticut*, III, 131–32.

21. "Diary of Lawrence Hammond," 145; "Journal of Rev. John Pike," Massachusetts Historical Society, *Proceedings*, 1st ser., XIV, 123.

22. This was probably the most severe of all epidemics in seventeenth-century New England. In February 1690 a merchant noted "smallpox increasing . . . at Boston." In December a minister in Milton counted "sixty-six visited with the smallpox in the town in about a year" (including thirteen fatalities). A few weeks later another minister, in southern New Hampshire, wrote that the disease "raged much at Piscataqua" through the winter. "Diary of Lawrence Hammond," 153; Diary of Rev. Peter Thatcher, in A. K. Teele, *The History of Milton, Mass., 1640–1887*, 2 vols. (Milton, 1888), II, 657; "Journal of the Rev. John Pike," 122.

23. Cotton Mather, writing from Boston in January 1698, noted "epidemical and pestilential colds . . . upon this whole town, and most of the neighboring plantations . . . [which] proved mortal to many, and grievous to most." Samuel Sewall's diary, for the same month, is full of deaths and funerals. ("Thus," he concluded, "the New England men drop away.") See *Diary of Cotton Mather*, 2 vols. (repr. New York, 1971), I, 247; M. Halsey Thomas, ed., *The Diary of Samuel Sewall, 1674–1729*, 2 vols. (New York, 1973), I, 386. A fast-day proclamation in Connecticut, in March 1698, noted "great sickness and mortality" there as well. (Trumbull and Hoadly, eds., *Public Records of the Colony of Connecticut*, IV, 242–43.) See also the comment by Gov. Roger Wolcott, noted in text, on p. 376.

24. Hosmer, ed., *Winthrop's Journal*, I, 155–56. William Hubbard's *A General History of New England* noted that "the monuments [of this storm] . . . were many years after visible" (p. 99). See also Morton, *New England's Memorial*, 127.

25. Hosmer, ed., *Winthrop's Journal*, II, 57, 264; "Rev. John Eliot's Records," 65.

26. Hosmer, ed., *Winthrop's Journal*, II, 259, 263.

27. Diary of John Hull, 203; "Diary of Lawrence Hammond," 160. Hammond described the floods of February and March 1692 as causing "abundance of damage in most parts of the country, carrying away bridges, mills, etc. [The] Connecticut River [was] 3 feet higher than ever it was known before. [It] destroyed many cows in the meadows, carried away some houses, and washed away in many places the very land with the English grain sown in it."

28. The hurricane of August 29, 1675, cut a swath across much of coastal New England. Thomas Minor, a farmer in Stonington, Connecticut, described "great . . . wind . . . [and] tide . . . [with] much loss of corn and hay . . . [and] multitudes of trees blown down." The Rev Simon Bradstreet of New London, Connecticut, noted widespread effects "at the east"—and, in particular "£2000 damage done . . . at Boston . . . in ships, smaller warehouses, etc." Sidney H. Miner and George D. Stanton, eds., *The Diary of Thomas Minor* (New London, Conn., 1899), 131; "Bradstreet's Journal," 329. See also Diary of John Hull, 240. On the storm of August 1683 (which seems to have been felt especially in Connecticut), see Miner and Stanton, eds., *Diary of Thomas Minor*, 179; Trumbull and Hoadly, eds., *Public Records of the Colony of Connecticut*, III, 131–32; Diary of Rev. Peter Thatcher, 650.

29. According to Thomas Hutchinson, "The winter of 1696 was as cold as had been known from the first arrival of the English, sleighs and loaded sleds passing great part of the time upon the ice from Boston as far as Nantasket." Thomas Hutchinson, *The History of the Colony and Province of Massachusetts Bay*, 2 vols., ed. by Lawrence Shaw Mayo (Cambridge, Mass., 1936), II, 76n. See also Thomas, ed., *The Diary of Samuel Sewall*, I, 363. The following winter, Sewall noted (of one particular sabbath in late January): "very thin assemblies . . . Mr. Willard prayed for mitigation of the weather." And again: "Mr. Wigglesworth preached . . . from these words, 'Who can stand before this cold?'" See *ibid.*, I, 384–88. Meanwhile, in Connecticut, a fast-day proclamation of mid-March specified "the sharpness and the long continuance of the winter season." See Trumbull and Hoadly, eds., *Public Records of the Colony of Connecticut*, IV, 242–43.

30. Hosmer, ed., *Winthrop's Journal*, II, 45, 92. See also the announcement of "days of humiliation" in the records of the church at Barnstable in Plymouth Colony, *New England Historical and Genealogical Register*, X, 37ff.

31. The summer of 1658 was described thus by one Massachusetts diarist: "season intemperate, rain immoderate, much wheat corrupted, the getting of fodder for cattle much hindered." See Records of Rev. Samuel Danforth, 198; also Diary of John Hull, 184, and Shurtleff, ed., *Records of the Governor and Company of Massachusetts Bay*, IV, part

one, 347. The summer of 1698 was described by the Rev. John Pike as "exceeding wet, to the great hindrance and damage of husbandry"; and there are references to "foulness of the weather," etc. scattered through the applicable sections of Sewall's diary. See "Journal of the Rev. John Pike," 132, and Thomas, ed., *The Diary of Samuel Sewall*, I, 396–98.

32. On these summer droughts, see Records of the Rev. Samuel Danforth, 203, 204, 209; Diary of John Hull, 221, 230; Morton, *New England's Memorial*, 207; "Bradstreet's Journal," 332.

33. The blight is noticed in virtually every diary and local chronicle from the 1660s. Moreover, it brought fast-days in each of the colonies affected; typical was the one proclaimed in Connecticut on May 29, 1668 for "our manifold sins, whereby we have caused the Lord to go out against us in these yearly judgements of blasting the increase of the field, the spoiling [of] the fruits of the trees," etc. (See Trumbull and Hoadly, eds., *Public Records of the Colony of Connecticut*, II, 89. For comparable Massachusetts examples, see Shurtleff, ed., *Records of the Governor and Company of Massachusetts Bay*, IV, part one, 118, 321.) The movement of the blight from wheat to other grains can be followed in Morton, *New England's Memorial*, 201, 205–6, 207, and in "Bradstreet's Journal," 327.

34. In the summer of 1663 John Hull noted a "blasting" of wheat-fields near Boston—"the first so general and remarkable that I yet heard of in New England." See his Diary, 208.

35. Morton, *New England's Memorial*, 201.

36. Diary of John Hull, 218.

37. "Bradstreet's Journal," 327.

38. For a general picture of these events, see Robert R. Walcott, "Husbandry in Colonial New England," in *New England Quarterly*, IX, 218–52.

39. "Rev. John Eliot's Records," 65. The same phenomenon was described by Edward Johnson and John Winthrop; see Jameson, ed., *Johnson's Wonder-Working Providence*, 253, and Hosmer, ed., *Winthrop's Journal*, II, 277.

40. Morton, *New England's Memorial*, 160; Diary of John Hull, 184; *ibid.*, 218; Records of Rev. Samuel Danforth, 204; fast-day proclamation in Shurtleff, ed., *Records of the Governor and Company of Massachusetts Bay*, IV, part one, 235.

41. Hosmer, ed., *Winthrop's Journal*, II, 348.

42. *Ibid.*, II, 158.

43. "Rev. John Eliot's Records," 64; Hosmer, ed., *Winthrop's Journal*, II,

44. "Bradstreet's Journal," 330; Diary of John Hull, 242; Thomas, ed., *The Diary of Samuel Sewall*, I, 28–29; Hubbard, *A General History of New England*, 648. According to local tradition, Increase Mather

had a premonition of this "dreadful fire," and preached a sermon on its providential meaning a week before it occurred. And Mather's own house was among those destroyed. See "Rev. John Eliot's Records," 414n.

45. "Bradstreet's Journal," 331. See also Diary of Rev. Peter Thatcher, 642; Diary of John Hull, 245; and Hubbard, *A General History of New England*, 649.

46. Diary of Rev. Peter Thatcher, 652; Diary of Noahdiah Russell, 59. Smaller but nonetheless damaging fires occurred at Boston in 1680 and 1681, as noted in the Diary of John Hull, 247, 248, 249.

47. The fire of 1690, "which consumed about 30 buildings," was noted in the "Diary of Lawrence Hammond," 155; see also Thomas, ed., *The Diary of Samuel Sewall*, I, 325, 330.

48. New England diarists seem to have been particularly impressed with death and destruction caused by lightning bolts; nothing else was quite so dramatically "providential." Thus, for example, a series of fatal thunderstorms in the summer of 1666 caused Nathaniel Morton to write as follows: "It was a great while, and many years spent, since the English came into these parts, before any considerable hurt was done by thunder and lightning, to either man or beast. . . . But now, how doth the Lord go on gradually in this, as in other, judgements here in New England; first by striking cattle, and then one person at a time, and this year diverse, to the number of seven. . . ." Morton, *New England's Memorial*, 206–7. Some particular episodes of this type evoked detailed descriptions (e.g. of the position of people and objects when struck—or barely missed). See, for example, Records of the Rev. Samuel Danforth, 202–3, and the "eminent deliverance" noted in the "Diary of Lawrence Hammond," 148. For other such episodes (more briefly described) see, e.g., Hosmer, ed., *Winthrop's Journal*, II, 63; Diary of John Hull, 184, 193, 218, 219, 222, 236; "Bradstreet's Journal," 325, 328; "Journal of the Rev. John Pike," 123. Hailstorms left a similar impression. One such broke windows in Samuel Sewall's house (an "awful providence") and caused him to remember an earlier occasion ten years before: "I mentioned to Mr. Mather that Monmouth made his descent into England about the time of the hail in '85, summer, that much cracked our southwest windows." See Thomas, ed., *The Diary of Samuel Sewall*, I, 402.

49. Hosmer, ed., *Winthrop's Journal*, I, 172, 176.

50. As noted by Edward Johnson; see Jameson, ed., *Johnson's Wonder-Working Providence*, 253. See also "Rev. John Eliot's Records," 65.

51. *Ibid.*, 236; Hubbard, *A General History of New England*, 524–25.

52. Hosmer, ed., *Winthrop's Journal*, II, 275–76, 286–87; "Rev. John Eliot's Records," 237; Hubbard, *A General History of New England*, 322, 526–27.

53. See "Rev. John Eliot's Records," 237n.
54. See Hosmer, ed., *Winthrop's Journal*, II, 6, 17, 82–83; Jameson, ed., *Johnson's Wonder-Working Providence*, 216ff.; Hubbard, *A General History of New England*, 246.
55. See Marion H. Gottfried, "The First Depression in New England," *New England Quarterly*, IX, 655–78.
56. Hosmer, ed., *Winthrop's Journal*, II, 6.
57. *Ibid.*, II, 82–83.
58. Diary of John Hull, 215.
59. Trumbull and Hoadly, eds., *Public Records of the Colony of Connecticut*, IV, 242–43.
60. See *ibid.*, 242–43n.
61. Morton, *New England's Memorial*, 198.
62. *Ibid.*, 198–99.
63. See Records of the First Church of Boston, Richard D. Pierce, ed., in Colonial Society of Massachusetts, *Publications*, XXXIX, 9–10. See also Records of the Rev. Samuel Danforth, 197.
64. Records of the First Church of Boston, 10.
65. This was an especially large and striking comet, noted in a variety of contemporaneous sources. The quotation in the text is from "Bradstreet's Journal," 325. The comet's progress across the heavens is described quite precisely in the Records of Rev. Samuel Danforth, 201. See also Miner and Stanton, eds., *Diary of Thomas Minor*, 65, 67; Diary of John Hull, 214; Morton, *New England's Memorial*, 198.
66. "Bradstreet's Journal," 325.
67. Shurtleff, ed., *Records of the Governor and Company of Massachusetts Bay*, IV, part two, 144. See also Records of Rev. Samuel Danforth, 202.
68. "Bradstreet's Journal," 325. Among the deaths which Bradstreet had specifically in mind were those of the Rev. Samuel Shepherd (of Rowley, Mass.), the Rev. Henry Flint (Braintree, Mass.), and the Rev. Jonathan Mitchell (Cambridge, Mass.) in the spring and early summer of 1668. The comet of that year attracted special attention because of its unusual shape: viz., "the form of a spear"; "very long and sharp at the lower end"; "a blazing stream . . . but the head or star was occult and hidden by reason of its propinquity to the sun." See Morton, *New England's Memorial*, 210; Miner and Stanton, eds., *Diary of Thomas Minor*, 83, 205; Records of the Rev. Samuel Danforth, 206.
69. "Bradstreet's Journal," 332. See also Diary of John Hull, 247; Diary of Rev. Peter Thatcher, II, 644; Miner and Stanton, eds., *Diary of Thomas Minor*, 163.
70. Diary of Noahdiah Russell, 56. See also Diary of John Hull, 249; Diary of Rev. Peter Thatcher, 649; Miner and Stanton, eds., *Diary of Thomas Minor*, 174; Thomas, ed., *The Diary of Samuel Sewall*, I, 53. A Massa-

chusetts fast-day proclamation of May 1683 noted "signs in the heavens" (among other "solemn warnings of Providence"); see Shurtleff, ed., *Records of the Governor and Company of Massachusetts Bay*, V, 388.

71. Diary of Rev. Peter Thatcher, 652. The same conjunction (of eclipse and President Rogers's death) was noted by Samuel Sewall; see Thomas, ed., *The Diary of Samuel Sewall*, I, 56.

72. *Ibid.*, I, 131.

73. Morton, *New England's Memorial*, 190.

74. Jameson, ed., *Johnson's Wonder-Working Providence*, 185. See also Hosmer, ed., *Winthrop's Journal*, I, 270–71, and Diary of John Hull, 172.

75. *Ibid.*, 185. According to Thomas Hutchinson, "the pewter in many places . . . [was] thrown off the shelves, and the tops of chimnies in some places . . . [were] shook down"; see his *History of Massachusetts Bay*, Mayo, ed., I, 80.

76. See Jameson, ed., *Johnson's Wonder-Working Providence*, 160.

77. *Ibid.*, 160.

78. Hosmer, ed., *Winthrop's Journal*, II, 91.

79. Diary of John Hull, 199; Records of Rev. Samuel Danforth, 199.

80. Diary of John Hull, 205; Morton, *New England's Memorial*, 189; Records of Rev. Samuel Danforth, 200. According to Danforth, this episode included some half a dozen discernible tremors spread over three days. The first (and apparently the largest) "shook men's houses and caused many to run out . . . into the streets"; but the only damage mentioned was to "2 or 3 chimnies."

81. *Ibid.*, 206; Diary of John Hull, 226, 228.

82. "Journal of the Rev. John Pike," 123.

83. *Ibid.*, 127.

84. *Ibid.*, 127.

85. Hosmer, ed., *Winthrop's Journal*, II, 155.

86. "Bradstreet's Journal," 329.

87. Hosmer, ed., *Winthrop's Journal*, II, 346.

88. *Ibid.*, II, 264.

89. Contemporary accounts can be found in *ibid.*, II, 195ff.; Hubbard, *General History of New England*, 280ff.; Morton, *New England's Memorial*, 133ff.; Thomas Shepard, *The Autobiography of Thomas Shepard*, Nehemiah Adams, ed. (Boston, 1832), 61ff. The fullest recent study is Emery Battis, *Saints and Sectaries: Anne Hutchinson and the Antinomian Controversy in the Massachusetts Bay Colony* (Chapel Hill, N.C., 1962). For a useful collection of writings from and about the controversy, see David D. Hall, ed., *The Antinomian Controversy, 1636–1638: A Documentary History* (Middletown, Conn., 1968).

90. Stephen Foster, *Their Solitary Way: The Puritan Social Ethic in the First Century of Settlement in New England* (New Haven, Conn., 1971), 81. Foster's is the best modern study of the "crisis." For contemporary accounts bearing on one or another aspect, see Hosmer, ed., *Winthrop's Journal*, II, 126, 140ff., 176, 211, 229ff., 271ff.; Jameson, ed., *Johnson's Wonder-Working Providence*, 223–24, 240ff.; Hubbard, *A General History of New England*, 347, 390ff., 417–19, 500ff.

91. For a summary of these complex and poorly documented events, see pp. 349–51.

92. The Quaker controversy began in the late 1650s; see Diary of John Hull, 178, 180, 188–89, 193, 200. On the Anabaptists, see *ibid.*, 219, 226; Records of Rev. Samuel Danforth, 203, 206.

93. There is a large modern scholarship of these events. See especially Edmund Morgan, *Visible Saints: The History of a Puritan Idea* (New York, 1963); Robert G. Pope, *The Halfway Covenant: Church Membership in Puritan New England* (Princeton, N.J., 1969); David D. Hall, *The Faithful Shepherd: A History of the New England Ministry in the Seventeenth Century* (Chapel Hill, N.C., 1972).

94. See Diary of John Hull, 216ff.; Records of Rev. Samuel Danforth, 201, 202.

95. For a lucid modern study of these various imperial difficulties and controversies, see Michael G. Hall, *Edward Randolph and the American Colonies, 1676–1703* (Chapel Hill, N.C., 1960).

96. The standard modern study is Douglas E. Leach, *Flintlock and Tomahawk: New England in King Philip's War* (New York, 1958). There are many pertinent and interesting passages in Richard Slotkin, *Regeneration through Violence: The Mythology of the American Frontier, 1600–1860* (Middletown, Conn., 1974). For original sources from and about the war, see Charles H. Lincoln, ed., *Narratives of the Indian Wars, 1675–1699* (New York, 1913).

97. See Alden T. Vaughan, "Pequots and Puritans: The Causes of the War of 1637," in *William and Mary Quarterly*, 3rd ser., XXI, 256–69; and Vaughan, *New England Frontier: Puritans and Indians, 1620–1675* (Boston, 1965). Some contemporary accounts can be found in Lincoln, ed., *Narratives of the Indian Wars*; see also Hosmer, ed., *Winthrop's Journal*, I, 213ff.

98. Contemporary references may be found in *ibid.*, II, 74, 135–36; Hubbard, *A General History of New England*, 446ff., 449; Diary of John Hull, 174, 176; Records of Rev. Samuel Danforth, 197.

99. See "Diary of Lawrence Hammond," 153–67; "Journal of the Rev. John Pike," 124–32; Thomas, ed., *The Diary of Samuel Sewall*, I, 251, 254, 287, 312, and *passim*.

100. As noted, for example, in Hosmer, ed., *Winthrop's Journal*, II, 204ff.; Hubbard, *A General History of New England*, 478ff.

101. See Diary of John Hull, 236–37; "Bradstreet's Journal," 329; Records of Rev. Samuel Danforth, 211; "William Adams: His Book," 20.

102. "Diary of Lawrence Hammond," 155–56; "Journal of the Rev. John Pike," 122; Thomas, ed., *The Diary of Samuel Sewall*, I, 269.

103. See, e.g., Hosmer, ed., *Winthrop's Journal*, II, 91; Diary of John Hull, 219, 220; Records of Rev. Samuel Danforth, 202–6.

104. Hubbard, *A General History of New England*, 604. Hubbard noted the deaths of ten Massachusetts ministers, within a four-year period, including such "eminent" figures as John Wilson (of Boston), Richard Mather (of Dorchester), and Charles Chauncy (president of Harvard College).

105. This viewpoint was strongly expressed, for example, in Cotton Mather, *The Wonders of the Invisible World* (repr. London, 1862), esp. pp. 12–16, 79–107. See also Deodat Lawson, *Christ's Fidelity the Only Shield against Satan's Malignity* (2nd ed., London, 1704).

106. The phrase is the title of an important book by Richard Bushman, *From Puritan to Yankee: Character and the Social Order in Connecticut* (Cambridge, Mass., 1967). The theme is brilliantly elaborated in Bernard Bailyn, *The New England Merchants in the Seventeenth Century* (New York, 1964).

107. The literature on and about the "jeremiad" is voluminous. See, e.g., the masterwork of Perry Miller, *The New England Mind: The Seventeenth Century* (Cambridge, Mass., 1939), and *The New England Mind: From Colony to Province* (Cambridge, Mass., 1953). For a brief but useful discussion of the relation between religious discourse and social reality in early New England, see Robert G. Pope, "New England *versus* the New England Mind: The Myth of Declension," in *Journal of Social History*, III, no. 2, 95–108.

108. This climate of feeling and opinion is well conveyed in Marion Starkey, *The Devil in Massachusetts: A Modern Enquiry into the Salem Witch Trials* (repr. New York, 1961); see esp. pp. 32–34.

109. Paul Boyer and Stephen Nissenbaum, *Salem Possessed: The Social Origins of Witchcraft* (Cambridge, Mass., 1974). This paragraph is the briefest possible summary of the interpretation so persuasively, even brilliantly, presented in the Boyer-Nissenbaum study.

110. On the aftermath of Salem, see Starkey, *The Devil in Massachusetts*, ch. 22; and Chadwick Hansen, *Witchcraft at Salem* (New York, 1969), ch. 13.

111. From the journal of Rev. Paul Coffin, of Buxton, Maine, as printed in Maine Historical Society, *Collections*, IV, 392.

112. Josiah Cotton, "Some Observations Concerning Witches, Spirits, and Apparitions, Collected From Diverse Authors," 49; manuscript essay, Houghton Library, Harvard University, Cambridge, Mass.

113. *Ibid.*, 53.

114. William Hooker Smith, "Remarkable Occurrences," no pagination, see section headed "March 21, 1799"; manuscript essay, New York Public Library, New York, N.Y.

115. C. C. Lord, "Two Witches," *The Granite Monthly New Hampshire Magazine*, XI, 33.

116. J. Hammond Trumbull, ed., *Memorial History of Hartford County*, 2 vols. (Boston, 1886), II, 51.

117. Ebenezer Turell, "Detection of Witchcraft," as printed in Massachusetts Historical Society, *Collections*, 2nd ser., X, 6–22. The author of this fascinating document was pastor in Littleton at the time of the "detection." As such, he was not only an eyewitness but also a key participant; indeed, he sought to play the traditional minister's role of assisting and supervising the victims. But he seems to have reserved judgment from the outset on the authenticity of the supposed "afflictions."

118. *Rhode Island: A Guide to the Smallest State*, Federal Writers' Project (Boston, 1937), 109.

119. Edgar Gilbert, *History of Salem, New Hampshire* (Concord, N.H., 1907), 348–49.

120. George F. Plummer, *History of the Town of Wentworth, N.H.* (Concord, N.H., 1930), 345.

121. Frederic P. Wells, *History of Newbury, Vt.* (St. Johnsbury, Vt., 1902), 337–38.

122. For an account (one among many) of Moll Pitcher's life and deeds, see Samuel A. Drake, *A Book of New England Legends and Folklore* (Boston, 1902), 142–46. The verse is from a poem by John Greenleaf Whittier, quoted in *ibid.*, 145.

123. See David Hackett Fischer, *Growing Old in America* (New York, 1977), chs. 2–3.

124. Some evidence of this change is found in C. Dallett Hemphill, "Face to Face: Etiquette and Male-Female Relations, 1760–1860," unpublished paper, Brandeis University, 1981, and in a forthcoming study by E. Anthony Rotundo, "Men and Masculinity in 19th-Century America," Ph.D. diss., Brandeis University, 1982.

125. John Hale, "A Modest Enquiry into the Nature of Witchcraft," in Burr, ed., *Narratives*, 405.

126. *Ibid.*, 402.

127. *Ibid.*, 401, 402.

128. Starkey, *The Devil in Massachusetts*, ch. 22; Hansen, *Witchcraft at Salem*, ch. 13.

129. Turrell, "Detection of Witchcraft," 6.

130. Smith, "Remarkable Occurrences," no page.

131. See, for example, the opinions expressed by Thomas Brattle, in a well-known letter of October 1692, as printed in Burr, ed., *Narratives*, 169–90. See also Robert Calef, "More Wonders of the Invisible World,"

in *ibid.*, 296–393. Among clergymen an early skeptic was the Rev. Samuel Willard, the man who presided at the "possession" of Elizabeth Knapp (see above, Chapter 4). Apparently Willard was the author of a little dialogue—published anonymously under the title "Some Miscellany Observations on Our Present Debates Respecting Witchcrafts" (Philadelphia, 1692)—in which the Salem trials were vigorously called into question. Willard is also supposed to have prayed with some of the accused (who were members of his own church in Boston) and even to have assisted in their escape from prison. See Calef, "More Wonders of the Invisible World," in Burr, ed., *Narratives*, 186n.

132. Keith Thomas, *Religion and the Decline of Magic* (New York, 1971), esp. ch. 22.

133. For a good, short introduction to this topic, see Stephen Thernstrom and Peter R. Knights, "Men in Motion: Some Data and Speculations about Urban Population Mobility in Nineteenth Century America," in Tamara K. Hareven, ed., *Anonymous Americans* (Englewood Cliffs, N.J., 1971), 17–47.

134. The classic contemporary description of this spirit is Alexis de Tocqueville, *Democracy in America* (1848; repr. New York, 1945, 2 vols.). See esp. second part, second book.

135. See, for example, the discussion in Marvin Meyers, *The Jacksonian Persuasion: Politics and Belief* (Stanford, Calif., 1957).

136. See Kirk Jeffrey, "The Family as Utopian Retreat from the City: The Nineteenth Century Contribution," in *Soundings*, LV (1972), 21–41.

137. See Irvin G. Wyllie, *The Self-Made Man in America: The Myth of Rags to Riches* (New Brunswick, N.J., 1954); Moses Rischin, *The American Gospel of Success* (Chicago, 1965); John G. Cawelti, *Apostles of the Self-Made Man* (Chicago, 1965).

138. The first scholarly study of this figure, now a little classic, was Barbara Welter, "The Cult of True Womanhood, 1820–1860," in the *American Quarterly*, XVIII (1966), 151–74.

139. Nancy F. Cott, "Passionlessness: An Interpretation of Victorian Sexual Ideology, 1790–1850," in *Signs*, IV (1978), 219–36.

140. See Richard W. Wertz and Dorothy C. Wertz, *Lying-In: A History of Childbirth in America* (New York, 1977), chs. 2–5.

141. See Joe L. Dubbert, *A Man's Place: Masculinity in Transition* (Englewood Cliffs, N.J., 1979), chs. 4–6; and Jeffrey P. Hantover, "Boy Scouts and the Validation of Masculinity," in *Journal of Social Issues*, XXXIV (1978), 184–95.

142. See Rotundo, "Men and Masculinity," *passim.*

143. See Bernard Wishy, *The Child and the Republic: The Dawn of American Child Nurture* (Philadelphia, 1968).

144. The leading contemporary statement of this viewpoint was Horace Bushnell, *Views of Christian Nurture* (Hartford, Conn., 1847).

145. See Joseph F. Kett, *Rites of Passage: Adolescence in America, 1790 to the Present* (New York, 1977).

146. See Nancy F. Cott, *The Bonds of Womanhood: Women's "Sphere" in New England, 1780–1835* (New Haven, Conn., 1977), ch. 5; and Carroll Smith-Rosenberg, "The Female World of Love and Ritual: Relations Between Women in Nineteenth-Century America," in *Signs*, I (1975), 1–29.

147. Yasukichi Yasuba, *Birth Rates of the White Population in the United States, 1800–1860* (Baltimore, 1962). See also Daniel Scott Smith, "Family Limitation, Sexual Control, and Domestic Feminism in Victorian America," in *Feminist Studies*, I (1973), 40–57.

148. A vast literature of child-rearing advice developed almost *de novo* in nineteenth-century America. Much of this material is cited in Wishy, *The Child and the Republic*.

149. Tocqueville, *Democracy in America*, II, 209.

150. See Kett, *Rites of Passage*; and John Demos and Virginia Demos, "Adolescence in Historical Perspective," in *Journal of Marriage and the Family*, XXXI (1969), 632–38.

151. See, e.g., Richard L. Bushmen, *From Puritan to Yankee: Character and the Social Order in Connecticut, 1690–1765* (New York, 1966).

152. The most sensitive student of this process (at least in its early phases) is Kenneth A. Lockridge. See his *A New England Town: The First Hundred Years* (New York, 1970), chs. 6–9, and also his "Land, Population, and the Evolution of New England Society, 1630–1790," in *Past and Present*, XXXIX (1968), 62–80.

153. The best synthetic statement on these broad-gauge trends is found in Richard D. Brown, *Modernization: The Transformation of American Life* (New York, 1976).

Subject Index

adolescence, and witchcraft accusations, 157–65, 397

affects, and witchcraft, 129, 149–50, 184–94

age, of witches, 64–70, 144, 272, 348, 391–92

agriculture, 224–25, 374–75

anorexia nervosa, and witchcraft, 159, 164–65

Antinomian controversy, 317, 379, 383

astrology, 61, 133

autonomy, as psychological issue in witchcraft, 148, 156–57, 179, 184, 199–200, 203, 205–6, 210, 396

blasphemy, 247

boundary-setting function, of witchcraft, 176, 277–78, 304–7, 398

cases of witchcraft, totalled, 11–12

cattle, attacked by witchcraft, 39–42, 45, 140, 142, 145–46, 171–72, 178, 185–86, 248, 252–54, 296

child-bearing, affected by witchcraft, 62, 170, 198, 218, 239

child-bearing experience, of witches, 72–73, 170

child-rearing, in early New England, 207–8, 396

comets, 377, 382–84

community action, against witchcraft, 116, 128–31, 172, 196, 305–12

comparative rates of witchcraft, 11–12, 310

confessions, of witchcraft, 8–9, 108, 345–46, 352

contentiousness, and witchcraft, 52–55, 86–89, 304, 319–20, 353, 359, 363

"conversion" symptoms, 117, 300

counter-magic, 8, 138–39, 147, 182–84, 193, 199, 217, 280, 331, 390–91

covenant, with the Devil, 6, 37, 69, 107–8, 116, 324, 345–46

crime, and witchcraft, 48, 76–79, 320–21, 346

cunning women, and witchcraft, 80–84

debt, and witchcraft accusations, 5, 40, 43, 295–96

"defenses" (psychological), 117, 122, 162–63, 194–97

Name Index